THE PAPERS

of

JOHN C. CALHOUN

THE PAPERS

of

JOHN C. CALHOUN

〖

Volume XXIV, 1846–1847

Edited by

Clyde N. Wilson

and Shirley Bright Cook

Alexander Moore, *Associate Editor*

University of South Carolina Press, 1998

*Publication of this book was made possible
by a grant from the National Historical Publications
and Records Commission.*

*International Standard Book Number: 1–57003–209–2
Library of Congress Catalog Card Number: 59–10351*

Manufactured in the United States of America

CONTENTS

◫

PREFACE

〖

This volume brings the Carolina statesman into the last, tumultuous, period of his life, a time of intransigent sectional conflict. The volume concludes with only two years and a few months remaining of a forty-year national career.

As always, we have made the record as complete as it can be. Besides the persons on the title page, Sean R. Busick and Jeffery J. Rogers contributed to the work of this volume. We have been, as always, assisted indispensably by the National Endowment for the Humanities, the National Historical Publications and Records Commission, the University of South Carolina, and the University South Caroliniana Society.

CLYDE N. WILSON

Columbia, May 1996

INTRODUCTION

Ⅱ

We come to the last few years of Calhoun's life, the period of the intransigent sectionalist so powerfully fixed in the American mind by post-Civil War historiography and popular lore—the obsessed fanatic full of dire forebodings and, it was often hinted, dark plottings, though as to whether the obsession was slavery or the Presidency the commentators do not agree.

It is perhaps well to remember that this was not the universal, or even the prevailing idea of Calhoun at the time Mr. Wilmot's mischievous Proviso burst on the Union—inaugurating the struggle between the North and South over the territories (future States) that would occupy the rest of Calhoun's public life and the attention of all right down to 1861.

Ellwood Fisher was an Ohio Democrat and a Quaker and one of Calhoun's many Northern admirers. Near the beginning of 1847 he published a widely reprinted description of Calhoun's place in the American dialogue that cast the slavery struggle in a somewhat different light than did the postwar explanations. Fisher approved of and agreed with Calhoun's preference for a Southern society based on domestic slavery over a Northern one based on "capital." "The money power," Fisher wrote, "like every other kind of power, aims to be paramount and exclusive. It aims at a showy form of civilization of its own, its habitation, its board—luxury collected from every clime where money finds its slaves."[1]

On December 19, 1846, (a Saturday), not long after the convening of the Congressional session, President James K. Polk requested Calhoun to call at the White House. In a long and, according to Polk, "frank and pleasant" conversation, they discussed

[1] "John C. Calhoun," by "F," first published in the Cincinnati, Ohio, *Daily Enquirer.* Quoted from the Tallahassee, Fla., *Floridian,* January 9, 1847, p. 1, reprinting from the *Enquirer.* Rufus W. Griswold, a New England scholar who published *The Prose Writers of America* in 1847, said there: "Mr. Calhoun is in many respects one of the most extraordinary men of the nineteenth century, and is undoubtedly one of the few for whom this period will be memorable in after times." (Quoted in the Charleston, S.C., *Southern Patriot,* April 22, 1847, p. 2.)

ix

measures for prosecuting the Mexican War and what terms should be asked for. Calhoun indicated that he was willing to settle for Upper California, but had no objection to Polk's insistence on New Mexico and Lower California as well and that he would support any war appropriation the President requested. But, as Polk recounted in his diary:

> He said he could not vote for it with the slavery restriction which had been attached to a bill with the same object in the House of Representatives near the close of the last session of Congress, and that if such a restriction were contained in any treaty with Mexico, he would vote against ratifying the treaty. I told him that such a restriction would be most mischievous, and would probably defeat the object in view. . . . I told him if such a treaty [acquiring the Californias and New Mexico, even without the restriction] was made slavery would probably never exist in these provinces. To this he readily assented, and said he did not desire to extend slavery; but that if the slavery restriction was put into a treaty, it would involve a principle, and whatever the other provisions of the treaty were, he would vote against it.[2]

The "principle" to which Calhoun referred and to rallying the South behind which he would devote much of his remaining energies, is not hard to discern and requires no dark explanation. It was laid forth simply in the three resolutions he introduced on February 19, 1847. The territories were the common property of the Union and Congress had no right to discriminate among States and deprive some of them of "full and equal right" in that common property. It was essentially the same position Thomas Jefferson had taken in his well-known letter of April 22, 1820, to John Holmes in regard to the Missouri question.

If one regarded the Union, as Calhoun did, as an agreement for mutual benefit of all the parts (and not as some sort of mystical, self-justifying entity), then the "fixed determination," now fully revealed, of one part to discriminate against another, had to be responded to by a determined and unanimous appeal to principle by the offended party.

Practically, the principle revealed itself in the insistence that the condition of future States not be predetermined by Congress. (The reasoning would later appear in the Dred Scott decision.) Neither Calhoun nor any other Southern spokesman ever denied that a State could make whatever decision it chose in regard to slavery or free-soil. But he had always insisted on the difference between the peo-

[2] Allan Nevins, ed., *Polk: The Diary of a President, 1845–1849* (New York: Capricorn Books, 1968), pp. 176–177.

ple incorporated in a sovereign state and the mere territory owned by Congress. (See his speeches of 1837 on the admission of Michigan.)

For Calhoun the proper spirit of the American Union was, or should be, the sectional comity of the Monroe years—cooperation and forbearance and not the seeking of advantage. The "fixed determination" to exclude the South from the benefits of the Union, dooming it to ever greater minority status, was a violation of this spirit.

And of course, Calhoun had no great respect for "the mere numerical majority," especially such a narrow and ambiguously motivated majority as that by which the House of Representatives had passed Mr. Wilmot's proposition. He had seen too many political deals. He was too well aware that the Proviso was in part fueled by Northern resentment at Southern resistance to the tariff, national bank, and internal improvements. Questions as great as the relations of the sections, the future of the South and of the Union, for him required a greater deliberation, a more open agreement, and a larger and firmer consensus, a "concurrent," majority.

Calhoun's stand evoked widespread if not unanimous agreement in the South. For Polk the issue was merely mischievous and essentially unreal—an embarrassment to his goals and his administration. His press, the Washington *Union*, would take the "practical" politician's instinctive stand in the middle. Condemn the Proviso and likewise condemn those troublemakers like Calhoun who were obdurate against it. Polk's position does not reveal superior political judgment, superior ethics, or superior patriotism—it reveals merely that he was taking in a shorter range of vision than Calhoun. Had he been able or willing to look ahead as far as Calhoun, he would have been forced to agree with him, as the whole South had come to do by 1861.

Calhoun does not seem to have been grim at this period despite the public trials and a persistent cough. Polk described him as in good humor. An Episcopal minister who was introduced to Calhoun when he passed through Charleston on his way to Congress in December, 1846, recounted in his diary:

> He is about six feet in height, or a little over, very thin and slim, stoops a triffle when walking accrost the room. Very affable and ready in conversation. He sat with his chair poised on the two back legs—his heels under the forelegs, and his hands in the arm holes of his Vest or in the pockets of his pants, with his upper lip raised almost continually. There is in his eye a glow—luster—

brilliancy or whatever it may be called—peculiar and striking. There appeared to issue from the center of them a flame of pure white light, that might cause objects before them to cast a shadow on the wall.[3]

Slavery in the territories was not the only major theme of Calhoun's last years. There was another theme which assumes a large place in this and subsequent volumes, a theme which also is reminiscent of an earlier, less boisterous era. That is Calhoun's attempts to avoid and to limit war, in which he achieved a great and perhaps enduring eloquence. As in his speech of February 9, 1847, in which he implored Americans to limit their aims and hostilities against the sister republic to the South.

This occasion drew much attention. The correspondent of the Cincinnati *Daily Enquirer* reported:

> The great point of attraction was the Senate, where Mr. Calhoun was the speaker. The galleries were crowded—the floor of the Senate and lobbies were crowded—indeed it was almost impossible to get near either door of the chamber. The various reports that had been in circulation as to the course he was likely to pursue—the interest of the subject and the great reputation of the speaker, drew a large crowd, which would have been intolerable had it not been made up so largely of beautiful women.[4]

Here is another description of the same occasion:

> While Mr. Calhoun was speaking, not a volume or scrap of paper was seen about him. He read no long extracts from books; he made no reference to notes or manuscripts of any kind. His notes and references were his own brain. His speech the offspring of his own mind. He handled his subject in a masterly manner. Every word was precisely the word, and had a purpose. Every sentence contained a truth and comprehended as much as weaker minds do in a speech. Mr. Calhoun talks rapidly, and his mind moves with so much vigor, and he goes so swiftly from the development of one great proposition to a second, that most minds are taxed to follow him. He has little action, and there is hardly any modification in the tones of his voice. Yet there is about him an air of deep earnestness, a complete devotion, and intense heartfelt enthusiasm of his whole soul, that he, on great subjects displays, to arrest the attention and bind, like a spell, all around them.[5]

Numerous small political motives could be and were assigned for Calhoun's stand here. But it was also surely a sincere lament for the

---

[3] "Diary of John Hamilton Cornish, 1846–1860," in *South Carolina Historical Magazine*, vol. LXIV, no. 2 (April, 1963), p. 74.

[4] Cincinnati, Ohio, *Daily Enquirer*, February 15, 1847, p. 2.

[5] Greensborough, Ala., *Alabama Beacon*, March 6, 1847, p. 2.

peril of republican virtue, as revealed in a letter to his beloved daughter Anna Maria:

> Certain it is, that the preservation of our institutions & liberty occupy but little of the attention of our Governm[en]t, Federal, or State, or that of the people. Wealth & power engross the attention of all. We act, as if good institutions & liberty belong to us of right, & that neither neglect nor folly can deprive us of their blessing.[6]

[6] To Anna Maria Calhoun Clemson, June 10, 1847, herein. Here is as good a place as any to put into the record the spurious Calhoun-Dumas correspondence that was ascribed to 1847, though not published until 1848. It was represented as an exchange of letters between Calhoun and Alexandre Dumas, père, (1802–1870), the French romancer who was already famous as the author of *The Three Musketeers* and *The Count of Monte Cristo* and who was of one-quarter African descent. Dumas writes Calhoun on 4/1/1847 announcing plans to visit the U.S. and asking if he will be in any danger of being "taken and sold as a slave." Calhoun's alleged reply, dated 8/1/1847, informs Dumas that his "African blood will subject you to imprisonment and slavery in this State." However, Dumas is assured, "you would, doubtless, experience no insult, but you would be politely turned out of town by our chivalry, as was lately the case in respect to a public agent sent hither by the State of Massachusetts." This feeble exercise in humor was apparently first published in the Boston, Mass., *Atlas*. It is printed in full, with commentary, in the *National Era*, vol. II, no. 59 (February 17, 1848), p. 26.

THE PAPERS

of

JOHN C. CALHOUN

▯▯

Volume XXIV

DECEMBER 7, 1846–
JANUARY 31, 1847

Ⅱ

Perhaps during his two days in Charleston on the journey to Washington, Calhoun had seen the "Democratic Letter Paper" that was for sale by Babcock & Co.'s bookshop on King Street. It was described as "Beautiful Letter Paper, each sheet having a correct and elegant miniature likeness of the illustrious J.C. Calhoun . . . ." (Charleston, S.C., Southern Patriot, *January 2, 1847, p. 4.)*

When the second session of the 29th Congress convened on December 7, the senior Senator from South Carolina was in his seat. Calhoun declined to serve on any standing committee.

On December 21 he presented the credentials of his newly-elected South Carolina colleague, Andrew P. Butler. The next evening, he was one of the distinguished guests invited by the New England Society of Washington to a gala celebration at Coleman's Hotel in honor of the 225th anniversary of the landing of the Pilgrims at Plymouth. He could not be present, of course, on the evening of January 1 for the "Annual Ball of the Calhoun Association" of New York City at Tammany Hall, tickets one dollar. In announcing this event, the redoubtable Mike Walsh editorialized: "It is of course utterly unnecessary for me to repeat that of all public men living, John C. Calhoun is my favorite. Soaring, as he does, triumphantly above and beyond all the low demagogueism by which he is surrounded, he is looked up to by the good and patriotic portion of his countrymen as one upon whom they can always depend in the hour of trial and danger." (New York, N.Y., Subterranean, *December 26, 1846, p. 2.)*

A further evidence of the Carolinian's popularity in New York was the election of his son Patrick, a lieutenant of the regular Army, as Colonel of the Second Regiment of New York volunteers.

During December Calhoun followed a watch and wait policy, writing to Franklin H. Elmore in a vein often repeated to others: "Things have not sufficiently developed themselves to form a correct opinion, as to the state of things here. The prospect is that there will be a warm session; and a good deal of distraction in the ranks of both parties." In fact, in the first weeks of the session Calhoun

3

showed more interest in encouraging a railroad connection from Charleston to Nashville than he did in addressing the Senate. He rose only a few times, to make suggestions on public lands and war finance bills, although on January 19 he had to respond to a bombastic attack by Thomas H. Benton. The press generally sided with Calhoun on that one.

The war went on, meantime, uncertainly, and with the shadow of the Wilmot Proviso, already reintroduced, hanging over its happy settlement.

It was during a quiet period just after Christmas that Calhoun wrote a note to his six-year-old grandson, John Calhoun Clemson, then sojourning at his father's post across the Atlantic. The note was in response to the child's first letter to his grandfather, who was "happy to learn . . . that you could write so pretty a letter."

Ⅲ

From HENDRICK B. WRIGHT

Wilkes-Barré [Pa.,] Dec. 8, 1846

My dear Sir, Your place and influence put it in your power to save the democracy of this State certainly & very probably that of the Union. By a modification of the tax laws discriminating in favor of the staples of this great State, coal and iron; our people would take the [tariff] law of '46 without complaints. As it is I fear the worst consequences to the party in the next effort. Our inter[es]ts in coal and iron are so important and they reach so many collateral measures, that an amendment of the law seems to be almost indispensable.

You, Sir, are the mediator in this case[?] ["matter,(?) &" *canceled*] if disposed to undertake the matter there can be no question of the result—and I am satisfied you can do it and compromise no principle. It would give you strength in Penn[sylvani]a and probably be the initiative of momentous questions her[e]after. I suggest this as your *personal* and *political* friend—for while I would disdain to say to you, what was not my honest opinion, you cannot bel[i]eve from past intercourse that I would do a thing or express a thought prejudicial to your inter[es]ts. And if the day should come when you were before the people as a candidate for their suffrages for the first office in their gift, no consideration arising from dif[f]erences of opinion would alienate me from your cause.

Bel[i]eving that you regard me sincere, I have taken the liberty to make the suggestion as to a modification of the tariff. And I should hope to see the movement originate with you. Our defeat in this State has been signal and I hope and pray that some slight legislation may prevent an occurrence of it again. This can be done by taking coal & iron out of the ad valorem list: and so long as the law does vary in *this*—can there be any objection to include these articles in that variation. I have no individual int[ere]st[?] in the matter—and am governed solely by the desire to save the party and increase its strength. Very truly your friend, Hendrick B. Wright.

ALS in ScCleA; PC in Boucher and Brooks, eds., *Correspondence*, pp. 363–364.

To Mrs. P[LACIDIA MAYRANT] ADAMS, [Pendleton]

Senate Chamber, 9th Dec[embe]r 1846
My dear Madam, I received your several notes by the mail of last evening, in reference to the debt due to Mr. Breckenridge, and regret, that there should be any mistake about it.

You mistake, in supposing that any thing was said about it, when you last saw me. The facts, according to my recollection, are as follows. When I first saw you, after my return from Washington, that debt & the one to Dr. [C.L.] G[a]illard became the subject of Conversation. I mentioned to you, that I was in advance in payment of the interest ["on the bond" *interlined*], & was not bound to pay any part of the principal, without six months notice; but as you were pressed, I would meet the debts for you, if ["I" *interlined*] could not obtain indulgence ["for you" *interlined*] until I sold my crop; but would prefer, if they refused indulgence, to raise the money by accepting an order from you for $1000, to meet that & some other small debts you owed, if the money could be raised that way; the order having six months to run. I saw the gentlemen & informed you, that indulgence could not be obtained. It is proper here to state, that in our first conversation, I asked you, if $1000 would meet all your immediate pressing debts, and understood it would, but that you would need $1000 more some time hence, & give me notice, so that I might be prepared to pay it under the bond. You either at the time ["or shortly after" *interlined*] I informed you that indulgence could not be had, asked me, if I would accept order in favour of Mr. [John S.]

5

Lorton for $1000 for six months, & I informed you I would. The next time I saw Mr. Lorton he spoke to me about it, & I informed him I would accept it. He presented it the next time I saw him, & I accepted it accordingly. I naturally concluded it was to meet the debts to Breckenridge & Dr. Gaillard, and the other small debts due by you, & did not suppose it was intended to meet the sum of $1000, which you informed me would not be needed for the present; & do not now know whether it was intended to meet that, or is an additional sum over and above ["that" *changed to* "it"] of which you gave me notice. I wish you to inform me on that point, without delay, that I may make my arrangements accordingly.

Nor do you state, what is the amount of the debt due to Mr. Breckenridge. I do not recollect the amount, but am of the impression it is about $170. I enclose a draft for $220, which I suppose is sufficient. If it be not, let me know, & the balance will be sent forthwith. I must ask you to acknowledge its receipt & credit the amount on the bond.

As to Dr. Gaillard's debt, if you cannot get indulgence on it, until my return, or raise the amount by a draft on me, until then, which I will accept, let me know, & it shall be met, but you will, I hope, see the absolute necessity, in making these heavy payments on the principal, of giving credit on the bond, &, I hope, you will take effectual steps to find it, if you have not already found it. With great respect I am & &, J.C. Calhoun.

[P.S.] The draft is on N. York & will be taken by Mr. [John] Hastie or [Enoch B.] Benson as it is above par in Charleston. All you have to do is to write your name [on] its back. J.C.C.

ALS owned by Mr. Holbrook Campbell.

To T[homas] G. Clemson, [Brussels]

Washington, 9th Dec[embe]r 1846
My dear Sir, I took your place [in Edgefield District] in my route here ["in my way" *canceled*], where I remained a day. I rode over the whole, & saw every thing; & found things in about as good a condition, as might be expected under circumstances. The negroes were all well, & looked well, except Susan, who had taken the chills & fever at Arthur Simkins['s]. They were also very contented & spoke well of the overseer [—— Mobley]. The Mules & horses were

in fair condition. The cattle very lean, which the overseer said was owing to the fact, that he could not pasture the harvest or corn field for the want of crop fences until the picking of cotton was finished, which he expected would be in a week. He added, that they would then be put in & would soon fatten, without being fed until nearly March. The sheep looked well. They numbered 48. The Hogs have not done well. The shoats all died last ["sp" *canceled*] fall & winter in good order, from some prevailing disease, which extended, as I understood through the neighbourhood, from old Mr. [John] Mobley. There were eight ["hogs" *interlined*] in the pen fattening, which would average about 150 pounds each; and several sows with 20 pigs. They were of a cross of the common hog of the neighbourhood. I find the opinion prevalent, that Berkshires will not suit the climate so far South. I directed the sows & pigs to be well fed & no pains to be spared to raise sufficient hogs for the supply of the place.

The corn has turned out pretty well. It has yielded about 1900 bushels, which is a good deal ["less" *canceled*] more than the place will require. With a much less crop last year there were sold 268 bushels. The oats were good. The cotton has not yielded equal to Col. [Francis W.] Picken[s]'s estimate. There are 32 bales packed & sent to Hamburgh; 8, by estimation, to be ginned & packed, & two or three to be picked out, making, say, in the whole 42 bales, weighing 400 to the bale, according to the estimate of the overseer, and equalling 16,800 pounds. The crop would have yielded well, but for the stand, which was very bad, owing to the cold wet spring. The field at the lower end, next to [Allen S.] Dozier's, would have yielded a bale to the acre had the stand been good. I directed the overseer to clear 20 or 25 acres adjoining to it, which will make a cotton field, with the other, of 40 acres of prime land. He will put in 20 acres more of cotton next year & also of corn. Your gang is yearly becoming stronger. There have been 6 added by birth, in the last 12 months. The fencing is not very good, & will, in places, require repairs, which can be made without preventing the clearing. I directed the overseer to pay particular attention to manuring & to add 8 acres more to cotton field near the barn, on account of the convenience of manuring. It will be added on the south side next to the low ground.

I wrote you that I had concluded to ["dismiss" *canceled*] get a new overseer; but found, that the information, on which I acted was not correct & concluded to continue him on the same terms for another year.

Tell Anna [Maria Calhoun Clemson], that I examined the furni-

7

ture, & found it in a good condition. Mrs. [Lucretia Simkins] Mobley has been very attentive. She expressed a great desire to hear from her, which I hope she will gratify ["her" *canceled*] by writing occasionally.

I ["left" *canceled*] all ["were" *interlined*] well [*sic*], when I left home. Willie [William Lowndes Calhoun] was gradually regaining his strength.

I enclose the President[']s [James K. Polk's] Message. It is a poor excuse for the Mexican war. Parties are in a state of distraction & disorganization. I have no time to say more at present on politicks.

The Caladonia [*sic*] has been in several days. I have got no letters either from you or Anna. I fear they went to Pendleton.

My love to Anna & the children [John Calhoun Clemson and Floride Elizabeth Clemson]. In haste. Your affectionate father, J.C. Calhoun.

ALS in ScCleA.

To F[RANKLIN] H. ELMORE, Columbia, S.C.

Washington, 10th Dec[embe]r 1846
Dear Sir, In consequence of your absence from the city [of Charleston], & not ["being" *interlined*] certain whether you would return, before the 1st Jan[uar]y, I addressed a letter, a few days since, to Mr. [Charles M.] Furman, the cashier [of the Bank of the State of S.C.], in reference to the note of my son [Andrew Pickens Calhoun] & myself in bank, and asking a renewal for six months, in the hope, that cotton may rise in price in the spring or early part of summer. The crop will certainly be a very short one from all I can learn. I have made particular enquiries since my arrival here, & find the opinion universal among the members from the South West, that it will be very short throughout all the great cotton region south of the 34th parallel. I do not think it can possibly exceed 1,800,000 ["bags" *interlined*], & if we make an allowance for the fact, that the falling off will be where the bags are very heavy, & the increase, where they are light, it ["will" *interlined*] not probably in reality exceed 1,600,000 fairly estimated.

We have been great suffer[er]s. Our crop [in Marengo County, Ala.] was good on the 1st August for at least 7000 bags ["at" *canceled*] averaging 500 pounds the bag; & has been reduced by the worms to

220. [*Marginal note:* "We are among the least of the sufferers in the vicinity."] I hope under these circumstances, the bank will not hesitate to [*one word canceled and* "in granting" *interlined; sic*] a renewal for six months. I informed Mr. Furman that you had the note of myself & son in blank. I gave you two when you were here last summer & one only I think was used. My son will remit a sufficient sum to pay the discount on the renewal. Let me hear from you on the subject.

Things have not sufficiently developed themselves to form a correct opinion, as to the state of things here. The prospect is that there will be a warm session; and a good deal of distraction in the ranks of both parties. Yours truly, J.C. Calhoun.

ALS in DLC, Franklin Harper Elmore Papers.

From CALVIN GRAVES

Raleigh N. Carolina
Senate Chamber
10th Decem[be]r 1846

My dear Sir, The relation which you sustain to the American people, and the Commanding position which you now occupy, will, I trust, be regarded a sufficient apology for this Communication from One, who has not the honor of your personal acquaintance.

Allow me, if you please, to Consult you, relative to a question now pending before the Legislature of this State, and one which deeply interests every true North Carolinian.

At the session of 1842–3 of this Legislature our State was arranged into Congressional Districts, (the democratic ["party" *interlined*], of which I have the honor of being a member, being in the ascendency). At the present Session, the Whig party proposed to repeal the Law of 1842–3, and re-district the State. By their Bill now before the House of Commons, they appropriate to themselves, *Six*, of the nine districts, into which the State is to be divided. A difference of opinion, amongst Our democratic friends, prevails, as to the *Constitutional power* of this Legislature to repeal the law of 1842, and disturbe the ["existing" *interlined*] arrangement until another apportionment of Representatives is made by Congress.

Will you be kind enough to favor me with your Opinion upon this Constitutional question? Accompanied by such views as you may find it Convenient to submit sustaining that Opinion.

9

The deep interest which [I] take in this matter, and the high authority of the Source from whence I seek the information, has alone pro[m]pted me to Make the Call. I have the honor to be Your friend & Ob[e]d[ien]t Ser[van]t, Calvin Graves of the County of Caswell.

ALS in ScCleA.

To "Col." J[AMES] ED[WARD] COLHOUN, [Abbeville District, S.C.]

Washington, 12th Dec[embe]r 1846

My dear Sir, The Mail of yesterday brought me your letter of the 30th Nov[embe]r, addressed to Pendleton.

From what I hear, I do not doubt, but your Tennessee correspondent is correct in his statement. It seems certain, that Col. [Thomas H.] Benton is to be the organ of the Administration in the Senate, which, as [Silas] Wright & he are bosom friends, would seem to indicate pretty certainly, that the latter is designed to be the successor, should [James K.] Polk dispair of running with success. Should such be the arrangement, the other portions of your correspondent[']s statement, that the press has already been subsidized & that the Post Master General [Cave Johnson] is in the movement, in all probability is true.

Willie [William Lowndes Calhoun] when I left home was still weak, and not free from the hazard of a relapse. He was reduced[?] exceedingly low by his last attack; & I fear his health will not be sufficiently restored until spring. Indeed, I am so uneasy about him, that I had concluded, should he get strong enough, to send him to Alabama to spend the winter ["in Alabama" *canceled*] with his brother Andrew [Pickens Calhoun; "for" *canceled*] to try the effects of limestone water & a warm, genial climate.

As to the state of parties here, I infer from all I can learn, that both parties are in a state of great distraction & disorganization. What will grow out of it, would be difficult to conjecture. I can see no immediate end of the Mexican War. It seems certain, that an attack is contemplated on Vera Cruz both by sea & land; but mainly by the latter. Great reliance seems to be placed on the success of the attack bring[ing] Mexico to terms. I doubt it; while it seems certain that a failure would tend greatly to prolong the War. I wish we could be fairly & honorably extricated from it. Its termination would be followed by great prosperity under the reduction of duties, while its long continuance, would be followed by many evil consequences, and among them the elevation of the whigs to power & the restoration of a protective Tariff. Yours affectionately, J.C. Calhoun.

ALS in ScCleA; PEx's in Jameson, ed., *Correspondence*, pp. 713–714.

From JOHN HOGAN

Utica N. York, Dec. 12th 1846

My dear Sir, I am rejoiced that you are again in the Senate. I hope now that your health is entirely restored and that you are as young as you were twenty years ago. There is no doubt that you will have a Stormy Session of it[;] indeed the country expects it. The Mexican question entangled as it is & has been will be a Source of trouble. Then to be added to that the Presidential question of '48 I am convinced will throw every thing into com[m]otion. The result of the recent Election in this State you were prepared to hear. Still we are in hot water in the State up to our waists. Mr. [Silas] Wright[']s friends in this State has entirely given up the contest for '48. Gen. [Lewis] Cass trys to make head way but he will be sorely defeated, even should he be the candidate of all the other States. You are aware that we have recently adopted a new Constitution in this State—by the terms of the Constitution we have just adopted *all* the offices in the State become vacant on the first of January 1847. Consequently all of those who heretofore occupied & held those offices and by which they exercised an undue influence in the State will all be thrown loose & without influence. Therefore it is idle to say that aney man or set of men will have much political power in the State. New men will spring up and those who heretofore exercised an undue influence will be laid on one side. The current of feeling in this State is becoming strong against the old office holders. They must one by one be put aside. From this state of affairs it is extremely difficult to say how matters will stand with us in this State in one year from this. Wright is substantially out of the question for the present—entirely so for '48. [William L.] Marcy & his friends still in a worse predicament and all others in same category and it is difficult to say who will be in the assendant. The few friends that Marcy has are in favour of Gen. Cass. The Cass party in the State no. about 15,000 out of 500,000 votes. I will not in this letter make a suggestion but will in a future one or when I have the pleasure of seeing you about the new year at which time I hope to be in Washington to take care of my matters there.

You will recollect that last winter when I was in Washington I mentioned to you that there were two Ladies near this City whose maiden name was Calhoun. They claim to be relatives of yours. They are advanced in years & both now have each a pretty property. Both those Ladies speak in the most friendly manner of you & make inquir[i]es for you when I see them. I suggested to each of them to make yourself or one of your sons their Hier to inherit their property which may be the case. At all events I hope that they will do so indeed I have no doubt but that they may. I will see them before I leave for Washington again. They may write you. I suggested to them to write & that I would see that the letters were delivered to you. I suggested to them in their letters to mention who their Father was & that you might be able to trace out your relationship. They claim to be cousins of your family. In my next letter before I leave I will be able to say more on the subject.

My health is nearly restored. I am as busy as a be[e] in my office keeping a close lookout as to the movements of the political waters.

I hope we will bring forward the Domin[ican] matters & have your little republic recognized. May I enquir[e] who will go with Mr. [John] Slidell to Mexico as Joint Com[mission]er to settle that matter. I doubt much whether he is the right man to[o] full of Bragadoceo to[o] pompous. Although residing in N. Orleans he knows but little of the Spanish character. Some Gent[leman] should be sent with him that the few Spaniards that reside in Mexico would have more confidence in and one who understands Mankind better than Mr. Slidel[l]. Rest assured that he will not succeed there. I hope my dear Sir that you will accept for yourself & family my best wishes for yourself & family. I am your Ob[edien]t Servant, John Hogan.

ALS in ScCleA.

From WILLIAM SLOAN

Columbia [S.C.,] Dec[embe]r 12th 1846
Dear Sir, Your favour of the 8th Inst. came to hand on last night. Mr. [Benjamin F.] Perry of Gre[e]nville has introduced a bill in the

[S.C.] Senate to Charter the Greenville & Columbia rail road which fixes upon Newber[r]y C[ourt] H[ouse], as a point by which the road shall pass, leaving the rout[e] above and below open to competition. Should the bill pass in its present shape, the road will certainly be located from this place by Newber[r]y and Laurance [*sic*] to Greenville. When the bill reaches the house [of Representatives] an amendment will be offered opening the rout[e] to fair competition which amendment I feel confident will be sustained.

The subject of giving the election of electors ["of" *canceled*] to the People has been discussed in the Senate and I understand that body is opposed to any change. In the house I am satisfied that a large majority are in favour of taking the election from the Legislature, but there is so much diversity of opinion as to the manner of doing so, that I apprehend the effect of which will be that the different plans will neutralise each other, and that the house will not agree to a change.

I am under the impression that this subject will become a verry exciting one, and that policy would suggest that it be settled upon a compromise on the federal basis by districts ["preserving the vote of the State as a unit" *interlined*].

I send you the bills of the various plannes before ["th" *canceled*] us, by which it is proposed to effect the proposed change. Very respectfully Your obe[dient] Servant, William Sloan.

ALS in ScCleA. NOTE: An AEU by Calhoun reads "Mr. Sloan." William Sloan represented Pendleton District in the S.C. House of Representatives during 1846–1847.

From V[ERNON] K. STEVENSON

Nashville, Dec. 12th, 1846

Dear Sir; In talking over the prospects of our contemplated railroad from Nashville to Chattanooga, to connect at that point with the great railroad improvements of Georgia and South Carolina, last winter, you agreed that if I would furnish the statistics of Tennessee, that you would write such articles upon the importance of the work to Georgia and South Carolina, and Charleston particularly, as the state of the case would justify; and I have not prepared this sooner, because I was anxious that your articles upon the subject should appear near the time of the publishing of the report on the railroad survey, which I expect will be ready for publication now in 10 to 20 days by J. Edgar Thompson, C[hief] Engineer, who inclosed to me your note in answer to certain inquiries, &c. stating that I had promised statistics, which I had not forgotten. Below you will find that I have, in addition to the statistics, taken the liberty of making a few suggestions upon the various subjects connected with it, which you can make such use of as you think best for the interest of the great work.

1st. I give the amount and value of all kinds of agricultural and manufactured articles produced and shipped from the line and immediate vicinity of the contemplated railroad line, and all nearly from Nashville, except the iron, which is produced mostly below Nashville, on the Cumberland river, and a large proportion of pork and bacon, which is now driven and wagoned off to the South.

* 30,000 hogsheads Tobacco, average weight 1667 lbs., 3 cents—making $50 per hhd.	$1,500,000
+50,000 bales of Cotton, shipped from Nashville, average weight 450 lbs., worth [$]33 per bale	1,666,666
500,000 sacks of Corn, mostly from Nashville, and all from the Cumberland river, 2½ bu. to the sack, 80c. per sack	400,000
350,000 fat Hogs, in all shapes, taken out of the railroad vicinity in Middle Tenn., average value $5 70 each	1,995,000
21,000 Beef cattle, chiefly driven out and boated from Nashville to market, $20 each	420,000
30,000 Horses and Mules, annually driven and sold from Middle Tenn., $60 each	1,800,000
—— Country made Jeans, linseys, and socks, shipped chiefly from Nashville south	200,000
There are 9000 bales of cotton manufactured in the different factories in Middle Tenn., one third of the goods and yards from which is shipped and sold out of the State, the estimated value of which is, I think, reasonably placed at	400,000
Wagons, carts, drays, carriages, gigs, &c., $350,000— one third exported from Nashville, &c.	116,000
Cedar, lumber, staves, hoop poles, and other products of the forest,	166,000
Iron in all shapes, estimated in a report of Mr. S[amuel] D. Morgan to our last Legislature, the capital being $4,100,000, and the products annually estimated as equal to the capital,	

14

makes it $4,100,000, and of this ¾ fully is made
and shipped from Middle Tenn., and the
largest part from the Cumberland river, below
Nashville, (there being 21 blast furnaces,
11 forges, and three splendid rolling mills,
the products of which is $800,000 per annum;
there are on the Tennessee river, in Tennessee,
12 furnaces and 8 forges and bloomeries;
estimating the 12 furnaces at 1500 tons to the
furnace, which is considered fair by our
iron men; and they make a grand total of
180,000 tons of mettle.)   (I send you with this
Mr. Morgan's report which was gotten up by
him with great care, at the request of our
General Assembly, and although this may
look large, I have no doubt but that it will be
doubled in ten years, for capital is being
invested in this branch of manufactures
constantly, from abroad as well as at home,
and our largest fortunes have been made

from it.)	3,075,000
600 tons of Hemp; raw and manufactured, at $80, being an average low enough, is	48,000
Poultry, shipped south from Nashville, in value	18,000
700,000 lbs. Feathers, worth at Nashville 23c. per lb.	161,000
180,000 Beeswax, do. 23c. per lb.	31,400
100,000 lbs. Genseng, do. 26c. per lb.	26,000
1,040,000 lbs. Wool, do. 18c. per lb.	189,000
15,500 bushels of Flaxseed, do. 70c. per bushel,	10,850
Dried peaches, apples, nuts and pea-nuts— apples, 40c. per bu., peaches, 60c., nuts, 100c., pea-nuts, 60c.	11,400
12000 bushels of peas and beans, at 60c. per bu.	7,200
23,100 gallons of Peach and Apple Brandy, country distilled, 60c. per gal.	13,860
1500 bbls. Whiskey, worth $8 00 per bbl., chiefly made in Nashville,	120,000
120,000 lbs. of Furs and Peltry, worth 12½c. per lb., from Nashville	15,000
Sadlery, harness, machines, cotton gins, cut stone, &c., from Middle Tenn.	360,000
	$12,642,576

Making a total of twelve millions six hundred and forty-two thousand five hundred and seventy-six dollars, nearly half of which is shipped from Nashville, and about 1-6 from Clarksville, about 40 miles below Nashville, and the balance hauled and driven to the States south of us.

The estimates below are taken from the report of the Commissioner of Patents [Henry L. Ellsworth] for 1846, except, as to cotton and tobacco, which I have taken the liberty of correcting; and it may be that New York and Ohio may have corrections to make that would take their products to a point largely beyond this. As it is, it presents a surprising state of facts, and such as I am certain would justify the belief that our railroad stock will be valuable, particularly when the contrast in prices here and at Charleston for all our products is taken into consideration. [*Chart belongs here.*]

[*Interpolation*: "*This is the amount ascertained from our steamboat manifests, and is consequently correct, though a greater amount than is set down by the Com. of Patents, for the whole crop of the State—yet this goes out of the Cumberland river alone."]

[*Interpolation*: "+This is estimated for this year from the best data to be had, and is allowing an increase upon the shipments from Nashville that year of 5000 bales, which is I think, not too large, as our crop of cotton is much better than last; this is also nearly as much as the Com. of Patents estimates the whole crop at; but in addition to this Memphis ships 150,000 bales."]

Thus it is seen that in agricultural products Tennessee stands in the front ranks with the great States of New York and Ohio, notwithstanding the former has a population of nearly 3 to 1, and Ohio nearly 2 to 1, and that this population has to be supported before there is a surplus; and further, that stock in either of those States have to be fed twice as long in the winter, our winters being but half the length of theirs; all which justifies the belief that if we had the same motives in price for our produce, that we would have nearly double as much to sell as either of those great States that are paying railroads so well.

Ten or twelve years ago, Tennessee purchased considerably of every kind of agricultural produce, chiefly from Kentucky, except cotton and corn, notwithstanding she stands now even ahead of that great State in the same products that she was dependent upon her for so lately; and I am well satisfied that with the additional inducements furnished by the better prices afforded to her by a railway to Charleston and Savannah, that she would double the amount of her products for sale in five years, for this great revolution in her prosperity has been created mainly by the fine McAdamized roads that

Comparative value of the products of agriculture in each of the following three States, placing each article at the same, and a fair, price or value.

	Quantity and value of the agricultural products of New York, her population being 2,626,000	Quantity and value of the agricultural products of Ohio, her population being 1,760,000	Quantity and value of the agricultural products of Tennessee, her population being 910,000
No. bushels wheat, 16,000,000, at $1 per bush.	$16,200,000	13,572,000, at $1 00 per bush. $13,572,000	8,340,000, at $1 00 per bush, $8,340,000
Do. barley, 3,574,000, at 50c. per bush.	1,787,000	15,400, 50 =	5,500, 50 = 2,950
Do. oats, 23,700,000, at 25c. per bush.	5,925,000	24,447,000, 25 =	8,625,000, 25 = 2,156,250
Do. rye, 3,560,000, at 50c. per bush.	1,780,000	2,548,000, 50 =	384,000, 50 = 192,000
Do. buck wheat, 3,347,000, at 50c. per bush.	1,673,500	950,000, 50 =	26,000, 50 = 13,000
Do. Indian corn, 13,250,000, at 50c. per bush.	6,625,000	57,600,000, 50 =	70,265,000, 50 = 35,132,500
Do. potatoes, 21,968,000, at 20c. per bush.	4,397,200	4,120,000, 20 =	2,256,000, 20 = 451,200
No. tons hay, 3,703,000 at $5 per ton	18,515,000	1,251,000, 5 00 per ton	42,500, 5 00 per ton 210,000
" hemp & flax, manufactured and raw	....	500, 80 00 =	1,500, 80 00 = 120,000
" pound tobacco	....	7,576,800, 03 per pound	60,000,000, 03 per lb. 1,800,000*
" cotton	....	....	113,000,000, 08 = 9,040,000+
" rice	....	....	9,000, 03 = 2,700
" silk cocoons, 7,850, at $2 per lb.	15,700	39,370, 2 00 =	30,110, 2 00 = 60,220
" sugar, 14,500,000, at 6c. per lb.	670,000	3,900,000, 06 =	520,000, 06 = 31,200
	$57,685,400	$57,899,394	$57,551,820

pass from Nashville to almost every rich neighborhood in Middle Tennessee. To give you an idea of the number, &c., I will state that we have running out of Nashville nine roads, and six branches leaving them within the county, and numerous others in the adjoining counties running in every direction from Nashville. Two of these roads reach to Louisville, Ky., taking different routes; another leaves one of these at Bowlinggreen, Ky., and runs through the richest counties in southern Kentucky, to Eddyville, on the Cumberland river, Bowlinggreen being at the head of slackwater navigation from the Ohio river. We then have various McAdamized roads of different lengths, reaching towards Alabama, but one of which reaches the line, a branch from which goes through a fine iron district to the Tennessee river, at Carrolville; and others running eastwardly in different directions to the highlands, from fifty to sixty miles off. In fact, every rich county in Middle Tennessee has its McAdamized road or roads to Nashville, but one, Franklin, lying on the line of this contemplated railroad. The Kentuckians propose that if we will make our railroad, they will extend a turnpike road that we have begun towards Russelville through that place, and to the Green river, at the mouth of Muddy river—it being slackwater to above that place from the Ohio river.

We will also slackwater the Cumberland to the Ohio, if we can get an amendment to a charter obtained at the last Legislature, which I have no doubt we will be able to do. We would have been at this work now, but for the defects in the charter being of so serious a nature that the commissioners (I being one of them) refused to open the books under it.

With this slackwater and our railroad to Charleston and Savannah finished, our system of internal improvements would be complete, so our river is south of the three point[s] where water freezes hard enough to impede steam navigation; it also empties into the Ohio below that point, which now gives us great advantages over our more northern neighbors, when their rivers are frozen over and ours open, in supplying New Orleans at full prices.

There is one fact with regard to the commerce of our country that will operate to give, at an important season, a very heavy trade to this railroad, if made, and that is this, at the breaking up of all of the northern waters, a vast amount of corn, pork, flour, and wheat is poured into New Orleans just as the cotton and tobacco from the more southern States is arriving, which, taken all together, gluts the New Orleans market and lowers the price of produce at the very time that the same cause creates a demand for shipping which raises the demands of ship owners, and the two causes, tending both to lower the price and raise freight, make it ruinous, many times, to holders of all kinds of produce, and more particularly those holding such articles as bacon, flour, and tobacco, that are so injured by the climate; and at the same time the canals of New York are closed up, and vessels are begging freight, and also at Charleston freight is lowest when highest at New Orleans—as an instance, last March freight from New York to Liverpool was ¼ penny per pound, and the same at Charleston, when it was the same day ⅞ at New Orleans, or $1 75 per 100 lbs. at New Orleans, and 50 cents at Charleston— giving an advantage of $1 25 per 100 lbs. to Charleston, and ready shipping. This $1 25 would more than pay the carriage from Nashville to Charleston, and place the produce from the upper Mississippi in market at Liverpool at least one month sooner, as well as afford a large saving in insurance; for a good steamer would reach Nashville from St. Louis, with good slackwater, in forty hours, when she would be five or six days to New Orleans, and the insurance thence to Liverpool is much higher than from Charleston, &c.

If the construction of this railroad line to Charleston should have the same effect upon the quantity of our produce taken to market that has been shown on what is called the eastern branch of the Belgian railway, (when the total amount of tonnage reaching the German frontier was twelve thousand tons in 1844, the amount transported after the railroad went into operation was sixty seven thousand tons; in 1842, before the railway took the traffic, the amount of light goods was one hundred and ninety-four thousand tons; in 1844 it exceeded five hundred thousand tons, &c.—see Edinburgh Review for Oct. 1846, page 264)—we will, with our present large productions and the great increase, expect to keep the road busy and supply Charleston with shipping of every variety in sufficient abundance to make her one of our largest cities. You will be greatly aided in coming to this conclusion by a reference to our Nashville price current, and that of Charleston or New York; and I am further satisfied that by making this railroad complete to Nashville, that we furnish Charleston with such an abundance of produce at all seasons as to bring the price at that point so much below the prices of New York as to induce vessels to load there for foreign ports.

You may be induced to think that our river is not so good as it really is, from what I have above stated. Therefore, I will here assure you that it is quite equal to the Ohio below Louisville, and is navigable usually eight months in the twelve for fine boats, and for the balance for smaller steamboats; but we intend it to be better than any navigation in the valley, by slackwatering it, and making six feet at all times in the channel.

If I have omitted anything, please call upon me; and if it is in your power to do so, please commence your articles immediately on this subject, as I find the public at Charleston are much alive to this subject, and fear, from late developments, that they may be diverted from this, as I think, main point. I should like to hear from you. Most truly, V.K. Stevenson.

P.S. At this date, (May 31, 1847,) flour at Charleston, for shipment to Europe, is worth $8.50 to 9.00 per barrel, when it is worth but $5.50 to $6.00 at New Orleans—leaving a margin of $3.00 per bbl. to induce St. Louis and Cincinnati to send their flour by Nashville to Charleston, which would not cost one dollar a bbl. more than to send to New Orleans, leaving $2.00 per bbl. in favor of sending by Nashville to Charleston. In wheat there is a difference quite equal—say $1.12 at New Orleans and $2.12 at Charleston or New York; and corn, 68 to 70 cents per bushel at New Orleans, and $1.12 to $1.16 at Charleston or New York. All of which proves that the Mississippi valley could gain 30 per cent., at least, by sending their grain and flour to market by Nashville, if this railroad were built; and Tennessee would gain double, and Nashville would have her return in warehousing, draying, and forwarding—all of this gain brought to our wharfs by the hundred steamers that it would then take to do our business. V.K.S.

PC in the Nashville, Tenn., *Whig,* June 12, 1847, p. 2; PC in the Charleston, S.C., *Mercury,* June 25, 1847, p. 2; PC in *Before Railroads. A Contemporary View of the Agriculture*[,] *Industry and Commerce of the South in the 'Forties* ([Nashville:] Nashville, Chattanooga & St. Louis Railway, [1929]), pp. 3–6; ALS (fragment) in NcU, Edward Vernon Howell Papers. NOTE: The ALS is missing its first half. Stevenson's postscript, dated 5/31/1847, may have been added to an unlocated retained version of his letter of 12/12 and never sent to Calhoun.

From CH[ARLES] AUG[USTUS] DAVIS

Newyork [City,] 13 Dec[embe]r 1846

My D[ea]r Sir, The "New England Society" has its annual dinner here on 22d inst. You have been invited and I sincerely hope you will come. If you have already written or sent a declination it will be suppress'd till I get a reply to this. On this point I speak "by authority" having been with the officers of the Society last evening all ["of" *interlined*] whom are most desirous you should come and *at whose pressing instance and solicitation I* n[ow] *address you.* The President of the Society is M[oses Hicks Grinnell?] brother of Mr. Joseph Grinnel[l] of House of Rep[resentative]s—and who is also at the head of one of our first Houses of Commerce here. The whole Society in fact is composed of and officered by our most active classes here.

I have long desired to have you visit this quarter and I can safely say I don[']t know a period or occasion when you could do so *under more agreeable and desirable circumstances.* It is in so [*sic*; no] way political—it is a mere assemblage of a *segment* of the great family *circle* of New Englanders. They will greet you enthusiastically partly because some of y[ou]r views are in a national point of view in accordance with theirs—partly because tho' not born among them *you were educated among* [them] and because they are always ready to do [*mutilation*] to eminent ability. Be assured therefore your acceptance and presence will give great satisfaction and pleasure. If you can remain a day or two after the dinner our City Authorities will be too happy to do you honor. Come to Balt[im]o[re] or Phil[adelphi]a the first day—and the next to N.Y. I w[oul]d advise that you come to Phil[adelphi]a the first day then leaving the next morning you will reach here by 2 o[']C[lock; "P.M." *interlined*]. This hour will enable y[ou]r friends to meet and escort you to y[ou]r rooms at the Astor House where the dinner comes off that ev[enin]g. There will be no exposure to weather—the travelling is perfect and once here you will not think of or know what the weather is. Y[ou]r whole time will be rendered agreeable.

You must come—we can't permit you to sa[*mutilation*] *on this occasion.* You shall have every thing y[ou]r o[*mutilation*] after you get here—go where you please do what you please—*Only Come.* Let me know your time of leaving and when you purpose arriving and you shall be met on the way & shown your way to our City.

If this was "high party time" and knowing y[ou]r reluctance to party junketing I should say don[']t accept—but it is not so, the public mind is calm and quiet—(tho' deep) and this is purely a Social meeting in which all conservative interest[s] join—an era of good feeling—just such a meeting as you will appreciate and enjoy—and I repeat my assurance to you it is just such an event as I could desire to see you here to meet and be met by. You will be surrounded by many old friends—and every one present will strive [to ex]press to you their warmest assurances of good [*mutilation*]. The weather is most favorable for the jaunt and you will be very happy all the time.

Do therefore be for once prevailed on to oblige *many* & none more than Y[ou]r Ob[edien]t Serv[an]t, Ch: Aug: Davis.

ALS in ScCleA.

To WILSON LUMPKIN, [Athens, Ga.]

Washington, 13th Dec[embe]r 1846
My old friend, Your letter reached our post office after I left home, & I received it at Aiken on my way. I have delayed answering it until I had time to understand something of the state of things here.

I see by the correctness of your views & remarks, that you keep well up with the course of events. You are right in thinking, that there is no immediate prospect of the termination of the Mexican war. Indeed, I cannot well see how it is to be terminated. Our administration cannot well agree to any treaty, which will not make large cession of territories without being utterly prostrated after taking, the grounds, they have; while, on the other hand, S[ant]a Anna cannot agree to make such cession, without his utter overthrow. But suppose that difficulty overcome, another still more formidable ["still" *canceled*] remains. Whatever may be the cession, it will be almost impossible, from present appearances, for the treaty to be ratified. If it should be silent on the subject of slavery in the ceded territory, the North will oppose it, & if it should prohibit slavery the South would; and in either event, there would not be a constitutional Majority. If to this ["it" *canceled*] be added, the danger of the interposition of England, Russia & France should the war be prolonged, the prospect is far from being a cheerful one, in reference to its termination, or the consequences like to grow out of it.

Entertaining these views, & believing that the war might have been easily avoided, & that it had its origin in an unconstitutional stretch of power on the part of the Executive [James K. Polk], I came here prepared to incur any responsibility and to make any sacrifice to bring it to an early termination, should I be able to see my way how it could be done. But I have looked in every direction without seeing any possible way by which it can be done. All I can do at present is to wait & see. It is easy to get into a war, but hard usually to get out of one. Had I been backed at the last session by a single Senator of any weight or influence on our side, or had a single day been allowed for deliberation, the war would have been averted. I go farther; had my solicitude to preserve peace with England not been greater than to preserve it with Mexico, I would have stopt the latter by moving a resolution to arrest the March of [Zachary] Taylor to the Rio Grand[e], & stopt the war thereby.

I know well the old spoils men will never forgive me. All the attacks you allude to comes from them. [David J.?] McCord, one of them, is the author of the article in the [Southern Quarterly] Review. He was a [William H.] Crawford man. I have not seen the article in the [Athens, Ga., Southern] Banner attacking my letter in reference to the mode of appointing electors in our State. But it comes from the same mint[?], I dare say. They may well be bitter. Their days are numbered; & they feel it. They are understood & the people have lost all confidence in them. Under their lead, should they attempt to force the party to follow it at the next election, they will be signally defeated. The party has fought too many battles for their exclusive benefit, and to its lasting injury. It is time they should stand aside & give way to more faithful & able leaders. You are right. Georgia, & not only Georgia, but ever[y] other State, which have been long under the control of the N. York school, is in danger of sink[ing] down under the old federal doctrines; and, if the leaders of that school shall longer have the control, the whole Union will.

You ask me to keep you informed of the undercurrent here. The most singular of these currents is a reconciliation & union of the administration & [Thomas H.] Benton. He is to be their leader in the Senate it is said & believed, and is in favour, I understand, of pushing the Mexican war to the utmost; notwithstanding the stand he took on the Texian question, as to boundary. This cannot, it is thought, po[i]nt, to [Silas] Wright as the successor, in case Polk cannot run again. He will carry but a very small portion of the party with him. The 54.40 [men] are decidedly opposed to him & the administration in feeling. Indeed there is little cohesion in the party. The whigs are not much better off. It will be difficult for them to rally, either as to men, or measures. The question under [David] Wilmot's resolution, which will be sure to come up this session, will throw both parties asundunder [*sic*], and tend strongly to draw a sectional line. Indeed, the Mexican question under all ["its" *interlined*] aspects, tend[s] strongly that way. The whigs can make nothing by opposing the Tariff act of the last session. I regard free trade as established, unless prevented by the expenditures of the Mexican war. It is only by that, and the disasters, which may accompany the war, that they have the least prospect of reaching power.

A word as to my own position. However much opposed to the decleration of the war, & the policy that lead to it, I shall give my support to bring it to a speedy & satisfactory termination. I must take things as they are, & not as I would have had them, had I possessed the control. To do my duty under whatever circumstances I may be placed, is the rule, which guides me, but I shall hold those, who have ["made" *canceled*] unnecessarily placed us in a state of war, accountable for consequences.

I shall at all times be happy to hear from you. Present me kindly to Mrs. [Annis Hopkins] L[umpkin] & your family. Yours truly, J.C. Calhoun.

ALS in NcD, John C. Calhoun Papers. NOTE: The article by McCord to which Calhoun refers was unsigned. It was a bitter attack on Calhoun's position at the Memphis Convention as abandonment of South Carolina principles. See "Mr. Calhoun and the Mississippi," *Southern Quarterly Review*, vol. 10, no. 20 (October, 1846), pp. 441–512.

From F[RANCIS] W. PICKENS

Edgewood [Edgefield District, S.C.,] 13 Dec[e]m[be]r 1846
My dear Sir, After I returned from selling some cotton in Hamburg I heard you had passed on down by Mr. [Thomas G.] Clemson's place. I am sorry you did not come by. I would have answered your last only that I was on the River and did not recieve it for some time after it was written and until near the time when you would be going on to Washington.

As the time is now past when those, who thought proper to prejudice you and yours ag[ain]st me, have done all they could do and have effected their purposes, I now take the opportunity to say that they gave the most extravagant, exaggerated, and false account of every thing I said and did at the public meeting held Saleday in June last at Edgefield.

The truth is that at the first meeting held the Saturday ["week" *interlined*] before Saleday I refused to attend upon the ground that I would not give any aid to any thing that might appear to conflict at that time with your position. And at the meeting of the committee afterwards that was then appointed I expressly said in advance that nothing must be suggested calculated to reflect on your course. I was appointed Chairman of the Committee. Mr. [Francis H.?] Wardlaw, N[athan] L. Griffin, Mr. W[hitfield] Brooks, Col. P[reston S.] Brooks & W[illia]m C. Moragne were all present and will recollect this fact. We could *hear nothing* authentic as to your course & the reasons from Washington. You *did not write a word* to me or to any one that we heard of.

The public meeting for Saleday in June was called and for several days previous I had been very sick, and on that day I was very unwell, more so than I had been for ten years, and had in the morning written in to say I would not attend. Mr. Brooks & Mr. Griffin both wrote to me and insisted that I should go in if merely to ["be" *interlined*] present and introduce the resolutions (which ["reflected" *canceled*] made not the slightest reflection on any human being). I did so in great pain and suffering. The whole object of the meeting was to get up ["volunteers" *canceled*] a war feeling and procure volunteers to sustain the Government. And what remarks I made were made entirely with this view. Immediately after I was done I was very sick—so much so that the Dr. had to give me laud[a]num. Col: [John] Bauskett was speaking and I left in my carriage without dreaming there was to be any opposition. After I left Col: [Louis T.] Wigfall ["introduced" *interlined*] the resolutions in relation to yourself and they were laid on the table by an almost unanimous vote as I understood. I *was not there* and never heard of what was done or said in reference to yourself until the next day, and yet I have been *made responsible for all that was said and done.*

Mr. Wardlaw was chairman of the meeting and he and his immediate friends were pleased with any thing that might injure me. I said the next day to those gentlemen who called to see me, that a full and true statement of the whole proceedings ought to be given. It was said that Mr. Wardlaw[,] Chairman[,] and Wigfall had come to an understanding that the rejected resolutions should not be published &c. I said then it was wrong and false impressions would be made. But after it was done, and the suppressed resolutions were informally published in a Hamburg paper with comments, I waited for Wardlaw to give a true account as Chairman. My relations to him were such that I could say nothing to him about it. The papers in this district being only weekly, in the mean time every sort of comment and rumor got out and Wardlaw made no statement. I then saw the object and how the matter was to be used. It was at the time privately known here to those actively engaged in it that Mr. [George] McDuffie would resign his seat. After all these occurrences I was too proud to come out and appear to explain with a view to ward off your powerful name and influence which had been, in the mean time, extensively invoked ag[ain]st me by letters as well as newspaper comments. It was true that I had differed widely with you on the course you thought proper to pursue on the Mexican war

bill &c, and had regret[t]ed that course more on your own account
and proper influence than any thing else, and this was all. But I was
awkwardly situated. It may be a weakness, but I have ever despised
to appear to court any man, and as for seeking popular favour under
the wing of any man living I scorn to do it. And nothing but strict
Justice & Truth ["now" *canceled*] induce me now to say any thing of
the past. Circumstances have now *transpired and been fully developed* which enable me to do so and preserve every manly sentiment which it has been my pride to cherish.

What proves that, the whole object was to effect local purposes,
is that Col: [Franklin H.] Elmore two weeks before the meeting at
Edgefield in June, at a meeting in Columbia uttered precisely the
same sentiments that I did, and advocated exactly the same resolutions in substance, and yet not a word of complaint has been suggested ag[ain]st him for his course. I have given you this full statement of what I did and the circumstances attending it freely and
candidly, and any thing to the contrary is false and was made for political effect by *anonymous scribblers.*

I have served ["the" *canceled*] a portion of the people of So.
Carolina in some capacity or other for the last fifteen years and I
have never yet approached any man or set of men to seek favour or
office. In the many trying and exciting scenes through which I have
passed, as God is my judge! I have never, for one moment, felt a single emotion or aspiration seperate from the honor and the interests of
South Carolina.

I could have recieved the Mission to Austria from [Martin] Van
Buren; and you recollect in the Summer of 1843, at your house, when
Mr. [Abel P.] Upshur Sec[re]t[ar]y of State wrote you on the subject
of presenting some friend of yours for the Mission to France, you
urged me to allow you to present my name and I refused it. And
when Mr. [James K.] Polk offered me the Mission to England I can
proudly say that I am the *only man* who ever refused such an office
expressly upon the avowed ground that "I could not accept it consistently with the feelings of allegiance I bear my own State." At
that time the Tariff was not adjusted and I would not have taken any
office from the Federal Government.

I have *been by you* when you *needed friends,* and when to *stand
by you* was *no gain* to any man. You have recieved more flattery
from others, but in our past intercourse I have nothing to regret.

As I never expect to have any concern in public affairs again I
felt it due to you as well as to myself that I should say what I have

in relation to this matter, and to let you know, that however seperated our spheres may be hereafter, yet you *shall,* as you have [*"ever"
canceled*] *ever* done, command my highest regard and admiration.
Very truly, F.W. Pickens.

ALS in ScCleA; variant ALS (retained copy?) in ScU-SC, John C. Calhoun
Papers; PC in Jameson, ed., *Correspondence,* pp. 1099–1102.

To CALVIN GRAVES, Raleigh, N.C.

Washington, 14th Dec[embe]r 1846
Dear Sir, I have given the subject of your note due consideration;
and must say, that I am of the opinion, that there is no Constitutional
objection to the legislature of a State altering the Congressional
Districts. The wording of the Constitution would seem sufficiently
broad to permit it; and it has often been done by different States,
without being objected to on constitutional grounds, as far as I am
informed.

But I regard alterations made with party views, without regard
to convenience or a fair & full expression of the voice of the State as
highly objectionable, and such, I believe to be the feeling of the great
body of the people. I have never known an instance of the kind,
which has not been followed by a reaction; and I am of the impression, that the best mode of opposing attempts to make such alterations is to point out clearly & fully their inconvenience & inequality.
With great respect I am & &, J.C. Calhoun.

ALS in ScU-SC, John C. Calhoun Papers.

From JOHN HASTINGS

New Garden, Columbiana C[ount]y Ohio
Dec. 14, 1846
Dear Sir, If you have a spare paper containing your opinion of the
People of your State choosing the Presidential Electors, instead of
the legislature, I would be much gratified if you would transmit it to
me. Much is said here about your sentiments on the subject, and I
am anxious to have it in my power (the article not having been pub-

lished here) to do them justice. Most respectfully Yours as ever, John Hastings.

[P.S.] We have not got the President[']s message yet.

ALS in ScCleA.

By Dr. William L. Jenkins, [Pendleton], 12/15. Jenkins recorded in his daybook a medical visit to the Calhoun household: "Hon. John C. Calhoun. To visit & prescription boy Ellick. [$]2.00." Entry in ScCM, Waring Historical Library, William L. Jenkins Daybook, 1840–1848, p. 61.

Memorial of the Charleston Chamber of Commerce, presented by Calhoun to the Senate on 12/15. This document, dated 12/4, requests construction of a new Custom House at Charleston. The existing building is inadequate, especially in the light of increased demands under the warehouse provision of the recent tariff law. The building now in use can be sold advantageously. The memorial is signed by Ker Boyce, President of the Chamber of Commerce, and attested by William B. Heriot, Secretary. (It was ordered to be printed and referred to the Committee on Commerce.) DS in DNA, RG 46 (U.S. Senate), 29A-G3.2; PC in Senate Document No. 8, 29th Cong., 2nd Sess. (Calhoun made unreported remarks in support of the petition: Charleston, S.C., *Mercury*, December 21, 1846, p. 2.)

Memorial of George Harvey, presented by Calhoun to the Senate on 12/15. In this document, dated 12/5, Harvey, of Charleston, agent for the owners and insurers of the British ship *James Mitchell*, asks to receive certain expenses due to him from an 1830 act for the relief of Alexander Claxton. That act was apparently related to a legal case in Fla. against Claxton, U.S. Navy officer who had seized the ship. Harvey encloses numerous supporting documents and states that the Treasury Department has declined to pay the sum due him. (The memorial was referred to the Committee on Claims.) DS in DNA, RG 46 (U.S. Senate), 30A-H2.

From JAMES LARNED

[Washington] 16 Dec[embe]r 1846

Sir, In behalf of the Committee of arrangements, for celebrating the 225th Anniversary of the Landing of the Pilgrims, I have the honor to invite you, as one of the Selected Guests, to partake of a dinner to be given at Coleman[']s [Hotel] on Tuesday the 22d inst. at 6 o[']cl[oc]k P.M. and, to ask the favor of an answer. With great respect Sir Y[ou]r mo[st] Ob[edient] S[ervan]t, James Larned, Ch[airman,] Com[mittee of] Arr[angements].

ALS in ScCleA. NOTE: An AEU by Calhoun reads "Invitation to celebrate the Landing of the Pilgrims."

To HENDRICK B. WRIGHT, [Wilkes-Barré, Pa.]

Washington, 16th Dec[embe]r 1846
My dear Sir, You mistake in supposing, that I have the power of making the modification in the act of the last session, which you suggest. I hold it to be one of those modifications, which would be opposed, not only by the free trade party, but the great body of the advocates of protection, with Mr. [Daniel] Webster at their head. Indeed, I understood him to declare in his place at the last session, that he would vote against that, or any other partial exception. The protective system can only stand on the ground of protection to all, or none of articles manufactured at home, and it is only on that ground, that the protective duty on sugar, molasses, Iron & coal has ever been supported by the New England States.

But were it in my power, it is due in candor to say, that I could not make it consistently with my views & principles. My conviction is strong, that the power to raise & collect taxes & & & & is a revenue power exclusively, & cannot be used as an instrum[en]t for protection, or any other purpose, without a dangerous perversion of the power. I am also of the impression, that what is called protection, when it is extended to all discription of articles made, or raised in the Union is no protection at all; but a great impediment to production, and that experience, if the trial should ever be fairly made, would prove it so.

It is true, at the last session, when the act was on its passage, I was willing to agree by common consent to a modification of the duties, on a principle, which I understood, would be acceptable to those interested in the coal & Iron business, as a present adjustment. I was willing, because I regarded it more important to effect less by the common consent of all parties, than more, to be followed by the continuance of the conflict between the parties. But it was soon found, that the difficulty of obtaining the consent of the party leaders on the whig side, was fully as great, as to obtain that of the democrats.

I have received your suggestions in the sperit they were offered, as coming from a personal & political friend, and I feel assured you will, as such, appreciate the perfect candour with which I have expressed myself. You will of course understand, what I have said, as intended for yourself. Yours truly, J.C. Calhoun.

ALS in PWbWHi, Hendrick B. Wright Papers; microfilm of ALS in NjP, Hendrick B. Wright Papers.

To Mrs. G. W. [ELIZABETH CLEMSON] BARTON, [Philadelphia]

Washington, 17th Dec[embe]r 1846

My dear Madam, I take the liberty of enclosing the within account of Cornelius & Co. with a check for the amount, as I infer that they are articles you got of them for Mrs. [Floride Colhoun] Calhoun. The check is made payable to Mr. Barton, and I will thank you to have it delivered to them with his name endorsed. I forwarded your letter to [Martha] Cornelia [Calhoun], which came under cover to me a few days since.

Present me kindly to Judge [George W.] Barton. With great respect yours truly, J.C. Calhoun.

ALS in ScU-SC, John C. Calhoun Papers. NOTE: Elizabeth Clemson Barton was the sister of Calhoun's son-in-law, Thomas G. Clemson.

To JAMES ED[WARD] CALHOUN, [Columbia, S.C.]

Washington, 17th Dec[embe]r 1846

My dear James, Some time before I left home, I enclosed a check to you on Mr. [John Ewing] Bonneau for $40. I have not since heard from you, & fear that my letter with the check has miscarried. I write now to request you to write me on the receipt of this, & to inform me, whether you received my letter & check; and if you did, whether you paid as I requested, two dollars for me to the

Editor of the [Columbia] Palmetto [State Banner; "as I requested" *canceled*]. I hope you are getting on well, & continue to be pleased with the Institution [South Carolina College]. I feel great confidence, that you will pass through with credit to yourself. You want nothing but application & perseverance to do so, and I do not think you will prove lacking in either.

Congress, as yet, remains in a state of quite [*sic*], & will continue so, until after the holy days. It is generally thought, it will be a stormy session; but I doubt it. It will, in my opinion, be characterized rather by confusion & distraction, as there is but little harmony in the ranks of either party.

We are now in the midst of a severe snow storm, which, I fear, will terminate in a cold & disagreeable winter. My health is good, & thus far, I have, in a great measure, escaped the colds to which I have been so subject to [*sic*] here in the winter. I hope your health remains good. When I left home Willie [William Lowndes Calhoun] was fast recovering from his severe attack. Your affectionate father, J.C. Calhoun.

ALS in ScU-SC, John C. Calhoun Papers.

From WILSON LUMPKIN

Athens [Ga.,] Dec. 17th 1846

My dear Sir, I have just read your favor of the 13th Inst. The views which you entertain upon the subjects to which ["you" *interlined*] advert, very nearly coincide with my own, perhaps entirely so.

But I drop you this hasty line, for the purpose of saying—that I foresee all the difficulties which you suggest, in bringing the war to a speedy & honorable termination. And to add, that nothing short of a vigorous prosecution of the war, on our part, can ["now" *interlined*] force the Mexican authorities to terms. For as you justly remark, we cannot now get out of the war with any degree of credit, except by large accessions of Territory—and such concessions will not be made by Mexico, but as a last resort to maintain her existance as a people. I should have rejoiced, if this war could have been avoided—but it is now, beyond our controul—except by prosecuting it to a final issue.

The responsibility of the war, & its consequences must & does rest upon the shoulders of, *the powers that be*, & time must & will

31

soon determine how much of good & evil will be the result. Secretary [of the Treasury Robert J.] Walker[']s report is an able one. Fully aware of the danger of *sectional* divisions in our confederacy, I fear they cannot much longer be avoided.

For myself, there are not one man in a thousand, in what is called the free States, that I would be willing to trust with the administration of the Federal Govt. Their unreasonable prejudices & assumptions, to me as an individual is altogether intollerable—I would make no compromises with them, except such as may now be found in our National Compact.

As far as you can in conscience, afford to the administration, the means of prosecuting the war—and while the war is still progressing, it may not be wise or prudent, to expose the errors in its prosecution. Truly y[ou]r friend, Wilson Lumpkin.

ALS in ScCleA; variant PC in Boucher and Brooks, eds., *Correspondence*, pp. 364–365.

From LOUIS MCLANE

Baltimore, Dec. 17, [18]46

My dear Sir, I have hesitated about writing you this letter, and yet, as I am quite sure you will acknowledge it to be disinterested, even if you should deem my suggestions not the soundest, I must believe you will not consider it altogether unworthy your attention.

I am sincerely desirous that you, and such as you, should maintain, if you cannot increase your power in the Country, and in the party; and as I have an impression that, in the latter at least, a crisis is approaching, I have felt a good deal of solicitude as to the position you may be induced to take.

I cannot be mistaken, I think, in supposing that for some time to come, the *war* will be the engrossing topic in the Country, and the course the opposition seems to have resolved upon must constitute it the absorbing criterion of our party divisions. Domestic measures will by & by come up, & have their share in our coming struggles, but, for the present session certainly, the policy of the government in regard to the war will be that of the deepest interest with the great body of the People. It is equally plain, that the great Democratic party to maintain its ascendency must rally cordially in support of the war, and that those leaders who exert their talents on the side of their Country will acquire the greatest popular advantages. It seems to me that the Country is too deeply involved and has too much at hazard to allow any public man to embarrass the administration, or to risk his power by casting doubt over the causes or policy which have brought ["it" *canceled and* "the war" *interlined*] on. The war is popular with the great masses, and public opinion will be very apt to visit those who are endeavouring to obstruct its progress with a [*one or two illegible words canceled*] condemnation scarcely less than ["those" *changed to* "that"] which followed the federal opposition to the War of 1813. I have no doubt that the war will strengthen the adm[inistratio]n and the party, and those whose talents and exertions may most contribute to defend and support it will, by the same means, confirm and strengthen their hold upon the popular support. Whatever may be thought of the reasonableness of it, I feel persuaded that the course of our eminent public men upon this subject will constitute the standard by which their claims upon the Country will be judged. I must confess to you that I cannot look upon this as a subject for regret. We suffer more in the estimation of the world ["from"(?) *canceled and* "from" *interlined*] our party divisions than from any other cause; and nothing tends more to weaken confidence in our institutions than the spectacle of one of our great parties uniformly taking part against the justice of our cause in all our disputes with foreign powers. I am, therefore, most solicitous that, in the present crisis, your vigorous support of the adm[inistratio]n in the prosecution of the war with Mexico, should be as prominent and effectual as in the memorable war with England in 1813; and that now as then, you should command for yourself and your friends the same approbation; especially as a cordial support of the war, and an efficient defence of the President [James K. Polk] in conducting it would leave you room for greater independence in regard to other matters in which you might desire to practice it. You need no hint from me to acquaint you with the course of other sections of the party who will not fail to see that the divisions growing out of the war, and of the conduct of the opposition are to afford them the means of action, and who will not fail to construe lukewarmness into hostility.

I am not now for the first time to tell you how deeply I have lamented the tendency of our party organization, aided to be sure by numerous untoward and adventitious causes, to set aside superior men, and weaken their legitimate influence in the Country; and I confess to you that I look upon the present crisis, as calculated, if wisely improved, to arrest that tendency. The period of war is calculated to call forth the wisest patriotism and the boldest talents, and I cannot be mistaken in believing that such a grade of talent, if properly exerted, will assert its proper ascendency, and tower above mediocrity. The people will feel both pride & affection for the men who stand preeminent in such a crisis, and will ["be" *interlined*] as apt to rally round the foremost of those in the civil departments as in the military ranks of the Country. I confess I should regard the war as fortunate if it lead to this result.

I ought frankly to state that I have in ["a" *interlined*] great degree been induced to take the liberty I am now taking from an apprehension, after conversation with my son [Robert M. McLane], that your inclination at present was to stand still upon the subject of the war, and at a suitable time to take an opportunity of reviewing its causes, and of expressing your disapprobation of them. Believing that such a course would be fraught with incalculable injury, I should not discharge my duty ["not to" *canceled and* "if I did not" *interlined*] express an earnest hope that further reflection would lead you to take a different view of the subject. I am, it is true, younger than you, and have had less experience of public life; but I cannot I think be mistaken in believing that such a course would lose you the advantages of your present position, and rank you among the opposition. The People at large, and the great body of the party are making great sacrifices, perhaps something of opinion, in support of the war, and they will expect their leading public men to do the same. Their power is now assailed on the ground of the war, and they will expect their eminent friends to stand by them. The opposition profess, while they condemn the origin of the war, and denounce its authors, to unite in its vigorous prosecution, but the great body of the Party will expect their friends to do [*one word canceled and* "much" *interlined*] more, and to exhibit a marked contrast with their opponents in this respect. I believe more over that a cordial union, and a steady perseverance ["among" *canceled and* "with" *interlined*] the Democratic party to use the war as the means of strengthening its popularity in the Country, will more than anything else give it the power of breaking down the abolition party and the other factions rising up in different parts of the Country. Indeed, without some such element, I am at a loss to conceive how these factions can be effectually overcome. They will be found to have gained strength just in proportion as the general party action in the Country has been, ["from any cause whatever," *interlined*] weakened; and if by using the present crisis to infuse into it new vigour, and create a new bond, we can bring the party out of the present as it emerged from the war of 1813, it may defy abolition and all other factions. The whigs might have avoided this; it is now too late, and if we have the wisdom to profit by their folly, the spirit of old times will be revived, and the men whose real talent & exertion have contributed to the results cannot fail to occupy their just position in the public mind.

Then again, is it not worth while to consider, whether the present crisis do not afford the occasion to efface once & forever all the divisions which have ["hitherto" *canceled*] hitherto tended to alienate some of our most eminent men from the great body of the party, and thereby enabled others of less pretension to recommend themselves to the popular support? I am sure this could be done; and that those who on the present occasion shall be most prominently & most effectual in sustaining their cause, will be the first to receive the proofs of their gratitude and confidence.

I feel however, Sir that ["where" *canceled and* "to one to whom" *interlined*] I should only be justified in giving intimations, I am swelling this letter beyond all reasonable limits, and I will therefore, bring it to a close.

In the hope, therefore, that I may have made you any suggestion worthy of your reflection, I add only the assurance of the sincere regard & esteem, with which I am, your friend, and obedient Servant, Louis McLane.

ALS in ScCleA.

From FRANCIS WHARTON

Phil[adelphia], Dec. 17, 1846

My dear Sir, I sent a package to you about a month's since [*sic*] containing a copy of a work on Criminal Law I have just published. It was directed to you at Columbia, but I have just learned that through some accident it is still in Charleston. I only hope that it will not arrive too late to secure your good will, and to awake your kind recollections.

I was labouring under a very severe attack of illness during the summer which incapacitated me from all business, and left me for some time unfit for active mental exertion. I prepared, however, a few remarks on your most admirable Memphis report, ["about" *interlined*] which I corresponded with Mr. [Freeman] Hunt, of the

Merchants Magazine [and Commercial Review], but which, from an alleged dread of their partisan character, but ["really" *interlined*] from ["a real" *canceled*] an increased political costiveness, he has delayed publishing.

You will receive from me in the course of a day or two a letter of introduction to young Mr. [Thomas L.] Kane, of Philadelphia, a gentleman of considerable talent and no little ambition. He is desirous of obtaining an appointment in the Mexican struggle, and though I do not suppose you take much supervision of the distribution of administration patronage, & I have promised to mention the subject to you & do so accordingly. Very truly your obliged friend, Francis Wharton.

ALS in ScCleA. NOTE: Wharton's work referred to was *A Treatise on the Criminal Law of the United States* . . . (Philadelphia: J. Kay & Brother, 1846).

To T[HOMAS] G. CLEMSON, [Brussels]

Washington, 18th Dec[embe]r 1846

My dear Sir, This will be delivered to you by W.C. [*sic;* William H.] Vesey Esq[uir]e to whom I take pleasure in introducing you.

He has been appointed Consul to Antwerpe, & will of course stand in intimate official relations to you.

My personal acquaintance with him is slight; but he comes recommended to me from quarters worthy of confidence; as an amiable, worthy & intelligent citizen. Yours truly, J.C. Calhoun.

ALS in ScCleA.

From WILSON SHANNON, [former Governor of Ohio]

St. Clairsville [Ohio], Dec. 18th 1846

My D[ea]r Sir, The name of my friend B.F. Brown Esq[ui]re of this State, has, or will be, presented to the President [James K. Polk] for the appointment of Secretary of the Territory of Oregon—an office which will be created and filled during the present session of congress. Mr. Brown is a democrat of the [Thomas] Jefferson school[,] is a firm and reliable friend and I should be pleased to see him rec[e]ive the appointment he desires. He is a young man of good character and high standing—has rec[e]ived a classical education, is an attorney of respectable standing and is familliar with western life. I have no doubt; should he be appointed, but he will fill the office with credit to himself and advantage to the country. If you can aid him in any way I would be gratified if you would do so.

I would be pleased to hear from you at any time your leisure will permit. Yours with great respect, Wilson Shannon.

ALS in ScCleA.

From [JAMES K. POLK]

Washington, Saturday morning, Dec[embe]r 19th 1846
The President presents his respects to Mr. Calhoun, and requests that he will do him the favour to call on him to day. If it shall be convenient to Mr. Calhoun, the President will be pleased to see him, between 4 & 5 O'Clock this afternoon.

ADU in ScCleA.

From R[ICHARD] K. CRALLÉ

Elwah Cottage [Lynchburg, Va.], Dec[embe]r 20th 1846
My dear Sir: I have not heard from you since we parted in the mountains; and am ignorant as to what is transpiring in the political world. Mr. [Vincent] Witcher who called on me yesterday, and who is just from Richmond, can give me very little information in regard to the under currents there. Though a member of the Senate, he is, (being a Whig) not let into the secrets of the opposite Party. From what he tells me, however, there can be no doubt that the friends of [William] Smith and [John W.] Jones are bitterly hostile and earnestly engaged. The result, he thinks doubtful; and inclines to the opinion that neither being able to concentrate the vote of the Party, some third man will have to be taken up [to support for U.S. Senator]. Should this be so, it is highly probable the contest will finally be between [James] McDowell or [George C.] Dromgoole on the one side, and [Robert M.T.] Hunter on the other. It is important that the two former should be defeated, a result which will

be certain if Hunter's friends remain firm; for he will assuredly carry the Whig vote, as being less obnoxious than either of the other two. Witcher tells me that, as yet no developements have been made as to the Presidency: but I have no doubt emmissaries are at work, and that we shall see more after the election of Senator. The late election of [William] Daniel to the Court of Appeals indicates an unhealthy state in the Legislature. He is a young man without the qualifications of information or experience. He is a Hunker in principle, and the only reason of his election, so far as I can see, is found in the fact that his name had been mentioned in connection with the Senatorial election. The fact illustrates the truth you once adverted to viz. the disposition every where to push older men out of the arenna [*sic*], as in the nomination of [James K.] Polk.

The Message of the President has been, I think, very generally approved, especially in regard to the main question, the Mexican war. He will be sustained in the *strongest measures*. This, I think, is certain, whatever may be the real merits of the controversy. It is stated in the papers that you, amongst others, have declined the appointment of Chairman of Foreign Affairs in the Senate; and the public are at fault as to the cause. So far as you are concerned I suppose that you have, very properly, declined to become the exponent of the Executive in a matter to which you were originally opposed. If Santa Anna pursue a wise course he will make the Government deeply regret it had not taken your counsel at first. Still it seems to me prudent and patriotic to sustain energetic measures; however unwisely we may have been precipitated into the war. This opinion I venture to express although I am fully aware that mere expenditure of blood & treasure is not the least of the evils likely to flow from it. The creation of popular *Heroes* are to be much more deprecated. Already an embryo President [Zachary Taylor] has been engendered at Monterey, and I fear more than one is in the process of parturition. But the state of public opinion is such that it will tolerate no counsels that look not to the vigorous prosecution of the contest. Wise warnings are in vain, as the past sufficiently proves.

I hear from many quarters of most favourable impressions left from your visit last summer. It has made you many ardent friends throughout the western portion of the State, and will exercise no small influence in the future. I am preparing to move up to my farm in early part of the next summer, where I shall probably spend the most of my time hereafter. I do not despair of some tolerable success in wool-growing after a year or so. Mrs. [Elizabeth Morris]

C[rallé] is not entirely reconciled to the seculsion [*sic*] of a mountain life; but I have no doubt that experiment will prove it to be less irksome than she at present imagines. She is now fast recovering from her confinement, after having presented [me] with a fine boy; and desires me to make her best regards to Mrs. [Floride Colhoun] Calhoun, yourself and family, and, at the same time to express with me, an united wish that you and they may consent to pass a portion of the summer with us every year. Our log cabins will be completed early in the next summer, and we shall wherewithal [*sic*] to offer you a hearty mountain welcome.

Appropos [*sic*], Capt. [George C.] Hutter whose nomination is now before the Senate, after having been for several years suspended from his command, begs me to ask you to examine his case. He is a meritorious man, as I hear, and has been badly treated. The citizens here intended to have held a public meeting for the purpose of urging his restoration to the service; but the nomination of the President renders it unnecessary. I wish it may be in your power to serve him.

When at leisure pray drop me a line, and believe me to be ever sincerely yours, R.K. Crallé.

ALS in ScCleA.

To JAMES LARNED, "Ch[airman,] Com[mittee of] Arr[angements]"

Washington, 21st Dec[embe]r 1846

Sir, I am highly honored by the invitation tendered by you, in behalf of the Committee of arrangement, to partake of a dinner, to be given on the 22d Inst., in celebration of the 225th Anniversary of the landing of the Pilgrims. I regret it will not be in my power to attend; but although absent, I wish you an agreeable & happy celebration.

Well may their de[s]cendants regard with pride the landing of their Pilgrim Fathers on the rock of Plymouth. Never was a colony commenced under appearently such unfavourable circumstances; and yet never has one grown with greater vigour, and attained, in so short a period, higher prosperity and greatness. It is now just two centuries and a quarter since they landed from a single small vessel on a barren coast, inhabited by feirce savage tribes, in the midest of winter, in a climate of almost artick severity, with scanty means & without the protection or countenance of the parent country. In spite of all these formidable difficulties, their de[s]cendants, in the short interval, that has intervened, have become a numerous, wealthy & highly cultivated people, constituting a large and distinguished portion of a federated Community extending from Ocean to Ocean, and already ranking with the first powers of the world, and still increasing in all the elements of greatness, with a rapidity beyond all former example. By what causes has so inconsiderable a begin[n]ing, under such formidable &, appearantly, almost insurmountable difficulties, resulted, in so brief a period, in such mighty consequences? They are to be found in the high moral & intellectual qualities of the Pilgrims; their faith, piety & confident trust in a superint[end]ing Providence; their stern virtues ["& courage" *canceled*]; their patriotism & love of liberty & order; their devotion to learning; & their indomitable courage & perseverance. These are the causes, which surmounted every obstacle & which have lead to such mighty results.

I avail myself of the occasion to offer the following sentiment.

The de[s]cendants of the Pilgrims; May they long continue to celebrate the Anniversary of the ["landing of their" *interlined*] Pilgrim Fathers, & preserve those high moral & intellectual qualities, which enable them to overcome all difficulties, & to lay the foundation of the prosperity & greatness of their posterity. With great respect yours & &, J.C. Calhoun.

ALS in ScU-SC, John C. Calhoun Papers; PC in the Richmond, Va., *Whig and Public Advertiser*, December 29, 1846, p. 4; PC in the Washington, D.C., *Daily Union*, December 30, 1846, p. 1. NOTE: An account of the proceedings of the celebration in the *Daily Union* indicates that Calhoun's letter was read and "received with applause," when the following toast was given: "*The Hon. John C. Calhoun*: A luminous star in the galaxy of American patriots; alike distinguished for intellectual brilliancy and power, as for the unblemished purity of his life, and the charms of his social intercourse." Isaac E. Holmes represented Calhoun at the event.

To F[RANKLIN] H. ELMORE, Charleston

Washington, 26th Dec[embe]r 1846

My dear Sir, I see no impediment to prevent the restoration of intercourse between Col. [William C.] Preston & myself. Indeed, I never regarded the fact, that we took different sides in politicks, while colleagues, as a sufficient reason for suspending our intercourse. As I assumed the right myself of independent judgement, I cheerfully accorded it to him; & left it to the unbiased decision of the State to decide, which was right, or which wrong. I, accordingly, kept ["up" *interlined*] our intercourse, until he suspended it. I left the last card & made the last bow, and never interposed the least obstacle in the way of his restoring himself to the favour of the State.

I got Judge [Andrew P.] Butler's letter [of 12/5], to which you refer, & responded [*not found*] to it in the same kind sperit in which it was written. I see no reason to doubt of harmonious feelings & action between us.

I hope the remittance of my son [Andrew Pickens Calhoun] of the sum necessary to renew the note will be received in time; but as it may not possibly, in consequence of the uncertainty, or delay of the mail, I hope it will not prevent the renewal. I am sure he will be punctual, but I know from experience the mail is subject both to considerable delay & uncertainty.

My estimate of the cotton crop [in Marengo County, Ala.] is founded on information derived through my son of the result of the crop in our neighbourhood, and of the members of Congress & others from the South West. I have not yet met with the first ["individual" *interlined*] that does not estimate the falling off in the Gulf ports at $1/3$, compared with last year. Below the 34th [parallel] it will greatly exceed that; while above, it will be hardly equal to last year's. Taking the two together, they all estimate the deficit of one third as ["a" *canceled*] moderate ["estimate" *canceled*]. If to this we add $1/3$ increase to the Atlantick ports, it will make, according to my estimate, less than 1,800,000 bales. Making, then, an allowance for the fact, that the bales, which fall off would average at least 450 pounds, while those, that will be added, will scarcely average 350, it will be found, that the true estimate, ["estimated"(?) *canceled*] in bales, compared with the last crop, will not exceed much, if any, 1,600,000. Such is my opinion, according to the best information I can obtain. The Western gentlemen tell me, that 500 pounds the bale would be a[s] near the truth for the Gulf bales than 450. They think the crop below 34 will be more than half short.

I enclose a letter [of 12/12/1846] of very considerable interest in reference to our rail road connection with Nashville, from Mr. [Vernon K.] Stevenson of that place. I have replied to him, that the information is too scanty for the Memoir, which I promised him I would prepare, if he would furnish me with the requisite information, & have indicated to him the additional information I would require; & informed him, that I would transmit ["it" *canceled and* "his letter" *interlined*] to you to be used to make a favourable impression in reference to the road, simultaniously [*sic*] with the appearance of the report of their Engineer. I would have sent it to [James] Gadsden, but I understand he is absent in Florida, knowing the great extent of your engagements. With the dattor [*sic; data*] contained ["in the letter" *interlined*], a suitable statement could easily be prepared. The road will give a great impulse to the business & growth of Charleston, & raise the stock of our road above par. Nothing ought to be omitted, calculated to rouse the attention of the Stock holders in our rail road and the citizens of Charleston to the importance of completing the connection between it & Nashville, as early as practical. Yours truly, J.C. Calhoun.

ALS in DLC, Franklin Harper Elmore Papers.

To A[NNA] M[ARIA CALHOUN] CLEMSON, [Brussels]

Washington, 27th Dec[embe]r 1846

My dear Daughter, The Cambria brought me Mr. [Thomas G.] Clemson's letter of the 14th Nov[embe]r, and yours to [Martha] Cornelia [Calhoun] of a corresponding date, which I forwarded to her immediately, after taking the liberty of reading it. I rejoice to learn, that you, & Mr. Clemson & the Children [John Calhoun Clemson and Floride Elizabeth Clemson] are in such good health, & that they continue to grow & improve so finely. After making all allowance for maternal partiality, I must believe, that they are all that could be desired. Indeed, all, who have seen them report them to be such. I enclose an answer to Calhoun's letter.

I also enclose a letter from your Mother [Floride Colhoun Calhoun], which will give you all the domestick & local news, I presume, of Pendleton & its vicinity.

Patrick [Calhoun] is now here, & looking remarkably well. He has been compliment[ed] by being elected the Col[o]n[el] of a Regiment of volunteers in the city of N. York, unanimously & and [*sic*] without solicitation. He is here in order to have it called into service, & he permitted to command it, without losing his commission in the line. Objections have been made by the [War] department, but he hopes to overcome them. However opposed to the declaration of the war, I cannot object to his going, & greatly prefer his going at the head of the Regiment, than as a subaltern in the line. He would be the youngest man, with a Col[o]n[el]'s commission, in service.

James [Edward Calhoun] continues to give good indications. He seems to be much attached to his studies & to be pleased with the institution [South Carolina College]. Col. [William C.] & Mrs. [Louise Davis] Preston have been very polite to him. I begin to have much hope of him.

Andrew [Pickens Calhoun] & family ["all" *canceled and* "were" *interlined*] well, when I last heard from them. He has three fine boys [Duff Green Calhoun, John Caldwell Calhoun, and Andrew Pickens Calhoun, Jr.]. He is very busey in preparing for a large crop to make up for the shortness of the present.

My own health is good, except, what is usual with me here, bad colds. I am very comfortably quartered at Hills, & have Mr. [Armistead] Burt & Martha [Calhoun Burt] in the joining room. The winter, thus far, has been pleasant.

Congress, as yet, has done nothing; but will, I suppose, begin in earnest after the 1st Jan[uar]y. The Mexican war is the great & absorbing question. Many now begin to see, that it is like to prove a very troublesome and embarrassing affair, to say no more; & to think, that I was right in opposing it. There is no seeing where or how it is to be ended. It is like to turn out as the war in Algeria has— a war between races & creed, which can only end in complete subjection of the weaker power—a thing not easily effected in either case. We have to boot the slave question mingled up with it. The present appearance is, that the ["North" *canceled*] scheme of the North is, that the South shall do all the fighting & pay all the expense, & they to have all the conquered territory. It is understood, that the North is united on [David] Wilmot's proposition to a man, & intend to act on it, when the country is conquered. What is to come of all this, time only can disclose. The present indication is, that the South will be united in opposition to the scheme. If they regard their safety they must defeat it, even should the Union be rent asunder.

As to myself, I am waiting for developements before I take my stand. My inaction & silence make [my] position more imposing. When ["the" *interlined*] time comes to act, I shall do, what duty requires be the consequences what they may. I desire above all things to save the whole; but if that cannot be, to save the portion where Providence has cast my lot, at all events. We never had a darker, or more uncertain future before us; and all from the rash ["& imprudent" *canceled*] step of rushing into war, when it could have been easily avoided, & when, if avoided, we had so clear a prospect before us. The Oregon question was as good as settled, & the settlement of that, would ["have" *interlined*] left little difficulty in settling the Mexican, ["leaving" *canceled and* "which would have given" *interlined*] a long & almost certain prospect of peace & prosperity.

Say to Mr. Clemson, that I have no farther intelligence about his place [in Edgefield District], since I passed by, & that Mr. [William A.] Harris has made another enquiry as to whether he would sell, through his father in law [John S. Jeter]. I forwarded his letter to his overseer as soon as received.

My love to him. Kiss the dear Children for their Grandfather, and tell them I wish to see them much. Your affectionate father, J.C. Calhoun.

ALS in ScCleA; variant PC in Jameson, ed., *Correspondence*, pp. 714–716.

To "Master" J[OHN] CALHOUN CLEMSON, [Brussels]

Washington, 27th Dec[embe]r 1846

My dear Grandson, Your letter made your Grand father very happy. He was happy to hear from you; happy to learn that you were well & to see that you could write so pretty a letter. He sent it to Grandmother in South Carolina, that she might be made happy too by reading it.

You must tell your sister [Floride Elizabeth Clemson], that she must learn to write too, & that I wish to get a letter from her. You must also kiss her for Grandfather. Your affectionate Grandfather, J.C. Calhoun.

ALS in ScCleA; PC in Jameson, ed., *Correspondence*, p. 716; PC in Cook, *John C. Calhoun–The Man*, p. 48.

To D[AVID] JOHNSON, [Governor of S.C.]

Senate Chamber, 29th Dec[embe]r 1846

My dear Sir, I have received two communications from you, in reference to the Staff officers of our regiment of volunteers, which I have laid before the delegation to be acted on. The papers are still with the President [James K. Polk], but I presume he will send in the nominations by Monday next [1/4/1847].

My principal object in writing now is, to state, that I learned last evening, that you had addressed to me, a recommendation of the Regiment in favour of Col. [Pierce M.] Butler for the place of Brigadier General, and to inform you, that it has not come to hand, as yet. I fear it has miscarried. With great respect yours truly, J.C. Calhoun.

ALS in ScU-SC, John C. Calhoun Papers.

Southern Rail Road Company to the public, [Vicksburg, Miss., 1846?]. This pamphlet describes the incorporation of the Southern Rail Road Company in Ala. and Miss. The company was capitalized at three million dollars to construct a railroad line from West Point, Ga., to Jackson, Miss. "with provisions to connect with, or . . . to own the links" between West Point and Montgomery, Ala. PC in *Southern Rail Road Company. Report of the Committee appointed by the Citizens of Vicksburg to obtain a Charter from the Legislatures of Alabama and Mississippi—Together with the Documents Accompanying the Same* [Vicksburg, 1846?] (a copy of which is among Calhoun's papers in ScCleA).

To S[amuel] C. Donaldson, [Baltimore, 1847?]. This two-page ms. was described as "an important political letter entirely about Henry Clay, and a firm establishment of the Republican party." ALS advertised for sale as Item 39 in *American Clipper: A Monthly Catalogue of American Historical and Literary Material* (Merion Station, Pa.: The American Autograph Shop), June, 1938, p. 211. (According to the advertisement the date of this letter was February 6, 1847, from Fort Hill. This must have been a misreading of the date since Calhoun was in Washington at that time.)

From A. P. STINSON

St. Joseph [Mich.,] Jan. 1, 1847
My dear Sir, After wishing you, in the true *Yankee Style,* a *"Happy New Year"* & many of them, I have to acknowledge the Rec[e]ipt of your verry [*sic*] interesting Letter of the 18 ultimo, which is *satis-*

factory as to the Interrogatories Propounded in mine to which this was the answer. I owe an apology for ["the" *interlined*] Blundering manner I wrote my Last as you have by It, been Led into an Error Just as I feared you would after I had Sent It Off & after reccollecting the Ph[r]aseology of It. The "Memphis Reports" were duly rec[eive]d & acknowledged at the time Order[e]d, But in a Subsequent communication you alluded to a *"Bill" you Intended to Introduce this Session,* touching the appo[i]ntment of Engine[e]rs compos[e]d of *"Experienced & Scientific Men"* to make *Surveys* where appropriations were needed for Harbors &c. This Is What I desire to See & to what I alluded in my Last In which I Said, or think I Said, *"Report"* Instead of *"Bill."* If therefore you Should Introduce Such a *"Bill"* I will be oblidged for a Copy *Earley as may be.* I thank you Sir, for the Assurance you gave me that I shall Earley be apprized of any movement of our friends, touching the *Presidential question.*

I fully Concur in the views contained in yours above referr[e]d to & only wait, Impatiently However, to *Act.*

Should there be any *Documents* or *Speeches* favouring the *Good Cause,* or any *Papers shadowing forth the wishes of our friends,* I will be greatly oblidged for Some. The Precaution you observed In getting the *"Frank"* of a friend (as I suppose) In which to Enclose yours to me, was *Judicious* & I avail my self, In Returning this answer, of the *Same Chan[n]el—Hon. A[rmistead] Burt* [Representative from S.C.].

So In future Should you have any thing to Communicate, may It not be well to Send under the "frank" of some friend; As this will avoid Suspicion? Your communication is, & Shall be, *Sacred.* No Eye human will See It. Though Personally It would be grattifying to me [to] Reveal Its Contents to Some of *our friends*—Still as enjoined I Shall not. Can[']t the *"Cau[c]us System"* the *Clique System* be Put Down? It occurs to me that Washington is the Place, This Session the time, *Your friends* the *verry Persons* to *Strike the Blow,* as If Delayed It may mature & become more Difficult of Putting Down. That the *System* is *Odious* with the *massees* [*sic*] & becoming daily more so, Is obvious to the most careless observer. It may not be proper for you, personally, to moot this question, as then you would be "mounted Rough Shod" by the "Cliques", your motives Impugned & your self villified from Maine to Georgia & from the Atlantic to the Pacific Oceans.

Still you have friends who may, & as I think *Should,* at the *Proper time,* make a *Demonstration.* Shew their Hands. The "wire workers" will thus see there is then a Disc[r]epan[c]y, a wide Differenc[e] between a Nomination & a[n Ele]ction[?] ha! I Submit then, whet[*ms. torn*]t the Best method of Remedying the [*ms. torn*] so Long & Justly complained of by *The People* & under which system they have become restive? After all you "Old Hands" & wise ones & being In the focal[?] Center of all that is going on, can best Judge & therefore with you I must Leave It Beseeching *an All wise Ruler,* who wields the Destin[i]es of men & Nations to guide & Direct In this Eventful Crisis. Believe me to be Sir, As I am, Yours Ever, A.P. Stinson.

ALS in ScCleA.

From BEN[JAMIN] RUSH FLOYD

Richmond, J[a]n[uar]y 2 1846 [*sic*; 1847] D[ea]r Sir, I take the opportunity afforded me by Mr. Johnston's trip to the City to ask the favor of you [to] write me upon the subject of our State Convention & the plan of her General internal improvements. In a conversation I had the pleasure of holding with you at Wythe last summer you remarked that "Space must be represented." I confess the idea was a novel one to me, and the more I have reflected on it the greater force it seems to have. Still I have not been able to comprehend how it is to be worked into the frame of Government as a component part of its basis. That it would neutralize the power of a dense population whose interests are the same, to some extent and give greater stability to a Constitution I think is obvious, but how ["it" *interlined*] can ["it" *canceled*] be made to harmonize with taxation & population I cannot well see. What would be the advantages are too indistinct to ["me" *altered to* "my"] mind to enable me to maintain a conclusion I feel to be true, but why I cannot tell so clearly. Why too should Legislative Elections be made by concurrent votes? What tendency would such restraints have upon the course of aspirants for State preferments? what, upon general subjects of improvement in the State—would it tend to change the Legislation from local to general questions—would it heal the dissentions between the East & West & in what way? I hope you will not give yourself trouble to write upon this subject if it withdraws your attention from any matter of more consequence to yourself.

47

Our body you will have seen is going on in true Virginia style slowly & I fear uselessly. The most engrossing subject is the approaching Senatorial election at last. I hope there are State rights men enough here who will stand fore, to effect something for the Cause. I am inclined to believe there will be no Caucus if there is I think it will be beaten by the impracticables.

The Hunkers are evidently alarmed even if they should not be beaten. [John W.] Jones I believe will be the competing candidate with [Robert M.T.] Hunter & in this event Mr. Hunter I think will be elected. If he is not it will not be the fault of Many of the State rights men. Some fall by the way side, but that was to be expected. As yet however nothing definitive is settled upon by the Hunkers that I can learn. I am pretty confident however that they will be beaten unless they can recruit largely from the Whig ranks. How this will be I cannot learn. I hope all will be for the best. In the mean time allow me to say How Sincerely I have the Honor to be your ob[edien]t Serv[an]t, Ben. Rush Floyd.

ALS in ScCleA. NOTE: Benjamin Rush Floyd was the son of former Governor of Va. John Floyd and the brother of future Governor John B. Floyd. Internal evidence indicates that this letter was probably written in January 1847 and accidentally dated 1846 by the writer.

By Dr. William L. Jenkins, [Pendleton], 1/3. Jenkins recorded in his daybook a medical visit to the Calhoun household: "Hon. John C. Calhoun. To visit & dressing boy[']s fingers. [$]2.50." Entry in ScCM, Waring Historical Library, William L. Jenkins Daybook, 1840–1848, p. 63.

From JOHN RAVEN MATHEWES

Habersham Co[unty, Ga.] Jan[uar]y 3, [18]46 [*sic*; 1847] My Dear Sir, It is some time since I have intruded upon your nationally precious time my scribbling propensity & would not now but that by the last Mail I rec[eive]d a letter from a young friend of mine who is anxious in case of an opening of new appointments in the Regular Army to obtain a commission. The number of officers in the present Army it is lamentable to notice ["is fast declining" *interlined*] and there may be an opportunity offering for your gratifying his wishes. His name is *Henry* Kershaw a grandson of one of our most respectable business houses in Charleston—Kershaw & Lewis. I have no hesitancy in saying that if the Govern[men]t desires efficiency in its appointments that he will not do injustice to its confidence. I have no other interest in making these remarks but "to render unto Caesar the things which are Caesar's" or in other words to promote the laudable wishes of a young man of respectability, good education[,] morals & worth in serving his country & a worthy ambition to succeed in life.

On the Subject of Politics we are in this State all adrift. The Democratic Party are committing suicide & the Whigs are exceedingly active. The former cannot let go their Old Hunkerism & the latter have played their last Card on "the Mill boy of the Slashes" [Henry Clay] with his gambling Political principles and it seems that they are so entangled in the mystification of principles declared & avowed over "a hasty plate of Soup" during the last Presidential campaign that it is hard for the Honest & Southern portion of the party to rally & emancipate themselves from their Abolition & ultra vexatious Bretheren. There is a great Portion of the Democracy too who are true & sincere—who wish to do what is right but their leaders are all looking after the loaves & fishes. Newspaper Editors, Teachers, Tradesmen, Lawyers &c. &c. all can boast of the principles laid down in a recent ["book"(?) *canceled*] Song—"We calculate *New England* will *always be our Home Sir*—Wherever *else* in *this broad Land*, it is our chance to roam Sir." The Legislature of So. Carolina has acted wisely, and a little longer endurance of her correct principles & the Storm of false Politics with which her sister States ["are" *canceled*; "surrounded" *altered to* "surround" *and* "her" *interlined*] will blow over & she will remain a beacon of deliverance. I was much pleased with the visit of Mr. [Richard] Pakenham to our [S.C.] Legislature &c. Altho I was not present so as to have paid my respects I heard those who convers'd with him speak in the highest terms of his Gentlemanly & sensible deportment. I think we will have to thrash the Mexicans into civilization and Anglo Saxon principles.

I have done very little in gold digging this winter being absent from home since the middle of October. My rice crop [in Colleton District, S.C.] has turned out abundantly and [I] am fixing up an expensive steam mill for Thrashing & pounding & expect to be at it 'till April next. I forgot to mention that Mr. Kershaw is between 25 & 30 years[,] is a South Carolinian—at present is in a commercial house in New Orleans—he would prefer hailing from So. Ca. but rather than lose a chance of preferment will waive his nativity. I see a Mr. [Henry A.] Clemson lost in the melancholy wreck of the Somers[;] is he a relative of our Friend Tho[ma]s G.—how were himself & family when you heard from them last & Do present my best respects. Believe me my Dear Sir Most respectfully & truly Y[ou]r friend, John Raven Mathewes.

[P.S.] I leave this day week for Charleston.

ALS in ScCleA.

From S[AMUEL] D[AYTON] BRADFORD

West Roxbury near Boston, 4th January 1847
My Dear Sir, I avail myself of the pleasant though brief meeting we had in Washington in Feb[ruar]y 1845 upon the subject of *Free Trade* to ask the favour of your powerful aid in the Senate in favour of the claims of Joseph Langdon Esq. to fill the place of American Consul at Smyrna [in Turkey]. I understand the President [James K. Polk] intends soon to fill the above named place in the usual way. Mr. Langdon is a nephew of Mrs. M.L. Greenwood of Boston[,] the mother of the late celebrated preacher of the same name [Francis W.P. Greenwood], and a lady universally respected and esteemed. I deviate from my usual custom in preferring a request of this nature on account of my great regard for her but I have not done so before first making every inquiry concerning Mr. Langdon, who, I learn, has long resided at Smyrna as an eminent merchant there; remarkable for his hospitality towards his countrymen, and respected highly by the people of the city where he resides. From the evidence before me I am satisfied that the appointment, should it be made will be one, of which the Government will never have reason to repent; but this is more than I would venture to say of some others, which have been made. On this account I would venture to ask your aid in case Mr. Langdon's name should be presented to the Senate for confirmation. I have already addressed the President and Mr. [James] Buchanan in particular upon the same subject.

I avail of this opportunity to renew the assurances of my great regard, and Remain very truly your friend & Ser[van]t, S.D. Bradford.

ALS in ScCleA. NOTE: An AEU by Calhoun reads: "Mr. Bradford relates to the Consulate at Smyrna."

From SARAH [MYTTON] MAURY

Liverpool, January 4th 1847

My dear Mr. Calhoun, Allow me to offer to you and Mrs. [Floride Colhoun] Calhoun the best and most affectionate wishes of the season on the part of myself and my husband [William Maury]. I hope the cough which inconvenienced you slightly last year has not been your companion during the present season. I am wearying to be at Washington for believe me I find the politics of England, (consisting solely of the best mode of feeding her hungered people,) very dull after the fresh and enlarged and various discussions I witnessed last year. I fear nothing from the Whig elections—the Mexican war, and local causes have produced them—not Free Trade; and consequently they are in *your* favour. The [copies of my book, *The*] "Statesmen" [*of America in 1846*] are in this packet. When you have had leisure to peruse my feeble attempt to describe your character my dear and admirable Friend, for such I hope you will ever permit me to call you, will you let me know if I have said what is true as far as regards your views and opinions. I read the sketch in Manuscript to General [Robert] Armstrong who was much delighted with it. He says "there is no word of panegyric that is not more than justified by the truth." He thinks I have said what you would approve of the principle of Nullification*—but if I have not, if you will point out any errors, I will rectify them in the ensuing work. [*Interpolation*: "*no one has assisted me in this or any part of the work."] How much I wish they knew you personally in England.

My husband at my request sends you a Circular—it is regarded here as an important document.

I have for ["the" *interlined*] last six weeks been a great invalid, and am now far from strong. I write lying down and am forbidden to use violent exercise. On Monday I go to London to consult Mr. [William] Lawrence. Had this indisposition not occurred I should have presented you with your little godchild in June.

My children are all well and full of promise, and our worldly affairs are prospering in such a way that I hope my husband may soon be able to retire from business. Then I shall hope to be soon in America a permanent resident—and often to see and hear you will be among my greatest pleasures.

Ireland is the stumbling block of our Government at present—there is nothing for it but Emigration as fast as possible. Lord John [Russell] is a great advocate of the system—but the task of legislating for the hungry is an awful one—and nothing that your Government have to encounter can compare with it.

I hope you will laugh at the detail of my interview with the Hon[or]able Joseph Grinnell [Representative from Mass.]. I have just heard that he has ordered a copy to be sent out to him—certainly he will have reason to rejoice in the distinguished position he holds among the "Statesmen of America".

I pray you, my dear Sir, to accept my grateful regard, and my most affectionate remembrances. Ever your friend, Sarah Maury.

[P.S.] Owing to the pressure of time, the binding is not so handsome and so neat as I wished—but I hope it may be overlooked. We had not time to print anew[?] the introductory title page.

ALS in ScCleA.

Memorial of marine insurance companies of New York City, presented by Calhoun to the Senate on 1/4. This document, undated and signed by officers of eight companies, opposes repeal of an act of 1837 concerning pilots, which act the pilots of the city are petitioning to amend or repeal. PC in Senate Document No. 26, 29th Cong., 2nd Sess. (The memorial was tabled, another Senator reporting that legislation was under consideration in committee.)

From R[ICHARD] E. MERRILL

North Conway N.H., Jan. 4th 1847

Dear Sir, Your favour of Dec. 26th was duly rec[eive]d & for your polite note I return you my thanks. I esteem even that a treasure, coming from such a source. I regret to find that you made a slight mistake by enclosing a copy of the "Congressional Globe," instead of your valuable "report upon the Memphis Convention," a document which has never reached us, notwithstanding I have made some effort to obtain a copy. Nothing save an intense desire to peruse that able paper would induce me to trouble you upon so trifling an affair, as it may appear to you, but be assured I esteem it as quite important to myself.

And now Sir, allow me to speak out with the freedom, of an American citizen to one so infinitely above me. I am a humble, respectable, member of the Democratic party, not beleiving [*sic*] however that Democracy is confined to *"fifty-four, forty men"* exclusively, but a decided advocate of "Free trade & low duties, no debt, retrenchment" &c & as such I advocated your claims to the Presidency in 1843, & as one means used circulated a scetch [*sic*] of your life by Hon. R[obert] M.T. Hunter (I beleive) as extensively as possible, which with other information created much inquiry as to the expediency of clinging to the rival candidate, come weal or come woe.

These treasonable, fanatical, political jugglers, create considerable prejudice against the South, noble, patriotic & forbearing as they have ever been, and the despicable faction led on by John P. Hale [Senator-elect from N.H.] take particular pains to abuse South Carolina in an especial manner. The course of your Legislature in regard to the N. Hampshire Resolutions was the most proper rebuke that could be administered. I have the pleasure of living in a town whose inhabitants are of a different character from the above. We honour the home of the Sumpter's Marions, Pin[c]kneys & Hayne's. "The union—it must be preserved," is our motto.

I have now troubled you too long, but you will excuse any improprieties I may have committed in my desire to give you an imperfect idea of the feelings of some portion of the friends of the South in this vicinity.

I have now a small favour to crave at your hands; if not inconsistent with your dignity and character I hope & trust you will comply. It is this—A copy of your Report on the Memphis Convention—and *from your own hand* the famous motto so often quoted, & to which I have refer[r]ed, "Free trade, low duties" &c, which once emenated from your pen.

Communications of any character will always be thankfully received. With respect, I am, Your ob[edien]t Serv[an]t, R.E. Merrill.

ALS in ScCleA.

From ROBERT WALSH, [U.S. Consul]

Paris, Jan[uar]y 4, 1847

My Dear Sir, The heirs of Major General [Johann,] Baron de Kalb have transmitted to Mr. John Carroll Brent of Washington their power of attorney to renew their petition to Congress for payment of what remains due to their ancestor. The power was accompanied by the enclosed statement, which I wrote at the request of the heirs. My feelings have been strongly moved by their case. A Mr. S[imeon] D. Bloodgood, of Albany, obtained from an agent whom they selected in Paris, a full authority to sell the lands which were granted to them in Ohio. He informed them in 1837, that he had accepted two thousand dollars! of which purchase money the half was paid and the other half to be paid to him in a few months. Since that period they have not heard of money or land, & Bloodgood, I believe, has become bankrupt. They are interesting, well educated gentry. The lady-grand[d]aughter of de Kalb has five sons; the grandson, a large progeny. I venture to send a copy of my exposition to you whose elevated spirit & whose quality of Senator of South Carolina will assure your attention to such a case, & whose patronage would be invaluable aid. The delegation of your liberal State, in the House of Representatives, may view it with special favor. I know that when this letter can reach you, the moment for a petition of the kind must be very inauspicious; this I mentioned to the heirs, but they are anxious to be at least presented again to Congress as early as possible. General [Lewis] Cass would, probably, from several considerations, assist. If Mr. [William R.] King [former U.S. Minister to France] has returned to the Senate, he might do the same. Their official residence in France brings a French claim nearer to their Sensibility. My agency is altogether gratuitous. I have not been able to ["obtain" *altered to* "procure"] a copy of your famous Report on Internal Improvements. The extracts which I found in the newspapers rendered me exceedingly desirous of obtaining the whole. It is some months since I desisted from corresponding with the [Washington Daily National] Intelligencer. The editors have represented *sickness* as the cause. It is true that I have been for a long time severely afflicted with imperfect indigestion and emaciation—occasioned by the intense and protracted heat of the summer. Yet I have constantly employed myself ten or twelve hours out of every twenty four either with official business or literary studies. My accumulation of materials literary, historical & social, has never been greater within the same tract of time. I might have managed as usual for the Intelligencer; but I was paralysed by the suppression of a number of my letters & the mutilation of others on the ground that the editors thought them likely to prejudice *national* interests—by which I understood *party* interests. Like Sancho [Panza], in counting the sheep that crossed the river, I must have my own way & latitude; otherwise it is impossible for me to scribble. It appears to me an injury to the country not to allow the freest expression of *fact* and opinion from an American disposed and situated as I happen to be abroad.

There is no danger of any change here until the death of [Louis Philippe] the King. Distress prevails throughout the realm, & it will increase for two or three months to come. When you wish to have any European politics or history from me, you can command them, & you must continue to regard me as alive to all that concerns you in any respect or region. I am, Dear Sir, with the liveliest esteem, Your faithful Serv[an]t, Robert Walsh.

ALS with En in ScCleA. NOTE: Walsh enclosed a statement by himself, dated 12/31/1846, in favor of the claims of De Kalb's widowed daughter-in-law, her son, and daughter. In preparing the statement, Walsh had examined letters and documents of De Kalb's written during the American Revolution and he quoted from them. He compares the obscurity and relative penury of De Kalb's descendants with the wealth and renown of Lafayette's. "All the members of Congress who have a large proportion of German constituents, must desire to remove from their minds and those of all American citizens of German origin and connection, any idea that the bounty of the Government is not as effectively extended, in the end, to German national benefactors, as it has been to the French, the Poles, and other foreign auxiliaries in the war of Independence." Walsh asserts that Congressmen from Md., whose troops De Kalb commanded, and from S.C., where he died, should take particular interest in the claims of his heirs.

From R. B. LEWIS

Dahlonega Ga., Jan[uar]y 5th 1847

Dear Sir, I should have written you some time ago, but Mr. [Benjamin M.?] Milner has not yet returned from his home in Pike County [Ga.]. I called on him for a settlement as you requested me ["to do" *interlined*;] he agreed to settle fairly, in fact he seemed willing to do what was right—but said he was going home[,] that it was not convenient for him to attend to the matter then but would return by Christmas, or sooner. He has not yet arrived, but is expected every day[;] when he comes I will call on him again for a settlement, and write you immediately. Messrs. Geo[rge] P. Bedford & Co. are still operating on lot 817, but the weather being very wet have not done well for some time past.

I have some money on hand received from them as tole [*sic*;

toll], and a small sum received of old Mr. Howell, from the O'Barr lot. Very respectfully, R.B. Lewis.

ALS owned by Bruce W. Ball.

REMARKS ON THE BILL FOR THE RELIEF OF THE WIDOW OF LT. COL. WILLIAM McRAE

[In the Senate, January 5, 1847]

Mr. Calhoun (who had been momentarily absent from his seat) rose and said that, although he had not heard the whole of the report, yet he believed he had a distinct recollection of this case. It was one in which it was proposed to give to the widow of an officer of the army, who died while in service, but not in battle, a pension for life. It was an entirely novel application, so far as the army was concerned, to ask for a pension for a widow under such circumstances; and it was an application which, if allowed, would lead to extensive innovation. It was assumed, he believed, to be proper to extend the practice of granting such pensions, because it had prevailed in regard to the widows of naval officers. There were gentlemen present who were more familiar with matters relating to the naval service than he was. But, if his impression was correct, this naval system had grown out of a law which passed through Congress in a hurried mannrr [*sic*], at the close of a session, and for which no one seemed willing to be responsible. There was, if his memory served him truly, a very large sum of money collected and set apart for a pension fund, out of prizes captured by the navy; and this fund, under the law to which he had alluded, received the direction of giving pensions to the widows of naval officers, equivalent to the half pay of such officers. There was a severe struggle made, in which he himself took part, to overrule this law, and he was under the impression that it had been modified; in this, however, he supposed he must have been mistaken. The case of Mary McRae might be, and he had no doubt was, a meritorious one; but a case of this kind would become a precedent, and would draw after it numerous other cases. If it should be granted in this instance, Congress would be beset with similar applications, and a general principle would be thus established. The question, in this view of it, was one of so much importance that he thought there ought to be a full Senate when a vote was to be taken upon it. Their pension list was already swelled beyond all reasonable bounds. There was not a nation of Europe which had so extensive a pension system as ours; it constituted a very large proportion of the expenditures of this Government, and he thought, if there were no other objection to its increase, that the present was a very improper period for commencing a further extension.

Under these impressions, he should vote against the bill; and, in order to have an opportunity to record his vote, he asked for the yeas and nays.

[*The yeas and nays were ordered, but Thomas H. Benton remarked that there was a more general bill on army widow's pensions pending, and suggested postponement until that was considered. This was agreed to.*]

From the Washington, D.C., *Daily National Intelligencer*, January 6, 1847, p. 1. Variant report in *Congressional Globe*, 29th Cong., 2nd Sess., p. 112. Other variants in the New York, N.Y., *Herald*, January 5, 1847, p. 3; the Washington, D.C., *Daily Union*, January 5, 1847, p. 2; the Alexandria, Va., *Gazette and Virginia Advertiser*, January 6, 1847, p. 3; the Charleston, S.C., *Mercury*, January 11, 1847, p. 2.

Remarks on the Michigan Land Bill, 1/5. "Mr. Calhoun remarked that he thought the same objections applied to this [internal improvements] bill as to the bill of last session. The vote he gave on that occasion he should give on this. He had no objection where a [rail]road passed through the public lands to give alternate sections to aid in its construction; but he understood that this bill required more than that; he did not believe himself justified therefore in voting for it." From *Congressional Globe*, 29th Cong., 2nd Sess., p. 113. Also printed in the Washington, D.C., *Daily National Intelligencer*, January 6, 1847, p. 2. (A variant report spelled out Calhoun's stated objections: "Where the alternate sections had already been sold, the bill proposed to give lands at the option of the State in other places, without reference to the advantage of the Federal government in their selection; but rather against it . . . ." From the New York, N.Y., *Herald*, January 7, 1847, p. 3.)

From WILSON LUMPKIN

Athens [Ga.,] Jan[uar]y 6th 1847
My dear Sir, I thank you for your favor of the 29th Ult. The mode suggested by you for the further prosecution of the war, is the one

which had not only occur[r]ed to me previous to the reception of your letter, but I have frequently suggested it to others, & I have never conversed with an intelligent man on the subject, that did not concur on the subject. The war would then be defensive on our part, & our citizens generally would be better reconciled to its long continuance. It really does appear to me, notwithstanding our signal success so far, that we have really not yet advanced the first step towards *subduing* the Mexican people—but the reverse, they are stronger & more determined than ever. The way we have so far prosecuted the war, must be changed, or it will be interminable. I have seen enough of the course of such men as [Representatives David] Wilmot of Penn[sylvania and Samuel] Gordon of New York & various others on the floor of Congress, to satisfy me, that both political parties ["at" *canceled*] in the non-slave-holding States, are firmly & fully united & resolved, to prohibit the introduction of any more slave States into the Union, formed of Territory which may be acquired from Mexico. It is true I have indulged some hope, that in the event of acquiring Territory, we might be able to form something like a reasonable compromise on the subject. But I begin to doubt now, that the time is rapidly approaching, when the great struggle between the slave & non-slave-holding States, must come up on an issue which will shake our glorious confederacy to its very center. My old friend, I love the Union. But I am ready to resist unto death, rather than to submit to the schemes, plans & policy, of the Abolitionist[s] & their friends & supporters throughout the non slave-holding States. Ardently as I love the Union, I consider it valueless, when it is used for my oppression & destruction.

From this time forward, we may expect the slave question, to be the great & vital one, which will over-ride every other question. Our divisions will be sectional. The names of Whig & Democrat, will loose [*sic*] their charms. My greatest apprehension is, that the South may not be as united in the day & hour of trial, as her Enemy. I fear, the lust for power & place, may have its influence, on many of our own people. And that portion of the Southern population, who own no slaves, generally feel very different on the subject, from the slave holder.

Nothing can preserve our rights in the approaching struggle, but union in the present Congress amongst Southern men, (or perhaps I should say, union in the next Congress). The South united, can face a frowning world. Work to the point of uniteing the South, regardless of party names.

I consider the new fangled scheme of Lei[u]t[enant] Gen[era]l

&C. perfectly ridiculous. It is nothing more, nor less—than a selfish, & base scheme—designed to benefit individuals, at the expense of the best interest of the Country.

If the press & Congress have become so debased, as to unite in keeping light from the people, have we not reason to fear, that the days of our Republic ["are" *canceled and then interlined*] numbered.

The unofficial people of this country are patriotic. Therefore they favor a vigorous prosecution of the war—Believing as they do, that no other way can be devised to procure a speedy & honorable peace.

From this to the close of the session, I shall look for proceedings in Congress with great interest. As ever y[ou]rs, Wilson Lumpkin.

ALS in ScCleA; variant PC in Jameson, ed., *Correspondence*, pp. 1102–1104.

From J[AMES] HAMILTON, [JR.]

Charleston S.C., Jan[uar]y 7th 1847

My dear Sir, I will be exceedingly obliged to you to have my nephew Charles K. Prioleau's name registered for a Lieutenantcy of Dragoons in the Regiment proposed to be raised. He is 20 years of age[,] of fine constitution, excellent understanding & possesses the necessary qualifications—courage, honor & truth.

I will thank you to register my son Oliver Perry Hamilton for a Captaincy of Dragoons. He is 25 years of age. As my own son I feel more reluctance in speaking of him. It will suffice to say that, in or out of the field he with his cousin will do no dishonor to our State, and this is saying much.

I beg your kind & friendly services in promoting the ardent wishes of these two young men. I remain With esteem My dear Sir Respect[full]y your friend & Ob[edien]t Serv[an]t, J. Hamilton.

LS in ScCleA. NOTE: O.P. Hamilton was appointed a Capt. on 3/5/1847, serving in the 12th Infantry Regiment. Under the Confederacy he commanded a cavalry battalion. Charles K. Prioleau apparently did not receive a commission for Mexican War service. During the Civil War he worked for the Confederate ordnance department in London.

Memorial of the Irish Emigrant Society of New York, presented by Calhoun to the Senate on 1/7. This document opposes the proposed repeal of a law of 1837 concerning pilots. It is dated 1/4/1847 and is signed by Gregory Dillon, President, and Florence McCarthy and M.J. O'Connor, Secretaries. The memorialists state that their sentiments are those "of the whole mercantile community," and that the act has prevented shipwrecks and loss of life. DS in DNA, RG 46 (U.S. Senate), 29A-H2.

Remarks in the Senate, 1/7. During debate on a bill to encourage enlistments in the Army, the question arose as to how long the Mexican Congress had been in session. Calhoun stated: "They met on the 6th [of December]." From the New York, N.Y., *Herald*, January 9, 1847, p. 3.

[JOSEPH J. SINGLETON] to Rob[er]t H. Moore, "Copy"

Dahlonega [Ga.,] 8th Jan[uar]y 1847

My Dear Sir, I feel bound as an Agent to be more particular with the business of my Principal [John C. Calhoun] than perhaps I would be with my own. Your memorandum being very imperfect, and not knowing Mr. [William G.] Lawrence in your Lease, I am bound to demand of you an assumsion of the Am[oun]t of the whole Toll from the two lots of Mr. John C. Calhoun which you have leased, or at least that part of the interest of the said Calhoun which he is entitled to under your lease, and I hope hereafter to hear no more of what Mr. Lawrence has made; be pleased to excuse this, as all I want to know in future is the monthly portion due Mr. Calhoun. A strict compliance with the terms of your lease I am compelled to exact, in which, should I fail, I now think I would prefer giving up the agency in preference to that of entering into a controversy with my neighbor whom I so highly esteem. It is possible that it may be for the want of a form is the reason of your imperfect return (consider I am only the agent and not the principal)[;] hence I will respectfully give you the following, which I hope will be strictly complied with in future, at the end of each month, beginning from the 1st of the present month (To wit)[.] Then follow the form &C giving greatly the preference to prompt payment &C. Signed &C.

ALU in ScU-SC, John C. Calhoun Papers. NOTE: This document, in the handwriting of Singleton, was addressed to Calhoun in Washington. Presumably, it was sent for Calhoun's information.

From H[ENRY] W. CONNER

Charleston, Jan[uar]y 9, 1847

The aspect of things at Washington is beginning to create much anxiety amongst us in Charleston. The Congress recently so unanimous in their precipitancy to declare the country in a state of war with Mexico appear now almost equally unanimous in abandoning the country in the time of its greatest need & unless some powerful influence is soon brought to bear we fear we shall stand forth discredited & degraded in the sight of all the world.

Your friends & the country as usual look to you in the emergency.

You opposed the war single handed & alone—pointed out its difficulties & its dangers & whatever may [be] the consequences the responsibility lies not with you.

At this distance we can of course know but little of the combinations or the currents or under currents that may be in motion in Washington & any suggestion we venture to make is of course in perfect defference to your better judgment—but it does appears [*sic*] to us that there is a crisis near at hand if not already arrived which will demand your interference.

Your course at the commencement of the difficulty—& the commanding position you occupy in the confidence & regard of the whole nation enables you alone—if it can be done atall to strike out a course to save the Honour of the nation which it appears [to] us now can only be done by a vigorous prosecution of the war but of this you are the better judge. It would besides in our humble opinion be the means of placing yourself in a still more enviable attitude before the people—a circumstance tho secondary in its importance with yourself we know still ought not to be lost sight of.

If you have time we would be glad to hear from you. It is possible we over[r]ate the difficulties in prospect.

I have taken the liberty of giving a letter of introduction to you in favour of Isaac Townsend a prominent merchant of New York & of much influence & more honesty & general intelligence, as a leading member of the democratic party of that city, than is usually to be found. In fact he is a gentleman of the purest character & I would be very glad if you could give him an interview. Very truly y[ou]rs, H.W. Conner.

ALS in ScCleA; variant PC in Boucher and Brooks, eds., *Correspondence*, p. 365. NOTE: An AES by Ker Boyce reads: "I have read the above and find, that it expresses my views fully and in order not to take up your valuable time I take this method, giving my views. Yours most Sincerely, Ker Boyce."

From Dr. T. T. Mann

435 Chesnut St. Phi[ladelphi]a, Jan[uar]y 9th/[18]47
Dear Sir, Yesterday while in conversation with a gentleman upon the results of Galvanism when applied to abnormal conditions of the human ["system" *interlined*] he spoke of a member of your family [Martha Cornelia Calhoun] whose affliction was incurable by the skill of your physicians.

Of a matter in which a man has no ulterior views except that of wishing to do good he may beg a hearing.

For a length of time past I have been directing many of my patients to use Galvanism, Generally in such chronic cases that if they would yield at all to medication it would ["be" *interlined*] slow and with reluctance. And I think where there is a loss of nervous power, unattended with organic disturbance And the muscles from inability to perform their office remain in a state of rigidity that I have found it to be of incalculable benefit.

Heretofore the means for applying Galvanism were so verry imperfect and painful (wires or iron rods) that but few persons could bear more than a verry slight current owing to the burning sensation communicated to the surface. To remedy this evil I have had constructed a "Flesh Brush" of soft bristles and silver tinsel so as to present to the skin a thousand different points instead of a single point as formerly, with the current so regulated as to ["be" *interlined*] thrown upon the surface with any degree of intensity.

With this as now used we can stimulate and warm the whole surface of the body increasing the cappillary circulation or with a stronger current bring on violent muscular contractions.

My f[rien]d wished me to draw your attention to this subject and if at any time you desire to know more of it I shall be happy to give all the information in my power. Yours respectful[l]y, T.T. Mann, M.D.

ALS in ScCleA. Note: An AEU by Calhoun reads "Dr. Mann[,] relates to impro[vemen]t[?] in the application of the Galvanick fluid."

From H[ENRY] O'RIELLY

Atlantic & Ohio Telegraph office
Philadelphia Exchange, Jan. 9, [18]47

Dear Sir, The interest you kindly manifested in my arrangements for the Telegraph System, when I last had the honor of presenting my presenting my [*sic*] respects to you, induce me now to enclose you some brief evidences of the progress & spirit of the enterprize. Against the efforts now making, & shadowed forth in the Postmaster General's [Cave Johnson's] Report, to increase the already enormous power of the Federal Govern[m]ent by the addition of the Telegraph System to the Post office Department, many look, as I confidently look, to *you*, Sir, for assertion now again of those doctrines which you boldly promulgated years ago on the subject of Govern[m]ental Patronage. Yours, H. O'Rielly.

ALS with En in ScCleA. NOTE: Enclosed is a printed broadside containing a "Memorial to the Legislature of Ohio," dated 1/7, from O'Rielly asking that all modes of telegraphing, not merely "Electro-Magnetic," be allowed equal opportunities; also containing a letter of 12/26/1846 from O'Rielly to the directors of the Atlantic & Ohio Telegraph Co., informing them of the completion of the line between Philadelphia and Pittsburg and pledging the completion of the "Atlantic, Lake and Mississippi Line."

To FRANCIS WHARTON, [Philadelphia]

Washington, 9th Jan[uar]y 1847

My dear Sir, I had requested one of the officers of the Senate to let me have a few copies of my Report [on the Memphis Memorial], which he informed me he had, & finding shortly after several sealed packages on my table, of about the same size, I concluded they were the copies I had requested, & remained under that impression until I received your note. On its receipt, I examined the remaining copies, & found them all to be Congressional Globes. I now enclose you a copy of my report, ["which" *canceled*] in conformity to your report.

I hope I may have ["during the Session" *interlined*] an opportunity to illustrate more fully the portion, which relates to rivers, whose navigable waters extend to two States, as I find that some of my friends & others do not seem to realise the full force of the reason in support of the opinion I maintain. I think when well understood it cannot be resisted. Yours truly, J.C. Calhoun.

ALS in ScU-SC, John C. Calhoun Papers.

REMARKS ON APPOINTMENT OF A PRESIDENT PRO TEMPORE OF THE SENATE

[In the Senate, January 11, 1847]

[*The Vice-President, George M. Dallas, was not present. The Senate had not yet elected a President Pro Tempore in this session. Dallas had given the chair to David R. Atchison of Missouri, who had been President Pro Tempore in the previous session. This precipitated a two-hour complicated debate over Senate rules and Constitutional interpretation in which more than a dozen Senators took part. John J. Crittenden of Ky. proposed to resolve the matter by a resolution appointing Atchison President Pro Tempore temporarily, until the return of the Vice-President.*]

Mr. Calhoun said the question obviously turned on the word "absent": and all precedent had decided that the Vice President could vacate his chair for a single day without being considered "absent." In so nice a question precedent should govern them. A plausible argument might be advanced on both sides, however, and perhaps the best way would be to alter the rule.

[*George E. Badger of N.C. questioned Calhoun's interpretation of "absent."*]

Mr. Calhoun said he would answer the question of the gentleman from North Carolina, if he would answer a question for him. Suppose the Vice President should go to the House [of Representatives] to see some friend, would he be present or absent?

[*There was further extended debate.*]

Mr. Calhoun said he would by no means attribute the course of the Vice President in this instance to any motive of party interests. He believed the Vice President had acted from the purest intentions. In reply to the interrogatory of the gentleman from Kentucky [Crittenden], he would say that he never appointed a substitute [when he was Vice-President], for during the whole period in which he presided over the Senate, he was not once absent.

From the Washington, D.C., *Daily Union*, January 11, 1847, p. 2. Variants in *Congressional Globe*, 29th Cong., 2nd Sess., pp. 162–164; the New York, N.Y.,

Herald, January 13, 1847, p. 3; the Charleston, S.C., *Mercury,* January 15, 1847, p. 2. NOTE: The first variant cited gives a much more detailed, but not necessarily more illuminating, account of the debate. In that variant, however, Calhoun is reported as replying, in the last part of his remarks, to a second question from Crittenden. Calhoun said: "Secondly, as to whether a person appointed by the Vice President would, in the event of the death of the Vice President, stand in his place with reference to the Presidency. To this, he would answer that he would not; because he would neither be the Vice President nor the President *pro tempore.*"

From Jos[eph] J. Singleton

Dahlonega [Ga.,] 12th Jan[uar]y 1847

Dear Sir, I rode over to the Obarr Mine this morning, where I remained the greater part of the day, with an expectation of meeting your two Lessees, [John] Pasco[e] & [John] Hockanoll. Neither of them came while I was there, so I am not yet prepared to give you any further information with regard to their views, tho' I am inclined to think they have changed somewhat since my last interview whith [*sic*] them from the fact that they have since been over and ordered the occupants out of the Cabbins for the purpose as they ["(the occupants)" *interlined*] informed me of moving into them this week. So soon as I hear of them being there I will visit the mine again, and will write you the result &C. I am at a loss to know what to do with Mr. [Robert H.] Moore; he gives me no satisfaction in regard to the rent he owes; if he does not do so very soon I shall ask your advice how to proceed; were it my property I should proceed to stop his operations under a forfeiture of his Lease regardless of the expense.

The Whigs in this part of the Country are lying on their oars waiting to hear whether Mr. [Henry] Clay will consent to be run for the next President or not; if he consents to run a large majority of them will support him; if he does not consent to his name being used as their candidate you certainly will be the choice of a very large majority of them provided you will consent to run. Now, should the "old Annexation opponent" consent to run, which I fear he will, and the Democratic party do not nominate you which I equally fear they will not; the next question for your friends to determine provided it meets your approbation, is, whether it will be prudent to run you upon your own merits regardless of Cliques or Caucus[e]s, relying upon the House of Representatives to choose their President. My humble opinion is, that in despite of all the intrigues of Demagogism the election might be carried into the House, if not secured through the Electoral College; in either event all will be right. A concert of action among your friends is all that is necessary which may be effected on the assembling at the respective seats of Government in the capacity of Representatives of the People. I will thank you to apprize me of your views on this subject by the 1st of March, as I have promised a number of voters to give them at our March Court an answer whether I will serve them in the Legislature or not, and our Court comes on the first Monday of the month, and I have no inclination to serve other than that of advancing the views ["of" *interlined*] such a friend as far as may be in my power, thereby conscient[i]ously promoting the best interest of not only my State, but that of the whole Union, and especially that of the Southern portion. I have not yet seen my friend [William C.] Dawson [former Representative from Ga.], but have received many verbal messages from him; he is afraid to write; he is closely watching ["the" *interlined*] current, with the view no doubt of availing himself of the strongest. I have the honor of being Your friend & humble Serv[an]t, Jos. J. Singleton.

ALS in ScU-SC, John C. Calhoun Papers.

To Governor [DAVID] JOHNSON

Washington, 13th Jan[uar]y 1846 [*sic*; 1847]
My dear Sir, I agree with you, that the materials of which our [Palmetto] Regiment is composed are not of a discription, which such a service requires. I never think of the men, and what is before them, but with deep feelings of regret. My consolation is, that I did my best to prevent the exigency, which has called them from their homes.

The state of things here is bad. Both parties divided & distracted, & neither with any confidence in the administration. The war, to appearance, is but just begun, and I can see no prospect of its immediate termination. The prospect is gloomy. I can see but one way to extricate ourselves from our difficulties, and avoid the disasters, which must accompany a protracted war; and that is to take a defensive position; to hold on to what we have got, or rather so much as may be required to indemnify us, & to say to Mexico we are ready to treat, if she is, & to settle our differences justly & liberally, and if she is not, we are content to hold what we have got. It would add but little to our ordinary force, or expenditure to take a defensive line, which would cover what would amply indemnify us. The adoption of such a policy would save millions, & thousands of valuable lives; & save us from many & great disasters. I will probably take some early opportunity to express my opinion fully on the subject.

Among other evils growing out of the war, is the renewal of the abolition question in a worse form than ever. Both parties at the North seem resolved, that we shall be excluded from whatever territory may be acquired. It seems to be their policy to let us spill our blood & expend our treasury, not to acquire additional treasury for the common benefit, but to be used, as an instrument to destroy us. Nothing but the united & determined resistance of the South can prevent the success of this base & dangerous plot against our peace & safety. Yours truly & sincerely, J.C. Calhoun.

ALS in ScU-SC, John C. Calhoun Papers.

From P[ierce] M. Butler

Montgomery Alabama, 14th Jan. 1847

Dear Sir, At the moment of leaving Hamburg Gov. [David] Johnson was kind enough to inform me of the purport of a Note he had received from you, on the Subject of a Brig. Gen[era]l, to be appointed for the volunteer Regiments, about being called into Service. In the spirit of a Carolinian & friend allow me a few words on this subject, at least as far as my name has been associated. I had known that the Field and Platoon officers of my Regiment were about recommending me, & that the Governor had concur[r]ed or united in a recommendatory letter to the War Department. If I had been consulted I would have invited an expression of the rank & file of the Regiment, & would have suggested that the letter had gone to the South Carolina Delegation. I have some reason for saying that the Governor so intended & regrets he had not observed this course. His character however is so direct—that it did not occur to him, that the other was the more appropriate etiquett[e]. Promotion is always desirable to a to a [*sic*] soldier—particularly, with the approbation of those to be commanded. I like others am as ambitious of the one, as I am solicitous of the other. I have some reason to believe that the volunteers themselves, are not wholly reconciled to the change, that this promotion would effect—while I am satisfied that they would be benefited by the increased rank, & equally if not materially benefitted, directly by the change—if they should think otherwise, it would be embarrassing to me, under all the circumstances.

I think South Carolina *entitled* to the Brigadier & I wish the Delegation *entirely united.*

In this state of things, rather than the State should loose [*sic*] *the officer,* I am willing & anxious to loose the office if another be more acceptable, or likely to unite the Delegation and the appointing power. In a word as my name has been tendered, I wish it now maintained, but if any other of our citizens be more acceptable or likely to succeed, no one more than myself will more heartily unite in his preferment. And among the var[i]ous distinguished Gentlemen that I have heard suggested, none would be more acceptable to me & I believe my Regiment than Gen[era]l James Jones of Edgefield District. He in a very eminent degree unites the duties of the Soldier of the Bureau & the Field.

You will please par[d]on the liberty I have taken, in writing you on the subject. I should more properly perhaps, have made Col. [Armistead] Burt [Representative from S.C.] the organ, as a conspicuous member of the military committee.

One half of the Regiment left here two days ago for Mobile, the other follow ["follow" *canceled*] this afternoon, & thence to Point Isabell. The good conduct & soldierly deportment of the Regiment since they left our own soil, is what all of us may well be proud of. I dread in advance, the suffering & loss of life incident to the climate, & the indiscretions of young men.

For one I hope this war will soon terminate at least before the warm season. I can but believe, if the energy & exertions we have a right to expect, be pursued, that it may close by May or June, or all obtained that it is ever practicable to attain. I will not pretend to put my judgement in contact, with others more capable of judging, that I learn have asserted that Vera Cruze cannot be taken. I *think* it can be taken with but little loss of life, and that the City of Mexico may follow in ten days. I am Dear Sir very very truly yours, P.M. Butler.

ALS in ScCleA. NOTE: Butler had been Governor of S.C. during 1836–1838 and was at this time Col. of the Palmetto Regiment of volunteers en route to Texas, in which rank he was killed at the battle of Churubusco on 8/20/1847.

To H[ENRY] W. CONNER, [Charleston]

Washington, 14th Jan[uar]y 1846 [*sic*; 1847]
My dear Sir, I have been inactive, but not indifferent in reference to
the Mexican War. On the contrary, I have been directing my attention closely to it, while waiting for developements, in order to enable
me to determine on my course. When the time comes, when I can
move with effect, I shall take the course, which duty may prescribe;
that is the course, which, in my opinion, is best calculated to extricate the country from the difficulties and dangers, which surrounds it.

It is at present in a sad condition. Never before was the prospect
so gloomy. Both parties are distracted & divided; and both without
confidence in the administration. The determination seems to be to
push the war with vigour, as far as words are concerned & voting of
men; but I see no disposition to raise the means for sustain[in]g the
war, unless, indeed, by ["raising" *canceled*] laying additional [tariff]
duties; that is by undoing the reduction of last session in whole or
part. To add to our difficulties, abolition is revived in a new and
more dangerous form. It seems to be resolved on by both parties at
the North, that no part of the territory to be acquired by the war
shall be for the benefit of the South. They are very willing that our
blood & treasury shall be ["in" *canceled*] expended freely in the war
to acquire territory, not for the common good, but as the means of
assailling and ruining us. We are to be made to dig our own grave.

Thus far my worst anticipations in reference to the war would
seem to be in a fair way to be realised. It dropt a curtain between
me & the future, which, as I told my friends at the time, I could not
penetrate, nor am I now able. I see no way to extricate the country
from impending calamities ["but" *interlined*] by turning the war
from an offensive to a defensive one, by holding what we have got,
or rather so much as would amply indemnify us; & say to Mexico that
we are ready to treat when she is & to settle differences on just &
liberal terms, but if she is not that we are content to hold what we
have got. A line might be taken, which would cover ["an" *interlined*] ample extent to indemnify us fully, that could be defended at
an expense, ["not" *canceled*] & by a force not much greater, than our
necessary peace establishment.

I shall take some early opportunity to explain my views. I know
not whether they will prevail or not; but if they should not, you may
regard the war as only just begun; that its end is uncertain, & that

should it be protracted, which would be probable, no man can tell what will come.

In the mean time our papers should be cautious & wait development here, ["&" *canceled*] except as to the slave aspect of the subject. On that, they should speak out unqualifiedly & boldly. ["Their" *canceled and* "Our" *interlined*] members here should be cheered by their sust[ain]ing voice. Ten days or two weeks will disclose much.

You may show this to such prudent friends as you may think proper. Truly, J.C. Calhoun.

ALS in ScC; photostat of ALS in DLC, Henry Workman Conner Papers.

From [Dr.] T. T. MANN

Philadelphia
435 Chesnut St., Jan[uar]y 14th 1847

Dear Sir, Yours of Yesterday came to h[an]d this morning. For your afflicted Daughter [Martha Cornelia Calhoun] I feel a deep sympathy, and would readily do anything in my power with even a remote prospect of ultimately restoring her.

As I wrote, those cases of loss of nervous power, when without *organic* ["leision" *canceled*] derangement the muscles remain in a state of rigidity, consequent upon the loss of nervous influence in the parts of the system so affected, that a current of Galvanic fluid passed in the direction of the nerves, will, I believe restore vitality to the nerves and action to the muscles.

Now how will this apply to the condition of your afflicted Daught[er]? I cannot tell. There are not sufficient symptoms before me. I know not the cause and nature of the complaint. The spinal colum[n] is liable to distortion from various causes, and at times without the vertebrae being ["at" *canceled*] much or at all diseased. At other times a verry serious affection is induced, the bones becoming carious and the cartilage connecting the bones ulcerated, followed verry generally by a *loss of power in the inferior extremities*, generally induced by a constitutional taint, showing a predisposition to *pulmonary* ["(Tubercular)" *interlined*] consumption.

In the first mentioned condition of the Spine I would most assuredly throw upon the centre of the bulk a strong current of Galvanic fluid with strong confidence of success.

At this moment I have in mind a patient raised from her back after 18 mo[nths?] close confinement—now well, attributes the cure to the fluid.

But should her case be attended with the last mentioned symptoms, then with internal remedies, issues, moxa, or blisters are strongly indicated, and the "brush" to be useful can only be so by the counter-irritation it will create by a long application in the direction of the spinal column.

The young Lady's nurse with directions can apply the Galvanism as safely and skillfully as I could. We all know that it is not attended with ["with" *canceled*] danger either to life or health, I have experimented on myself for four weeks each day in succession for 2 hours without the least evil arising from it.

I have ordered to be made a verry fine apperatus small, yet of sufficient strength for all ordinary purposes. If you wish your child to make trial of it I will have it sent on. Cost for all complete in mahogany case & Brushes $25.00.

Allow me the honor to be My dear Sir Your ob[edient] S[er]-v[an]t, T.T. Mann.

P.S. The apperatus mentioned was ordered for myself and you will not feel either by courtesy or otherwise bound to take it if you are not disposed to use it. T.T.M.

ALS in ScCleA.

From [James L. Edwards, Commissioner], Pension Office, 1/15. No law directs that a Revolutionary pensioner's pension shall be continued to his widow. Joseph Righton was pensioned under the statute of 6/7/1832. If his widow was married to him before 1794 and can submit proof of that fact in accordance with regulations, she can be pensioned under the statute of 6/17/1844 until its expiration on 3/4/1848. FC in DNA, RG 15 (Veterans Administration), Letters Sent, 1831–1866.

From Ja[me]s H. Ladson & Co.

Charleston, 15 January 1847

D[ea]r Sir, We have been requested to send the enclosed Petition to you. It is very desirable to have an appropriation for two bouys [*sic*] at each of the Santee bars, a light at Bull's Bay, and more efficient lights for Charleston Harbour, the present beacons being almost worthless. It is suggested instead of these last, to mark out the North Channel by a light at our new Fort Sumter, and another at the point of the Battery. We are aware that this is an unfortunate time to make this application, but we are confident you will do the best you can for us, and remain Very Respectfully, Y[ou]r ob[edien]t Serv[an]ts, Jas. H. Ladson & Co.

DS with En in DNA, RG 46 (U.S. Senate), 29A-G3. NOTE: The enclosed petition, dated 1/12, is signed by 61 citizens, officials, firms, and ship captains of Charleston. It was presented by Calhoun to the Senate on 1/19 and was referred to the Committee on Commerce.

From ELIZABETH A. R. LINN

St. Genevieve [Mo.,] Jan[uar]y 15th 1847

Will my ever kind, and dear Cousin, the truly great Mr. Calhoun permit me, to solicit his powerful influence, in obtaining a Commission, in the army for my Son, William Augustus Linn. For his capacity, to fill any station, in which a young man, could be placed, to defend his Country, permit me, to refer you, to Gen[era]l [Edmund P.] Gaines, Gen[era]l A[ugustus C.] Dodge, & my good Brother, Dr. [James H.] Relfe, of the House of Representatives. From the commencement, of our war, with Mexico, my Son, has been intens[e]ly anxious, to join the Army, but my health, has been so very bad, that I could not consent, for him, to leave me. Finding however, there is but little prospect, of my regaining health, I feel, that it will be too selfish for me to detain my Son, from a situation, on which he, has fixed his heart. Therefore I will be profoundly grateful, if you will, get him a Commission in the Army.

For several months, I have been striving, at different times, to address you, a long letter, to explain to you, my *True situation*, as it respects, this dreadful Law Suit, between Gov[erno]r [Francis] Thomas [of Md.] & Col. [Thomas H.] Benton, but Alas, I am so feeble, from continued illness, that it requires, the most painful effort, to write you these few lines. That the least blame, in your pure, & lofty mind, should rest, on the memory, of my Sainted Husband [Lewis F. Linn, former Senator from Missouri], or on myself, in this sad affair would be a source of *deep sorrow* to me, when I am fully aware, if the facts were *all known* to you, that you would *approve* of the course; that we were *compel[l]ed to take.* I have written to

Doctor Relfe, to inform you *all* about this matter, as I have not the strength, to write, to you fully, on the subject, & your good opinion is too dear to me, to silently let misrepresentation take its course against me. I hope dear Mrs. [Anna Maria Calhoun] Clemson, & all your interesting family are enjoying good health. If Mrs. [Floride Colhoun] Calhoun is with you, please to give her my respectful Compliments & for yourself, receive the warmest Regard, & The most exalted Esteem of Your sincere Friend, Elizabeth A.R. Linn.

ALS in ScCleA.

To Ja[me]s Ed[ward] Calhoun, Ju[nio]r, [Columbia, S.C.]

Washington, 16th Jan[uar]y 1847

My dear James, I enclose, agreeably to your request, a check on the bank of Commerce of New York [City] for $60, which I hope you will receive in time. As soon as it comes to hand, acknowledge its receipt, so that I may know it has arrived safely.

I hope you ["keep" *interlined*] your accounts square by paying as you go & having no debts. I feel confident you will use every economy. It is absolutely necessary this year in consequence of our Alabama crop being cut so very short by the worms. I will find it difficult to get through the year.

I am glad to hear such good accounts of your progress & standing. Willie [William Lowndes Calhoun] writes, that the members of the Legislature from Pendleton report you to be at the head of your class. Go on my son. Acquire knowledge & good habits & cultivate honorable sentiments. Willie I suppose is now on his way to Alabama.

The bill to create a Lieut[enant-]General has just been voted down by a considerable majority in the Senate & may be considered as killed. It is an important stept [*sic*] towards bring[ing] the war to a close. I have thus far kept silence, but will seize some early opportunity to express my opinion in full in reference to the war and our future military operations.

I have no time to add more. Write me as often as leisure will permit. Let me know what you are stud[y]ing & how you are please[d] with the particular branch of knowledge which you are stud[y]ing & all that you may think interesting about the College. Your affectionate father, J.C. Calhoun.

ALS in NcD, John C. Calhoun Papers.

J[ohn] C. Calhoun and Others to [J A M E S K. P O L K]

[Washington, *ca.* January 16, 1847?]

Dear Sir, We beg leave to recommend to you for an appointment as a Captain of Dragoons, Edward Manigault ["of Charleston, South Carolina" *interlined*]. Mr. Manigault we believe is fully qualified by education, and character for such an appointment. [*Signed:*] J.C. Calhoun, R[obert] B[arnwell] Rhett, Armistead Burt, J[oseph] A. Woodward, R[ichard] F. Simpson, I[saac] E. Holmes, A[lexander] D. Sims, A[ndrew] P. Butler.

LS with En in DNA, RG 107 (Secretary of War), Personnel Papers, 1838–1912: Applications for Appointment, No. 44. Note: Enclosed was an ALS of 1/11/1847 from Daniel E. Huger, [former Senator from S.C.], to Butler, recommending Manigault. Calhoun and Butler were the Senators and the other signers of the LS were Representatives from S.C. The undated LS is given an approximate date by its En which has an EU indicating it was received [in the War Dept.?] on 1/20. Manigault was appointed Capt. of Infantry on 3/5/1847 and had risen to Major when mustered out in 1848. Later, as a Confederate Major he served in the defenses of Charleston.

Remarks on an amendment to the graduation bill, 1/18. Under consideration was a bill to reduce the price of public lands unsold after a period of years to the minimum. It was proposed that a briefer period and a lower price be stipulated for poorer "pine lands" in four States on the Gulf of Mexico. "Mr. Calhoun said if he could believe that this amendment could be adopted without other discriminations, he would vote for it: but he concurred entirely in the views of the Senator from New Jersey [William L. Dayton], that a discrimination in one case would lead to endless confusion. Under these impressions, he should vote against the amendment [which subsequently failed of adoption]." From *Congressional Globe*, 29th Cong., 2nd Sess., p. 201. Variants in the Washington, D.C., *Daily Union*, January 18, 1847, p. 2; the Washington, D.C., *Daily National Intelligencer*, January 19, 1847, p. 2.

From R[ichard] K. Crallé

My dear Sir: I read your last letter with much interest, and entirely concur in the views it contains. I took the liberty of stating them to your warm friend, Judge [Daniel A.?] Wilson a day or two since, who cordially approved of them throughout, and begs me to say to you that the position you have taken must and will be sustained by the Country, if we would save ourselves from ultimate disgrace.

The remarks of Preston King [Representative from N.Y.], which fully confirm your anticipations have been received and read here with indignation by men of all parties. If he speak the sentiments of [Silas] Wright, it seems to me that the *stratagy* of the school will most likely turn against the contrivers. The annunciation must rouse and concentrate the whole South and South-west, which, in my view, is more important than any thing else. The want of this union has heretofore presented an insuperable obstacle to every effort at reform. United, we shall be able to throw of[f] the machinery of Party which has kept the Country in thrall for the last fifteen years. There is a manifest inclination on the part of the People to be rid of the Caucus machinery which has so long enslaved them. Amongst us here the Hunkers are already driven to the wall; or if the system be resorted to at all, its powers are directed against themselves. This may be inferred from the nomination of [William] Smith [Governor of Va., as Democratic candidate for U.S. Senator], as he is not regarded as the Candidate of the Hunkers. We have not yet heard of the result of the election, but from the small vote of [John W.] Jones in the Caucus (15 only as I hear) there is not much probability that he has been chosen. He, it is understood represented the Hunkers in the Legislature. I do not yet despair, however, of [Robert M.T.] Hunter's election as I am told this morning by an intelligent friend just from Richmond, that the Whigs will unite with his friends in preference to any other Democrat.

But as to the movement of Wright through King, Is it not probable that the main design is to drive you into an open opposition to the war, whether carried on offensively or defensively? I can well imagine the policy which might dictate such a movement. The war itself is, notwithstanding the blunders committed ["is" *canceled*] popular. The ardent, acting, aspiring portion of the Country, the army, the navy, and the horde of Contractors must needs be in favour of it. To break you down with the powerful and active interests, and at the same time to separate you from the Party, and throw you into a false position, might well suggest itself to such a mind as Wright's—and no more effectual a schism could have been devised than the one proposed by King. Now, while I do not in the least doubt that the plan you suggest of *conducting* the war is the only wise one, and that, if Santa Anna be the man I take him to be, the Government will be compelled to adopt it ultimately to save itself from defeat and disgrace; still I should be very sorry to see you play into their hands by opposing the war itself on account of the course of those scoundrels as respects the acquired territory. I doubt whether, in the present war spirit of the Country, you could be sustained to this extent, though I doubt not you would be as to the mode you propose of conducting it.

Again—as to the final settlement of the question, should we hold on to the conquered territory, can it be possible that the South would submit to the danger and degradation proposed? If these men be serious in their avowed purposes, and attempt to carry them out, the time will have fully arrived when a separation will be inevitable, and separation will be the result. But I doubt the sincerity of the movers, so far as Wright and his clique is concerned. I fear it is only a fient [*sic*]—a *russe de guerre*, having for its present and principal object the cutting off of you and your friends from the Party, and placing you in direct opposition to the Administration and the war.

These are hastily considered views, suggested in the absence of facts and circumstances, without a better knowledge of which no accurate judgment can be formed. So far as I have been able to learn, I think this movement has injured the New York managers more than any other act of which they have been guilty. God send it may totally prostrate them in the South.

We are here in the midst of arrangements for the spring Canvass for Congress; and, in this District you may form some idea of the progress of events when I tell you that not a single candidate has been named who is not an open and avowed friend of yours. Indeed it is admitted on all hands that none other could either be nominated or elected, so strongly is public sentiment setting in your favour. The old Hunkers here are themselves talking quite favourably. The same change, I think, is observable in every portion of the State, and your course will be looked to with much interest.

At the earnest request of Capt. Otey, the father of the young man [Van Rensselaer Otey] mentioned in it, I send you the enclosed letter—a copy of which has been forwarded to the President [James K. Polk]. Capt. O[tey] is one of our wealthiest and most influential men; and though he is aware that you do not concern yourself with such matters, he begs me to enclose this to you under the hope that an occasion might occur when you might be able to ["serve" *canceled*] do something for his son [*ms. torn*]s a very exalted opinion of you, and I verily believe would be more flattered to hear that you had *spoken* in his behalf, than that another had obtained a Lieutenancy for him. He has just returned from Point Comfort where he offered to give a thousand Dollars for a substitute, but his son refused to listen to it. The fact is, he is a daring, and adventurous youth, and will cut his way to distinction if an occasion presents himself [*sic*]. I wish much, if you are on terms with [William L.] Marcy [Secretary of War], and an occasion should offer, you would endeavour to procure him a Lieutenancy. By so doing you would oblige a powerful interest in this section. But the Father is aware that you take no part in [*ms. torn*; m]atters, and does not anticipate anything at your hands. He [*ms. torn*] your once having applied in behalf of a young man of his [*ms. torn*]nd considered it so high an honor, that, with the feelings of a [*ms. torn*] he begs me to send it to you.

It is thought that Mr. Willis Bocock of Buckingham will succeed Mr. [Edmund W.] Hubard [Representative from Va.] in Congress. He is I learn a fast friend; and far more *active* than his predecessor. I am, myself, nominated in the Papers this morning, but, even were the ["nomina" *canceled*] convention to concur, (which I have no idea they will do, as I never mingle with the People), my engagements are too numerous and urgent to allow me to canvass the District.

I will send you by the Friday's mail a number of the [Lynchburg, Va., Daily] Virginian containing an extract from a work lately published by Prof[essor George] Bush of the University of New York, which presents some of the most extraordinary *phenomena* in Psychology, that have yet come to my notice. I should like to know what you think of them.

With best respects to Mrs. [Floride Colhoun] Calhoun and the members of your family that may be in Washington, I remain yours truly, R.K. Crallé.

ALS in ScCleA. NOTE: The writings of George Bush mentioned in Crallé's penultimate paragraph relate to his interest in Swedenborgianism.

From BENJ[AMIN] Y. MARTIN

Abbeville C[ourt] H[ouse,] So. Ca., 19 Jan[uar]y 1847
My Dear Sir, My father, Jacob Martin, has a son, his youngest, a volunteer in the Palmetto Regiment. He is a private in Capt. [J. Foster] Marshall's Company raised from this District. Without the knowledge either of my father or Brother, I have deemed it my duty to write to you, & bespeak your kind services, if any opportunity presents itself, of presenting his claims to the President for an appointment.

My brother [John J. Martin] is a youth about 20 years of age & has been reading Law in my office for about a year. He has the intelligence & spirit to discharge & perform faithfully & gallantly any duties which may be assigned to him.

My object was simply to bring this subject to your notice—Knowing that if the occasion should arise you might ["would" *interlined*] be able to serve my brother. I remain with great respect & high esteem your ob[edien]t Servant, Benj: Y. Martin.

P.S. I rec[eive]d your letter on the subject of your demand against Dr. W[illiam] H. Calhoun & shall reserve in my hands about the amount you mentioned. There is nothing new or important here. Our eyes are turned alternately with anxiety to Washington & Mexico. It is the opinion here that the war should be vigorously prosecuted & unless it is brought to a close this Campaign, that we will have a second Spanish Gue[r]rilla on our hands. B.Y. Martin.

ALS in ScCleA.

REMARKS IN DEBATE WITH THOMAS H. BENTON ON A REPORT OF THE MILITARY AFFAIRS COMMITTEE

[In the Senate, January 19, 1847]
[Benton, the committee chairman, reported a bill granting bounty lands to members of the Army. He was criticized by John Macpherson Berrien of Ga. for having, contrary to the Senate's previous instructions to the committee, omitted officers of volunteers from the bounties. Berrien moved to amend the bill. There was a warm discussion among Berrien, Benton, and several other Senators.]

Mr. Calhoun asked for the reading of the instructions to the committee.

They were again read.

Mr. Calhoun said he was not in favor of the amendment now proposed, and he doubted very much whether he should be able to bring himself to vote for any such provision for granting bounty lands. They had had a good deal of experience on this subject, and the result of that experience was, that it was the very worst mode, both for the treasury and for the soldiers and volunteers for whose benefit it was intended. But he rose to say that, in his humble opinion, it was due to the mover of this proposition—it was due to the authority of the Senate itself, that the amendment should be put in, so that the bill should stand precisely where it would have stood if the members of the committee had recollected that there had been such instructions. He was disposed to throw no censure upon the committee; there were a great many amendments moved, and it was not extraordinary that this particular matter should have been overlooked. But, most undoubtedly, if the committee had known there were such instructions, and omitted to put them in, it would be an act of the deepest disrespect to the Senate. Under this impression, though opposed to the proposition, he, for one, should give his decided vote to put the amendment where it would have been if the committee had remembered the instructions.

[*Benton expressed "astonishment" at Calhoun's remarks and asserted that if Berrien's motion were adopted, the amendment would become a part of the bill "and could not be again dissented from." He moved to send the bill back to committee.*]

Mr. Calhoun said he was not in the habit of doing anything without due reflection. He might have been mistaken as to the stage in which this bill was now. But he had spoken under the impression that it was before the Senate as in committee of the whole; if so, an amendment could be inserted, and the Senate would have an opportunity to strike out that amendment; or, at least, to record its vote upon it when the bill was taken out of committee. It was a point, however, which he never could yield, that the bill should be made to conform to the instructions given to the committee.

[*Benton said Calhoun had made "a question of revolt" and ridiculed the notion that an amendment be inserted in order to strike it out. He referred to children building "cob-houses" to knock down or putting wood chips on each others' heads to knock off.*]

Mr. Calhoun. I am not apt to be excited or to be puerile. There is no puerility about it; there is no accusation of revolt. The majority of the committee themselves sustained him in the view he took. But it was the Senator from Missouri himself who set up the authority of the committee, and justified his disobedience to the instructions of the Senate. The Senator himself seemed to take the responsibility. I only said that if the disobedience was intentional, it was a disrespect to the Senate. I only claim now that we should do what would have been done if the committee had not made an oversight. This is due to the Senate.

[*Benton claimed that he had been "arraigned before the world for neglecting the business of the Senate." He demanded the yeas and nays on his motion and Berrien's amendment. If the latter carried, he would move immediately to strike out the amendment.*]

Mr. Calhoun said that, as the Senator himself agreed to do the thing which he deemed puerile, he (Mr. C[alhoun]) should vote for his proposition when in order.

[*There was further discussion among several Senators, during which Benton said that, though he felt compelled to make the motion to recommit, he would vote against it.*]

Mr. Calhoun said, if the Senator did not support his own motion, he (Mr. C[alhoun]) certainly would not do it.

[*Benton's motion to recommit was defeated 0 to 50. The vote on Berrien's amendment was 26 to 26. The presiding officer then voted in the negative and defeated it.*]

From *Congressional Globe*, 29th Cong., 2nd Sess., pp. 206–207. Also printed in the Washington, D.C., *Daily National Intelligencer*, January 20, 1847, p. 2; the Charleston, S.C., *Mercury*, January 25, 1847, p. 2; the Edgefield, S.C., *Advertiser*, February 3, 1847, p. 2. Variants in the Washington, D.C., *Daily Union*, January 20, 1847, p. 2; the New York, N.Y., *Herald*, January 21, 1847, p. 4; the Alexandria, Va., *Gazette and Virginia Advertiser*, January 21, 1847, p. 2 (reprinting the Baltimore, Md., *American* of unstated date); the Alexandria, Va., *Gazette and Virginia Advertiser*, January 23, 1847, p. 2. NOTE: In the second variant report cited, Benton was described as "considerably excited." The third variant described Benton as "the principal belligerent" who had responded to Berrien and Calhoun "by an unusual display of ill-nature." The fourth variant cited concluded its report with the observation: "Mr. Calhoun replied mildly and with dignity, and Mr. Benton was up again several times lashing himself into a towering passion, and exhibiting himself in the light of a chafed bull, bellowing and pitching at every one who came near him."

From BENJ[AMI]N HUGER CAPERS

Retirement [near Durhamville, Tenn.,] January 20, 1847
Dear Sir, Though I have not the pleasure of a *personal* acquaintance
with you, I have always greatly admired your *character*; and, therefore, I address you this communication, without apology. The *political opinions* of my Brother, the Rev. Bishop [William] Capers,
with whom you are acq[uaint]ed, are such as I have cherished as my
own, for the last twenty years. About ten years ago, I located my
family permanently in the western part of Tennessee, in order that
Mrs. [Rebecca Greaves] Capers might be near her Parents. Since
that time, while I have been engaged in the ministry of the Methodist
Church, I have also looked with care and attention to the important
questions, which, from time to time, have agitated our beloved country. Permit me to say, that the course you have taken, on all those
important subjects, [*one word canceled and "has always" interlined*]
met my *cordial approbation.* My object in this Note, is to request
that you will send me, all your *Speeches*, during the present session
of Congress, [and] such other *Documents* as you may think will interest me. Dir[ect] your communications to *Durhamsville, Lauder-
dale County, Tennessee.* I send this by a friend to be mailed in
Memphis, believing it will reach you sooner. You have a *host* of
friends in my neighbourhood, and in the surrounding country; and
should you, at any time, visit the western part of Tennessee, you will
find a *warm Carolina welcome*, at the residence of your friend, and
obedient servant, *Benj[ami]n Huger Capers.*

ALS in ScCleA.

Remarks on the military bounty lands bill, 1/20. "Mr. Calhoun
rose not to detain the Senate a moment. He simply proposed to
state the ground on which he should place his vote. He should give
his vote for that which would make the bounty most valuable to the
soldier or the volunteer; and as he believed restrictions would make
it less valuable, he should vote for that which had the least restrictions. Governed by these views, he should vote, in the first instance,
for the amendment of the Senator from Ohio [Thomas Corwin, which
gave unrestricted grants to all who served in the war honorably and
their heirs]; and if that succeeded, he should vote for the amendment
of the Senator from Texas [Thomas J. Rusk, which provided for the
award of scrip rather than bounty land warrants]." From *Congressional Globe*, 29th Cong., 2nd Sess., p. 215. Variants in the *Wash-*

ington, D.C., *Daily Union,* January 21, 1847, p. 1; the New York, N.Y., *Herald,* January 22, 1847, p. 4; the Charleston, S.C., *Mercury,* January 25, 1847, p. 2.

From J[AMES] H.[?] FRY

Richmond, 21 Jan[uar]y [18]47

My dear Sir, Permit me to congratulate you upon the election of the Hon[orab]l[e] J[ames] M. Mason to the Senate of the U.S.—who is one of y[ou]r best friends—as well as Mr. [Robert M.T.] Hunter. This election is an evidence of y[ou]r growing popularity upon the people, for y[ou]r late course in sustaining the country instead of that party which has brought such distress upon the U.S.

We have great confidence and hope that you may yet be instrumental in restoring *peace*; and putting a stop to the unnrighteous[?] war which we have now existing.

I cannot see how this government can go on without the repeal of the Sub Treasury—The Tarriff of [18]42 again brought to pass & a duty on Tea & coffee.

Excuse this hasty scrawl. With my best wishes for y[ou]r success I am dear Sir Y[ou]rs truly, J.H.[?] Fry.

ALS in ScCleA. NOTE: Fry was a member of the Va. Senate at this time.

From RUFUS W. GRISWOLD

Philadelphia, Jan. 22, 1847

Dear Sir, It is intended immediately (unless you should discourage the undertaking) to renew efforts to have the American author placed on the same footing with the foreigner, as a teacher of the American people. It is hoped that you will take charge of the subject in the Senate. With your support no doubt is entertained of success. Unwilling to trouble you with the reading of a long memorial, I take the liberty of stating a few of the positions maintained in one that has been prepared, and of asking whether if all these positions were established to your perfect satisfaction, you would approve of a law of International Copyright.

1. American authors lose now in Europe nearly as much as the

foreign authors lost here, by the unlicensed republications of their works. (Over 300 American books were reprinted in Great Britain during the last year.)

2. The American author is almost excluded from his own market by the influx of foreign books, under the present system. The better class of our authors therefore retire from the field, in which they are excluded from a fair competition, and the education of the people is thus in a very large degree surrendered to teachers opposed to our country and its institutions.

[*Printed clipping*: "A short time before Mr. Washington Irving was appointed Minister to Spain, he undertook to dispose of a production of merit, written by an American who had not yet established a commanding name in the literary market, but found it impossible to get an offer from any of the principal publishers. 'They even declined to publish it at the author's cost,' he says, 'alleging that it was not worth their while to trouble themselves about native works, of doubtful success, while they could pick and choose among the successful works daily poured out by the British press, *for the copyright of which they had nothing to pay.*' And not only is the American thus in some degree excluded from the audience of his countrymen, but the publishers, who have a control over many of the newspapers and other periodicals, exert themselves, in the way of their business, to build up the reputation of the foreigner whom they rob, and to destroy that of the home author who aspires to a competition with him."]

3. The present system shuts out from our country nearly all the good foreign literature of the present age, and gives us a vast increase of the baser sort.

[*Printed clipping*: "*For the information of readers unacquainted with the operation of the present system, it may be necessary to state more particularly than has been done in the text, some of the ways in which it tends to weaken the mind and deprave the heart of the nation. Its literature is the richest boon we receive from the Past, and the literature of the Present, if fairly represented in the republications, would, upon the whole, no doubt, have a most salutary influence. But the denial of copyright to foreigners effectually deprives us of most of the really great works with which the presses of Europe are teeming, while it gives us nearly all they produce that is frivolous and vicious. It costs a great deal of money as well as labour to prepare the market for large works; there must be much advertising, a large distribution of copies, elaborate abstracts in reviews and journals, and many other means to create a demand; and the expenses of these means must be added to those of the mechanical manufacture. Yet now, as has been shown by numerous instances, as soon as a house with enterprise and capital has issued a readable impression of a work, and secured for it such a circulation as promises a fair remuneration, some base fellow is sure to bring out on dingy brown paper and small type a deluge of cheap copies, with which he reaps all the advantages of the first publisher's efforts, and leaves him with his stock unsold, and his investment unreturned. It is true that, notwithstanding these dangers, a few of the more indispensable histories and other fruits of true cultivation are reprinted here: but they are generally issued in the most compact and cheap style, sometimes much abridged, and nearly always without those charts and plates which add so much to the value of many foreign editions. A recognition of the foreign author's right of property would at once remedy this part of the evil entirely.

On the other hand, there is extraordinary activity in the republication of the light and licentious literature of the time. It is sickening to lean over the counters of the shops where cheap books are sold, and survey the trash with which the criminal folly of the government is deluging the country. Every new issue deepens the wide spread depravity, and extends the demand for its successor. As but little capital is required for the business, and the returns are quick, these leprous spots are constantly springing up in the cities; and to gratify the prurient tastes which they create, the literary sewers of Paris and London are dragged for the filthiest stuff which floats or sinks in their turbid waters. The demoralization increases, and the novels of Paul de Kock, disgusting as they are, in the original, (in which a racy style and sparkling wit render them attractive, despite their moral deformity,) are made worse by the addition of gross obscenity by the translator; and from those of Eugene Sue the reflective portions, which serve to neutralize the effects of the narrative, are left out. All private morals, all domestic peace, fly before this withering curse which the Congress persists in sustaining, by its refusal to recognise the rights of the foreign author. For, if the respectable publishers could be protected in their business, they would furnish good editions of good books, that would give a healthy tone to the common sentiment, and drive this profligate literature into oblivion; if the foreign author were protected in his rights, he would be but a competitor of the native author, and would have an inducement to support those liberal principles of society which are here established, thus strengthening them here, and diffusing them in his own country; and if the American were thus admitted to a competition in his own market with the European, our best intellects would be busy with the instruction of the people, which is now in so large a degree surrendered to the supporters of aristocracies."]

4. The books of real value that are reprinted here, under the present system, are almost all abridged or otherwise mutilated, and are printed in the worst possible manner.

5. The recognition of the foreign author's right of property would not to any considerable degree increase the prices of books, while it would insure an improvement in the selection of them, and in their manufacture.

The extracts on the preceding page are from a book of mine in the press in this city, which treats but incidentally of the subject. They are inserted as being more easy to read than my poor MS.

I am not ignorant that your attention is now very much engrossed by public affairs, and I should accuse myself of a wont of patriotism as well as of courtesy if I sought for any common purpose a moment to divert your mind from its present intents. But I trust you will think upon the subject of this letter with the large number of persons most immediately interested. It seems to me that a statesman could by no other means advance the interests of our country, more than by that protection of the foreign author, which would bring his books into a direct competition with those of our own writers. With the profoundest respect I have the honor to be Your ob[edien]t Serv[an]t, Rufus W. Griswold.

ALS in ScCleA. NOTE: The two printed clippings inserted by Griswold are from his work, *The Prose Writers of America*, one from the Preface and the second from a note on p. 48. An AEU by Calhoun reads "Mr. Griswold[,] refers to international copy right."

From S. A. LAURENCE

New York [City,] 22d January 1847

Dear Sir: In the administration of Mr. [Martin] Van Buren, I suggested to you some crude thoughts on the subject of an independent Treasury, having previously submitted them to him, and which I think were among the *first* that called his attention to the subject. The present Law embraces the fundamental principles of those suggestions, with the exception of a provision I deemed important, and which, had it been retained, would probably have silenced much of the clamour raised against the act, without affecting unfavorably the am[oun]t of Specie deposites of the Treasury, or the favorable results expected to be derived therefrom—viz: That the issue of Treasury drafts at sight for $100 and upwards without Interest, be authorised in payment of public dues receivable at the option of the applicant, redeemable only where issued, and Specie to that am[oun]t reserved for their redemption. Such a provision would save much of the trouble and expence of counting and transporting Specie, and the risk attending it; the drafts would always be in demand, being a safer and less expensive remittance than specie. But the Law, as it stands, may answer a good purpose, and I hope it will not be repealed, at any rate until after a fair trial. I know the opposition to the Law and the influences that will be brought against it are powerful, consisting of Officers, Directors, borrowers & dealers of Banks, with their friends and connections, Importing and Shipping-merchants, Manufacturers and their respective influences, the New-England States in mass—all resident foreign Bankers, Merchants and Agents, with their numerous dependents & influence; and all similar classes of influence in England. The influence of Banks and Bankers, must be curtailed and brought within legitimate bounds. To that influence may be attributed the panics, pressure in the money market[,] embarrassment, and failures constantly occurring—to the detriment of the Treasury and the mercantile interest of the Country. The Independent Treasury is the only remedy, and will, if fairly tried, cure the evil in a short time. It will divert from Bank deposites, a large amount of specie to the vaults of the Treasury, and place it beyond the reach of Bank-Loans or operations; thus reducing their influence to that extent, while it prevents the shipment of that am[oun]t of Specie to foreign ports.

The Banks of this Country are said to be more or less connected with and influenced by foreign capitalists; and so long as the revenue of the Country is deposited with Banks, it will measurably be subject to foreign influence, or at any rate to the vicissitudes of trade, which often result in losses so extensive as to effect the credit & standing of the Banks—thus rendering the safety of the deposite less secure, than it would be under the immediate charge and control of the Government. In resisting this act, the Business-men of this Country do not show their usual foresight. Most of their troubles for a long series of years, have been caused by the action & undue influence of Banks on the money market: They have brought on every crisis, & to secure themselves & promote their own interest, they will continue to do so, so long as they retain the power, irrespective of individual embarrassment or ruin, or the security of public deposites. It is often asserted & believed that our merchants trade in British Capital. It is not true—on the contrary, the British merchant has the advantage of our Capital—the value of our exports invariably exceed the am[oun]t of their advances. Take a case: The American merchant consigns produce to the British merchant to the am[oun]t of $100, draws against it for $75, leaving in the hands of the British merchant 25 P[e]r Cent of the investment—thus furnishing him Capital to that extent—And, as to the Business transacted by British Agents resident in this Country, it is injurious both to the American merchant & the Government. He floods the market with a refuse Stock of worthless goods (paying of course a small duty) sells them at auction for cash, takes the proceeds in specie from the Banks, & remits it to England: thus lessening the importation of the sound article, which would pay a full duty, & cramping the regular merchant's means of payment by the constant drain of Specie from the Banks, which of course reduces their means of granting facilities to the regular merchant. Had the independent Treasury been in operation the last two Years, most of the troubles, herein alluded to, would have been avoided; while the Capital of the Country would probably have increased One hundred & fifty millions of Dollars.

It is to be hoped, the Mexican War will be settled before the sickly season commences; it will save many valuable lives, & much treasure; and render the individual, most prominent in effecting it, popular beyond all former example! What think you of the proposed plan of holding the conquered possessions—securing them by military posts, withdraw the forces, & waite the pleasure of Mexico to sue for peace?

The issue of Treasury notes with Interest, convertible into Stock within a given period, is the best, if not the only, mode of securing the Loan to pay the expence of this war; and I hope the Bill will pass.

There is one subject in which I feel a deep interest—the next Presidency. Will you do me the favor to write to me on that subject, and state, *in extenso*, the plan of operations. We have many strong friends here, ready to co-operate and act; also a strong paper (Journal of Commerce) to aid the cause. Hoping for an early answer I remain, Dear Sir Truly & respectfully, Yours, S.A. Laurence.

ALS in ScCleA.

From HENRY MCKEE

Saint Louis, Jan[uar]y 22, 1847

Dear Sir, Since I had the pleasure of seeing you at the seat of government, I have watched with no little interest, the agitation of the slave question, merging itself into every subject of national character: let the Spartan band from the South & West remain firm to the Missouri Compromise and the puny and pussilanimous bravadoing of the northern fanatics cannot prevent us from acquiring territory in Mexico under constitutional principles. Should the rights of the slave holding States ever be violated by misguided men, I would meet them as the enemies of our country, with the sword in one hand and the Torch in the other & if possible the entrenchment of our liberties should be their graves. When moral force is exhausted my principle is neither compromise nor concession.

Although partial strangers to each other, I approach you for a favor with the utmost confidence, owing to indulgence & kindness ["*of*" *altered to* "to"] friends. Means to a considerable extent have passed hence, times are precarious & dangerous to do business without sufficient capital. In pursuance of all this, I ask (respectfully) the Executive of the U.S. through you for the appointment of Captain, Paymaster or Commissary in one of the new regiments to be raised for service in Mexico. If called into service it is my opinion that I would not tarnish either the flag of our Country or that of my *ancestry*, in addition should civil & peaceable relations be prosecuted the government might find in me an efficient & faithful representative. The Hon[ora]ble Ja[me]s H. Relfe [Representative from Mo.] will join you in this and here let me observe that his Excellency has a letter from Gov. [John C.] Edwards which I handed him while at Washington City.

Now Sir whether you exert yourself or do not exert yourself, whether sucessfull or unsuccessfull, it will not abate my disposition to honor & elevate your name. I will conclude by invoking the aid of providence in consum[m]ating your wise & virtuous acts, and that the American people from Maine to Florida & hence to the Pacific Ocean ["pray"(?) *canceled and* "rise" *interlined*] with one voice & do you the justice so richly deserved & so honorably earned.

My old friend Major Alphonse Wetmore, who so nobly fought on the N.W. frontier during the late war is an applicant for a Colonelcy in one of the new regiments. The Major lost his arm and is otherwise highly deserving. I most respectfully ask for his application your attention. Please write to me at this place. I have the honor to Remain Your friend, Henry McKee.

ALS in ScCleA. NOTE: An AEU by Calhoun reads "See Gen[era]l [David R.] Atchison[?]." Henry McKee was the brother of William McKee, owner of the St. Louis *Democrat* and became a Confederate partisan in Missouri. However, no record of a commission in the Mexican War has been found.

From HAROLD SMYTH

Wytheville Va., January 22nd 1847

Dear Sir, Having no *chance* of access to the present Administration, thro my *immediate* Representative [George W. Hopkins], and there being at this time, no Democratic Senator in Congress from this State, thro whom to apply: I venture to request the favor of you to place the name of one of my son's before the Secretary of War [William L. Marcy], as an applicant for a Cadet's Warrant at West Point. His name is Alexander Smyth. Aside from a father's predilections, I think I may say, he is worthy of such appointment. I do not hope for much of personal favor from this Administration, why, I do not know. Nevertheless I wish to gratify my son in making the application.

From the recent selection of the Post Master General [Cave Johnson] of newspaper's in Southwestern Virginia thro which to circulate proposals for carrying the mails in Virginia, I think, I am justified in the expression, that I do not expect much from this Administration. There are two Democratic papers published in this quarter of the State. One, printed at Wytheville [the *Republican and Virginia Constitutionalist*] which I edit; the other printed in Abingdon [the *Virginian*] edited by a man who was a [William G.] Brownlow whig in 1840. This latter paper is under the patronage of Col. G[eorge] W. Hopkins and has a circulation not reaching *Three Hundred*, exclusive of exchanges. The paper which I edit has a circulation to subscribers of over *Six hundred*. Now if it is deemed proper and economical to publish the proposals in a newspaper in this quarter of the State; would it not be more just & useful to publish in a newspaper with a circulation of Six hundred, than in one with a circulation of Three hundred subscribers? The price of publishing will reach near Six hundred dollars.

It may be, that, neither Mr. [James K.] Polk nor the Post Master

General is aware of this crying injustice to one, who bore some part in the struggle of 1844. The man who has been chosen for favor and patronage, took no part whatever in that struggle. He was nothing other than a compositor in the Office of the Banner a newspaper then published at Abingdon owned by a company of gentlemen, and edited by Robert Lathem.

The vote in this Senate District at the election of 1844, when compared with that of 1840, exhibits an increase of the majority, of four hundred and fifty three votes. The County of Wythe (my native County,) the Spring of 1844 [*sic*; 1840?] elected a whig by 3 votes. I returned to the county (having been from it some six or seven years,) in November 1843, commenced the publication of a Democratic paper on the 25th Dec[embe]r of 1843. Wythe gave Mr. Polk *Two hundred and forty four* votes of a majority. In 1840 Wythe gave Mr. Van Buren 195 votes of a majority.

I feel anxious to know if a *certain class* of the ["members of the" *interlined*] Democratic party are to be put to the ban. If they are not, then I desire that the President, and the Hon. Post Master General be informed of the injustice, first to the public, and to myself last, done thro the information, advice, and influence, as I presume of Col. Hopkins.

Will you please consider this matter. Very Sincerely Your friend, Harold Smyth.

ALS in ScCleA. NOTE: An AEU by Calhoun reads "Gen[era]l Smyth." Harold Smyth was the son of the late Alexander Smyth, Brig. Gen. in the War of 1812 and Representative from Va.

From A[LEXANDER] H. EVERETT, [U.S. Commissioner to China]

Macao, Jan. 24, 1847

Dear Sir, I received yesterday your letter of the 8th of October last. It will give me great pleasure to co-operate with you and your friend, so far as it may be in my power, in introducing the culture of tea into the United States. From the general similarity, or rather, as you say, identity of the climate and other physical characteristics of the two countries, I see no reason, why the plant, with proper management, should not thrive as well with you, as it does here.

I avail myself of the opportunity, afforded by the overland mail, which is just about leaving, to acknowledge the receipt of your letter; and will immediately take measures for procuring and transmitting the seed. I have not time, before writing for this occasion, to make any inquiry upon the subject, and do not know, how far the habitual jealousy of the Chinese government in regard to foreigners may interpose obstacles: but you may, at all events, depend upon my best exertions. If I obtain the seed, I will send, at the same time, such information, as I may procure, in regard to the cultivation of the plant and the preparation of the leaf for market.

Accept my best thanks for your kind inquiries in regard to my health. It is not, and probably never will be, entirely restored; but does not seem to have been injuriously affected by the voyage, or the change of climate. My complaints do not prevent me from attending to business, although they impair, in some degree, my activity and enjoyment of life. If I were perfectly well, and, especially, were at liberty to visit, at discretion, all parts of the Empire, I should consider a residence here as exceedingly interesting.

My wife [Lucretia Peabody Everett] joins with me in cordial regards to Mrs. [Floride Colhoun] Calhoun. I shall be most happy to hear from you, at all times, upon this or any other subject. When are we to get the first volume of your Political Philosophy? I trust that your senatorial avocations will not prevent you from giving a few days occasionally to this enterprise. Cicero, you know, was in full practice in the Forum, and a leader in the Senate, at the time, when he wrote the celebrated six books on the Republic.

We have good news, so far as the success of our arms is concerned, by the overland mail, which has just arrived, & brings accounts of the taking of Monterey. I had hoped, however, and almost believed, that we should have received the still better intelligence of the conclusion, or, at least, probability of peace: so that I am, on the whole, rather disappointed. Faithfully yours, A.H. Everett.

ALS in ScCleA. NOTE: Everett's declining health led to his death in 7/1847.

From JOHN R. PETERS

New York [City,] 24 Jan. 1847

Dear Sir, It may be interesting & usefull for you to know that the letter which first appeared in the [New York Morning] Express & from thence is republished in all the papers is from a genuine manuscript from old Rough & Ready dated Monterey 9th Nov[embe]r

1846 and addressed to an *old distinguished & gallant* friend of his now *stationed* in this City. Wheather Gen[era]l [Zachary] Taylor intended this letter for publication or not he must be aware of of [*sic*] what is well known that this eratic old Gentleman dare do any thing that he may deem for public good, & that he is not embarrassed by feelings of responsibility to any body. Whatever effect this extraordinary letter may produce at Washington or in Mexico it will be eagerly sought & read by our entire reading population & its influence upon their minds will exceed that of any other man or body of men. On the subject of the war & our relations with Mexico he is the highest authority ["with the people" *interlined*] nor can their confidence in him be shaken by the acts of others. What has occasionally hap-[p]ened in all time has occur[r]ed again—["an" *changed to* "a"] respectable obscure Colo[nel], known only to a few thousands has ["unconsciously" *interlined*] come up in a few months to be ["known &" *interlined*] regarded by 20,000,000 as their Hero, Sage[,] Statesman & oricle. Every man[,] woman & boy views him as our most prudent[,] safe & competant General & that he has [*one word changed to* "earned"] a debt of gratitude from each by peraling[?] his life repeatedly for his country. The President [James K. Polk] having omit[t]ed to mention his name in official dispatches, the masses wait only for what they may deem evidence of intentional persecution to astonish him & the wise men of the nation by sliding him into the Presidency as quickly as we have been slid into a war of conquest. The people spread over such a vast extent of country are generally slow in coming to correct & fixed opinions upon great national questions but it often happens that our executive officers & leading representatives ["are" *canceled*] require more time to assertain public opinion & public policy. My extensive acquaintance with all the States makes me confident in my opinion that a large majority of the people desire this war of uncertain ["of" *canceled*] objects & ["uncertain" *canceled and* "doubtfull" *interlined*] results to be terminated by the present Congress on some such plan as suggested by Taylor & others. Nobody wants all Mexico & verry [*sic*] few expect to reap glory or money from ["crushing" *interlined*] an ignorant numerious hord[e] of obstinate distracted paupers—& then surrendering to them most of their impoverished ter[r]itory. The Chinese never squeeze a pauper ["to get money" *interlined*] nor does the arrogant & rapacious Britton expend their blood & treasure to conquer countries to be surrendered at the end of the contest. Our administration is generally esteemed to be composed of industrious labor[i]ous, men of good intentions—but at present the reliance of the people is ["principally" *interlined*] upon Congress. I belong to that numerous class of the democracy who look to Mr. Calhoun to steer the ship intoport [*sic*] when by unskilfull management she is ["in"(?) *canceled*] threatened with disaster. Indeed a great portion ["of the whigs" *interlined*] look to the same quarter, when they get alarmed.

If you have forgotten that I had the honor of your acquaintance some years ago, please to refer to my old friend W[illia]m R. King if present Gens. [Samuel] Houston [and Thomas J.] Rusk or Gen[era]l [John A.] Dix &C. With profound respect Your Ob[edien]t Servant, Jno. R. Peters.

P.S. I am precluded from giving the name of the gent[leman] who rec[eive]d the letter from Gen[era]l Taylor.

ALS in ScCleA. NOTE: The letter of Zachary Taylor referred to had been widely reprinted after being released by the recipient, Gen. Edmund P. Gaines. It was dated 11/9/1846. Taylor defended his actions at Monterey and expressed his disapproval of carrying the war further into Mexico and of annexing Mexican territory.

REMARKS ON THE TREASURY NOTE AND LOAN BILL

[In the Senate, January 25, 1847]
[*Dixon H. Lewis of Ala., chairman of the Committee on Finance, brought forward a bill from the House of Representatives to authorize a loan and an issue of Treasury notes. He asked immediate consideration. There was considerable debate.*]

Mr. Calhoun said he regretted exceedingly to hear that the state of the treasury required prompt action on this bill. He certainly felt disposed to give as prompt aid as any man in the Senate, in providing for the necessities of the treasury, but he could not agree to take up this bill to-day. He was, himself, he presumed, in the same condition as many other Senators. He had not examined the bill, and the reason why he had not done so was, that, in regard to all bills which originated in the other House, he considered it useless to examine them until their passage through that body, because, previous to their passage, they were liable to be amended, and materially changed in their provisions. He thought it was due to Senators, upon all sides, that there should be a postponement of the bill for one day at least; and his opinion was, that if pushed forward now, it would cause much more delay than if suffered to lie over for examination for one day. With this view, he should vote against the motion of the honorable Senator from Alabama. He hoped, however, that the Senator from Alabama would not press his motion.

[*The vote on immediate consideration of the bill was 24 to 24. The presiding officer voted affirmative, carrying the motion, and consideration proceeded. During discussion of complicated provisions of the bill, differences of opinion were expressed about the meaning of a section authorizing the purchase of State stock by the Secretary of the Treasury.*]

Mr. Calhoun presumed the proviso would authorize them to purchase it at par if it could not be obtained under par.

[*There followed lengthy debate, at the end of which the Senate voted 24 to 20 to adjourn for the day without voting on the bill.*]

From *Congressional Globe*, 29th Cong., 2nd Sess., p. 248. Also printed in the Washington, D.C., *Daily National Intelligencer*, January 26, 1847, p. 3. Variants in the Washington, D.C., *Daily Union*, January 25, 1847, p. 2; the New York, N.Y., *Herald*, January 27, 1847, p. 3; the Charleston, S.C., *Courier*, January 29, 1847, p. 2.

Further remarks on the Treasury Note and Loan Bill, 1/26. The Senate had adopted a proviso requiring that the Treasury notes to be issued should not be hypothecated or exchanged for less than the principle and interest due. It was objected that the return of the bill to the House of Representatives for concurrence in this amendment would cause too great a delay. "But, Mr. Calhoun, in two or three words, influenced the Senate very properly to agree to it [the retention of the proviso]. He said, let me tell the Senate that if this proviso be not agreed to, the notes may be hypothecated at much less than their value upon their face, as was the case in the late war with Great Britain." From the Charleston, S.C., *Courier*, January 30, 1847, p. 2. (Twice more in this debate Calhoun made barely reported remarks on amendments to the bill. *Congressional Globe*, 29th Cong., 2nd Sess., p. 261.)

From [Capt.] William Blanding

Mobile [Ala.], Jan. 27, 1847

Sir, I enclose you a letter from the Commissioned officers of Seven Companies of the So. Ca. Regiment of volunteers, which they have instructed me to forward to you. Three Companies departed yesterday from this port, with sealed orders, which will account for its not being signed by the whole Regiment. It is sufficient perhaps to say that ["they" *interlined*] concur with us.

This is intended as no idle compliment to Col. [Pierce M.] Butler, and it will not be regarded as such, We trust. It has been written without any previous conference with Col. Butler and in consequence of information which has reached us, that the Executive of our State [David Johnson] has stated to you that We desire to retain Col. Butler, under all circumstances, at the head of our Regiment. We desire his promotion and believe that as Brigadier he will be able still to advance our Regiment. I am with great respect Your ob[edien]t Ser[van]t, William Blanding.

P.S. The rest of the Regiment is now embarking.

[Enclosure]

Headquarter of Palmetto Regiment
Camp Deas Mobile [Ala.,] January 27th 1847

Sir, As the Commissioned officers of the Palmetto Regiment of South Carolina Volunteers, We desire ourselves rightly understood and our wishes fully expressed in relation to the appointment of a Brigadier General to command the forces of which our Regiment will constitute a part. It will be a source of the highest gratification to us that Col. P.M. Butler should remain at the head of our Regiment. He possesses in the greatest degree the confidence and regard of the Commissioned officers and of the rank and file and we are sensible that the honor of our State could not be trusted to safer hands.

Yet whilst his removal from his present post would be the cause of deep regret to us all We write in an earnest recommendation of him for the Post of Brigadier General. We believe from his long experience and high qualities of head and heart that no appointment could be made with more honor to our Country and benefit to the service.

Be pleased, Sir, to lay this letter before the President [James K. Polk] at your earliest convenience—Hon[orab]l[e] J.C. Calhoun. We are very Respectfully your ob[edien]t Ser[van]ts, F[rancis] Sumter Captain com. A, A[lbertus] C. Spain 1st Lieut. "A," C[yrus] S. Mellett 2nd Lieut., Thos. M. Baker, 2d ", Keith S. Moffat Capt. Comp. (C), Jos. B. Kershaw, 1st Lieut., Adj[utan]t & Lieut. James Cantey, J[ames] W. Cantey Jr. 2 Lt. ", Preston S. Brooks Capt. Com. (D), W[illiam] C. Moragne 1st Lieut. ", Wm. P. Jones 2 Lieut. " ", Joseph Abney, " " ", L[eroy] Secrest Cappt. Com. J., A[ndrew] J. Secrest 2nd L[i]eut. Com. J, K[ennedy] G. Billings 2

Lieut. Comp. J, Wm. Blanding Capt. Comp. (F), A[rthur] M. Mani-
gault 1st Li[e]ut. " ", Lewis F. Robertson 2nd Lieut. ", Ralph Bell
2 Lieut. ", W[illiam] D. DeSaussure Capt. Comp. (H), Wm. B.
Stanley 1st Lieut. " H, M[ichael] R. Clark 2nd Lieut. " H, T[homas]
W. Moye 2nd Lieut. " H, J[ohn] B. Cousart 1st Lieut., J. Foster
Marshall Capt. Comp. E, J[ohn]B. Moragne 1st Lieut. ", F[rederick]
W. Selleck 2d Lieut., Alexr. A. Roberts 2nd Lieut[ena]nt ", James
D. Blanding Capt., Asst. Comry., S[amuel] McGowan Capt[ai]n
Ass. Qr. M.

LS with En in DNA, RG 107 (Secretary of War), Personnel Papers, 1838–1912,
Applications for Appointment, no. 10, box 5. NOTE: Thirteen signers of this
enclosure were later members of the South Carolina General Assembly. Gens.
Joseph B. Kershaw, James Cantey, Arthur M. Manigault, Samuel McGowan, Col.
William D. DeSaussure, Lt. Col. J. Foster Marshall, and Capt. James D. Blanding were all officers in the Confederate States Army. While the Palmetto Regiment was in camp at Mobile it was treated to a barbecue at which one of the
speakers was Andrew Pickens Calhoun. (Columbia, S.C., *South-Carolinian,*
February 3, 1847, p. 3.)

Remarks on the military bounty lands bill, 1/29. Under discussion was the proposal of Thomas J. Rusk of Texas to award scrip in
lieu of bounty land warrants. James F. Simmons of R.I. proposed
that such scrip should be made interest-bearing at six per cent. "Mr.
Calhoun said he hoped the Senator from Texas would permit the
question to be put upon the proposition as at first offered. He
thought there was great objection to scrip bearing interest. It would
be in fact a creation of a new debt." From the Washington, D.C.,
Daily National Intelligencer, January 30, 1847, p. 2. Variant in *Congressional Globe,* 29th Cong., 2nd Sess., p. 287.

To T[HOMAS] G. CLEMSON, [Brussels]

Washington, 30th Jan[uar]y 1847
My dear Sir, The Hibernia brough[t] me yours of the 28th Dec[em-
be]r; with one to Col. [Francis W.] Pickens & a letter from Anna
[Maria Calhoun Clemson] to her mother [Floride Colhoun Calhoun]
& another to [Martha] Cornelia [Calhoun]. I was delighted to hear
that you were all well.

Since I wrote you last, I had a letter from your overseer [——
Mobley]. He says all are well & that things were going on well on
the place. He writes, that he was requested to inform me, that there

is a note presented against you of $125.59 by Mr. Levy Wilson. That it is a note, which Rob[er]t Umphris [*sic*; Humphreys], your former overseer held on you; that he is dead, & that his business has passed into the hands of Mr. Wilson, & that he wanted the money, and requested him to get information from me how it should be paid. I informed him to say to Mr. Wilson, that I knew nothing about it, but that I would write to you to take your direction about it, & that if the note was justly due, it would be promptly paid on hearing from you.

The letters inclosed will give all the news from home. The price of food & cotton has risen considerable in consequence of the news by the last steamer. There is now, I think, a fair prospect, that the latter will sell at fair prices for several years to come. Nothing stands between the country & unbound[ed] prosperity in all branches of its industry, but the unfortunate Mexican war. All now acknowledge its folly, & desire most heartily to get out of it, as soon as possible; but it is hard to do that, without the lead & cooperation of the Administration. If they had sufficient sense & nerve, it could be easily accomplished. I have pointed out the way, & offered my best efforts to aid in conversation; but they hesitate; & will I fear, until plunged into inextricable difficulties.

I have thus far been silent & inactive, in hope some opportunity would offer to enable me to act with effect. None has yet offered, & I fear none will. If none should, I will take the first good occasion to express my opinion fully, as to the course, which ought to be pursued.

My friends think I never stood higher, or stronger than I now do. Time has justified the wisdom of my course, in reference to the Mexican war; & the caucus machinery, which has ever been opposed to me, is evidently giving away. The election of [Robert M.T.] Hunter & [James M.] Mason to the Senate is proof conclusive, that it ["is" *interlined*] rapidly on the decline in Virginia. I hold it to be now certain that there will be no more Baltimore nominations, or if there should be, the nominee, will be assuredly defeated.

The Administration has been endeavoring to build up, through [Thomas H.] Benton, the old [Martin] Van Buren party, but all in vain. They will probably next try the [Lewis] Cass party, but, I think, with as little hope of success. We hold the balance, and it is felt.

My health, with the usual exception of cold & cough, during the winter here, has been pretty good—fully as much so, as I could expect with the little exer[cise] I take, & the course of living in such a place as this.

My love to Anna [Maria Calhoun Clemson]. Kiss the dear children for their grandfather, & tell them how much I want to see them. Your affectionate father, J.C. Calhoun.

[P.S.] I intended to send this by Mr. [Cornelius?] Hoyt, but mislaid his address at New York. I saw him several times. He spoke often of you, & Anna & children & in the kindest terms. Explain to him if you please, why I sent directly by the steamer & not through him. J.C.C.

ALS in ScCleA; PEx in Jameson, ed., *Correspondence*, p. 717.

J[ohn] C. Calhoun and Others to WILLIAM L. MARCY, [Secretary of War]

House of Repr[esentative]s, Jan[uar]y 30 1847
Sir: We beg leave to submit the claims of Col. J[oseph] B. Kershaw for the post of Capt. of Dragoons or of Infantry in the Regiments expected to be raised.

Mr. Kershaw became acquainted with your excellency some weeks since. He is the grand son and only descendant of Col. [Joseph] Kershaw of the Revolution, who sunk ["an enormous" *changed to* "a very large"] estate in sustaining the cause of our independence. The grand son is worthy of the grand sire. [*Signed:*] A[ndrew] P. Butler [Senator from S.C., and] J[oseph] A. Woodward, A[lexander] D. Sims, Armistead Burt, R[ichard] F. Simpson, James A. Black, R[obert] B[arnwell] Rhett [all Representatives from S.C., and] J.C. Calhoun.

(See next page) [for further signatures:] Th[omas] H. Bayly [Representative from Va.,] F[ranklin] W. Bowdon [and] Henry W. Hilliard [Representatives from Ala.].

LS (in Woodward's hand) in DNA, RG 107 (Secretary of War), Personnel Papers, 1838–1912: Applications for Appointment, No. 14. NOTE: Joseph Brevard Kershaw (1822–1894) was subsequently an able Maj. Gen. of the Confederate States Army. The reference to him as "Col." perhaps refers to militia rank. Kershaw did not receive the appointment solicited. He had joined the Palmetto Regiment as a Lt.

Remarks on the Oregon public lands bill, 1/30. "Mr. Calhoun said he was in favor of a thorough examination of this subject. They were about to legislate for the first time upon the subject of the lands in Oregon, and it was necessary to inquire how far this legislation would affect the existing relations between ourselves and the Indian tribes; and also how far it would affect the more important questions growing out of the relation existing between ourselves and Great Britain. He thought it very doubtful whether they ought to grant donations of land to those who might choose hereafter to emigrate to Oregon. As to those who had already gone there in the expectation of receiving grants of land, such grants ought certainly to be made." From the Washington, D.C., *Daily National Intelligencer,* February 1, 1847, p. 1. (In another report, Calhoun said, additionally: "As the bill to establish a Territorial Government in Oregon was now before the Committee on the Judiciary, the best way would be to recommit this bill, and let the two bills be considered together [which suggestion was adopted]." From *Congressional Globe,* 29th Cong., 2nd Sess., p. 293.)

FEBRUARY 1–MARCH 3, 1847

॥

The Wilmot Proviso, barring the South from the fruits of the Mexican War and dooming her to be an ever dwindling minority in the Union, was making its way through the House of Representatives. Calhoun's son Andrew, writing on February 4, reported strong feelings in Mobile where he had just been trying unsuccessfully to sell cotton. Andrew's opinion was probably typical: "that the present crisis cannot be gotten over honorably by the South, without bringing the North to its senses. . . . I am getting heartily sick of the whole yankee tribes."

On February 9 Calhoun rose to give the Senate and the country his view of the war, the occasion being consideration of "the three millions bill," an appropriation to facilitate the speedy prosecution of hostilities to victory. "Never, Mr. President," began Calhoun, "since I have been on the stage of action, has our country been placed in a more critical situation than at present." There followed a multi-layered and profound examination of the existing situation, how it had come about, and what was best now to be done. The ex-Secretary of War advocated a defensive policy. Cease further advances, hold what had been gained, and bring the enemy to a settlement. And he elaborated his reasons. His stand was consistent with the restrained policy he had shown for many years now.

On February 12 Calhoun replied to the inevitable non sequitur charges that his position on the war was motivated by "ambition," this time charges floated by a Polk point-man in the Senate, Hopkins L. Turney.

On February 15 the Wilmot Proviso was passed by the House as an amendment to the war appropriation bill. The vote was 115 to 106. The next day Calhoun attended a public meeting to raise funds for relief of sufferers from the Irish famine, and was elected a vice-president of the proceedings.

On February 19 Calhoun offered resolutions in response to Wilmot—affirming that the territories were the common property of all the States; that discrimination against the immigration of citizens of some States was unconstitutional; and that the people of every State had the right to form their own constitution without any condition imposed by the federal government except that it be republican. The resolutions brought a series of attacks by Benton, who damned Calhoun for pursuing "abstractions." "All the great rules of life are abstractions," replied the Senator from South Carolina.

On February 20 Calhoun defended his resolutions at length and on February 24 elaborated his position on the war, again in reply to Benton who had devoted a whole speech to a personal attack on Calhoun. According to the Senator from Missouri, recently disappointed in his hopes for appointment as commanding general of the field army, Calhoun had single-handedly caused the war by his actions as Secretary of State.

Calhoun's resolutions did not come to a vote, but the sides had been drawn in the critical struggle for the territories. The Senate killed the Proviso by a vote of 21 to 31 and sent the war appropriation bill back to the House without it. On the last day of the session, March 3, the House took up the Senate version in Committee of the Whole and passed it 115 to 81.

Calhoun's mail indicated growing uneasiness in the South, which he undoubtedly shared. He departed southward almost at the last sound of the gavel of the 29th Congress.

〖〗

REMARKS ON POSTPONING THE THREE MILLIONS BILL

[In the Senate, February 2, 1847]
[*Under consideration was a bill for appropriating three million dollars "to bring the existing war with Mexico to a speedy and honorable conclusion."*]

Mr. Calhoun said this was a matter of great importance, and one requiring time and deliberation. He thought it always proper that the Senate should have some opportunity of expressing their opinions on the state of the nation generally, and that on some commensurate subject. On reviewing the position of the session which had passed, he thought more time had been consumed on their side [the Democrats] of the chamber than on the other [the Whigs]. He did not think the proposition to postpone until Thursday [2/4] an unreasonable one. Debates commenced after due reflection, too, were generally more concise than those pressed on without time for consideration. He thought a week devoted to the discussion of this question would not be too long a time, and he trusted that the delay until Thursday would be agreed to. He should probably address the Senate himself on this question.

From the Charleston, S.C., *Mercury*, February 6, 1847, p. 2. Variant in *Congressional Globe*, 29th Cong., 2nd Sess., p. 309; Benton, *Abridgment of Debates*, 16:41–42. Other variants in the Washington, D.C., *Daily Union*, February 2, 1847, p. 2; the New York, N.Y., *Herald*, February 3, 1847, p. 3.

REMARKS ON A RESOLUTION OF THANKS
TO ZACHARY TAYLOR

[In the Senate, February 3, 1847]

[Under consideration was a resolution ordering a gold medal and expressing the thanks of Congress to Maj. Gen. Taylor for the capture of Monterey. Discussion centered upon one qualifying sentence: "Provided, That nothing herein contained shall be construed into an approbation of the terms of the capitulation of Monterey."]

Mr. Calhoun said he should vote to strike out this proviso, and he would briefly state his grounds for doing so. He would do so, in the first place, upon the ground which had been stated by his honorable colleague [Daniel Webster], as a mere matter of taste and propriety; and, in addition to that, he would vote for striking it out because he considered that a vote of thanks, when accompanied by the slightest censure, was entirely cancelled. He would vote for striking it out because, to his mind, there was a palpable contradiction between giving a vote of thanks and a medal to General Taylor and the army, and the exception by which those thanks and that medal were accompanied.

If the exception, if the capitulation itself to which the exception referred, constituted a part of the battle, then, according to the conception of those gentlemen who entertained this idea, they ought not to vote for a medal at all. If it did not constitute a part of the battle, why should that which was irrelevant be made a part of the resolution? The naked question was this: Was the battle of Monterey such a one as deserved that the thanks of Congress and a medal should be bestowed? If it were, let them be granted, and granted unanimously, without condition; and if it were not, let both be withheld.

[*Arthur P. Bagby of Ala. criticized Calhoun's position and stated he wished to be able to distinguish between what he approved and what he disapproved.*]

Mr. Calhoun corrected a misunderstanding of his position in which the Senator from Alabama had fallen.

[*The Senate struck out the offending proviso by a vote of 33 to 15, all the negative votes being Democrats.*]

From *Congressional Globe*, 29th Cong., 2nd Sess., p. 318. Variant in the Washington, D.C., *Daily Union*, February 3, 1847, p. 2, and the Columbia, S.C., *South-Carolinian*, February 10, 1847, p. 2. Another variant in the New York, N.Y., *Herald*, February 5, 1847, p. 3.

From A[NDREW] P[ICKENS] CALHOUN

Tulip Hill [Marengo County, Ala.,] Feb[ruar]y 4th 1847
My dear Father, On my return from Mobile a few days since I re-c[eive]d yours of the 12th last month. I am surprised that you have not heard from me as I had written two letters to you at Washington. I found every thing at Mobile excited about the rapid rate that cotton was going up, but no sales were taking place in consequence of the daily expectation of steamer news. Since I left, news has reached us via New Orleans, up to the 15th Dec[embe]r from Liverpool bringing a rise of 2 pennies and immense sales. Our cotton was worth when I left Mobile 11 cents and I expect will now command 12 cents or more. I had limited our cotton at 12½ cents—but as soon as I heard the last Liverpool accounts I wrote forthwith to raise my limit—if we can hold on I want now to get 15 cents. I scarcely think our cotton was even offered for sale, for I left the day before the news reached Mobile and our samples were then rolled up and had not been placed on factors['] shelves for sale. I little thought then that the rise would be so great, or so sudden. I have had to draw for a part of our expenses, and such funds as I required, but we will have no difficulty in holding on to our cotton as long as we desire. I will have the interest on the [Ann Mathewes] Ioor note remitted in time. I wrote you I had sent a draft of $500 dol[lar]s to the Bank [of the State of S.C.]. I have rec[eive]d no receipt for it as yet. I will remit the money for your carriage when I go down, to J[ohn] E[wing] Bonneau as directed. You wrote me to sue upon a credit, and I dislike to press

untill cotton is sold as I know it will then be promptly paid. As soon as our cotton is sold I will remit the ballances ["a/"(?) *canceled*] over and above our liabilities here, as you may think best.

I did not take a turn in Mobile but I was asked what you were a going to do. I never knew so much anxiety as there is to hear from you. I feel anxious myself—*very*. My own opinion is, that the present crisis cannot be gotten over honorably by the South, without bringing the North to its senses. I firmly believe the whole affair is agitated as much to keep the South from electing her champion at the next election—in other words to bear upon your prospects; and I fear it may succeed. We ought to take the stand, *if it is constitutional*, that we of the South will close our ports to the productions of any State that permits incendiary anti slavery doctrines to be promulgated, or their citizens to come amongst us. I am getting heartily sick of the whole yankee tribes. They are mean in all things, and cheat at all, and certainly they have discovered the philosopher[']s stone for they turn every thing to gold, and make it out of all things[,] religion, politicks, law ["politicks" *canceled*]. I profess as strong a regard for the Union as any man but certainly there are some things superior to it, and if our individual and collective safety is not, then the South had better be distroyed—swallowed up by an earthquake, than that this Union should be disseered. I know how you have expended a long life to avert this catastrophe and whoever looks to the principles you have laid so clearly down, must see that the only chance to save this Union is in the admission of your doctrines. Properly administered it is the best model of a gover[n]ment the earth has ever seen; but changed as it has been from a mild, persuasive, and progressing one with increase of population and means, to an aggressive, turbulent, and conquering community, it seems to me, without a miracle, we must loose [*sic*] the conservative principles of our gover[n]ment and undergo some great radical change, and I seriously begin to think dissolution will be the only remedy to preserve *life*[,] *liberty* or *honor*. Therefore it is I look to your course in common with others with such intense interest. Have you a hearty supporter in [Senator from S.C. Andrew P.] Butler[?] He is a man of great obliquity of vision, and *judgement*[,] I have always thought. His brother [Pierce M. Butler] the Col. of the Carolina regiment extolled you above all statesmen the other day in Mobile. The citizens of that place gave a barbacue to his regiment and there was an immense assembly. I reached town that morning and attended. Butler was toasted and and [*sic*] after recapitulating the great men of our State, past and present, *almost in silence*, and when I thought he was a going to omit yours entirely, he pronounced it, and I thought there never would be silence again for him to proceed—he then went on and as I said I never he[a]rd such eulogy, at every sentence of which he was stopt with huzzas. I was called out and spoke for half an hour I am told with effect. My object was to do away with an impression that I have no doubt many of your op[p]onents take advantage of, that South Carolina is governed personally by you—without taking in consideration that it is your position—planted upon truth—and the great moral effects must be responded to by So. Ca. or she degenerates at once. Hence it is I took the position that while other States are more populous and wealthy[,] So. Ca. occupied the front rank of the republick, which could only be accounted for by the fact that she had erected a higher intellectual and moral standred [*sic*] and they who came nearest up to it entitled themselves in proportion to her approbation and support. This constituted her present greatness and that her fall would be in proportion as *her standred was lowered.* This was one of the *points.* All I *said* was *discreet.* Butler told me that I exercised a wonderful control of the assembly and congratulated me upon my great success.

Our plantation is in superb order—all thoroughly drained and nearly all ploughed. I shall clear some land, but will not cultivate it, as we already have a full crop. It will be in fine order for another year.

While I think of it Col. Butler told me that he had rec[eive]d a letter signed J[ohn] C. Calhoun Jr. asking for a place in his regiment to go to Mexico[?]—he said he could not tell exactly what the writer wanted but wrote him that he might come and mess[?] with him, altho' he had no post that would be a salaried office. John should be cautious. I am delighted that Pat[rick Calhoun] has been so highly honored. So are all your friends out here. He should with the eyes of the country upon ["him" *interlined*] discard every feeling but *one,* and that is to come up to the expectations of his friends. We are all well, and join in love. Your affectionate son, A.P. Calhoun.

ALS in ScU-SC, John C. Calhoun Papers. NOTE: The ms. is badly faded, and the punctuation is at some points conjectural.

To Dr. JA[ME]s A. HOUSTON

[Washington, published February 4, 1847]
MY DEAR SIR: I take pleasure in saying that I have the highest opinion of your talent as a reporter. During the long period I have been a member of Congress, no reporter has ever reported me with greater satisfaction to myself. Indeed, considering my manner of speaking, I have been surprised that you have on several occasions been able to report me with so much accuracy; and among them, on that to which you refer—the Oregon speech [of 3/16/1846]. With great respect I am, &c., J.C. CALHOUN.

PC in the Washington, D.C., *Daily Union*, February 4, 1847, p. 3. NOTE: During the month of 2/1847, Houston came under attack in both the Senate and the House of Representatives for alleged distortions in reporting debates on Mexican War appropriations. These attacks came from Northwestern Democrats opposed to the Polk administration, for whose organ, the *Union*, Houston was chief Congressional reporter.

J[ohn] C. Calhoun and Others to W[ILLIAM] L. MARCY, [Secretary of War]

[Washington, *ca.* February 4, 1847]
Sir, We respectfully recommend Mr. Perry Butler of South Carolina to you ["for" *interlined*] the appointment of Lieutenant in one of the Regiments to be raised for the Mexican War.

He is a young Gentleman of good health & robust constitution, the grand son of Gen[era]l [William] Butler of Revolutionary memory and a nephew of the gallant Com[m]odore Oliver H. Perry.

We have no doubt, if in this position, he would sustain the honor of his country either in peace or war. And we will be much gratified if this appointment can be made. [Signed:] R[ichard] F. Simpson, J.C. Calhoun, R[obert] B[arnwell] Rhett, J[oseph] A. Woodward, I[saac] E. Holmes, James A. Black, A[rmistead] Burt.

LS in DNA, RG 107 (Secretary of War), Personnel Papers, 1838–1912, no. 9. NOTE: The signers are all members of the S.C. Congressional delegation. Perry Butler's uncle, Senator Andrew P. Butler, did not sign, perhaps from considerations of propriety. The letter is given an approximate date from a letter of Simpson to Marcy of 2/4/1847 that is found in the same file. Christopher Raymond Perry Butler (1829–1853) became a Lt. in the 2nd Artillery, subsequently dying of yellow fever at Tampa, Fla.

From Jos[eph] J. Singleton

Dahlonega [Ga.,] 4th Feb. 1847

My Dear Sir, I have just returned home after an absence of between 2 & 3 weeks where I found yours of the 22d Ult.; The contents of which, as a Southern man, I feel a deep interest, and I am sure setting aside our unimportant divisions the whole South should be equally so. I have been as low down as Lagrange (Troup County) for the benefit exclusively of my youngest Daughter, where one of [the] best female schools in our State exist[s], and returned by the way of Athens[,] a distance in route of near 400 miles. I made it my business in an obscure, or disinterested manner to assertain as near as I could the political feelings of Georgians, and I can assure you, that I did not converse with one single Democrat, except Gov. McDonnold [that is, Charles James McDonald], (who, by the by, I consider at the head of the Democratic party of Georgia) but what were your friends, and his only objections to you were the constitutional grounds you occupied in your Memphis Report as it is so called here; he said he intended to write you a long letter on the subject. He is as you may understand one of our most strenuous Democrats, who will descend as low as any other, without the shadow of an effort to improve the doctrine.

The Whigs, if they cannot run their choice Mr. [Henry] Clay[,] you may expect to be nominated by them so far as Georgia is concerned. They will certainly sustain the South and its interest, and will not be ashamed to recognise you as their Champion; ["and I" *interlined*] am sure the Democrats should be equally as willing, as the weight of testimony is on their side.

Your Memphis Report which you left with me I lo[a]ned to Gen[era]l [William B.] Wofford under a promise to return it; for fear he may not do so, I would be glad you would send me another, as I may thereby be enabled to understand your views more fully on that subject, and as it appears that this is to be the most vulnerable point of attack by our anti-constructionist. Our views in regard to the Mexican War, so far as I have been enabled to assertain them in my travels, are in favor of securing their seaports both on the Gulph, and on the Pacific this winter, make them Ports of entry under the same restrictions of our own, then strike a line of demarkation so far as we have conquered, and make it a defensive, in the place of an offensive war, with the view principally of relieving our Troops of the deleterious effects of the climate in summer & autumn.

I have not had time since my return to visit your mines, but will do so in a few days, and write you again.   As ever yours &C, Jos. J. Singleton.

ALS in ScU-SC, John C. Calhoun Papers.

From F[RANKLIN] H. ELMORE

Charleston, Feb[ruar]y 5, 1847

My Dear Sir, The Southern [Quarterly] Review is about changing hands & can be put on a solid & safe foundation, if we can get help. Mr. [Daniel K.] Whitaker's necessities put him in the market.   You know how unreliable he is—but we can get it for a very moderate sum, by way of safe loan.   It is published by Messrs. Burgess [*sic*; James S. Burges] & [Robert] James who are creditors[?] $2600. Whitaker asks $6000.   Burgess & James are willing to buy & thus they must raise $3400.   The[y] offer to buy if they can be helped to raise $3400.   They say they are willing to take half or the whole—and offer either to take in partnership or on their own account.   I submit both schemes to you & for your opinion at the request of your friends here.

The first is to lend Messrs. B[urges] & James in sums not less than $100 from such as will come forward.   For these loans they will give sealed notes & a mortgage to Trustees to secure repayment.

The property is as follows—Sub[scriptio]n list is 2300 at $5 each. There is due $8000 of which at least $5,000 is good & these go with in the purchase—and will be applied to pay off as collected these notes.

The second plan is to make it [a] joint stock concern[,] we taking half in these subscriptions of not less than a share apiece of $100.

This gives us control.

The Editorship is to be exclusively & solely with Mr. J[ohn] M[ilton] Clapp late Editor of the Mercury.   In his hands we feel that the rights, principles & interests of the South & of the Republican Party will be safe.

We wish your opinion—your aid in giving us moral influence to carry it out.   If you agree with us cannot you write to Mr. [Ker] Boyce, [Henry W.] Conner & such other friends as you think may help us.

We shall write in a day or two to each of the Delegation.   In the mean time will it not be well for you to confer with them, [Robert

M.T.] Hunter [Representative from Va.] & such other friends as you judge best on this subject[?]

I write in the utmost haste & after a short consultation with those who are moving. They desire me to let you know the movement at once & it is only now begun. In great haste Yours truly, F.H. Elmore.

[P.S.] The Cotton market is firm & steady altho we are bare of shipping. Exchanges down to 5¼. Cotton has been sold at 12¾–12½ & down to 10. Rice is rising.

ALS in ScCleA.

From J[OHN] Y. MASON, [Secretary of the Navy]

Navy Department, February 5th 1847

Sir, Your note of yesterday enclosing a letter of Mr. John C. McGehee has been received. Under the law of 1845 assigning Midshipmen to the several States, Florida is entitled to one and a very large fraction. She has now three on the Navy list and can therefore receive at present no additional appointments.

Mr. C[olumbus] Smith[']s name will however be registered and whenever an opportunity shall occur to make an appointment from Florida, his claims will be respectfully considered. Mr. McG[ehee's] letter is herewith returned. I am respec[tfull]y yours, J.Y. Mason.

FC in DNA, RG 45 (Naval Records), Miscellaneous Letters Sent by the Secretary of the Navy, 1798–1886, 37:374 (M-209:14).

Remarks on the "Three Million Bill," 2/6. During a speech by Reverdy Johnson of Maryland, Calhoun twice interjected brief remarks from his seat. Johnson stated that on the day of the declaration of war against Mexico, President [James K. Polk] had authorized Santa Anna to return to Mexico, though without informing the Congress. Calhoun queried: "Is the Senator certain of this?" He received an affirmative reply. Later Johnson asked Calhoun to clarify a point about the declaration of war in 1812: whether the causes and objects of the war were stated in the war declaration itself. Calhoun replied: "In the accompanying report." From *Congressional Globe*, 29th Cong., 2nd Sess., Appendix, pp. 312–313. Variant in *Congressional Globe*, 29th Cong., 2nd Sess., p. 337.

From J[AMES] HAMILTON, [JR.]

Oswichee Bend [Ala.,] Feb[ruar]y 7[t]h 1847
My Dear Sir, I have long designed dropping you a line but really my private & domestic occupations have been such that I literally have not had a moment at my disposal. And now just on the eve of my departure to visit my Plantation in Texas I have not time to do more than to say that ["amidst" *canceled and* "in spite" *interlined*] my silence & ["amidst all my" *interlined*] distracting ["whilst" *canceled and* "cares" *interlined*] you are yourself the object of my unbounded confidence & ["confidence" *canceled and* "esteem &" *interlined*] your fortunes & success as the *first* public man in this Country are the objects of my unceasing solicitude.

Altho the presidency could not add to your fame, and probably not to your happiness yet for the honor of the country & for the repute of its virtue & discernment I ardently desire your elevation. But recently I have been desponding a good deal, from the profligacy of the Northern Democracy & the s[t]upidity of the Southern Whigs who seem to want the sense to perceive that there [*sic*] true policy ["is" *interlined*] to unite with us in rallying on yourself.

Such is the insti[n]ctive ingratitude of Republics that your great & incomparable services on the Oregon ["Question" *canceled and* "difficulty" *interlined*] appear to have been forgotten & I fear without you can give some turn to the Crisis of our War with Mexico that you will suffer the prejudice ["from the belief" *interlined*] of being inimical to the Administration on the subject of the War with Mexico.

Now I believe no man in the U.S. has suffered so much in his fortunes as I have by the accursed War yet I feel the necessity of standing by those who are waging it that we may get out of it with the least possible delay.

That the War has been feebly conducted as far as the Govt. ["was" *canceled and* "is" *interlined*] concer[n]ed, without a combination & comprehensiveness of views necessary to such a great public exigency I believe and certainly the late move to place a civilian [Thomas H. Benton] at the head of the Army (& such an Individual too)!! shows that [James K.] Polk & his Cabinet are as ignorant of the sensibilities ["of" *canceled and* "which belong to a just" *interlined*] military pride as the object of their favor is of military knowledge.

If our Army had submitted to such an outrage, they ["would" *interlined and* "deserved" *changed to* "deserve"] certainly to be flogged even by such enemies as the Mexicans. You certainly de-

110

serve the thanks of the Country & our little Army for having blown up this absurd *project* & the inflated Bladder who was to have been the object of its honors. The discretion with which you acted is as worthy of praise as the object of your labors.

I have not the smallest idea when it comes to the push that the North will have the nerve to break the line of the Missouri Compromise short off when we cross the Rio Grande. If they do if the South submits we are far worse slaves than our Vassals. If we do not raise the standard of resistance we are the basest Paltroons that ever lived to be frightened into slavery & debasement. Let the issue I say be made the moment the War is at an end if our [*"domestic" interlined*] enemies desire. Its descussion would now weaken the Country in the prosecution of hostilities. That[?] descussion when Peace takes place will nerve[,] animate & fit us *for the struggle which must come.*

When I reach New Orleans I will [*one word canceled and "see" interlined*] your [*"devoted" interlined*] friends in the Legislature of New Orleans & endeavour to ascertain whether we cannot carry thro a movement in your favor sufficiently authoritative by our majority to give an impulse to your nomination South & West. If this cannot be triumphantly effected we must wait[,] abide our time & look out at some more propitious moment.

I will write you from New Orleans where address me to the care of Messrs. Dick & Hill.

I can do nothing more now My Dear Sir than assure you of the esteem with which I am ever faithfully, respectfully & cordially your friend & ob[edien]t Ser[van]t, J. Hamilton.

P.S. The election of Mr. [Robert M.T.] Hunter to the Senate [from Va.] on which I ardently congratulate *you* & all our friends and the military appointment of your Son [Patrick Calhoun] in the New York Reg[imen]t are both favorable Tokens from those two great States.

The first was elected with a perfect knowledge of his being your devoted friend & the last without doubt in kind reference to your repute as well as his own merits.

ALS in ScCleA; PEx in Boucher and Brooks, eds., *Correspondence*, pp. 366–367.

From ELLWOOD FISHER

Steamer Dominion from Louisville to
Cin[cinn]a[ti], 2 mo[nth] 8, 1847

Dear Friend, I expected to have been before to day on my return to Washington, but business will delay me a few days longer, probably until the 12th Inst.

I find the state of opinion in this region much sounder than I expected. The War is felt and acknowledged by many democrats to be a great blunder as well as evil and I think there are but few that would oppose, any reasonable effort to bring it to a prompt conclusion. I have stated thy views on the subject to a number of gentlemen high in the confidence of both parties, and have met with but one unfavourable to it. The Louisville Journal goes entirely counter to the course of [John J.] Crittenden [Senator from Ky.], and will continue to do so. The Editor of the Democrat who returned from Washington a few days before me and who has supported the Administration in every thing says that it is not he knows in favour of carrying the War to the city of Mexico. And I have no doubt he had assurances to that effect.

The Journal has the largest circulation by far of any paper in the Southwest—and as that is the region most liable to err on this question, I have thought it important to take some pains to have ["the" *canceled*] it discussed boldly and frankly.

The Administration again as at the close of last session assumes a somewhat pacific aspect, as would seem from a renewal of the demand for money to treat, and from the announcement of [Ambrose H.] Sevier [Senator from Ark.] that only New Mexico and California will be insisted on. But as the professions of the Administration cannot be trusted at all, and as it might even negociate to obtain further pretexts for the continuance of the War it will devolve again on the Senate to define the position of the country as in reference to Oregon, even if against the views of the Executive. Indeed the latter stands so low abroad as well as at home, that its own course especially if in opposition to the Senate, or the character of the Senate, would be but little respected. I should not think that Santa Anna or any other leading Mexican could have faith enough in ["the good faith of" *canceled*] overtures from the President [James K. Polk] to compromise himself in the opinion of the people there by acceding to propositions to treat—and I am well satisfied that the people here ["are" *canceled*] will insist not loudly but effectually at the ballot box ["for" *canceled and* "on" *interlined*] the adoption of a policy to ensure peace. I am even afraid that the plan thee proposes, will, since it is to be executed by the men in power not be considered adequate, and I trust it will be presented so definitely as to leave them the least possible discretion. It is true that it seems monstrous to suppose that the President can now be in favour of prosecuting the war much longer. Perhaps he is not—but if so, the slightest incident that might occur to encourage it, the faintest hope of doing something brilliant would be enough to lead him on.

The people here are now realizing the free trade policy—and the Whigs are silent about restoring the Tariff of 1842. Still the ["very" *canceled*] speculations now arising from the foreign demand and consequent high price of produce, and also from the expenditure of a considerable part of the government loans in the country which come from abroad may, by the [*partial word canceled*] revulsion liable to occur when the foreign demand declines and when foreign loans are no longer made, furnish a pretext for the restoration of that policy similar to what existed in 1842. I think it would be well to keep the country prepared for such a change so as not to be confounded by it.

The indications of party incoherency are strong on both sides[,] Whigs as well as Democrats. Nothing but the certainty of being able to overthrow the Democrats will keep the Whigs together, and it is doubtful even if that will, since there is so much discrepancy of opinion as to the selection of Candidates. With greatest regard thy friend, Ellwood Fisher.

ALS in ScCleA. NOTE: This letter was postmarked in Cincinnati on 2/10.

Petition of the Irish Emigrant Society of New York, presented by Calhoun to the Senate on 2/8. The petitioners ask that Congress amend an 1819 law so as to provide further measures for the health of immigrant ship passengers. The petition is dated 1/26/1847 and is signed by Gregory Dillon, president, and Florence McCarthy and M.J. O'Connor, secretaries. The petition was referred to the Committee on Commerce. DS in DNA, RG 46 (U.S. Senate), 29A-G3.2.

REMARKS ON THE TEN REGIMENT BILL

[In the Senate, February 8, 1847]
[*Under discussion was a provision allowing the President to appoint the officers of the regiments during the recess of the Senate (begin-*

113

ning on March 4), the nominations to be submitted to the Senate when it reconvened (in December). The provision was supported by John A. Dix of N.Y., chairman of the committee of conference on the bill with the House of Representatives.]

Mr. Calhoun said it would not be possible for him to vote for this report. The question as it was presented to him was, that the President should, during the recess, appoint all the officers of these regiments; and it was to be done on the ground of expediency. It was said that they could vest in the President power to appoint inferior officers, and by some construction of the constitutional provision, it was to give sanction to this proviso. But it could not be sustained by any fair construction. Another ground had been presented by the Senator from Michigan [Lewis Cass], who put it on the ground that these officers could not be appointed in the time remaining before the end of this session. He [Calhoun] briefly examined the arguments urged on the Senate, and concluded that the course recommended was neither expedient, nor constitutional, nor consistent with the dignity of the Senate. By the term "inferior officers," he had always understood those persons connected with the departments of the Government, such as clerks, an interpretation which he proceeded to defend and enforce.

From *Congressional Globe*, 29th Cong., 2nd Sess., p. 349. Variants in the New York, N.Y., *Herald*, February 10, 1847, p. 3; the Charleston, S.C., *Courier*, February 12, 1847, p. 2; the Greenville, S.C., *Mountaineer*, February 19, 1847, p. 1. NOTE: The first variant cited indicates that Calhoun and Cass "continued to debate a constitutional point involved in these appointments as proposed," a debate which was not reported.

From JOHN B. SITTON

Pendleton S.C., 8th Feb[ruar]y 1847

Dear Sir, Will you please to buy a check or Draft on New York for $84^{52}/$_{100}$ dollars, and remit the same to—

S.P. Smith Esq[ui]r[e]
Newark
New Jers[e]y.

I am due him that much for varnish purchased on the 25th ult. & have no chance to purchase a check here, & suppose you can readily obtain it in Washington. If you can spare time from the arduous duties you have to perform to do this favour for me, I will credit your ac-co[u]nt by the same amount, and feel much obliged by your kindness. With the high[e]st considerations &c I am very truly &c &c, John B. Sitton.

[P.S.] If you remit Mr. S[mith] ask him to return an acknowledgment or receipt for the amount.

ALS in ScU-SC, John C. Calhoun Papers. Note: An AEU by Calhoun reads, "18th Feb. Transmitted draft no. 1756 drawn by the bank of the metropolis on the bank of Commerce for $84 52⁄100.

Speech on the War with Mexico

[In the Senate, February 9, 1847]

The bill making further appropriation to bring the existing war with Mexico to a speedy and honorable conclusion, being under consideration—

Mr. Calhoun rose, and thus addressed the Senate. Never, Mr. President, since I have been on the stage of action, has our country been placed in a more critical situation than at present. We are not only in the midst of a very difficult and a very expensive war, but we are involved in a domestic question of the most irritating and dangerous character. They both claim our serious and deliberate consideration, and I do trust that before this session closes, late as it is, they will both receive a full discussion. It is due to our constituents that the actual state of things in reference to both should be fully understood. For the present, I propose to consider the question which is more immediately pressing—how shall the war be conducted to bring it most advantageously to a successful termination? Or, to express it a little more fully, how shall it be conducted to enable us most advantageously to effect all the objects for which it was made? For it is only by effecting those objects that the war can be properly said to be successful.

There are two ways in which the war may be conducted. The one is, to push on offensive operations until Mexico is compelled to yield to our terms. The other, to take a defensive position and to maintain and secure the possession of the country already in our military occupation. The question which I propose to consider is, which of these two plans of operation ought to be selected. It is a grave question; in my opinion, next in importance only to the war itself. I have given it my deliberate consideration, and the result to which I have come is, that we ought to choose the defensive position. I shall now proceed to state the reasons upon which that conclusion is founded.

I believe it is the policy best calculated to bring the war advantageously to a successful termination; or, to express it more fully and explicitly—for I wish to be fully comprehended on this important question—to bring it with *certainty* to a successful termination, and that with the least sacrifice of men and money, and with the least hazard of disastrous consequences and loss of standing and reputation to the country. If I rightly understand the objects for which the war was declared, I feel a deep conviction that, by assuming a defensive attitude, all of them may be effected. I say, if I rightly understand, for, strange as it may seem, those objects, even at this late day, are left to inference. There is no document in which they are distinctly enumerated and set forth by the Government, and of course they can only be ascertained by viewing the messages of the President [James K. Polk] in reference to the war, in connection with the acts of Congress recognizing its existence, or for carrying it on. I have examined them, and particularly the message of the President to Congress, recommending that Congress should make war, for the purpose of discovering the objects for which it was made, and the result is that they were threefold: first, to repel invasion; next, to establish the Rio del Norte as the western boundary of Texas; and thirdly, to obtain indemnity for the claims of our citizens against Mexico. The first two appear to me to be the primary, and the last only the secondary object of the war. The President, in his messages, did not recommend Congress to declare war. No. He assumed that war already existed, and called upon Congress to recognise its existence. He affirmed that the country had been invaded, and American blood spilt upon American soil. That assumption was based on the position that the Rio del Norte was the western boundary of Texas, and that the Mexicans had crossed that boundary to the American side of the river. This he affirmed was an invasion of our territory.

The act of Congress reiterated the declaration that war had been made by the Republic of Mexico, and thus recognised the Rio del Norte as the western boundary of Texas, and the crossing of that river by the Mexicans as an act of invasion. Hence, both the Executive and Legislative branches of this Government are committed to the fact that the Rio del Norte is the western boundary of Texas, and that crossing it was an invasion on the part of the Mexicans. To repel the invasion and establish the boundary were then clearly the primary objects of the war. But having got into the war, the President recommends it to be prosecuted for the other object I have mentioned—that is to say, indemnity for our citizens—a recommendation, in my opinion, proper; for while we are engaged in war all the differences between the two countries ought, if possible, to be settled. These appear to me to be the objects of the war. Conquest is expressly disavowed, and, therefore, constitutes none of its objects. The President, in addition, recommends that we shall prosecute the war in order to obtain indemnity for its expenses, but that in no sense can be considered as one of its objects, but a mere question of policy; for it can never be supposed that a country would enter upon a war for the mere purpose of being indemnified for its cost.

I hold, then, Mr. President—such being the objects of the war—that all of them can be accomplished by taking a defensive position. Two have already been thoroughly effected. The enemy has been repelled by two brilliant victories. The Rio del Norte is held, from its mouth to its extreme source, on the eastern side, by ourselves. Not a Mexican soldier is to be found there. As to the question of indemnity to our citizens, such has been the success of our arms that we have not only acquired enough for that, but vastly more, even to comprehend, great as they already are, the expenses of the war, if it should be judged to be wise and and [*sic*] just policy on our part to make Mexico responsible for them. Here arises the question—shall we hold the line we now occupy, and which we cover by our military forces, comprehending two-thirds of the whole of Mexico, embracing the valley of the Rio del Norte, on the west side, as far as the Sierra Madre, and on the north to the southern limits of Lower and Upper California and New Mexico—shall we hold all this, or shall we select some other position better calculated for the object in view? I am not prepared to discuss this point. I have not the requisite information, and if I had, it would not be necessary, with the object I have in view. What I propose to discuss, in the absence of such information is, what considerations ought to govern us in selecting a defensive line. These must be deducted from the objects intended to be effected by taking a defensive position.

The first and leading consi[dera]tion that ought to govern should be to select a line that would fully accomplish the objects to be effected in making the war; avoiding the appearance, however, of taking any portion of the country on the mere principle of a war of conquest. But what may be required in reference to this consideration may be enlarged by the other considerations he would now proceed to state.

117

The first and most important of them is, that in selecting a defensive line, it should be such as to possess, in the greatest degree, such natural advantages as would require the smallest sacrifice of men and money to defend it; and among others, such as would afford every facility for drawing promptly supplies of men and provisions from the adjoining country. The next consideration in making the selection is, that the country covered by it should be convenient and desirable for us to possess, if in the ultimate adjustment of the difference between us and Mexico, it should become the established boundary of the two countries. I go further, and add, that it should be such as would deprive Mexico in the smallest possible degree of her resources and her strength; for, in aiming to do justice to ourselves in establishing the line, we ought, in my opinion, to inflict the least possible amount of injury on Mexico. I hold, indeed, that we ought to be just and liberal to her. Not only because she is our neighbor; not only because she is a sister republic; not only because she is emulous now, in the midst of all her difficulties, and has ever been, to imitate our example by establishing a federal republic; not only because she is one of the two greatest powers on this continent of all the States that have grown out of the provinces formerly belonging to Spain and Portugal; though these are high considerations, which every American ought to feel, and which every generous and sympathetic heart would feel, yet there are others which refer more immediately to ourselves. The course of policy which we ought to pursue in regard to Mexico is one of the greatest problems in our foreign relations. Our true policy, in my opinion, is not to weaken or humble her; on the contrary, it is our interest to see her strong, and respectable, and capable of sustaining all the relations that ought to exist between independent nations. I hold that there is a mysterious connection between the fate of this country and that of Mexico, so much so, that her independence and capability of sustaining herself are almost as essential to our prosperity, and the maintenance of our institutions as they are to hers. Mexico is to us the forbidden fruit; the penalty of eating it would be to subject our institutions to political death.

The next consideration is, that the line should be such, in the event of its being ultimately established between us, as would lead to a permanent peace between the two countries; and, finally, that it should be such as would lead to as speedy a peace as possible, and for this purpose it should be eminently coercive. Neither of these requires any illustration.

Such being the considerations that ought to govern us in selecting a defensive line, the next question is, what line would best fulfil them; and here again, I am not prepared to pronounce definitively. It requires a more exact knowledge of the country than I possess or can derive from any of the maps, all of which, there is reason to believe, are more or less imperfect; but while I do not feel myself prepared to pronounce definitively, I am prepared to suggest a line, which, in my opinion, to a very great extent, will fulfil most of these considerations; and what recommends it more strongly to me is the fact, that it is substantially the one which the Executive themselves, as I infer from the declaration of the chairman of the Committee on Foreign Relations [Ambrose H. Sevier], contemplate establishing even in the event of a successful offensive war. The line to which I refer is the following: beginning at the mouth of the Rio del Norte, and continuing up the same to the Pass del Norte, or southern boundary of New Mexico, about the thirty-second degree of north latitude, and thence due west to the Gulf of California, which it would strike, according to the maps, nearly at its head, and thence down the Gulf to the ocean.

I now propose to turn back and compare this line, with the considerations which I have laid down, as those which ought to govern in selecting a defensive line. It will secure all the objects for which the war was declared. It will establish the Del Norte as the western boundary of Texas throughout its whole extent, from its mouth to its source; it will give us ample means of indemnity, even if the cost of the war itself should be deemed proper to be included in the indemnity, which, as at present advised, I am far from being disposed to countenance. The next consideration is, that the line should be such as would involve in its maintenance the least sacrifice of men and money. In reference to this the one suggested has great advantages. In the first place, on its east side, the Del Norte would constitute the line, a broad, rapid, and navigable stream, of which we would have the entire command, and in the next it would be near to the settled parts of Texas, from whence, in an emergency, the forces and the means of supply necessary for its defence may be promptly derived. The whole extent of this portion of the line is less than four hundred miles, measured on the map. I have consulted the opinions of military men of judgment and experience, in reference to its defence, and they inform me that three forts properly located, one not far from the mouth of the Del Norte, another somewhere near Camargo, and a third at the Pass del Norte, properly constructed, and garrisoned with a suitable force, would be sufficient for its defense. The fort at the Pass del Norte would, from its position, not only defend the river itself, but protect New Mexico, by commanding the only passage through which the Mexicans could invade it. Four regiments would be ample to garrison the forts, after the first year, when they would be completed.

The other portion of the line, extending from the Pass del Norte to the Gulf of California, and thence through the gulf to the Pacific Ocean, would be still more easily defended. The part which extends from the mountains that border New Mexico on the west, and which seperates the waters of the Del Norte from those which fall into the Colorado and the Gulf of California, passes through a country inhabited on both sides by Indian tribes through its whole extent, and requires neither men nor forts for its defence. It is in length about three hundred and fifty miles. The residue is covered by the Gulf of California. A few small vessels, which could be furnished under the peace establishment, with a single regiment, would be ample for its defence, and the protection of California. Hence, five regiments, with a small naval force, supported by the contiguous population, would be sufficient for the defence of the whole line against any force which Mexico could bring against it.

The next point to consider is, what would be the expense of maintaining this force, in addition to what the peace establishment would require. On this, too, I have consulted officers of experience, and they are of opinion that two and a half millions of dollars annually would be sufficient.

The next consideration is, that the country to be covered should be convenient and desirable to be held by us, if, as has been stated, on the settlement of our differences with Mexico, the line should be established as the permanent boundary. And here again it possesses striking advantages. It is contiguous to us. It has on its eastern side the Rio del Norte as the boundary between it and Texas, and on its northern, the southern boundary of Oregon, through its whole extent. But what makes it still more desirable, and what is of vastly more importance to us, is the very circumstance which makes it of little value to Mexico, as it regards its strength or resources; and that is that it is almost literally an uninhabited country. It covers an area of 600,000 square miles, with a population of less than 100,000, of all complexions and all descriptions, being but one inhabitant to each six miles square. It is indeed as sparsely settled, and even less so, than the country in the possession of the neighboring Indians. It is this very sparseness of population which renders it desirable to us; for if we had the choice of two regions of equal extent, and in other respects equally desirable, the one inhabited and the other not, we would choose the uninhabited, if we consulted the genius of our government and the preservation of our political institutions. What we want is space for our growing population, and what we ought to avoid is, the addition of other population, of a character not suited to our institutions. We want room to grow. We are increasing at the rate of 600,000 annually; and in a short time the increase will be at the rate of 1,000,000. To state it more strongly, we double once in twenty-three years, so that at the end of that period we will number forty millions, and in another twenty-three years, eighty millions, if no disaster befal us. For this rapidly growing population, all the territory we now possess, and even that which we might acquire, would, in the course of a few generations, be needed. It is better for our people and institution[s], that our population should not be too much compressed.

But the very reasons which make it so desirable to us, make it of little advantage to Mexico. Her population is nearly stationary, and will not, at her present rate of increase, within the period I have specified as that within which our population will have twice doubled, be but a few millions more than at present. Indeed, so far from being valuable to Mexico, it is directly the opposite; a burden and a loss to her. It is, in the first place, exceeding remote from her. California is as far from the city of Mexico as it is from New Orleans, and New Mexico is not much nearer to it than it is to Washington. They are both too remote to be defended by so weak a power. It is a remarkable fact in the history of this continent, that the aborigines in this and the adjacent portions of Mexico, encroach upon the European occupants. The Indians are actually gaining ground upon the Mexicans, not but that they are brave and capable of defending themselves with arms, but the jealousy of the central government had in a great measure disarmed them, while from its feebleness and remoteness, it is incapable of affording them protection. It is said that there are not less than three or four thousand captives from New Mexico and the neighboring States, in the hands of the Indians. Such being the state of things, it is manifest that while the acquisition would be of great importance to us, it would, instead of being a loss to the Mexicans, be a positive gain. The possession by our people would protect the whole of the adjacent portions of Mexico from the incursions and ravages of the Indians, and give it a greater degree of security and prosperity than it ever has experienced from the commencement of her revolution, now more than a quarter of a century ago.

The next consideration is, that the line should be such, if it should be established as a boundary, as would lay the foundation of a permanent peace between us and Mexico; and here again it has remarkable advantages—it is impossible for us to prevent our growing population from passing into an uninhabited country, where the power of the owners is not sufficient to keep them out. In they will go. We may pass laws heaping penalty upon penalty, but they will be of no avail to prevent our pioneers from forcing themselves into the country, unless efficiently resisted by the power in possession. Of this we have abundant proof from experience in our relations with the Indians. Many and severe laws have been passed to prevent intrusion upon them, with little effect. In the end, the only remedy has been found to be, to purchase their lands, and remove them to a greater distance. If such is the case with the Indians, where the population is more dense, and our means of preventing intrusion much greater, it would be vain to expect that we could prevent our people from penetrating into California, or that the government of Mexico would be able to prevent their doing so. Even before our present difficulties with Mexico, the process had begun. Under such circumstances, to make peace with Mexico without acquiring a considerable portion at least of this uninhabited region, would lay the foundation of new troubles and subject us to the hazard of further conflicts—a result equally undesirable to Mexico and ourselves. But it is not only in reference to a permanent peace with Mexico that it is desirable that this vast uninhabited region should pass into our possession. High considerations connected with civilization and commerce make it no less so. We alone can people it with an industrious and civilized race, which can develope its resources and add a new and extensive region to the domain of commerce and civilization. Left as it is, it must remain for generations an uninhabited and barren waste.

This brings me to the final consideration that the line should be such as to cover an extent, ample for the purpose of coercing a settlement, and in this respect, the one suggested leaves nothing to be desired.

But while I suggest this as a definite line, if a better cannot be found, it would be very far from my views to hold the country which it covers absolutely. My opinion is, that it ought to be held as the means of negotiation. We ought to say to Mexico, that such is our intention, and that if she is ready to negotiate, we are; and not only to negotiate, but to settle fairly, justly, and liberally, and with a view to a permanent peace between the two countries; and if, for that purpose the part held by us should be considered more than an indemnity, to pay liberally for the balance.

But in order to render the means of coercion more effectual, I would hold, not absolutely, but also subject to negotiation, the ports of Mexico now in our possession, and which we could retain without too great a sacrifice of men and money. These ports I would open to the commerce of all countries, subject to a rate of duty that would barely cover the expense of maintaining the line.

I have now fully shown that we may certainly maintain this line, and thereby accomplish all the objects for which the war was declared, and that with little or no sacrifice of men or money, or without hazard or loss of reputation; and I may add, with a fair prospect of laying a foundation for a permanent peace between us and Mexico, on the final settlement of the differences between us. What would be its fruits? A speedy reduction of a large portion of the expenses of the war, by discharging the whole of the volunteers as soon as a defensive position is taken, which may be in the course of a few months. It would make a saving of fifteen or twenty millions of dollars during the year; the necessity for additional taxes would be avoided; credit would be immediately restored; a considerable portion of the loan might be dispensed with; and last, though not least, a measure which many of us on this side of the chamber have so much at heart, I mean that of free trade, would be rescued from great and impending danger. The short experience we have had of its operation holds out the prospect of almost unbounded prosperity to the country; not so much in consequence of the reduction of our own duties, as that made by Great Britain, which has opened her ample market for grain and other provisions of every description.

But it may be objected to the policy, that, with all its benefits, it would not bring peace. I think otherwise. What reason would Mexico have for holding out? None that I can perceive. On the contrary, she would see that we had undertaken to do what we could certainly perform—what our strength was abundantly adequate to go through with, without hazard or difficulty—she would also see that she had everything to loose [sic] and nothing to gain by holding out, and that if she obstinately persisted in refusing to treat, she might lose the of territory covered by our line, without compensation, instead of being liberally paid for its value beyond full indemnity for our claims against her.

But there are other and powerful reasons which would induce her to come to terms. By assuming a defensive position, and ceasing to push offensive operations against her, the feelings of the people of Mexico would in a short time undergo a great change. They now regard the war as a war between races and religions, and thus regarding it, they are under the excitement of the strongest and the profoundest feelings of our nature. Every nerve is braced, and every arm strengthened in resistance to us. The resolution of the whole country is to oppose us to the utmost of their power and resources. A defensive attitude on our part would tend powerfully to abate these deeply excited feelings. The war would no longer be regarded as a war of races and religions. They would no longer dread the extinction of one or the other. The ordinary, every day business of life would gradually absorb their attention. Add to this the effect which the possession of their ports would have upon their finances, by cutting off the most prolific branch of their revenue, and there would seem to be fair grounds for believing that, within a short period, much shorter probably than could be effected by offensive operations, she would be ready to negotiate and settle the differences between the two countries by a permanent peace. But, suppose in all this I am mistaken, and that Mexico will persist in holding out with her characteristic obstinacy, what would be the result? We will have war without expense or hazard—a war partaking much more of the character of peace than of war, so far as we are concerned. Our population would flow into the territory covered by our defensive line, and enable us to reduce the military establishment which would be necessary in the first instance. Above all it will once again place us on *terra firma*, and enable us to see beyond the dark curtain which is now suspended between us and the future.

I have now stated the reasons why I am in favor of taking a defensive position. I have, I trust, shown that we can by it bring the war to a successful termination, with little or no sacrifice of men and money, and without hazard of any description whatever. It remains to be shown, what are the grounds of my opposition to the continuance of an offensive war, and if I am not greatly mistaken, they are as strong as can well be conceived. I am opposed to it, for the very reverse reasons to those I have stated. There is no certainty, in the first place, that it will bring the war to a successful termination; and in the next, if it should, it would be at a vast expense of men and money, and with no inconsiderable hazard of disastrous consequences, and loss of national reputation.

In order to understand fully and correctly the force of the objection to continuing and pushing offensive operations, it is indispensable that the object *intended* to be effected should be distinctly and clearly perceived, for until that is understood, we can form no decisive opinion in reference to it; and here I premise, that its object is not conquest, or the acquisition of territory, for that is expressly disavowed. I further premise, that it is not to acquire additional means of indemnity, for I have already shown that we have ample means now in our hands to effect that purpose. If then it is for neither the one nor the other, I ask what is its object? But one answer is given; to obtain peace; or to use the language most commonly employed, to conquer peace. But how is peace to be obtained? It can only be by treaty. War may be made by one nation, but peace can only be made by two. The object then is to obtain a treaty; but what treaty, one that will suit Mexico? That can be obtained at any time. No, the treaty which is wanted is one that will suit us; but how can that be effected, but by compelling Mexico, by force of our arms, *and at our dictation*, to agree to such terms as we may dictate; and what could these terms be, but to secure all the objects for which the war was declared; that is, as has been shown, to establish the Rio Del Norte as our western boundary, and to obtain ample territory as the only means of our indemnity?

The intention, then, is to compel Mexico to acknowledge that to be ours which we now hold, and can, as I have already shown, easily hold, without her consent. This is all—more or less cannot be made of it. But how is Mexico to be compelled to sign such a treaty[?] We are informed that, for that purpose, the intention, in the first place, is to take Vera Cruz, and the Castle of San Juan de Ulloa, and then to march to the city of Mexico, and there to dictate the treaty. Now, with this object in view, I ask the Senate, is it worth while to pursue a vigorous war to compel Mexico to acknowledge that to be ours, which we hold, and can easily hold, against her consent[?] Is it worth while, even if we were perfectly certain of complete success by taking Vera Cruz and marching to Mexico, and there dictating a treaty at the end of this campaign? What would be the sacrifice, in effecting this, of men and money? The army authorised to be raised is about seventy thousand men, and the expense of the campaign may be put at thirty millions of dollars. It will probably exceed it by several millions, but I desire to be moderate. Suppose the active force in the field be 50,000 men, what then will be your sacrifice under this supposition? the loss of thirty millions of dollars. And what the sacrifice of life will be, may be judged of by looking at the past. One-third must be put down as certain to perish, not by the sword only, but by disease. Sixteen thousand lives then must be sacrificed. Now, I put it home to you Senators. Is it worth while to make this immense sacrifice of money and men for the mere purpose of obtaining the consent of Mexico to hold what we can so easily hold in despite of her? I put a graver question. I appeal to the conscience of every Senator who hears me, can you as a Christian, justify giving a vote that would lead to such results? Nay, is there one of you, who would give thirty millions of dollars, and sacrifice the lives of sixteen thousand of our people, for the two Californias and New Mexico? I answer for you, there is not one; and yet we propose to pursue a war, which, if terminated in a single campaign, and most fortunately, would lead to these sacrifices.

But is there any certainty our forces would reach Mexico [City] by the end of this campaign; or if they did that a treaty could be dictated? These are the questions that next demand our serious consideration.

An offensive war, such as we propose to carry on, looks as a possible event ultimately to subduing the country. Viewing it in that aspect, the war is but barely commenced. It is true we have acquired two-thirds of the territory of Mexico, but let it be remembered, these two-thirds are adjacent to us; let it also be remembered that it is sparsely populated. To give a vivid conception of its extent, the portion of Mexico held by us is almost 100,000 square miles more than the whole extent of the magnificent valley of the Mississippi, embracing the entire region between the Alleghany and Rocky Mountains. But although such is the immense extent of the territory, there are but six or seven hundred thousand inhabitants scattered over its surface.

It is this adjacent country, thus sparsely inhabited, which we have overrun, and now hold by military occupation. We have met, in conquering it, but little resistance, except from the regular army of Mexico, and as yet have gained in reality but little in a military point of view. Instead of conciliating the inhabitants they are reported to be more hostile than ever, and not an inconsiderable portion of our army will be required to hold and defend the country we occupy. As yet we have scarcely approached Mexico proper, consisting of the elevated plain on which the City of Mexico stands, and the hot regions extending on the east, along the Gulf of Mexico to Yucatan, and along the borders of the Pacific and the Gulf of California, on the west. Within these comparatively narrow limits, consisting of one-third of all Mexico, there is at least seven millions of people, fully ten times as many as the portion of Mexico we occupy. Here, too, is the seat of her wealth, and power, and civilization. The character of the country, and its climate, present formidable obstacles to an invading army. The approaches to the table land are few, passing through narrow defiles, and up steep acclivities, and the region itself is mountainous and rough in the extreme. It may be compared, in a military point of view, to Mount Atlas, in Africa, or the Caucasus, in Europe. To this may be added a scanty supply of food for men, and forage for horses, of an invading army. The climate of the hot regions, both on the Pacific and on the Gulf, is extremely sickly, especially that of the Gulf, to which our military operations in reference to the City of Mexico will be directed. Perhaps there is none on earth more so. It may be said to be the native home of the yellow fever, one of the most terrific of diseases. It prevails during eight months every year, and not unfrequently during ten months; and what adds to the difficulty in the way of an invading army, is the prevalence of sudden and violent storms, during the period of the year when the fever does not prevail. April itself is a sickly month, and March doubtful. We are now near the middle of February, and may have in the field force sufficient to take Vera Cruz; but I appeal to all sides, have we force enough, or can we have force enough in time to avoid the vomita, and march to the City of Mexico during this campaign? I will not say we have not, but I say with confidence that there is no certainty that we have or will have sufficient for such an enterprise.

But if we fail to reach the city this campaign, what will be its effects? We shall be worse off than we now are; a year will be lost; Mexico will be encouraged and we discouraged; she will add to her fortifications and defences, and increase her supplies of arms, in which she is now especially deficient.

But suppose we should be so fortunate as to be able to reach the City of Mexico? Is there any certainty that we should be able to dictate a treaty such as we desire? With whom have we to deal? A race of people renowned above all others for their obstinacy, and the pertinacity of resistance—a people whose hereditary pride is, that they rescued their country when over[r]un by the Moors, after a war of seven or eight centuries—a people who for eighty years waged war for the maintenance of their dominion over the Low Countries—a people who, for twenty years carried on the war against her own colonies, before they would recognize their independence. Such are the people with whom we are contending, and is it certain that such a people will be compelled by our occupying the City of Mexico, to yield to our terms? We must remember that the city is not to Mexico what Paris is to France; on the contrary, all her internal struggles, with almost no exception, prove that the City of Mexico, in a military point of view, has very little control over the country.

But, if there be no certainty either that we can reach Mexico, or reaching it, can compel her to yield to our terms, we may have another campaign before the war can be concluded, by what is called vigorous measures; and here the question presents itself, shall we have the means—can we raise the men and money to carry on the third campaign? Remember, it must be much more costly, and require a greater force than what is required for the approaching campaign. It will be carried on at a greater distance from us, and every step as we advance will require a larger detached force to occupy and cover our rear. Bear in mind also, that it will be of a different character from either the past or the approaching campaign; for if we conquer the city without obtaining peace, one of two results will follow, her government will withdraw or be dispersed, and we shall, in either case, be compelled to subdue and hold the country in military subjection. In either case, we shall have a guerrilla war, such as now exists between France and the Arabs in Africa, and between Russia and the Circassians in the Caucasus. Shall we be able to raise the men and the revenue which will be required to carry on the extensive military operations incident to such a war? Can you rely upon raising volunteers? Will not the first flush of feeling which accompany [*sic*] the commencement of a war, and which leads to the spirit of volunteering, expire by the commencement of the third campaign? Is it not probable, that the many volunteers who will return with broken constitutions—who went for glory, but return with shattered health—will greatly discourage the ardor of volunteering, strong as the impulse is in the breasts of our young and patriotic countrymen. The probability is, that we must mainly rely for men on the ordinary process of recruiting; and can we certainly calculate in that way to raise fifteen or twenty thousand men for the third campaign, for that number at least will be required?

But, suppose this surmounted, a far more difficult question presents itself; can you raise the ways and means? The resources from treasury notes will have been exhausted, and we shall have to resort to loans and taxes as our only means. Can you borrow a sufficient amount to meet the demands of the campaign, probably not less than twenty-five or thirty millions of dollars, but at an enormous rate of interest? Can you impose taxes to a great amount? On what will you lay them? On imports? The duties on them may be increased, but to no great amount; additional duties on many of the articles would diminish instead of increasing the revenue. Will you lay direct or internal taxes? The resources of the country are great, beyond almost any other, but there are two circumstances which will interpose to prevent their being reached. The first is, that many of the States are deeply in debt, and have imposed very onerous taxes to meet their own obligations. Can you impose additional taxes without greatly overburdening the people of those States? Remember, that by the constitution, all taxes must be uniform throughout the United States, and of course, what is imposed upon one must be equally imposed on the other. Will the people of the indebted States bear additional taxes? Will Pennsylvania, with forty millions already on her shoulders? Will the imposition not compel her and other of the indebted States to suspend the payment of interest on their debts? Will it not prevent Maryland, Indiana, and other States deeply in debt, from the resumption of the payment of interest on theirs? Will not the effect be to widen the sphere of repudiation, so as to comprehend most of the indebted States? Is there the slightest chance with this prospect before us, that internal taxes to any considerable amount will be imposed by Congress for the further prosecution of an offensive war? Can any one answer in the affirmative, who has witnessed the strong indisposition to impose additional taxes at the present session?

But suppose this difficulty, interposed by the indebtedness of many of the States, to be removed? There is another still remaining, not less formidable. Is there sufficient unanimity and zeal in favor of the war to warrant the belief that Congress would impose internal taxes to carry on offensive operations? Does this session furnish any evidence of any such zeal or unanimity? On the contrary, does it not furnish ample evidence that there is great division and want of zeal in reference to the war? We would be blind not to see that a very great portion of the people honestly believe that the war might and ought to have been avoided; that it was commenced by the Executive without the sanction of Congress or the Constitution, and that it is highly inexpedient and injurious. What my opinions are on all these points, I would be glad to explain on a suitable occasion; but I do not regard this to be the proper one, to mingle my own private views and sentiments in reference to the causes of the war, and the manner in which it was commenced, with the deeply important subject under consideration—how the war shall be conducted, so as to terminate it most favorably to the country.

But suppose all these difficulties to be removed, there remains another still deeper and more alarming to be met—one touching the very foundation of our Union; how shall the territory be disposed of if any should be acquired? Shall it be for the benefit of one part of the Union to the exclusion of the other? We are told, and I fear that appearances justify it, that all parties in the non-slaveholding States are united in the determination that they shall have the exclusive benefit and monopoly—that such provisions shall be made by treaty or law, as to exclude all who hold slaves in the South from emigrating with their property into the acquired country. If the non slaveholding States having no other interest but an aversion to our domestic institutions, (for such is slavery as it exists in the South,) if, I repeat, they can come to the conclusion, to exclude the South from all benefit in the acquired territory, with no other interest but that, I turn to their representatives on this floor and ask them, what they suppose must [be] the feeling of the slave-holding States, to whom this question is one of safety and not of mere policy, to be deprived of their rights, and their perfect equality secured by the Constitution, and to be assailed in their most vulnerable point? Be assured, if there be stern determination on one side to exclude us, there will be determination still sterner on ours, not to be excluded.

Now if I may judge from what has been declared on this floor, from what I hear on all sides, the members from the non slaveholding States, if they were sure that slavery would not be excluded from the acquired territory, would be decidedly opposed to what they called a vigorous prosecution of the war, or the acquisition of a single foot of territory; can they then believe that the members of the slave-holding States, on the opposite supposition, would not be equally opposed to the further prosecution of the war and the acquisition of territory? And how can this war be vigorously carried on for a third campaign, with this known pointed division of opinion between these two great portions of the Union as to the ultimate disposition to be made of the territory to be acquired[?]

But I will suppose, that all these difficulties are surmounted—that men and money may be had, and that unanimity and zeal existed on all points—the question then presents itself, can you, should you not obtain peace in the city of Mexico, can you bring this war to a successful termination by subduing the country? Can you certainly—not probably? That is the question. Look at the history of such wars carried on by powerful and highly civilized nations against others poor and less civilized, in mountainous regions like Mexico—the wars of Russia against the Caucasians, and the war of France against the Arabs in Algeria—and take warning. In both there has been powerful and effective resistance against the best troops in Europe, under the lead of their most experienced Generals. And are we to expect to subdue the country without encountering like difficulties? Are you certain that you will not, and that the war will be brought to a termination at the end of the third campaign; that you can effect in a single campaign what has cost France already in Algeria, sixteen—and has cost Russia in the Caucasus, I knew not how many? And it may be added, which cost us against a paltry band of Indians in Florida, five campaigns and thirty millions of dollars? Well then, if we are not certain; this war may go on, if offensive operations are to be continued, to the fourth, fifth, sixth, seventh, and I know not what number of campaigns. I say may, for the mere possibility, ought to be sufficient to deter a wise people from a policy which would lead to such disastrous results, as would a long and protracted war, in attempting to subdue Mexico, and where especially so little is to be gained. What can we gain, if success should finally crown our efforts by subduing the country? What would we do with it? Shall we annex the States of Mexico to our Union? Can we incorporate a people so dissimilar from us in every respect—so little qualified for free and popular government—without certain destruction to our political institutions? And can we bring into our Union eight millions of people all professing one religion—and all concentrated under a powerful and wealthy priesthood, without subjecting the country to the most violent religious conflict, and bringing the government in the end under control of a single sect? No. These difficulties are insurmountable. The question then recurs, what shall we do with the country? Shall we hold it as a subject province? Consequences not less fatal will result from this disposition of it. It would end in the loss of liberty, as it ever has, where free States undertake to hold in subjection extended provinces. The process would be short and easy. It would be followed by enormous patronage, and that again by a corresponding increase of the power and influence of the Executive, and end finally in despotism, by making that department absolute. Such would be the inevitable results, if you should undertake either to incorporate them into the Union, or to hold them as subject provinces, unless indeed the stern conflict between the slave-holding and non-slave-holding States, as to the disposition to be made of the territory, should give a different turn to the conquest, and terminate the whole in a disrupture of the Union.

But if the dread of these results should determine us to abandon, after we had subdued it, what we shall acquire by a further prosecution of the war—as we certainly would, if we acted wisely—how strongly it would illustrate the folly of what is called a vigorous prosecution of the war. It would, on that supposition, leave us, as far as the acquisition of territory is concerned, after all our mighty sacrifices and the hazards and disasters to which we may be exposed, where we now stand, and where we may stand and maintain ourselves with perfect certainty, with little or no sacrifice of men and money, and without any hazard of disastrous consequences.

We would be fortunate, among these sacrifices, to escape without an appalling loss of human life, and an immense burden in the shape of a public debt, to be followed by a permanent and irretrievable loss of free trade, for generations to come; to say nothing of the disastrous consequences which the vastly increased patronage of the Government may have upon our free institutions, and the loss of reputation and standing as a government and a people, should we, after putting forth all our efforts to subdue the country in a vigorous war, be baffled in the attempt.

When I said there was a mysterious connection between the fate of our country and that of Mexico, I had reference to the great fact that we stood in such relation to her that we could make no disposition of Mexico, as a subject or conquered nation, that would not prove disastrous to us; nor could we conquer and subdue her without great sacrifice and injurious effects to our institutions.

Hence my opinion, already expressed, that it is our true policy not to weaken nor humble her, but to desire to see her under a safe and stable government, and capable of sustaining all the relations which ought to exist between independent nations. Situated as the two countries are to each other, my conviction is deep, that the prosperity of each, and the maintenance of free and popular institutions on the part of both, depend greatly upon our pursuing towards her a just and liberal course of policy. In this view I hold this war to have been a great departure from our true line of policy, and therefore, deeply to be deplored. Should we be so unfortunate now as to commit the error of determining to prosecute offensive operations vigorously, instead of taking a defensive position, we shall take a step which I fear we shall long have to rue. Thus thinking, I regard it a paramount question—party is nothing to it; but, let me say to whatever party may advise it, that they stake their fate upon a cast which may end in their overthrow and ruin, to say nothing of the higher consideration of disasters to the country, on which I have so fully dwelt.

There is but one way of escape, as far as I am capable of seeing, and that I have suggested. I might say much more to enforce its adoption, but forbear consuming the further time of the Senate. The way I have suggested is not the result of recent reflection, for I have long looked upon the subject with intense interest. Nor is it the first time I have suggested it in my place. During the last session, in a discussion while our doors were closed, on the bill appropriating two millions of dollars for a like object, I suggested, but more briefly, the same plan of policy as the most advisable course, and the only one, as far as I could see, likely soon to bring the war to a certain and successful termination.

With a few observations in reference to myself, I shall close my remarks. I shall feel myself compelled, as the Senate will readily perceive from what I have said, to vote against the amendment of the Senator from Michigan [Lewis Cass]. In reference to that amendment and the bill itself, I reserve an expression of opinion until I see further developments, both as to the course of policy intended to be pursued in conducting the war, and the great domestic question to which I have alluded. My vote may depend upon developments as to both.

From *Speech of Mr. Calhoun, of South Carolina, on the Bill Making Further Appropriation to Bring the Existing War with Mexico to a Speedy and Honorable Conclusion, Called the Three Million Bill. Delivered in the Senate of the United States, February 9, 1847* (Washington: printed by John T. Towers, 1847). Also printed in *Congressional Globe,* 29th Cong., 2nd Sess., Appendix, pp. 323–327; Crallé, ed., *Works,* 4:303–327; Wilson, ed., *The Essential Calhoun,* pp. 129–133 (part). Variant in the Washington, D.C., *Daily Union,* February 9, 1847, p. 2; the Charleston, S.C., *Mercury,* February 15, 1847, p. 2; the Charleston, S.C., *Southern Patriot,* February 15, 1847, p. 2; the Columbia, S.C., *South-Carolinian,* February 17, 1847, p. 1; the Columbia, S.C., *Southern Chronicle,* February 24, 1847, p. 1; the Edgefield, S.C., *Advertiser,* February 24, 1847, pp. 1, 4; the Huntsville, Ala., *Democrat,* February 24, 1847, pp. 2–3. Another variant in the Washington, D.C., *Daily National Intelligencer,* February 10, 1847, pp. 2–3; *Congressional Globe,* 29th Cong., 2nd Sess., pp. 356–359; Benton, *Abridgment of Debates,* 16:56–60 (part). Another variant in the Charleston, S.C., *Courier,* February 13, 1847, p. 2; the Tallahassee, Fla., *Southern Journal,* February 23, 1847, pp. 1–2 (reprinted from the Baltimore, Md., *American and Commercial Daily Advertiser*); the Greenville, S.C., *Mountaineer,* February 26, 1847, pp. 1–2. Still other variants in the Alexandria, Va., *Gazette and Virginia Advertiser,* February 10, 1847, p. 3; the New York, N.Y., *Herald,* February 13, 1847, p. 3; the Petersburg, Va., *Republican,* February 12, 1847, p. 2; the Charleston, S.C., *Mercury,* February 13, 1847, p. 2.

REMARKS ON A QUESTION OF PRIVILEGE

[In the Senate, February 10, 1847]

[David L. Yulee of Fla. introduced resolutions to bar reporters of the Washington, D.C., Daily Union from the Senate, and to condemn the editors of that paper "for a public libel upon the character of this body." The resolutions referred to the Union's report, published on February 9, of the Constitutional debate on the President's appointing power that had taken place on February 8. The Chair, (Vice-President George M. Dallas), ruled that the resolutions should lie over. George E. Badger of N.C. and others protested that it was a question of privilege and thus had immediate priority.]

Mr. Calhoun expressed his hope that the Senator from North Carolina would withdraw his appeal. It was desirable, in his opinion, that the subject should lie over until to-morrow, so that Senators might have an opportunity to examine the article referred to, which contained, it is alleged, attacks—for it was not a single attack, but several—on this body. It was also desirable that opportunity should be given to look into the character of the report alluded to in the resolution, and to see to what extent it was garbled. There could be no doubt that an insulting attack had been made on this body; and that the report on the amendment to the army bill had been one-sided, not a word having been published of what had been said on the side of those who interposed a constitutional objection to the amendment, while two speakers on the opposite side are fully reported. He hoped the whole subject would be allowed to go over until to-morrow.

[There was further debate.]

Mr. Calhoun said he did not entertain the least doubt of the correctness of the position taken by the Senator from North Carolina, that a question of privilege always takes precedence. He had merely suggested the postponement in order to give time for an examination, but he would not press it.

[After further debate on the point of order, the resolutions were postponed until the next day by a vote of 23 to 16.]

From *Congressional Globe*, 29th Cong., 2nd Sess., p. 367. Variants in the Washington, D.C., *Daily Union*, February 10, 1847, p. 2; the Washington, D.C., *Daily National Intelligencer*, February 11, 1847, p. 2; the New York, N.Y., *Herald*, February 12, 1847, p. 3.

FURTHER REMARKS ON THE
WAR WITH MEXICO

[In the Senate, February 10, 1847]
[Lewis Cass of Mich. delivered a speech in favor of the bill appropriating a further three million dollars to conclude the war.]

Mr. Calhoun explained that the Senator from Michigan had not truly represented him, when he attributed to him a declaration [in his speech of 2/9] that we had not the means to carry on this campaign. In this, that Senator was entirely incorrect. He had merely put it to the Senate, if the means could be drawn out—and there would doubtless be a difficulty in getting the men, and there would be a great increase of expense—he put it to the Senate, if, when obtained, it would be worth all this sacrifice of money and of lives. The Senator from Michigan had also alluded to an expression that there was a mysterious connexion between Mexico and the United States. Mr. C[alhoun] explained that he spoke of the contiguity of the two republics, and the danger to this country if it should absorb the neighboring republic. He also entered into some explanation in relation to the line which he desired to see this country maintain from the Gulf of Mexico to the Pacific; and maintained that it could be protected by the small force he had before mentioned.

From *Congressional Globe*, 29th Cong., 2nd Sess., p. 374. Variant in the New York, N.Y., *Herald*, February 12, 1847, p. 4. NOTE: In the variant report, Cass pointed out that the frontier to be defended was 1,950 miles. Calhoun replied that only 480 miles of this required direct defense.

FURTHER REMARKS ON THE
TEN REGIMENT BILL

[In the Senate, February 10, 1847]
[Sidney Breese of Ill. alleged that Calhoun's position against the President's power to appoint officers after the recess of Congress was inconsistent with his votes in 1813 in the House of Representatives.]

Mr. Calhoun replied that the act of 1813, to which the Senator from Illinois had referred, did not absolutely raise the regiments, but gave a discretionary power to the President to raise not exceeding twenty regiments. It was therefore impossible to appoint officers until the offices were created.

Again, in reference to the allusion to him by the Senator from Illinois, he observed that he was the chairman of the Committee on Foreign Relations during that session, and it would certainly be extraordinary if he should be held amenable for every act then passed. On the passage of the act in question there was no division, and therefore he might have voted against it. He was surprised that the Senator from Illinois should be so anxious to fix inconsistency on him, for which there was not the slightest shadow. His opinions remained unchanged, that if these appointments were to be vested in the President, they must be vested as now recommended by the committee of conference—in him alone, if they were inferior officers. On this point, however, he could not agree with other honorable Senators.

In relation to the precedents quoted by the Senator from Illinois, he said there had been doubtless, in the course of fifty years, much loose legislation, and yet the gentleman could not bring more than four or five cases to sustain his position. He retained the opinion that "inferior officers" were those connected with the departments. Were it otherwise, they might depute to the heads of departments or to courts of justice the appointments of brigadier generals; but the framers of the Constitution never intended any such incongruous or absurd exercise of power.

He would not consume further time than to say, that his constitutional opinions remained unchanged; and, retaining such opinions, he must vote against the report.

[*There was further debate during which Breese repeated his contentions.*]

Mr. Calhoun briefly replied. He thought the Senator from Illinois was taxing a young man rather too much when he required him to find out all the constitutional difficulties which interpose to obstruct the passage of acts of legislation. At the time of which the honorable Senator spoke, he was chairman of the Committee on Foreign Relations in the other House, and he might not have been present when these measures were adopted.

From *Congressional Globe*, 29th Cong., 2nd Sess., pp. 376–377. Variant in the New York, N.Y., *Herald*, February 12, 1847, p. 4.

From W[ILLIAM] GILMORE SIMMS

Woodlands, [Barnwell District, S.C.,] Feb. 10, 1847

My dear Sir, I can well conceive that, just at this juncture, your time is very much employed, and I beg you therefore to choose your own leisure in according me an answer to the subject of this Letter. During the last session there was submitted in your body a resolution voting a bust or statue to Mr. John Rutledge of South Carolina. I should like to be put in possession of the report upon this matter, & to be informed of the course which the proposition took, and whether anything was done in it. We are all looking very anxiously to your course on the subject of our Mexican relations. That the South desires the territory we have gained—that the public mind everywhere is fully resolved that we shall keep it—I have little question; but the point with us ["is" *interlined*] to make the conditions preliminary, by which our domestic institutions will be made secure. I think the popular greed will put down the abolitionist faction at the North, if once satisfied that the acquisition of territory cannot be made unless the South is pacified. How far the South, by a temporary coalition with the opponents of Government, can succeed in withholding supplies &c. is a question. But I prattle something too idly, and write this only to let you see the direction which our minds take in my obscure neighbourhood. I am, Sir, with great respect Your ob[edien]t Serv[an]t &c, W. Gilmore Simms.

ALS in ScCleA; PC in Oliphant, Odell, and Eaves, eds., *The Letters of William Gilmore Simms*, 2:267–268. NOTE: An AEU by Calhoun reads: "Gilmore Sims" [*sic*]. Calhoun's reply to Simms has not been found. However, in a letter to James H. Hammond on March 29, 1847 (*The Letters of William Gilmore Simms*, 2:292) Simms stated that he had received a letter from Calhoun which he was now forwarding to Hammond. Simms gave his critical opinion of Calhoun's letter, asserting that he "makes a stronger case against the South in the present condition of affairs, than he did in his speech in Charleston." Calhoun, according to Simms, was motivated by the hope of being President, but "does not seem disposed to play for the high stake a bit more sagaciously today than twenty years ago. . . . Does he not acquire his great metaphysical powers at the loss of others by which he fails duly to appreciate the nature of the very animal to whom he most appeals."

Further remarks on a question of privilege, 2/11. Discussion continued on George E. Badger's appeal from yesterday's decision of the Chair (Vice-President George M. Dallas) against Badger's point of privilege. "Mr. Calhoun rose to make a single observation. There was (he said) great impatience on the part of the Senate to proceed with the consideration of the important questions which awaited the action of the Senate, and he hoped that no further time would be wasted upon the matter now before them. It was a very narrow question, amounting only to this: whether it was such a question of privilege as ought to take precedence of all other business. This, after the discussion which had already taken place, he thought the Senate was quite prepared to decide." Later "Mr. Calhoun suggested that the Senator from Ohio [Thomas Corwin, who was scheduled to speak next on the "three million bill"] should be consulted as to whether he desired to proceed." From *Congressional Globe*, 29th Cong., 2nd Sess., p. 382. Also printed in the Washington, D.C., *Daily National Intelligencer*, February 12, 1847, p. 2. Variant in the Petersburg, Va., *Republican*, February 17, 1847, p. 2.

Speech in Reply to Hopkins L. Turney

[In the Senate, February 12, 1847]

[*The Senate was engaged in extended debate on the resolutions condemning the Washington* Daily Union *for its reportage of Mexican War debates. Turney of Tenn., an administration supporter, remarked that "there are aspirants here for the Presidency of the United States," including one Democrat who, "when he carries his forces to the Whigs, gives them a majority." "Now if he insists on my giving names," said Turney, "I will point to the leader to whom I refer, but I would rather not go into this matter." He added more to the same import and suggested that the leader to whom he referred, having the balance of power between parties, was responsible for the measures passed or not passed by Congress.*]

Mr. Calhoun. If the Senator speaks of me as an aspirant for the Presidency, he is entirely mistaken. I am no aspirant—never have been. I would not turn on my heel for the Presidency; and he has uttered a libel upon me—

The President. The honorable Senator must be aware that—(the remainder of the sentence was lost).

Mr. Calhoun, if he supposes that I am capable of voting upon any question with reference to the Presidency, or any other consideration but a regard to truth, justice, and my country. No, sir. The whole volume of my life shows me to be above that. There are men, Mr. President, who cannot believe that an individual is influenced by a single circumstance but party considerations or presidential elections, and who attribute all motives to one or other of these; and I am the most misunderstood man in the world by that portion of this and every other party. No, sir; I want no Presidency; I want to do my duty. No denunciations here, or out of this House, can deflect me a single inch from going directly at what I aim, and that is the good of the country. I have always acted upon it, and I will always act upon it. If he means to say that there is any organized opposition here, as far as I am concerned, or my friends, which affects the votes here, irrespective of public duty and conviction, never, never was a man more mistaken—never! And I think it will be very hard for him, or any other Senator here, to specify a single measure that we have either delayed or defeated that is necessary to the conducting of the war. Now I ask him—I pause, and ask him, if he can point to a single one?

Mr. Turney. I will try when you get through.

Mr. Calhoun. No, sir, no! Not a single one. I voted several times for adjournment with gentlemen on the other side when I considered that adjournment was proper; but I have no concert with them, no more than I have on this side. Mr. President, in thus acting without concert of action I performed my duty. What we do want above all things on earth in our public men is independence. It is one great defect in the character of the public men of America that there is that real want of independence; and in this respect a most marked contrast between public men in this country and in Great Britain. But this is not the proper occasion on which that difference is to be pointed out; but I will say that it is in part the wretched system of caucussing, which has created in every State a party of men who work in concert to get offices for purpose of plunder, and who exercise too great a control over the measures of Congress. I am glad the Senator thought proper to refer to me in this pointed manner. I have seen these insinuations in various quarters, and in different presses; but they are to me as nothing. If I know myself, if my head was at stake I would do my duty, be the consequence what it would. Sir, they could not urge me upon this war. Why so? I hope upon some occasion I shall have an opportunity to state the reasons more in detail. But, amongst other reasons, I saw in this very war what every man now begins to see—consequences which deterred me. And we are not at the bottom yet. I stood upon tha[t] occasion alone, separated from my respected and esteemed colleague, (Mr. [George] McDuffie). I voted here in my seat against it; and can he (Mr. Turney) suppose that I was governed by the paltry and miserable consideration of being President of the United States? The position is respectable, but there are other positions infinitely more so. I would rather be an independent Senator, governed by my own views, going for the good of the country, uncontrolled by any thing which mortal man can bring to bear upon me, than to be President of the United States, put there as Presidents of the U. States have been for many years past.

[*Turney spoke; then Calhoun resumed, as follows:*]

I am really obliged to the gentleman from Tennessee for giving me an opportunity to repel a great many insinuations which I have seen upon this very subject, and the endeavor to fix upon myself and friends the responsibility of which he has spoken. He has got up and made a grave charge, that there was on this side of the house a party combined together, in reference to Presidential elections, who controlled all measures in reference to that. I have already denied that I was any candidate for the Presidency. I appeal to every friend—to my friends upon this floor, upon either side of the house, and to every one in the State of South Carolina—if my whole course of conduct has not been this: that I would not accept the Presidency unless it comes to me by the voice of the American people; and then only from a sense of duty, and taken as an obligation. At my time of life the Presidency is nothing; and for many a long year, Mr. President, I have long aspired for an object far higher than the Presidency—that is, doing my duty under all circumstances, in every trial, irrespective of parties, and without regard to friendships or enmities, but simply in reference to the prosperity of the country. If my life be reviewed hereafter, I leave to those who may review it the settlement of this question. What charge has he made out against myself and the few of my friends who have voted with me during the present session? Where has he shown that we have rejected or abandoned any measures connected with the conduct of this war? One single act only, and that is, not voting for the proposition for a lieutenant-general. Now, Mr. President, on this we need no apology. That vote needs no defence.

If the American people have been unanimous on any one subject, they have been on that. Now this is only one act, and I am happy that here, in my place, in the presence of this large audience, I have an opportunity to repel this charge, so that the whole truth may go forth in regard to it. But not a single other vote can be shown on which to rest this charge. For if there had been another, it would have been added to the long catalogue which the Senator from Tennessee has drawn up against me upon other and irrelevant subjects. But there is another, which he suspects. He suspects that I will not vote for the three million bill; and that because I said, when I spoke on the subject [on 2/9], I waited further developments. Was there any thing, Mr. President, in that—was the Senator ignorant that a proposition had been made in the other House, and probably would be made here, to stick the Wilmot proviso on it? I put it to him—I put it to Senators on both sides who represent Southern portions of the Union—whether he or any of them will vote for the bill if that amendment be appended? And because I choose to make this reservation—(and there are other reasons, not necessary to be stated at present, equally powerful)—because I choose to make this reservation, I am to be held up as embarrassing Congress, consuming its time, and opposing measures necessary to carry on the war! Well as to that consumption of time, it is one of the most unfounded insinuations. Is there any Senator at all, who takes part in the debates, who has consumed less time than myself? I have made but a single speech, the other day, and that but an hour; and besides that, I have not made a speech that has occupied five minutes; and yet on these grounds, amounting to nothing, we are told that we are to be responsible for every thing connected with the session, done or not done! Well, that shows a very deep feeling working within. It may be there are aspirants to the Presidency who think something may be gained by making these charges. I know not. Or it may be the individual feeling of the Senator himself, from some personal considerations, although I do not know how this can be, as I have never had the slightest personal difference with him. Well, he accuses me of voting against the bill the other day upon the ground of some constitutional objection, and that I had given a different vote in the year 1813. There was a bill passed in 1813, but is there any evidence that this question was made or presented? I believe the Senator from Massachusetts, (Mr. [Daniel] Webster,) was then a member of the House. He may be able to tell. It is a long time ago. I have forgotten all about it. But, to the best of my knowledge, I never heard the question presented as to the constitutionality of the provision till it was raised by the Senator from Connecticut (Mr. [Jabez W.] Huntington) in the discussion here.

Mr. Webster here said, whether it was discussed earlier than May, 1813, I know not; but I know the question was not raised then, nor since, till now.

Mr. Calhoun. So I thought. But does not the Senator know that, in these complicated measures, often very important constitutional questions may not present themselves? Now I am to be charged, on such grounds, as having changed my opinions—pleading infancy at one time, and dotage in another; for such is the language which the Senator applies. But again: he spoke of the responsibility for the war as arising from the annexation of Texas. I did take a deep interest in that measure of annexation, and to no act of my life do I revert with more entire satisfaction. Annexation at that time, according to my opinion, was a question of pure necessity. I might go into this matter if it would not occupy the time of the Senate. (Cries "go on.")

According to my view, the time was not propitious in one aspect. The then President [John Tyler] had no party in either House. I am not certain that he had a single supporter in this, and not more than four or five in the other. It appeared to me to be a very unpropitious moment, under such circumstances, to carry through so important a measure. When it was intimated to me that I would be nominated for the office of Secretary of State, I strongly remonstrated against it to my friends here; but before my remonstrance reached them I was unanimously appointed, and was compelled to accept. I saw that the Administration was weak, and that the very important measure would be liable to be defeated. But circumstances made action on it inevitable. I ascertained, from sources perfectly reliable, that at the World's Convention the American delegation suggested to the abolitionists of England that then was the time to act, and if they wished to aim a fatal blow at slavery, it must be in Texas; and, in order to do that, England must obtain control there. I received information—I will not say official, but from a quarter [Ashbel Smith] in which there could be no mistake—that an interview had taken place between Lord Aberdeen and a deputation of the World's Convention. I was then at home in South Carolina, and immediately transmitted to the Secretary of State [Abel P. Upshur] that information, accompanied by my opinion that it demanded instant attention. I suppose that letter and my communication formed one of the reasons for the movement then made for annexation. What was then the condition of Texas? She was weak, and could not long remain without the support of England or the United States. The British Government saw this, and commenced its operations under the suggestion of the World's Convention, by pressing Mexico to recognise her independence on condition of abolishing slavery. The time had come to act, and for consequences to be met, be they what they might. I accepted the office, with all these difficulties before me. I said: ["]This office is unacceptable to me. I go in with no small share of reputation, if I may judge from appearances. I shall experience great difficulty in accomplishing the object for which I have been appointed, and may lose much reputation; but I must do my duty.["] I undertook it, and when I undertake a thing I go straightforward to it. I placed the question on its true ground, that this movement was intended to bring Texas under the control of England, with a view to abolish slavery there, and, through that, abolishing it throughout the country. A treaty was formed, and it shared the fate that might have almost been expected from the weakness of the Administration. It was defeated. But the Senator says I had stipulated in that treaty that the Rio Grande was the boundary.

Mr. Turney. I remarked that I had never read the treaty, but I understood that its terms went to the Rio Grande.

Mr. Calhoun. The Senator is just as wrong in that as in all his understandings. No such thing; the line was intentionally left open. The two respectable commissioners from Texas [J. Pinckney Henderson and Isaac Van Zandt] will bear me testimony as to that. It was expressly left open, in order that the boundary might be subsequently established by negotiation with Mexico. I know that a Senator of this body [Thomas H. Benton] put a construction on it similar to that of the Senator from Tennessee, and strongly assailed me on that assumption. But it was so far from true, that as soon as the treaty was signed, I communicated directly with the Mexican Government, through our Chargé d'Affaires [Wilson Shannon], and stated that I was ready to settle all questions of difference, and amongst others the boundary, upon the most liberal principles. I did not apprehend that war would follow. But I am held responsible, on the ground that if Texas had not been annexed, we should not have had a Mexican war. Is he sure of that? Why, this is an attack on Mr. [James K.] Polk. What is the whole staple of the message, but that the real cause of war was injuries committed on American citizens long before annexation? Has the gentleman overlooked that? And did not General [Andrew] Jackson and Mr. [Martin] Van Buren declare that those injuries were a just cause of war? The immediate cause of the war, if he desires to know, was the marching of our forces from the frontier, (A Senator: Corpus Christi)—from Corpus Christi to the banks of the Del Norte. To repel that on the part of Mexico, is what the President calls an invasion, assuming that the Rio Del Norte was the boundary. But can that be justly charged to annexation? If General [Zachary] Taylor had remained where he was, there would have been no invasion. The evidence is clear. The fact is, and cannot be denied, that General [Mariano] Arista communicated to General Taylor, either by letter or a trusty agent, that if the American troops would remain where they were, (at Corpus Christi,) the Mexican troops would remain where they were, on the west side of the Rio del Norte. That both might send out detachments to the Salt Colorado, (a stream about midway between the two places,) for the purpose of guarding the frontier and preventing smuggling, and that there would be no conflict between them. If I am not mistaken, this was communicated to the Department, and a call upon it would bring it forth, if it should be required. I think something to the same effect was recently published in the Southern papers. (A Senator: Yes!) So, then, we have clear evidence that the war was made by the order to march to the Del Norte. That the President believed that to be the boundary I do not question.

But the great question comes up, Has the Executive the right to determine what our boundary is? When we have a disputed boundary question—and we have had many—does it belong to the Executive or to Congress to determine it? There are two ways to do it. One is by negotiation and treaty, to be performed by the Executive and this body, in case the two nations agree to negotiate. The other is, if the party disputes the boundary and will not come to terms, for Congress to declare where the boundary is, and maintain it, if need be, at the hazard of war. How long did the boundary of Maine remain unsettled? From the acknowledgement of independence in 1783, down to the time that the Senator from Massachusetts [Webster] closed it by treaty. But did any of the Presidents ever think of marching troops upon the line? The British held Detroit and Fort Stanwix after the treaty of peace until Jay's treaty in 1784. Did General [George] Washington undertake to establish the boundary by marching troops to the St. Lawrence, which was our boundary? If war, then, has followed annexation, it is not to be traced to one from South Carolina, but to one from Tennessee [Polk].

I might say more on this subject, but I will not detain the Senate. The gentleman has made a great many charges upon my political course. He has charged me with inconsistency, and represented me as voting on different sides of all questions. The gentleman's understanding on this point is just as correct as on all others. I leave that all to history. I will not say that I have not changed my opinions on many things—very little on constitutional points—and not many on questions of policy. My mind is indeed rather rigid. Like all young men coming to Congress, I had my opinions both as to principle and policy, but had much to learn as to the actual working of our system, which could only be had from actual experience: before they could be firmly and fully established, I had to go through the process of experience. At that time, the great question was the war with Great Britain, in reference to which I took a bold and decided stand. I continued in Congress but two years after the war; and, after filling the office of Secretary of War and Vice President, returned to Congress, and took my seat in this body in 1832–3; and, from that day to this, the volume of my life is known to the country; and I challenge the Senator, or any Senator on this floor, to show, from that day to this, wherein I have changed my views. He says that when the question came up on the recognition of Texas, I belonged to the opposite side of the house. No. I belonged to neither side. Several Senators—the Senator from North Carolina nearest to me [Willie P. Mangum], and the Senator from Massachusetts—can testify as to that. I never met in caucus in consultation with either side of the house. I took my own independent course, standing nearly alone for some years, voting what I believed to be the true interest of the country, irrespective of party. And let me say, I have never attended those meetings for the purpose of deliberation with gentlemen on this side of the House, except during the period of excitement in the extra session called by General [William Henry] Harrison in 1844 [*sic*; 1841], and part of the next session. I attended then, because the Democratic party had been overthrown in the preceding elections, and there were at that time great questions involved in the issues between the parties, in which I agreed with them and was opposed to the opposite party. I met only in reference to the arrangements to sustain the Democratic party in those issues, but not on subjects of legislation on which the party was divided.

Mr. President, I have been a long time a member of this body. It is the first time in which an assault has been made upon me, and without the slightest provocation. It seems to me that if the gentleman had answered yes, when asked if he referred to me, it would have been more manly. But he pointed to me, and I could not remain silent.

It is painful to me, sir, to come out on these occasions; I desire rather never to speak of myself; but I pardon the gentleman, for he has given me an opportunity to set myself right on certain points, in relation to which I wish to stand right, and may take another opportunity to make myself more fully understood. As to the war, I have deplored it. I have deplored it for its consequences. I have deplored it for the manner of bringing it on. As to my views in reference to the war, I have kept silent; assailed here and throughout the country, my friends urged me to come out and explain at the last session. I intended to remain silent until I saw a suitable opportunity for explanation. And here let me say what just now comes to my mind. It may be asked, thinking as I do, as to the causes of the war, why I did not take some step to arrest the march of General Taylor? In the first place, I never heard that the march was ordered until a long time after the order was given. The Senator from Delaware (Mr. J[ohn] M. Clayton) gave me the first intimation that the order had been issued. I replied that it was impossible, and could not believe it until the fact was certainly ascertained. After General Taylor had actually commenced his march, I said to several of my friends he ought to be stopped, it will bring on war. I said also, if my memory serves me, the same thing to the Senator from Delaware, from whom I first derived my information. (The Senator assented.) I said to him and others that the Oregon and Mexican questions are intimately connected; that a war with England, in reference to Oregon, would certainly involve in its consequences a war with Mexico; and that a war with Mexico might also involve a war about Oregon, or at all events prevent the settlement of our difficulties with England in reference to it. That, thus viewing it, Gen. Taylor, in my opinion, ought to be stopped; and that I would lay a resolution on the table calling for the order under which he marched, and would follow it up by a resolution to arrest his march, were I not prevented by the position which I occupied. Of the two, I considered it more important to avoid a war with England about Oregon than a war with Mexico, important as I thought it was to avoid that. That it was important I should maintain the kindest and most friendly relations with the President, in order that I should have some weight in bringing the Oregon question to an amicable settlement; and that, if I were to move in reference to the order given to Gen. Taylor, it would, I feared, place me in hostile relations to the Executive, and destroy any weight I might have with it on the Oregon question. This, with the hope that the Oregon question might be settled before an actual conflict between the forces under Gen. Taylor and those under Arista, prevented me from acting. Otherwise, I would certainly have taken a move to arrest the march, and thereby arrest the war. I have much more to say in reference to the cause of the war, which I must postpone until some suitable occasion. I could state some facts in relation to Oregon, but I am not at liberty, and therefore forbear. I thank the Senate for the kindness with which it has now heard me.

From *Speech of Mr. Calhoun, of South Carolina, in Reply to Mr. Turney, of Tennessee. Delivered in the Senate of the United States, February 12, 1847* [Washington: 1847?], pp. 1–7. Also printed in Crallé, ed., *Works*, 4:328–339.

Variant in *Congressional Globe*, 29th Cong., 2nd Sess., pp. 395–400; the Alexandria, Va., *Gazette and Virginia Advertiser*, February 15, 1847, p. 2; the Washington, D.C., *Daily National Intelligencer*, February 17, 1847, p. 2; the Columbia, S.C., *Southern Chronicle*, February 24, 1847, pp. 1–2. Other variants in the Washington, D.C., *Daily Union*, February 12, 1847, p. 2; the Washington, D.C., *Daily National Intelligencer*, February 13, 1847, p. 3; the New York, N.Y., *Herald*, February 14, 1847, p. 3; the Charleston, S.C., *Mercury*, February 16, 1847, p. 2; the Cincinnati, Ohio, *Daily Enquirer*, February 17, 1847, p. 2; the Petersburg, Va., *Republican*, February 17, 1847, p. 2; the Greenville, S.C., *Mountaineer*, February 26, 1847, p. 4.

From MANSFIELD TORRANCE

Columbus [Ga.,] 12th Feb[ruar]y 1847

Dear Sir, I wrote Col. [Seaborn] Jones [Representative from Ga.] some time since, that through the selfishness of some & the timidity of others, our people were ruining themselves, & what was worse, ruining our cause, the cause of liberty & equality. What people ever attempted before, to carry on an expensive war by loans? There is much more propriety in taxing Tea & Coffee than salt & iron. I suppose the Tariff Democrats want to force us back on the high duty system, & some of the rest are afraid of a clamor by the old women, about their tea & coffee. All parties here are for taxing the whole free list, in preference to borrowing. Is there no shame to get our people to lay a sufficient duty on tea & coffee to pay the interest on our loans? Capitalists would come forward more freely, if they saw some certain provisions for paying interest. I wish we had *more statesmen & fewer Politicians* in Congress. A large majority of them think of nothing beyond themselves or their party. Partys except to carry out great principles are a curse. I was truly glad to see that some of you in the Senate had the good sense to rebuke the foolish party zeal of the House in relation to the vote of thanks to Gen[era]l [Zachary] Taylor. Such traps are contemptible & should be denounced by every honest strait forward man in the country.

When is the war to terminate, & are we to retain California? If we are, are the free States, determined on excluding us from going there, by making them all free States? This last is a momentous question. Will the South remain true to their rights, or will they permit themselves to be bullyed out of them? I ["had a" *canceled*] spent the last evening with Major [John H.] Howard & he thinks with me, that we might have avoided the war, but as we are in it, we

147

should levy war taxes, & carry on the war vigorously, until we "conquered a peace" & that we should make the Mexicans pay the *costs of suit.* If we do we shall have to take pay in lands.

Some think this would not be magnanimous & others say we have territory enough already, & that our Govt. is spreading too widely. If Congress would confine itself within its proper sphere, the extent of our Govt. cannot effect its durability. If Charles Pinckney[']s proposition in the Convention, had passed, requiring two-thirds to pass revenue laws our Govt. might have extended over the whole Continent with safety. As it is I believe that Direct taxation is all that can save us. Let the people *know* & *feel* what they pay & fifteen millions will in time of peace defray our expences. I rec[eive]d a letter dated Victoria Mexico, 14th Jan[uar]y, stating that Gen[era]l Taylor had been ordered to Monterey. Can it be possible that Gen-[era]l [Winfield] Scott or the President [James K. Polk] would send him to perform garrison duty, when active operations are expected? It would be exceedingly unpopular & I think justly so. I fear the President has some weak advisers. When I read his first message I gave him meek credits for talents & his vetoes satisfied me he was *firm.* He writes well but I fear like Mr. [James] Madison he is not suitable for warlike times. Some one has been to blame. Congress gave plenty of men & money, & with the money provisions & transportation should have been ready before the men were sent on. $20 more or less in the hire of mules & wagons was a small matter, when the army was lying idle in the sun & rain for the want of them; each day[']s expence making the difference in the cost of 500 teams or more.

Has not too much been said on both sides about Gen[era]l Taylor[']s letter? It appeared to me as harmless as Scott[']s *soup* letter.

If you have the time to spare from your duties I should like to have your views (Confidential if you prefer it) on our affairs generally. Knowing the number of similar requests I fear you cannot comply with mine. Howard & myself would however be much gratified to hear from you.

My respects to Mrs. [Floride Colhoun] C[alhoun] & for yourself accept the assurances of my profound respect, Mansfield Torrance.

ALS in ScCleA.

From JAMES GADSDEN

Charleston S.C., Febr[uary] 13[?], [18]47

My Dear Sir, I have just risen from the perusal of a very imperfect report of your speech [of 2/9]. In the General views of which I heartily concur. Gen[era]l [Waddy] Thompson[']s remarks likewise in the [Washington] Intelligencer are strong. I made two efforts in both the [Charleston] Courier & Mercury to awaken public attention to this subject, but I regret to say that with the exception of the [Columbia] So. Carolinian, no other paper seems to have noticed or republished them.

The Boundary you fix being the pretext of the war is no doubt correct in principle, and accords with the repeated avowals of the Administration that Conquest was not our aim—but as we have been involved in war and great efforts have been made to inflame the Community against the Mexicans, I fear the influence of opinions, "that they deserve chastisement & we must have indemnity" will be used against your views. It is not Truth & Right, which in these days Politicians seek, but what can they convert most to their Individual ag[g]randizement. So you may expect on this as on the Oregon Question all the opposition operated on by the same influences. Each one, witness [Thomas H.] Benton & [Samuel] Houston & now [Lewis] Cass want to be considered the Leader in the policy adopted & by taking the war side of the Question they have with them all those who are most clamarous & who in making most noise impress others that they are the majority. That the war is decidedly unpopular & that all require Peace on honorable terms is evident, but there are too many who mistake what honor means and who are desirous to inflict chastisement as imposed on us, as well to secure ample indemnity for even the expences of the war. It may probably be more magnanimous for the present, & more certain of inducing negotiation on the part of the Mexicans for Peace, to assume the Boundary & for the reasons you name, but if with Peace, our line should be transferred from the River to the Mountain—Say commencing at Solo Marina [sic], or Barra del Santanda, to the Mountain & along the same to the Great Bend, at Alamo, on the Rio Grande & then by that River to the Pass del Norte & from thence on the 32° degr[ee] of Latitude to the Pacific, would be the most natural Boundary & best calculated to preserve Peace between the Two contiguous Powers.

The Valley of the Lower Del Norte must belong to the same People—different Races, under different Institution[s] cannot occupy opposite sides. The Mountains, with their desolate elevations form much better barriers. These are mere suggestions however. I go for honorable Peace, and all the harmony & prosperity which Free Trade brings. You have commenced the work. Don[']t let Congress adjourn without closing it. Yours Truly, James Gadsden.

[P.S.] It has been intimated to me that some effort will be made by Mr. Eulee [*sic*; Fla. Senator David Levy Yulee,] to defeat Dr. W[illia]m Simmons['s] renomination as Register of the U.S. Land Office at St. Augustine. I cannot believe that so much injustice will be attempted against a Gentleman of his high character and retireing aimable deportment. Will you look into it[?]

ALS in ScCleA.

Remarks in the Senate, 2/13. In the course of a speech, John M. Clayton of Del. referred to Calhoun's remarks of the previous day on his position in regard to the beginning of the Mexican War. He corroborated Calhoun's account of their conversations at the time. Calhoun interjected briefly: "The first conversation was in January [1846], when you announced that fact [of the Army being sent toward the Rio Grande]; and the second conversation was in February." Clayton replied, "Yes, the Senator is right," and continued his speech. From *Congressional Globe*, 29th Cong., 2nd Sess., p. 412.

REMARKS ON THE LIBERTY OF THE PRESS

[In the Senate, February 13, 1847]

[*Debate continued on the resolutions barring representatives of the Washington* Daily Union *from the Senate. Andrew P. Butler of S.C. suggested that instead of exclusion and censure, a committee be formed to allow the editor, Thomas Ritchie, to present his defence.*]

Mr. Calhoun said he very highly appreciated the high and delicate sense of justice which his honorable colleague was known to possess, and which induced him to make this motion. It was made, he knew, with a sincere desire to afford Mr. Ritchie an opportunity to make some explanation, if he desired to do so, in regard to these publications, upon the high ground that any person who is charged with an offence ought to have an opportunity to exculpate himself. But he did think (and he trusted that his honorable colleague would agree with him) that the progress of this thing had clearly shown that nothing available could be done in this way. In the first place, the editor of the Union, since the proposition of his honorable colleague had been submitted, had reiterated his charges, showing an entire obstinacy; and, in the next place, gentlemen upon this floor who vindicated him placed their vindication on the ground, not that the libellous article was published without the knowledge and consent of the editor, but upon the ground that our action in relation to it would have the effect of invading the liberty of the press. It did appear to him that it was better to come at once to a vote upon the resolution, and this he thought was the general sense entertained on all sides.

Being up, he would say that it struck him that the grounds upon which they put this matter presented a most serious issue between what was assumed to be the liberty of the press on one side, and the rights of this body to control the conduct of an individual occupying the position of printer to this body, on the other. It was put upon the ground that our printer had business relations to the Senate which required him to come there and hold intercourse with the members of that body; and, let his offence be what it might, if they undertook to withhold from him the privilege of coming there, we would have done him a wrong, and that that wrong was tantamount to an invasion of the liberty of the press.

[*James M. Mason of Va. said that if Ritchie's privileges were taken away "on account of any thing published by him," it would be "striking at the freedom of the press."*]

Mr. Calhoun. Precisely. If you take away certain privileges which are considered proper to be enjoyed for the conducting of his business of public printer it will impair the liberty of the press. Now, if you carry out this principle, where will it end? Suppose he comes into this House and insults a member upon this floor. Suppose he proves to be noisy, and disturbs us in the exercise of our high prerogative, would it not be a proper exercise of power on our part to prevent the continuance of such disturbance? But if the liberty of the press is to be set up as an excuse for our forbearance in the one case—in the case of an atrocious libel upon the Senate—it may also in the other. Where is to be its limit? The limit is not to be found in any assumed liberty of the press. It is to be found in our sole discretion. This is just as much our domicil as the home of a citizen is his; and we are equally entitled to exercise our discretion as to whom we will admit and whom we will exclude from this place, as the citizen has in regard to his home. Here we are supreme; and who shall enter and who shall not, is a matter of pure option with us.

As to the accidental results, as to whether it may affect the interests of Mr. Ritchie, that can have no possible bearing upon the question before us. If he shall have sustained an injury by the violation of any existing compact, he has a right to appeal to our sense of justice. But to deprive him of any right that he may have to enter this Chamber is no more an infringement of the liberty of the press than it would be for a subscriber to a newspaper to withdraw his subscription if he were insulted. No, sir; the liberty of the press, as secured by the Constitution, is another and a very different thing. The Constitution declares that no law shall be passed which shall interfere with the liberty of speech or the freedom of the press.

Now, let me say, there are two ways by which we may lose a right: one, by yielding it, whether with or without just cause; the other, by pushing that right too far. In my opinion, nothing more tends to destroy the liberty of the press than to push it to extremes, as I have perceived is the policy in this Chamber. It is not the liberty of the press at all that is involved in this question. It is a mere question of discretion on our part. But to come back to this privilege which the editor has here. That privilege is twofold: one, as regards the management of the printing, and the other as regards giving an account in his paper of what takes place here. Now, sir, there can be no possible reason for his coming into this Chamber on account of the printing, for there is another than the editor who has charge of that department of the business connected with their public duty. But it is the editor who is admitted here, and why? Because, being the editor, the man more immediately interested in our proceedings, it is supposed that he should have an opportunity to know and to converse with members here, and to know what is going on, in order to give a correct and true, full and exact account of these proceedings. Beyond this his relations of business with us ceased. The great aggravation in this case is, that the senior editor of the Union was here on the very day [2/8] on which the debate respecting the constitutional objections to the amendment proposed to the army bill was going on, and he knew the bill was lost upon that ground; yet, knowing this, knowing the constitutional scruples [in regard to the appointing power] which gentlemen entertained, he came out with a full report of the speeches made on the other side, without a single word being reported of those who entertained doubts as to the constitutionality of the measure. For this, however, the stenographer is not blameable, but the business man of the publishing department. The senior editor, then, knowing these facts, publishes this atrocious libel upon the Senate. Was this fulfilling the object for which the editor was admitted here, and can he now come and claim that a deprivation of the privilege extended to him by this body would be a violation of the liberty of the press?

Sir, I am myself a strong advocate for the liberty of the press, but when I undertake to defend the liberty of the press, I do not turn my mind in such a direction as this, where may be seen a train of mercenary editors bought up by Government money—a train more terrible than an army with banners, proclaiming in a high tone the liberty of the press is sacred; they themselves, meanwhile, pronouncing their own contradiction. Sir, I am obliged to speak freely on this subject. Now, the question is, what are we to do? Gentlemen say, if you take away this privilege, you will make the editor more popular. Be it so; that is no consideration of ours. It is ours to do our duty, be it what it will. I do not admire these questions of expediency. I do not hold to inquiring how it is going to operate on public opinion, if we do this, or do that. Do that which is right, and take the consequences. Now, we have an important duty to perform; we are the representatives of the sovereign States; we are bound to protect our respectability and standing, because upon that respectability depends our influence upon the affairs of the nation. Now, ask if an individual were insulted in this outrageous manner, would he leave his door open for the entrance of him who had insulted him? No, sir. He would very justly refuse him admission. But you do not take this course; you publish to the world that your editor may say what he pleases of you, and you will not resent it. I put it to gentlemen, would you act so in your own case? And, if not, would you act upon less high principles in regard to the representatives of the sovereign States than you would in regard to yourselves individually? Sir, I have no hesitation in this matter. I am prepared to give my vote firmly, strongly. I shall not trouble the Senate any further in regard to it.

[*Debate continued on until the Senate voted to bar the editors, though not the reporters, of the* Union *from the chamber. The vote was 27 to 21, Calhoun voting with a majority made up largely though not entirely of Whigs.*]

From *Congressional Globe*, 29th Cong., 2nd Sess., p. 415. Also printed in the Washington, D.C., *Daily National Intelligencer*, February 15, 1847, p. 3; the Washington, D.C., *Daily Union*, February 15, 1847, p. 2, and February 16, 1847, p. 1. Variants in the New York, N.Y., *Herald*, February 15, 1847, p. 3; the Charleston, S.C., *Courier*, February 17, 1847, p. 2; the Columbia, S.C., *Southern Chronicle*, February 24, 1847, p. 2.

From F[ITZ] W[ILLIAM] BYRDSALL,
"Private"

New York [City,] Feb[ruar]y 14th 1847

Dear Sir, I have long observed an abuse growing up in the Senate of the U.S.—of Senators arraigning one another for the political acts or sentiments of former years. In my humble opinion this is not consistent with the dignity of the Senate, or the rights of Senators, because personalities should not be exhibited in that body, and because that as every Senator is the representative of a sovereign State, he is only accountable to the State he represents.

In the recent Tournay in which Mr. [Hopkins L.] Turney [Senator from Tenn.] in the Senate tilted himself against you, I am much pleased with the manner in which his onset was met. It afforded a happy oppertunity of placing yourself in a just point of view before the popular mind of the Country, for you of all public men have been misrepresented ["to" *interlined*] and therefore misconceived by the people. There is no man who knows you believes that your elevation to the presidency would be any personal acquisition or elevation ["to yourself" *interlined*] but the friends of Constitutional principles desire to see you in a position where those principles could be declared and evidenced with greater effect. This, as regards you and the presidency is the whole story.

But your speech [of 2/9] on the three millions Bill in its very severity of truth and analysis—in its strict harmony with the best rules of composition and total absence of imaginative or dictional ornament—in its grouping of facts existing and illustrative, has struck a blow which cannot be resisted or returned in any other way than in personalities. The mercenaries of patronage in this city, many of whom went for [William Henry] Harrison in 1840, others who went from [Martin] Van Buren to [James K.] Polk in 1844 and nearly ["all" *interlined*] of whom will go from Polk to any successful candidate in 1848 accost me in the streets "Well what do you think of Mr. Calhoun now?" I can assure you ["however" *interlined*] that the best and largest portion of the people do not express themselves as these mercenaries do.

The Telegraphic news in the [New York] Herald reports Mr. [James D.] Westcott [Senator from Fla.] as having said in the Senate on the 13th that "the democracy of this administration consisted of nothing more than loaves and fishes from the Lieutenant General down to a mere second lieutenant. If the people of the U.S. were only aware of the corruption which exists at the seat of Government they would tumble the President and his departments—the Congress and the Whigs and Democrats heels over heads together into the Potomac, and they would do right."

This is very strong—stronger I suspect than the Senator expressed himself, but I am forced ["to believe" *interlined*] from what I see and feel around me here, and it is painful to myself to see and feel it, that there is no difference in the principles of democrats and whigs but that which governs Ins and Outs. Either party will resort to any means right or wrong, true or false, holy or wicked, pro or anti that will gain votes.

I see that you are averse to the acquisition of territory from the populous country of Mexico, or that ["portion" *interlined*] which would grow cotton and sugar. Were you to go in favor of more territory in that direction, what an outcry would be raised that you wanted the whole of Mexico for slave States. There would be a wo[e]ful howl among those politico philanthropists who really have as little regard for the negro as they have for republican institutions or the Constitution of the United States. A few years ago many of our Barnburning Democratic Abolitionists were "Northern men with Southern principles." If Messres. Van Buren & [Silas] Wright had not made a miscalculation upon the Texas annexation question, we should not have now the Preston King [Representative from N.Y.] movement, or the Wilmot proviso. The Albany dynasty ["had" *interlined*] calculated that the unpopularity or weakness of the [John] Tyler administration would quash annexation for some time.

I don[']t hear a word about nullification in these days. Who are the nullifiers now in the worst sense of that term? There is a vast difference between the nullifiers of an unconstitutional tax law, and the nullifiers of our system of Government.

An old man once said to his son, that if he wanted revenge upon his enemies to pray for long life and if granted, he would see enough respecting all of them to satisfy his desire. I think that if your life is spared a few years longer, you will see all those men overthrown who for nearly a quarter of a century have systematically and by corrupt political machinery operated to pervert the democratic party and the legislation of the Union. You were an obstacle in their way upward, therefore they injured you in every possible manner, and it would seem to be a trait of human nature that the injurer never forgives.

I rejoice to learn by the papers that Senator [Dixon H.] Lewis is recovering his health. I have felt much anxiety about him and would have written to him but feared that it might be ["more of" *canceled*] an intrusion upon a sick man.

In conclusion—Every day's experience and reflection satisfies me that if the Governmental principles advocated by you shall not prevail—our system of Government will not be of long duration. Yours with profound Respect, F.W. Byrdsall.

ALS in ScCleA; PC in Jameson, ed., *Correspondence*, pp. 1104–1106.

Remarks on a Naval pension bill, 2/15. "Mr. Calhoun said this bill was one of very great importance. He hoped some explanation of its provisions would be given." Later, "Mr. Calhoun intimated the necessity for great caution in passing bills which enlarged our pension system. Great additions to it had originated in small beginnings like this. If he understood the matter, these pensions were payable out of a fund raised from prize money, for the benefit of the widows of officers of the navy. Originally, it was designed that this should be confined to the widows of officers killed in battle. Then it was extended to the widows of officers generally. It also had been extended to the military service; and now, if any officer died, whether in battle or not, his family was provided for." After further explanation by two supporters of the bill, "Mr. Calhoun said, if it was not intended to introduce new cases, he would withdraw his objection." From *Congressional Globe*, 29th Cong., 2nd Sess., p. 422. Variant in the Washington, D.C., *Daily Union*, February 16, 1847, p. 1.

Remarks on a joint resolution on the Washington monument, 2/15. Jacob W. Miller of N.J. was pushing for action toward authorizing selection of a site for the monument. "Mr. Calhoun submitted to the Senator from New Jersey that it would be regarded as discourteous to the Senator from Missouri [Thomas H. Benton], who was not in his seat, to urge the passage of this joint resolution in his absence. That Senator, it would be recollected, had opposed this measure at the last session, and expressed his intention to produce some new facts when it should be again brought forward. As an act of courtesy to the Senator from Missouri, therefore, he moved to lay the joint resolution on the table for the present. The motion was agreed to; ayes 17, noes 16." From *Congressional Globe*, 29th Cong., 2nd Sess., p. 422. Also printed in Benton, *Abridgment of Debates*, 16:72.

Remarks on the bill to build four additional war steamers, 2/15. "Mr. Calhoun said the impoverished state of the treasury would not justify this extraordinary expense at this time. The vessels could not be brought into service during the war, and therefore, the building of them could be deferred till the war was over." From the New York, N.Y., *Herald*, February 17, 1847, p. 3. Variant in *Congressional Globe*, 29th Cong., 2nd Sess., p. 423.

From MARTIN CORYELL

Eagle River, Lake Superior, Feb. 16, 1847

D[ea]r Sir, My Father [Lewis S. Coryell] intimates to me your desire to have a description of this mineral region. I feel a delicacy in making the attempt, because my information is confined to a small circuit of the [Upper] Peninsula [of Mich.].

That it is rich in mineral wealth no one can doubt since the late developements, but that it will yield large returns to every man or company who own one or more Locations or Shares of stock, is doubtful, and yet by a judicious expenditure of large capital, and in a few instances small amounts, large profits will be realized, but not under five or more years. I do not of course, have reference to Stock operations, but to the producing of the mineral.

The Company in whose employ I am, is from Boston & Detroit. Hon. D[avid] Henshaw one of the Trustees, and a master spirit in the Co., is well known to you; the Location is 3 miles square and seems most admirably selected, having Eagle River flowing through it from the East & a Branch from the west, at the foot of a Bluff some 300 feet in height and nearly perpendicular, extending diagonally from the western to the Eastern line of the Location, with nine good veins shewing within a mile, but undeveloped, and 2 miles more of Bluff unexplored.

The vein upon which we are now working is on the northern slope of the Trap range and one mile from the Lake Shore, and ["are" *canceled*] 212 feet above its surface, we have sunk 187 feet from the surface and have drifted 600 feet, but the most singular feature of our present workings is a chasm, or as we term it the "opening," having accidentally discovered ["it" *interlined*] by breaking through the rock and mistaking it for a cavity; It is 35 feet beneath, and directly below the bed of the river, it is filled with angular and boulder

157

Rocks of large size, Sand & Gravel; in this deposite, some times one, but more frequently from one to four feet above the bottom (and top of the vein) we find the copper Boulders & some silver. The largest copper mass weighed 1757 pounds but the greater quantity is small lumps of 5 pounds & less—the largest mass of silver weighed nearly 8 pounds. We have found 2 pits sinking some 20 feet below the general level which yield much copper.

The amount of Pure native copper sent to Boston was 9670 pounds [and we] have now on hand 9000 [pounds, totaling] 18670 pounds. Owing to the deficiency of the machinery there has been but little done in reducing the Rock that contains the native Copper, but we hope next season to effect something. The mine that stands highest ["in value" *interlined*] at present, is the Cliff, owned by the Pittsburg & Boston Mining Co., and is situated within three miles of the Lake Shore (mouth of Eagle River) on the same Range of this Co. and ¼th of mile from the western line, but on the south side of the Bluff; they are working 70 miners and 80 Laborers and mechanics, they are erecting Steam Machinery for Stamping, & think they will erect a furnace for smelting, finding it too expensive to transport the crude ore to Boston notwithstanding its richness; this mine was also famed for its silver but that has nearly all disappeared from the vein. A Smelting Furnace has been erected by a Co. from Newyork called the Pioneer, which will buy all the ores from the various locations, it having none of its own. They expect to put it in Blast next week.

The Copper Falls Co. join this Location on the East, and is celebrated for the large mass of native copper found in the vein, estimated to weigh 22 tons, part has been removed[,] the remainder being difficult to manage retains its place. Their works are in good condition & promise well. Three Locations so far, only yield the Grey sulphuret ores they are on the south side of the point & Slope; two are near Lake La Belle and are rich & well defined the other 7 miles South of the Mouth of Eagle River, and not yet fairly developed.

Many other Companies might be mentioned that have good "prospects" and are preparing for active operations in the spring but I would refer you to the War Department, as the mineral agents make monthly returns from all the Cos. for details respecting each. In regard to the Geological character of the country the Report of Dr. [Douglass] Houghton, Late State Geologist of Michigan, which was reprinted by order of Congress is considered correct, and the only new facts made known by recent developements is, that veins are more productive of native Copper in the Amygdaloid trap than in any other kind, and the top of the range is capped by a strata of GreenStone (Trap) which entirely cuts out the copper & supplies its place with qua[r]tz and calcareous spar or entirely effacing all traces of a rich vein, the dip of this strata is northwesterly and at an angle of 45 degrees and as yet its thickness is undetermined.

It is South and under this Strata that the Cliff mine makes so rich and productive.

The Climate is far from being disagre[e]able[;] we have had the Thermometer down to 12 Below Z[ero] but generally 18 above[;] the snow is now about 4 feet deep in the woods; myself & family have enjoyed excellent health being more free from colds than when in Penn[sylvani]a. If mining progresses it will become a grazing country & will produce wheat, oats, Potatoes & Peas & many other similar productions.

We are anxious that the Lands should be sold and become the property of the various Companies & individuals that improvements may be made of a more substantial kind; nobody caring now, for the future, mines will be more surely developed, and capital and Labor bestowed with a prospect of return at a future day.

Should this prove pleasing to you, be assured that I am always ready to serve, and thus partially compenssate for many favors I have received. With great respect Your ob[edien]t Se[r]v[an]t, Martin Coryell.

ALS in ScCleA.

Remarks on the "Three Millions" bill, 2/16. Lewis Cass of Mich. declared that he intended to bring up in the Senate a certain letter which had been alluded to frequently by opponents of the administration. [This was a letter of Isaac D. Marks to Gen. Zachary Taylor in 9/1845, containing information of the Mexican Gen. Mariano Arista's proposals for mutual abstention from troop movements.] "Mr. Calhoun said the authority was in the late letter of Mr. Marks; but there was no doubt the Senator from Michigan could get all the information on the subject by application at the State Department." From the New York, N.Y., *Herald*, February 18, 1847, p. 4.

To T[HOMAS] G. CLEMSON, [Brussels]

Washington, 17th Feb. 1847

My dear Sir, I was happy to learn by the [ship] Sarah Sands that you, & Anna [Maria Calhoun Clemson] & the children [John Calhoun Clemson and Floride Elizabeth Clemson] were well. I forwarded your letters to your overseer [—— Mobley] as you requested, after perusing them, & the letter of Anna to John [C. Calhoun, Jr.], to Charleston, where he expects to be on his return from Florida in a few days. He accompanied his Uncle John [Ewing Colhoun] there in an excursion, which he took for his health.

I hope you will succeed in doing much better in the planting business this year, than you have heretofore done. Prices of all ["kinds of" *interlined*] agricultural produce have risen, and negroes with them. Men, I hear, command $1000 & weoman [*sic*] $7 or 800, which, if correct, adds greatly to your capital. When I last heard from home, all were well. Willey [William Lowndes Calhoun] had gone to Alabama & Mrs. [Floride Colhoun] Calhoun was making arrangements to leave home to meet me on my return in Charleston.

I enclose two copies of my speech [of 2/9] on the Mexican war. It has been well received; and has made a deep impression. The best proof of the depth & strength of the impression is the fierce war it has drawn down on me from the [James K. Polk] Administration through its organ here. Those in power see that they have involved themselves & the country in a war fraught with the most disasterous consequences, & from which it will be difficult to extricate themselves. They begin to feel, that their doom is sealed, & hence their bitter & malignant attacks under the garb of defending the liberty of the press.

The Country is, indeed, in a sad Condition, & the principles & doctrines of the Republican party, are in a fair way of being permanently subverted through the weakness & folly of the administration. Should the war continue scarcely the vestige of any one of them will be left; free trade will ["be" *canceled*] sink under an oppressive debt to be paid by the impost; the sub-treasury will end in a more intimate connection of the Govt. with the paper system than ever; economy & retrenchment will be lost in the vast & irregular expeditions of the war, & the patronage of the Government will be extended beyond all former examples.

I shall meet the assaults on me with perfect composure & with every confidence of rising above them in the end. The war cannot be continued; and a defensive position must be ultimately assumed.

You must excuse a short letter. The pressure of my engagements is great. I have scarcely a spare moment.

My love to Anna; & kiss the children for their Grandfather. Your affectionate father, J.C. Calhoun.

ALS in ScCleA; PEx in Jameson, ed., *Correspondence*, p. 718.

From J[AMES] GREGG

Columbia, 17th Feb[ruar]y 1847

My Dear Sir, I can not forego the gratification of telling you what extreme pleasure your reply to that fellow [Hopkins L.] Turney gave me.

You have fully confirmed what I have thought all along and said frequently in my family though I did not care to say much about it out of doors whilst the war was going on, that if Gen. [Zachary] Taylor had not been ordered from Corpus Christi to the Rio Grande we should have had no war and that Mr. [James K.] Polk had very injudiciously and imprudently dragged us into it as there was no kind of necessity whatever for that ill fated movement.

The Abolitionists & northern members generally objected and predicted that the annexation of Texas would lead to a war with Mexico but we all Mr. Polk & all insisted on it that this would not necessarily follow, nor would it had it not been for Mr. Polk's utter lack of judgment and unaccountable indiscretion.

You have however put that matter like a demonstration in Euclid and I do not see how any one in his senses can after that entertain a doubt about it.

Mr. Polk has done pretty well in some things but he began with one most capital blunder which for a while put me altogether out with him, and he has followed it up with at least three others and would have added a fourth in the appointment of his Lieutenant General if you had all allowed him.

After the three extraordinary victories gained by Gen[era]l Taylor no man in the Union whether from the army or the Senate should have been sent to supercede him.

After what I have said I need scarcely add that if you could have looked into my thoughts with the eye of the Almighty you could not in your great Speech which I read with equal pleasure have expressed with greater exactness my opinions so far as they extended and beyond that I agree with you perfectly, and if I am not grossly mistaken, although many [an]d especially young persons may have hitherto been lead [*sic*] astray, yet the whole country will settle down upon what you have so clearly pointed out.

I trust you will pardon this hasty scrawl from yours most Sincerely, J. Gregg.

ALS in ScCleA; PC in Boucher and Brooks, eds., *Correspondence*, pp. 367–368. NOTE: An AEU by Calhoun reads "Col. Gregg." James Gregg (1787–1852) was a prominent Columbia lawyer, a regular member of one or other house of the S.C. General Assembly during 1822–1845, a Col. of militia, and held many other public offices. He had married Cornelia Maxcy, daughter of Jonathan Maxcy who had been president of S.C. College and a brother of Calhoun's close friend Virgil Maxcy. Among the Greggs' children was Maxcy Gregg (1814–1862), at this time an officer in the Palmetto Regiment and later a Brig. Gen. of the Confederate army.

From F[RANCIS] W. PICKENS

Edgewood [Edgefield District, S.C.,] 17 Feb[ruar]y 1847
My dear Sir, I have just this moment recieved [*sic*] yours with the enclosures from Mr. [Thomas G.] Clemson.

I suppose you will soon be returning home unless the Senate be retained in extra Session. If you expect to reach Aiken any day before the 10th March and *will let me know* the exact day I will send my carriage for you and bring you this far on your way home. And, if it suits your convenience, we shall be very happy to have you spend a day or so with us before you go on. The reason why I mention the 10th March is, that after that I have an engagement in Charleston which I will be obliged to attend to by the 16th or 17th March.

I recieved your letter dated in last December, but as it required no answer, I never acknowledged it before.

We have had a bad winter and been exceedingly busy.

Mrs. [Marion Antoinette Dearing] Pickens begs her respects. Yours very truly, F.W. Pickens.

ALS in ScCleA.

REMARKS ON RECEIVING A PETITION FROM A BRITISH SUBJECT

[In the Senate, February 17, 1847]
[Vice-President George M. Dallas said that he had been given a petition from a British subject, John A. Barry, asking for legislative action to extend the appellate jurisdiction of the U.S. Supreme Court to certain "controversies" not now covered. Dallas said it was for the Senate to decide whether the Senate would receive it or not. Daniel Webster argued that there "could not be the slightest doubt as to the propriety of receiving petitions from citizens of a foreign country."]

Mr. Calhoun said he did not hear the first part of the remarks of the Senator from Massachusetts; but, judging from his concluding remarks, he believed that that honorable Senator and himself differed somewhat in regard to this question of receiving petitions from citizens or subjects of a foreign country. He had always considered it a fundamental principle that the affairs of this Government, so far as they related to foreigners, were to be conducted by the Executive Department, and that all applications of this kind must come through that branch of the Government. In his opinion, the proper course in this case would be for this British subject to present his petition, in the first instance, to his own Government, and, if deemed proper, it might then be forwarded either through our Minister there, or the British Minister residing here. This appeared to him to be the regular and effectual mode, and one which would prevent many consequences it was desirable should be avoided. He referred to a case of this kind which occurred in the last war [of 1812], in which, if his recollection served him, he said it was almost unanimously decided that the proper course to be pursued was the one he had now indicated. There was no good reason, he thought, why foreigners should not make their applications, in the first instance, to their own Government, that it might be determined by them whether the application proposed to be made to this Government ought to be made at all or not. He was inclined to consider, however, that aliens residing within the country should be exempt from the rule, because they were, for the time, subject to our laws, and bound to obedience; but an application such as the present, proceeding from an alien residing abroad, was unsustained by precedents. He thought the petition ought not to be received.

[Webster and others spoke further, Webster referring to the case of "General Boyd" (that is, John Parker Boyd, an American soldier

of fortune) who had petitioned the British Parliament for $50,000 compensation for services in India, the petition having been received and granted. Webster raised issues both of precedent and reciprocity.]

Mr. Calhoun begged to remark, before the question of postponement was taken, that the conclusion to which he had come, instead of resting on General Boyd's case, arose out of the case to which he had referred as having occurred during the late war. The cases were very different from each other. General Boyd was a general in the British service. British precedents could not govern us. We must make our rule conform to our institutions. He thought it would be well for the Senate to take further time to deliberate before deciding this matter.

[*Webster spoke again.*]

Mr. Calhoun said he alluded to the case which took place in the other House during the late war.

Mr. Webster. Ah! that was the petition of an alien enemy.

[*After further discussion the question of reception was postponed.*]

From *Congressional Globe,* 29th Cong., 2nd Sess., pp. 434–435. Also printed in the Washington, D.C., *Daily National Intelligencer,* February 18, 1847, p. 2; the Washington, D.C., *Daily Union,* February 18, 1847, p. 1. Variants in the New York, N.Y., *Herald,* February 19, 1847, p. 4; the Charleston, S.C., *Courier,* February 22, 1847, p. 2.

To Mrs. Sarah [Mytton] Maury, [Liverpool, England]

Washington, 18th Feb. 1847

My dear Mrs. Maury, The Statesmen of America is before me on my table, and has been there for several days; and yet, I have had so little leisure in consequence of my incessant engagements, that I have only read the part allotted to myself. With that, I have every reason to be pleased. You have said all I could desire you to say & said it well. I hope after times will not think you have drawn a lik[e]ness too flattering. I shall reserve the rest of the volume until after the close of this short & busey [*sic*] session, when I shall be able to read at my leisure. I anticipate much pleasure from the perusal.

I can well conceive, what distressing feelings the incessant demands of the hungry must excite in the breast of the benevolent on your side of the Atlantick. We even feel it here at this great distance; but while I feel in common with the rest of my fellow citizens great sympathy for the distress with you, I rejoice to witness the strength of the kindred feeling between two people, between whom, I hope, peace & friendship will ever prevail.

I am happy to hear of the welfare of your family & the prosperous condition of your husband's [William Maury's] affairs; but greatly regret to learn, that you have been so much indisposed, and since[re]ly hope that your health may be completely restored under the advice & treatment of Mr. [William] Lawrence.

My health, generally, has been good; notwithstanding the continuance of my cough, which has been much the same it was last winter.

The Mexican war has proved as pregnant of evils as I feared it would be. It was a great mistake—one of the greatest ever made in my time. It might have been easily avoided. But as we are in it, we must get out of it as we best can. How the war should be conducted to effect that, you will find is now the subject of deliberation in the Senate. You will find my views in reference to it disclosed in a speech [of 2/9], of which I enclose two copies; one for yourself, & the other to be placed in the hands of any of your editors, should any one be disposed to print it, in whole or part. It is more full & correct, than that printed in either of our journals here.

It has been well received and has made my friends say a deep impression. I hope it may do something to arrest the war, at least so far as it relates to its expenses & the sacrafice [sic] of life ["are concerned" *imperfectly erased*].

It is to be feared, if nothing is done, we shall lose all we have gained in the way of free trade, to the great detriment ["of both" *canceled*] of both countries.

Mrs. [Floride Colhoun] Calhoun is not with me this winter. She was well, when I last heard from her.

With kind respects to Mr. Maury & your family I am yours truly & since[re]ly, J.C. Calhoun.

ALS in El Paso, Texas, Public Library, Southwest Collection. NOTE: *The Statesmen of America in 1846* was published in 1847 in London and Philadelphia. Mrs. Maury's husband, William Maury, was a son of James Maury, late U.S. Consul to Liverpool, and was engaged in mercantile pursuits in England.

From A. D. Phelps

Boston, Feb[ruar]y 18, 1847

Sir, Enclosed, I have taken the liberty to hand you a bill of European Agriculture &C.—it being the balance due on your subscription.

Please to remit me the amount of the same, (3.00) by mail, at your convenience, in current money, & Oblige Resp[ectfull]y &C. Yours, A.D. Phelps.

ALS with En in ScU-SC, John C. Calhoun Papers. NOTE: The enclosed bill was for six issues of *European Agriculture and Rural Economy.* An AEU by Calhoun reads, "Mr. [Henry] Colman's bill, Mr. Phelps agent. 30th April enclosed a post office Draft."

Remarks on a bill to regulate the carrying of immigrant passengers in merchant vessels, 2/18. "Mr. Calhoun said he was in favor of the amendment. A few days since [on 2/8] he had presented a petition from the Irish Emigrant Society of New York. He was not sure that the amendments proposed by the committee [of Commerce] met all the views of the petititoners. He would therefore ask the Secretary to read the petition to which he referred." From *Congressional Globe*, 29th Cong., 2nd Sess., p. 446. Variant in the New York, N.Y., *Herald*, February 20, 1847, p. 4.

From John D. Gardiner

Sag Harbor [N.Y.,] Feb. 19th 1847

My Dear Sir, I have just read your recent speeches in the Senate; the one on the subject of the Mexican war, and the other in vindication of your course—And I have read both with much pleasure. The policy of stop[p]ing further aggressive movements, in this unhappy war, and of taking our stand in future on the defensive, is, in my estimation, the most correct and desirible. It will prevent the effusion of blood & and [*sic*] the waste of treasure; and at the same time, accomplish the objects of the War, and bring it to a successful termination. I have long thought so; and your very able speech upon the subject has fully established my previous opinion. I can see no possible advantages that can accrue from a further continuance of the War, but many, very many serious evils. We do not wish to subjugate, or dismember the Mexican Empire, if we could by lifting the finger. It would be no less unjust than impolitic. That she has treated us ill, there ["is" *interlined*] no doubt; but that a vigorous prosecution of the contest, is the best method of obtaining a satisfactory redress of these wrongs, is what I do not and cannot believe. It is also the ["believe" *altered to* "belief"] of many of the people in this quarter, and throughout the whole Union. Unhappily the Government is committed to a vigorous prosecution of the war, for the purpose of conquering peace; and there is too often, in Governments as among individuals, a sort of pride of opinion, that forbids any ["in" *erased*] change of Policy whatever be its consequences, and however contrary to the public interests and welfare.

To convince those at the head of affairs, acting under such influence, is at all times extremely difficult, if not impracticable—Having fixed their plans, they are determined to carry them out, without looking with calmness and impartiality, at their results; Unlike true philosophers, and wise Statesmen, they become impatient of contradiction, and deem greater and better men their enemies, merely, because they oppose their schemes, and exercise the right, of declaring, their own veiws and sentiments, with fearlessness and independence. But whatever be the veiws and feelings of those ["in" *interlined*] power, in regard to your late speech on the present war, sure I am, that it has been haialded [*sic*], by the great mass of the people, of this republic, as a noble and timely effort, to arrest the evils of war, and effect an adjustment of our difficulties in a more reasonable and pacific manner. And were the course you have ["so" *interlined*] ably pointed out, adopted by the Government, the clouds that now hang over the Country would soon be dispersed, and honorable and amicable relations between the two sister republics, restored. As a great & powerful nation, it becomes us, in the present crisis, to exhibit, a spirit of true magnanimity; and hold out the olive branch. This is true national honor, about which so much is said. It would be received in this light, by all sober minded men and by all civilized nations. War, in itself, is an evil & curse morally, religiously, Politically and physically; and to be deprecated by every friend to God or man; and can never be ["Justified" *interlined*] except against tyrants seeking the destruction of ["our" *interlined*] liberty and rights. Self defence, is ["the" *interlined*] only justifiable ground of its existence—And when it exists, he is the greatest philanthropist, and the best patriot, who contributes most to bring it to a speedy and honorable termination. To promote this object, it does appear to me that your late speech is calculated to do much; and whether your veiws are adopted or not by the Powers that be, you will enjoy the satisfaction of having faithfully discharged your duty ["to" *interlined*] the Country and to the government; and will therefore have your reward. I am happy to learn that you have been reelected to the Senate. This is a renewed expression of the Confidence of the good people of S. Carolina, in your faithfulness[,] ability & integrity, and cannot fail to sustain and cheer you on in every conflict; to yield support in every trial.

I am in the enjoyment of health; surrounded with many blessings, with children & friends. I often think of you, and ["your" *interlined*] name is ever associated with the pleasing reminiscences of early life and College days; which often rise in memory as fresh as the scenes of yesterday; and will continue there while life shall last.

Please to excuse my troubling you with this letter, prompted by true respect and esteem. If you can find time before congress adjourns, please to favor me with a few lines, with your veiws of public matters ["&" *interlined*] things. That the best of heaven[']s benedictions may rest upon ["you" *interlined*] in whatever sphere, public or private, you ["may" *interlined*] be called to act, is the sincere desire of your ancient friend & Classmate, John D. Gardiner.

ALS in ScCleA. Note: An AEU by Calhoun reads "Mr. Gardiner."

Remarks on the New Hampshire and New Jersey antislavery resolutions, 2/19. Joseph Cilley of N.H. presented resolutions from his legislature calling for the exclusion of slavery from the Territories and for "every effort, consistent with the Constitution of the United States, for the extermination of slavery." Calhoun asked: "By what majority were these resolutions passed?" Cilley replied that the majority was large and composed of both parties. Then Jacob W. Miller of N.J. presented resolutions from his legislature endorsing the Wilmot Proviso. Calhoun asked: "By what majority were these passed?" Miller replied that the vote in one house was unanimous and in the other nearly so. From *Congressional Globe*, 29th Cong., 2nd Sess., p. 453. (In a variant report, James D. Westcott, Jr., of Fla. demanded a vote on the reception of the N.H. petition, in response to which Calhoun said: "They are from a sovereign State; let them go." New York, N.Y., *Herald*, February 21, 1847, p. 3.)

Speech and Resolutions on the
Restriction of Slavery
from the Territories

[In the Senate, February 19, 1847]
Mr. Calhoun rose and said: Mr. President, I rise to offer a set of resolutions in reference to the various resolutions from the State legislatures upon the subject of what they call the extension of slavery, and the [Wilmot] proviso attached to the House bill, called the three million bill. What I propose before I send my resolutions to the table, is to make a few explanatory remarks.

Mr. President, it was solemnly asserted on this floor some time ago, that all parties in the non-slaveholding States had come to a fixed and solemn determination upon two propositions. One was, that there should be no further admission of any States into this Union which permitted by their constitution the existence of slavery; and the other was, that slavery shall not hereafter exist in any of the Territories of the United States; the effect of which would be to give to the non-slaveholding States the monopoly of the public domain, to the entire exclusion of the slave-holding States. Since that declaration was made, we we [sic] have abundant proof that there was a satisfactory foundation for it. We have received already solemn resolutions passed by seven of the non-slaveholding States—one-half of the number already in the Union, Iowa not being counted—using the strongest possible language to that effect; and no doubt in a short space of time similar resolutions will be received from all of the non-slaveholding States. But we need not go beyond the walls of Congress. The subject has been agitated in the other House, and they have sent up a bill "prohibiting the extension of slavery" (using their own language) "to any territory which may be acquired by the United States hereafter." At the same time, two resolutions which have been moved to extend the compromise line from the Rocky mountains to the Pacific, during the present session, have been rejected by a decided majority.

Sir, there is no mistaking the signs of the times; and it is high time that the Southern States, the slaveholding States, should inquire what is now their relative strength in this Union, and what it will be if this determination should be carried into effect hereafter. Already we are in a minority—I use the word "we" for brevity sake—already we are in a minority in the other House, in the electoral college, and I may say, in every department of this government, except at present in the Senate of the United States—there for the present we have an equality. Of the twenty-eight States, fourteen are non-slaveholding and fourteen are slave-holding, counting Delaware, which is doubtful, as one of the non-slaveholding States. But this equality of strength exists only in the Senate. One of the clerks at my request has furnished me with a statement of what is the relative strength of the two descriptions of States, in the other House of Congress and in the electoral college. There are 228 representatives, including Iowa, which is already represented there. Of these, 138 are from the non-slaveholding States, and 90 are from what are called the slave States, giving a majority in the aggregate to the former of 48. In the electoral college there are 168 votes belonging to the non-slaveholding States, and 118 to the slave-holding, giving a majority of 50 to the non-slaveholding.

We, Mr. President, have at present only one position in the government, by which we may make any resistance to this aggressive policy which has been declared against the South; or any other that the non-slaveholding States may choose to take. And this equality in this body is one of the most transient character. Already Iowa is a State; but, owing to some domestic difficulties, is not yet represented in this body. When she appears here, there will be an addition of two senators to the representatives here of the non-slaveholding States. Already Wisconsin has passed the initiatory stage, and will be here the next session. This will add two more, making a clear majority of four in this body on the side of the non-slaveholding States, who will thus be enabled to sway every branch of this government at their will and pleasure. But, if this aggressive policy be followed—if the determination of the non-slaveholding States is to be adhered to hereafter, and we are to be entirely excluded from the territories which we already possess, or may possess—if this is to be the fixed policy of the government, I ask what will be our situation hereafter?

Sir, there is ample space for twelve or fifteen of the largest description of States in the territories belonging to the United States. Already a law is in course of passage through the other House creating one north of Wisconsin. There is ample room for another north of Iowa; and another north of that; and then that large region extending on this side of the Rocky mountains, from 49 degrees, down to the Texan line, which may be set down fairly as an area of twelve and a half degrees of latitude—that extended region of itself is susceptible of having six, seven, or eight large States. To this, add Oregon which extends from 49 to 42 degrees, which will give four more, and I make a very moderate calculation when I say that, in addition to Iowa and Wisconsin, twelve more States upon the territory already ours—without reference to any acquisitions from Mexico—may be, and will be, shortly added to these United States. How will we then stand? There will be but fourteen on the part of the South—we are to be fixed, limited, and forever—and twenty-eight on the part of the non-slaveholding States! Double our number! And with the same disproportion in the House and in the electoral college! The government, sir, will be entirely in the hands of the non-slaveholding States—overwhelmingly.

Sir, if this state of things is to go on—if this determination, so solemnly made, is to be persisted in, where shall we stand, as far as this federal government of ours is concerned? We shall be at the entire mercy of the non-slaveholding States. Can we look to their justice and regard for our interests? I ask, can we rely on that? Ought we to trust our safety and prosperity to their mercy and sense of justice? These are the solemn questions which I put to all—this and the other side of the chamber.

Sir, can we find any hope by looking to the past[?] If we are to look to that—I will not go into the details—we will see from the beginning of this government to the present day, as far as pecuniary resources are concerned—as far as the disbursement of revenue is involved, it will be found that we have been a portion of the community which has substantially supported this government without receiving anything like a proportionate return. But why should I go beyond this very measure itself? Why go beyond this determination on the part of the non-slaveholding States, that there shall be no further addition to the slave-holding States, to prove what our condition will be?

Sir, what is the entire amount of this policy? I will not say that it is so designed. I will not say from what cause it originated. I will not say whether blind fanaticism on one side, whether a hostile feeling to slavery entertained by many not fanatical on the other, has produced it; or whether it has been the work of men, who, looking to political power, have considered the agitation of this question as the most effectual mode of obtaining the spoils of this Government. I look to the fact itself. It is a policy now openly avowed as one to be persisted in. It is a scheme, which aims to monopolize the powers of this Government and to obtain sole possession of its territories.

Now, I ask, is there any remedy? Does the Constitution afford any remedy? And if not, is there any hope? These, Mr. President, are solemn questions—not only to us, but, let me say to gentlemen

171

from the non-slaveholding States, to them. Sir, the day that the balance between the two sections of the country—the slaveholding States and the non-slaveholding States—is destroyed, is a day that will not be far removed from political revolution, anarchy, civil war, and wide-spread disaster. The balance of this system is in the slave-holding States. They are the conservative portion—always have been the conservative portion—always will be the conservative portion; and with a due balance on their part may, for generations to come, uphold this glorious Union of ours. But if this scheme should be carried out—if we are to be reduced to a handful—if we are to become a mere ball to play the presidential game with—to count something in the Baltimore caucus—if this is to be the result—wo! wo! I say to this Union!

Now, sir, I put again the solemn question—does the Constitution afford any remedy? Is there any provision in it by which this aggressive policy—boldly avowed, as if perfectly consistent with our institutions and the safety and prosperity of the United States!—may be confronted? Is this a policy consistent with the Constitution? No, Mr. President, no! It is, in all its features, daringly opposed to the Constitution. What is it? Ours is a Federal Constitution. The States are its constituents, and not the people. The twenty-eight States—the twenty-nine States (including Iowa)—stand under this Government as twenty-nine individuals, or as twenty-nine millions of individuals would stand to a consolidated power. No, sir. It was made for higher ends. It was formed that every State as a constituent member of this Union of ours should enjoy all its advantages, natural and acquired, with greater security, and enjoy them more perfectly. The whole system is based on justice and equality—perfect equality between the members of this republic. Now can that be consistent with equality which will make this public domain a monopoly on one side—which, in its consequences, would place the whole power in one section of the Union to be wielded against the other sections of the Union? Is that equality?

How then do we stand in reference to this territorial question—this public domain of ours? Why, sir, what is it? It is the common property of the States of this Union. They are called "the territories of the United States." And what are the "United States" but the States united? Sir, these territories are the property of the States united; held jointly for their common use. And is it consistent with justice—is it consistent with equality, that any portion of the partners, outnumbering another portion, shall oust them of this common property of theirs—shall pass any law which shall proscribe the citizens of other portions of the Union from emigrating with their property to the territories of the United States? Would that be consistent—can it be consistent with the idea of a common property, held jointly for the common benefit of all? Would it be so considered in private life? Would it not be considered the most flagrant outrage in the world—one, which any court of equity would restrain by injunction, or any court of law in the world would overrule[?]

Mr. President, not only is that proposition grossly inconsistent with the Constitution, but the other, which undertakes to say that no State shall be admitted into this Union, which shall not prohibit by its constitution the existence of slaves, is equally a great outrage against the Constitution of the United States. Sir, I hold it to be a fundamental principle of our political system, that the people have a right to establish what government they may think proper for themselves; that every State about to become a member of this Union has a right to form its government as it pleases; and that, in order to be admitted there is but one qualification, and that is, that the government shall be republican. There is no express provision to that effect, but it results from that important section, which guarantees to every State in this Union a republican form of government. Now, sir, what is proposed? It is proposed, from a vague, indefinite, erroneous, and most dangerous conception of private individual liberty, to overrule this great common liberty which a people have of framing their own constitution! Sir, the right of framing self-government on the part of individuals, is not near so easily to be established by any course of reasoning, as the right of a community or State to self-government. And yet, sir, there are men of such delicate feeling on the subject of liberty—men who cannot possibly bear what they call slavery in one section of the country—although, (not so much slavery as an institution indispensable for the good of both races)—men so squeamish on this point, that they are ready to strike down the higher right of a community to govern themselves, in order to maintain the absolute right of individuals in every possible condition to govern themselves!

Mr. President, the resolutions that I intend to offer present, in general terms, these great truths. I propose to present them to the Senate; I propose to have a vote upon them; and I trust there is no gentleman here who will refuse it. It is manly, it is right, that such a vote be given. It is due to our constituents that we should insist upon it; and I, as one, will insist upon it that the sense of this body shall be taken; the body which represents the States in their capacity as communities, and the members of which are to be their special guardians. It is due to them, sir, that there should be a fair expression of what is the sense of this body. Upon that expression much depends. It is the only position we can take, that will uphold us with any thing like independence—which will give us any chance at all to maintain an equality in this Union, on those great principles to which I have referred. Overrule these principles, and we are nothing! Preserve them, and we will ever be a respectable portion of the Union.

Sir, here let me say a word as to the compromise line; I have always considered it as a great error—highly injurious to the South, because it surrendered, for mere temporary purposes, those high principles of the constitution upon which I think we ought to stand. I am against any compromise line. Yet I would have been willing to acquiesce in a continuation of the Missouri compromise in order to preserve, under the present trying circumstances, the peace of the country. One of the resolutions in the House, to that effect, was offered at my suggestion. I said to a friend there [Armistead Burt], "let us not be disturbers of this Union. Abhor[r]ent to my feelings as is that compromise line, let it be adhered to in good faith; and if the other portions of the Union are willing to stand by it, let us not refuse to stand by it. It has kept peace for some time, and in the present circumstances, perhaps it would be better to be continued as it is." But, it was voted down by a decided majority. It was renewed by a gentleman from a non-slaveholding State [William W. Wick of Ind.], and again voted down by a like majority.

I see my way in the Constitution. I cannot in a compromise. A compromise is but an act of Congress. It may be overruled at any time. It gives us no security. But the Constitution is stable. It is a rock. On it we can stand, and on it we can meet our friends from the non-slaveholding States. It is a firm and stable ground, on which we can better stand in opposition to fanaticism, than on the shifting sands of compromise.

Let us be done with compromises. Let us go back and stand upon the Constitution!

Well, sir, what if the decision of this body shall deny to us this high Constitutional right, not the less clear, because deduced from the entire body of the instrument, and the nature of the subject to which it relates, instead of being specially provided for? What then? I will not undertake to decide. It is a question for our constituents— the slaveholding States. A solemn and a great question. If the decision should be adverse, I trust and do believe, that they will take under solemn consideration what they ought to do. I give no advice.

It would be hazardous and dangerous for me to do so. But I may speak as an individual member of that section of the Union. There is my family and connexions. There I drew my first breath. There are all my hopes. I am a planter—a cotton planter. I am a Southern man and a slaveholder—a kind and a merciful one, I trust—and none the worse for being a slaveholder. I say, for one, I would rather meet any extremity upon earth than give up one inch of our equality—one inch of what belongs to us as members of this great republic! What! acknowledged inferiority! The surrender of life is nothing to sinking down into acknowledged inferiority!

I have examined this subject largely—widely. I think I see the future. If we do not stand up as we ought, in my humble opinion, the condition of Ireland is prosperous and happy—the condition of Hindostan is prosperous and happy—the condition of Jamaica is prosperous and happy, to what the condition of the Southern States will be if now they should not stand up manfully in defence of their rights.

Mr. President, I desire that the resolutions which I now send to the table be read.

(The resolutions were read as follows:)

Resolved, That the territories of the United States belong to the several States composing this Union, and are held by them as their joint and common property.

Resolved, That Congress, as the joint agent and representative of the States of this Union, has no right to make any law, or do any act whatever, that shall directly, or by its effects, make any discrimination between the States of this Union, by which any of them shall be deprived of its full and equal right in any territory of the United States, acquired, or to be acquired.

Resolved, That the enactment of any law which should directly, or by its effects, deprive the citizens of any of the States of this Union from emigrating with their property into any of the territories of the United States, will make such discrimination, and would, therefore, be a violation of the Constitution, and the rights of the States from which such citizens emigrated, and in derogation of that perfect equality which belongs to them as members of this Union, and would tend directly to subvert the Union itself.

Resolved, That it is a fundamental principle in our political creed, that a people in forming a constitution have the unconditional right to form and adopt the Government which they may think best calculated to secure their liberty, prosperity, and happiness; and that in conformity thereto, no other condition is imposed by the Federal

Constitution on a State in order to be admitted into this Union, except that its Constitution shall be republican; and that the imposition of any other by Congress would not only be in violation of the Constitution, but in direct conflict with the principle on which our political system rests.

I move that the resolutions be printed. I shall move that they be taken up tomorrow; and I do trust that the Senate will give them early attention, and an early vote upon the subject.

From *Speech of Mr. Calhoun, of South Carolina, in Reply to Mr. Turney of Tennessee* . . . [Washington: 1847?], pp. 7–11 under the half-title, *Remarks of Mr. Calhoun, on Presenting His Resolutions on the Slave Question. February 19, 1847*. Also printed in *Congressional Globe*, 29th Cong., 2nd Sess., pp. 453–455; the Washington, D.C., *Daily Union*, February 19, 1847, p. 2; the Charleston, S.C., *Mercury*, February 23, 1847, p. 2; the Columbia, S.C., *South-Carolinian*, March 3, 1847, p. 1; the Camden, S.C., *Journal*, March 3, 1847, p. 1; the Edgefield, S.C., *Advertiser*, March 3, 1847, pp. 1–2; Crallé, ed., *Works*, 4:339–349; Benton, *Abridgment of Debates*, 16:82–86; Lence, ed., *Union and Liberty*, pp. 513–521; Wilson, ed., *The Essential Calhoun*, pp. 382–389. CC of resolutions in DNA, RG 46 (Senate), 29A-B10. PC's of resolutions in *Senate Journal*, 29th Cong., 2nd Sess., pp. 209–210; Senate Document No. 152, 29th Cong., 2nd Sess.; *De Bow's Commercial Review*, vol. IV, no. 2 (October, 1847), pp. 557–558; the New York, N.Y., *Herald*, February 21, 1847, p. 4; the Petersburg, Va., *Republican*, February 22, 1847, p. 4; the Columbia, S.C., *Southern Chronicle*, February 24, 1847, p. 3; the Vicksburg, Miss., *Weekly Sentinel*, March 3, 1847, p. 3; the Charleston, S.C., *Mercury*, August 11, 1847, p. 2; the Oregon City, Ore., *Oregon Spectator*, September 8, 1847, p. 1. Variant speech reports in the Washington, D.C., *Daily National Intelligencer*, February 20, 1847, pp. 2–3; the New York, N.Y., *Herald*, February 20, 1847, p. 3, and February 21, 1847, p. 3; the Alexandria, Va., *Gazette and Virginia Advertiser*, February 20, 1847, p. 2; the Charleston, S.C., *Courier*, February 23, 1847, p. 2; the Greenville, S.C., *Mountaineer*, March 5, 1847, p. 1.

Remarks in Debate with Thomas H. Benton after Presenting His Resolutions

[In the Senate, February 19, 1847]

[*When Calhoun sat down after presenting his resolutions on slavery in the Territories, Benton arose immediately and declared that he was not "going to lay aside the necessary business of the session to vote on such a string of abstractions."*]

Mr. Calhoun. The Senator says he cannot take up abstractions. The Constitution is an abstraction. Propriety is an abstraction. All the great rules of life are abstractions. The Declaration of Independence was made on an abstraction; and when I hear a man declare that he is against abstract truth in a case of this kind, I am prepared to know what his course will be! I certainly supposed that the Senator from Missouri, the representative of a slaveholding State, would have supported these resolutions. I moved them in good faith, under a solemn conviction of what was due to those whom I represent; and due the whole South and the whole Union. I have as little desire as any Senator to obstruct public business. All I want is a decision, and a decision before the three million bill is decided. If the Senator from Missouri wants [to speak on other business] tomorrow morning, very well. The resolutions can be taken up on Monday [2/22].

[*Benton declared that he would never neglect public business "to take up firebrands to set the world on fire."*]

Mr. Calhoun. The Senator does not at all comprehend me. I expressed a hope that he would be found ready to support the principles presented in my resolutions.

Mr. Benton. I shall be found in the right place. I am on the side of my country and the Union.

From *Congressional Globe*, 29th Cong., 2nd Sess., p. 455. Also printed in the Washington, D.C., *Daily Union*, February 19, 1847, p. 2; the Charleston, S.C., *Mercury*, February 23, 1847, p. 2; Benton, *Abridgment of Debates*, 16:86. Variants in the Washington, D.C., *Daily National Intelligencer*, February 20, 1847, p. 3; the Alexandria, Va., *Gazette and Virginia Advertiser*, February 20, 1847, p. 2; the Charleston, S.C., *Courier*, February 23, 1847, p. 2.

Further Remarks on the Mexican War

[In the Senate, February 19, 1847]
[*In the course of a long speech Samuel Houston of Tex. attacked Calhoun's position on the war, contrasting it with his position as Secretary of State. In support Houston put into the record Calhoun's letter of 4/11/1844 to the Texan commissioners in the U.S. concerning the protection of Texas while annexation was pending. Houston also disputed Calhoun's suggestion of an easily defensible line to be maintained.*]

Mr. Calhoun said, the Senator from Texas had endeavored to make certain words which he had used in a communication to the

Texas Commissioners cover more ground than he had intended. For himself he had no such intention as the Senator's interpretation would imply. The Commissioners from Texas [J. Pinckney Henderson and Isaac Van Zandt] naturally required protection, having just ground to apprehend that Mexico might take advantage of the circumstances and position in which she would be placed, but they asked for more than this Government could comply with. All that the [John Tyler] Administration could then do, was to place a fleet on the Gulf, and to send General [Edmund P.] Gaines on the frontier; and if Mexico should make any hostile movement, to bring the subject before Congress. The Administration was aware that the question of war was with Congress and not with itself. The Administration was resolved to do all that it could constitutionally do; but on the question of war it could only make a recommendation to Congress, and that it would have done.

The Senator from Texas said that those movements did more to endanger the peace of the country than the marching of General [Zachary] Taylor from Corpus Christi to the Rio Grande. But that movement at last produced no war. The truth was, that although there was a possibility that Mexico might interfere when the negotiations were known; although she might have a strong desire to do so, yet her condition at that time was such that she had little capacity to make any war, and his impression was, that if we had stood on the defensive—if we had maintained Texas as we found Texas, there would have been no danger of war. That was his impression. And on that impression he had all along acted. He would not go into this subject; but the Senator had said that the line he proposed was an extensive one, and that it would take ten thousand men for its maintenance. But he supposed there was a part of that line which would require no considerable defense.

A brief conversation ensued between the Senators from South Carolina and Texas, respecting that line, and the possibility of protecting it without a large force.

[*Houston again rendered his interpretation of Calhoun's 1844 letter.*]

Mr. Calhoun explained, that his meaning was in case of an emergency—the invasion of Texas by Mexico—that the subject would be submitted to Congress. He again insisted that the line which he had designated could be maintained with a small force. Part of it was occupied by Indians, and other part to the Pacific was covered by water, and therefore would require but a small naval force. To this (he said) this Government would have to come, unless some extraordinary circumstance should occur. He called upon the advocates of the opposite policy to consider it. Their view of dictating a peace was an event which no man could yet see; and it might be so far postponed that the nation would get tired of the war and abandon it, or take this defensive line. He believed it would be found the best for the whole country.

[*Houston asked whether aid would have been rendered to Texas in an emergency in 1844 when Congress was not in session.*]

Mr. Calhoun said that was provided for. Congress was to be called together with all possible despatch.

[*After this discussion, Lewis Cass brought up the question of a report of Isaac D. Marks, U.S. Consul at Matamoros, Mexico, made to Gen. Taylor in 9/1846, concerning the pacific intentions of the Mexican commander Mariano Arista. (This letter had been used by Polk administration opponents to suggest the avoidability of the war if Taylor had not been ordered forward from Corpus Christi.)*]

Mr. Calhoun said the fact was clear, that Generals Taylor and Arista acted on that information. And from September to May, General Arista acted only on the defensive; thus the facts corroborated the statement of Mr. Marks, who was a highly respectable citizen.

From *Congressional Globe*, 29th Cong., 2nd Sess., p. 460. Variants in the New York, N.Y., *Herald*, February 21, 1847, p. 4; the Charleston, S.C., *Mercury*, February 23, 1847, p. 2; the Cincinnati, Ohio, *Daily Enquirer*, February 25, 1847, p. 2. NOTE: In the *Herald's* report of the day's debate, the "brief conversation" between Houston and Calhoun mentioned in the *Globe* report above was rendered in more detail. In order to support his position that only a small force was needed to defend, Calhoun questioned Houston about the defenses of Texas prior to annexation. Houston's replies elicited the information that there had been two invasions, both of less than a thousand men, and that these had not caused serious harm despite the fact that Texas had no standing army. The text of Calhoun's letter of 4/11/1844 is in *The Papers of John C. Calhoun,* 18:208–209.

From F[REDERICK] HOLLICK

Barnum's [Hotel,] Baltimore, Feb. 20, 1847

Dear Sir, I would not intrude upon you now, when I know your time is so fully occupied, if the matter I write about was not of some consequence, at this particular time, to the country at large, and of interest to yourself on that account if on no others.

You will probably recollect that about 12 months ago, I saw you and spoke about some investigations which I had made, and which I wished to extend, as to the result of Hybridising between the Whites and Negroes. You were so kind as to give me many facts, and to suggest new observations. I was not able then to follow out my intentions and ideas fully, as to Lecturing on this subject, though I have to some extent, but it has run in my mind ever since, and I am now determined to prosecute my inquiries further and make the results of them known. It strikes me that at this particular *crisis* in the affairs of the country, when we have such fanaticism as the *"Wilmot proviso"* exhibited, that the real relation of the two races to each other should be generally known, and their proper positions pointed out. I feel confident that this matter may be so laid before *the people* in *any Part* of the Union, as to annihilate Abolitionism altogether. There is no question as to the fact that Comparative Anatomy and Physiology, as well as the past history of man, prove incontestibly that the Negro race *always has,* and almost *must,* occupy a servile position when the two races live together. I will undertake to prove this, & maintain it against all the world. Since I saw you I have been very busy with my profession, in Philad[elphi]a, but have found time to Lecture on this subject a time or two, and on each occasion have found that *nine tenths,* at least, of the Audience ["where" *altered to* "were"] convinced by my facts & reasonings. I am now on my way to Norfolk and Richmond, to Lecture on Physiology generally, and this subject in particular, but more especially to gather all the *facts* I can in relation to it. You gave me a Letter to Mr. [Littleton W.] Tazewell, for which I thank you, and hope now to avail myself of; and I should also be still more indebted, if you think the matter of sufficient importance to be encouraged, if you will recommend me to any one else likely to assist. I will deal frankly with you Sir, and tell you my desires & intentions. I want to collect such a body of *indisputable facts,* by examining living Negroes, ["and" *canceled*] mulattoes &c. and dissecting their bodies when I can do it, ["in" *altered to* "as" *and* "conjun" *canceled*] shall in conjunction with their Social history, past & present, put this matter *beyond Cavil or question.* I will then Lecture upon it in the chief Cities, and publish my Lectures. I feel confident that in the present state of the relations between the North & the South, this is the only mode by which the South can make her position be properly understood, and effectually counteract the influence ["of" *interlined*] the Abolitionists. Indeed Sir, I do think this matter is of *paramount* importance just now. To carry my project out fully however, I must be *assured* of having the assistance of Southern gentlemen, owners of Negroes particularly, and their encouragement of my Lectures. If you countenance the scheme, and recommend it, I have no doubt of its success. I should therefore like to hear from you, if you can find time and feel sufficient interest.

I have just now been speaking with *Mr. George [R.] Gliddon,* who has been pointing out to me the real position of the Negro among the Ancient Egyptians, and he has proposed, in case you countenance the idea, that we should *both* go on the expedition—he taking the *historical* facts, and me the *Anatomical!* We could then challenge, & I feel confident, (without egotism) overcome any opposition to our positions. There should be no shirking the matter, nor meeting it *half way only.* The position should be *maintained* that Slavery is the *natural, constant,* and *inevitable* state of the Ethiopian race, when living with the ["race" *canceled and* "whites" *interlined*]. Of this I am convinced myself, & also that *we two* could *prove* it, and convince other people of its truth. But, as I remarked before, I cannot afford to do it as an *amateur* only. If I know that the parties really interested, (the Southerners) will assist and encourage me, I will do it, and so will Mr. G[liddon]. This Is why I write to you, & request an early reply. Probably I may come on to Washington; but please send to me at the *National Hotel, Norfolk Va.,* as it is uncertain. Respectfully Yours, F. Hollick, M.D.

P.S. Unless detained here too long I shall go on to *Charleston* now, but if I am detained too long I must defer it till next fall—and then I will go to Boston & N. York after. F.H.

ALS with Ens in ScCleA. Note: Hollick apparently enclosed an advertisement for lectures by George R. Gliddon on Egyptian archeology and another for *Chronos. Outline of a Grand Chronological Atlas,* by Henry Venel, translated and edited by Gliddon. Hollick was a prominent and widely-published authority on anatomy and human reproduction.

Remarks on the appointment of officers of volunteers, 2/20. Under discussion was an provision of an Army bill that would allow the President to fill vacancies in the officers of the volunteer regiments. David R. Atchison of Missouri argued that the regiments were State troops whose officers had so far been appointed by the States. "Mr. Calhoun thought the power to the President was unconstitutional." Later, Calhoun explained that the "volunteers now in the field—were, in the constitutional sense, militia, and the appointment of the officers it was therefore not competent for the President to make." From the New York, N.Y., *Herald,* February

23, 1847, p. 4. Variant in *Congressional Globe*, 29th Cong., 2nd Sess., p. 464. (In the variant Calhoun was reported as saying: "When vacancies occur, the next in command might take the place without taking the rank of the senior officer.")

SPEECH ON HIS SLAVERY RESOLUTIONS IN REPLY TO JAMES F. SIMMONS

[In the Senate, February 20, 1847]

[*Simmons, a Rhode Island Whig, delivered a speech arguing against the position taken in Calhoun's resolutions introduced the previous day.*]

Mr. Calhoun said he desired to make one or two remarks in reply to some portions of the speech of the honorable Senator from Rhode Island. I intend now and hereafter to argue this question with calmness. It is not one to be argued in a spirit of excitement. The Senator from Rhode Island rests his reasons against the resolutions which I have offered, in the first place, on the fact that there was no territory belonging to the United States at the time of the adoption of the Constitution, from which slavery was not excluded. Now, whether that be an argument of any force or not, I do not, in the first instance, intend to inquire; but what I do intend to say is, that the fact that there was no territory belonging to the United States at that time which did not exclude slavery, reads a lesson to us that we ought never to forget. How did the United States get possession of that magnificent territory between the Mississippi and the Ohio, now swarming with an intelligent and most numerous population? It was by the magnanimous cession of the oldest and leading Southern State. It was she that ceded it to the Union in the spirit of that generosity and patriotism which has ever characterized Virginia, and, let me add, all the Southern States of this Union. Now, how did it happen that Virginia and the other Southern States came to be excluded from that territory? It was by an act of the old Congress, in which the Senator very properly told us that the non-slaveholding States had a majority.

Mr. Simmons. Every one of the slaveholding States voted for it.*
[*Footnote:* "Mr. Simmons was in an error. The States were divided in passing the ordinance."]

Mr. Calhoun. The non slaveholding States had a majority, and that Congress passed a law excluding slave-owners from the territory. Virginia was thus deprived of all participation in that magnificent territory, without the slightest authority under the old articles of confederation. It was a palpable violation of that instrument, and was so represented by Mr. [James] Madison himself in "The Federalist," if I do not mistake. It is some time since I looked into it. Now, here we have a warning. I trust that the South never will forget that an act of unlimited generosity, almost without precedent, was converted, through the force of a majority of the non-slaveholding States in the old Congress, into a monopoly of this territory from which Virginia herself was excluded, and all done without authority of the articles of the old confederation, and in violation of them. What has been the consequence? There have grown up in that territory, five States, from which we are not only excluded, but they are made a receptacle, contrary to the Constitution—I am giving facts, solemn facts—of our fugitive slaves, and are thus made the medium of depriving us of them, directly in violation of the Constitution, which provides that all fugitive slaves shall be delivered up on claim of the owner. Organized companies have been formed in Ohio and other States—Illinois, Indiana (Mr. [Edward A.] Hannegan (in his seat.) No, not Indiana.) I was in error then; but organized companies have been formed at least in Ohio, for the purpose of transporting our slaves into Canada, where they are beyond the reach of this constitutional provision, and expressly with a view of defeating it. They are known to exist, they act openly, and yet the legislature of that State refrains from any action on the subject. Now, I put it to the candor of the Senator from Rhode Island and to every other Senator on this floor, if this does not read us a lesson, which we ought long, long to remember?

This has resulted from a violation of the articles of confederation, by passing the ordinance already alluded to—passed by a body in which we are informed by the Senators, the non-slaveholding States had a majority. It is the natural result of a power exercised by a single body, controlled by a numerical majority, without an antagonizing power in the Constitution to counteract it. I care not what the form of the Government is—it is nothing if the Government be despotic, whether it be in the hands of one, or of a few, or of many men, without limitation. It belongs to the human heart that the power will be abused; and what is most extraordinary, those abusing it will often not be conscious of the abuse.

I come to the next ground taken by the Senator from Rhode Island, that the United States, at the time of the adoption of the

Constitution, had no territory from which slavery was not excluded. From this fact he concluded, that it was the intention of the framers to exclude slavery from all territories to be acquired. Now I put it to the Senate, is that a legitimate conclusion? Is there any principle from which we could infer from a mere naked fact like that, that it was the intention of the framers of the Constitution to prevent the slaveholding States from having any participation in any territory thereafter to be acquired, either by purchase or conquest. I confess I can see none.

The next argument relied upon by the Senator is this, that at that time there was a certain proportion between the number of non-slaveholding and slaveholding States which gave the former a majority in the old Congress, and that as they had a majority when the Constitution was framed, it was intended they should maintain it forever afterwards. I have shown how the power was exercised by the old Congress, while they possessed this majority, in reference to the very question now under consideration, and that it affords us sufficient warning to guard us against a predominance of such a majority in every branch of this Government, as will be the case if we do not resist the aggressive policy of excluding slavery from all the territories of the Union.

But suppose this argument of the Senator to have any force, it is as good for us as it is for him. It would follow that the disproportion which then existed in favor of the non-slaveholding States ought never to be increased, and yet the resolutions adopted by his and other States, propose that we should be excluded hereafter from all the territories of the United States, and that no other slaveholding State should ever again be admitted into the Union.

Mr. Simmons. There is no such proposition in the resolution from my State.

Mr. Calhoun. Well, that is the proposition of other States. If we are to be excluded, what will be the result? Instead of having this disproportion of six to eight, we will have a disproportion of fourteen to twenty-eight! Double, precisely. That will be the end of it. And if ever any portion of Mexico should fall under the authority of the United States, and come to be our property, and if we should apply to it the same principle, where, I ask, would it end? What has led the Senator from Rhode Island into these extraordinary conclusions? I have great respect for that Senator. I believe he intends fair. But let me say to him that he has viewed all in reference to this question one-sidedly. He has considered it in a single aspect, and viewing it thus partially, his clear and strong intellect has been brought to very erroneous conclusions. His error originates in the belief that this is a national Government—that we are a nation—that we are one people, and not a union. And to prove that we are a nation, what documents does he furnish? A single resolution by the State of New York calling the convention that framed the Constitution.

Mr. Simmons. I quoted the language of the resolution simply for the purpose of showing the use of the word "nation," at that time, which the Senator has so pertinaciously refused to employ. But it was not at all to sustain my general position.

Mr. Calhoun. Well, then, it was no argument at all! All the rest was bare assertion; and yet he threw up his hands and expressed his amazement that any one should hold the doctrines that we hold! I will follow the Senator however. It is true that the resolution of the State of New York used the word national; and what is further true, that there was a large body in the United States, at that time, in favor of a a [*sic*] national Government. The three States which took the lead on that side were Massachusetts, Pennsylvania, and Virginia. They were the three largest, and were actively and strenuously in favor of a national Government. The two leading spirits were Mr. [Alexander] Hamilton, of New York, probably the author of the resolution, and Mr. Madison, of Virginia. In the early stages of the convention there was a majority in favor of a national Government. But in this stage there were but eleven States in the convention—Rhode Island never appeared there, and New Hampshire had not yet appeared with her delegates. In process of time New Hampshire came in—a very great addition to the federal side, which now became predominant; and it is owing—I speak it here in honor of New England and the Northern States—it is owing mainly to the States of Connecticut and New Jersey, that we have a federal instead of a national Government—that we have the best Government instead of the most despotic and intolerable on the earth. Who were the men of these States to whom we are indebted for this admirable Government? I will name them. Their names ought to be engraven on brass and live forever! They were Chief Justice [Oliver] Ellsworth, Roger Sherman, and Judge Patterson [*sic*; William Paterson] of New Jersey. The other States further South were blind. They did not see the future. But to the sagacity and coolness of these three men, aided by a few others, but not so prominent we owe the present Constitution. So completely did the national party succumb, that during a large portion of the latter part of the sittings of the convention the word "national" was not named. The "Federal," the

"Union," became the favorite names. The national party was completely overthrown; and what is remarkable, the very men who took the lead of the national party, assumed the name of "Federalists," clearly showing that it had become the favorite name. Honest and great men they were; and as such were disposed after they were overruled to give an honest and a fair trial to a system, to which at first they were opposed, and under the name of "Federal," they recommended that Constitution to the adoption of the people of the United States; conclusively proving that the scheme of a national government first proposed had been overruled, and a federal government adopted in its place. Now, if the Senator's eyes had been properly directed, he would not have been ignorant of this, and not being ignorant, would not have made the extraordinary declaration he has made; that the idea that we constitute a Union of States, and not a nation, was so absurd, that nothing but the extraordinary ability with which it had been advocated could rescue it from ridicule.

But this is not all. Many of the original federal party in the convention assumed the name of republican, after the "national["] party had assumed that of federalist, from an apprehension that the original bias of the former in favor of a national government, would tend to give it a direction that way, in carrying out the power of the government in practice. Under the name of republican, and the lead of Mr. [Thomas] Jefferson, and maintaining to the utmost the federal character of the government, they achieved a great victory, which carried him into power in 1801, and thus established in practice, the federal theory of the government, as I have shown it was, in the convention that adopted the Constitution. These facts show the deep feeling of the people in favor of the federal theory, in opposition to the national, in the early stages of our government, and afford conclusive proof, that if the latter had been adopted in forming the Constitution—if that instrument had been based upon the national, instead of the federal theory, it never would have been adopted by the people of the States.

But the federal character of the government may be established from its internal structure, as well as from historical evidence. It affords ample proof that it is a federal Union of States, and not a national government—a constellation of nations, and not a single nation; a far more brilliant and thinking conception—much more philosophical and better calculated to carry out the great object for which it was formed. If we had no other proof that the object was to preserve perpetual the Union, as it existed under the old articles of confederation, and not to destroy it by erecting a national, consolidated government, the letter of General [George] Washington to the old Congress, submitting for its consideration the present Constitution, which he signed as president of the Convention, would be conclusive. He calls it the "general government of the Union," and states as its leading objects, a consolidation of the Union. The word Union is significant. Politically speaking, it is never applied to individuals as united under a government, but always to States, as constituting separate and distinct communities, and implies of itself the idea of a federal or confederated government.

Thus regarded it is obvious that in using the word consolidated, it was not intended to be understood that the object in adopting the Constitution was to destroy the Union, but to strengthen and perfect it, with a view of preserving and perpetuating it.

The Senator made a remark in this connection, which it is proper I should notice. He dwelt for some time on the interpretation which I gave to the term United States, in what I said in introducing my resolutions; I said it meant the "States United"; my object was to get clear of the geographical idea, which in common parlance, is attached to the term United States. As commonly used, it is intended to designate that portion of this Continent which Providence has allotted to us, and has come to receive this meaning, because there is no specific name to express it. But that is not its meaning in the Constitution. As used in that instrument, it is intended to designate all the States that are members of this Union. Indeed, if my memory serves me, in the first plans of the Constitution submitted to the Convention, the preamble commenced with "we the people of New Hampshire, Massachusetts," and so on, enumerating all the States, as in the Declaration of Independence, but afterwards the phraseology was changed, and the expression, "we the people of the United States," as it now stands in the preamble, adopted in its plac[e;] from which, those who think with the Senator infer, that the Constitution was ordained and established, not by the States as separate and distinct communities, but by the people of the whole, as constituting an aggregate mass of individuals. It becomes important in this view to inquire why a change of phraseology was made. Were the names of the States dropped, and the present phraseology adopted, with the intention to support this interpretation, or with some other motive? The Constitution itself will answer the question. The very last article provides, that the ratification by nine States shall be sufficient for the establishment of the Constitution between the States so ratifying the same. Then, as it could not be known, whether all the twelve States would ratify, or if all should not ratify, which of the twelve would, it became impossible to retain the original phraseology which enumerates all the States, after the words "we the people," and yet from this change made indispensably necessary, from that provision of the Constitution, it is attempted to subvert the federal government, plainly established by it, and rear in its place, a great national consolidated government—to expunge the word "Union," and insert in its place that of "Nation." In illustration of the foresight in making the change, it is proper to remark, that Rhode Island and North Carolina, in the first instance, refused to ratify, and that the Constitution went into operation without them. We are as devoted to the Union as any portion of the American people; I use the phrase as meaning the people of the Union, but we see in a national consolidated government, evils innumerable to us. Admit us to be a Nation and not a Union, where would we stand? We are in a minority. We have peculiar institutions and peculiar productions, and shall we look to a mere numerical majority of the whole—the unsafest of all governments for protection? I would rather trust a sovereign, rather an aristocracy—any form of government, than that. I hold that whenever the idea becomes fixed, that the mere numerical majority have an inherent and indefeasable right to govern, constitutional liberty must cease. It is Dorrism. Rhode Island has had some experience of what that is, and the last man I should suspect of advocating this do[c]trine, as applied to the Union, is the Senator from Rhode Island. It is bad enough when applied to a State, but when applied to our Union, it is ruinous. The true idea of a constitutional government, is the reverse; a government of the whole, a government which should fairly and fully express the sense of every portion, and thereby the sense of the whole, and not one that expresses simply the voice of the numerical majority, or the numerical minority. Either of them would be the government of a part over a part and not the government of the whole.

Now let me tell the Senator, that the doctrines which we advocate, are the result of the fullest and most careful examination of our system of government, and that our conviction, that we constitute a Union, and not a nation, is as strong and as sincere as that of the Senator, or any other in the opposite opinion. We are as good judges of our interest and safety, and the means of preserving them, as the non-slaveholding States are of theirs, and rather better than they can be of ours.

The argument which the Senator based on the annexation of

Texas, clearly proves how far the mind may be deflected from sound conclusions by a partial view of the subject. He asks, where I, as a strict constructionist, find any right to annex Texas to the Union.

Mr. Simmons. I said that this movement began on the part of this government to prohibit the abolition of slavery in a foreign nation, and I desire to know the constitutional authority for that.

Mr. Calhoun. I intended so to state the position of the Senator. A "foreign nation," then—that is, Texas. He asks, then, where I would find any authority in the Constitution for that measure. The Senator must remember that the British Minister himself, Lord Aberdeen—whom I greatly respect as a man and as a statesman—had the candor to send us a communication to be read by the British Minister to the Secretary of State, whose office I then filled, announcing that their object was not only to see slavery abolished in Texas, but in the United States and throughout the world. Now I think nothing is clearer than this, that the United States are bound, under the highest guarantee, to protect the States of the Union against domestic violence, be it what it may, and that, being thus bound, whenever it is within the sphere of their power to take measures to prevent the causes leading to it. This government has the exclusive control of our foreign relations, and is of course bound to take measures to prevent the operation of any cause originating in a foreign State, and which may in its consequences threaten to disturb the internal peace and security of any of the States of this Union, or to express it more strictly, to guard against the exciting of domestic violence from abroad.

The only question then is, whether the movement contemplated by Great Britain in Texas, would not, if permitted to be carried out, lead to insurrectionary movements almost necessarily in Louisiana and the other States bordering on Texas. Was it not, then, specially the duty of this government, when it was informed from an authentic source that the American delegate to the World's Convention, had informed that body that the most effectual mode to abolish slavery in America, was to abolish it in Texas, and that then was the time for doing it. Was it not, I ask, our duty to take effectual steps to counteract it—especially was it not, when it was known that a committee was appointed by the convention to wait on Lord Aberdeen on the subject, and that it had received a favorable response? Add to this the communication from Lord Aberdeen above referred to, and I ask the Senator, whether a case is not made out, when this government, under the solemn guarantee of the Constitution, entered into by all the States, to protect the government of each other against domestic violence, was not bound to adopt the most efficient measures to prevent the policy of the British government in reference to Texas, and which must have ended in insurrectionary movements in the neighboring States, from being carried into effect? I also ask how could that have been effected but by the course which was adopted?

A word as to our motives. If we are opposed to the course of policy which the [non]slaveholding States have announced that they are determined to pursue in reference to slavery, and the interpretation of the Constitution on which they are prepared to rest that determination, judging by the remarks of the Senator, our opposition rests on the ground that they will be ruinous to us, if not effectually resisted. We know what we are about; we for[e]see what is coming, and move with no other purpose but to protect our portion of the Union from the greatest of calamities—not insurrection, but something worse. I see the end, if the process is to go on unresisted—it is to expel in time the white population of the Southern States and leave the blacks in possession. I see beyond what the Senator sees, because he has not viewed the subject from the proper point. I have moved my resolutions from no party view—no design to embarrass any side, but simply that the slaveholding States, which I in part represent, shall know what is the sense of this body in reference to their constitutional rights touching this important point. If you believe we have none, tell us so. If we are doomed to remain forever restricted to our present numbers, whilst the other States are to spread out and fill the continent, tell us so. Let us know the worst. We love and revere the Union, it is the interest of all—I might add the world—that our Union should be preserved; but the conservative power is in the slaveholding States. They are the conservative portion of the country. Where wages command labor, as in the non-slaveholding States, there necessarily takes place between labor and capital a conflict, which leads, in process of time, to disorder, anarchy, and revolution, if not counteracted by some appropriate and strong constitutional provision.

Such is not the case in the slaveholding States. There labor and capital are identified. There the high profit of labor, but increases the means of the master to add to the comfort of his slaves, and hence in all conflicts which may occur in the other portions of the Union between labor and capital, the South will ever be found to take the conservative side. Thus regarded, the non-slaveholding States have not much less interest, fairly understood, in upholding and preserving the equilibrium of the slaveholding States, than the latter themselves have. I was, in this connection, much struck many years ago by a remark made by one of four young English gentlemen, who in passing through this city spent some evenings with me—of whom Lord [E.G.G.S.] Stanley [Earl of Derby] was one. We were conversing about the cause which for so long a time had kept this Union together in peace and harmony. It was regarded as a wonderful phenomenon that a country of such vast extent and of such numerous population, should have passed through so many years under free and popular institutions, without convulsion or a shock. Lord Stanley, without any suggestion or leading remark of mine, said that it was owing to the Southern States, and that it was their conservative tendency that preserved us from disorder. Let gentlemen then be warned, that while warring on us, they are warring on themselves. Acting thus on the defensive, and restricting ourselves simply to repelling attacks, I regard it as hard—as unjust, that we should be accused of creating excitement, whilst those who have brought forward these aggressive measures, are held up in quite a different light—as the advocates of harmony and quiet. If excitement has been created, they, and not we, are the authors. We mean none and will cause none; all we ask is to be let alone, but if trampled upon, it will be idle to expect that we will not return it.

From *Speech of Mr. Calhoun, of South Carolina, in Reply to Mr. Turney of Tennessee* . . . [Washington: 1847?], pp. 12–16 under the half-title *Mr. Calhoun's Reply to Mr. Simmons, on His Resolutions. February 20, 1847.* Also printed in the Charleston, S.C., *Mercury*, February 24, 1847, p. 2; Crallé, ed., *Works*, 4:349–361; [Eugene Musson], *Lettre à Napoleon III sur l'esclavage aux états du Sud, pur un Créole de la Louisiane* (Paris: Dentu, 1862), pp. 154–155 (part). Slightly variant report in *Congressional Globe*, 29th Cong., 2nd Sess., pp. 466–467; the Washington, D.C., *Daily Union*, February 20, 1847, p. 2; the Washington, D.C., *Daily National Intelligencer*, February 22, 1847, p. 1; the Alexandria, Va., *Gazette and Virginia Advertiser*, February 23, 1847, p. 2; the Charleston, S.C., *Courier*, February 24, 1847, p. 2. Other variant reports in the New York, N.Y., *Herald*, February 23, 1847, p. 4; the Greenville, S.C., *Mountaineer*, March 5, 1847, p. 1.

From P. S. Buckingham

Wytheville, Va., Feb[ruar]y 21, 1847

Dear Sir, I beg to claim the privilege which you had the kindness to grant me during your short sojourn among us last summer, of applying to you for such speeches &c as I might desire.

Your recent speeches on the subject of the Mexican War are looked to with universal interest, and I hope you will excuse me for requesting ["you" *interlined*] most earnestly to be so kind as to send me a copy of your speech on the Mexican War delivered on the 9th if I remember correctly—also your reply to [Hopkins L.] Turney of Tennessee.

Your friends here preserve the most affectionate remembrance of you personally, and as a statesman and politician we all feel most grateful to you, not only for averting the war with England, which was likely to grow out of the Oregon Question, but for the high and impregnable moral ground which you have taken on the subject of our Mexican difficulties. The people regard the war as Mr. Polk's war.

Mr. Polk, the Administration, the management and conduct of the War in the *department*, are universally condemned here by both parties. A sentiment—a very strong sentiment of indignation pervades the public mind, for the unjust and unsoldierly treatment of Gen. [Zachary] Taylor.

There is but a single individual in all this Country who has been heard to say a single word in disparagement of the Gen.

Allow me to hope that we shall on some early occasion in the future, again have the pleasure of extending to you the hand of hospitality & friendship of our Town & County.

Your attention to my request as to your speeches referred to, will greatly oblige Your Friend & Most Ob[edien]t Serv[an]t, P.S. Buckingham.

ALS in ScCleA; PEx in Boucher and Brooks, eds., *Correspondence*, p. 368.

To W[illiam] W. Corcoran, Washington, 2/21/[1847?]. "Mr. Calhoun has the honor to accept the invitation of Mr. Corcoran to dinner on Thursday next, the 25th Inst." ALU in DLC, William Wilson Corcoran Papers.

From F[ITZ]W[ILLIAM] BYRDSALL, *"Private"*

New York [City,] Feb[ruar]y 22d 1847

Dear Sir, The Resolutions presented by you to the Senate of the U.S. on the 19th inst. with your introductory remarks have arrested my deepest attention. In my opinion the war with Mexico—the Tariff question—the presidential succession, are triffling matters in comparison with the principles and subjects comprehended in the mighty grasp of those Resolutions. The man [Thomas H. Benton] who in the slang phrazeology of small politicians called them a "string of abstractions" did not ["at" *interlined*] all comprehend them, or if he did, his language on that occasion was a resort to evasion or something worse, unworthy of a representative of a sovereign State.

I honor you more and more since you presented those Resolutions. As one I take my stand upon every word of them as essential to ["the" *interlined*] maintainance of Our Union. I have no language to express my appreciation of them. They are brought forward at the proper conjuncture of public affaires—they speak without sophistry in plain classic Anglo Saxon that all can understand. They are as important to the north as they are to the South.

Never was any social institution more unfairly vilified than that which is termed Southern slavery. It is the very best institution that could be devised for the negro race of Africa—a race which for the last two or three thousand years has advanced as little in the land of its origin as the horse or cow—a race which has improved both in moral and physical condition under the patriarchal system of the South, beyond any other condition it has ever been placed ["in," *interlined*] upon this earth. It is an inferior race and must ever be subject to the superior as a menial one. Social & political equality is the worst position for itself it can be placed in, because duties are then required of it which it is not mentally qualified to perform—it cannot provide for the future nor protect itself in a community where there is no patriarchal system to provide & protect.

We had a public meeting here at Vauxhall Garden, which was understood by many of the signers to the call to be for the purpose of condemning the abolition movements in Congress which interrupted the proper measures for the prosecution of the [Mexican] War. Ex Chancellor [William T.] McCoun when placed in the chair opened the meeting by declaring that he would not sanction any proceedings condemning "the northern Democracy for the noble stand it had taken in Congress against the extension of Southern Slavery." This announcement excited a tumult of the most violent kind of hisses and plaudits, and Vauxhall garden became exactly like the House of Representatives at Washington, but on a larger scale as to numbers, with more vociferation and excitement. The democracy here did not sanction Mr. McCoun's remarks and he had to sit down.

I say for the sake of our Union—for the sake of the well being of humanity, God speed you in the noble self-sacrificing stand you are taking in preservation of the Constitution of the United States and consequently of Republican Institutions. I am Dear Sir Yours with increased Respect, F.W. Byrdsall.

ALS in ScCleA; PEx in Boucher and Brooks, eds., *Correspondence*, pp. 368–369.

From G[EORGE] F. LINDSAY

Mobile [Ala.,] Feb[ruar]y 23 1847

Hon. Sir, Amid the factious storms raging around you, for the fearless & honest discharge of your duty, permit a humble but ardent friend to send you his gratitude & thanks. I need not presume to bid you *go on*. Your God & your conscience will tell you that. But I must say that although *the Press* in this city would represent it differently, every honest intelligent citizen in Mobile approves and applauds your course. To the *Whig* paper we do not wish to look for your defence. The *Tribune* is *Neutral*, and the *Register*, the Dem[ocratic] paper, is in the hands of a man (S.F. Wilson) who *gloats* over every opportunity to strike at you. But your *friends* here—the thinking intelligent, *honest* men of both parties stand firmly by you in this howling tempest of corruption.

Excuse the liberty I have taken, but while I *know* that you are neither deterred from duty, or urged to it by the popular voice, I could not restrain myself from telling you that the Newspapers of this City belie ["&"(?) *canceled*] public opinion, & deceive the ignorant. I even requested the Democratic paper to publish the short speech of [Edward A.] *Hannegan* [Senator from Ind.], & it was refused!

May the God of Heaven sustain & reward you in *time* & Eternity for your Independent Patriotism! You once in New Orleans heard me say it, & I now repeat it

"You'll leave a name[,] a Light, a Land-mark, on the cliffs of *Fame*."

Hon. Sir, from the gushings of my heart have I penned these incoherent phrases—but again let me assure you I am but the mouthpiece of those in this city whose approval you covet. Your youthful but ardent admirer, G.F. Lindsay.

ALS in ScCleA.

Remarks in reply to Thomas H. Benton, 2/24. In a long speech Benton attacked Calhoun as responsible for the Mexican War, "the undisputed author and architect of that calamity." He quoted from a letter allegedly from the "official journal" of the John Tyler administration [that is, the Washington *Madisonian*] giving clandestine political direction to administration supporters. Calhoun asked: "Does he intend to say that I ever wrote such a letter?" Benton replied: "I read it [aloud]. I say nothing." Calhoun said: "I never wrote such a letter as that!" Later, Calhoun said: "I take this occasion to say that I never exercised the slightest influence over that paper. I never had the slightest connexion with it. I never was a subscriber to it, and I very rarely read it." From *Congressional Globe*, 29th Cong., 2nd Sess., p. 497.

Speech in Reply to Thomas H. Benton on the Mexican War

[In the Senate, February 24, 1847]

[*Benton spoke at length, ostensibly on the subject of the bill to appropriate a further three million dollars to bring the war to a conclusion. The entire speech was a pointed attack on Calhoun, who, according to Benton, had personally caused the war when he was Secretary of State but "now sets up for the character of pacificator!"*]

Mr. Benton having concluded—

Mr. Calhoun rose and said: One thing, Mr. President, at least, may be inferred from the unprovoked attack of the Senator, and the great solicitude he evinced to trace the authorship of the war to me—and that is, that the war is unpopular. There can be no mistake. He felt that the tide of public sentiment had turned against it, and hence the anxiety exhibited to place its responsibility on my shoulders, and take it from those on whom it ought justly to rest. Had he supposed the opposite—had he believed that the war was necessary and unavoidable, and that its termination would be successful—I am the last man to whom he would attribute any agency in causing it. I am gratified that the Senator has furnished this evidence. It affords reasonable hope, that those who are responsible for it will exert themselves, and I hope with success, to bring it to a speedy termination.

He traces the authorship to me, because, as he asserts, I am the real author of the annexation of Texas, and that annexation is the real cause of the war. I trust, Mr. President, there will be no dispute hereafter as to who is the real author of annexation. Less than twelve months since, I had many competitors for that honor: the official organ here [the *Daily Union*] claimed, if my memory serves me, a large share for Mr. Polk and his Administration, and not less than half a dozen competitors from other quarters claimed to be the real authors. But now, since the war has become unpopular, they all seem to agree that I, in reality, am the author of annexation. I will not put the honor aside. I may now rightfully and indisputably claim to be the author of that great event—an event which has so much extended the domains of the Union, which has added so largely to its productive powers, which promises so greatly to extend its commerce, which has stimulated its industry, and given security to our most exposed frontier. I take pride to myself as being the author of this great event.

But the Senator objects that I so conducted the question of annexation as necessarily to lead to the war. On what does he rest this charge? He rests it on the ground that I selected the resolution as it came from the House of Representatives, as the basis of the annexation, instead of giving the Texan Government the choice between the House resolution and the amendment of the Senate originally moved by the Senator himself. He complained bitterly that the Senate resolution passed at the very heel of the session, under the expectation that it would be carried into effect by the present Administration, then just coming into power, and not by Mr. Tyler's Administration, then about to expire, had not been adopted.

He seemed to think that the then Administration had no right to act upon it, and that, undertaking to do so, was depriving its successor of some of its rights. He accused me of acting with the greatest promptness. The fact is so. The resolution, if I recollect, was signed by the late President [Tyler] about the first of March [1845]. I saw the importance of acting promptly, and advised the President to act without delay, that he had the constitutional right of doing so, and that I deemed it necessary that he should act in order effectually to secure the success of a measure which had originated with his Administration. His Cabinet were summoned the next day, and concurred in the opinion. That night I prepared the despatch for Mr. [Andrew J.] Donelson, our chargé in Texas, and the next day, late in the evening of the third of March, it was forwarded to him. It was my last official act of any importance as Secretary of State.

I selected the resolution of the House in preference to the amendment of which the Senator from Missouri was the author, because I clearly saw, not only that it was every way preferable, but the only certain mode by which annexation could be effected. My reasons for thinking so were fully set forth in my despatch, which may be found among the public documents accompanying the first annual message of the present Executive. They will speak for themselves; they never have been controverted, and never can be successfully. Indeed, I never considered the Senator's amendment as expressing the deliberate sense either of the Senate or House of Representatives. It is well known that he, and a few of his friends, had the power of greatly embarrassing the passage of the resolutions of the House, if not of defeating them; and that his amendment was moved, not so much as an improvement of the resolutions, as to gratify him and them. That the course I adopted did secure the annexation, and that it was indispensable for that purpose, I have high authority in my possession—that which all would admit to be the highest, if I could with propriety introduce it; and for this prompt and decided act, if for nothing else, I might claim the authorship of annexation.

Now, can anything be more absurd than the assertion that the war with Mexico resulted from selecting the House resolution, instead of the amendment of the Senator? He has ventured the bold assertion, without the shadow of an argument to sustain it. What possible difference could it make with Mexico, whether the annexation was made upon one or the other? Why should the one not be as offensive to her as the other? Indeed, I doubt much whether, even to this day, the Government of Mexico knows whether the resolution was passed with or without an alternative. Such is the baseless ground on which he has charged me with being the author of the war. I had heard, for several days past, that he had prepared to make an elaborate attack on me. Some of my friends asked, rather jestingly, if I did not expect to be annihilated. After these givings out, and such laborious preparation, I did suppose the Senator would make some show of a formidable charge; but of all the attacks I have ever witnessed, in this or any other legislative body, I have never known one so empty and ridiculous. Every one of his charges is founded either in gross error or partial statement of facts, or on some forced and absurd conclusion. I may begin with the very first that he made. He had the assurance to assert, in the presence of the

Senate, that I was the first to introduce the question, who was the real author or cause of this war. Now, I appeal to every Senator, and every other individual who was present on this occasion, whether the Senator from Tennessee (Mr. [Hopkins L.] Turney) did not first charge me with being the author of this war, and whether I did not limit myself to repelling his charge, by showing that it originated in the order to General [Zachary] Taylor, to march from Corpus Christi, and take position on the Rio del Norte? I go further and ask, is there a Senator here ignorant of the fact, that the question of, who was the author or cause of the war, had been long before elaborately discussed in this body—in the House of Representatives, and throughout the whole country, from its declaration up to that time[?] In the face of all this, the Senator rises up in his place, after a long and laborious preparation, and asserts that it was I who originated the inquiry as to who was its author. This is a fair sample of the accuracy of the Senator, in his numerous allegations to show that I was the author of the war. I might go on and take them up one by one, and show that every one of his positions and deductions is equally unfounded in fact or false in conclusion. I do not deem it necessary. A large portion of his speech was but the stale repetition of what he said in the session of 1842–'43 [*sic*; 1843–1844], upon the treaty which I had concluded with Texas, then under discussion in this body. All the documents now brought forward, were then before the Senate, and he went on with the same topics very elaborately, and with more power than on the present occasion, without making any impression on the country. The country was against him then, and still remains against him, and it is in vain that he undertakes to disturb its settled conviction. It will remain ever unchanged, in spite of all that he can do. Under this conviction, I will not weary the Senate by repelling assaults then made and then repelled. The most prominent of the charges—the orders given by the Administration to place a fleet in the Gulf of Mexico, and a portion of the Army on the frontier of Texas—was repelled by my then colleague, (Mr. [George] McDuffie,) of whom he speaks so highly on this occasion. In repelling it, he said, that if the orders to which the Senator then and now objects, had not been issued, the Executive would have been guilty of great dereliction of duty.

The Florida treaty [of 1819], forming another subject of attack, figured also on that occasion, in connexion with annexation; and what he has said now is but a repetition of what he said then. He then, as now, made me responsible for that treaty, although I was but one of six members of Mr. [James] Monroe's Cabinet, and the youngest of its members—responsible, without advancing a particle of proof that I even gave it my support or approbation. He rests the charge on some disclaimer, as it seems, that the then Secretary of State (Mr. [John Quincy] Adams) has, at some time, made, that he was not responsible for the treaty. The Senator may be right as to that; but how can that, by any possibility, show that I was responsible? But I am prepared to take my full share of responsibility as a member of Mr. Monroe's Cabinet, without having any particular agency in forming the treaty, or influence in inducing the Cabinet to adopt it. I then thought, and still think it a good treaty; and so thought the Senate of the United States; for, if my memory does not deceive me, it received every vote of the Senate. (A Senator: "Yes, every vote.") It then received the unanimous vote of the Senate, promptly given. Of course, if that treaty was the cause of the war with Mexico, as the Senator seems to suppose, this body is as much the author and cause of the war, as the individual on whom he is now so anxious to fix it.

I have said it is a good treaty, not without due reflection. We acquired much by it. It gave us Florida—an acquisition not only important in itself, but also in reference to the whole southwestern frontier. There was, at that time, four powerful tribes of Indians, two of whom—the Creeks and the Choctaws—were contiguous to Florida, and the two others—the Chickasaws and Cherokees—were adjoining. They were the most numerous and powerful tribes in the United States, and, from their position, were exposed to be acted on and excited against us from Florida. It was important that this state of things should terminate, which could only be done by obtaining the possession of Florida.

But there were other and powerful considerations for the acquisition. We had, a short time before, extinguished the Indian title to large tracts of country in Alabama, Mississippi, and Georgia, lying upon streams and rivers which passed through Florida to the gulf—lands in a great measure valueless, without the right of navigating them to their mouths. The acquisition of Florida gave us this right, and enabled us to bring into successful cultivation a great extent of fertile lands, which have added much to the increased production of our great staple, cotton. Another important point was effected by the acquisition: It terminated a very troublesome dispute with Spain, growing out of the capture of St. Marks and Pensacola by General [Andrew] Jackson, in the Seminole war; and, finally, it perfected our title to Oregon, by ceding to us whatever right Spain had to that territory.

Such is the treaty on which the Senator has lavished so much of his abuse; but there were other reasons for adopting the Sabine [River] as the boundary, and of which I was ignorant at the time the treaty was formed, and to the knowledge of which I have come within the last few years. Mr. Monroe, if I am correctly informed, in adopting that line acted under circumstances which left him little option. I am not at liberty to state them—the information I received confidentially. It is sufficient to state that he had ascertained that the Senate would not ratify a treaty with a boundary farther west. It was communicated to him by Senators of first respectability. Their reason for refusing to ratify a treaty which would extend the boundary beyond the Sabine, I do not choose to go into, although it was communicated to me with information to which I have alluded.

But if we take out of the speech of the Senator what he has stated in relation to annexation, and the Florida treaty, in which, as I have stated, he has but repeated old and stale charges, that made not the slightest impression on the country at the time, What is there left of his present attack upon me? It is surprising that a man of his experience and sagacity should suppose that the repetition of these threadbare charges, regarded as futile when first made, should make any impression now. Indeed, I may consider myself obliged to him for repeating them, after such elaborate preparation, as it affords the most conclusive proof how exempt my course has been from any just censure during the long period of time in which he has attempted to trace it.

To make good his allegation that I am the author of annexation, and that annexation caused the war, he asserts that I was in favor of the annexation of Texas as far back as 1836, immediately after the battle of San Jacinto, and the capture of [Antonio Lopez de] Santa An[n]a; to prove which, he read an extract from the speech [of 5/23/1836] which I delivered on resolutions from Mississippi, presented by her Senator, now Secretary of the Treasury [Robert J. Walker], instructing the Senators to obtain an immediate recognition of the independence of Texas.

It is true that I then advocated an early recognition of the independence of Texas, and its admission into this Union; but I was not alone in that, nor did I take a leading part in the discussion; the two most prominent advocates of her cause at that time were the Senator from Mississippi [Walker] and my then colleague [from S.C.], (Mr. [William C.] Preston); but they were seconded by a large portion of this body at the time. The distinguished Senator from Massachusetts [Daniel Webster] bore a part in the debate, and expressed his opinion in favor of recognition at an early period, and of the vast importance of the future condition of Texas to our country. I have not had time to examine the discussion; but find that I was among those who advised delay until further information could be obtained, and many were for prompt action; but the Senator from Missouri has thought proper, in the face of these facts, to hold me up as the only individual disposed for a prompt and immediate action. He has done more. He has suppressed the fact, very important to be known, that before the close of that very session the report of the Committee on Foreign Relations, recommending that the acknowledgment of the independence of Texas, as soon as satisfactory information could be obtained that it had successfully established a Government, was adopted by the unanimous vote of the Senate, including the Senator himself, and that at the very next session, her independence was recognised.

Sir, I admit, even at that early period, I saw that the incorporation of Texas into this Union, would be indispensable both to her safety and ours. I saw that it was impossible that she could stand as an independent power between us and Mexico, without becoming the scene of intrigue of foreign Powers, alike destructive of the peace and security of both Texas and ourselves. I saw more: I saw the bearing of the slave question at that early stage, and that it would become an instrument in the hands of a foreign Power of striking a blow at us, and that two conterminous slaveholding communities could not co-exist without one being wielded to the destruction of the other. The Senator is right. What I then said was intended to shadow forth the future, that future which actually came, when I was called, by the unanimous voice of the country, to take charge of the State Department, in reference to these very events. I saw, with General Jackson, that the golden opportunity had occurred when annexation must take place in order to avoid interminable difficulties and great disasters; and, seeing it, I did not hesitate to undertake the duty which had been assigned me, notwithstanding the difficulties, from the weakness of the Administration at that period. I succeeded, in despite of them, and that, too, without war; and all the elaborate efforts of the Senator from Missouri, never can deprive me of the credit to which I am entitled in reference to the great question of annexation.

On a review of the whole, my course, I may say, exhibits not only some foresight in reference to it, but also some powers of averting the dangers, and securing the end which I desired.

Every measure towards the accomplishment of annexation had been consummated before the present Administration came into power. No war followed, although the act of annexation had been completed more than a year before the rupture between us and Mexico took place; nor would war have followed at all, had we acted with ordinary prudence. That Mexico was chafed, chagrined; that she threatened much, and blustered much; talked about war and even the existence of hostilities—are all true. It was, however, but talk. The strong should always permit the weak and aggrieved to talk, to bluster, and scold, without taking offence: and if we had so acted, and exercised proper skill in the management of our affairs, Mexico and ourselves would by this time have quietly and peaceably settled all difficulties, and been good friends. We have chosen to pursue the opposite course, and are in war.

Every Senator knows that I was opposed to the war; but none knows but myself the depth of that opposition. With my conceptions of its character and consequences, it was impossible for me to vote for it. When, accordingly, I was deserted by every friend on this [Democratic] side of the House, including my then honorable colleague among the rest, (Mr. [George] McDuffie,) I was not shaken in the least degree in reference to my course. On the passage of the act recognising the war, I said to many of my friends that a deed had been done from which the country would not be able to recover for a long time, if ever; and added, it has dropped a curtain between the present and the future, which to me is impenetrable; and for the first time since I have been in public life, I am unable to see the future. I also added, that it has closed the first volume of our political history under the Constitution, and opened the second, and that no mortal could tell what would be written in it. These deep impressions were made upon my mind, because I saw, from the circumstances under which the war was made, a total departure from that course of policy which had governed the country from the commencement of our government until that time; and that, too, under circumstances calculated to lead to most disastrous consequences. Since then less than a year has elapsed; but in that short period enough has already been developed to make what was then said look like prophecy.

But the Senator charges, entertaining as I did these impressions, that I did not take a stand, and arrest the march of General Taylor to the Rio del Norte. I have already stated the reasons on another occasion why I did not; and however unsatisfactory they may be to the Senator, they are satisfactory to myself, and I doubt not they will be to the community at large. He also intimated that I ought to have communicated my views to the President. I was guilty of no neglect in that respect. I did not fail to state in the proper quarter explicitly what I thought would result from the order given to General Taylor, but I found very different views from mine entertained there. Those in power were quite as confident that the march of General Taylor to the Del Norte would not in its consequences involve war as they were that notice without compromise in reference to the joint occupancy of Oregon would not involve war with England.

In looking back upon these matters, I have the satisfaction to feel that I fully performed my duty both here and elsewhere with reference to these important questions.

With my view of the character and consequences of the war, I have forborne much. I have suffered not a little in the estimation of my friends, both in and out of Congress, for refusing to vote for the bill recognising the existence of a war asserted to be made by the act of Mexico. I have been urged by them to explain the reasons for my course on that occasion; but I persisted in declining to do so, because I could not see that it would be of any service to the country, while it might weaken the hands of those who are charged with the prosecution of the war. I adopted the only course which, according to my opinion, I could with propriety—to take no active or leading part in reference to measures intended for carrying on the war, but to give a quiet and silent vote in favor of all which did not seem to me decidedly objectionable; but, in the meantime, to look out for the first favorable opportunity of presenting my views how the war should be conducted to bring it most advantageously to a successful termination. I accordingly embraced the opportunity on the discussion of the three-million bill now before the Senate to present my views, not in the spirit of opposition, but of kindness to the Administration, reserving to myself the expression of my opinion as to the causes of the war for some suitable occasion. It seems, however, that the friends of those in power were not satisfied with this course on my part: it became an object of assault both in this Chamber and without its walls. The Senator from Tennessee immediately on my right (Mr. Turney) commenced the attack here by directly charging me with being the author of the war, and it has since been followed by the Senator from Missouri on this occasion. I have thus been forced, in self-defence, to depart from the line which I had prescribed for myself, and to enter into the question, Who is the author or the cause of the war? The responsibility is not on me, but on those who have compelled me to make the departure. Thus far I have limited what I have said strictly to self-defence, as I shall also do on the present occasion.

In looking to the causes which led to the war, I go one step further back than the Senator from Maine, (Mr. [George] Evans,) who discussed the subject in this aspect with great accuracy and ability. He began with Mr. [John] Slidell's mission and negotiation. I go a step further back, to the management of the negotiation prior to that period. When this Administration came into power there were two great questions on hand connected with our foreign relations—the Oregon and the Mexican. As different as they were in their character, and as remote as the two Powers were from each other, there was an intimate connexion between them which could not be overlooked in conducting the negotiation, without falling into a great and dangerous error. Such at least is my opinion. I wish to say nothing to wound the feelings of the distinguished individual [James Buchanan] who had charge of the negotiation, but it seems to me that he fell into a great error in consequence of overlooking this connexion between the two subjects. To my mind it is one of the clearest of propositions, that there could be no well-founded hope of adjusting our difficulties with Mexico until the Oregon question was finally settled. Why so? The reason is obvious. Mexico knew that we had heavy claims against her which she was little able to pay. Debtors without means are usually shy of their creditor. She could not but see that there was a chance of escaping our demands against her, provided a conflict should ensue between us and England in reference to Oregon. She could not but see more—that it might possibly afford her an opportunity of recovering either a part or the whole of Texas by an alliance with England, and availing herself of the aid of British strength and resources in waging a war against us. At all events, she would look with confidence to her being protected as an ally of England in the treaty by which the war should be terminated. Whatever objection may be made to England, she never deserts an ally in war. It seemed to me, under these circumstances, that it was a great error to suppose that the differences with Mexico could be adjusted while those with England were pending. Our true policy, then, according to my opinion, was to suspend all attempts at opening negotiation with Mexico until that question was finally settled. When that was effected, and Mexico could no longer look to the support of England in her controversy with us, she would see the folly of declining to adjust the differences between us, and enter[ing] into conflict with a Power every way so vastly her superior.

There would, then, be another advantage which would greatly favor a settlement of our difficulties with Mexico. The eloquent Senator from Louisiana [Pierre Soulé] has truly said that Mexico, at least so far as capital is concerned, was a British colony. The immense interest which England has in the country, would have inlisted her on the side of peace, and the whole of her vast influence would have been exerted to induce Mexico to enter into a satisfactory arrangement with us. I cannot doubt that, under the influence of these powerful causes, with a little forbearance and prudence on our part, all the causes of difference between the two countries would, ere this, have been settled by a treaty satisfactory to both.

An opposite course was, however, unfortunately taken; both negotiations were pushed at the same time, and that with Mexico, with as much zeal, and as strong a pressure, as that with England. The then President of the republic of Mexico ([José Joaquin] Herrera) was friendly to the United States, and anxiously disposed, on that account, as well as others, to settle the differences with us. Acting under these feelings, he acceded to the proposition to receive a commissioner, without duly reflecting, as the events proved, on these great impediments in the minds of the Mexicans against treating with us. The result was as might have been anticipated. [Mariano] Paredes took advantage of the error, and hurled Herrera from power; and the effect of this premature attempt at opening negotiation, was to overthrow a friend and place an enemy in power, deeply committed against settling the differences between the two countries, and thereby—as ought to have been foreseen—greatly to increase the difficulty of any future settlement of the questions. What followed from this unfortunate step, until it ended in war between the two countries, has been so clearly traced by the Senator from Maine, as to supersede the necessity of my touching upon it.

The overlooking of the intimate connexion of these two questions was not only the first link in that series of causes which finally terminated in this war, but it came near preventing the settlement of the Oregon question. Had the action of Congress, which finally led to the settlement of the Oregon question, been delayed until it was known that skirmishes had taken place between our forces and the Mexicans on the Rio Grande, (but a short period,) there is every reason to believe the Oregon question would not have been closed. I speak upon high authority—the escape was a narrow one.

Fortunately, the British Government promptly acted upon the notice, and tendered a proposition to our Minister on which the settlement was finally made, which he received and forwarded to our Government but a few days before news was received in England of the skirmishes on the Rio Grande. But while they fortunately occurred too late to prevent a settlement of the Oregon question, they unfortunately occurred too soon to preserve peace with Mexico. But if the policy which the Administration first adopted after annexation had been pursued, to occupy the frontier of Texas with our military forces to the extent of country which she held at the time of annexation, and no further, there is every reason to believe that on the settlement of the Oregon question the peace of the two countries would have been preserved.

It is true Mexico claimed the whole of Texas; but it is equally true that she recognised the difference, and showed a disposition to act upon it, between the country known as Texas proper and the country between it and the Del Norte. It is also true that we and Texas recognised the same difference, and that both regarded the boundary as unsettled, as the resolution of annexation, which provides that the boundary between Texas and Mexico shall be determined by the United States, clearly shows. It is worthy of remark in this connexion, that this provision in the joint resolution is understood to have been inserted in consequence of the ground taken at the preceding session by the Senator from Missouri on the discussion of the treaty, that the Nueces [River] was the western boundary of Texas, and that to extend that boundary to the Rio del Norte would take in part of Tamaulipas, Coahuila, and New Mexico. What, then, ought to have been the course of the Executive after annexation under this resolution? The very one which they at first pursued—to restrict the position of our troops to the country actually occupied by Texas at the period of annexation. All beyond, as far as the Executive was concerned, ought to have been regarded as subject to the provisions of the resolutions, which authorized the Government to settle the boundary. There are but two modes of settling a disputed boundary—one by the joint consent of both parties, that is, by treaty, of which the President and the Senate are the organs; the other, by the determination of one of the parties for itself, after failing to obtain the consent of the other, and that, under our Government, can only be done by Congress. Indeed, when we speak of our Government, it is understood to mean Congress and the Executive, acting jointly— the one by passing an act or resolution, and the other by its approval. And in Congress, taken in this sense, all discretionary power under our system of Government is invested. It is only by this power that a disputed boundary can be determined by the Government for itself, and without the consent of the other party. The President had no more right to determine on his own will what the boundary was than I had, or any other Senator. Such, indeed, appeared to be the conviction of the President himself. It is only on such a supposition that we can explain his course in attempting to open a negotiation with Mexico, with a view of settling all differences between the two countries, among which the settlement of the boundary was considered a paramount question. Why negotiate, if it were not an unsettled question? Why negotiate, if the Rio del Norte—is, as it was afterwards assumed—was the clear and unquestionable boundary? And if not, upon what authority, after the attempt to open negotiation had failed, could he determine what was the boundary, viewing it as an open question? Was it not his plain duty, on such an occurrence to submit the question to Congress, which was then in session, and in whom the right of establishing the boundary and declaring war was clearly invested? Had that course been adopted, I greatly mistake if the sense of this body would not have been decidedly opposed to taking any step which would have involved the two countries in war. Indeed, I feel a strong conviction, that if the Senate had been left free to decide on the question, not one-third of the body would have been found in favor of war. As it was, a large majority felt themselves compelled, as they believed, to vote for the bill recognising the existence of war, in order to raise the supplies of men and money necessary to rescue the army under General Taylor, on the Del Norte, from the dangers to which it was exposed.

But to bring the matter home, the Senator himself is in no small degree responsible for the war. I intend no attack on him. I have made none, and will make none. The relations between him and myself, personal and political, have long been such, that self-respect and a sense of propriety forbid my alluding to him, except when unavoidable, and then in a courteous manner; and I now allude to his course only because it is necessary to explain mine, and the motives which governed me on the occasion.

The Senate will remember, that when the President's message was received recommending Congress to recognise that a war existed between us and Mexico, and to raise the necessary means for its prosecution, the Senator from Mississippi, whose seat is immediately on my right, but who is now absent, (Mr. [Jesse] Speight,) moved to print twenty thousand copies of the message and documents. The scene was a solemn one, and what occurred will long be remembered by the members of the body. I rose and objected; and said that we were on the eve of great events, and expressed my hope that we would proceed calmly and deliberately. I suggested that the printing of so large a number of copies would be construed into an endorsement of the message; adding, that I was unwilling either to endorse or condemn, until the message and documents were printed, and carefully perused by me. A debate ensued, and the Journals of the Senate will show what took place. The Senator from Missouri was the individual who made the discreet and appropriate motion to separate the recommendations of the message into two parts, and refer that which related to recognising the existence of war to the Committee on Foreign Relations, and that which related to the raising of men and supplies, to the Committee on Military Affairs, of which he was chairman. The latter, it was expected, would report immediate measures for the support of General Taylor. I seconded the motion, and it was carried by a large majority. I saw in it that which gave me hope, and that I should be able to effect the object I had in view, and which I will hereafter explain.

The House of Representatives acted with much more precipitancy; it passed a bill the very day the message was received, recognising the existence of the war, and providing means for its prosecution. It was late in the evening when it passed the House, and I am of the impression that the Senate had adjourned; and it was not reported to it that day; but be that as it may, the next day the Senator, as chairman of the Committee on Military Affairs, reported the bill to the Senate as it came from the House, with both provisions in it; directly contrary to the order of the Senate, made on his own motion, to refer the part of the message relating to the recognition of war to the Committee on Foreign Relations. To that, and the fact that a caucus had been held of the party which agreed to sustain the report, may be traced the precipitate (to use no stronger word) action of the Senate, and the recognition of the war. It emphatically made the war. Had the order of the Senate been respected—had the Senator from Missouri, in conformity with it, and as he was in duty bound to do, moved to strike out all that related to the recognition of the war, and referred it to the Committee on Foreign Relations, and confined his report to raising the necessary means of rescuing General Taylor and his army from the pressing dangers which surrounded them, the possibility is, that the war might have been averted, and the two countries at this day have been at peace. Sir, I say possibility, because, even then, after the skirmishes between our forces had occurred, I did not despair of escaping war, if sufficient firmness and prudence were used on the part of this body. I had deeply reflected on the subject in advance, and great as were the difficulties, I still saw a gleam of hope.

The intelligence of the skirmishes on the Rio Grande was received here on Saturday. I at once saw the danger, and turned my mind to the subject. I anticipated that a message would be received on Monday from the Executive, and formed not an incorrect opinion as to what would be its character. Casting my eyes over the whole, with a view of avoiding war, I came to the conclusion in my own mind, what course was best to effect that object. Next morning I communicated the conclusions to which I had come to two of my colleagues, who were boarding with me; I said to them, that there was but one way of escaping war, but I am not certain that it would be successful. It will, however, place us in the chapter of accidents, and thereby afford a possibility of escape. I was asked what it was, and replied, that it depended on separating the question of war from that which relates to the rescuing of General Taylor and his forces. Let the means necessary for the latter be immediately granted, but let time be taken for due and deliberate consideration of the former. Had that been done, it was my intention to throw my whole weight against the immediate declaration or recognition of war; treating what had occurred as mere hostilities between the two armies, without authority of the Congress—the war making power of either Government.

We had not a particle of evidence then, or even now, that the Republic of Mexico had made war against the United States. Indeed, we are in the anomalous condition of the two countries being at war during and [*sic*] almost an entire year, without either having declared it, although the constitutions of both expressly provide that Congress shall declare war.

Instead, then, of recognising war, I would have taken the very opposite ground—that what had occurred was mere hostilities, and not war, as the Congress of Mexico had not authorized it.

To provide for the contingency of the Congress of Mexico approving of what had occurred, and refusing to treat for the settlement of our difficulties, I would have advised the raising of ample provisional force, to be collected at some convenient and healthy point, where they could be trained during the interval, and be fully prepared to meet such decision; but even in case such decision should be made, instead of advising a formal declaration of war, I would have advised, as General Jackson recommended, giving authority to the Executive to make reprisals for seizing and holding such portion of the Mexican territory as would afford ample indemnity, to be retained until the differences between the two countries were settled; but, in the meantime, would have taken measures to repel the attacks made upon our army by the Mexican forces, and to drive them far beyond the limits of our borders.

Had this course been pursued, we should have had all the glory and reputation of the two brilliant victories at Palo Alto and Resaca de la Palma without being involved in the present indefinite and expensive war waged against Mexico. We would also have had the advantage of the chapter of accidents—of Mexico disavowing hostilities, and indemnifying our citizens—either from a sense of weakness, or of returning justice on her part, or from the influence of other Powers, which have an interest in preserving peace, from their commercial or other relations with her, and thereby save a resort to arms on our part. But, at all events, failing in that, we would have avoided, by resorting to reprisals, the enormous expenses, the sacrifice of men and money, and the disasters to which the war has exposed us. I have now met, and, I trust, successfully repelled, all the charges made by the Senator from Missouri, except those relating to the Missouri compromise, and the abolition question of that period, for which I am in no ways responsible. I was not then in Congress. I filled the office of Secretary of War at the time, and had no agency or control over it. His charges are as light as air—old and stale, without even plausibility, and I have not the slightest fear of their having any weight, either here or in the community.

From *Congressional Globe*, 29th Cong., 2nd Sess., pp. 498–501. Also printed in the Washington, D.C., *Daily Union*, February 27, 1847, p. 1; the Alexandria, Va., *Gazette and Virginia Advertiser*, March 2, 1847, p. 2; the New York, N.Y., *Herald*, March 2, 1847, p. 1; the Charleston, S.C., *Mercury*, March 4, 1847, p. 2; the Columbia, S.C., *Southern Chronicle*, March 10, 1847, p. 1; the Edgefield, S.C., *Advertiser*, March 17, 1847, pp. 1–2; the Huntsville, Ala., *Democrat*, March 17, 1847, pp. 2–3; the Washington, D.C., *Daily National Intelligencer*, April 1, 1847, p. 2; *Speech of Mr. Calhoun, of South Carolina, in Reply to Mr. Benton, of Missouri. Delivered in the Senate of the United States, February 24, 1847* (Washington: printed by John T. Towers, 1847); Benton, *Abridgment of Debates*, 16:96–103; Crallé, ed., *Works*, 4:362–382. Variants in the Washington, D.C., *Daily National Intelligencer*, February 25, 1847, p. 2; the Alexandria, Va., *Gazette and Virginia Advertiser*, February 25, 1847, p. 3; the New York, N.Y., *Herald*, February 25, 1847, p. 4, and February 26, 1847, p. 4; the Charleston, S.C., *Mercury*, March 1, 1847, p. 2; the Cincinnati, Ohio, *Daily Enquirer*, March 1, 1847, p. 2; the Charleston, S.C., *Courier*, March 1, 1847, p. 2; the Greenville, S.C., *Mountaineer*, March 5, 1847, p. 3. NOTE: The New York, N.Y., *Mirror*, March 13, 1847, contains a long and colorful discussion of the Calhoun-Benton conflict at this time.

From R[OBERT] F. W. ALLSTON

Matanza near
Georgetown So. Ca., 25th Feb. 1847

My Dear Sir, In the absence of a public meeting (one of the right sort is not easy to get up here, & they are apt to be perverted too to some other purpose; there are, in little Georgetown a great many yankees) I have confer[re]d with many of my neighbors at social meetings, and am happy to be able to offer you, with my own, their common congratulations on your course of conduct in the debate on the "3 million bill" and in that more personal one which succeeded it; I allude to the attack made by the Senator from Tenn. [Hopkins L. Turney].

In the course of your remarks on this latter occasion, you said what I have long wish[e]d you could proclaim for yourself in connection with the canvass for chief magistrate. Never can a citizen of So. Carolina occupy the post of President without resorting to truckling & intrigue, and I trust in God, I may not live to see one of our old party do that. Your sentiments express[e]d on this occasion together with the developements then made, must place you on higher ground than ever before the thinking & reflecting public. I glory in this! I can understand it. I feel it all—and from my heart, I tender you the sincerest sympathy of an humble individual.

Whilst talking over this with my friends I received the paper containing your Resolutions (brought forth by the action of the House on the "Wilmot proviso") and your remarks [of 2/19] on presenting them. With one consent my friends pronounced "Well done! good & faithful servant."

The action you propose will embarrass many an aspirant & many an opponent. I see how Mr. [Thomas H.] Benton is gall[e]d by it, he is not ready for such a question! But you have chosen, doubtless, the proper time. If such is to be the determination of Congress, let us know & sound the alarm. Let the question with all its responsibilities—with all its ultimate tendencies be met by us—twere folly, worse, to avert our eyes, when danger is nigh. The better course, the more manly, & the safer is to look it full in the face, and meet it calmly & firmly, with all our faculties about us—if overcome, we have but fallen in the path of duty—and the longest & most brilliant & successful career, can terminate in no end more successful, more satisfactory or more noble.

I trust our delegation will act unitedly and with the utmost harmony. I warn[e]d your colleague [Andrew P. Butler] & J[ames]

A. Black [Representative from S.C.] of this before they left Columbia. [Isaac E.] Holmes' impulses are noble but he is rash & indiscreet. Black is politic ["but very efficient & untiring" *interlined*]—
but you know them all. Excuse me my Dear Sir, for presuming to
write to you thus. But my anxiety, impels me, that you should not
be foil[e]d in any one step that you may find it necessary or expedient to take.

[*One word changed to* "Conveying"] to you, as I am happy to
do, the approbation of us all as to the bold & plain manner in which
you have treated the question of our institutions under the Constitution, as well as the question, to us all important, of our relative
strength, in the scale of the Union, my reflections on this subject, in
the midst of a careful & very active planter[']s life, have for the two
last years caused me much disquietude, & I have found it impossible
to shut out sometimes a sad foreboding. But you are the only human
being to whom I have said as much. With best wishes for your
health & success, I am very Respectfully, R.F.W. Allston.

ALS in ScCleA.

Amendment to the civil and diplomatic appropriation bill, 2/25.
"Mr. Calhoun moved to amend the amendment by making an appro-
priation of $30,000 for the erection of a custom-house at Charleston."
This amendment was agreed to, and Calhoun made further unre-
ported remarks in opposition to another amendment to the bill, which
would refund certain sums to the public printers Thomas Ritchie and
John P. Heiss. From the Washington, D.C., *Daily Union*, February
26, 1847, p. 2. Variant in *Congressional Globe*, 29th Cong., 2nd
Sess., p. 506; the Washington, D.C., *Daily National Intelligencer*,
February 26, 1847, p. 2.

To [William W. Corcoran, Washington, *ca.* 2/25/1847?]. "I
regret exceedingly that owing to a severe indisposition on the part
of Mr. [Armistead] Burt [Representative from S.C.] and an engagement connected with my official duties, it will not be in his or my
power to dine with you today." ALS in DLC, William Wilson
Corcoran Papers.

From THO[MA]S FITNAM

Washington, Feb. 24 [*sic*; 25?] 1847

Sir, Permit me to say, that the premeditated attack of Senator [Thomas H.] Benton upon you yesterday [*sic*] in the Senate, was, in my opinion, an utter failure. Such, too, was the impression of all the Reporters with whom I conversed at the time on the subject.

I will not make any remark upon the *impropriety* of Mr. [James K.] Polk's Cabinet backing Mr. Benton up by their presence at such a moment; public opinion will set that matter right in the proper way. *I think it has already done so here.*

If you will allow me to say a word on the course you ought now to adopt towards the administration—and it is but the echo of universal public sentiment, you should, without delay, *this session,* flagellate them with ["out" *interlined*] mercy. It requires but a very slight touch to turn the whole batch of *imbeciles* over into that everlasting oblivion, from whence they ought never to have been taken. Benton has broken his own neck, and in his fall, has dragged the *Cabinet conspirators* down, down to his own unmanly level, where they are now floundering in the mire of their own making. There let them stay, if you be not disposed to act upon the hint, that I have thrown out above.

They are like, in their relation to public affairs, to use some of my own doggerel,

When *asses* meet upon the self-same plain,
Which *nobler* beasts have tried to reach in vain;
Prick up their ears, and antic capers cut,
And *common sense* without the pale of wisdom put.

I have the honor to be, Sir your Ob[edien]t Servant, Thos. Fitnam.

ALS with En in ScCleA. NOTE: Enclosed is a ms. extract in Fitnam's hand from Benton's speech of 6/12/1844 in which Benton criticizes the President's [John Tyler's] stated intention of allowing Mexico "ample recompense" for any "loss she might sustain" as a result of a U.S.-Texas treaty. Fitnam notes: "I would like to learn if Mr. Benton intends to *pay* Mexico for her territory *before* any treaty be made between her and the United States?"

Remarks on his resolutions, 2/25. "Mr. Calhoun rose to call up the resolutions submitted by him some days since, and which he gave notice yesterday he should ask for the consideration of during the morning hour to-day." George Evans of Maine pleaded that the morning was needed to complete amendments to the civil and diplomatic appropriation bill. "Mr. Calhoun then waived his motion for

the present, giving notice, however, that he should call up the resolutions after the Senator from Massachusetts (Mr. [John] Davis)
should get through, or during the morning hour to-morrow." From
Congressional Globe, 29th Cong., 2nd Sess., p. 505. Also printed in
the Washington, D.C., *Daily National Intelligencer,* February 26,
1847, p. 2. Variant in the Washington, D.C., *Daily Union,* February 26, 1847, p. 2. [Later in the day's proceedings Calhoun once
more waived his motion at the request of Edward A. Hannegan of
Ind. *Congressional Globe,* 29th Cong., 2nd Sess., p. 509.]

Remarks in reply to John Davis of Mass., 2/25. Several times
during a speech by Davis on the "three million bill," Calhoun interjected comments. "Mr. Calhoun begged to correct the honorable
Senator. So far as he was concerned, he had never said that annexation was the cause of the war." Later, Calhoun said: "It may have
been the occasion of the war, but not the cause." Still later, in reference to the Wilmot Proviso, Calhoun said: "his impression (if the
Senator would allow him to interrupt him for a moment) was, that,
if slavery was abolished in that territory, it would be abolished in all
the States." From *Congressional Globe,* 29th Cong., 2nd Sess., p.
506. Also printed in the Washington, D.C., *Daily National Intelligencer,* February 26, 1847, p. 2. Variant in *Congressional Globe,*
29th Cong., 2nd Sess., Appendix, pp. 416–417.

From R[ICHARD] K. CRALLÉ

Lynchburg [Va.,] Feb[ruar]y 26th 1847
My dear Sir: I thank you for a copy of your Speech [of 2/9] on the
Three Million Bill, which I have read with much satisfaction. The
substance of your remarks on the Resolutions on Saturday last [2/20],
has also reached us, and much interest is felt in regard to your expected speech on Monday last. I have rarely seen more anxiety
than exhibits itself amongst the masses, and we have reached a turning point in public affairs. The late meeting here, called by the
Hunkers for the express purpose of condem[n]ing you numbered
only 25, out of a population of 7,000. It has done more good than the
managers contemplated; and I think will recoil on them with great
force. Another meeting is contemplated next week, though not absolutely determined on. One good effect of the vote has been to
separate your friends entirely from the Plunderers; and if I am not

deceived the consequences will be felt in the coming elections. We are firm and unshaken as you may see from the Richmond proceedings. The organization of an independent Party is what I have long desired; and I should not be surprised to see this result throughout the State. I am not, however, certain. Your friends have been so long accustomed to yield, that mere habitude may possibly operate as a law. I hope not, however; and rejoice at the prospect of a separate and independent organization. This seems to me the only ground left for honest and patriotic men; and I am grossly deceived if the opinion do not gain ground with the reflecting of both sides. I have already heard that the Whig Candidate for Congress in the District, (Mr. [Henry P.] Irving) one of your old friends, has openly taken grounds in your defence [*ms. torn*; His?] brother [Joseph K. Irving] the former opponent of the Democratic candidate—and a man of much influence, is warmly enlisted in the cause. He was of the Nullifyers in 1832; and in a conversation to day I find him as he was in better times. From various other quarters of the District I hear favourable accounts. Whigs, as well as Democrats, are much excited; and though I am not confident in regard to [Thomas S.] Bocock, who is the candidate in the place of [Edmund W.] Hubard, I, by no means despair that he will take a satisfactory position. He will be with me next week; and I can then better ascertain his purposes.

But as to the main point. We have come to a *direct issue.* The administration is openly against you, as I long ago anticipated—as I told you would be the case before you returned to the Senate. They leave you no other ground but open opposition in return. It seems to me you have nothing to do but to defend the position you have taken, regardless of consequences. On the grounds assumed in your resolutions, you can *command* the entire South. Press them to the last extremity. Yield not one jot or tittle. I do not doubt the result so far as the public sentiment is concerned. If the proviso be not stricken out, it is, of course, expected that you will vote against the Bill. We look with great interest for to-night's mail, as we expect to hear what is the result of Monday's discussion. I reserve a portion of my paper for tomorrow, after we shall have heard of the result. I write now in great haste, and hardly intelligibly. By all means, if you can find a moment of leisure, let me hear from you before you leave the City. We had a private meeting to-day in reference to the establishment of a Press here—the present one having sided with the Hunkers [it] can, I hope, succeed.

Sunday 28 Feb[ruar]y '47

The failure of the mails leaves us in entire ignorance as to the fate of your Resolutions, and the course which certain Senators have taken. I hope you will succeed in getting a direct vote upon them, tho' I doubt it, especially if the Whigs be anxious to give it the go-by. At all events you have nothing to fear from pressing them to the utmost. The subject is becoming every day more and more the topic of political circles.

Let me hear from you before you leave the city. With the highest regard & esteem yours truly, R.K. Crallé.

ALS in ScCleA.

From F[RANKLIN] H. ELMORE

Charleston, Feb[ruar]y 26, 1847

My Dear Sir, I wrote to you some time ago in regard to an arrangement which was proposed for the Southern [Quarterly] Review. It was sprung on us at a moment, which required *immediate action.* We had no time to consult as to what was best or to learn the views of our friends. Not hearing from you, I do not know how far it has met your opinions. I trust—indeed I feel assured the change has not been in any respect without advantage & in some greatly for the better.

Mr. [Robert] James one of the new Proprietors goes to Washington to see & confer with the friends of the work. He desires to do so with you especially & I have given him a letter of introduction which he will deliver to you on his arrival. He leaves today or tomorrow.

We are looking with intense interest at the course of events at Washington. I have heard a good deal said in regard to your course—on the war & its mode of being conducted the principles are approved & the details in the main agreed to. Your resolutions & speeches upon them have the undivided approval I think of the people. I do not think I have ever seen you sustain yourself with more power.

I write in the utmost haste in Bank [of the State of S.C.] & in the midst of business, to apprise you of the move for the Review & of Mr. James['s] intended visit. Mr. [Robert Barnwell] Rhett [Representative from S.C.] can probably inform you of the particulars in case you desire more information. I am My Dear Sir yo[ur]s truly, F.H. Elmore.

P.S. The new Editor of the Mercury [John E. Carew] feeling a fear of these new questions or rather of his own inexperience, applied to me to aid him. I wrote two or three of his headers on the Resolutions &c. Pray say if the course we took was such as to satisfy you.

ALS in ScCleA.

Remarks on the proposal to compensate further the public printers Thomas Ritchie and John P. Heiss, 2/26. "Mr. Calhoun thought there was a material difference in the position which these printers occupied in relation to the Senate, and that in which they stood with regard to the House. He would therefore vote for the motion to strike out the words relating to the Senate." From *Congressional Globe*, 29th Cong., 2nd Sess., p. 514.

Remarks on compensation to Texas, 2/26. Thomas J. Rusk of Tex. offered an amendment to the civil and diplomatic appropriation bill to pay $70,000 to the State of Texas for certain long-standing claims for U.S. infringements on a Texas Republic military force and customs house. "Mr. Calhoun thought that the claim at least for the restitution or payments for the arms seized, was a fair one." From the New York, N.Y., *Herald*, February 28, 1847, p. 4.

Remarks on his resolutions, 2/26. "Mr. Calhoun remarked, that if the honorable Senator from Massachusetts [Daniel Webster] was not desirous of being heard to-day upon the subject of the resolutions, he would not call them up; but if he were desirous of doing so, he would feel it his duty to insist upon the resolutions being taken up in accordance with the arrangement which was made yesterday. He would be governed altogether by the wishes of the Senator." Webster replied, and Calhoun asked: "I understand the Senator from Massachusetts as not being desirous of proceeding with his remarks?" Webster assented, and other Senators pressed other business. From *Congressional Globe*, 29th Cong., 2nd Sess., p. 517. Also printed in the Washington, D.C., *Daily National Intelligencer*, February 27, 1847, p. 2. Variant in the New York, N.Y., *Herald*, February 28, 1847, p. 4.

From ALFRED SHUCKING, "Private"

Washington, Febr[uary] 26 1847
Dear Sir: Permit me to interrupt for a moment your highly valuable time, for my own satisfaction.

I have made it a pleasure to render into German (with but few transitions, it fills 16 pages) your speech of the 9th inst., which you were kind enough to hand me in pamphlet form, for the "Weser-zeitung" at Bremen, a very liberal paper and in consequence inter-dicted in Prussia, but so much the more sought after. Things that are printed in Germany are of much more effect when they are read here, than what is published in partizan papers here—and rightfully so, because they generally take an independent view. Besides I wished to make it apoint [*sic*], to explain to the German people (and their intelligent character deserves respectful appeal) on this occasion of the war and the [Thomas] Ritchie incident—your own elevated position and its bearing *conservative* of the Union & Con-stitution—that in fact the South, the more it is pressed upon and the more strongly it resists, becomes the more firmly the conservative *keystone* of these States united.

I have found my enthusiasm for men in many instances very quickly cool down, as time revealed common inconsistencies & foibles. With regard to you it has risen in the same degree, as vulgar clamor was loud against you—and I have come out triumphant (though irresistibly) out of the last trial—the Ritchie question. If I have become more indoctrinated in the spirit of your public life, it is because I have been more attracted by it and because I admire greatness, boldness, independence & originality wherever I find it. These are the features which, in whatever manner, humble or high, exhibited, assimilate man to his divine Prototype—all inculcated, authoritative, imitated action levels him to his other relationship—the Orang-Outang.

Like every great & philosophic mind you are too far above and in advance of the average intelligence of what is called the "people" (that is those, who are influenced by the caucusing wire-pullers) to be appreciated, or even remotely understood by the *mass*—witness the successful *palming off* for an attack on the liberty of the press (by you! who incurred the fierce assaults of another administration [that of John Quincy Adams] by vindicating the liberty of speech!) of a simple *State-rights castigation* upon a usurping executive editor. You who would long ago have been called to preside, by acclama-tion, in a highly intellectual nation—such as perhaps the German, will, I fear, never be made President by the *multitude*. My aspirations for the glory of these United States would be crowned with seeing you at the head of them. I would desire ["not" *changed to* "no"] more, and be contented to use language similar to that of Simeon in the bible.

I have also drawn from your speech, in which ["historical" *interlined*] reference is made to the *federal*, & not *national*, institution of this government.

I should feel greatly honored & obliged to receive copies of all your speeches, printed in pamphlet form. I am sorry to find that most of the German papers totally misconceive & misconstrue your position & bearing. They too do not *understand* you—and it would be desirable, that they should be furnished with your speeches in extenso, so as to inform themselves of your true policy. I take the liberty to enclose a list of the principal papers. A copy of the Bremen paper I shall do myself the honor to send you, when I receive it.

I should apologize for the liberty of my language towards you, if *I* had ever seen reason to take you to be an enemy of it. On this subject I had proposed to write for the Intelligencer one or two philippics under the signature of "Onslow *Jr.*" in which in particular I intended to draw a parallel betw[een] your position in the Ritchie affair and the [John] Randolph question—but I, wisely I suppose, distrusted my powers for so high a flight and the announcement of the Editors, that they declined to publish articles on the subject, fully prevented me. I am, Sir, with sincere & unfeigned admiration Your obed[ien]t Serv[an]t, Alfred Shucking.

ALS in ScCleA.

From S. W. DALTON

N. Orleans, Feb[ruar]y 27th [18]47

Dear Sir, I need not say, that as a preeminent American Statesman, I have long and intimately known John C. Calhoun. But until the winter of 1833–4, I had not the honor of your personal acquaintance, nor seen you since, except as you passed through this place on your way to the National Convention at Memphis, Tenn.; when, with many of your friends, I called to pay my respects to you personally, as well as for the distinguished services which your genius and talents have rendered our common country. On this occasion, you favoured me

219

with an interview and your opinion on the subject of the practicability of the American Party—you may not recollect either the occasion or myself, but the expression of your opinion I have not forgotten. You at once pronounced the project of a third party, a political impracticability; and added that the Federal and State Rights parties, would always and exclusively divide the American people: meaning thereby, as I understood you, the two old political parties, Whigs and Locofocos, that have long distracted and dangerously divided the great American family. At that time, as you may perhaps remember, an effort was making in this State to organize the American Party—not Native American, with which I was then, and had been for some time, identified; being long since convinced, and by late events, satisfied that the detestible and distructive party strife of whiggery and locofocoism would lead to consequences, from their desperate schemes for President-making, the most startling and dangerous to the peace, the honor, if not the integrity of the Union!

To avert from our beloved country, these fearful consequences with which it is now threatened, to an alarming degree, the great collective body of the *American people*, should at once rise up in their majesty and power, so long abused—and crush the monster Party, as it now exists. The blood and treasure, the *honor* and *glory* of the Nation demand it. The orphan[']s cries, the widow[']s tears, an aged father and mother's anguish, will long deplore the present consequences, the curse of Party. History will weep over its innocent victims who have already or may yet fall, gallantly fighting its battles, and record in letters of blood, the curse of party.

Sir I believe that the time has arrived when the American people are waking up to a fearful apprehension of the national curse of Party; that they are not only ready but *willing*, in a most exemplary and indignant manner, to rebuke its rampant spirit. Why Sir, the very name of party is odious and disgusting to the good and intelligent citizens of New Orleans: It stinks in their nostrils ["like" *canceled and* "as doth" *interlined*] the smoke of a candle that is blown out. True, there are some, such as you may see, whose names are attached to a call for a meeting, to night, in the locofoco papers of our city, for the purpose of expressing *their indignation* at the expulsion of [Thomas] Ri[t]chie and general conduct of the United States Senate!! Men Sir without influence or any weight of character. One an overseer of the streets, another an irish drayman, a third a drunkin irish pettifogger &c men who would sacrifice every thing for party and the crum[b]s which fall from their master[']s table. But sir, they are not the people, nor will that meeting, express the voice of the people of this place. Here and elsewhere, the *American people*, the *true democracy of this country*, the *sensible lovers* of her *honor* her *institutions* and her *prosperity*, begin to see and feel the force and truthfulness of your independent and noble position on the important subject of our war, or rather the President's [James K. Polk's] war with Mexico. They begin to see through the mist, the vail which hitherto has concealed, or left to inference, the object of the vigorous prosecution of the President[']s war with Mexico: a war from the further prosecution of which, he and his partizans would at this moment be glad to escape if they could in anywise justify themselves before the people in the short sighted and miserable policy which brought it on, and has continued it up to the present time. They know it cannot be, and they have not the magnanimity and moral courage to acknowledge their blunder. They would rather sacrifice the lives of our countrymen, exhaust our treasury and jeopard the national honor, than submit to the degradation and shame, to which a candid confession of their political crimes and sinister objects, would necessarily subject them, before the American people. Either horn of the dilemma is fatal to the locofoco succession to the presidency. If they go forward to conquer peace, or "war" with Mexico, the consequences must be disasterous to the Party; if they ingloriously fall back upon the Rio Grande, as laid down by yourself, clear and convincing as "words of holy writ", though it would be a fortunate event for the country and must eventually take place, yet it would be equally fatal to the party, thus driven to such an alternative. To a statesman of your political sagacity it were idle if not presumptious [*sic*] in me, to say, that a crisis is at hand in the organization of political parties among us. They must and will be dissolved. The people need not go Washington City to be convinced, as Mr. [James D.] Westcott [Jr., Senator from Fla.] plainly tells them, "of the firulent [*sic*] reeking corruption of this administration," that the institutions of their country "are used, but as a machine to plunder them for the benefit of office beggars"— the tainted streams from the fountain head of party have searched every portion of the Country: spreading the bitter waters of party strife and discord every where—and into these streams the people will find it much more convenient to "tumble the President and heads of departments, head over heels,["] than into the Potomac. And will do it. They only want a man of the people and not of a party, to accomplish this, a man of elevated character, talents and patriotism. And now Sir permit me, an humble individual, to say to you without flatary [*sic*], that when I read your late speech in the U.S.

Senate, in which you so nobly denounce party and its detestable schemes for president-making, declaring "that you would not turn upon your heel" to be president of the U.S. as they have been made for several years past, that if at all it must come from the people and not a party—a noble American Sentiment—I, in an instant, felt an instinctive conviction that to you Sir the American must and would look for their next president, and for reasons already alluded to, I believe that by being properly brought before them, as the People's candidate, you must succeed against all caucus or party candidates that may oppose you for the next presidency—a station for which you are so eminently qualified.

I presume your personal and intimate friends here and elsewhere are, or should be already moving in this behalf, therefore, as comparatively a stranger, I forbear making any suggestions, but rather beg that you will excuse the liberty, which in the sincerity of my heart, I have thus taken, in addressing you this long and uninteresting letter, and believe me to be most sincerely Your humble Servant, S.W. Dalton, M.D.

P.S. Reference Hon. Henry Johnson U.S. S[enator from La.]
" [Isaac] E. Morse H[ouse of] R[epresentatives]
" S[eth] Barton U.S. Solicitor.
Should any thing transpire to night worthy your attention I may trouble again.

ALS in ScCleA. NOTE: An AEU by Calhoun reads "Mr. Dutton."

From Jos[eph] W. Lesesne

Mobile, Feb[ruar]y 27th 1847
Dear Sir, I have taken the liberty of enclosing you to day an article signed "Vindicator." I hope it will afford some evidence that you will always have friends who appreciate your motives and are never more ready to make sacrifices for you than when party proscription is the penalty they pay for it.

The article was hastily prepared; and moderate as its tone and language is, I could only smuggle it into the paper [the Mobile *Register*?] through the aid of another devoted friend who ["fathered" *canceled*] stood fairly with one of the Editors and was kind enough to father it for me.

Our poor Southern States have no voice *at home*. Our News papers controlled by narrow minded yankees speak only the sentiments of northern men. This is a great misfortune and has done and is doing more to ruin the South than all other causes combined.

Your friends here feel no further anxiety on your account, than that you should be able amidst the "whips and stings of fortune"— the most difficult and trying circumstances in which you are placed to preserve that calm self possessed temper which up to this time has given such advantage to your position. Your moderation in replying to the vulgar assault made on you has taken your opponents by surprise; but they expect a *scene* with Mr. [Thomas H.] Benton. I hope you will disappoint them. Believe me, sir, your fame is beyond their malice. You may be pained, mortified and vexed at these things. But they are harmless and will pass away like the names of their authors. No good man ["who" *canceled*] who ever had confidence in you has had it at all shaken by recent events.

Our policy is to keep ourselves as far as we can from being suspected of having any ["party" *canceled*] interested views for you. I am sure we have not—none that you yourself would not avow. The Presidency at present is certainly not an object of Ambition to any great or good mind. And ["if" *interlined*] this ["is" *canceled*] the miserable "Phantom" which these men invoke perpetually ["impair" *canceled and* "invoke" *interlined; sic*] break the force of your talents and impair the value of your noble exertions for the public ["as it must be in" *canceled*] were half as frightful to them as it must be indifferent to you they would be the first to shun allusion to it. No man I fear will ever again be President of the United States who is not a mere party tool, unless some violent change in the moral constitution of both the great parties in the Country should take place. To me the future of our country looks very dark and gloomy. I fear we have become frightfully corrupt as a peoples [*sic*]. The operations of Banks, the pernicious influence of the Bankrupt Law—the influence of a legislative sanction of bad faith—and ["the long practice and popular approval of" *interlined*] "the spoils maxim" by both the political parties that divide us, have all conspired to ["render" *canceled*] bring public and private morals to the lowest state of degradation. Time, possibly, may cure the evil. But in Republics the downward tendency of the popular mind once decidedly given is seldom arrested. Very truly your f[rien]d &c, Jos. W. Lesesne.

ALS in ScCleA.

Petition of James Miller, presented by Calhoun to the Senate on 2/27. The legal representatives of Miller & Robinson, Charleston merchants, asked indemnity for French spoliations prior to 1800. The petition was tabled. Abs in *Senate Journal*, 29th Cong., 2nd Sess., p. 234.

Remarks on the Post Office appropriation bill, 2/27. "Mr. Calhoun said he should vote in favor of the motion" [to restrict the patronage power of Deputy Postmasters in selecting newspapers for advertising]. From *Congressional Globe*, 29th Cong., 2nd Sess., p. 528.

Remarks on further compensation to public printers Thomas Ritchie and John P. Heiss, 2/27. "Mr. Calhoun, on account of a [previous] pledge from Ritchie and Heiss, to stand in their election, subject to any law of reduction which the Senate might adopt, moved to exclude the printing of the Senate done before the reduction from the extra per centage of the old prices." (The motion failed on the casting vote of the Vice-President, George M. Dallas.) From the New York, N.Y., *Herald*, March 1, 1847, p. 3.

Remarks on the annexation of Texas in reply to John M. Niles, 2/27. Niles, of Conn., made a speech on the Mexican War, in which he referred to Calhoun's "precipitate haste in the annexation of Texas, in order to prevent . . . the entering wedge" to abolition. "Mr. Calhoun intimated that this was his position." Later, "Mr. Calhoun again explained his objects in hurrying forward the annexation of Texas. England, in concert with the World's [Antislavery] Convention, was moving to the abolition of slavery in Texas, with the avowed object that this movement was designed to promote the ultimate object of the extinction of slavery in the United States. The necessity of averting the consequences of this movement, he believed to be a paramount duty, and a duty that admitted of no delay." From the New York, N.Y., *Herald*, March 1, 1847, p. 3.

Remarks on the "Three Million Bill," 2/27. "Mr. Calhoun said that it was known that the Senator from Delaware [John M. Clayton] had for several days attempted to obtain the floor, and therefore he hoped that honorable Senator would have ample opportunity to address the Senate. But it would be unreasonable to expect him to go on at this late hour. He suggested that the Senate should adjourn with the understanding that the vote [on the three millions bill] should be taken definitely on Monday [3/1]." This was agreed to. From *Congressional Globe*, 29th Cong., 2nd Sess., p. 533. Variant in the Washington, D.C., *Daily Union*, February 27, 1847, p. 2.

REMARKS ON THE IRISH AND
SCOTCH RELIEF BILL

[In the Senate, February 27, 1847]
Mr. Calhoun made some remarks, but in so low a tone that he was very indistinctly heard in the gallery. He was, however, understood to say, that he was as happy as any gentleman on that floor to coöperate in measures of relief for the suffering people of Ireland, but he wished very much that they had more time at their disposal to give it more consideration. It was not so much the amount they should contribute—for the British Government was amply competent to take care of her own people—as the feeling they would exhibit towards the people of Ireland. If, however, they had more, they might extend its operation, for it was not the people of England, Ireland, and Scotland alone, that were suffering. France, too, was in a suffering condition. He had seen a letter from a highly respectable source, which stated that France would be without food before the harvest time. The people of Europe generally were suffering more or less. He suggested that a national vessel should be sent to Great Britain and to France, to carry the bounty of this country, and he was understood to say that no constitutional difficulties interposed to prevent it.

[*Several other Senators spoke.*]

Mr. Calhoun, in reference to some remarks made by the Senator from Indiana, (Mr. [Edward A.] Hannegan,) explained why he had no constitutional objection in this case. He drew a distinction between the foreign and domestic policy of this Government. Entertaining these views he had voted for the appropriation for the relief of the people of Caraccas in 1812. He, however, suggested that this appropriation was a very heavy one to make, when the country was in a state of war and subject to the demands upon our treasury which resulted from warlike operations. He, however, should gladly vote for the bill.

[*James M. Mason of Va. said he had Constitutional scruples and proposed as a substitute that the Navy be authorized to carry to Eu-*]

225

rope such private relief as might be provided by the people of the U.S.]

Mr. Calhoun inquired what the freight of grain was?

Mr. Mason replied, sixty cents per bushel.

Mr. Calhoun said, the plan, then, of the Senator from Virginia might give more actual relief than the proposition as contained in the original bill.

[*Mason spoke again.*]

Mr. Calhoun said, that was the very course which England herself had taken, by throwing open her ports to the vessels of all the world. He signified his intention to vote for the amendment.

From *Congressional Globe*, 29th Cong., 2nd Sess., pp. 533–534. Variant in the Charleston, S.C., *Mercury*, March 4, 1847, p. 2.

From Tho[ma]s J. Butler

Mobile, March 1/ [18]47

My dear Sir: As I do not think the report of y[ou]r speech [of 2/9], in the [Washington] Union, upon the 3 million appropriation as complete as any publication of it that may be made, under y[ou]r revision, in pamphlet form, I have to beg the favor of you to forward me a copy in pamphlet.

And I will make the further request of you to put my name on any list you may have of persons to whom you may be in the occasional habit of sending public documents &c.

I do not not [*sic*], my dear Sir, make these requests out of idle curiosity, but because I feel a deep interest in public matters, and because further, in all that concerns you, whether as the great political, or moral exemplar of the South, I feel a personal & peculiar pleasure, growing out of political adherence, and my earnest & sincere admiration, and which I may add without being accused of manworship, has "grown with my growth & strengthened with my strength."

Since writing the above I have seen & read the remarks [of 2/19] made by you preliminary to the presentation of y[ou]r Resolutions upon the subject of slavery. Should that speech, or any other of yours upon the subject, be published, and should you make distribution of them, will you have the kindness to forward me copies?

And now as it may be a matter of interest to you to know how those of your friends here whose attachment to you seems not only political, but personal, feel upon the subject of y[ou]r position in relation to the war, I would state that there has come under my own personal observation, (and I know personally almost the entire number of those who are denominated your *peculiar friends,*) but a single individual, who thinks and *says you are wrong,* & *who has felt himself constrained to give you up!*

Alas! that a single passenger on the vessel should lose confidence in the pilot in the midst of such a tempest, & upon a dangerous coast!

Sir, he will come back! He is young, ardent, impulsive—experience will teach him wisdom. He will look again to you—to our pilot—for hope & safety!

It is strange Sir that a single Southerner should lose confidence in you in this emergency! Strange indeed, that your friends, who have so long clung, not only to your wisdom & genius, but your *virtue,* should, now, in the very midst of the crisis, lose their confidence, & abandon their friend!

Now I have been accused of following you blindly, and by the very person who has seen fit to abandon you—but I have answered that it ["was" *interlined*] natural and proper I should follow y[ou]r lead—or the lead of some one, as [*partial word canceled*] my avocation, did not qualify me to be the best judge in all political expediences: that, first of all, in your personal worth—in the noble example you have set us all of what a good man ["is" *interlined*] by the illustration of y[ou]r whole life, I have abiding confidence—in y[ou]r talents their [*sic*] could be no doubt—your identity of interest was unquestionable—you had long, long experience—your judgement was ripe, y[ou]r wisdom was profound, you were prudent, thoughtful, vigilant; that it was natural for me to rely upon you—you were a Southern man, and a Slaveholder: that nature, interest prompted you to do the best you could for your country & y[ou]r section. Thus have I answered—and further that I was upon the beach, that you were upon the top of the light-house, that I had but my eyes which embraced but a narrow scope of sea, that, besides your elevation, your experience, your integrity & y[ou]r judgment, you had a glass, which extended your horizon, and the better enabled you to discharge the duties of a watchman! But, it has been replied, "you follow blindly!" Well, if I do, I have answered, thank God! I have a staff to lean upon in which I have all confidence.

I do not write Sir in a spirit of adulation. I feel that profounder are the impulses of my heart, and that, in the midst of the rencounter, the cheers of one's friends add to his comfort & confidence. You will therefore Sir, set down the motive prompting me to indite this letter, not only to my ardent attachment as a man, but my sense of duty as a citizen, and accept from ["me" *interlined*] the prayer that Providence may watch over & protect him, whom He has raised up for our shield. Thos. J. Butler.

ALS in ScCleA. NOTE: An AEU by Calhoun reads, "Mr. Butler[,] Send Speech."

From F[ITZ] W[ILLIAM] BYRDSALL

New York [City,] March 1st 1847

Dear Sir, I have read with deep interest in the newspapers your Speeches [of 2/12, 2/20, and 2/24] in the Senate in reply to Senators [Hopkins L.] Turney[,] [James F.] Simmons and [Thomas H.] Benton. If you have revised and got put up in pamphlet form any of them, I should be much gratified to obtain from you a copy of each or any of them, and also a few extra numbers to place in the hands of others for their instruction.

I am delighted with your exposition of our federative system of Government or union of nations, in contradistinction from the national and consolidated Government which many men erroneously conceived ours to be. I read many years ago "New Views of the Constitution" by John Taylor of Caroline Va. and one remark of the author in that work, was so self evidently clear to me, that I have been a States rights Republican ever since. It was in substance, that if any State of the confederation opposed or resisted an unconstitutional act of the General Government, the opposition in such a case would be the act of a Sovereign State, and as such, would command consideration and respect, while if the Government was a national and consolidated one, the conduct of the State would be rebellion and treason.

The session is near a close when you will return to the State you represent. Never have you deserved better of her than you do now, and not only your own State but the whole of the Southern States are under deeper obligations to you than they can ever adequately return.

But after all, the consciousness of doing right is the highest the purest and most gratifying reward that a man can receive. I am Dear Sir Yours more deeply, F.W. Byrdsall.

ALS in ScCleA.

From ROB[ER]T L. DORR

Dansville, Liv[ingston] County
N. York
March 1, 1847

D[ea]r S[i]r, The interest which I in common with many other of my fellow citizens have manifested in your behalf I think will be a sufficient justification for this communication at this time. I have been reading with no little interest the debate in the Senate on your resolutions in relation to slavery in which Senator [James F.] Simmons of Rhode Island participated, and must confess that I was somewhat confounded at some of the notions advanced by you on that occasion. It may be that on reading your remarks I misapprehended their purport, or am so dull of apprehension that I cannot see their rationality. The Rochester papers make you say "that you would prefer a Despotic government or an Aristocracy to a government where the numerical majority govern, and then you say this is Dorrism, and that the Senator from Rhode Island was the last person in the world from whom you expected such doctrines because Rhode Island had tasted of its bitter fruits." Now I happened to be one of those who were opposed to the "Wilmot Proviso" and was waiting with some anxiety to see your views upon the subject; but I can assure you it was with great surprise and astonishment that I read the above language from one enjoying so much respect and confidence. I was one of those too who believed in an extension of the right of suffrage in Rhode Island, and a constitution securing it call it Dorrism or what you please but differed with the movers in the means resorted to, to attain that end. When such a constitution was wrung reluctantly from the opposing party the question as to which party was right it seems to me is thereby foreclosed. I cannot see with the limited information I possess into the correctness of any other theory of republican government but in the admitted right of the majority to rule. Any other theory substitutes a sort of *Divine right* in a less number to rule the residue[,] a proposition to which a free people will never assent. If you are to attempt to transfer the sov[e]reignty by drawing a line of distinction between your fellow men pray tell how and where you are to draw it? Will you undertake to say that the rich[,] the Bankers or the monopolists shall alone exercise the sov[e]reign power and exclude the poor man because he is poor? Would you transfer the sov[e]reign power into the hands of professional men and exclude the Farmers and Mechanics because they are Farmers & Mechanics? Would you transfer the sov[e]reign power into the hands of good men alone and exclude the bad? If so who would you select as the Umpire but Omnipotence itself to decide in such a case? It seems to me that the very moment we depart from the conceded right of the numerical majority to govern that very moment we depart from the republican system itself. I am now speaking with reference to the rights of our own free white citizens & not slaves & to such also I suppose you referred in your debate with Simmons of Rhode Island. I think that if an attempt were made in the State of New York or any other State to deprive the numerical majority of the right to govern there would be such an uprising of the people in the shape of Dorrism as you call it that it would long be remembered by the people of U.S. and the movers and abettors of such a plot would be consigned to an oblivion darker than that which shrouds the name of [Benedict] Arnold. And in such a result unless I much mistake the discernment[?] of the people nine tenths would most heartily concur. The notion is intolerable and outrageous, and cannot be sustained for a moment without changing fundamentally the very structure of the government. Who is prepared for or who desires such a change? I am aware that there are many eminent men in the U.S. who are doubtless honest in their opinions, who steadfastly adhere to the old state of things—cling with remarkable tenacity to the errors of the past—to the laws[,] usages an[d] customs of antiquity however oppressive or inconvenient they may be and they look upon human progress and gradual changes which that progress demands as unwise, inexpedient and revolutionary! There are however a vast majority of the people who honestly differ with them in opinion upon this subject. If scientific researches are authority on this point they certainly prove that since the Creation man has intellectually been a progressive animal, and that even the laws of nature have changed to accommodate his progressive state. If Omnipotence then has stooped so far to aid in his elevation it would indeed appear strange if the inclinations or institutions of man should possess the capacity to impede or thwart his progress. Whatever our notions may be I insist that the thing is impossible. The interest I have always manifested in your behalf I here urge as an excuse for the boldness expressed in this letter, and how it is that the advocate of "free trade" of a strict construction of the Constitution, and hitherto of the sov[e]reignty of the people, and the great adversary of concentrated political power should advance sentiments so anti republican in theory is a mystery the solution of which I shall look for with some considerable anxiety.

I have already spun out this communication much longer than

I intended, and nothing but the extraordinary position you seem to occupy will justify its prolixity. Resp[ectfu]lly, Robt. L. Dorr.

ALS in ScCleA; PC (from the Rochester, N.Y., *Daily Advertiser*) in the New York, N.Y., *Evening Post*, April 14, 1847, p. 1; PC in the Charleston, S.C., *Southern Patriot*, April 19, 1847, p. 2; variant PC in the Edgefield, S.C., *Advertiser*, April 21, 1847, p. 2; PEx in the Charleston, S.C., *Mercury*, April 17, 1847, p. 2; PEx in the Pendleton, S.C., *Messenger*, April 30, 1847, p. 1.

From JOSEPH C. HART, "Private"

New York [City], March 1 1847

My Dear Sir: This letter is intended to be private and confidential, unless for the purposes contained in it you choose to refer it to some one or more of your political friends.

I have been endeavouring for some time past to start and establish a free-trade Journal in this city, having in view the connection of your name as a Democratic Candidate for the presidency. I have not been able to enlist men enough in the enterprise who have capital to spare. It is upon this subject, therefore, that I have concluded to address myself to you personally and directly, without the consultation with or advice of any person whatever. It will cost ten thousand dollars, at least, to establish a *Daily* Journal permanently; and that sum will be sunk in the enterprise, as I have known by previous experience, before it can support itself. This is a large sum—too large, perhaps, to propose to you or your friends; and certainly too large for me to raise without your or your friends' aid. I therefore propose, in order to keep the subject alive and before the people, as well as to form a nucleus around which your friends here may rally, to establish a paper of the first order which shall be issued weekly for some 6 months to come, and then, if possible, to start a daily paper. Our Democratic friends here are mostly of a class who can hardly afford to take and *pay* for a paper: therefore it will mainly have to be circulated gratis for a time. The consequence will be, as I predict from some twenty years' experience, that we will prevent their going off and splitting up upon other candidates. You are decidedly their favorite in the city of New York, and they lack but a paper, expressing their views, to settle down permanently for you. Mr. [Silas] Wright, with his "abolition tail" and propensities, is not now their man; and strong exertions are constantly but privately made for

Mr. [Lewis] Cass. We must therefore strike at once or lose our advantage.

If your friends can perceive the necessity of acting now, as I do, I may, without offense I hope, propose that they join with me either in a daily or weekly paper here, to be conducted in a fearless and vigourous manner. It would not be worth a pin if conducted otherwise.

With these views I propose that the sum of 2,500$ be raised. 500$ of this sum will be necessary to begin with, for preliminary arrangements; and, after the paper is started, then 50$ per week will be ample for its support for one year. I offer my editorial services ["for" *canceled*] without charge. My writings have mainly appeared in Mr. [Levi D.] Slamm's Plebeian & Globe. From the beginning of his latter paper I wrote the articles that appeared therein on our Negro question, which I believe have been greatly instrumental in preventing the adoption of negro suffrage in our new constitution—much to the discomfiture of Mr. Wright and his covert abolition friends. Added to this, although a professional man, I ["have" *canceled*] am a practised editor. In all these matters, if you have no objection, reference may be made to Mr. Slamm, who is now in Washington, regarding myself and my ability.

It has been stated to me that the Hon. Mr. [Franklin H.] Elmore, of your State, would be the proper person to consult with in regard to my proposition; but, as I have no acquaintance with him, I know not the avenue of approach to that gentleman except through yourself. My acquaintance even with you, personally, is so slight that I am rather afraid to presume upon it; but the object, which is that of doing you service, will form my excuse. You may remember my introduction to you by Mr. [Clinton?] Roosevelt and Mr. Slamm some two years ago, on the evening before your departure to the South. It was at your Hotel in Washington; and the pleasure I derived from the interview, although casual, will not soon be forgotten.

I leave this subject now with you. If I hear from you, well; if not I must contrive some other way of carrying my object into effect. But in either case believe me respectfully Your friend: Joseph C. Hart, 31 Wall St., N.Y.

ALS in ScCleA.

Remarks on the Missouri Compromise, 3/1. William L. Dayton of N.J. stated that William Lowndes had supported the compromise and therefore restriction of slavery. "Mr. Calhoun here said that Mr. Lowndes was sick when the compromise was made. Mr. L[owndes] had made a speech to show that Missouri was a State, and could alone decide the question of the admission of slavery." From the Charleston, S.C., *Courier*, March 5, 1847, p. 2. Variant in the Washington, D.C., *Daily National Intelligencer*, March 19, 1847, p. 2; *Congressional Globe*, 29th Cong., 2nd Sess., Appendix, p. 432.

Remarks on a resolution "to provide for full and accurate reports of the proceedings and debates of the Senate," 3/2. "Mr. Calhoun (who spoke with much difficulty, owing to hoarseness) rose and observed that he had no agency in this business further than, when asked his opinions, he had stated that he believed it would be of the greatest advantage to have the debates in the Senate reported promptly, fully, and with accuracy. He thought so still. But if he thought the proposition had any connexion with the establishment of a political paper, he would be the last man to give it his support. The great object, he thought, was to disconnect the reports from the party presses." From the Washington, D.C., *Daily National Intelligencer*, March 6, 1847, p. 3. Variants in *Congressional Globe*, 29th Cong., 2nd Sess., p. 567; the New York, N.Y., *Herald*, March 4, 1847, p. 4; the Charleston, S.C., *Courier*, March 6, 1847, p. 2.

Remarks in reply to William Allen, 3/3. On the last day of the session Allen tried to get consideration of a bill to organize a government in Oregon Territory, in the course of which he hinted that Calhoun was an enemy to Oregon. "Mr. Calhoun was so very hoarse as scarcely to be able to speak, and yet he desired a single word. He regarded the imputation of the Senator from Ohio as light as air. He was opposed to the consideration of the bill. The Senate was too thin; and we have not now the time." From the New York, N.Y., *Herald*, March 5, 1847, p. 3. Variants in the Alexandria, Va., *Gazette and Virginia Advertiser*, March 4, 1847, p. 3; the Charleston, S.C., *Courier*, March 8, 1847, p. 2.

MARCH 4–APRIL 30, 1847

◫

*Calhoun usually spent only a day or two in Charleston when return-
ing from Washington and then hurried home to Fort Hill. This time
he prolonged his stay. Arriving on the morning of March 6 on the
steamer from Wilmington, he was received formally by the Mayor,
City Council, and a deputation of citizens. "The hospitalities of the
City were tendered to him, and he was escorted to the Carolina Hotel
in Broad-street, where lodgings had been previously prepared for
him, as the Guest of the Citizens." (Charleston, S.C., Mercury,
March 8, 1847, p. 2.)*

*Calhoun was to address a public meeting on Monday, March 8,
but he felt so unwell it had to be postponed until the next evening.
An overflow crowd filled the spacious New Theatre long before the
7 p.m. convening time, including the city leaders and the State's entire congressional delegation. Two tiers of boxes were reserved for
ladies. When "Calhoun made his appearance upon the stage, such
a shout of rapturous welcome was sent up as made the walls re-echo
with its gladness, and it was long before the outbursts of feeling,
again and again reiterated, could be sufficiently repressed to enable
Mr. Calhoun to return his acknowledgments for his kind reception."
Isaac W. Hayne led the meeting in adopting forceful resolutions
against the Wilmot Proviso, and then Calhoun spoke, despite a severe
cold and hoarseness. (Charleston, S.C., Mercury, March 10, 1847,
p. 2.) His subject was "our peculiar domestic institution" and the
"fixed determination" of a majority of both parties in the North to
appropriate all the territories of the Union to themselves, to the exclusion of the South. Were this not resisted, the South was doomed
to subservience and exploitation.*

*Calhoun was at Columbia on March 15 and home at Fort Hill late
the next day. On March 19 he wrote his son-in-law Clemson about
his pleasure with the condition of the farm.*

*The statesman's correspondence was heavy and concerned many
matters. On March 21 he wrote a questioning New Yorker an ex-*

*planation of the "concurrent majority." On April 9 he explained
fully to a North Carolinian his feelings about the situation of the
country. For Calhoun, aggressive warmaking, free-soilism, the spoils
system, party chicanery, debt, and the exploitive tariff were all consequences of the same malady—the degeneration of what he always
called "the Republican party." The party, he wrote, "is again in a
fair way, I apprehend, to lose power, because it has greatly departed
from its original faith, & embraced the principles & policy of its opponents to a far greater extent than is supposed by those who have
not carefully watched the course of events."*

*While in Charleston Calhoun had had his photograph taken, so it
would appear from an announcement carried by that city's papers
on March 24. A "Mr. [Sterling C.] McIntyre," who advertised himself as a maker of high quality likenesses "(not cheap Daguereo-
types)" reported that he had likenesses of Calhoun on hand. And
the* Mercury *of April 28 announced that word had been received
from the sculptor Hiram Powers in Italy that his commissioned statue
of Calhoun was almost complete.*

〖〗

From DUFF GREEN

Washington, 4th March 1847

Dear Sir, I send you enclosed a copy of my prospectus as corrected.
I will not distribute or publish it until I hear from you. I have inserted "the Telegraph" because I believe that it will tend to rally my
old subscribers and in that respect tend greatly to strengthen my
position and yours. I know that there are persons who have endeavored to persuade you that I was unpopular as an editor, and did
prejudice to you, but the truth is that I have had but few enemies who
were not made so by my supporting you and the effort of all those
who were disposed to desert and betray you was to distroy your confidence in me, lest I should denounce and expose them.

I have to day agreed upon terms with the parties who came on
to purchase my mineral land [in Md.], and they assure me that in
the course of ["this" *altered to* "a"] week they can comply with their
contract. This will put me comparatively easy in money matters,
and enable me to appropriate something in aid of the cause but the

press should be put on a footing to defray its own expenditure, and that must be done by contributions.

If Charleston gives a decided impulse and influential men in the State will take upon themselves to obtain subscribers I will venture to proceed, for we should not lose a moment. The members going home will make an impression against us unless we move promptly and with energy.

It is necessary to sustain our friends in Virginia in the April elections. They will feel stronger if they know that they be sustained by the Telegraph.

I have written frankly. Write me so in return. If you prefer "the Statesman" or any other name say so, and I will adopt your suggestion, but it seems to me that a change of name indicates a sense of weakness, whereas we must maintain the propriety of the past.

I again repeat that my desire to serve you as much or more than any thing else prompts me to take my pen. All I ask is that my motives [*one word canceled and* "may be" *interlined*] properly appreciated. If you and those in whom you have confidence or on whom you rely can find any other person who will be more acceptable, I will cheerfully yea gladly retire and contribute in money as much as he who gives most.

Let no delicacy toward me prevent you placing the press in the hands of any you or they prefer. I know that I must make great sacrifices, which like what I have already undergone, will not be appreciated, but I am willing to make them if my motives are duly appreciated *now*. The past is forgotten, and the future must take care of itself. Yours truly, Duff Green.

[Draft Circular]
Prospectus
For publishing at the City of Washington a daily paper
to be called
The Times

The inevitable consequence of human agency is an abuse of the powers of government, and a struggle, which, acting on the interests, passions and prejudices of society enables designing men to form combinations dangerous to public liberty. The most dangerous are those founded on sectional interests or geographical divisions.

Where the powers and duties of Government are prescribed by a written Constitution, and its officers & agents are responsible for the manner in which public trusts are performed, a free and enlightened press is indispensable to a proper discharge of those duties which devolve on the people themselves. The function of the press is the true interpretation and right direction of public events, and this should be accomplished by a free, full, fair, and truthful discussion of the conduct of public men and of the measures which they propose. It is thus and thus only that the people can ascertain how far public men, or public measures deserve their support.

Such has been the tendency of party conflicts that the people of the United States have become nearly equally divided and organizations have been formed in both parties for the purpose of controlling the party to which these ["sub" *canceled*] subordinate organizations belong. The basis on which these organizations rest is that Union is necessary to success & that the minority of the party must submit to the will of the majority. The effect of this principle is to enable a bare majority of a majority to control the will of the dominant party, and by that means place all the power and patronage of the Government in the hands of a small minority of the whole people.

If as we have asserted the tendency of human agency is an abuse of ["the" *interlined*] power ["of Government" *interlined*] it is apparent that a minority of the people holding ["those" *interlined*] powers acquired through the agency of an organized party will endeavor to subsidize the press, and all must see that a party Government sustained by a venal & purchased press must become a fraud upon the people operating by a system of false pretenses.

A free press should be independent of the Government[;] it should hold the Government itself in check by a free and full and fair discussion of public measures and a fearless censure of public abuses. How else can the people know when to approve or when to condemn an administration. Viewed in this aspect the establishment of a press ["by the administration" *interlined*] for the avowed purpose of defending all its measures, and the open avowal of its servile and prostituted condition prove that the present state of the press and the present state of parties are such as to make it the imperative duty of the people themselves to whom the Government belongs to establish a press which shall be their organ, and which shall for them speak to and of the Government.

Does any one doubt this truth? If so we refer such to the efforts now making to destroy the independence of the senate, by a false clamor against the action of that body and the bitter denunciation and proscription of such of the democratic party as refuse to unite in that false clamor to show that ["they" *canceled*] those now in power seek to govern the Country by the force of party patronage and party proscription, & yet such is the condition ["of the press" *canceled*] of parties and of the press, that these truths which all must see and feel, cannot be discussed or understood.

["The party in" *canceled*] Those now in power came in as the advocates of free trade, and a sound currency, Yet they are surrounded by men who are clamorous for a *vigorous* prosecution of the war with Mexico, which is in truth but another term for an *expensive* prosecution of the war—the effect of which will be ["to" *interlined*] create a great public debt, and abrogate free trade and the subtreasury by driving the duties above the ["protective" *canceled*] point of protection, and substituting a government paper [*one or two words changed to* "currency"] instead of the specie currency.

Again the adoption of the Wilmot proviso, and by the House of Representatives, ["and" *canceled*] the passage of ["a" *canceled*] resolutions of a similar character, by seven of the non slaveholding States and the declaration that parties in those States are hereafter to be formed in reference to that question, proves that in that section, a reorganization of parties has taken place, and that whatever may be their local divisions upon this question all ["parties" *canceled*] will unite in denying the political equality & Constitutional rights of the south.

["To us it is therefore" *canceled*] It is a melancholy truth that such is the force of party influence and ["of" *interlined*] public patronage, that on the questions thus presented, the worst enemies of the south are from the south. He that is not for us, in such a crisis is against us, and there are southern men who are false to the ["southern interest sectio(*ms. torn*)" *canceled and* "south because a (*ms. torn*)" *interlined*] and subsidized press, ["threatens" *canceled*], presents to them ["party" *canceled*] party proscription and party denunciation on the one hand and government patronage on the other.

["At best Our presidential elections have become a lottery for the distribution of one hundred and" *canceled.*] Under the combined influence of an organized party and a venal press, our Presidential Elections have become, lotteries for the distribution of one hundred & twenty millions of dollars, ["and" *canceled and* "in which" *interlined*] party ["services" *canceled*] electioneering services are the price paid for tickets. A *vigorous* prosecution ["of the war, in the mann(?)" *canceled*] which as we have said means an *expensive* prosecution of the war, will double if it does not quadruple the sum to be distributed, as this large ["fee" *canceled*] sum must be disbursed by the party in power, it is apparent that those who are to be enriched by the war, will not be content with increasing the expenses but they will prolong ["the" *canceled*] its duration. For our part we are for peace—Peace between the United States and Mexico, and Peace between the north and the south. Peace between the United States and Mexico as soon as practicable consistently with the honor and interests of both. Peace between the north and the south, upon the only basis on which it can be preserved—a rigid adherence, to the compromises of the Constitution and a perfect equality in all respects between the slave holding and non slave holding States.

We desire peace with Mexico to avoid the many disasters to which a continuance of the war will expose us and we desire Peace between the north and the south, as indispensable to the preservation of the Union. It is because we are satisfied that neither of the two leading Journals of this City meet these great issues with the fullness, fairness and decision they demand, and especial[l]y that which relates to the conflict between the north and the south that we deem it necessary to establish "The Times."

Of the Journals to which we refer one [the *Daily National Intelligencer*] stands silent, looking on as if afraid to take part, while the other [the *Union*] is busily engaged in confounding all distinction between those who introduced and supported the Wilmot proviso and kindred measures and those who have given them a patriotic resistance. There can be but one explanation, of a course so extraordinary on the part of these influential Journals. They represent the two great parties to which we have referred, and [*two words canceled*] consider, the interests of the parties which they ["they"(?) *canceled*] represent as paramount to all other considerations.

We wish to be distinctly understood. We believe that ["the" *canceled*] as both the great political parties in the north, are in the process of reorganization on the basis of denying the political equality, ["of the" *canceled*] and constitutional rights of the south, the only means of preserving the union itself is to unite the south in defence of the rights and interests thus assailed. We believe that, in truth, the north is no less interested in preserving the rights, interests and political ["equality" *interlined*] of the south, than the south itself—for the Prosperity and security of the North, depend upon the maintenance of order and good government. The south is essential[l]y conservative. Our past history proves that this is the ["result of the" *interlined*] existence of slavery in that section ["which must" *canceled*] & that it must be so as long as slavery continues. Abolition ["agitation" *interlined*] tends to unite and strengthen the south; it has precisely an opposite tendency in reference to the north. There it divides and adds to the many other causes, which create in that section a state of perpetual agitation affecting injuriously the relations of society and the tenure of property.

In the north capital & labor are in conflict, and as population, ["increases" *canceled*], and the demands of labor increase that conflict will become more active. In the south capital and labor are united, and no such conflict does or will ["exist" *canceled*] exist. Hence abolition ["agitation" *interlined*] will strengthen the south, and add to its stability and security. It weakens the north and adds to its instability and insecurity.

Thus it is clear that the north has a deep interest in putting down abolition, and as a united stand on the ["south" *canceled*] part of the south, is the most effectual means of doing so the north is deeply interested in supporting a paper, whose object is to produce that result.

We know the North too well to doubt for a moment that many of its intelligent and patriotic inhabitants of both parties, are ready to rally with the south, as soon as the south is rallied in support of the Harmony, union & equality of the States.

Admonished by past experience nothing less than the peculiar crisis in which the country is now placed could induce the undersigned to assume the arduous labor and weighty responsibility of conducting a public press, and they tender their services with the understanding and belief that efforts will be made in all parts of the Union, and especial[l]y in the south, by contributions and subscriptions to establish "The Times" on a basis equal to the crisis in which we are placed and the great interests which it will support and defend.

Our appeal is made to the south, and we expect, the men of property and influence in that section, and elsewhere ["who desire" *interlined*] that such a press should be established, to take upon ["themselves" *interlined*] the task of ["obt ob" *canceled*] obtaining contributions and subscriptions. Contributions are called for because such a press can expect no Government patronage, and because those for the protection of whose property and interests the paper will be established are in duty bound to defray the expense of publication and compensate the able and experienced associates and contributors whose services will in that case be obtained.

With these remarks and explanations the undersigned submit this prospectus: if it is received and acted on as in their opinion it should be their talents[,] energies & experience will be faithfully and fearlessly exerted. If otherwise they will have the consolation to know that they have discharged their duty in an emergency ["frau" *can-*

celed] fraught with results the consequences of which no one can now foresee.

The Times will be published daily for six dollars ["per annum" *canceled*], semiweekly, during the recess and triweekly during the session of Congress for ["five" *canceled and* "four" *interlined*] dollars, and weekly, for one dollar & fifty cents ["per annum" *interlined*] payable in advance. ["All contributions & subscriptions necessary to the publication of the paper will" *canceled*; "should be" *interlined and then canceled*; "The publication" *interlined and then canceled*; "The Times will be commenced immediately under a belief that" *interlined*] All contributions and subscriptions ["necessary to" *canceled*] sufficient to secure its permanent publication will be made. ["If not the paper will" *canceled*.]

ALS in ScCleA; En (draft) in NcU, Duff Green Papers (published microfilm, roll 22, frames 467–474). NOTE: The precise document enclosed by Green with this letter has not been found. However, it must have resembled the draft, found among Green's papers, which is transcribed above.

DUFF GREEN to R[ichard] K. Crallé, Lynchburg, Va.

Washington, 5th March 1847

My dear Crallé, Mr. Calhoun received your letter just as he was starting last night and I write at his request to say that he [will] answer it when he gets to Pendleton.

It was impossible for him to get a vote on his [slavery] resolutions. He prepared an address to be signed by the representatives and senators from the southern States but it was too late to accomplish it, and they adjourned without doing any thing.

He left in good spirits and under a belief that the democratic members are disposed to conciliate *him*, but in this he was wrong— never did they feel more hostile to him. He is, as they believe, the only obstacle to the consummation of their plans of power and patronage and hence they will wage an unrelenting war on him. Their purpose is to drive the party into a convention and his sin is that his influence will be exerted against it. The movement in Virginia is for the purpose of intimadation and it will have its effect in your State and elsewhere.

We want a press. It will be greatly to my prejudice but I am about to publish "the Telegraph" again and will treat Mr. [James K.]

Polk and the war with fairness & candor, and in the spirit of kindness but I will show that [Thomas] Ritchie and [James] Buchanan are guilty of the war and much more. Upon them I will wage a war as bitter as that which they wage on Mr. Calhoun.

One of the most efficient means of attack on them will be a history of the Convention and of the Caucus system—in all the States. I know no man who can give the history of the Richmond Junto as well as you can and I must assign you that duty.

I am going into the matter in earnest if I find the country prepared to respond, to me, and I trust that you will write to me, frequently and with candor. Yours truly, Duff Green.

ALS in DLC, Duff Green Papers; PC in Moore, ed., "Calhoun as Seen by His Political Friends," *Publications of the Southern History Association*, vol. 7, (1903), p. 424.

From DUFF GREEN

Washington, 6th March 1847

My dear Sir, I have just seen Mr. J[ohn] S. Barbour and find that he is panic stricken. He says that [Shelton F.] Leake and [Henry] Beddinger [*sic*; Bedinger, Representatives from Va.] both refused to frank your speeches upon the ground that it would injure them in their elections. He told me that he saw [James A.] Black [Representative from S.C.] at the State Dept. and that he said that you were trying to take South Carolina to the Whigs but could not do it, and spoke in a most hostile manner. He said that Simms [*sic*; Alexander D. Sims, Representative from S.C.] was also hostile to you. So much for the Democracy of Virginia and South Carolina. I learn also that [William B.?] Preston [Representative from Va.] is consulting and planning and that his room at Gadsby's [Tavern] is a rallying point for some of the most bitter and proscriptive Whigs.

I spent some time to day with J[ohn] M. Clayton of Delaware, and from him I learn that the Whigs will probably rally on [John J.] Crittenden or [Zachary] Taylor. He sees that there are objections to both, but said that the Whigs never had made the same preparation to act on public opinion that they are now making, and that he had never seen them so resolved on success. They are to hold their national convention in Phila[delphia] and the Whigs of that city have pledged themselves to provide accommodation for 150,000.

These facts are important as they prove, first the debased and degraded condition of Virginia, and next that it is more than probable that the Whigs will have a slave holding candidate for the Presidency.

It is now distinctly understood that [Lewis] Cass has not only become reconciled to the administration but that he is the candidate for the time being of those who wish to plunder the Treasury. Under this state of thing[s] it becomes the more necessary that your friends should have a press here. An able press will enable us to control events. It will make us, in truth the balance of power party, but without a press we are gone. Crittenden is yielding and our adversary is wise. All that they now require is a step—they go a step at a time, and what we have to fear is that he may compromise the slave holding interest more than an open and avowed abolitionist could do.

I hold myself in readiness to aid, but ready to give place to any other. I know what I have to go through. I have no hope that what I have done will be appreciated, & admonished by the past I fully appreciate the future, but I am prepared for ingratitude and injustice. I will labor for the cause of my country, and do my duty if I am sustained as I should be. But I must know soon what you and your friends will do. I can take no step until I hear from you. Yours truly, Duff Green.

ALS in ScCleA. NOTE: This letter was addressed to Calhoun at Charleston with the note: "If Mr. C. has left send to Pendleton. To be forwarded if Mr. C. has left."

From JAMES L. RANSONE

Gapview near Charlestown
Jefferson County [West] Virginia
Mar[ch] 6 1847

My dear Sir, The object in obtruding this letter is to express my sincere regret, in not being able ["to" *interlined*] avail myself, of the pleasure & the honor, of calling upon you, agreeably to your kind invitation lately given to me in Washington.

Perceiving that the business of Congress, left to you, not one moment—I postponed my call, until the morning after the adjournment, when to my surprise & lasting regret, I was informed that you had left immediately, on the adjournment of Congress!

During the recess of the Senate, on the day of our brief interview,

I was in one of those eating Houses in the basement of the Capitol; alone with my friend [James M.] Mason of the Senate—when the *Venerable* editor of the [Washington] Union [Thomas Ritchie] came in. Mason introduced us, as a matter of course. Having long since drifted out of the channels of political life, & never having been, in any public service, save that of the *defence of my Country*, Mr. R[itchie] was at a loss *whare* [*sic*] *to place me*.

In the evening—seeking to avoid the crowd in the other Galleries, I went to the Reporter[']s Gallery & from thence ["was" *interlined*] looking in upon the Senate the venerable father of the *Seven principle* party, entered, and took his seat just before me. Very soon he observed me, & commenced remarking upon the proceedings then passing in the Senate. Both having to rise & lean over the back, of his partition, as a Reporter, to our mutual discomfort, I, or he, suggested the want of an additional Reporter, &, I *volunteered*, & jumpted [*sic*] over, & took my seat by his side.

Passing over the incidents that passed between us, in the *Eating room*, before adverted to, & which if ever ["you" *changed to* "we"] should meet, I shall be *too apt*, to tell you—Mr. R[itchie] remarked, to me, as soon as seated by him—we shall have a *scene*, here to night, & it is all wrong. Yes, I replied, the *wild Boor, out* of the woods, [g]nashing *his teeth* & *gnarling*[?], at a noble *patriot & statesman*, & seeking to destroy him if he can—to which, he replied, there might be a difference of opinion, *on that subject*. To which, I replied—I knew there was, I feared ["there was" *interlined*] a wide difference between him & myself, & by way ["of" *interlined*] not letting him be *deceived* as to *my position*, I would repeat that I looked upon [Thomas H.] Benton, as a wild beast *out* of the woods, seeking to destroy *all* that, lies his way. He replied, "Benton has a *undying hatred* of C[alhoun]." But this proceeding to night, I cannot understand—& think it all wrong &c." And then added, "*that he did not care a Dam*[*n*] for all the great men," snap[p]ing his fingers over the *Eagle*, & over the Senate, so loud, that ["the attention of" *interlined*] many persons was attracted. When Benton had the Rule read, requiring all Senators present to vote, & after you had made a few remarks showing your physical inability to speak—&, had voted, I *again*, said to Mr. R[itchie] I look upon Benton as a *wild Boor* out of the wood *seeking* to *destroy* all that lies in *his* way. Who do you allude to? said Mr. R[itchie] as, *in his way.* I pointed to *you.* He added yes it was true—&, all wrong." I added one will *perish* like the beast, & the other, *live* forever—&, history ["will" *interlined*] record his name, on her highest pages, as the purest patriot & greatest statesman of his ages. Whereupon Mr. R[itchie] repeated his former remark, "there might be a difference of opinion, ab[ou]t that"—& so we parted.

I regret not obtaining the promised copies of your speech [of 2/24/1847], in reply to Benton. Pray send to me as many as you can spare. I saw Boyer—& he read me your note & showed me, Keenan[']s letter—neither one *trust*-worthy—& I required of Boyer, to deliver the ["no. of y(ou)r" *interlined*] speeches he had, to me—&, not to circulate one, till we met in Winchester. He is not in *good order*—having but little *perception*, of any sort. You have my Dear Sir, my best wishes ["& prayer," *interlined*] for your speedy restoration to health, the loss of which, it grieved me to perceive. May a kind providence restore that inestimable earthly blessing, & long spare you as ["a faithful" *interlined*] sentinel upon the watch towers of our Country[']s liberties, Prays, y[ou]r ardent admirer, & humble Serv[an]t, James L. Ransone.

ALS in ScCleA.

From Jos[eph] J. Singleton

Dahlonega [Ga.,] 6th March 1847
My Dear Sir, We have just gotten through the busy scen[e]s of the week[']s superior Court, and I am a candidate for the Senate of our State, and so far as present prospects indicate, my chance for success is very good. We have had Democratic speech[e]s, and Whig speeches, the former intended with much violence to operate against you, and the lat[t]er much to your credit and fame as the ultimate saviour of the South and its Institutions. The tro[u]bled ocean of Democratic politics must, and will give way to the wafting breeze of Southern rights, or I am greatly deceived. The pinch of the game will be this year, and by the next, I am much in hopes we will all be confiding with the utmost reliance upon the only landmark of our political saf[e]ty, The Constitution of the United States; how long it will continue to be the landmark, is not for us even to predict (sufficient for the day is the evil thereof)[;] hold on, hold on, hold on, and never "give up the ship" should be our dying motto, and preemptory demand of others only, that which we would, they should in like manner demand of us, similarly conditioned. I am in hopes to see you in this Country during the spring or summer ensuing. The winter has

been so excessively bad that there has been but little done on your mines, and that only by way of preparations for the opening of the spring. Every manifestation to do right on them, is now apparent, which I hope will continue. May this letter find you at home in the full enjoyment of your domestic circle. And I would be glad to know what paper of your State enjoys your fullest confidence. I have the honor sir of being yours respectfully &C., Jos. J. Singleton.

ALS in ScU-SC, John C. Calhoun Papers.

From A[sa] Whitney

Richmond Va., March 6, 1847

Sir, It appears clearly to my mind that the greatest and most important subject for the attention and action of the Statesman and Capitalist is the speedy developement of the great internal resources of our Country by the means of railroads from the Atlantic Cities, into the great Basin of the Mississippi, producing a speedy and frequent intercourse and communication with a cheap transportation for all the products of the earth. I know this cannot, nor would I have it a subject for Legislative action but should be done by individual enterprise yet any man of influence by his opinions upon the subject can urge the people on to the full extent of their energy and ability when the great object will be accomplished.

The Basin of the Mississippi can produce enough to feed nearly the entire human family and at lower prices than any other part of the Globe but the expenses of transportation to the Atlantic Cities takes nearly all the produce will sell for even when in demand and at high prices, but little or nothing is left to the producer, and the now only channels of communication natural or artificial can be used only for that part of the year when the produce is least in demand for foreign markets.

All Europe is interested in this subject. The scarcity of food I fear must continue untill the surpluss population can be placed where they can produce for themselves from the soil, and a surplus to exchange for the Manufactures of Europe, and here they must be placed, there is none other country for them. By railroads Flour may be transported from the Ohio to the Atlantic Cities for from 50 to 75 cts. and from the upper Mississippi for $1 p[e]r bbl. and meats for half a cent p[e]r pound. Animals would be slaughtered where fattened, sent to the Atlantic Cities and then packed. The supply would at all seasons of the year equal the demand for home and abroad, at reasonable prices, and the producer would receive all the benefit from the diminished cost of transit—therefore enable him to consume twice or thrice the amount of Manufactures. The attention of [the] European capitalist as well as Statesman is being turned to this as I think highly important subject, and I think will soon see they can find no relief for their overpopulation and no increased foreign demand for their manufactures untill the surpluss can be placed here and become producers and consumers, thereby an exchange will take place, to the relief and advantage of all and capital must be furnished to complete several great thoroughfares from the Atlantic to the Mississippi river. For the purpose of explaining this subject in all its bearings, and for procuring capital to carry out the object, it has been proposed to me to go to Europe. Considering your State and Section of Country deeply interested, has induced this letter. If your railroad could be continued to Memphis, and, on, to the Ohio it would open to a communication with your market at a cheap rate of transit, an immense tract of fine corn and Cotton Country, now too remote from means of communication with market to be of little or no value—and bring to your City nearly all the produce which now from necessity goes down to New Orleans. At rates of tolls which will sufficiently support Railroads, with the saving in time, and expenses less at your port than New Orleans, ["and" *interlined*] with your ["and" *canceled*] better communication with Europe, this result would be forced and make one of the greatest and most important thoroughfares for the Commerce of our Continent. Should my views meet your approbation and should you think I can do any thing to further the interest of your State, it will give me great pleasure so to do. Permit me to say, I shall be most happy in knowing you have arrived home safely with improved health. With highest Considerations of Respect I am Truly Yours, A. Whitney, 41 William Street, New York [City].

ALS in ScCleA. Note: An AEU by Calhoun reads "Mr. Whitney, ["Including" *canceled*] enclosing a rough draft of my Answer."

From Geo[rge] N. Sanders

New York [City,] 8 March 1847

My Dear Sir, I did not receive Col. [Caleb] Cushing's letter of which I send you a copy until after you left Washington. It is important, in as much as we may infer that if the war should suddenly terminate, he would gladly embark in the enterprise. But should the war continue, I know of no one that can fill Col. Cushing's place. Whatever funds fortune may place in my hands, will be held until Col. Cushing's return, or until some other superior man shall offer. With high regard Your ob[edien]t Serv[an]t, Geo. N. Sanders.

[Enclosure]
C[aleb] Cushing to Geo. N. Sanders, "Copy"

Boston, Febr[uary] 26, 1847

My dear Sir, I have found it impossible to leave my duties here for the purpose of visiting Washington, & am busily engaged in preparations for my departure by sea to Mexico. But for this the enterprise which you have proposed to me would present great attractions, in reference as well to its general as its personal objects. The circumstances however, under which the command of the Massachusetts Regiment, & the expectations of the State in consequence, have constituted a demand on my services which it was impossible to disobey. I should not [have] time, nor would it be proper for me, in Mexico, to write for the public eye, nor could I give any attention to an undertaking having its seat in New York. I think your plan is an excellent one; & that it supplies a manifest & pressing public desideratum; & therefore I hope & believe you would be successful if you undertake it, as I trust you will; & I beg you & your friends to accept my grateful acknowledgments of the high honor you have done me in making this proposition.

I shall anticipate the pleasure of meeting your brother [Maj. John Sanders] in Mexico, & I am Very truly & respectfully (signed[ ),] C. Cushing.

ALS with En in ScCleA. NOTE: Cushing, who had held and would hold numerous important public offices, had raised a regiment at his own expense and would join the army in Mexico where he would become a brigadier general. Which of Sanders's numerous projects is referred to is not clear, though it may have had to do with land speculation around Chicago and the Great Lakes on behalf of N.Y. capitalists.

SPEECH AT A MEETING OF CITIZENS OF CHARLESTON

Tuesday Evening, March 9, 1847

Fellow Citizens—In complying with the request of your committee to address you on the general state of our affairs, in connection with the Federal Government, I shall restrict my remarks to the subject of our peculiar domestic institution, not only because it is by far the most important to us, but, also, because I have fully expressed my views, in my place in the Senate, on the only other important subject, the Mexican war.

I fully concur in the address of your committee, and the resolutions accompanying it. The facts stated are unquestionable, and the conclusions irresistible.

Indeed, after all that has occurred during the last twelve months, it would be almost idiotic to doubt, that a large majority of both parties in the non-slaveholding States, have come to a fixed determination to appropriate all the Territories of the United States, now possessed, or hereafter to be acquired, to themselves, to the entire exclusion of the slaveholding States. Assuming, then, that to be beyond doubt, the grave, and to us, vital question is presented for consideration: have they the power to carry this determination into effect?

It will be proper to premise, before I undertake to answer this question, that it is my intention to place before you the danger with which we are threatened from this determination, plainly and fully, without exaggeration or extenuation, and, also, the advantages we have for repelling it, leaving it to you to determine what measures should be adopted for that purpose.

I now return to the question, and answer, Yes, they have the power, as far as mere numbers can give it. They will have a majority, in the next Congress, in every department of the Federal Government. The admission of Iowa and Wisconsin, will give them two additional States, and a majority of four in the Senate, which heretofore has been our shield against this and other dangers of the kind. We are already in a minority in the House of Representatives and the Electoral College; so that with the loss of the Senate, we shall be in a minority in every department of the Federal Government; and ever must continue so, if the non-slaveholding States should carry into effect their scheme of appropriating to their exclusive use all the Territories of the United States. But, fortunately, under our system of government mere numbers are not the only element of power. There are others, which would give us ample means of defending ourselves against the threatened danger, if we should be true to ourselves.

We have, in the first place, the advantage of having the Constitution on our side, clearly and unquestionably, and in its entire fabric; so much so, that the whole body of the instrument stands opposed to their scheme of appropriating the Territories to themselves. To make good this assertion, it is only necessary to remind you, that ours is a Federal, and not a National, or Consolidated Government— a distinction essential to correct understanding of the Constitution, and our safety. It ought never to be forgotten, or overlooked. As a Federal Government, the States composing the Union are its constituents, and stand in the same relation to it, in that respect, as the individual citizens of a State do to its government. As constituent members of the Union, all the Territories and other property of the Union belong to them, as joint owners or partners, and not to the Government, as is er[r]oneously supposed by some. The Government is but the agent intrusted with the management. And hence the Constitution expressly declares the Territory to be the property of the United States—that is the States united, or the States of the Union which are but synonymous expressions. And hence also Congress has no more right to appropriate the Territories of the United States to the use of any portion of the States, to the exclusion of the others, than it has to appropriate the same way the Forts, or other public buildings, or the Navy, or any other property, of the U. States. That it has such a right, no one would venture to assert; and yet, the one is placed exactly on the same ground with the other by the Constitution.

It was on this solid foundation that I placed the right of the slaveholding States to a full and equal participation in the Territories of the United States, in opposition to the determination of the non-slaveholding States to appropriate them exclusively to themselves. It was my intention to urge them to a vote, but I was unable to do so, in consequence of the great pressure of business during the last few days of the session. It was felt by those opposed to us, that, if the foundation on which I placed my resolutions be admitted, the conclusion could not be successfully assailed; and hence the bold, but unsuccessful attempt, to assail the foundation itself, by contending that ours is a National or Consolidated Government, in which the States would stand to the Union, as the counties do to the States, and be equally destitute of all political rights. Such a conclusion, if it could be established, would, indeed, place us and our peculiar domestic institutions, at the mercy of the non-slave holding States; but fortunately it cannot be maintained, without subverting the very foundation of our entire political system, and denying the most incontrovertible facts connected with the foundation and adoption of the Constitution.

But, it may be asked, what do we gain by having the Constitution ever so clearly on our side, when a majority in the non-slaveholding

States stand prepared to deny it? Possibly such may be the case: still we cannot fail to gain much by the advantage it gives us. I speak from long experience. I have never know[n] truth, promptly advocated in the spirit of truth, fail to succeed in the end. Already there are many highly enlightened and patriotic citizens in those States, who agree with us on this great and vital point. The effects of the discussion will not improbably greatly increase their number; and, what is of no little importance, induce a still greater number to hesitate, and abate somewhat in their confidence in former opinions, and thereby prepare the way to give full affect to another advantage which we possess. To understand what it is, it will be necessary to explain what is the motive and object of this crusade, on the part of the non-slaveholding States, against our peculiar domestic institution.

It is clear, that it does not originate in any hostility of interests. The labor of our slaves does not conflict with the profit of their capitalists, or the wages of their operatives; or in any way injuriously affect the prosperity of those States, either as it relates to their population or wealth. On the contrary, it greatly increases both. Its product, those which mainly stimulate and render their capital and labor profitable; while our slaves furnish, at the same time, an extensive and profitable market for what they make. Annihilate the products of their labor—strike from the list the three great articles, which are almost exclusively, the products of their labor—cotton, rice, and tobacco, and what would become of the great shipping, navigating, commercial and manufacturing interests of the non-slaveholding States? What of their Lowel[l]s and Walthams; their New York and Boston, and other manufacturing and commercial cities? What, to enlarge the question, would become of the exports and imports of the Union itself; its shipping and tonnage, its immense revenue, in the disbursements of which millions in those States, directly or indirectly, live and prosper? Fortunately, then, the crusade against our domestic institution does not originate in hostility of interests. If it did, the possibility of arresting the threatened danger, and saving ourselves, short of a disrupture of the Union, would be altogether hopeless; so predominant is the regard for interest in those States, over all other considerations.

Nor does it originate in any apprehension, that the slaveholding States would acquire an undue preponderance in the Union, unless restricted to their present limits. If even a full share of the Territories should fall to our lot, we could never hope to outweigh, by any increased number of slaveholding States, the great preponderance which their numbers give to the non-slaveholding States in the House of Representatives and the Electoral College. All we could hope for would be, to preserve an equality in the Senate, or, at most, to acquire a preponderance in that branch of the Government.

But, if it originates neither in the one nor the other of these, what are the real motives and objects of their crusade against our institution? To answer this, it will be necessary to explain what are the feelings and views of the people of the non-slaveholding States in reference to it, with their effects on their party operations, especially in relation to the Presidential election.

They may, in reference to the subject under consideration, be divided into four classes. Of these, the Abolitionists proper—the rabid fanatics, who regard slavery as a sin, and thus regarding it, deem it their highest duty to destroy it, even should it involve the destruction of the Constitution and the Union—constitute one class. It is a small one, not probably exceeding five per cent of the population of those States. They voted, if I recollect correctly, about 15,000, or at most 20,000 votes in the last test of their strength in the State of New-York, out of about 400,000 votes, which would give about five per cent. Their strength in that State, I would suppose, was fully equal to their average strength in the non-slaveholding States generally. Another class consists of the great body of the citizens of those States, constituting at least seven-tenths of the whole, and who, while they regard slavery as an evil, and as such are disposed to aid in restricting and extirpating it, when it can be done consistently with the Constitution, and without endangering the peace or prosperity of the country, do not regard it as a sin, to be put down by all and every means.

Of the other two, one is a small class, perhaps not exceeding five per cent of the whole, who view slavery as we do, more as an institution, and the only one, by which two races, so dissimilar as those inhabiting the slaveholding States, can live together nearly in equal numbers, in peace and prosperity, and that its abolition would end in the extirpation of one or the other race. If they regard it as an evil, it is in the abstract, just as government, with all its burdens, labor with all its toils, punishment, with all its inflictions, and thousands of other things, are evils, when viewed in the abstract, but far otherwise, when viewed in the concrete, because they prevent a greater amount of evil than what they inflict, as is the case of slavery as it exists with us.

The remaining class is much larger, but still relatively a small one, less, perhaps, than twenty per cent of the whole, but possessing great activity and political influence in proportion to its numbers.

It consists of the political leaders of the respective parties, and their partisans and followers. They, for the most part, are perfectly indifferent about Abolition, and are ready to take either side, for or against, according to the calculation of the political chances; their great and leading object being to carry the elections especially the Presidential, and thereby receive the honors and emoluments, incident to power, both in the Federal and State Governments.

Such are the views and feelings of the several classes in the non-slaveholding States, in reference to slavery, as it exists with us. It is manifest, on a survey of the whole, that the first class—that is, the Abolition party proper—is the centre which has given the impulse, that has put in motion this crusade against our domestic institution. It is the only one that has any decidedly hostile feelings in reference to it, and which, in opposing it, is actuated by any strong desire to restrict, or destroy it.

But, it may be asked, how can so small a class rally a large majority of both parties in the non-slave holding States to come to the determination they have, in reference to our domestic institution? To answer this question, it is necessary to go one step further, and explain the habitual state of parties in those, and, indeed, in almost all the States of the Union.

There are few of the non-slaveholding States, perhaps not more than two or three, in which the parties are not so nicely balanced, as to make the result of elections, both State and Federal, so doubtful, as to put it in the power of a small party, firmly linked together, to turn the elections, by throwing their weight into the scale of the party, which may most favour its views: such is the Abolition party. They have, from the first, made their views paramount to the party struggles of the day, and thrown their weight where their views could be best promoted. By pursuing this course, their influence was soon felt in the elections, and, in consequence, to gain them soon became the object of party courtship: first by the Whigs; but for the last twelve months, more eagerly by the Democrats, as if to make up for lost time. They are now openly courted by both; each striving by their zeal to win their favour by expressing their earnest desire to exclude what they call slavery from all the territories of the United States, acquired or to be acquired. No doubt the Mexican war, and the apprehension of large acquisition of territory to the slave-holding States, has done much to produce this state of things; but of itself it would have been feeble. The main cause or motive, then, of this crusade against our domestic institution, is to be traced to the all-absorbing interest, which both parties take, in carrying the elections, especially the Presidential. Indeed, when we reflect that the expenditure of the Federal Government, at all times great, is now swelled probably to the rate of seventy million of dollars annually, and that the influence of its patronage gives it great sway, not only over its own, but over the State elections, which gives in addition a control over a vast amount of patronage, and the control of the Federal patronage, with all its emoluments and honors, centre in the President of the United States, it is not at all surprising, that both parties should take such absorbing interest in the Presidential election; acting, as both do, on the principle of turning opponents out of office, and bestowing the honors and emoluments of Government on their followers, as the reward of partizan services. In such a state of things, it is not a matter for wonder, that a course of policy, so well calculated to conciliate a party like the Abolitionists, as that of excluding slavery from the Territories, should be eagerly embraced by both parties, in the non-slave holding States, when by securing their support, each calculates on winning the rich and glittering prize of the Presidency. In this is to be found the motive and object of the present crusade against our domestic institution, on the part of political leaders and their partizans in those States.

It would be a great mistake to suppose that it is the less dangerous, because it originates mainly in mere party considerations, in connection with elections. It will be on that account but the more so, unless, indeed, it should be met by us with promptitude and unanimity. The absorbing, over-riding interest, felt by both parties to carry the elections, especially the Presidential, would give such an impulse to their efforts to conciliate the Abolitionists, at our expense, if we should look on with apparent indifference, as would enlist in their favor the large portion of the non-slaveholding States, estimated at seven tenths of the whole, which are as yet well affected towards us, and utterly dishearten the small but intelligent class, which, as yet, is perfectly sound. The former would conclude, in that case, that we ourselves were ready to yield and surrender our domestic institution, as indefensible; and that the non-slaveholding States might carry their determination into full effect, without hazard to the Constitution or the Union, or even disturbing the harmony and peace of the country. Indeed, such has already been our apparent indifference, that these opinions have been expressed, even on the floor of Congress. But, if we should act as we ought—if we, by our promptitude, energy, and unanimity, prove that we stand ready to defend our rights, and to maintain our perfect equality, as members of the Union, be the consequences what they may; and that the immediate and necessary effect of courting Abolition votes, by either party, would be to lose ours, a very diffe[re]nt result would certainly follow. That large portion of the non-slaveholding States, who, although they consider slavery as an evil, are not disposed to violate the Constitution, and much less to endanger its overthrow, and with it the Union itself, would take sides with us, against our assailants; while the sound portion, who are already with us, would rally to the rescue. The necessary effect would be, that the party leaders and their followers, who expect to receive the Presidential election, by the aid of the Abolitionists, seeing their hopes blasted by the loss of our votes, would drop their courtship, and leave the party, reduced to insignificance, with scorn. The end would be, should we act in the manner indicated, the rally of a new party in the non-slaveholding States, more powerful than either of the old, who, on this great question, would be faithful to all of the compromises and obligations of the Constitution, and who by uniting with us, would put a final stop to the farther agitation of this dangerous question. Such would be the certain effect of meeting, with promptitude and unanimity, the determination of the non-slaveholding States to appropriate all the Territories to their own use. That it has not yet been so met is certain; and the next question is: Why has it not been, and what is the cause of this apparent indifference in reference to a danger so menacing, if not promptly and unitedly met on our part?

In answering this important question, I am happy to say, that I have seen no reason to attribute this want of promptitude and unanimity to any division of sentiment, or real indifference, on the part of the people of the slaveholding States, or their delegates in Congress. On the contrary, as far as my observation extends, there is not one of their members of Congress, who has given any certain indication of either. On the trying questions connected with the Wilmot proviso, the votes of the members from the slaveholding States, at the last and present sessions, were unanimous. To explain what is really the cause, I must again recur to what has already been stated; the absorbing interest felt in the elections, especially the Presidential, and the controlling influence which party leaders and their followers exercise over them. The great struggle between the parties is, which shall succeed in electing its candidate; in consequence of which, the Presidential election has become the paramount question. All others are held subordinate to it by the leaders and their followers. It depends on them to determine whether any question shall be admitted into the issue between the parties, in the Presidential contest, or whether it shall be partially or entirely excluded. Whether it shall be one or the other, is decided entirely in reference to its favorable or unfavorable bearing on the contest, without looking to the higher considerations of its effects on the prosperity, the institutions, or safety of the country. Nothing can more strongly illustrate the truth of what I have asserted, than the course of the parties in relation to the question which now claims your attention. Although none can be more intimately connected with the peace and safety of the Union, it is kept out of the issue between the parties, because it is seen that the Presidential vote of New York, and many others of the non-slave-holding States, will in all probability depend on the votes of the Abolitionists; and that the election of the President may in like manner depend on the votes of those States. And hence the leaders in them are tolerated by many of the leaders and their followers in the slaveholding States, in openly canvassing for the vote of the Abolitionists, by acting in unison with them, in reference to a question, on the decision of which the safety of their own section, and that of the Union, itself may depend. But while it is seen that the Presidential election may be secured by counting [*sic*; courting] the Abolition votes, it is at the same time seen, that it may be lost, if the consequence should be the loss of the vote of the slaveholding States: and hence the leaders are forced to attempt to secure the former without losing the latter. The game is a difficult one; but as difficult as it is, they do not despair of success, with the powerful instrument, which they have under their control. They have, in the first place, that of the party press, through which a mighty influence is exerted over public opinion. The line of policy adopted is, for the party press to observe a profound silence on this great and vital question; or, if they speak at all, so speak, as to give a false direction to public opinion. Acting in conformity to this policy, of the two leading organs at the seat of Government, one [the Whig *Daily National Intelligencer*] never alludes to the question, so that as far as its remarks are concerned, no one could suppose that it was the cause of the least agitation or feeling in any portion of the Union. The other [the Democratic *Daily Union*], occasionally alludes to it, when it cannot well avoid doing so; but only to palliate the conduct of those who assail us, by confounding them with our defenders as agitators, and holding both up equally to public censure. It is calculated, by pursuing this course, that the people of the slave-holding States will be kept quiet, and in a state of indifference, until another and still more powerful instrument can be brought into play, by which it is hoped that Slaveholders and Abolitionists will be coerced to join in nominating and supporting the same candidate for the Presidency. I allude to what is called a National Convention, or Caucus, for nominating candidates for the Presidency and Vice-Presidency. Already the machinery has been put in motion, in order to coerce [Virginia] the oldest and most populous of the slave-holding States; and no doubt, will, in due season, be put in motion to effect the same object in all of them. Should it succeed—should party machinery for President making prove strong enough to force the slave-holding States to join in a convention to nominate and support a candidate who will be acceptable to the Abolitionists, they will have committed the most suicidal act that a people ever perpetrated. I say acceptable; for it is clear that the non-slave holding States will outnumber in Convention the slave-holding, and that no one who is not acceptable to the Abolitionists can receive their votes, and, of course, the votes of the States where they hold the balance; and that no other will be nominated, or, if nominated, be elected. And yet, there are not a few in the slave-holding States, men of standing and influence, so blinded by party feelings, or the prospect of personal gain or advancement by the success of their party, who advocate a step which must prove so fatal to their portion of the Union, under existing circumstances. Can party folly, or rather madness, go farther?

As to myself, I have ever been opposed to such Conventions: because they are irresponsible bodies, not known to the Constitution; and because they, in effect, set aside the Constitution with its compromises, in reference to so important a subject as the election of the Chief Magistrate of the Union. I hold it far safer, and every way preferrable, to leave the election where the Constitution has placed it: to the Electoral College to choose; and if that fails to make a choice, to the House of Representatives, voting by States, to elect the President from the three candidates, having the highest votes. But, if I had no objection to such Conventions, under ordinary circumstances, I would regard the objection, as fatal, under the existing, when all parties of the non-slaveholding States stand united against us, on the most vital of all questions, and when to go into one would be, in effect, a surrender on our part. As both parties there have united to divest us of our just and equal rights in the public domains, it is time that both parties with us should unite in resistance to so great an outrage. Let us show, at least, as much spirit in defending our rights and honor, as they have evinced in assailing them. Let us, when our safety is concerned, show at least as firm a determination, and as much unanimity, as they do, with no other interest on their part but the temporary one of succeeding in the Presidential contest. Henceforward, let all party distinction among us cease, so long as this aggression on our rights and honor shall continue, on the part of the non-slaveholding States. Let us profit by the example of the Abolition party, who, as small as they are, have acquired so much influence by the course they have pursued. As they make the destruction of our domestic institution the paramount question, so let us make, on our part, its safety the paramount question. Let us regard every man of our party, who stands up in its defence; and every one as against us, who does not, until aggression ceases. It is thus, and thus only, that we can defend our rights, maintain our honor, ensure our safety, and command respect. The opposite course, which would merge them in the temporary and mercenary party struggles of the day, would inevitably degrade and ruin us.

If we should prove true to ourselves and our peculiar domestic institution, we shall be great and prosperous, let what will occur. There is no portion of the globe more abundant in resources—agricultural, manufacturing and commercial—than that possessed by us. We count among our productions the great staples of cotton, rice, tobacco and sugar, with the most efficient, well fed, well clad, and well trained body of labourers for their cultivation. In addition to furnishing abundant means for domestic exchanges among ourselves, and with the rest of the world, and building up flourishing commercial cities, they would furnish ample resources for revenue. But far be it from us to desire to be forced on our own resources for protection. Our object is to preserve the Union of these States, if it can be done consistently with our rights, safety, and perfect equality with other members of the Union. On this we have a right to insist. Less we cannot take. Looking at the same time to our safety and the preservation of the Union, I regard it as fortunate that the promptitude and unanimity, on our part, necessary to secure the one, are equally so to preserve the other. Delay, indecision, and want of union among ourselves, would in all probability, in the end, prove fatal to both. The danger is of a character, whether we regard our safety or the preservation of the Union, which cannot be safely tampered with. If not met promptly and decidedly, the two portions of the Union will gradually become thoroughly alienated, when no alternative will be left to us, as the weaker of the two, but to sever all political ties, or sink down into abject submission. It is only by taking an early and decided stand, while the political ties are still strong, that a rally of the sound and patriotic of all portions of the Union can be successfully made, to arrest so dire an alternative.

Having now pointed out the danger with which we are menaced, and the means by which it may be successfully met and resisted, it is for you, and the people of the other slaveholding States, to determine what shall be done, at a juncture so trying and eventful. In conclusion, it is my sincere prayer, that the Great Disposer of events may enlighten you and them to realize its full extent, and give the wisdom to adopt the best and most efficient course for our own security, and the peace and preservation of the Union.

From the Charleston, S.C., *Mercury*, March 23, 1847, p. 2. Also printed in the Charleston, S.C., *Southern Patriot*, March 23, 1847, p. 2; the Washington, D.C., *Daily Union*, March 27, 1847, p. 2; the New York, N.Y., *Herald*, March 28, 1847, p. 1; the Edgefield, S.C., *Advertiser*, March 31, 1847, pp. 1–2; the Columbia, S.C., *South-Carolinian*, March 31, 1847, p. 1; the Greenville, S.C., *Mountaineer*, April 2, 1847, p. 1; *Niles' National Register*, vol. LXII, no. 5 (April 3, 1847), pp. 73–75; the New York, N.Y., *National Anti-Slavery Standard*, April 8, 1847, p. 1; the Columbia, S.C., *Southern Chronicle*, April 14, 1847, p. 1; the Camden, S.C., *Journal*, April 14, 1847, p. 1; the Washington, D.C., *Daily National Intelligencer*, May 27, 1847, p. 2; *Remarks of Mr. Calhoun, at the Meeting of the Citizens of Charleston, Tuesday Evening, March 9, 1847* (n.p., [1847?]), 8 pp.; Crallé, ed., *Works*, 4:382–396; Anderson, ed., *Calhoun: Basic Documents*, pp. 253–265; Lence, ed., *Union and Liberty*, pp. 525–537. Variant in the Washington, D.C., *Daily Union*, March 15, 1847, p. 2; the Alexandria, Va., *Gazette and Virginia Advertiser*, March 16, 1847, p. 2. Another variant in the Washington, D.C., *Daily National Intelligencer*, March 16, 1847, p. 3; the Cincinnati, Ohio, *Daily Enquirer*, March 24, 1847, p. 2. Another variant in the Georgetown, S.C., *Winyah Observer*, March 17, 1847, p. 1; the Columbia, S.C., *Southern Chronicle*, March 24, 1847, p. 1. NOTE: Crallé's version of this speech (upon which all later printings have been so far based), is slightly variant in incidentals and a few words, though not substantively so. The Charleston, S.C., *Mercury*, March 10, 1847, p. 2, describes in full the occasion of this speech, including the public proceedings that led to and followed from it. The meeting adopted resolutions that "submission to the proposed exclusion from an equality of benefits in the Territories of the United States, beyond what is already yielded by the Missouri Compromise, would be unwise, dangerous, dishonorable and debasing"; that "this is a question paramount to all considerations of party, or mere temporary policy"; and that strong endorsement was given to resolutions recently adopted by the House of Delegates of Virginia. (The Virginia resolutions avowed that the federal government had no control over slavery; that a prohibition of slavery in any territory would not be recognized, being an invasion of every citizen's natural right of property; that it was the duty of all lovers of the Union to oppose any such prohibition; and that the slaveholding States should take "firm, united and concerted action in this emergency.") The resolutions having been adopted at the Charleston meeting, "Mr. Calhoun was loudly called for." According to the *Mercury*, he addressed "an unusually large and enthusiastic meeting of the citizens of Charleston District assembled at the New Theatre." When Calhoun's speech had concluded, "the whole assemblage manifested their concurrence in its sentiments by the most enthusiastic cheering." The *Mercury* of March 10 also noted: "Our Reporter took copious notes of Mr. Calhoun's remarks, but, from their important character, it is deemed advisable not to publish them until they have the benefit of his revision, when we will lay them before our readers." According to at least one account, a similar meeting was held at Columbia on 3/15, at which Calhoun was reportedly present but Senator Andrew P. Butler was the speaker.

To DUFF GREEN, [Washington]

Charleston, 9th March 1847

My dear Sir, I have just returned from addressing a very large and enthusiastick meeting. It is said to be the largest ever held here. I find perfect unanimity here, including Whigs and democrats. I never have been received even here with greater unanimity and enthusiasm than ever. I got your letter [of 3/4?] and prospectus. I placed the lat[t]er in the hands of several intelligent friends. It met their entire approbation.

I find the impression here is, that $25,000 would be necessary to place a daily paper at Washington on a solid foundation. I have had a full conversation with several capitalists, who are firmly attached to the cause, in order to ascertain what portion of it can be raised here. They required time to consider and decide. They are to inform me as soon as their decision is made, when, if it should be favorable, I will write to leading friends in other States. I think the indications here favorable but it will take time to make arrangements. The fate of the Constitutionalist [*sic*; the Washington *Constitution*] has cast a damp. Ten thousand dollars was raised here to support it. The whole has been lost without doing any good.

The selection of the editor, you know, must depend on the leading contributors. I suggested your name, as if sounding; and I am bound in candour to say, there was no re[s]ponse. Nothing was said in disparagement of you, but I was forced to infer that it did not meet with approbation. As to myself, I am inclined to think that the course your prospectus indicates, to restore the old organ [the *United States' Telegraph*] and its editor, under its proper name, would be a very successful move; perhaps the most successful, which could be made; but it is, I fear, too bold to obtain the assent of the timid, who constitute so large a portion of any party. I would individually be glad; nay rejoice to see you restored to your old position. I have confidence in your friendship, and am grateful for your support in passing through some of the eventful periods of my life; but I feel confident you will see that the relation I bear to you of a private character and the position I occupy in the party put it out of my power to speak in anything like a tone of authority on the subject.

I have written you in the sperit you requested, but it is proper to add that I do not consider that there is anything yet settled in reference to the paper or its editors, and that I would be most gratified to see your great experience and talents associated in conducting it, should it be established.

As to myself, I look wholly to the cause and would really rejoice to see some one take the lead and receive the appropriate honors of leadership instead of myself. I am most anxious to retire to the quiet of private life, after my long and laborious publick service; but it seems to me the more I do, the more I am compelled to do, and the farther I recede from retirement.

I shall write you again, when I hear from my friends from Charleston about the paper.

Mrs. [Floride Colhoun] Calhoun joins her kind regards to yourself, Mrs. [Lucretia Maria Edwards] Green and family.

I enclose this to Mr. Bull to avoid the espionage of the post-office.

PC in Jameson, ed., *Correspondence*, pp. 718–720.

From Cha[rle]s N. Webb

Halifax, N.C., March 9, 1847

Dear Sir: You will please accept my thanks for the Speeches you sent me—A notice of which you will see in to-day[']s "Republican"—a copy of which has been forwarded to your Address, with the article *marked.* In that article I speak the sentiments of my heart. And although I have been opposed to you in politics ever since you joined the "fallen fortunes" of Mr. [Martin] Van Buren; at all times, I would have been willing to have seen you in the Presidential Chair—but not as the Loco foco, or Party President.

When you turned against General [Andrew] Jackson, the Hero of N. Orleans, and South Carolina nullified, I was with you. I have been opposed to the "powers that be" ever since. I thought you never would leave me—but suppose you done so from the promptings of an honest heart. I have been in your company—have conversed with you freely—my wife, once, had the pleasure of your company from this place to Petersburg in the Stages. She frequently speaks of Mr. Calhoun—and says "he is a great man—Can it be possible that he differs with us in Politics[?]" We were opposed to the Administration then—we are now. I was then an Editor and am now. My wife frequently assists me in the Editorial department.

Sir I have been an Editor ever since 1834, and have never applied for any office—and if I can succeed as well hereafter as I have heretofore, in all probability I never will: but fat offices are very enticing. I have resisted, or rather declined solicitations to become a candidate for a Seat in our State Legislature. But I have no political aspirations to gratify—save that of an honest discharge of duty as Editor; and so long as I can obtain a comfortable living by that I shall stick to it.

Sir: I love you—and would rejoice to see you President of these United States. (But not the President of a Party.) Can[']t the thing be brought about?

It would afford me great pleasure to receive a letter from you and if you deem me worthy of notice, when at leisure I hope you will write me. You have many warm friends here. But they don[']t belong to the [James K.] Polk or Van Buren Party—Tom Benton, [Lewis] Cass or [William] Allen Party—But the Nullifiers—the friends of Henry Clay—the friends of [William Henry] Harrison.

I write this letter in great haste and send it off without giving it a reading. I am, Respectfully Yours, Chas. N. Webb, Editor of the "Roanoke Republican."

ALS in ScCleA. NOTE: There appear to be no extant files of the *Roanoke Republican* for 1847, making it impossible to identify the article mentioned. Calhoun's AEU on this letter reads: "Editor of the R[oano]ke Republican."

From JOHN HEART

Charleston, March 10, '47

Dear Sir, The "Evening News" has published a sketch of your remarks [at Charleston on 3/9], and as it is something like the "tracks" I used to furnish, and preserves the order in which you made your points, I have thought it might be useful to you in writing out. I think it very important that the "remedy" should be enlarged upon, and the abuses of the "Convention" system exposed. I think, from the tone of the Southern press, that the public mind is open to information, and the question connecting itself with the great Southern question, makes the present moment especially opportune for the exposition. I have suggested to some of the ["South" *canceled*] gentlemen here the propriety, when we receive your speech, to republish the entire proceedings in their proper connection, and to have it printed in pamphlet form for circulation, and it is probable that it will be done. The Augusta "Constitutionalist" of this morning takes the "back track" decidedly, as to some of its hard sayings, about you, and what is even more important, gives the present National Convention System a hard hit, and says that your system of electing delegates by Congressional districts is "decidedly preferable." Very truly & respectfully your friend & serv[an]t, Jno. Heart.

ALS with En in ScCleA. NOTE: Heart enclosed an article, "Remarks of Mr. Calhoun," from the Charleston *Evening News* of 3/10.

From M. A. ALLEN BROWN

Wilkesboro N.C., March 11th 1847

It is with feelings of deepest sorrow and most poignant regret that I have learned through the public Gazettes of the country that you have alienated your affections and withdrawn your support from the great Republican party of the Union and associated yourself with the selfstyled Whig but more propperly termed the Federal and anti-american party of the United States. In as much as I have heretofore been one of your firmest supporters and most ardent votaries, I deem it ["but" *canceled*] no more than a fixed duty for me to communicate to you what I have heard and to solicit from you an answer under your own hand and seal, explanatory of your present position in order that I may know in what way to shape my future political course as I cannot think of withdrawing my support from one whom I have allways regarded as my political Savior. With high regard & esteem I have the honor to subscribe myself your ob[edien]t Servant, M.A. Allen Brown.

ALS in ScCleA. NOTE: Mailed at Wilkesboro on 3/14, this letter was addressed to Calhoun at Greenwood, S.C.

From WILSON LUMPKIN,
[former Senator from Ga.]

Athens [Ga.,] March 11th 1847

My dear Sir, I stop a moment from my busy, but humble cares, to thank you for your three speeches rec[e]ived yesterday. I was truly anxious to see your reply to [Thomas H.] Benton, as I had not met with it, in any paper which I read.

Your reply to Benton[']s, low, vulgar & impudent attack, is such as I should have expected from you—and wherever read by well informed men, will be considered a complete vindication on your part. But I suppose you are apprized of the fact, that at this time, that almost the whole press of the Country, seem to be combined to destroy your influence with your Countrymen. Moreover, almost every office seeker, of both parties, unite with the subservient presses to do you all the injury they can. True, there may be found some few honorable exceptions, both of the press & politi[ci]ans—but the voice of these few, ["are" *canceled*] is overwhelmed, by the many who ride upon the tide of the storm, which they have designedly created. I hope justice may [be] done you during your life—& if not you must look to Posterity.

It was impossible for you longer to avoid, your late conflicts in the Senate. It was forced upon you, by [Thomas] Ritch[i]e, [Hopkins L.] Turney, Benton &C.[;] indeed I have no doubt, but you were doomed by the councils of the leaders of the present dominant party, to be forced into your present position.

In regard to your course, upon the expulsion of Ritch[i]e [from the Senate], I think he deserved, richly deserved, expulsion. Yet I think it was, unwise in the Senate, to take any notice at all, of the *Old hack.* His *libels* could never have injured the Senate, & their proceedings have only served, to give him a consequence, which he could have acquired in no other way. And the whole press, have united with him, to pervert the whole transaction, to the injury of those who expelled him, from his priviledges in the Senate chamber.

In regard to Turney, Benton & Co. as far as I am informed, it appears to me, that your course has been dignifyed & correct.

After all, I suppose Benton will be placed at the head of the Army—whether for good, or evil—let time develope. I see from the tone of the press here, an effort will be made, to place Gen[era]l [Lewis] Cass, at the head of the Southern Democrats. His late War speech has been extensively circulated here.

Your peace policy throughout has been right. The settlement of the Oregon question, on the 49° has met the approbation of the wise & the good every where. If the Mexican War, could have been avoided, it certainly ought to have been done.

Under any circumstances, many evils will result from the War—I fear more than will be counter-balanced by good. For myself, I can do nothing but stand still & wait for the Salvation of God. The opinions of men of experience & age, are not respected, as they once were. Politics have become a *trade*—& office seekers are ever war[r]ing against the influence of the Patriotic, the wise & the good.

There is ["no" *interlined*] way permanently calculated to benefit & save the Country, but to lessen the patronage & power of the Federal Government.

Patrick Henry was the great man of his day—& was under the influence of a far seeing view of things, approaching a Prophetic spirit. The Mexican War, cannot last long. The people are tired of it.

My family join me in great respect & best regard for you & y[ou]rs. Wilson Lumpkin.

ALS in ScCleA; PEx in Boucher and Brooks, eds., *Correspondence*, pp. 369–370.

From DUFF GREEN

Washington, 17th March 1847

My dear Sir, Do you recieve [*sic*] the [Washington] "Union"? If you have read the daily attacks made upon you th[r]ough that paper you must see that the managers now expect to consolidate the [Democratic] party by denouncing you, and thus, by intimidation, prevent any desertion from their ranks. The correspondence between [James K.] Polk and [Thomas H.] Benton, & the editorials in the Union leave you no alternative, but submission or resistance[;] if you are resolved to submit, then I will be a very unfit person to take charge of the paper here, if you are resolved to vindicate your own character, and to rally your friends then I do not hesitate to say that you cannot find a single person in the United [States] so competent in all respects as I am.

I say this because ["be" *canceled*] the time has come when it is not only proper but necessary that we should understand each other. In your letter [of 3/9] from Charleston you say, "The selection of the Editor you know must depend on the leading contributors. I suggested your name, as if sounding, and I am bound in candor to say there was no response. Nothing was said in disparagement of you but I was forced to infer that it did not meet with approbation." And after speaking of your own views you say, "I feel confident that you will see that the relation I bear to you of a private character and the position I occupy in the party put it out of my power to speak in any thing like a tone of authority on the subject."

I have found some difficulty in replying to your suggestion. So far from seeing as you suppose that there is any thing in our private relations or in your position to the party making it improper for you to *insist* on my being the Editor, I see precisely the reverse.

Our private relations are those of confidence and friendship. I have demonstrated that friendship by sacrifices personal and pecuniary such as no other personal friend has ever made or ever will make for you or the cause in which we have both labored. I have never pretended to you, as some who have done much less, that those sacrifices were made for you alone, but you must be aware that my respect and attachment for the man, were blended with my devotion to the principles for which those sacrifices were made.

When your false friends in 1834, impatient of delay were preparing to betray you and your principles they commenced their operations by efforts to persuade you that, you could be benefitted by substituting another Editor. I then warned you of their real purpose, but unwilling to impede your prospects in any manner I surrendered my press into the hands of an Editor selected by them and paid him out of my own pocket the salary which they pledged themselves to pay.

When [Francis W.] Pickens and [Dixon H.] Lewis formed their coalition with [Francis P.] Blair & [John C.] Rives in 1840 I foresaw what would come of it and then refused to be a candidate for printer to Congress because I would not have you appear in a false position or seperate you from friends in whom you had confidence.

I need not now repeat what then passed between us, but I refer to the past, that I may say that no act of your public life has done you so much prejudice with the people as the impression that you have not given me that support which I had a right under the circumstances to expect, and that that is one reason why my support is more important to you than that of any other person.

I write thus frankly because it is proper that we should understand each other distinctly on this point. If there be any thing in our private relations which in your opinion makes it improper that you should *insist* that I should be the Editor of a paper which is to be organ of a party of which you are the acknowledged head it is proper that I should know it. I have now been proscribed for many years, by [Andrew] Jackson, [Martin] Van Buren, [John] Tyler & [James K.] Polk because they all feared that any influence I might obtain would be exerted for you. If your *friends* can persuade *you* that I should be proscribed for any cause, knowing me as you do, and committed to me as you are upon the subject of this paper it is time that I should know it. ["You and they only let(?)" *canceled*] I only await your reply to determine my course. I am resolved to vindicate your character against [Thomas] Ritch[i]e[']s attacks. If your friends establish a paper with a view to your nomination as a candidate for the Presidency and wish me to edit it, & give me the guarantees of support I am willing to undertake. If they prefer another, I can be at no loss as to the motives and will be at no loss for the means to establish a paper ["and in that case you will be no longer embarrassed by our 'private relations' because I shall ("take" *interlined*) special care to let it be known that I am no longer your political partisan" *canceled*]. Yours truly, Duff Green.

ALS in ScCleA; PC in Boucher and Brooks, eds., *Correspondence*, pp. 370–372.

From Geo[rge] Montgomery

New York [City,] March 18th 1847
Dear Sir, The enclosed are the Sentiments and views Lately expressed at a Meeting of several of your friends, in this city, among whom, I recognized [Charles A.] Clinton, McKracken [*sic*; John L.H. McCracken], Brady, [George E.] Baldwin, and others, who are ever ready to advance your interest, when an opportunity offers. With the greatest respect I remain Your friend and ob[edient] S[ervan]t, Geo. Montgomery, No. 9 Third St., New York.

[Enclosure]
This is the question. On what common ground can Northern & Southern men meet as supporters of Mr. Calhoun for the Presidency? What can the North say to Slavery? What can we do about it? This is the difficulty, and if we solve it there is none behind. We want a clear intelligible and acceptable explanation on this point, and we want that only, to unite this nation as one man.

Nobody pretends now, but the mad and mischievous abolitionist, that we are to meddle with existing Slavery. But we want new Territory, and some of us want a great deal, and events just now seem to favour their views who want most. Is the Congress of the U.S. by law or resolution, or the President and Senate by Treaty, to debar forever the existence of slavery in such Territory? Is Government to meddle with the question at all? for if so, then the Slavery question becomes an element to be considered among the reasons for preferring one candidate for office to another. It is to be presumed that every man in office will act in accordance with the principles he has professed before election, at all events we know Mr. Calhoun will, and we know what his principles are. Nevertheless there is a difference of position which must and will have its effect, and that effect an important one. The Senator is the advocate of a section of the country, forced to be so by the interests and opinions of other sections, pressing on all sides against him. The President is the representative of the whole people, set above debate, to act calmly for the views[,] wishes and interests of the whole.

But in this matter what can President or Congress do? They can refuse to acquire this Territory in question perhaps, though that I doubt, as public opinion appears at present. But will that prevent Slavery from invading it? Not at all. The South and South-west are ready to rush in there, to acquire and use the land, whoever may be its nominal sovereigns, and Mexico can no more keep out the Slave immigration than the free. She may preserve a nominal sovereignty for a few years, and then an independent nation will rise up and shake her off as Texas did, and in that nation there will be Slavery wherever the soil makes it profitable. Are we to take the land then by Treaty, and bind ourselves to Mexico in the treaty itself that we will preserve it forever free from slavery? We should thus confer on our neighbour a strange right of supervisorship, but suppose it done; or suppose what is less offensive that we took the country without stipulation, but passed an act in the spirit of the Wilmot proviso, and attempted to enforce it. And then suppose, what might very probably happen, that a large body of emigrating planters should set our law at defiance. Suppose some thousands of well armed resolute men possessing and cultivating a district beyond the Rio Grande with their slaves, holding them without law, or against law, but resolved to hold them to the last. Are we prepared to make war upon such a population? Let us think of it in time and decide calmly, for such is the alternative before us. The slave population will find its way in spite of us and in spite of Mexico, to the districts suited for its use. Mexico can do nothing about it, if we leave her the country, slavery will be legalised in the whole of it. If we take it from her, then our northern views, if urged with moderation, will effect a reasonable compromise, and will thus narrow down the inevitable slavery, to the smallest possible confines. But even if all this were to be denied, if we were to argue on the idea of an effectual prohibition by Congress, so long as this is Territory, what can we do when States are formed. Congress admits a State on conditions regarding slavery; but what if that free and independent State, the next year, casts off those conditions, can Congress enforce them? or expel her from the Confederacy? The idea is absurd. Slavery is a matter of geography, of soil and climate, and so long as there are slaves to be bought, wherever they are profitable they will be used. In new countries and southern climates they are eminently profitable, and legislation might as well attempt to turn the Gulf stream, as to prevent their employment.

With regard then to Territory, (unincumbered with the Spanish race) let us first acquire all we can, in the clearest conviction that its chances are better on anti-slavery principles than they can be if it be left to itself. Secondly let us not legislate for this territory till we have acquired it; and lastly when we have it, let us not attempt anything which we are morally certain of not being able to effect. As much as we can effect, every northern man will join in attempting against the extension of Slavery, and should we differ with Mr. Calhoun on that point practically then as we differ from him theoretically now, that difference must be referred to our great arbiters, majorities. We have points enough of agreement with him ["fixed," *interlined*] to quiet our fears in leaving this one open.

ALS with En in ScCleA. NOTE: Included in the number of Calhoun's New York supporters were James T. Brady, John H. Brady and James H. Brady.

To T[HOMAS] G. CLEMSON, [Brussels]

Fort Hill, 19th March 1847

My dear Sir, I received yours by the last steamer but a short time before I left Washington.

On my return, I meet [*sic*] Mrs. [Floride Colhoun] Calhoun in Charleston waiting my arrival. My reception by the ["citize" *changed to* "city"] authorities & the citizens generally was warm, & even enthusiastick—never more so. I remained four days, and addressed a crowded meeting in the theater the evening preceeding my leaving. It was literally cram[m]ed, and hundreds had to retire from the impossibility of getting in. I was unfortunately labouring under a severe cold, accompanied by hoarseness; but I succeed[ed] in making my self heard, in a short address of about 30 or 40 minutes. I dwelt wholly on the slave question, its danger and our means for resisting it. The time is come when it must be brought to a final decision. The next session will indicate what that will be. From present appearance it will be one of the most important sessions since the commencement of the Government.

We took your place [in Edgefield District] in our route home, and remained two days; but unfortunately the first was one of incessant rain, & the next cloudy & rain. The [Saluda] river, in addition, was all over the low grounds. The overseer [—— Mobley] said it was higher, than it had been for years; but, fortunately, it did no damage. It fell rapidly & left the oats uninjured. They were just coming up.

I, of course, had no opportunity to look at the place, except what was adjacent to the house & road; but I made careful enquiry about every thing. The overseer informed me, that he had cleared & would put in corn, about 40 acres of new ground, the best on the place, which another year will make a field, taking in the good cotton land adjacent, of upwards of 50 acres, which ought to give 50,000 pounds of seed cotton, one year with[?] another. He also informed me, that he had put in all the oats & had manured between 30 & 40 acres of land. He was backward in ploughing, owing to the excessive wetness of the winter. I found that to be the case all along the road, & even on my own place here. The stock, he informed me was in good order. The hogs had greatly increased, & what, I saw of them, & the mules looked well. The negroes, with the exception of colds, which have been common & severe, were well, & [*one word canceled*] contented. The only ["po" *canceled*] ill fortune that had occur[r]ed, as far as I could learn, was the death of one of the negro children, Joe's son, about 7 or 8 years old. It died shortly after our arrival at the place. The disease was worms. Every care seems to have been taken of it. It passed a great number of worms. Orders were given to attend to the other children in time by giving verminefuge [*sic*] ["medicine" *interlined*].

I have not yet gone over my own place, except the field intended for cotton, (Speed[']s field) now containing, with the addition made to it, ["of" *canceled*] 120 acres. I find it in very fine order, thoroughly ditched, with hill sides drains, well ploughed, & freed, to a great extent, from rocks. About 30 acres of it has been manured. The other portion of the plantation, I had put in order before I left home. The whole of my up land is now secured[?] by Hill side drains, which, I trust, by the aid of sub ploughing & a rotation of crops, will be effectually saved from washing. I doubt whether there is a place in the State, out of the region of the Sea Island cotton & rice, in as good order.

My cold, or rather cough, still continues, but is better, & I hope, I may get, in a great measure clear of it, as warm weather approaches.

The family is well. Mrs. Calhoun writes to Anna [Maria Calhoun Clemson] by the same conveyance with this, & will give all the news.

All join their love. Your affectionate father, J.C. Calhoun.

ALS in ScCleA; PEx in Jameson, ed., *Correspondence*, p. 720.

From W[illia]m M. Morton

Athens [Ga.,] 19 March 1847
Dear Sir, The Citizens of this place held a meeting this day on the subject of getting a good road from Pendleton Villedge to Athens, At which meeting I had the Honor of presiding as Chairman ["& Mr. (Asbury?) Hull Secretary" *interlined*]. The meeting resolved to Appoint Com[m]issioners on behalf of the people of this place to meet such Com[m]issioners of Pendl[e]ton as May be appointed to examine the Country and look out for the best route. We are exceedingly anxious for this Com[m]unication to be open[e]d which we flatter ourselves will be for the mutual benefit of both. Our Com[m]issioners will be ready to act as soon as we are informed of the readiness of any which may be appointed on your side. They will meet them in Pendleton[,] Athens or any intermediate point designated by yourself. Yours very respectfully, Wm. M. Morton, Ch[airman].

[Enclosure]
["myself & Mr. B.F. Sloan was s" *canceled*]. At a Meeting of the citizens of this place held a short time since we ["myself & Mr. B.F." *canceled*] Sloan [*sic*] have been appointed to act ["with" *canceled*] as commissioners with those ["appointed" *altered to* "chosen"] by the citizens of your place for the purpose of selecting the most practicable route ["from this place to Athens" *canceled*] between the two places.

We beg ["leave" *canceled*] that you would inform the commissioners on your part that we are ready at any time to meet them at

271

a suitable point & would suggest that we meet ["them" *interlined*] at Fords Store Formerly Dr. Eustis['s?] residence which is 9 miles S.E. of Carnesville [Ga.; "on the Road leading" *canceled*] & about 6 or 8 miles from the Madison Springs [Ga.; "or at" *canceled*]. Hoping to hear from them at an early date We remain Y[ou]rs Resp[ec]t-f[ul]ly, T.R.C.

ALS with En in ScCleA. NOTE: The En, written in a different handwriting from Morton's, appears to be a rough draft of a formal notice. EU's in an un-identified handwriting upon the enclosure read "Wrote 23 Ap[ri]l[,] 1847, also T.S. Reese & J.A. Cherry" and "23 Ap[ri]l Answ[ere]d[,] also T.S. R[eese], J.A. C[herry], W[?]. B. Cherry."

To "Col." JAMES ED[WARD] COLHOUN, [Abbeville District, S.C.]

Fort Hill, 20th March 1847

My dear Sir, I returned home on Tuesday last with your sister [Floride Colhoun Calhoun], who met me in Charleston, & had the pleasure of finding all well, except old Peggy, who has been quite dangerously ill, & my place in as good a condition, as I could expect, in all respects.

I received your last letter at a period of the session, when I was so much engaged, that I had not time to answer it. The sittings of the Senate were exceedingly laborious towards the end of the session, & I was forced to take a very active & prominent part.

The grievance of which you speak, in reference to the proposed substitution of a horse mail from Abbeville to the double wells on the Georgia rail road, admits of no remedy, but the repeal of the act of Congress passed three years since, which makes it the duty of the Post Master General to have the mail carried in the cheapest manner, without reference to the mode of conveyance. It was to go into operation with the respective lettings [of contracts] in the several portions of the Union, and as this is our turn, it will be put into operation on all our routes, and among others to the present stage line from Pendleton to Hamburgh. The act was passed by the North, to carry out the scheme of reducing the postage so low, as to charge a large annual burthen on the revenue from the imposts, & that ["it" *canceled and* "the income of the Dept." *interlined*] might not be reduced so greatly, as to cause reaction, the plan was adopted to cheapen the transportation of the mail by breaking up the mail stage accom[m]odation, in which it had but little interest, comparatively. There is I think no hope of its repeal, so that we must grin & bear it, as well as we can. The only remedy will be ["to" *canceled*] for some one to bid for the line sufficiently low to take it, & establish a hack. It is the way we propose to do to Athens, which must hereafter be our route to Augusta, Hamburgh & Charleston.

Can you not come up this spring? We would all be very glad to see you. All join their love. Yours affectionately, J.C. Calhoun.

ALS in ScCleA; PC in Jameson, ed., *Correspondence*, pp. 721–722.

To C[HARLES] N. WEBB, [Editor of the Halifax, N.C., *Roanoke Republican*]

Fort Hill, March 20, 1847

Dear Sir—I received with your letter [of 3/9] the paper you were so kind as to send me.

I see that notwithstanding your kind feelings towards me, you have greatly misjudged me in thinking I ever joined "the fallen fortune" of Mr. [Martin] Van Buren. The truth is, that I have not been able, with my principles and policy, to act with either party, except occasionally, for the last 17 years. I differ from both on several important questions, and among others, the proscriptive policy of turning opponents out of office indiscriminately, and bestowing their places, as rewards for partisan services, on the least meritorious of the respective parties, and agree with each in some particulars. Mine has been an independent course throughout; and hence I have been compelled to separate from the party in power and act with those out of power, during the long period mentioned. I have never separated from the weak to join the strong, but from the strong to join the weak. I seek no office, and desire none, and only continue to represent the State in the Senate because it is unwilling I should decline. I would not accept the Presidency but from the people, and then from a sense of duty only. Nothing can induce me to sacrifice my independence, not even to retain favor of my native State. If I, in 1837, supported Mr. Van Buren, it was because he was forced to sustain the measures I had supported against him and General [Andrew] Jackson, and because the whigs took ground against them; and not because I joined him or his fallen fortunes. I had no motive to do either, while I had strong ones to support the measures which I approved. It would have been highly censurable in me to turn against them because he had been forced to support them. With great respect, I am, &c., J.C. CALHOUN.

PC in the Charleston, S.C., *Courier*, April 23, 1847, p. 2; PC in the New York, N.Y., *Herald*, April 25, 1847, p. 2; PC in the Alexandria, Va., *Gazette and Virginia Advertiser*, April 26, 1847, p. 2; PC in the Columbia, S.C., *Southern Chronicle*, April 28, 1847, p. 2; PC in the Edgefield, S.C., *Advertiser*, April 28, 1847, p. 3; PC in the New Orleans, La., *Daily Picayune*, April 29, 1847, p. 2; PC in the Athens, Ga., *Southern Banner*, May 4, 1847, p. 3; PC in the Camden, S.C., *Journal*, May 5, 1847, p. 3; PC in the Pendleton, S.C., *Messenger*, May 7, 1847, p. 1; PC in the Nashville, Tenn., *Whig*, May 11, 1847, p. 2; PC in the Richmond, Va., *Enquirer*, May 11, 1847, p. 1; PC in *Niles' National Register*, vol. LXXII, no. 14 (June 5, 1847), p. 210; PEx in the Tallahassee, Fla., *Florida Sentinel*, May 4, 1847, p. 3; PEx in the Hillsborough, N.C., *Recorder*, May 6, 1847, p. 3; PEx in the Harrisburg, Pa., *Democratic Union*, May 19, 1847, p. 2. NOTE: All the printed versions of this letter were derived from its original publication in an unknown, not extant, issue of the Halifax, N.C., *Roanoke Republican*.

To FRANCIS WHARTON, [Philadelphia]

Fort Hill, 20th March 1847

My dear Sir, Such has been the extent of my engagements, that I have not had a leisure moment to look into your volume. I shall devote the first spare time, after bring[ing] up my correspondence, which fell much in the rear towards the close of the session, to its perusal; after which I will write you again. I have not a spare copy left of [John C.] Fremont[']s tour, or I would send it to you with pleasure. Yours truly, J.C. Calhoun.

ALS in ScU-SC, John C. Calhoun Papers. NOTE: Fremont's "tour" was probably his *Report of the Exploring Expedition to the Rocky Mountains in the Year 1842, and to Oregon and North California in the Years 1843–'44* (Washington: Gales and Seaton, printers, 1845), also printed as Senate Executive Document No. 174, 28th Cong., 2nd Sess.

To ROBERT L. DORR, [Dansville, N.Y.]

FORT HILL, 21st March, 1847

Dear Sir: I see by your letter [of 3/1], that you have formed your opinion on a very imperfect report of what I said; and in order that you may see what I did say, I enclose the within, which contains a corrected copy of my reply [of 2/20] to Mr. [James F.] Simmons [Senator from R.I.], with my reply [of 2/12] to Mr. [Hopkins L.] Turney [Senator from Tenn.], and my speech [of 2/19] on my resolutions. You will see that if I am opposed to a government based on the principle that a mere numerical majority has a right to govern, I am equally opposed to the government of a minority. They are both the government of a part over a part. I am in favor of the government of the whole; the only really and truly popular republican government—a government based on the concurrent majority—the joint assent of all the parts, through their respective majorities, and not the mere government of the majority of the whole.

Such is the constitution and government of the United States, and such are all really and truly constitutional governments. The government of a mere majority or minority is not popular enough for me, they are both in their nature despotic and not constitutional governments. I do not object to extended suffrage. I have ever advocated it. By Dorrism I mean the right claimed for the numerical majority, that it has the inherent and absolute right to govern, a sort of right to govern, a sort of right divine, like that claimed by Sir Robert Filmer for Kings. Such a right has no foundation, and is inconsistent with the very idea of a constitutional government. With respect, I am, &c, J.C. Calhoun.

PC (from the Rochester, N.Y., *Daily Advertiser*) in the New York, N.Y., *Evening Post*, April 14, 1847, p. 1; PC in the Charleston, S.C., *Mercury*, April 17, 1847, p. 2; PC in the Charleston, S.C., *Southern Patriot*, April 17, 1847, p. 2; PC (dated 3/31) in the Edgefield, S.C., *Advertiser*, April 21, 1847, p. 2; PC in the Pendleton, S.C., *Messenger*, April 30, 1847, p. 1; PC in *Niles' National Register*, vol. LXXII, no. 10 (May 8, 1847), p. 148; PEx in the Alexandria, Va., *Gazette and Virginia Advertiser*, April 28, 1847, p. 2; PEx in the Charleston, S.C., *Mercury*, June 11, 1847, p. 2; PEx in Wilson, ed., *The Essential Calhoun*, p. 50.

From Thomas McMillan

Beaufort [S.C.,] March 22d 1847

Respected Sir, Permit me to present to your penetrating mind a few Observations on a subject that deeply interests our country. In observing your views of this present Mexican war, and the most probable consequences to the Union, and particularly to the south, it appears to me, that in this instance, as in all such critical occasions in this country; and in particular with Great Britain in former critical emergencies, that the Almighty Ruler of the Universe raises up men competent for the occasion to fulfil his wise purposes. On this most critical and dangerous emergency (excuse me for my opinion) It has long appeared to my mind, and more so Lately that by your coolness and deep devotion to the wellfair of this Union, and particularly to the South, that we most look to you as our pilot and helmsman. Under this impression (you will) I believe and flatter myself, that you will excuse me in thus writing to you on this occasion. My object in doing so, is to bring to your notice ["a singular prophecy" *interlined*] perhaps, which has not been presented to your mind; and if you see this subject as it appears to me, it may have a bearing on your future deliberations. The subject is certainly worthy of notice and consideration and if it applies to the present state of affairs of our nation we will certainly by knowing it, be more prepared to meet it. My mind is so deeply impressed with the present state of affairs and the probable consequences arising therefrom, that the following passages of prophecy, are to all appearance applied to the Rise, to the present, and the future destany of this country. Indeed it is to be Lamented that so Little notice is genarly taken of the ways of providence in governing the nations, or individuals. I am no minister of the gospel, yet I cannot be blind to the Operations of providence compared with past history and when I see in the prophecies so singular a denounciation as I am about to bring to Your notice. I again would repeat that I do beg you will excuse me for addressing you and if you shall deem it worthy of your consideration; I would deem it an honour conferred by acknowledging the receipt of this, as a satisfaction that you have received it. I feel assured that it will not be beneath your notice, singular as this step may appear, which I have taken.

To introduce the subject to your notice I would reffer you to the XVI & XVII Chapters of Isaiah. The first Chapter contains the denouncinations against the Land of Moab which we see how completely it has taken place by the conditions of that country and Idumia adjoining it. Towns and villages in ruins and deserted of its inhabitants; and all for pride. The XVII Chapter contains the denouncinations against Syria and Israel, and particularly the Capatol of Syria. These nations were doomed to destruction "Because they had forsaken the God of their Salvation and the Rock of their stren[g]th," excepting the city of Damascus which was doomed "to become an heap" we see how fearfully these predictions are fulfilled. These nations were all called by name and they still retain that same

name, their fate is a warning to other nations. ["which" *canceled*]
I have brought forward the foregoing preleminary remark, which
will illustrate in some degree what follows, and the certainty of its
fulfillment. Chapt[er] XVIII. The Prophet here fore tells of a
country that would exist, no name being given to it. First, he mentions its Locality and pronounces a "Wo" upon it—2dly he mentions
its Characteristics, as a nation of fast sailing ships that most [*sic*]
cross the sea or the Atlantic—3dly That it would be a nation of
Christian people bearing the fruits of Christianity saying to their
ships "go ye swift sailing messingers carry Ambassadors or Mission-
arys &c," 4thly This would be at an age of the world when the
Ensign or the Banner of the cross would be Lifted upon the mountains ["or nations" *interlined*] and when the gospel Trumpet would be
blowen. These are some of the characteristics. As to the application
of these features, there cannot be any reasonable doubt but that it is
applied to the United States, before we proceed farther we will glance
at that portion of the subject. The prophet was in the land of Canaan
at the head of the Mediteranian Sea[;] he is supposed to look west-
ward to where his prediction pointed, and he said, "Wo to the Land
shadowing with wings (or sails) which is beyond the rivers of
Ethiopia" (or Africa). Therefore this Land is not in Asia, Europe or
Africa but beyond Africa a Land of Sails[,] of fast sailing ships that
go by sea (not the rivers) "But that sendeth Ambassadors by *Sea*["]
or the Atlantic ocean, here is not only its locallity at once portrayed
but its commercial Character and its Christian Character bearing
fruit such as the Missionary ["&" *interlined*] the Bible cause. It was
to be in Later years and not cotemperanious with any of those
nations which he had denounced. For the Prophet call upon all the
inhabitants and dwellers on the earth to witness the operations of
God's providence with this nation at that particular period of time.
"When ye see the ensign (of the Cross) Lifted upon the mountains
See Ye, and when hear the (Gospel) Trumpet blowen, *Hear Ye*." We
cannot be at a Loss therefore to mark the period of time, it was not
to be a heathen nation, but when the mountains or nations which
were then heathen in the days of the prophet. When they "should
lift up the insign," here is one mark. "And when ye hear the
Trumpet blowen." Take particular notice all the inhabitants of
the earth *and see* that nation, appearently bearing the fruits of
rightiousness, a vine of the Lord's own planting full of fruit rushing
up to perfection as "a clear heat on herbs" or as ["]a Cloud of dew
before the harvest." Here the Prophet has spread the picture of this
western Land before us, and calls on all to look at it, and Observe.

Here the prophet at this stage pronounces the "Wo" that was about to take place on the appearently happy and flourishing Land.

"And the Lord said unto me, I will take my rest and consider in my dwelling place Like a clear heat upon herbs and a cloud of dew ["before the" *canceled and* "in the heat" *interlined*] of harvest when the bud is perfect and the sour grape is ripening in the flour, he [*one word altered to* "shall"] both cut off the sprigs (Territories) with prunning hooks, and take away and cut down the branches," (States). Admitting then that the application of the Locallity is America and that the Characteristics of the people are those of the United States—and that when all the former heathen nations of Europe should assume the Christian name, Then and at that time this country would be just at that state of perfection which is described in the foregoing predictions. God compares it then to a fl[o]urishing vine rushing up under his owen peculiar consideration and care full of Grapes the bud perfect as just before harvest, full growen fruit but not matured, and still sour. And the singularity of the case causes the prophet to call all the inhabitants of the world and dwellers on the earth to witness this Signal of God's providence. We are left to infer the cause Why this "Wo" is to be poured out on so ["a" *canceled*] prosperous and seemingly God fearing people. But it ["is" *interlined*] no doubt under the same head as the former predictions against Moab, Syria & Isreal. "Because thou hast forgotten the God of thy salvation and hast not been mindfull of the rock of thy stren[g]th." In whatever way this has taken place, in what shape it may be discerned, there is none more probable than the warlike Spirit now manifested, or the party spirit of rancur of the north to the south, or whateaver it may be, we are informed very plainly that such denouncination will assuredly take place, and no man can heal and close the breach when providence opens it, for his all wise purposes.

It would be wisdom therefore to provide and be prepared for the Crisis—it is well that we are informed of it so plainly before it falls upon us ["or" *interlined*] that it meet us unexpectedly and unprepared. Now Let us see what the Lord is about to do to this vine of his "consideration" and care, full of grapes, full growen and perfect, but sour as just before the harvest. "He shall both cut of[f] the sprigs with prunning hooks (violence) and take away and cut down the branches. They shall be Left together unto the *fowls* of the *mountains* (Eagles, birds of pray, Armies of the nations) and the *beasts* of the earth." (In scripture Language, mountain is Nation or government, *Beasts* of the earth, is Nations in their civil and milatary capacity, the same mountains are spoke of as raising the ensigns of the cross ie Christian nations, their milatary powers, birds of pray). "They shall be Left together (twigs & branches) unto the fowls of the mountains and to the beasts of the earth and the fowls of the mountains shall summer upon them, and the beasts of the earth shall winter upon them." It does appear to me that the above figureative Language indicates a separation of the union, into small or Larger confederices, at all events severed from the root or general gover[n]ment—that the nations of Europe will rule, or have a ruling influence[,] a certain political power and their armies either as conquerors, or protectors from internal convultions and civil war will be called in for a season only; "The fowls of the mountains or nations shall (only) summer upon them.["] But their political or Civil influence appears to continue Longer; "shall winter on them." And to confirm the period more positiv[e]ly he adds looking back to the operations of providence with his own people, the dispersed ten tribes of Isreal, to what ["would" *canceled and* "will" *interlined*] be taking place in the eastren hemisphere at that period, he says "*In* that time a present will be brought to the Lord of hosts of a people scatt[e]red and peeled, *From* a people terrible from their begin[n]ing hitherto"—Al[l]uding to the Babylonians had been a terrible peopel for punishing and spoiling the Hebrews, up to that date in which he was speaking. What I beg to notice in this, is, that the prophet does not say (at that time) or that, the ten tribes restoration should not be commenceurate with the fall of this Republic, But he says "*in that time* &c" this tends to confirm the period of time, that when the western Republic attains to that character given it, a commercial nation having Missionary and Bible and all such enterprises as to form its character and fl[o]urishing like a prosperous vine—branches or States bearing fruit—twigs or young Shoots without fruit, and at the same time the nations formerly heathen in the prophet's time proffessing Christianity and sounding the gospel Trumpet. All these are conspicuous at this present day, and the present portentious aspect of our civil, Religious & milatary affairs seems to forebode some Great catastrophey at hand. "Rightiousness exalteth a nation" but if she depart from it, the terrible warnings that we read of, and that we see visibly arround us. Let us but look at the state of Mexico—Spain, Portugale, Italy and especially Ireland, is not the hand of God becoming evidently more and more visible in his Gover[n]ment in his dealings with men. But what has been said of our own country, is a phenomenon that "all the inhabitants of the world, and dwellers on the earth are called to witness.["] You may think it

279

singular, and even absurd in me an humble and Obscure individual to presume to address such a Letter to you, but I do it through the High esteem in which ["I" *interlined*] admire and respect you, supposing that you have had Little Leasure for the study and contemplation, particularly of the prophecies. My mind was so deeply impressed with the subject, that I conceived it to be a duty to present it to your notice in the humble garb of an unlettered man. Letters, or Litreture is excel[l]ent, but Truth, plain simple Truth is better. If you should discover that the above is applicable to the nation, I have attained all ["that" *interlined*] my anxiety desires in this instance, feeling confident in your ability to guide the south safely into a settled state, while others that may not be aware of the destany pointed out by an all wise and Ruling providence and make vain attempts to struggle against adverse fate, and make shipwork[?], you may, by keeping an eye to the unalterable decrees of the Almighty Ruler as they transpire, and anticipate that which is to come, may cooperate with him, for what ["he" *interlined*] does, is and must be best. May he guide you in your Councels and bless all your Laudable undertakings and spare you Long on earth not only to reap the fading Laurels of men, but a Rich Crown of reward in that inheritance which is uncoruptable and und[e]file[d?] and fadeth not away, is the petition of your unworthy and Humble Servant, Thomas McMillan.

ALS in ScCleA.

From M[ITCHELL] KING

[Charleston] Tuesday morning, 23d March 1847
My Dear Sir, I have just finished the reading of your remarks to the citizens of Charleston, on the evening of the 9th Instant, and under the immediate influence of the deep convictions which these remarks have produced in my mind, I cannot refrain, as a Citizen of South Carolina, from tendering to you with the highest respect & deference, my earnest acknowledgments for the light which you have shed on a subject of the profoundest interest to the whole South—and not to the South only—to the whole union. May God in mercy grant, that the voice of the Prophet may not have been raised in vain—that the language of truth and wisdom and forethought may work these desired effects—that it may rally every enlightened mind amongst us,

to the protection of the fences and compromises of the Constitution—and tend to bear onward this great confederacy, in all its vigor and purity with all its blessings, to the latest posterity. Then whatever may be the changes and chances on the political chessboard—the freshest laurels will cluster around your brow—and your ["name" *interlined*] will be transmitted to future ages as the Father of your Country. I am with the sincerest respect Dear Sir Very faithfully yours, M. King.

ALS in ScCleA.

From JOHN TYLER

Sherwood Forest
Charles City County Va.
March 23, 1847

My Dear Sir, I feel it to be due to myself to enclose you the New York Mirror of the 13th Inst. and to direct your attention to that portion of an article which I have designated by ink lines. I do this for the single purpose of declaring the entire falsity of the publication, most especially so far as it ascribes to me any unfriendly intentions towards you while you were a member of my Cabinet, or the knowledge of any plot or machination on the part of others of a character injurious to you. So far from this I do not hesitate to say that from the time of your acceptance of the Secretary-ship of State to the close of my Administration, you possessed my entire confidence, and that had it been otherwise you would have been informed of it from my own lips. I held no consultations as to Cabinet appointments and most generally they were not announc'd to others until they were irrevocably made. Such was the fact in your own case. My object throughout was by calling the highest talents to my Cabinet, to secure myself through great public measures an honorable mention in history. Whether this object has been accomplish'd or not the future alone can determine. The ascription of motive which is made to me by this libellous writer for calling you to the Cabinet, you are as well aware as myself to be wholly unfounded.

I have abstained from noticing the numberless attacks which have been made upon me as well since as before I left Office, but in this instance I have deem'd it proper to break my uniform silence.

With best wishes for your health and happiness I am y[ou]rs &c, John Tyler.

ALS in ScCleA; PC in Jameson, ed., *Correspondence*, pp. 1106–1107. NOTE: An AEU by Calhoun reads, "Ex P. Tyler." The article referred to by Tyler was doubtless that which appeared in the New York, N.Y., *Mirror*, vol. V (March 13, 1847), p. 366. The anonymous writer assumes to have inside knowledge of the Tyler administration. Using Calhoun's recent dispute with Thomas H. Benton in the Senate as a starting point, he relates circumstantially alleged events during that time. He absolves Calhoun from knowledge of clandestine instructions to newspapers "in the pay of the State Department." However, he states that Calhoun was only appointed to the Cabinet to remove a rival for the Presidency and that six months after the appointment Tyler was desperate to get rid of Calhoun.

To "Cadets" C. B[AKER] SIGWELL, J. S. W.[?] HUBBARD and W[ILLIAM] M. MORGAN

Fort Hill, 27th March 1847

Sirs, I have just received your note; and in answer state, that it would be perfectly useless, at this late period, when there are so many applications already on file, to present yours for the places you desire. There is no hope of them receiving the least attention. Respectfully, J.C. Calhoun.

ALS in TNJ, James G. Stahlman Collection. NOTE: Those addressed by Calhoun were apparently students of the S.C. Military College who had hoped for commissions in the Mexican war forces.

From THO[MA]S G. CLEMSON

Brussels, March 28th 1847

My dear Sir, The Cambria brought your letter of the 17th of February and a file of [Thomas] Ritchie's scurrilous paper the [Washington] Union in which you are not spared. I was perfectly prepared to see this & expected no less from Ritchie. He has always been opposed to you because part & parcel of the old hunkers—[Silas] Wright[,] [Martin] Van Buren &c, & has done the South incalculable injury. He has, since I have seen his papers, done his best to damn you with insidious remarks in his own peculiar style. For one I am happy to know that he has been refused the entrance of the senate. His attacks & course towards you will from being covert now become open, and less injurious on that account. I only regret that this crisis had not taken place ten years since, it would have placed it out of his power to injure you & through you the south to the extent he has heretofore done. I am unable to judge how it will act on him, whether it will raise him into martyrdom & concentrate the action of the old Hunkers again but of one thing I feel assured, that is that you did right & you have placed him towards you in his true light. I repeat that I regret that it has been so long postponed. I agree with you that this war has been most disastrous & might have been avoided. It is the height of folly to suppose that we can carry our arms easily to the city of Mexico. It will I fear prove as disastrous to us as the Russian campaign did to the French. The natural obstacles[,] distance[,] climate &c will prevent our success. Nothing is more certain than your statement that war will have to become defensive. One thing I regret that is mixing[?] of the slavery question[;] it appears to have been unavoidable & will perhaps unite the south & thus enable them to hold on to the advantages they have recently gained.

The Cambria also brought me a long letter from Col. [Francis W.] Pickens. I copy the following extract, as it regards a subject which you mentioned some time since in a letter to Anna [Maria Calhoun Clemson], of course it is entirely gratuitous on his part, for I never mentioned the subject to Col. P[ickens]. He says[,] "I take but little interest in ["politics now" *canceled*] public matters now. They circulated all kinds of falsehoods last summer when I had gone travelling North about my splitting from Mr. Calhoun &c &c. I merely regretted he had not supported the supplies for the Mexican war as it was commenced & this was all; & yet when I left home Col. [Louis T.] Wigfall circulated it in the papers that I had denounced Mr. Calhoun. Through Mr. [Armistead] Burt in congress he got Mr. Calhoun to believe it before I knew any thing at all of it. He had received information that Mr. [George] McDuffie was to resign his seat & he being bankrupt in fortune & character hated me exceedingly because I would not sustain his falling fortunes. He was known here to be without a particle of principle or truth & has since left in disgrace for N. Orleans being entirely sold out by the sheriff & his wife [Charlotte Maria Cross Wigfall] having gone to Providence to live with her relations. Yet this was the man who from the most malignant motives cont[r]ived when I was in Canada to insinuate himself into Mr. Calhoun[']s friendship to produce the most false impressions. It so disgusted me that I had not the slightest interest in politics since." He also makes another remark which I add. "Mr. Calhoun[']s friends (who by the by are no real friends of his in this

State) have injured him very much. They have advised for their selfish purposes & not for his interests." I have made the above extract not of course that I should in any way be mentioned as having written you on the subject but merely to put you in possession of Col. P[ickens']s feelings on the subject. In speaking of Cotton Mr. P[ickens] thinks that the defect in last year[']s crop came from the heretofore considered, the best cotton region in the United States. The worm & mist which has destroyed the Cotton below the falls of the rivers on the Gulph [of Mexico] is thought to be a permanent production of that region, owing to the great moisture & heat towards the Gulph, & it is begin[n]ing to be supposed that country will be permanently uncertain for Cotton. This consideration has stopped emigration and land is rising in this country (Carolina). My impression is that my land will increase in value for some time to come & I have no doubt that negroes will do the same, but I have no idea that they will continue to command present prices for a long time. What ever value my property may have in So. Carolina, it has yielded me no income, other than the increase of the negroes, & the prices may continue to increase. I see no ["relative" *canceled*] prospect of a relative increase in my moneyed income from planting. I feel however perfectly safe as I owe no money & my property is entirely unincumbered. I hope that your anticipations (expressed last summer about your crop) were realised & that you have held on to your crop. I do not know what your intentions are with regard to the debt you & Andrew [Pickens Calhoun] owe me, but if you do not intend paying the amount due me ["(which I am willing to leave in your hands until I have need for the money)" *interlined*] I think it would be better for you & for myself that the whole amount due me should be expressed in some more permanent shape ["or" *interlined*] form than the notes which you gave me at the last settlement. You are aware that the time for the payment of those notes has gone by & they on that account become invalidated. I have often felt particular gratification in feeling that my salary sufficed (or nearly so) the wants of myself & family & I was thus enabled to give to you every facility as to the payment of the money in your hands. I have also had satisfaction in knowing that the increase of my property would be to their future advantage & enable us all to do much that would have been denied us on our return had it not been for this increase. My health has much improved since I came to Europe & for the last six months I have been diligently employed in perfecting myself in studies that will allways be a resource at least of pleasure.

It is strange that my lawyers [J.B.] Crockett & [D.C.] Briggs in

Missouri never write about my affairs, it appears as if no one in the West could be trusted.

My impression that the course you have taken with the administration & the old Hunker party will do you more service than evil. You never could expect any thing at their hands. They would use your influence if they could, but you never could expect their support. They can do you less injury now than when seemingly friendly to you. Their success never would have added to you & I doubt if they can do you the least injury. They never would have aided you under any circumstances & I again congratulate you upon the issue. You stand far above the assaults. I inclose you a letter cut from the columns of the [London] Morning Chronicle, it will give you some idea of the letters that are written from Washington & published in the English papers.

The spring thus far has been very fine, and the crops of all descriptions most promising. We are all well, the children [John Calhoun Clemson and Floride Elizabeth Clemson] are improving daily. Floride if any thing grows too rapidly. Anna joins me in sending love to all the family. Your affectionate son, Thos. G. Clemson.

ALS in ScCleA; PEx in Boucher and Brooks, eds., *Correspondence*, pp. 372–373.

To DUFF GREEN, [Washington]

Fort Hill, 28th March 1847

My dear Sir, I see by the contents of your letter [of 3/17], that you have misunderstood me on a point, where I had supposed my meaning was very obvious. By *private* relations, I had no allusion to our personal relations, either of confidence, or friendship. It would, indeed, be absurd to make either of them a cause of delicacy in giving a preference to you. I alluded to our family connections through the tie of marriage.

Nor do you seem to understand, what I intended by the expression of my position to the party, who support me. It is not that of a leader aspiring to the presidency, but that of an individual, who, in the discharge of his publick trust, looks only to his duty and only expects their support from their concurrence in opinion with him. Occupying that position towards them, as associates and equals, and not as partisans, or followers, I assume no right to dictate, nor do I admit the right on their part to dictate to me. It is the relation of independence on both sides; and I feel it to be a matter of delicacy, to respect it especially when they stand in the relation of contributors to the support of a cause, which I would advocate without reference to their support, or opposition.

Having explained my meaning, I deem it proper to repeat, that I neither doubt your friendship, or capacity. On the contrary, I place a high estimate on both. I know of no one, who in my opinion, would conduct a paper with more ability, or greater fidelity. I go further. As you lost an honorable and profitable position by your adherence to the cause, I would rejoice to see you again in the same position and in the conduct of a paper of the same name. The triumph would be that of truth and justice; and as far as I can contribute to it, consistently with a due sense of propriety, and the success of the cause, I will do so. Further I cannot go. I cheerfully yield my own claims to such consideration, and no friend can ask me to go further. I ask no sacrifice of any friend, which I would not cheerfully make myself. Indeed, I would much rather make the sacrifice, than ask a friend to make it.

But when the funds are raised, it will, then, be the time to consult as to the editorship of the paper. Whether they will be or not, I fear is doubtful, from the reason I alluded to in my letter [of 3/9]. I have not yet heard from my Charleston friends with whom I conversed on the subject. A word as to myself.

You seem to think, that I permit other persons to prejudice me against you, and that I have not given you the support I ought. As to the first, you greatly mistake. When I know a man, no one can influence my opinion, and what is more, very few undertake to do so. I take care to check it at once, when attempted, as I know to what unfounded conclusions, the jealousy of the mutual friends of a prominent individual will lead them. In addition, I am of that temper that I would rather be betrayed, than to suspect on light grounds. Besides, I feel, that I may be deserted, but cannot be betrayed: having, as I always have, had truth for my only guide; and no motive for concealment. I entertain not a thought, which I am not willing should be known to the world; and have not ever written a letter, which I am not willing it should be published. It is hard to betray one, who can with truth say as much.

As to my want of giving you due support, I know not when I have had the power of doing so, and abstain[ed] from doing it, when it could be done with propriety. Indeed I might ask when have I ever had the power to wield any portion of the patronage of the Government, since the termination of Mr. [James] Monroe's administration! During the short period, I was in Mr. [John] Tyler's administration, he engrossed the whole; and I came in under circumstances, which did not permit me to take a stand against it.

The only instance you allude to, is that of 1840, when by uniting with the Whigs, I might have made you in connection with [Joseph] Gales and [William W.] Seaton the printers, against [Francis P.] Blair and [John C.] Rives. I now think as I did then, that standing opposed to the Whigs on all the great questions of the day, as I did, that I could not without loss of character and confounding my position, do other than I did; and had hoped that such would be your own conclusion, when you came coolly to reflect. I deeply regretted to be placed in the position, but thinking as I did, and still think, had you been my brother, I would have acted as I did. I acted on my own conception, uninfluenced by any others. As highly, as I value friendship, and as much disposed, as I am, to support my friends, I cannot yield my conception of what is right, or wrong to either, while I would cheerfully make any personal sacrifice for the purpose. Had I withheld my support on the occasion, from any motive on my part of personal ambition or advancement, I would have been inexcusable; but that I suppose, you can hardly think, although I [am] forced to infer, that as long as you have known me, you have never fully realized how subordinate I hold such considerations, when they come into conflict with what I believe to be right. Even in early manhood, when I felt their impulse far stronger, than I now do, they could never over rule my sense of right. I regret, that one, who ought to know me, as well as you ought, should under estimate my character, as I am forced [to] think you do, on such a point.

Let me add in conclusion, that while I think, there is a great opening for a truly independent and able paper at Washington (never greater in my opinion) and that no one is more able to conduct such an one than yourself, I would be very sorry to see you undertake editing a paper there, unless on calculations founded on the prospect of its ultimate profit. But if you can see your way looking to it, clearly, and can find the means to start one, even a weekly sheet at first, on your own independent hook, avowing your object to be, to restore the principles of the party, which brought Gen[era]l [Andrew] Jackson into power, but which were defeated by the introduction of the spoils principle and the party machinery of the Albany Junto, and the treason of Mr. [Thomas] Ritchie and others like him, and assuming the old name of the [United States'] Telegraph, you would preoccupy the ground, and rally the whole South and a large po[r]tion of the old party everywhere to your support. The prospectus you prepared, would be the proper basis, modified to suit the suggestions made. Place it on the high ground of an independent press, holding principle paramount and never subordinate. In my opinion, it would stir up the South, and hasten its efforts to raise funds to establish on a firm foundation, a press at Washington.

You ask me if I read the [Washington] Union. I do not take it and rarely see it. I expect him [that is, Ritchie] to do his best in the way of abuse. He sees, that my overthrow is necessary to save the hunkers.

PC in Jameson, ed., *Correspondence*, pp. 722–725.

From CHA[RLE]S J. FOX and Others

Charlotte [N.C.,] March 29, 1847

Sir, The friends of the Rail Road proposed to be constructed from some point on the South Carolina Rail Road to this place, have resolved to hold a convention at this place on the 27th of April next. The purpose of this convention will be to exchange views with the various sections in North & South Carolina interested in the work and to secure some plan of cooperation by which they enterprize may be rendered successful. Believing that you duly appreciate the importance of the undertaking both in its immediate effects on the prosperity of the two States directly interested but also in regard to those more enlarged consequences which may grow out of it when considered in relation to other works now projected or in progress to the north of us and with which it may some day be connected, we respectfully solicit your presence at the proposed convention. We the more earnestly make this request as we are convinced that the enterprize may in some great degree depend on the result of its deliberations. Very Respectfully &c, Chas. J. Fox, Jos. W. Hampton, Joseph H. Wilson, W[illiam] Johnston, Jas. W. Osborne, Committee.

LS in ScCleA. NOTE: An AEU by Calhoun reads "Rail road meeting at Charlot[t]e."

From Cha[rle]s N. Webb

Halifax, N.C., March 29th, 1847

Dear Sir: Yours of the 20th was received yesterday, and I can assure you that so far from its weakening my affections for you, it has had a great tendency to strengthen them.

I took the liberty of shewing your letter to me, to a few of your particular friends; who were highly gratified. They see in every line, the Republican, Statesman, good and great man—and *desire its publication.* And it would afford me great pleasure to have it appear in the columns of the "Roanoke Republican," as well as to see it copied in *every* paper in the Union. May I be permitted to give it publicity?

For your independent course upon the Oregon & War questions, I see that you are denounced by many of the Democratic presses, not only of my own State; but of other States composing the Union.

I repeat sir, in this letter, what I wrote before—that you have many warm friends here (nullifiers:) and they brightened up on hearing the nature of the letter you had written me—they still entertain the hope that you will be President; but not in opposition to Whig policy—or the President of a party.

Dr. Robert C. Bond, in whose memory you have ever occupied a green spot, wishes to be remembered to you. Hoping to hear from you soon, I remain, your Friend &c, Chas. N. Webb, Editor of the "Roanoke Republican."

ALS in ScCleA.

To A[sa] Whitney

Fort Hill, 29th March 1847

Sir, I entirely concur with you, in the opinion, that one of the greatest objects to which capital can be ["employed," *canceled and* "directed," *interlined*] whether regard be had to its profit, or to the general benefit, that would result from its application, is the opening of rail road communications between the Atlantick and the great & fertile valley of the Mississippi. Its capacity for producing, especially food, can hardly be overestimated, and the opening of cheap, certain, safe & rapid communication ["by rail roads" *interlined*] between it, and the older & more advanced portion of the Union & the old Continent ["*generally*" *interlined and* "by rail roads" *canceled*], would do more for commerce, & the advancement ["*of commerce*" *canceled and* "of the" *interlined*] wealth, population, & prosperity of ["the world generally" *canceled and* "both" *interlined*] than can well be conceived. It would effectually & for ever establish free trade, with all its blessings, economical, political & moral. I agree with you, that all Europe, &, it might be added, the world is concerned ["in it" *canceled and* "in effecting so desirable an object" *interlined*]; and I regard ["*your*" *interlined*] intention of going to Europe with the view of attracting attention to it, as highly laudable. I wish you much success.

As to the advantages possessed by the Southern Atlantick States, in reference to such communication, I regard them as very great. A glance at the Map of the U. States will show how much nearer they approach to the centre of the great Valley, taking the mouth of the Ohio as the centre. If to this, we add the roads from Charleston & Savannah would turn the Alleg[h]any mountains & all its chains, except the Cumberland; that it is cut by the Tennessee River near where the two Roads united would strike ["that River" *canceled and* "it" *interlined*]; that the country passed through is remarkably favourable for the construction of rail roads, to the two proposed termini, NashVille & Memphis; that it would pass, ["throughout" *altered to* "through"] its whole extent, a productive country; that any link would pay ["& each make the other more profitable" *interlined*]; that the run would be continuous; that it would be unobstructed winter & summer; & that it would terminate at points, where navigation would be open ["all winter, & summer" *canceled and* "both seasons" *interlined*], unimpeded by the ice of the ["former" *canceled and* "winter" *interlined*] or the droughts of the ["latter" *canceled and* "summer" *interlined*], their great ["& superior" *interlined*] advantages would seem unquestionable. ["It" *canceled and* "They" *interlined*] will ["add to them when" *canceled and* "appear still more striking when we take into consideration" *interlined*] the facility, which the Island of Bermuda, & the Azores would afford to Steam Navigation between Charleston & Savannah ["on one side" *interlined*] & ["the" *interlined*] European ports ["on the other, including its" *interlined and* "with its exemption" *canceled*] comparative ["exception" *interlined*] from storms & Ice in Winter & Spring ["is taken into consideration" *canceled*].

In connection ["with this subject" *canceled*; "therewith" *interlined*; "it" *interlined and then canceled*], I enclose a copy of my

Memphis Report, & a copy of the Report of the Engineer, on the subject of ["the" *canceled*] extending ["of" *canceled*] the Georgia rail road from its terminus on the Tennessee, at Chat[t]anooga, to NashVille, which will throw much light on that important ["extension, which" *canceled and* "project. When completed it" *interlined*] would make ["a" *canceled and* "an uninterrupted" *interlined*] continuous run from Charleston & Savannah to NashVille. ["The navigation of" *canceled and* "It stands on the Cumberland river, which runs" *interlined*] almost directly to the centre of the vall[e]y. Its navigation from ["of the Cumberland, on which NashVille stands" *canceled and* "Nashville to its mouth" *interlined*] can be made at a small expense equal to the Ohio between its ["mouth" *canceled and* "junction" *interlined*]. From NashVille the road would be certainly extended to LouisVille, through a fine country & ["very" *canceled and then interlined*] favourable to the construction of a rail road.

If you can favour me with a reliable statement of the cost of transportation of any given amount of Merchandize; freight, insurance & all expenses included & the time necessary, from Boston, N. York, Philadelphia & Baltimore or either to the mouth of the Ohio, you would greatly oblige me. I would be glad to have it accompanied with a statement of the average interruption during the year from Ice, snow, & droughts. I would be glad to hear from you while in Europe. With great respect I am & &c, J.C. Calhoun.

ALS (draft) in ScCleA.

From Jos[eph] J. Singleton

Dahlonega [Ga.,] 30th March 1847

Dear Sir, I have very recently been an eye witness to the operations on your own lot, as well as those in which you are interested; on the former, (or the Obarr lot) I am not pleased with the start your Lessees [John Pascoe and John Hockanoll] have made. I am apprehensive that there will be some difficulty in forcing upon them a strict complyance with the terms of agreement entered into by them. They have as yet only placed a Brother of John Pasgo's [*sic*], with a large family of Children, and only two laborers besides himself upon the Obarr lot; hence there is but little done towards developing the resources of the mine. I urged, and explained the necessity of prompt, and energetic action, both as regards their own interest, as well as that of yours. They speak of giving up their Lease. I shall not receive it, until I am instructed to do so by yourself, which instructions I hope will not be given, until I have some opportunity of tisting the efficasy of a solemn contract.

[Robert H.] Moore & [William G.] Lawrence have done very little recently either in the vein or deposite; hence there is but very little more toll added to my last report. I sent you by Mr. [Francis W.] Pickens a letter which I received from Mr. W[illia]m C. Dawson [former Representative from Ga.]; after you read it, be pleased to return it, as I have not yet answered it. I have the honor of being Your humble Servant, Jos. J. Singleton.

ALS in ScU-SC, John C. Calhoun Papers. NOTE: In an AEU Calhoun commented: "Dr. Singleton, Authorized him to act for me as he would for himself."

From RICHARD M. YOUNG, Comm[issione]r

General Land Office, March 31st 1847

Sir, I have the honor to return, herewith, as requested, the letter referred by you to this office, which was addressed to you by your nephew, Mr. B[enjamin] A. Calhoun, in reference to his preemption claim, in the Columbus dist., Mississippi.

In reply to your request on the subject, I have to state, that subsequent to the entry made by him, of the $E\frac{1}{2}$ N W$\frac{1}{4}$ Sect. 6 T. 10 R. 19, E. under the act of 4th Sept. 1841, the *whole* of that quarter section was claimed by W[illia]m J. Darnall, under the same law as the first settler, and induced (as you have been heretofore advised) directions from this office for the investigation of said conflicting claims, by the land officers after notice to both parties, that such investigation was had, and the testimony elicited was transmitted to this office with the decision of the land officers in favor of the right of Darnall & against that of Calhoun—that said papers & decision were referred to the Secretary of the Treasury [Robert J. Walker] on the 28th Sept. last for his decision under the 11th Sect. of the Act of 4th Sept. 1841, and returned by him on the 7th October last with a confirmation of the decision of the land officers—that said confirmation was communicated to said officers on the 9th of the latter month, and advice thereof given by them to Mr. Darnall, who subsequently appeared, paid for and entered the land claimed, which entry was filed for patenting and the prior invalid one of Calhoun cancelled.

The appeal from the decision of the land officers has been submitted to the Secretary of the Treasury and determined by him according to law. The case is therefore regarded as finally settled.

Your nephew, who is desirous, under the latter circumstances to have his money refunded can accomplish that object by forwarding an application to this office for the same, accompanied by the duplicate receipt and an intimation where he desires the Treasury warrant for the same to be sent.

In reference to the expenses (amounting to $80) which were incurred, as stated by your nephew, in the prosecution of his claim, I have to state, that this office cannot take any steps, which would recognize the principle of any indebtedness on the part of Government for expenses incurred by unsuccessful claimants by preemption. The entry by Mr. B.A. Calhoun of the half quarter claimed by him, was allowed upon testimony exhibiting upon its face prima facie evidence of a valid claim, but in due time the whole of the quarter section was claimed under the same law, by another person, alleging himself the first settler, and therefore, under the law, alone entitled to the right—an investigation of the subject, after due notice, resulted, in the establishment of that fact to the satisfaction of the Register & Receiver and their decision in favor of said first settler, as would have been originally done had the two claims been brought together to their notice, prior to Mr. Calhoun's entry. The latter, in his letter to you speaks of the claimant having been living on the land for some two years, and his entry of but the half quarter would seem to have been made, so as to avoid an interference with the improvements of the opposing claimant on the other half. The law gives the right to the quarter section, and under it the claimant, Darnall, proved up & paid for the full quarter. There would not appear to have been any error of action or of construction by the Land officers, when all the facts in the case were presented, and the expenses incurred by your nephew were such as he deemed necessary in support of his presumed rights, like thousands of others engaged in contests for public land. With much respect, Your ob[e]d[ien]t Serv[an]t, Richard M. Young, Comm[issione]r.

FC in DNA, RG 49 (General Land Office), Letters Sent: Preemption Bureau, 23:166–167.

From P[ATRICK] CALHOUN

American Hotel
New York [City,] April 5th, 1847

Dear Father, I wrote Mother [Floride Colhoun Calhoun] a few days since and have therefore delayed writing you a short time. I have not heard one word from home since parting with you in Washington—which I regret the more, as I was quite uneasy about your health when you left Washington, and very anxious to hear how you were on reaching home. I am in hopes that you have entirely recovered from the severe cold from which you were suffering when we parted.

I judge from what [William] Ransom [Colhoun] informs me in a letter lately received from him, that Mother did not meet you in Charleston, as you had hoped and supposed she would. I trust that her failing to meet was not caused by any ill health on her part.

Nothing is talked of here but the recent victories gained by General [Zachary] Taylor in Mexico—they will surely make him President unless some unforeseen misfortune should occur to mar his increasing popularity. Whigs and Democrats go for him here— that is the portion of the Democratic party which carries the election. Every labourer, foreigner or otherwise, you meet in the street throws up his hat and hurrahs for General Taylor. Military fame and glory is everything with the people and carries all before it. It is really melancholy to me to see how entirely the people—at least those of this City—are influenced by these things. Such feelings cannot but injure the public tone.

The Administration appears to be at the lowest ebb. Scarcely anyone speaks of it but in terms of contempt. I do not see, if the President [James K. Polk] continues to decrease in popularity as he has in the last few months, how he will be able to sustain himself.

I shall visit Kentucky probably between the 1st and middle of May—and may be married—depending upon circumstances which I may not be able to control. My inclinations and feelings certainly lead me to do so—but I must confess, I approach the married state with great reluctance. I have certainly never felt the same degree of affection for any lady, as I do for Miss Tibbatts, and I believe her in every way suited to make a good wife. Notwithstanding this, it is difficult for me to bring my mind to it. My course of life has been such, as in some degree to destroy my suitableness for quiet life; and therefore for married life. I feel however that it would be in many respects beneficial to me. I shall certainly go to Kentucky, and if Col. [John W.] Tibbatts [former Representative from Ky.] is ordered to Mexico, I may be married. At all events I must prepare myself for it. My funds have run very low and some additional means will be necessary to me. If ["therefore" *canceled*] you will therefore advance me such an amount as you may deem proper, it will be a great relief to me. It would be just as convenient if you will authorize me to draw on brother Andrew [Pickens Calhoun] through his Factors—and notify him of it. If you conclude to do so, let me know who they are. I can manage it through Cousin [James] Edward Boisseau.

My love to all. Your affectionate son, P. Calhoun.

ALS in ScCleA.

From WYNDHAM ROBERTSON, JR., "Private"

Memphis Tenn., April 5 1847

My D[ea]r Sir, A letter from this flourishing and quite important point on the Mississippi may not be unacceptable. Very recently I have taken occasion with my friend the Hon. Mr. [Frederick P.] Stanton [Representative from Tenn.,] to travel through the western district of this State for no other purpose than to learn the public Sentiment on the exciting questions which are engaging public attention. I take occasion in my own behalf as well as in that of many of your ardent friends to congratulate you on your interesting and instructive remarks made at a meeting of the citizens of Charleston on the 9 of March last. The views and opinions expressed by you are heartily concurred in and strongly approved by a majority of the people in Tennessee, breathing as they do a spirit of conciliation ["but" *canceled and* "and" *interlined*] at the same time *firmness*, which if observed cannot fail to preserve harmony and good order in popular elections. The Slavery question is almost too delicate for news paper discussion. I have been always of opinion that if the union is ever dissolved this subject will be at the bottom of it, it is necessary therefore, when touched upon to avoid such expressions as are calculated to widen the breach which is now so threatening. Allow me to assure you that your Speech at the Memphis Convention has won for you "golden opinions" and conciliated the opposition to an astonishing degree. As far as I can learn previous to its delivery your position was not so popular as your many ardent friends had believed—there were ill-founded prejudices existing based upon the merest pretences but which were calculated to do you injury. They have been all however removed and there is but one opinion as to your orthodoxy in the great party issues. In this part of the country we commend you for your firm and manly stand on the resolution to remove Mr. [Thomas] Ritchie from the gallery of the Senate Chamber. While it is necessary to preserve the freedom of the press as guaranteed by the Constitution, yet when it is converted into a corrupt engine of *mischief*, to vilify and defame the highest authorities of the land, it is the duty of our legislators to regulate and restrict it and to set examples worthy of imitation. I have known Mr. Ritchie well for many years. I was a resident of Petersburg Va. as you know up to 11[?] months since when I located here and there has never been but one opinion as to the vanity and self-sufficiency of this old creature. The most zealous democrats in the Va. Legislature have often remarked it and I speak advisedly when I say that body even would have proscribed him had it not been for his years and influence with the people. He has obviously presumed too [much] upon his Knowledge of Executive affairs and has made confident predictions expressed with great earnestness which have never to this day come to pass! proving beyond doubt that he did not know *quite* as much as he had the credit for.

In locating here my expectations in all respects have been more than realized—my professional union with the oldest and most distinguished member of the bar in west Tennessee, Judge [Valentine D.] Barry has been the means of giving me a lucrative practice. Should a national convention be held to nominate Candidates for the Presidency & Vice Presidency which I deprecate on the grounds taken by you at Charleston, it is my purpose to advocate your Claims for that office which you should have long since filled. In modern times a custom of electing obscure men to the office seems to prevail. It is much to be regretted and speaks but little for the pride of the American people.

It will afford me great pleasure to hear from you when your time and circum[stan]ces will allow. Believe me Very Truly Y[ou]r friend, Wyndham Robertson, Jr.

ALS in ScCleA.

From DUFF GREEN

Washington, 6th April 1847

My dear Sir, Yours of the 29th [March 28] is before me. It is, under the peculiar circumstances, most gratifying to me to be thus assured of your confidence and regard. If I know my own heart, its first wish, connected with public affairs is to see you, in the position for which your superior qualifications, your eminent public services, and public and private virtues give you claims greater than any other person— I need not say to you, that no one, has a higher respect for your character, and that no one places a higher estimate on your friend-ship. Knowing that I have at all times suffered persecution, because your political adversaries feared that my influence would be exerted for your advancement, the suggestion that those who are recognised as your friends, wanted confidence in me, was calculated to wound me, in ["the" *canceled*] proportion to the claims which my fidelity, my services and my sacrifices gave me upon them. No one else could so well urge those claims because no one else so well knows on what they rest, as you do. You know that I have never permitted my own private interests or personal preferences to control my sense of public duty. In the case to which you refer in 1840 you know that when I found that [Francis P.] Blair and [John C.] Rives had induced both [Dixon H.] Lewis & [Francis W.] Pickens to become candidates for Speaker, with an understanding that your friends were to vote for them as printers[,] I told you that I would not ask you to aid my Election as printer. I saw then and told you that your young friends in Congress were making a position for themselves in the dominant party at your expense and at the expense of your principles[.] I have since seen the selfishness of others, and I am frank to say that one of the inducements with me to [*one word canceled*] publish a paper is to counteract that tendency, on the part of those who have acted with you, towards being absorbed by the majority. I would now, while ["your" *interlined*] influence is active ["give" *canceled*] create an interest which will control for good, the future elements of party.

I have always known that you acted then (1840) as you have on all other occasions, from a high sense of your duty to the country—I appreciate the influence which the bias of your political associates ["gave" *canceled and* "had upon" *interlined*] your own judgment, and altho I regretted then & have ever since, [*one word canceled*] your reconciliation with [Martin] Van Buren, I have abated nothing of my attachment, confidence or respect for you, personally and politically.

After writing to you I saw G[e]n[era]l [James] Gadsden, and conversed with him on the subject of the paper, and he suggested that my best plan was to issue a prospectus and call upon the South to aid me. He said that the objection had been made in Charleston that all was quiet until *you* came, and that their movement had not been responded to in any other place. I wrote by him to Mr. [Isaac E.] Holmes and have not heard from either of them. I confess that it does appear to me that the South are a doomed people, and I am compelled to ask myself, why should I who have so little in common with them, take upon ["the" *canceled*] myself the advocacy of their interests? I confess to you further that I cannot ["fail"(?) *canceled*] close my eyes to the fact that this lethargy in the South indicates a state of indifference, which, with the fixed opposition to you in influential quarters, greatly discourages me.

I can see that to avail ourselves of Gene[ra]l [Zachary] Taylor[']s position and popularity we may by uniting your friends and his give a direction to the next Presidential Election greatly to strengthen the position of the South, but I am unwilling to take on myself the responsibility of such a movement. Taylor is a slave holder, and should the Va. Elections go against them the Whigs will nominate him. This will probably be followed by the nomination of an abolition Candidate. It is our interest to commit the Whigs against Abolition and we should hold a position which will prompt all parties to look to us as controlling the future.

It has been suggested that the people should in primary assemblies nominate you & Taylor. If your friends were to do this, the Whigs might nominate Taylor and thus complicate our position. My own view is that as yet we should hold the nomination in reserve, put the questions in issue fully & forcibly before the people, and select our candidate for the South, when public sentiment is more fully developed.

I have closed a satisfactory arrangement for the sale of a part of my mountain property. The parties reside in Phil[adelphi]a and are highly respectable and wealthy. They go to see the property this week and make the pay[men]t upon the report of the Geologist, which can not be otherwise than satisfactory. I will then be in funds and can publish a paper on my own account but, before I act in the matter, wish to hear from you relative to Gen[era]l Taylor[']s position. Yours truly, Duff Green.

ALS in ScCleA; FC in NcU, Duff Green Papers, vol. 12, pp. 15–17 (published microfilm, roll 25, frames 53–54); PC in Jameson, ed., *Correspondence*, pp. 1107–1109.

To W[ILSON] LUMPKIN, [Athens, Ga.]

Fort Hill, 6th April 1847

My dear Sir, I would have been blind not to see, that the corrupt of both parties would be opposed to me, as they have been in reality at all times for ["these" *canceled*] 20 years passed. My offense is, that I am opposed to the system of plunder, which has corrupted both, & in a great measure, the whole country, and the caucus machinery by which it has been fastened on the people, I fear never to be thrown off. God grant, that my apprehension may prove unfounded; for if not, there will come a day of retrabution [*sic*], the like of which, the world has rarely witnessed. My offence is opposition to this debasing & corrupt system, with its machinery. If I could be made to bow down to it, I might oppose the Mexican war, or any other particular measure, with perfect impunity, and ["without" *interlined*] loss of party cast. If at any time, I had intimated, that I would with draw all opposition to the Baltimore caucus for nominating a President, or, as he may now be denominated, the chief of the banditti, every sin would be for given.

You are right in supposing, that I could not, with my principles, longer avoid the recent occur[r]ences. Mr. [James K.] Polk, & those who act with him, ["never" *canceled*] never intended to have any relation with me, but that of hostility, secret or open, on their part, or subjection on mine. Indeed, how could we act together with the different principles & objects, which governed us? He & they looked to power & retain[in]g it, with the view of enjoying its honors & emoluments; I, on the contrary, looked to the country and its institutions, with the view of perpetuating them. His scheme for retaining power was to secure each of the great sections of the country, by addressing himself [to] the favourite policy of each—War for the west; spoils for the North, & free trade for the South. No one can read, impartially the documents, in relation to Mexico, without seeing, that war with her had been resolved on long before it occur[r]ed. Indeed, the line of policy pursued, in reference to her, was almost the only one by which it could have been brought about. It was certainly the very one best calculated to bring it about. Nothing was more easy, than to avoid the war, if it had been desired.

Now what has become of free trade, with which we were to be soothed & satisfied? The expense of the war, should it ["even" *interlined*] now terminate, settles that question. The whole will fall on the impost & by far the greater part of course on us, & ["amount" *canceled and* "a rate" *interlined*] of duties will be required to pay the debt & its interest, & the enormous expense of the government, from its increased military & naval establishments, that would satisfy the most rabid protectionists. Indeed, every thing for which the party has been, apparently, contending for the last dozen of years; low duties; no monopoly; no debt; moderate patronage; & seperation of the government from the paper system, will be lost—lost I fear forever, by the corrupt & deceitful line of policy, which has been pursued. It will obliterate the line between the two parties. Hereafter, there will be little distinction between ["them" *interlined*] in reference to principles or policy. They already stand on the same ground, as to the slave question. Their struggle hereafter will be a naked struggle for the spoils, undignified by a single principle, or question of policy.

I enclose a copy of my Charleston address [of 3/9], which will more fully illustrate this point. That we shall be the victims ["in the first instance" *interlined*] of this most wicked & debased condition, to which parties have sunk, if it is to go ["on" *interlined*], is as certain as we exist; & ["that" *interlined*] the country ["will in the end," *interlined*] is not less so. Our fate & that of the whole Union rest on us. If we meet & repel the attack on our domestick institution, as we ought, ["our" *canceled*] we may, with the blessing of Heaven, save ourselves & the Union, & restore the Constitution & reform the government; but, if not, our doomed [*sic*] is sealed. If we go into ["con" *canceled*] caucus to make a President with abolitionists, or those who court them, we shall be lost, even with the avowed intention, not to abide by its dicission, unless a sound individual shall be nominated. The Convention will be the judge of that; & will take care, to select the most equivocal & treacherous of the candidates, who, in the end, will be to us, the most dangerous. He will be, what may be called a moderate & judicious man, as [Andrew] Jackson was on the Tariff.

I have taken my course. Nothing can drive me from it. This State is with me, more unitedly, than ever. I hope, even your [Ga.] papers, will [be] giving me a hearing by republishing my Address. Truly, J.C. Calhoun.

ALS (microfilm) in NcU, Southern Historical Collection, Barrow Papers; ALS (photostat) in GU, David C. Barrow Papers.

To [M. A. ALLEN BROWN, Wilkesboro, N.C.]

Fort Hill, Ap[ri]l 9, 1847

Dear Sir; Regarding you to be one entertaining strong political attachment to me, as you state yourself to be [in your letter of 3/11], I answer you as a friend. If to be devoted to popular institutions, if to believe in the principles which brought the Republican party into power under Mr. [Thomas] Jefferson, if to prefer country to party & dare to oppose party when party deviates from its principles or policy is to be a Republican, then am I one, & ever have been, & never more so than now. I had supposed I had given too many & trying proofs of my Republicanism, Judged of these tests, to have my Republicanism doubted at this late day. I have often before opposed the party when in power, to save both it & the country. I have often before been denounced by partisans & party papers for doing so; but time has ever, as it will now, prove[d] me to be in the right. It has been my fate to oppose the party when in power & full strength, & to come to its rescue when fallen or out of power. It is again in a fair way, I apprehend, to lose power, because it has greatly departed from its original faith, & embraced the principles & policy of its opponents to a far greater extent than is supposed by those who have not carefully watched the course of events. The Republican party would ever triumph, & never be in danger if true to its principles & policy. I would say to you & other political friends who may have given too hasty an ear to the abuse of mere partisans & party papers who go with the party, right or wrong, wait & see. To time I always appeal against their clamours.

I enclose you a copy of my address [of 3/9] to the citizens of Charleston. With great respect, I am &c., J.C. Calhoun.

Transcript in T, Correspondence—By Author, accession 319; PC in Jameson, ed., *Correspondence*, pp. 725–726.

To C[HARLES] N. WEBB, [Halifax, N.C.]

FORT HILL, APRIL 9, 1847

DEAR SIR—The letter [of 3/20] I wrote to you, and which you desire permission to publish [in the *Roanoke Republican*], was written with the feelings called forth by the letter [of 3/9] from you, to which it is the answer. I have not kept a copy, and cannot say whether it is of a character, either from manner or matter, which would make it right to publish it. As a general rule, I ever avoid appearing in the public press when I can well avoid it; but as I have never written a line containing a sentiment in my life, that I would be unwilling the world should see, I leave you to act as you please in relation to it. With respect, I am, &c., J.C. CALHOUN.

PC (from the *Roanoke Republican*) in the Charleston, S.C., *Courier*, April 23, 1847, p. 2; PC in the Edgefield, S.C., *Advertiser*, April 28, 1847, p. 3; PC in the New Orleans, La., *Daily Picayune*, April 29, 1847, p. 2; PC in the Athens, Ga., *Southern Banner*, May 4, 1847, p. 3; PC in the Camden, S.C., *Journal*, May 5, 1847, p. 3; PC in the Pendleton, S.C., *Messenger*, May 7, 1847, p. 1; PC in the Richmond, Va., *Enquirer*, May 11, 1847, p. 1.

From F[RANKLIN] H. ELMORE

Charleston, Ap[ri]l 10, 1847

My Dear Sir, Shortly after my return to the City after I saw you[,] Mr. [Henry] Gourdin[,] Mr. [Henry W.] Conner, Mr. [Ker] Boyce, Mr. [Moses C.] Mordecai & myself met & had a consultation respecting the [news]paper. We have had several others since. The result of our conference was that it was very desirable to have the paper. Col. [Isaac W.] Hayne was also called in & concurred. Several others have been spoken to & also concur. The conclusion amongst us is that it can be done, if it is done well & aid can be got elsewhere in proportion with what we will do in So. Carolina.

Col. Hayne at our request embodied the ["foll" *canceled*] letter of which I send you copies. Our idea at first was to send these immediately out to confidential persons—but Col. Hayne suggested what I think was a sound plan—to send you copies of the letter which you might use as you deemed best in the other States. That you might write to such persons as you rely on & know what they could do in their States. If they approve this letter as a common platform, then we would at once commence our measures to raise our quota. If they do not like the letter & think it can be amended, suggest their amendments. Or if they think it best to act in each State on its own basis, while we combine on the common point to establish the press, we are content.

Our opinion is that it is worse than useless to go on with this scheme unless two things are provided. An Editor equal to the position—and ample means to sustain the press.

All my reflections confirm my first suggestion to you of Col. Hayne, if he could be got. His name—the Revolutionary & Senatorial associations—his own high character[,] fearless spirit yet calm temper & discreet character—& sound judg[men]t all recommend him. In information & talants [*sic*] he is fully equal to it. I fear he cannot be got—but I have not ventured to suggest it. All of us here concur in designating him.

Might not [Robert Barnwell] Rhett be induced? He designs leaving Congress I understand. I have not heard it from himself, having only seen him for an hour or so. He would do most admirably.

But no man can get on efficiently if he is not amply provided with means. Less than $30,000 can hardly do—$40,000 would be far better. If the balance could be got elsewhere, it seems to me we could raise $10[,000] & possibly ["$20,000" *canceled and* "more" *interlined*] in this State. With such a basis, a paper edited by Hayne or Rhett or some such man w[oul]d render powerful aid & protection to us.

We have fallen behind somewhat in our action from my inability to give the matter the attention & services it requires. Not only do my own affairs personal & official press very much & engrossingly on my time, but I have, for ten days preceding the last three or four, been incapacitated by influenza in my head for almost every thing. I am only now getting fairly over it.

We also think a letter from you personally to Mr. [Nathaniel] Heyward—Judge [Daniel E.] Huger [former Senator from S.C.]—and some gentleman about Georgetown (Rob[ert] F.[W.] Allston, for instance) would do much to aid us. One also to Maj. [John M.] Felder [former Representative from S.C.]. Inclose them to us & we will use them. One also to W[hitemarsh] B. Seabrook.

Could you sound Rhett as to the paper? I mean editing it. He is in favor of establishing it. I talked that over with him.

If the letter we send you does not meet your views in any respect or can be amended, we wish you to write us freely & correct it or amend it.

I have since writing the above shown it to Gourdin & Conner. A suggestion has been made that strikes me as sound—that Rhett may be & is, most probably, not acceptable to the Western men. His manner has not pleased them & he is not so popular with them as a leading Editor ought to be. What do you think?

Mr. [R.B.] Smith who edits the Southern Journal of Florida seems to be a spirited writer. Do you know any thing of him?

I go to day to Washington. [Dixon H.] Lewis [Senator from Ala.] is there & has recovered his health. Yo[ur]s truly, F.H. Elmore.

ALS in ScCleA. NOTE: The enclosure drawn up by Isaac W. Hayne, mentioned in Elmore's second paragraph, has not been found among Calhoun's papers. However, a copy is in DLC, James Henry Hammond Papers, with the letter of 3/31/1847 from Hayne to Hammond. It is a briefer version of the printed circular dated 8/2/1847, transcribed below with Calhoun's letter of 9/15/1847 to Eustis Prescott.

From ANNA [MARIA CALHOUN] CLEMSON

Brussels, April 11th 1847

My dear father, Tho' you have not written me a letter in a long time, I will be a good child, & not give your turn to any one else. I am quite jealous of Mr. [Thomas G.] Clemson. To be sure I read all of your letters to him, but that is no reason you should never write to me; But I know you have so much to do, that I will not scold you too much, only whenever you can find the time, remember how much pleasure your letters always give me, & I am sure you will waste a half an hour on me occasionally.

At present that the steamers have commenced running twice a month regularly, we shall hear more frequently, which is always a great happiness to me, & when all of you cannot write, you, sister [Martha Cornelia Calhoun], & mother [Floride Colhoun Calhoun], can take it by turns to give us a letter every mail.

You are now I suppose quietly at Fort Hill, where I wish I was also, for now especially, that the fine weather is commencing, I long so much for fresh air & the country for the children & myself, that I am even more homesick than usual. I find such a constant residence in a town very disagreeable, but it is inevitable. We cannot afford to travel, for it is all we can do with the greatest economy to live, without running in debt. We do not even keep a carriage, which we found impossible, & as we must hold on to & pay for our house whether we are in town or not, travelling is out of the question. However we are in an airy part of the town near the boulevards, & almost in the country, so that the children do not suffer, tho' they cannot be all the day in the open air as I would like them, for we have not even a garden to our house. All this is but trifling, as long as they are so well & hearty as they thank heaven! continue to be, & for myself, when one can[']t have a thing they must do without it,

& I remember too well your lessons, & example, not to content myself with things as I find them, but I long for the day when Mr. Clemson will think it possible for him to live at home, & I hope the high price of cotton, & the prosperity of the South, of which Col. [Francis W.] Pickens speaks in his last letter, may soon bring that happy time for me.

We had, the middle of last month, some fine weather, but with the usual uncertainty of the climate in this country, it has since been very cold & disagreeable again, but to-day is fine, & I hope spring has come at last. The winter has been long & severe, & the suffering among the poorer classes very great, & even did I find Europe much more to my taste than I do, the thoughts that I was surrounded by so many suffering fellow beings, would render a residence here painful. The contrast of the luxury of the rich, & the misery of the poor, causes always a sense of injustice. I am far from saying that those who amass money have not a right to it, but that system which causes such an immense disproportion in the classes of society, must be wrong, & when I leave the magnificent residences of the rich, & find the streets crowded with beggars, I no longer wonder, as I once did, at the excesses of the french revolution nor do I feel surprised at the fear of the great, for every thing which approaches reform, or change in the state of things. If I am so struck with all this in Belgium which is confessedly the most liberal country in Europe, (more so than England in some respects,) & where the charity of the rich is really very great, what must it be in other countries?

I hope you found all well & doing well at home. Mother complains, in her last letter, of suffering from her teeth. She should have them out, it is the only remedy, as I found last year. It seems all of the family are dispersed, & only mother, yourself, & sister, remain to keep the old fireside warm. One of these days I hope we may all be re-united once more, but the time seems long.

The children continue to give me satisfaction in every way; I begin even to see some progress in learning, about which however I was never uneasy, for they evince to[o] much talent not to be able to learn whenever they are set seriously about it. [John] Calhoun [Clemson] really writes uncommonly well, better than Willy [William Lowndes Calhoun] did when I came to Europe. You cannot judge of his letters to mother & yourself, which are worse written than anything else, first because he always writes on the slate, & the change to paper worries him, & also his very endeavour to do better than common, makes, as is often the case, one cause of failure. The children are brought up good Americans you may be assured.

They already love their country dearly, & I take every pains [*sic*; to] encourage the feeling, for I feel daily more & more convinced, that if patriotism were not a virtue, it would be worth cultivating as a source of happiness. They talk constantly of you & their grand-mother, & only yesterday Floride [Elizabeth Clemson] asked her papa, if he would not take her to America *"tomorrow"* to see her dear gandfather & grandmother. They constantly ask to kiss their grand-mother's miniature—your likenesses, being only engravings, do not strike them so much. I do wish, if it be possible, you would have a good likeness of yourself taken for me, about the size of mother's. I need not tell you how I should prize it. I don[']t know whether I ever asked you to put by a copy of your life & speeches for Calhoun, with his name written in by you. The copy you gave him, is so often borrowed, & so much sought after, that it is a good deal injured. We dined at the Palace a day or two ago. I sat next the King [Leo-pold I], & as usual he asked after you, & said something complimen-tary of you. Amongst other things he said, that your counsels were always wise, & differed entirely in spirit from the time serving spirit of too many of the public men in America. He is I should think a man of considerable natural capacity & much cultivation but so filled[?] up with indolence, & egotism, that he is a mere nullity in his kingdom. All the better perhaps you will say, but I don[']t know. If one must have a monarch, one who by example & precept takes a lead, has great influence on the moral of the country, more than *we* can possibly believe could be the case. However unfortu-nately the reverse is equally true, & bad monarchs are much more common than good.

My love & that of Mr. C[lemson] to mother, sister. I shall write mother shortly. I wrote sister last mail. The children send many kisses to all. Your devoted daughter, Anna Clemson.

ALS in ScCleA.

To T[HOMAS] G. CLEMSON, [Brussels]

Fort Hill, 11th April 1847

My dear Sir, The last steamer brought me yours of the 27th Feb.; and I am happy to hear that you and Anna [Maria Calhoun Clemson] & the children are well, & that they are growing so finely.

I have since written to Mr. [John] Mobl[e]y to inform Mr. [Levy]

Wilson, that your note to [Robert] Humphrey's, which he holds, will be paid by Mr. [John E.] Bonneau, & requested Mr. B[onneau] to take it up on presentation. It was too late, when your letter was received to give order to change [*or* charge] your cotton seed.

The melon seeds came safely, and I am much obliged to you for them, & shall take great care in planting them. If they should succeed in producing, as fine fruit, as some I received many years ago from Commodore [John] Ro[d]gers, they will be a great treat.

Since I wrote you last, I got a letter from Mr. Mobley, your overseer, informing me, that his health was so bad, that he did not think he could do justice to you in attending your business, and proposing to give up his place, provided another could be had to take it, & that he could be paid for the portion of the year he has been employed. I, immediately, wrote to Col. [Francis W.] Pickens, requesting him, if he could find a suitable person to take his place to employ him for the residue of the year, & to give an order on Mr. Bonneau for what would be due to Mr. Mobley. I also wrote to Mr. Mobley, and informed him what I had written to Mr. Pickens, & referred him to him to make the arrangements. I hope he may succeed in getting a good substitute.

The spring has been very backward; but the weather has been warm & dry since the commencement of the month, & vegitation has pushed forward with great rapidity. The woods begin to assume their summer garb, and every thing seems gay & cheerful. This morning is a lovely one, of the most agreeable temperature. The birds are sending up their joyous notes in every direction. We, however, begin to want rain, to bring up our corn & cotton, & give vigour to the growth of small grain.

As to politicks, things as yet, continue much as they have been, when I last wrote you. [Thomas] Ritchie continues his abuse, to which I have no objection. He has been long my secret foe, he is now & [*sic*] open & bitter one. Whatever impression, he may make against me for the time, will in a short time react. I do not think, that there is the slightest prospect, that the old Hunkers of which he is the organ, can ever again be resuscitated. They are incurably corrupt—alike destitute of honor, or honesty. They know, that I have sustained the democratick party for the last ten years, & that without my support, they would have been prostrated for ever by the explosion of 1837. They know, that my support has been of the most disinterested character; & yet they hate me, with a deeper hatred, than what they do, their professed opponents, simply because of my opposition to the spoils principle & the caucus Machinery—the only

cohesive power, that holds them together. But their days are numbered, & they see it; & hence the gnashing of the teeth, & bitter curses.
I take it with perfect calmness. They shall have more cause for
["their" *canceled*] Wailling before I am done. The last session is
but the prelude to the next, when the day of rec[k]oning will
commence.

I enclose a letter from her mother [Floride Colhoun Calhoun] &
another from [Martha] Cornelia [Calhoun] to Anna, which I suppose
gives all the family & local news. I had, since they were written, a
letter from ["Andrew" *canceled*] Willie [William Lowndes Calhoun],
who writes that his health is greatly improved.

All join their love to you & Anna & children. Kiss them for their
grandfather & tell them how much I want to see them.

I have in a great measure recovered from the effects of the Influenza. Your affectionate father, J.C. Calhoun.

ALS in ScCleA; PEx in Jameson, ed., *Correspondence*, p. 726.

From ELLWOOD FISHER

Cincinnati, 4 mo[nth] 11, 1847
My dear friend, I have been so much engaged with private affairs
since leaving Washington, as to have learned little of public opinion
in this quarter on the recent aspect of politics. We have however
just had a city election here which throws some light on the subject.
There is in this place now a democratic majority estimated at a few
hundred—and the regular hunkers undertook by a caucus to organize
the party and distribute the spoils—some sixty officers including the
Mayor to be elected. The result was the triumph of the Whigs generally, their mayor by a majority of about six hundred. The hunkers
were confident of success, and are much mortified—having never
witnessed a greater contempt of their system. Independent candidates were generally prefer[r]ed.

I am happy to find that so far as I have enquired our friends are
unshaken—notwithstanding the pusil[l]animous conduct of so many
in Virginia. And I think we shall shortly establish a paper here of
the most independent character. Our friends whilst they have despised the public honours in this part of the State heretofore in the
gift of the hunkers, have been successful in private undertakings and
were never in a better condition to act effectively.

The Whigs and Democrats are much at a loss as to their next candidates for the Presidency. The [John] McLean men are acting with more vigor than the friends of [Thomas] Corwin, but both classes of Whigs as well as the Hunkers are alarmed at the prominence which the battle of Buena Vista has given to [Zachary] Taylor.

The news of [Winfield] Scott[']s success however in the capture of the city of Vera Cruz and the Castle, which has just arrived will probably create a diversion in his favour. I am however apprehensive that if peace be not now immediately made the War will be protracted indefinitely, and will be paramount to all other subjects—and so long as this part of the country remains so prosperous from the foreign trade as to be unaffected sensibly in its finances by the War there is great danger that it will acquiesce in its continuance. And after all that has been achieved in Mexico what guarranty have we of a speedy peace?

How are the religious and political duties of a christian Republican system like ours to be harmonized? The tenets of Christianity are too pure to be observed with much fidelity by the mass: certainly it is not [to] be expected after the toleration extended to this unrighteous War. And yet if public morality be insisted on among a people no better than ours, how can political ascendancy be acquired? We cannot acquiesce in the wrong—can we prevent it without power? The true principles of Religion must remain militant until the millenium. So we are taught in the New Testament—and in fact when we examine the subject closely we can scarcely find it possible for pure principles of religion to be otherwise than militant. If triumphant—if their exercise were followed by immediate reward, the prospect of the reward would taint with selfishness the motives of the righteous. Their kingdom is not of this world. Can we then if those principles are carried into political life as they must be, expect success, or any thing more than occasional and uncertain success? I admit that if the true doctrine of our federative system prevailed—if the majority of the people of the States and not a majority of the people of the Union were to govern we should approach much nearer to the standard of moral rectitude, for the unity of interests and even of passions and prejudices so diversified must be in much stricter conformity to the moral government of the Universe than the local and transient sentiment of a mere numerical majority. For certainly the universal interest of men is conformable to the universal law which is given them. That is the evidence of our Creator[']s wisdom and goodness. But does not the low grade of morals which pervades the mass operate as a perpetual and impassable obstacle to the adoption and observance of our federative principle? Is there not always or generally an appetite for plunder or for wrong of some sort too strong to be controuled or restrained by the limits which our Constitution imposes? And must not the friend of our fundamental political as well as of our fundamental religious law expect to remain generally militant? and for similar reasons as to both? We must indeed triumph ultimately in precise proportion to our fidelity to both—but probably not in our day. The struggle in both cases developes the greatest virtues and the noblest faculties—the greater and the nobler from the very remoteness and uncertainty of success. Power and Fame the most effective and exalted must ensue, but they will be for coming generations to feel and to proclaim.

Power if acquired in this country must be administered in accordance with public opinion, which is the mere compound result of the subsisting principle and intelligence of the several members of our system—in which of course much wickedness and ignorance must mingle to alloy and pervert it. But what is thus required to satisfy the present age, must for that reason offend posterity which will be exempt to a considerable degree from the causes that pervert the conclusions of our days. Can a great man and a good one therefore administer government, without losing reputation? The most popular of our Presidents have been among the least able—some of them among the least good.

These considerations have heretofore prevented me from being sanguine of political success—and I confess I was agreeably surprized when in the election of [James K.] Polk I thought we had accomplished such great progress in the establishment of sound principles. Subsequent events have remitted me to my original views. I therefore have not generally indulged in the hope of power. But I have ever considered our system as the finest the world ever presented for the development and exercise of the greatest of our faculties, and for accomplishing the greatest ultimate good by political action. The extent of our population and territory and ["the" *canceled*] of our civilization, brings into action and demand a greater proportion of general moral principle than any other, and must give us a greater sympathy and influence with posterity than any other government that ever existed. In such a case political and moral or religious duties assimilate—and their consequences are similar.

I have read with all the pleasure and instruction thy speeches usually give thy address to the people at Charleston.

Remember me cordially to thy Wife [Floride Colhoun Calhoun] and family. Very truly thine, Ellwood Fisher.

[P.S.] My wife also sends regards.

[Marginal P.S.] What is the aspect of ["the" *canceled*] affairs in the South Atlantic States?

ALS in ScCleA.

To "Col." A[NDREW] P[ICKENS] CALHOUN, [Marengo County, Ala.]

Fort Hill, 12th April 1847

My dear Andrew, The last mail brought me your's of the 2d Inst., & I am happy to hear, that you are all well & that your business is in so forward a condition, & your place ["is" *canceled*] in such fine order. I regard it, as you do, as one of the finest plantations in the whole country, and that ["nothing" *interlined*] short of necessity ought ever induce us to part with it. I hope the time never will come, when that will compel us. I agree with you in the advantage of early preperation & planting, but there is one of the inducement[s] for it, that I am of opinion, ought to be entirely dispensed with; I mean fodder pulling. I regard it as well established, that it is an entire dead loss. One of our neighbours, a very careful & exact man, made last year an experiment in order to test how much the corn lost by pulling ["the" *interlined*] fodder, and ascertained on a fair trial, that the corn lost in weight an amount exactly equal to the weight of the fodder. I have been so well satisfied ["from observation" *interlined*] that the loss was great, that I have for several years ceased in a great measure to pull fodder. I am also satisfied, that the injury done to the land by a corn crop is in a great degree owing to the same cause. I have, also, come to the conclusion, that the shucks cut & moistened, is not ["much, if" *interlined*] any, inferior to fodder, as food for Horses; & such I find is the opinion of one of our most experienced stage contractors. To make up the deficiency for fodder, I sow rye & cut the straw; & to cut it & the shucks, I have a cutter, which I put in motion by the gear of my gin, that would in a few hours cut what will do me for a week. Either of them, with corn, or rye meal, makes excellent food.

Our season has been fine since the 1st of the month, very warm & sufficiently dry. If it has been as good with you, your crop must look well. I am still confident, that cotton will ["con" *canceled*] rise, before the mid[d]le of June, & hope you will hold back.

I am distressed, that your mother [Floride Colhoun Calhoun] should write to William [Lowndes Calhoun], as she does, in reference to you. She has spoken several times about Izey to me, & I have expostulated with her in strong terms about the impropriety of her course. The truth is, she is not satisfied with her own course in reference to her. Nothing would do at one time, but that I must sell [h]er, which I refused to do. Then she took up the plan of taking her to Alabama to be sold, which I also opposed; & finally changed her mind not to sell her, because [Martha] Cornelia [Calhoun] objected, which by the by she did from the first; &, in her eagerness to get her back, throws the blame of her not being returned on you. If in her letters to Willie, she has said any thing, that looks, as if, I partook of her feelings, in reference to ["her" *canceled and* "Izey" *interlined*], or the carriage & horses, or Shark, the plantation Horse, John [C. Calhoun, Jr.] rode out, I hope you have not permitted it to have the least weight with you. So far from it, she has never alluded to either with me, without rebuke. I have not felt the least inconvenience for the want of Shark, & do not doubt you have done your best to dispose of the Horses & carriage. If you cannot sell the Horses without too great sacrifice, keep them for plantation horses, unless there should be an opportunity of sending back the one, that does not baulk. He is a fine buggy horse & we have one, in which we could use him.

In reference to the difficulty you might have with her & Mr. [Thomas G.] C[lemson] about my estate, & particular[ly] Tulip Hill place, in which we are jointly concerned in case of my death, [it] has not escaped my reflection. I intend to guard against it, & wish to consult with you about it. I hope it will be in your power to make us a visit this summer or fall, with your family, when an opportunity would be afforded to consult you & to make my arrangement. As life is uncertain, it ought not to be delayed.

I hope Margaret [Green Calhoun] has by this time passed the critical event, which you state was near at hand; & that she is doing well. She would in a few months be able to travel.

As to the suspecions & unfounded blame of your Mother, you must not only bear them, but forget them. With the many good qualities of her Mother [Floride Bonneau Colhoun], she inherits her suspecious & fault finding temper, which has been the cause of much vexation in the family. I have borne with her with patience, because it was my duty to do so, & you must do the same, for the same reason. It has been the only cross of my life.

I hope William will have fortitude enough to have his tooth extracted. Tell him, that I received his last letter, & that I am happy to hear his health has improved so much. I would answer it, but wrote to him not long since.

All join their love to you & Margaret, the children & William. Your affectionate father, J.C. Calhoun.

[P.S.] Marengo is in fine order & proves to be an excellent riding horse. It would have been most unreasonable for me to complain about Shark not being returned, when one so much his superior & more needed by me, was sent.

ALS in NcD, John C. Calhoun Papers. NOTE: Margaret Maria Calhoun, daughter of Andrew Pickens and Margaret Green Calhoun, was born on April 30, 1847.

From JOHN FOX

Doylestown[,] Bucks Co[unty, Pa.,] 12 April 1847
Dear Sir, Stephen Moylan Fox, a nephew of mine, is now ["as" *canceled*] an engineer on the Gadsden railroad in South Carolina. He is desirous of being employed in others which are contemplated in your State. His precise object I have told him to state to you by letter.

I am very desirous to assist him if I can do so, and I am satisfied no man is better qualified for such a situation than he. He is now about 35 years of age and has a family. His early education was very good and he was about two years at West point. For many years he has ["been" *canceled*] been employed in Pennsylvania on Railroads and other public improvements and I believe is universally considered as a very able and efficient officer.

Being much interested for him and his family I have enquired from time to time from those in whose employ he was as to his standing, and I have always heard high encomiums upon his capacity, industry, and integrity. I can refer to some names known to you— James Clarke, Canal Commissioner for many years. He told me repeatedly that Moylan Fox was one of the very best Engineers in the State. Samuel D. Ingham knows his general reputation. Lewis S. Coryell knows his character as an officer and personally well. Simon Cameron [Senator from Pa.] knows his character as an Engineer & personally. He will refer you to the names of the principal Engineers under whom he has served. If it should be in your power to advance his interest in the way he desires it will gratify us much if you can consistently with your own views assist him.

313

Our *Clay men* here are all [Zachary] Taylor men. I suppose "War, pestilence, and famine" are different matters now and a military Chieftain may conscientiously be supported. From what I see I have no question that Penn[sylvani]a will go for Taylor if he is a Candidate. I wish he would decline on the ground that sound patriotism requires him to do so—and take the ground that a successful military chief ought not to be supported for the Presidency. It would elevate his character & the example would be most useful. But I know no man who throws the Presidency aside but yourself. I am most sincerely your friend & Servant, John Fox.

ALS in ScCleA. NOTE: An AEU by Calhoun reads "Judge Fox."

From E[DWARD] TURNER

Franklin Place near Hamburgh Mi[ss].
Ap[ri]l 12 1847

Dear Sir, I have your several speeches, recently delivered in the Senate of the U.S. under your *frank*, & thank you for your kind attention.

I have looked on, with deep concern at the rise & progress of this Mexican War, and allow me to say to you that no man rejoiced more than I did at your re-election to the Senate, or more highly approved of your acts & speeches since you took your seat in that distinguished body. If at any time I disapproved of a *single* vote, (on [John M.] Berrien[']s resolutions, for instance) yet upon the whole I feel grateful as an American citizen & a Southron man at your general course, & wish you had the management of the Executive department of our Government.

Poor old [Thomas H.] Benton! What a figure he cuts, in his recent correspondence with the President [James K. Polk] about the Major Gen[era]ls commission!

Our brave & skillful Major Generals [Winfield] Scott & [Zachary] Taylor, have settled that matter I trust, by their recent victories. With such men as these, & [William O.] Butler, [John A.] Quitman, [William J.] Worth, [John E.] Wool, Keary [*sic*; Philip or Stephen W. Kearny] & [Jefferson] Davis in the field, how could the President make such appointments, as B[enton] & others! With great respect, & esteem I have the honor to be y[ou]r mo[st] ob[edient] s[ervan]t, E. Turner.

ALS in ScCleA.

314

From A[LEXANDER] BOWIE

Tal[l]adega, Ala., 13 Ap[ri]l 1847

My dear Sir, I trust that you will not feel it as a cruel infliction to receive a letter, now & then, from an old & constant friend—more especially as I shall not write but when something connected with your own prospects, or those long cherished principles which I first learned from you, bears heavily on my mind.

The events of the last winter in Washington, have made a deep & lasting impression upon your friends here—& I presume every where. Such has been the effect produced here, that already we begin to feel that we no longer belong to the Democratic party—indeed, the party has, substantially, ostracised *us*, as Tom Richey [Thomas Ritchie] "& id omne genus" have served or endeavored to serve *you*. What shall we do? We can never be Whigs, until *they* repudiate the political doctrines which they have heretofore advocated. If we should attempt a party organization on our own principles, we should find ourselves a third party, weaker than either of the others, and an object of bitter hostility, to both. Indeed, our political creed would differ but little, if any, from that professedly embraced by the Democratic party—it would, however, as I think, be more honestly professed & more faithfully acted out. I have long been satisfied that the present organization of parties in the United States has been an unfortunate one. Thousands of those who were a few years ago most excellent State rights republicans, are now Federal Whigs. Many, who fifteen years ago, were prepared to peril life, property & every thing but freedom, in opposition to a protective tariff, have since found themselves battling, side by side, with the champions of the restrictive policy. Such, however, is the unavoidable consequence of party organization. Accident often determines the adoption of a ["principle" *canceled and* "measure" *interlined*], when party obligations compel us to espouse it, even though it be opposed to our preconceived & most cherished principles. In our government, it seems to me, the only sensible & legitimate division of parties is by the line which separates the State rights doctrine from that of consolidation. Upon this base, were parties first organized in our country, and I think it is deeply to be deplored that *that* organization was ever broken up. If we could have a reorganization of parties, assuming the old names, or new names with the old principles, many whigs here (and I doubt not, elsewhere) would join us. In this county, you have some strong friends in the whig ranks; but they are old State rights men, who find that they are in a false position. It is all important that upon the Slavery question the South should be united—and it is one of the most melancholy effects of our present party divisions that even a common danger will hardly produce a cordial union. If we were now, as we once were, either Republicans or Federalists, there would be but little division in the South.

But it is vain, I fear, to talk about new-organizing parties—*we* have not the power to do it, & I suppose we must submit to things as we find them. My object in beginning this letter was to assure you of the unabated confidence of your friends here; and to ask you, if it will not be too great a tax on your time, to give me your views as to the proper policy to be pursued, in the present state of things, by those who have been heretofore called "Calhoun Democrats." There is no political event we desire more than to see you elevated to the presidency—yet, with your known principles & feelings, we scarcely believe such an event to be possible. By the by, I have often, of late years, been reminded of a prophecy upon that subject uttered to me, by the late [Senator] Felix Grundy of Tennessee, some thirty five years ago. He spent a night with us at old Mr. [James?] Wardlaw[']s where I boarded. He was on his return from Congress during the last war with England. I was indulging in a little enthusiastic admiration both of you & Mr. [Henry] Clay, & predicting that you would both fill the presidential office. Mr. Grundy, agreeing with my encomiums, said, in very nearly these words, "I think you will find yourself mistaken—neither Mr. Calhoun nor Mr. Clay will ever be President of these United States—and I now predict further, that after the last Revolutionary character, who is qualified for the station, shall have filled the office, a first rate statesman will never attain it— such a man will never sell himself to a party; and therefore can never be elected." So far his prediction has been verified; and although I do not believe that the mantle of Elijah fell upon *his* shoulders; yet I have awful fears that he guessed the truth.

May we not hope to see you at our house next autumn? You promised me you would make your next trip to Alabama by this route. Excuse this rambling epistle, and with kind regards to Mrs. [Floride Colhoun] Calhoun, believe me your sincere friend, A. Bowie.

ALS in ScCleA; variant PC in Jameson, ed., *Correspondence*, pp. 1109–1111.

From WILSON LUMPKIN

Athens [Ga.,] April 13th 1847

My dear Sir, I am in receipt of your favor of the 6th Inst. Your views in regard to the political prospects of the Country—and the present state and condition of the two great political parties very nearly coincide with my own. I have no confidence whatever, in either of the party organizations as they at present stand. Nor do I believe that either party can be purifyed, by honest men chiming in with them. Parties in this country have degenerated ["into" *canceled*] into political organizations, for mere purposes of gaining power & office. For many years ["past" *interlined*] I seen, ["felt" *with the* "I" *interlined*] & deplored the corruption to which you advert. But have not yet been able, to devise an efficient remedy, for the formidable evil, which has taken such deep hold upon our beloved country. The press is awfully corrupt, & will give nothing to the people, which will enlighten them to see, the designs of the Leaders & aspirants for place & power. Most of the papers in Ga. are closed against light.

Without even intimating it to you, or any one else, I have tryed in the most courtious & kind manner, to get several papers, to publish your late speeches in Congress—but have not been able to succeed, but to a very limited extent. Your views upon almost every subject, are misapprehended, & misrepresented. And whatever you may think, I assure you, that the power of the press, for evil, as well as good, is almost irresistable—especially when conducted by unprincipled and corrupt men—pampered by the smiles & patronage of those filling high Offices. I know not, what the honest & patriotic of the present day can do, while the people & press, are in the hands of the leaders & aspirants of the two great parties—Except it be, to stand still, & wait for the salvation of God.

In politicks as well as other matters, I have always found it, the most successful course, to do ample justice to my antagonist—never to strike blows, against that which is invulnerable. Therefore, I think we of the South, who aided in bringing Mr. [James K.] Polk into power, should not on account of other errors, fail to give him all due credit, for his course, on many subjects connected with the internal policy of the country. As far as I have seen, the administration has been true to its pledges on the subject of the Tariff, & the management of the financial & commercial affairs of the country. And the President[']s vetoes of the log rooling [*sic*] internal improvement Bills deserves the approbation of the country. And although I dislike the manner of bringing on the War with Mexico, I am disposed

317

to treat the errors on that subject with forbearance. But in conducting the War, I see much to censure. From the begin[n]ing & throughout, I can perc[e]ive a littleness of spirit, in trying to make *party* capital, out of the War, at the expense of the best interest of the country. From the time, the President[']s "Exalted friend" Col. [Thomas H.] Benton, became the Magnus Apollo, of the admin[istra]tion, I have seen with deep mortification, that the President of the U.S. was a mere *play-thing*, in the hands of more designing men. Every thing connected with the Lieut[enant] Gen[era]lship, was most ridiculous. Col. Benton[']s vindication of the ["presiden"(?) *canceled*] President &c all made the matter worse.

At present the true men of Ga., can only stand still. They have no idea of joining caucus conventions. They will make no compromises, with Protectionist—abolitionist—or antislavery men. The whigs count them in vain. The Democrats abuse them. They have no power over the press. They see their fellowmen misled. And may at last, be forced to join the multitude, in favor of some millitary cheiftain [*sic*]. Y[ou]r fr[ien]d as Ever, Wilson Lumpkin.

ALS in ScCleA.

From JOHN E. CAREW

Charleston S.C., 14 Apr[il] 1847

Dear Sir, I have just rec[eive]d a letter from Ex Gov. [William] Aiken who is at present at his plantation requesting me to ask the favor of you to send him some letters of introduction to persons in Europe.

He leaves the United States early in May and is anxious to obtain letters to Sir Robert Peel, Mr. [Richard] Cobden, in London and Marshall [Nicolas] Soult, Monsieur [F.P.G.] Guizot & [Louis A.] Thiers in Paris or any others that you may choose. As the intercourse between this place and his plantation is by no means regular, and as he will be here in a few days, You would greatly oblige both him and myself by directing to me in Charleston. I trust we are not obtruding too much on your valuable time.

There is nothing new. Old Mr. [Thomas] Ritchie is out this morning in a long article on Gen[era]l [Zachary] Taylor's nomination for the Presidency. It is a sore Subject with the Editor, and the course of the [Charleston] Mercury has I am sure added nothing to his comfort. He is very restive under our questions and says that he will not have his devotion to the South called in question by the Mercury.

Hoping it may suit your convenience to let me hear from you soon I remain Sir With great consideration and regard Y[ou]r mo[st] ob[edien]t S[ervan]t, Jno. E. Carew.

ALS in ScCleA.

From Walker & Bradford, Hamburg [S.C.], 4/14. They present a statement of Calhoun's account from 9/1/1845 to date, showing a balance due of $311.71. "For your convenience we shall draw upon you at sight in a few days in favor of Mr. J[ohn] S. Lorton [of Pendleton], and, as we are in much need of money, we trust that you honor our draft upon presentation." An AEU by Calhoun reads: "Bradford & Walker ac[coun]t. Paid[.] See order within." ALS with En in ScU-SC, John C. Calhoun Papers.

From ALLSTON GIBBES

Philadelphia, April 16th 1847
Sir, I will not aggravate the trespass I am about to commit on your time and patience by the addition of an apology. You will perhaps find one in the subject—in your own position—and in the penalty which great men are required to pay for their elevation. As the delegated Representative, in the Senate of the United States, of my native State, (God save her!) my public interests are, so far, in your charge. I seize the leisure, if leisure it be, of a recess, as the most opportune time, to invite your consideration of the claims which a free, just, and liberal Government may, and ought to, allow to its citizens affected *personally* by its own acts of *national* policy. In the ["acquisition" *canceled and* "annexation" *interlined*] of Texas, with the acquisition of its large territory, and the absorbption [*sic*] of its commercial revenues, there may seem to be some consideration due to the holders of its obligations of debt, and to the pledges of "Public Faith," for their redemption, based upon its former means of revenue, now transferred, with its allegiance, to a community of States. But I do not intend to offer a word, either of argument, or compliment, on this matter. You, Sir, may well be spared both. I only beg to state necessary facts.

I hold Bonds of the State of Texas, bearing on their face an acknowledgment of debt to the holder, of about $10,600, with arrears of interest due of about $4000. They came into ["my" *interlined*] hands for valuable consideration, at some sacrifice of other and productive securities, and, allow me to add, at the cost of some credulous tribute to that arch-deceiver "Public Faith." I have been impoverished by unfortunate investments, for want of better knowledge, in Bank Stocks &c. of my own, and, unhappily, some sacred "Trust" funds, which latter however I have replaced, at my loss. I look now to this plank of Texas for escape from shipwreck—not for myself— for broken health, and a half century of years, give me warning to quit—shortly I think. But Sir, I have two sisters—one unmarried, whose poor pittance is in my unlucky keeping—the other the worthy widow, with a helpless family, of a worthy man, Major John Wilson, who earned the cause of his death in the service of the State of South Carolina, as Civil and military Engineer. She too has been ruined by the failure of a son in mercantile business, and is now dependant on the frail tenure of his life, (in the West Indies,) for her daily bread. Pardon me these painful details—and the extent of my trespass on your patience. I feel assured that you will, for no man, believe me, holds in higher or juster estimation the character of him whom I venture thus to address, than, Sir, your most humble Servant, Allston Gibbes of South Carolina.

Texas Bonds.

P.S. It may perhaps be proper to "annex" some brief description of the Bonds. They are of three kinds, viz.

1. No. 5304 issued to Tho[ma]s Toby for "Fifty Shares, each $100 in the Consolidated Fund of Texas, created by an Act of Congress approved 7th June 1837"—"redeemable at the convenience of the Government after 1 Sept[embe]r 1842" bearing interest at the rate of 10 per cent p[e]r an[num] from 1 May 1839 payable semi-annually. "For the payment of this Stock the Public Faith is hereby pledged; and so much of the revenue arising from imposts and direct taxation as may be necessary is appropriated for the payment of the interest." Dated at Houston 30 April 1839. Signed by Tho[ma]s Gales Forster, Stock Com[missione]r and J.W. Simmons, Comptroller.

2. "Certificate of Stock in the ten per cent consolidated fund, created by Act of Feb. 5th 1840. Be it known that there is due from the Republic of Texas to —— —— dollars, payable to Order"—"the Principal redeemable at the pleasure of the Government after 30 June 1845"—interest payable semi-annually from 15 June 1840—with warrants for the same duly signed. Dated, Austin June 15th 1840.

Signed, Cha[rle]s De Morse, Stock Com[missione]r, J.W. Simmons, Comptroller. Six Bonds, each $500. Five bonds, each $100 with interest warrants duly signed, ten on each.

3. "Government Bond, payable to holder, Receivable for all Government dues: eight per cent fund of $1,500,000 created by Act of Congress, Feb. 5th 1840. The Republic of Texas promises to pay to —— or order —— dollars, with interest at the rate of eight per cent p[e]r an[num] from date hereof, payable semi-ann[ual]ly." The Principal redeemable at the pleasure of the Government after 1 Jan[uar]y 1846. This Certificate, including the instalments of interest which may have become due, shall at all times be receivable in collection of the revenue, and in the payment of *any dues* to the Government: the revenue from License Tax, and Tax on Personal Property is set apart, and specially appropriated for the payment of the interest on this fund. Treasury department, Austin, Oct. 1, 1840. (Signed) W[illia]m Serey, Act[in]g Sec[retar]y of Treas[ury], Mirabeau B. Lamar, Pres[iden]t. *Quere.* Might not these bonds be made available in any reclamation of the State of Texas against the U.S. I hold three Bonds, each $500. Six bonds, each $100, with Interest warrants, duly signed, ten on each.

Sir, if you could find time, at your leisure, to give me a word of opinion or advice in this matter, it would be gratefully received, as charitably conferred.

ALS in ScCleA.

From H[ENRY] W. HILLIARD, [Representative from Ala.]

Montgomery, Ala., 16th April 1847

My dear Sir, But for my absence from home I should before this have replied to your interesting letter.

I cannot for a moment doubt that your views, so fully expressed upon the question touching slavery, will be the views of the whole South. I shall see that your speech at Charleston is spread through this State, or at all events this part of the State, if I can effect it. You have many friends here, and indeed throughout this District, and your views of a great public question so deeply affecting the South, ought to be known.

So far there has not been much feeling upon this question, manifested by the people of this State, but I am confident there is a deep and settled sentiment in regard to it, which requires only some exciting cause to call it out in great power.

I shall be most happy to hear from you at all times, and in the meanwhile am Very respectfully & very truly Yours, H.W. Hilliard.

ALS in ScCleA.

To C[HARLES] J. Fox and Others

Fort Hill, 17th April 1847

Gentlemen, It will not be in my power to attend the proposed Convention to be held at Charlotte on the 27th Inst. by the friends of the projected rail from some point of South Carolina rail road to that place. But I heartily wish you, & its other friends may succeed, in accomplishing the object of the meeting. I regard the projected road among the most important of those, which have been suggested in the southern Atlantick States, excepting those intended to connect them with the great valley of the Mississippi. There is no portion of those States, in my opinion, lying east of the Mountains, equal to that watered by the upper portion of the Catawba & the Yadkin ["rivers" *interlined*] taking extent, fertility & every other thing into consideration, except its remoteness from market. Remove that, and it would become one of the most productive & the finest portions of those States; but that can only be done by a rail road of which the first link would be the ["one" *canceled and* "road" *interlined*] you have projected. Should it be completed to Charlotte, I do not in the least doubt ["it would extend" *interlined*] to all the interior portion of your State, quite up to the foot of the mountains, that seperate it ["your" *canceled,* "State" *interlined and then canceled*] from the Western counties of Virginia, ["in its North eastern direction" *canceled.*]

That a road to ["a region" *interlined*] so extensive & productive ["a region" *canceled*], and which from its direction & the character of the country ["through which it would pass" *interlined*] could be so cheaply made, would pay han[d]somely, if economically ["executed" *canceled,* "made" *interlined and then canceled, and* "constructed" *interlined*], seems to me highly probable. ["Not only a great amount" *canceled and* "It would be much used not only for the transportation" *interlined*] of produce & merchandize ["would pass over it, but a great number of travellers" *canceled and* "but for travellers" *interlined.*] With great respect I am & &, J.C. Calhoun.

Autograph draft in ScCleA. NOTE: Other committee members to whom this letter was to be addressed were J[oseph] W. Hampton, W. Johnston, James W. Osborne, and J[oseph] H. Wilson.

From S[TEPHEN] MOYLAN FOX

Gadsden So. Ca., April 17th 1847

Sir, At the request of my uncle, John Fox of Penns[ylvani]a, I write to you to ask your influence in obtaining the place of Chief Engineer of the comtemplated rail road from Greenville—for which I propose making application.

As evidence of my abilities to perform the duties of the office, I would state, that I have been constantly and actively employed in the profession since 1828; from which time I have been engaged upon most of the Railways and Canals in Penns[ylvani]a.

I would respectfully refer you, for evidence of my qualifications to Edward Miller & S[olomon] W. Roberts of Philadelphia & C[harles] L. Schlatter of Harrisburg Penn[sylvani]a civil engineers; and H[enry] D. Bird Pres[iden]t of the Peterburg Rail road Co. & Edw[ar]d Gratz of Philad[elphi]a Pres[iden]t Lykens valley rail road Co. I have the honor to be Your Ob[edien]t Serv[an]t, S. Moylan Fox.

ALS in ScCleA.

To DUFF GREEN

Fort Hill, 17th April 1847

My dear Sir, The mistake, which I think you and the most of my friends make in reference to myself is, that you do not fully realize how completely I hold my own advancement subordinate to what I deem my duty to the Country. Even in the ardour of youthful aspiration, when the Presidency was an object of desire, I never could bring my mind to yield to a measure, or course of policy, which I thought wrong, to obtain that high office; much less can I now, when it is no longer to me an object of desire. Had I arrived at the Presidency by any other way, than an upright, and fearless discharge of what I conscientiously believed to be my duty, I would have been much more flexible, and under the influence of friends; but as it is, when I do not agree with any one portion, they have been too apt to suppose, that I had been influenced by those, with whom I happen to agree. You make this mistake as to my course in 1840. It may be, that the motives of those on the occassion, to which you refer, was such as you suppose; but, be that as it may, in making up my opinion, I had no consultation with them, nor had their opinion in relation to the subject to which you refer, the least influence with me. I am always happy to hear the opinion of my friends and often avail myself of their suggestions, in modifying my course; but rarely ever in taking it. I have said thus much, because, I think, you not infrequently fall into error, in attributing, what is the result of my deliberate judgement to the influence of others.

I entirely agree with you, that the Presidential election ought to be held in reserve, with the restriction, that no one of the old hunkers or their nominee by the Baltimore convention, shall get our support. I regard that portion of the party, as incurably corrupt. In their folly and profligacy they made the Mexican war, without seeing, that the successful general will ever be sure to turn the party, in this country, out of power, which makes a war. They began to see it, when it was too late, and hence their desire to have a Lieu[tenan]t General and to strike a blow at Gen[era]l [Zachary] Taylor during the last session. And hence, also, the sending of Gen[era]l [Winfield] Scott, in the hope of exciting their mutual Jealousy and dividing their political friends on the Presidential question. Indeed, the movements on the part of both parties, have looked to that exclusively. It is to be hoped, that the very few, who look exclusively to the country, by taking an independent stand, and keeping in reserve their influence, may finally throw it, where something may be done to advance the publick good.

I am glad to learn, that you have closed a satisfactory arrangement, about your mountain property, and I hope that your expectation will be realized, but let me repeat my hope, expressed on a former occasion, that you will not engage in publishing a paper, unless you can see your way clearly. Your first duty is to your family.

My Charleston friends appear disposed to make an effort to raise the necessary funds to establish a paper for the support of the South, on a solid basis, provided the other Southern States will cooperate, or at least a part of them. But, I fear, that their attention is so much absorbed in the events of the Mexican war, and that they are so much entangled by their party connections, that nothing will be done.

PC in Jameson, ed., *Correspondence*, pp. 727–728.

From R[ichard] K. Cralle

Elwah Cottage [near Lynchburg, Va.,] April 18th 1847
My dear Sir, I have delayed answering your favour of the 22nd ult. until I could hear and see more from various sections of the State as to the probable course of public affairs. Enough is now developed to warrant the conclusion drawn in your note of the 6th inst. which has just reached me. Ignoble cowardice and an inordinate love of office have prevailed over every honorable sense—truth, justice, consistency and patriotism. The dread of being in a minority is far more powerful than the love of truth; and manly independence succumbs to the hope and expectation of plunder.

Such is the spectacle presented by the State of Virginia. Her Politicians, with some few honorable exceptions, have been so long under the controul of [Thomas] Ritchie, that abject subserviency seems to have become a part of their very natures. Had your friends maintained firmly the stand they took at the meeting in Richmond, I have no doubt the State could have been preserved from the fatal tyranny of a National Convention; but the time when the meeting was held was most unpropitious—immediately preceeding an election in the result of which, many of its members had a direct and strong personal interest. Without organization, or the means to make their influence to be felt immediately, and uncertain of the final result of an open and bold stand, they were foolishly led to compromise every thing by yielding that which gives to their enemies complete controul now and for the future. [Lewis E.] Harvie and [James A.] Seddon, and [Thomas S.] Bocock [Representative from Va.] seem alone to have maintained themselves.

This is all most shameful, nay, disgraceful—and is enough to make a man forswear politics altogether. But the end is not yet. The result of the election next Thursday will present some reliable data for future calculations. If it go against the Hunkers (and I am strongly inclined to this opinion,) it may present hopes favourable to a future and more auspicious organization of Parties. The dominant Party will perceive its need of our assistance, and may be induced to reconsider its stringent and exclusive rules of discipline—principles they have none. But if they carry the State, it seems to me that no favourable calculation can be made on the State for the future. We must be put down as the servile and obedient vassals of the Albany Regency; unless, indeed, some new question arise to arouse the public mind from the stupor that enthrals it—or some popular favourite ["arise"(?) *canceled*] to sever the bonds that bind us.

As to the former, I had entertained hopes from the great issues involved in the Wilmot Proviso, and presented in your Resolutions. But as you well observe in your note of the 6th inst. these are virtually surrendered, when the Election of the Chief Magistrate is given up to the Cabal called a National Convention. Their selection determines the person, and their *imprimatur* endorses the principles of the candidate. So that even this tremendous question gives place to the engrossing matter of power and plunder. Indeed it is much to be doubted, (I speak of course in reference to this State alone—as to the other slave States it may be otherwise) whether the naked issues involved in the Wilmot Proviso, would, of themselves, suffice to overthrow the despotism of Party—for a very large portion (the trans-Allegheny,) of the State is, I fear ripe for the measure, however the fact may be concealed from motives of Party prudence. The fear of losing the vote of the State in the Presidential Election alone, I am inclined to think, prevents both factions in the west, from showing their hands. As to the Richmond Junto, looking as they do solely to the possession of power and the plunder it secures, I hesitate not to express the opinion that they will side with the majority, even should that threaten the safety of our domestic institution as it exists—much less its extension to new Territory. Indeed, so completely have they stultified the public mind, that you cannot even bring intelligent men to look the question fully in the face. They are too much engaged about the election of Presidents to think or to reason like men. This is true of both factions—and if the disease exist to the same extent in other States we shall pass easily under the yoke, without even sufficient virtue to enter a protest; much less to resist as becomes men the daring assault on ["their" *canceled and* "our" *interlined*] rights, honour and liberty.

The other alternative presented in the moral weight of some popular favourite is hazardous in the extreme, as our own past history sufficiently proves; to say nothing of the histories of other popular Governments. That favourite *must be* a *military Chief.* None other, without some great change in the temper and spirit of our People, can ever hope again to wield sufficient power over the masses. If such a man be taken up, and through his influence the vile machinery of the Factions that infest the State be deranged or broken up, what security have we against the common destiny of all Republics? [Andrew] Jackson might have fixed the Government on a firm basis for a century at least had his virtue kept pace with his popularity, or his judgment been equal to his energy. But while he overthrew the Federal oligarchy, he allowed himself to be used as the tool of the worst of all factions—*the Spoils Party*—the very men who had most bitterly denounced him—and left us as a legacy ignorance, vice, insolence and anarchy.

It is true, we may all entertain better hopes of Gen[era]l [Zachary] Taylor, who, it seems is fast rising into notice and threatening the aspirants of the present corrupt and imbecile dynasty. I see it stated in the Public Papers that you have retired from the contest and advised your friends to rally to his support. Is this true? I shall not attempt to dissuade you or offer counsel; but while I feel it to be absolutely necessary for the safety of our institutions that the present infamous dynasty should be utterly overthrown and extirpated, I am by no means certain that the election of Gen[era]l Taylor will secure it. Should the Plunderers find him too strong to be resisted, they will, as in the case of Jackson, immediately sheath their poisoned poignards, and salute him with a kiss, though it be that of Judas. This they will certainly do; and looking forward still to the future, will endeavour at the same time to preserve their vile machinery of Conventions and Caucuses for future use. If he be of the tone or temper of Jackson, he will, like him, pass through the fire to Molech, and leave corruption and despotism as our perpetual heritage.

On the other hand, if they stand out, and the opposing faction take him up, as they will do, it will be with aims not very dissimilar. Already you see, from the late nomination in Philadelphia when John Sargeant [*sic*; Sergeant] and others of that ilk, figured most prominently, that a *National Convention* is to pass its final and authoritative judgment. Thus you perceive that they too are for preserving, *in the first place*, the same iniquitous machinery, and doubtless for the same iniquitous purposes. The fact is, that little and bad men cannot rise without the use of *this lever*; and therefore little and bad men, (and who amongst the low and debased Leaders of the two Factions can be placed out of this category,) will stand by it to the last. In fighting for it, they are contending for their very existence.

In no case, therefore, could we, I think, safely or consistently support Gen. Taylor, but as a Candidate distinctly opposed to these infernal machines, which have already corrupted the public virtue and prostrated the most conservative principles of the Constitution. That he will have it in his Power as President to reform, to a great extent, the abuses and corruptions of the Government, I have no doubt; but the sincerity of his purposes should be tested by an open and undisguised denunciation of that vile system of President-making &C. which, more than all other causes combined, has led to these abuses and corruptions. If he will do this, his election, with your support, will be certain; and the consequent benefits to the Country incalculable. Will he do this? Will he throw himself upon the People, instead of the ignoble knot of political hucksters who have sold and enslaved them?

If you retire from the contest, however, and under the present aspect of affairs I cannot undertake to dissuade you, I, for one, shall have no more to do with public matters; but retire forever from [the ar]ena, to the calm pursuits of literary and agricultural labour. I see the ten[dency of the public fee]ling is towards Taylor every where. It is eminently so in this section. Thi[s is what (*one word missing*) and predic]ted in my letter to you the Session before the last. This Mexican war, I felt a[ssured was destin]ed to produce a new litter of military *Heroes* and *Presidents*. The prophecy is [in a] course of fulfilment. For your *own* reputation I never believed that the Presidency was worth [the] pursuit; or that patronage and power could add anything to your fame. Still, for the sake of the Country and its Institutions, I desired much to see you in the Chief magistracy. Your retirement, if indeed, you have retired from the contest, will not deprive me of the hope; for with your regular and temperate habits, I do not doubt but that your physical and mental energies will remain unimpaired for many years to come. I shall, therefore, still live under the hope that *when I vote for a President*, it will still be for John C. Calhoun. I shall, *most surely*, vote for no other, though the dead rise to bid me.

[William M.] Blackford will publish your remarks next week [in the Lynchburg *Virginian*]. They would have appeared before but for the pressure of local electioneering matter, and military despatches.

I wish most ardently that you and your family could spend the summer or fall months with us in the mountains. I have had considerable additions made to my House, and, by August, could give you very passable accommodations. Such a trip would serve much to strengthen and recreate you. Write to me as soon as this reaches you, as I am very anxious to know your views and purposes after seeing the Papers last night. Mrs. [Elizabeth Morris] C[rallé] joins me in affectionate regards to yourself, Mrs. [Floride Colhoun] C[alhoun] and Miss [Martha] C[ornelia Calhoun]. Mary [Crallé] is at school in Richmond. Very truly yours &c., R.K. Crallé.

ALS in ScCleA; variant PC in Jameson, ed., *Correspondence*, pp. 1112–1116. NOTE: A few words have been supplied in brackets where the ms. is torn.

From THO[MA]S CURTIS

Limestone Springs, S. Car[olina], 19 April '47
Sir, While I resided at Charleston, I had the honor of being personally introduced to you twice, I think—and will take the liberty of believing that the purport of this Letter will not be uninteresting to you as a public man, and a South Carolinian.

My son [William Curtis] and myself have made the purchase of this place, with a view to establishing a superior Female School. We have held it about 18 months, and are well satisfied with the countenance that has been afforded us in all parts of the State. We now number over 90 pupils.

But in this, as in most other Southern enterprises, we meet continually with an eye askance, Northward; and have the strong desire—we think the means—of rectifying this, in our particular pursuit. That is, we wish to exhibit a species of Female College in S. Carolina (whether called by that name or not) that shall compete, for advantages, with any of the Northern Schools, and fairly *settle* the pref[e]rence of the State for educating its own daughters. Our position is retired and healthy; our premises unusually large and well adapted to our object.

Once a year (the first week in June) we hold a Commencement and invite our leading Literary friends. Shall we presume too far on your sympathy with our object, to request your attendance on the approaching occasion? The Governor [David Johnson] is our neighbor, and will address the pupils. It would be a great impulse to excellence with some fine young minds around us, if you, Sir, would attend and favor them with an Address. A visit of this kind from Mr. [Joel R.] Poinsett, last year, did us all great good.

I will no further intrude on your time than to say, that I trust to have the honor of making a call upon you at Pendleton, in the early part of next month. You will give this matter, I am sure, due consideration. I am, Sir, very respectfully, Your most obed[ien]t Servant, Thos. Curtis.

ALS in ScCleA. NOTE: Thomas Curtis (1780–1858) was an Englishman and Baptist minister who came to the U.S. in 1833. The Limestone Springs Female High School became an outstanding educational institution.

From SARAH M[YTTON] MAURY

Liverpool, April 19th 1847

My dear Mr. Calhoun, I cannot refrain from expressing the gratification which your letter of approval afforded me. Some of my friends tell me that my effort to stem the infatuation of the Abolitionists has in some degree been serviceable—if so I have every reason to congratulate myself. I have read your Speech at Charleston on the 9th of March, and I think you take the wisest possible course by exposing their real wishes and intentions. It is really curious how the humbug (forgive the word) of Emancipation has gained proselytes both in England and in America; but in both countries I have found that their complete ignorance of the relative and of the individual positions of the Southern States in a great measure accounts for it. In England many people believe that slavery is universal throughout *America* by which they mean every part but Canada. They have no idea of the complexity of a political struggle which under the glorious denomination of Liberty and Emancipation turns upon the pivot of a Presidential election. They have also no idea of Slavery, except a picture of a gang of negroes with an overseer with a whip in his hand, who follows and drives them on to impracticable tasks, beneath a burning sun, and his lash steeped in their blood. Their ideas of a Planter are also amusing enough—it is believed by some that in the drawing room a Planter is a perfect gentleman—but that like the Council of Ten at Venice he could sit at table with his guests, and listen at the same time to the groans of his tortured slaves in the dungeon beneath his feet. Of course these ideas are encouraged by the Abolitionists here, and until much familiar intercourse takes place between England & the Southern States, I do not see how such impressions can be eradicated.

I hope that your cough has banished with the chills of winter, and that you will be able to go through the arduous session before you without suffering. I cannot disguise from myself that you will be attacked on all sides—but you are very strong on the Mexican affairs. In a letter which I lately received from Governor [William H.] Seward [of N.Y.] he says—"Mr. Calhoun is winning golden opinions, and justifying the enthusiastic admiration you express of him.["]

This is much from a friend of "protection[,]" of "Abolition," and of John Q[uincy] Adams, but Seward is innately noble, and passionately admires genius.

With regard to my "Statesmen" they have made me both in England and in America far more notorious than I ever anticipated. Here they have been extensively read—in Liverpool I hear that *every man* has perused them—the universal opinion seems to be that "the Statesmen is a work of great genius on the *worst* of subjects—viz. Slavery, Popery, and the Americans." Twelve english newspapers eight of which are London Journals have poured upon me the phials of their wrath—but decidedly the book has made an impression on public opinion, and especially in L[iver]pool—for my husband [William Maury] says that he no longer hears the sneers against the Americans which used to annoy and mortify him. Some persons have observed that the Journals have also in a great measure ceased to ridicule & vituperate America but I dare hardly flatter myself that so feeble an instrument as I could have so desirable an influence. I have however made many new friends, and I believe that the candour of the english induces them to regard with favour those who boldly combat their prejudices, when the first fit of passion is over.

I was fully prepared to be condemned by the Press in America as well as in England—because I have praised men of all parties without reference to their politics. This is unhappily a cause of great offence in the United States because party feeling is so violent that men regard their political opponents as utterly vile, stupid, & wicked. I could not, my dear Mr. Calhoun, stoop to such baseness, nor would you have approved such a course, if I had. Besides a closer scrutiny will shew that I have never praised any man for any thing which was not his. I have left much *un*said for prudent and I hope for praiseworthy reasons, but I have exalted no man at the expence either of truth or of my own principles. The condemnation therefore of the American Press concerns me as little as the abuse of the English Journals. From Boston I have several very gratifying letters, though "you are too democratic for all in this our Whig city"—And they tell me that the circulation has been extensive.

But I am writing a volume, and you will receive this at a moment

331

when you will be intensely occupied. Pray remember me most kindly to Mrs. [Floride Colhoun] Calhoun, and believe me always most faithfully your friend, Sarah M. Maury.

[P.S.] I have sent your speech [of 2/9/1847] on the Three Million Bill to the London Times some time ago—but they are so jealous that I greatly fear they will not publish even an extract from it. Would you believe that not a single Journal has ever taken the slightest notice of any of the extracts contained in the "Statesmen." This meanness is really contemptible. My Husband and I also were shocked the other day to hear the exultation that prevailed when a premature account was received, & it was asserted that the Americans had been beaten in Mexico—and at the very moment when the Macedonian arrived in Cork!

ALS in ScCleA.

Sight draft from Walker & Bradford, Hamburg [S.C.], 4/19. Calhoun is called upon to pay $311.71 to the order of J[ohn] S. Lorton [of Pendleton] "for value Received (being for am[oun]t of our account to 13 Inst.) . . . ." DS in ScU-SC, John C. Calhoun Papers.

From EDWARD DIXON

Warrenton [Va.], April 22nd, 1847

My Dear Sir, A rumor is going the rounds in the papers that you have written a letter in which you express an unwillingness to be brought out for the Presidency, and also indicate your purpose to support General [Zachary] Taylor for that office, in the event of his name being placed before the people. Of course, it is well understood that Taylor must be brought forward without reference to those strong lines of *party* distinction which would involve in his support, a sacrifice of political principles, before you can lend your cooperation to elevate him to the Chief Magistracy of the nation. I take the liberty of writing to you upon the subject on account of the great sensation which the rumor has produced throughout the country, manifested in the croaking of the "Old Hunkers," the lively gratification of the people generally without reference to party, and the deep interest of your friends in all that appertains to yourself. Your friends in Virginia are as united and firm as ever—they still believe that the highest honors of the country are due to you for your patriotic and valuable services, and that the public interests demand that you should be placed at the head of the Government. But a people are very much controlled by events; and as you cannot assume any position which does not bear directly upon the destinies of the country—and as unforeseen circumstances have directed public attention to General Taylor as "the people[']s candidate," it is altogether natural that there should be, even thus early, a very general speculation in regard to your position. As soon as the rumor to which I have referred reached this section, some of the first men of the community paid the highest compliment to your patriotism, and expressed the greatest degree of gratification. The people are sick of "Old Hunkerism," and are impatient for an opportunity to purge the Government of its licentiousness and corruption. Of course, your friends do not *know* that you have taken any ground either for or against Taylor, but since the late rumor they are exceedingly anxious to ascertain, in order that they may decide upon the proper line of action to adopt. If you are in favor of Taylor, they will cordially acquiesce, but if, as yet, you have expressed no views upon the subject, they will stand firm and wait for further developments. Since the late indications of hostility to you at the seat of Government, your friends are more closely bound to you than ever. For the present, however, as I have already intimated, the popular enthusiasm created by Taylor's achievements in Mexico, seems to unite the country in his favor; and it is certainly highly important for the public welfare, that you should occupy a position which will secure a controlling influence with the next Administration. We would be highly gratified to hear from you, and that you should give us permission to use your letter as we may think proper, but upon that subject, your wishes will be strictly observed. Very respectfully and sincerely yours, Edward Dixon.

ALS in ScCleA.

From J[AMES] D. B. DE BOW

New Orleans, Ap[ri]l 23, 1847

My dear Sir, This is the second time within a year that I have taken the liberty of troubling you and of adding something to the oppres[s]ive correspondence with which as an eminent public man you must be afflicted. I hope ["you" *altered to* "however"] you will pardon me from my connection with that old State which is to you dear as life & which & every son of which regards your reputation & glory as a common inheritance.

Gen[era]l James Hamilton [Jr.] was with us the other day—he spoke much & warmly upon that great question of slavery which has come at last to be of first concern to us at the South. He stated his intention to request from you a paper, embodying fully your views upon the Wilmot Proviso & the true course to be pursued by the whole South. Gen[era]l Hamilton also requested me to write you upon the subject. I know how much your time has been & is still occupied & how fully you have discussed this matters [*sic*] in your Washington & Charleston speeches—but I have thought it not improbable that there is material within your reach & views not yet urged which if embodied & published would fix public attention more completely & advance the great cause. There appears an apathy in this quarter of the world at present upon the subject altogether unaccountable & the truth is my dear Sir the people have not been kept well informed upon it. Neither of your speeches were republished by any of the papers of this city.

Should my suggestion not seem inappropriate & should you consider it in every respect consistent with your position & duties & other avocations I should be most pleased to have something from you for publication in my Review which has come now to have an extensive circulation all over the Union & most particularly at the South. Mr. [Levi] Woodbury of New Hampshire has promised me a paper upon ["a" *interlined*] kindred subject & Gen[era]l Hamilton is preparing for me notes upon Texas &c.

I regret that you had no occasion to take up the Memphis Report at the last Congress. I received your kind letter upon it & was flattered with the consideration. It is my intention before long to publish the Report in the Review—that all may understand its great principles—it has never been published here.

There is nothing new from Mexico—the report for several days has been that you will throw your influence into the scale of Gen[era]l [Zachary] Taylor for the Presidency on the great issue of the South— for one whatever your course I shall believe it the high & noble one of the patriot citizen & statesman. Excuse my liberty. Y[ou]rs with high consideration, J.D.B. De Bow.

ALS in ScCleA.

From R[ICHARD] PAKENHAM, *"Private"*

Washington, 23 April 1847

My dear Sir, You may remember that you had the goodness to give me a few copies of your speech on the three Million Bill, in order that a correct impression of your sentiments on the subject of the Mexican War might be conveyed to H[er] M[ajesty']s Govt.

I forwarded the speech by the "Sarah Sands," and it reached its destination safely. I am now directed by Lord Palmerston to express to you His thanks for your kindness. Mr. [Henry U.] Addington also desires to be cordially remembered to you and to Mrs. Calhoun— "for both of whom He says," He feels a very great "regard."

I have to add that I have, at length, received by the "Cambria" the drawings & Instructions about Artesian Wells. I forward them to [William Ogilby] our Consul at Charleston to be presented, as you desired, to the Mayor. I am quite ashamed of the delay that has occurred in this affair, but I am sure you will do me the justice to believe that the fault has not been mine.

I hope that you and Mrs. Calhoun are in the enjoyment of good health. I am upon the point of going home on leave of absence— and it will afford me great pleasure to attend to any thing in which you may wish to employ me while on the other side of the Atlantick. I have the honor to be, with great esteem & regard, My dear Sir, faithfully yours, R. Pakenham [British Minister to the U.S.].

ALS in ScCleA.

From J[AMES] HAMILTON, [JR.]

Charleston, April 24 1847

My Dear Sir, If I have not written you before it has been the result of my having been for the last two Months on the move in my Journey to Texas & on my return home. Your course, the vindictive attacks which have been made on you, the admirable ability with which you have sustained the one & the firmness & dignity with which you repelled the other have commanded my alternate sympathy and augmented Regard.

On my return home, I found with few exceptions the Democratic press of Georgia, was in full cry against ["you" *interlined*], and among the most ["rabid &" *interlined*] clamorous was the Columbus Times edited by [John Forsyth] a Son of the late Mr. [John] Forsyth.

You have some very devoted friends in Columbus who happen to comprise the most intelligent & respectable people in that place. As soon as they learnt my return from Texas they sent for me to come up to Columbus and to consider how these attacks were to be repelled. At their suggestion I went to the Hotel & sketched an article ["which I send you" *interlined*; *not found*] which however militant in its tone the Editor was compelled to publish. It is only an introductory Fire vindicating your your ["character" *canceled and* "motives" *interlined*] from the unworthy imputations cast upon them. The defence of your *course* & *opinions* I reserve for a moment of greater leisure & a more convenient season under proper provocation. I mean when I take it in hand to make it effective if I can.

I am just from N. Orleans the focus of all the Rays which are there converging from the Valley of the West to make Gen[era]l [Zachary] Taylor President. His partisans are almost universally your friends and the most intelligent surrender or rather are inclined to surrender your claims rather from *necessity* than choice because they believe that the popularity of the old Gen[era]l will *alone* enable the Country to relieve itself of the conjoint & infamous burdens of Hunkerism & abolitionism.

A Relative of Gen[era]l Taylor's came to see me when I was in New Orleans and frankly told me that he greatly prefer[r]ed you to his kinsman for the Presidency but under your recent rupture with the Democrats & the total alienation of the Northern Whigs from you ["on a/c of your position on the Wilmot Proviso" *interlined*] your election was altogether hopeless altho if Gen[era]l Taylor was out of the field he had no doubt you would get a majority of the Slave States in the Union.

In these opinions I entirely concur. He then went on to say that Gen[era]l Taylor would not accept he believed a *party* nomination or even the nomination of a national convention. If elected by the spontaneous Will of the people he might serve. This Gentleman moreover remarked with some emphasis—If without specific guarantees but under ["a" *interlined*] pledge to do his duty to the whole Country according to ["his" *canceled and* "the dictates of his own" *interlined*] conscience the old Gen[era]l received the support of the highly talented party of Mr. Calhoun (the most talented & chivalrous as he was pleased to say in the Country) ["they woul" *canceled and* "he & his friends would" *interlined*] have a fair share in the Govt. of the Country & in the direction of its public measures. My reply to him was that next to yourself, I should certainly prefer the election of Gen[era]l Taylor, because I believed he was an honest man with a kind heart & a clear head. But I could give no assurances of support without consulting ["our" *canceled*] my Carolina friends with whom I was resolved to act *under all circumstances & contingencies.*

Now My Dear Sir what are we to do? With Gen[era]l Taylor in the Field you cannot be elected and even if he is withdrawn (of which there is not the smallest prospect for his friends will force ["him" *interlined*] into the canvass) your election would be doubtful & could only be consummated after a tremendous struggle in the H[ouse] of R[epresentatives].

The Question then arises shall we stand off & permit the Gen[era]l to pass into the hands of the Whigs or by a timely tender of our adhesion endeavour to organize a new national Republican ["party" *interlined*] on a broad basis sufficiently broad under the adjustment of the tariff[,] internal improvements[,] Bank, & rejection & negation of the Wilmot provisio to admit of [John J.] Crittenden & yourself taking part in the Govt. of the Country[?]

I shall write to two of Gen[era]l Taylor[']s friends (in immediate communication with ["him" *interlined*]) to take the ground that he will accept *no party nomination* nor will he entertain for one moment a consideration whether he would accept the Presidency *until the War with Mexico is closed.* This will give us time to shape our measures but the question again presses home what shall these measures be? We must ["not" *interlined*] lag too far in the rear or we shall lose all influence in controlling public measures. Or shall we let this military tempest rage, stand aside and take no part in its power or its agitations?

I cannot perceive how a Man of your power whether in or out of Congress can take no part in the public affairs of the Country. Your influence would be as *certain* altho *as silent,* as the Laws of Gravitation. It is the irresistible destiny of Genius, & it remains for you to decide how you will use that power in an entirely new state of things. Write immediately in reply directed to Savannah Geo[rgia]. I remain My Dear Sir with esteem faithfully & respec[tfull]y Yours, J. Hamilton.

ALS in ScCleA; PC in Jameson, ed., *Correspondence,* pp. 1117–1119.

From PETER SKEN SMITH

Philadelphia, Ap[ri]l 24, 1847

Dear Sir, Admiring and approving your recently published Sentiments with reference to the elections of future Presidents from and by the People, at the instance of the American Executive Committee of the State of Pennsylvania of which I have the honor to be Chairman, I respectfully inquire whether, should it be tendered to you and that unanimously, you are disposed to accept the nomination of President of the United States from the National Native American Convention to assemble at Pittsburg[h], Pa. on the second tuesday of May ensuing, for the purpose of designating Candidates for President and Vice President of the United States?

The Candidates to be nominated as the Peoples' Candidates and to be supported by the great American Party of the Country, as the standard-bearers of the National principle, that to preserve and perpetuate our Republican Institutions, *The American Born must Rule America.* I am Sir, very Respectfully your friend, Peter Sken Smith.

ALS in ScCleA; PC in Jameson, ed., *Correspondence*, pp. 1116–1117. NOTE: An AEU by Calhoun reads "Mr. Smith—wishes to know whether I would accept a nomination of the Native American party. Rec[eive]d to[o] late to answer in time." Smith was editor of the *Native Eagle and American Advocate*, a weekly magazine published in Philadelphia. He was also a militia captain and played a prominent role in the nativist riots in Philadelphia in 1844.

From MARIA D[ALLAS] CAMPBELL, "Private"

Philadelphia, April 26th 1847

My dear friend, A too intense application to his profession, has so much impaired the health of my son St. George, that his physicians and friends have advised & persuaded him to try the efficacy of a short trip across the Atlantic, & he purposes leaving this [country] on the 10th of May, to return by the 1st of Sept: You will understand my solicitude under these circumstances, and also the confidence I have in your friendship, when I request for him a letter from *you*, to Mr. [Thomas G.] Clemson, and any other letters you may deem as likely to be serviceable to him. Of course in so short a visit, he neither desires nor expects to make acquaintances, beyond those of our own immediate friends, who if he be sick, (which may

God avert) in a foreign land, will extend to him *kindness*, & if he be well, will guide him in the best way to attain information of *other places & things*. I can of course obtain all essential letters, to our Ministers & Chargés abroad, from Mr. [James] Buchanan [Secretary of State], who has ever testified cordial good will towards me & mine; but I value your name, so highly myself, that I should feel proud that my son should bear with him that passport. Will you therefore as promptly as possible enclose me letters for him[?] It is his intention to visit England, perhaps Scotland, & then cross over to the Continent, where his travels will depend in a great measure upon his health & strength. Any letters therefore that you may feel inclined to confide to him, *to use*, if he finds necessary will be most gratefully acknowledged by me, & I think I may add not unworthily bestowed upon my son. I have followed your course of last winter, with the deepest interest, & with *almost* my usual *complete* approbation. I wrote to you once but upon consideration *waited*. God bless you all—ever your Sincere friend, Maria D: Campbell.

ALS in ScCleA.

From R[obert] Toombs,
[Representative from Ga.]

Washington Ga., April 30th 1847

D[ea]r Sir, Your note & the newspaper containing a copy of your Charleston speech [of 3/9] reached here during my absence from home. I thank you for them. As soon as the speech appeared in the Charleston papers, it was immediately printed in all the Whig papers of the State which have met my eye. Your very just & impartial classification of the people of the north on the slavery question has met with general commendation, & has excited anxious enquiry among the people, as to the best mode of arresting ["the" *interlined*] antislavery action, & (if possible), tendencies of the north.

I begin to fear that the question is fast approaching a crisis. It seems our successes in Mexico have greatly raised the pretensions of [James K.] Polk & his cabinett & the weakness & divisions of Mexico will in all probability induce ["th"(?) *canceled*] her to accede to terms which we ought not to demand & which will ["be" *interlined*] disgracefull to her & ruinous to us. You are aware of my early & uniform disrelish of the idea of ["the" *interlined*] appropriation of

Mexican Territory. I can see nothing but evil to come of it. And now I do not clearly see how it can be well avoided to some extent. Our policy upon this whole Mexican question it is now evident will be in your hands. The Whigs & your friends will undoubtedly be able to control the next house of Representatives & upon that question I think the Senate. The people of the South are now anxiously waiting to see what direction you will give it. It is perfectly clear that the Present administration & its supporters have lost all character with the Country & all that it hopes from them is to do as little mischief as possible. I should be glad at all times to hear from you. Present my best respects to Mrs. [Floride Colhoun] Calhoun & your daughter [Martha Cornelia Calhoun]. Mrs. [Julia DuBose] Toombs desires to be remembered to you & Mrs. C[alhoun] & your daughter. I am very respectfully Your ob[edien]t ser[van]t, R. Toombs.

ALS in ScCleA; PC in Boucher and Brooks, eds., *Correspondence*, pp. 373–374.

MAY 1–JUNE 30, 1847

〖

This spring, from Fort Hill, Calhoun's third son, John Jr., wrote to the War Department, unsuccessfully it turned out, for permission to raise a company of volunteers for the coming campaign in Mexico. Whether his father knew of this is not clear. He had twice before applied for a commission. Though President Polk was willing to appoint sons of the Whigs Daniel Webster and Henry Clay, he had no place for a son of John C. Calhoun.

Calhoun doubtless enjoyed the summer's farm work and family weddings. He perhaps noticed without much caring that Webster made a visit to Charleston on May 8, enjoying a reception and a speech-making opportunity. On May 11 Calhoun wrote to his English friend, Mrs. Sarah Maury, about his delight at the progress that enlightenment—that is, free trade—had made on both sides of the Atlantic.

He showed in his correspondence his usual interest in railroads; a desire to rally Southerners to the need for a firm and common defense; and encouragement for the establishment of a reliable newspaper in Washington for the latter purpose. All of his Southern and many Northern correspondents agreed with him in these goals, including, increasingly, Southerners from those circles where he had not been particularly beloved.

As always, Calhoun disclaimed "ambition," as when he wrote Duff Green on June 10: "But political advancement has ceased to be for a long time any object to me, personally. I would accept the Presidency on no condition but to reform the Government and carry out the principles and policy with which I am identified; and I have no idea that it will ever be tendered to me for that purpose."

〖

From J[OHN] L. SCOTT and Others

William & Mary College [Williamsburg, Va.], May 1, 1847
Sir, Permit us through those we represent on this occasion to express
the wish that you would be present with us on the 4th of next July,
around the festive board ["and" *canceled*] to mingle with the hospitalities of the citizens of our old Town and the students particularly,
of this time honoured institution. Hoping that you will be present
with us on that day, allow us to express our wishes individually, and
collectively, that you be with us on the 4th of next July. With sentiments of the warmest esteem, we are yours, J.L. Scott, J[ohn] E.
Friend, W[illiam] H. Mitchell, C.R. McAlpine, Committee.

LS (with letter and signatures in one handwriting) in ScCleA. NOTE: An AEU
by Calhoun reads "Invitation to attend 4th [of] July, W[illiam] & M[ary]."

To RICHARD RUSH, [U.S. Minister to France, Paris]

Fort Hill, 2d May 1847
My dear Sir, This will be delivered to you by my friend Mr. Aikin
[*sic*; William Aiken], to whom I take pleasure in introducing you.

He recently filled the place of chief Magistrate of the State, &
ranks among the most wealthy & esteemed of our citizens, for his
many good qualities.

He visits Europe with the view of seeing & becoming better acquainted with that interesting quarter of the globe.

He is desireous, while in France, of being introduced to some of
her prominent publick men, particularly to Marshal [Nicolas] Soult
& Mr. [F.P.G.] G[u]izot & Mr. [Louis Adolphe] Thiers; & I feel
assured you will take pleasure in meeting his wishes in that respect.
With great respects Yours truly, J.C. Calhoun.

ALS in NjP, Rush Family Papers (published microfilm of The Letters and Papers
of Richard Rush, reel 20).

From A. P. STINSON

St. Joseph [Mich.,] May 3, 1847
My dear Sir, Your Esteemed favour of the 3d ult. accompanied by the
"Pendleton Messenger" contain[in]g your address to the Citizens of

Charleston on the 9th of March, has safely Reached me & for which please accept my thanks. What was contained in the Messenger however I had Long since Read I think in [James Gordon] Bennett's "New York Herald." It met my approbation then & on a reperusal does now. So I suppose I must be dub'd, as I have for years been ["]a Northern man with Southern Principles." Well be it so. I sometimes am Led to fear, I may be "Read out["] of the Party, whose motto is "Principles not men," but who is to be *re[a]d in!* The Party, If I can Judge, have none to Spare, or will not Long If things go on as every thing now Indicate[s]. The course persued by the *fanatics* & Suc[c]umb'd to by the Aspirants to popular favor at the *North* & West, Never has, or will, find a Response in my breast. I Know men in the Halls of Congress from New England the Last Session who Catered to the Abolitionist to Secure their votes who have not *One feeling* In common with them, If Indeed the Liberty Party have any feeling for the Southern Slave themselves[,] a problem yet to be Solved. I have Often thought of a Remark in a Late Letter of yours to me, wherein you Speak of "How Little Independence Public men have." It is so & Sorry am I for It. What the end of all this "truckling for Power & Place" may result ["in" *canceled*] In I know not, nor dare hazard a *guess,* Proverbial as are We "Yankees" for "Guessing." That the fr[i]ends of [Lewis] *Cass* are hard at work (secretly however somewhat) for '48 I believe, & that It will be made a question Based on "Masons & Dixons Line" is also Equally Entitled to Credence. This then being the Case, what is due to the *South* & to *your self* will Readily suggest It Self to you I think. Self Preservation is the first Law of our Natures. It behooves the South then, in this Crusade upon her & her Institutions, by the fanatics & their Allies the "Office Seekers," to Prepare for the Contest & Present a *Bold*[,] *Determined* & *United front* & say to these fanatics & Aspirants, The *South must* & *Shall* be Respected. How this Demonstration can best be made is perhaps not so easily told. It Strikes me your address & Speeches are to the Point & If the Press at the *South* only reiterate It, & manifest a disposition to adhere to It—you will put to flight those Aliens[,] those Sowers of Dissentions in Our Common Country. The N.Y. Herald occassionally is "Putting It to them with Sharp Sticks" and is, as I Infer, In Your Interest. All your Speeches are Reported for (& Publish'd In) that Paper & oft accompanied By Editorial Remarks. So much So that It is Called Here "Calhoun's Organ"! Well So be It. I had Rather have the N.Y. Herald on my side than any 10 Papers at the East as all It contains is *Practical* Common sense & consequently appeals to the Judgment of Men of understanding. As I

343

have before Said, so I Repeat It, the Press, the Subsidis[e]d Press, In the West, do not shadow forth Public Sentiment as I understand it. They Sing Peans of Praise to those In Power & who have *Patronage to bestow!* Most Heartily have I become Disgusted with this *truckling* to power, on the Part of the *Press* & Aspirants for Place. I am not prepared to say, but It would be a "God Send" to the Republican Party to be "Whipt out" in '48 & thereby Releive the Country of some of these "Bargain & Sell Politicians" who have hung Like an Incubus upon us of Late years & with whom It has been, "me & my wife, my Son John & his wife us four & no more" wrapt up in *self* & *Self alone.*

I say I am not prepared to say It would not be the very best thing for us to get decently Drub'd & thus teach the Office Seekers that they are Mortal—& their Lives, Politically, in the Hands of the People, a fact they Seem to be Ignorant of. In Short Sir, In "weal or woe" I am the friend of *J.C. Calhoun* Ready to "do or Die." Yours ever truly, A.P. Stinson.

P.S. June 3. To day I took up this Letter which I Supposed I finished at its date. How I neglected It cannot for the Life of me tell, but So It is & which Please excuse. Nothing new Since the Date worthy of note. Truly Yours ever, A.P.S.

ALS in ScCleA.

To [THOMAS G. CLEMSON, Brussels]

Fort Hill, 6th May 1847

My dear Sir, I am very happy to hear by yours by the Cambria, that you are all well.

The views you take ["in" *interlined*] reference to the course of [Thomas] Ritchie, & the position in which it has placed me in reference to the hunker portion of the party are perfectly correct. They are incurably corrupt; & I am glad to be seperated from them by their own act. It places me on grounds perfectly independent of either party; to act according to the dictates of my own judgement. The days of hunkerism is numbered. Mr. [James K.] Polk is the last of the dynasty. It never ["can" *interlined*] rise again to power. The folly & the vice of the party have destroyed ["it" *interlined*]. He sought by the Mexican war to perpetuate the power of the party, but it will prove the means of his & their overthrow. As things now stand, he will make [Zachary] Taylor his successor by making the war. It has made him the available candidate, & that of itself will be sufficient to rally a majority around him. Indeed, it would seem to be an established principle with us, that the party in power, which makes war, will be sure to be turned out of power by it—if successful, by the successful general; & if not, by the opposition. When that comes to be understood, as it will be, if Taylor should be elected, we never again shall have a war, when it can be avoided. Had the administration ["had" *interlined*] sufficient sagacity to see it, Taylor never would have been ordered to the del Norte, & there would have been no war. As much as I am opposed to military chieftains for presidents, I shall, thus thinking, be content to see him elected ag[ai]nst Mr. Polk, or any one, who contributed to make the war; and, let me add ag[ai]nst the nominee of a convention, either democrat, or whig. But I go no farther. I shall stand fast on my own doctrines, & act in conformity to them, in any emergency, including the Presidential. It is the only way, by which I can serve the country & preserve my ["own" *canceled*] character.

I informed you, in my last [dated 4/11], that I had a letter from [—— Mobley] your overseer, stating that his health was bad, & he wished to withdraw; and that I had written to Col. [Francis W.] Pickens & left it to him to act according to his discretion. Since then, I received a letter from him, immediately after his return from Alabama. He had not then seen Mr. Mobl[e]y, & as I have not since heard from him, I hope his health has been sufficiently restored to remain. By the by, it is strange, after giving you the opinion he has of the cotton region of the South west, that he should immediately after ["proceed" *canceled and* "go" *interlined*] to Alabama & purchase a large plantation, hands and all, in that very region, & plant this year 700 acres of cotton there, as he wrote me he has done. He must have undergone a very sudden change of opinion.

The extract from his letter to you, in reference to his course towards me, surprises me much. I am, in the ["first" *interlined*] place, at a loss to understand his object in writing to you in reference to the subject, and in the next, that he should make the statement he has. It is wide of the facts of the case. He represents, that the falsehoods, as he calls them, were circulated, while he was absent in Canada, when in fact, the statements, be them false or true, were made openly & circulated widely through the papers by ["Whi" *canceled*; Louis T.] Wigfall and others, immediately after the meeting, & long before he left for Canada, without contradiction then, or ever to this day in publick, although he denied them to me, when in Washington on his way; through friends before I would call on him,

&, after I did, personally, & since by letter. In [*"assining" canceled and "giving" interlined*] my reason to him, why I gave the [*"statements" interlined*] credit, I put it expressly on the ground, that they had been widely circulated, without being contradicted by him.

As to what he says, in reference to Mr. [Armistead] Burt, there is not the slightest foundation for it. So far from opposing his election to the Senate, he expressed himself decidedly in favour of [*"him" canceled and "it" interlined*], [*"before" canceled*] before the occurrence, and before it was known, that he had any connection with the article in the Southern Review, or my speech at Memphis. No one knows better than Col. Pickens, that I cannot be acted on by insinuations against one, for whom I entertain friendly feelings. I deeply regret, that he should, after, as he knew, I had made up my mind to forget the passed in relation to him. You could not do less than you did, in sending the extract. It shall remain with myself.

We shall not want to pay off, what we owe you, until after the growing crop. We hope to apply a part of the next succeeding [crop] to your debt, & in the meantime, will be ready to renew the notes, in single note, or give our bond for the amount, as you may desire. I hope Andrew [Pickens Calhoun] will be able to make us a visit this summer or fall when it can be done.

With love to Anna [Maria Calhoun Clemson] & the children. Your affectionate father, J.C. Calhoun.

ALS in ScCleA; PEx in Jameson, ed., *Correspondence*, pp. 728–729.

To Mrs. L[UCRETIA CALHOUN] TOWNES

Fort Hill, 6th May 1847

My dear Ni[e]ce, I am happy to hear, that your daughter is about to form a connection, which, as I learn, is every way eligible & agreeable to you & Doctor [Henry H.] Townes.

We shall be in attendance on the interesting occasion. William [Lowndes Calhoun] is not yet returned from Alabama, but is shortly expected. Should he return in time he will accompany us. Your affectionate Uncle, J.C. Calhoun.

ALS in ScCleA. NOTE: Kate Floride Townes married James P. Graves of Washington, Ga., at Abbeville, S.C., on 5/19/1847. Lucretia Calhoun Townes was the daughter of Calhoun's elder brother William.

J[ohn] C. Calhoun, Jr., to W[illiam] L. Marcy

Fort Hill, May 7th 1847

Sir, Seeing recently by the papers, that the President [James K. Polk] is about to call seven thousand more men into the service of the country, to fill up the vacancies occasioned by the disbandment of several of the Regiments, whose term of enlistment has transpired, I take this early opportunity of addressing to you this letter, to enquire, whether companies will be seperately received, and if so, whether you will not give me permission to raise one, which I am confident I can do in a very short time, as there is in this vacinity, at least one hundred young men, anxiously awaiting the opportunity, to render their country all the service which gallantry affords, and it is through their strong solicitation, that I am prompted to address you this communication.

I have been an applicant for a commission in the Army or Navy since the commencement of the War, but owing to the want of energy of my friends, I have not been able to procure a situation. I took the liberty to address a letter to the President some time since, asking him for a commission under the ten Regiment bill, but he did not do me the honor to answer it, so I concluded that my application was made too late.

I have been anxiously wishing for a long time to procure some situation in the Army; this District is not represented in the Regiment from this State, we raised a fine company but were too late to be attached to it, but I hope that you will yet give us an opportunity to serve our country to the best of our abilities. For refference I will give you the names of the Hon. J[ohn] Y. Mason, I[saac] E. Holmes, and the Hon. D[ixon] H. Lewis.

I have a very good kno[w]ledge of Infantry and Dragoon Tactics, a great deal of which I acquired, whilst on a tour, on the north western Pra[i]ries in 1844, with a detachment of the 1st Dragoons, commanded by Capt. [James] Allen. I attended all their reviews, and together with what I have read, I feel confident that I could command a company. I will feel much honored, if you will give this as speedy an answer, as circumstances will admit of. I remain sincerely yours &c, &c, J.C. Calhoun, Jr.

ALS in DNA, RG 107 (Secretary of War), Letters Received by the Secretary of War (Main Series), 1801–1870, C-132 (M-221:139). Note: On 10/18/-

1846, John C. Calhoun, Jr., had written to Secretary of the Navy John Y. Mason, inquiring about a commission in the Marine Corps or the dragoons. ALS in DNA, RG 45 (Naval Records), Applications (Unsuccessful) for Commissions in the Marine Corps (Mexican War Period), File A–D. Mason had replied on 11/-2/1846 that he had an "anxious desire to see your wishes gratified" and would bring the subject to the notice of the President. FC in DNA, RG 45 (Naval Records), Miscellaneous Letters Sent by the Secretary of the Navy, 1798–1886, 37:92 (M-209:14).

To Col. J[AMES] ED[WARD] COLHOUN, [Abbeville District, S.C.]

Fort Hill, 7th May 1847

My dear James, We intend to be at the Wedding of Kate [Floride] Townes, & your sister [Floride Colhoun Calhoun], [Martha] Cornelia [Calhoun,] John [C. Calhoun, Jr.,] & myself, and William [Lowndes Calhoun], should he return in time from Alabama, will be with you on the night of the 17th Inst. & stay the next day with you.

I write to let you know, in order you may be at home. Affectionately, J.C. Calhoun.

ALS in ScCleA.

From H[ENRY] W. CONNER

Charleston, May 7, 1847

My Dear Sir, It was premature I have thought for *us here* to take up the selection of an Editor of the paper we propose to establish at Washington until we had at least taken some practical or efficient steps to raise the means necessary for its establishment. It appears however that we have got ahead of our subject as I perceive by a letter of yours to Col. [Franklin H.] Elmore of the 18th ult. & which has been just shewn me & that Mr. [Robert Barnwell] Rhett has been recommended to your consideration for the Editorial department. This recommendation does not meet the concurrence of the Gentlemen who have been interesting themselves here to get up the paper & is directly contrary I know ["to the views" *interlined*] of nearly every friend you have in this City. He is considered to be a rash & ultra man in his politicks—frequently bent upon extreme & desperate courses—very excitable & unstable—& intollerant & contemptuous of all about him—with neither tact or discretion & without sympathy or popularity with the great mass of men—whether right or wrong, this is the feeling of the public with regard to him & it would surely be neither the part of wisdom or discretion to force him or any other person so little acceptable upon the people in any capacity, much less as Editor of so important a paper.

Of these objections I do not partake in the whole myself. I only mention them to you as evidence of the feelings entertained by the great majority of those upon whom a paper would depend for its support & its influence, but I entertain other objections that to my mind over[r]ule the others.

I distrust Mr. Rhett[']s friendship to yourself not but that I believe he respects & admires you greatly—but his ambition is of so exceedingly selfish a character as to leave no doubt in my mind that he would without hesitation sacrifice you & all the world besides—if the least in the way to his own advancement & I refer to prominent acts of his own life in confirmation of what I say. He strove to get you out of the Senate to make way for himself. He again not only opposed but denounced you on another occasion when you discountenanced his wild & desperate attempt to precipitate this State into rash action three years ago, & if we are informed correctly stands ready now to oppose you on the improvement of the Mississippi & to seperate with you on that subject if necessary. I have no unkind feeling toward Mr. Rhett & never had—on the contrary I appreciate to the full his talents—his energy—industry & elevated private character—but he is in every way else, disqualified for the post that it has been proposed to be assigned ["him" *interlined*] & if it be known that it is in contemplation to get up this paper for Mr. Rhett, his name kills it dead on the spot—but if it did not, he & his paper would kill the party as sure as fate—that is as far as it is possible to kill a party occupying the strong ground they do.

If this subject had come up fairly before us here, I should have contented myself with opposing it on its true grounds, & I now only present myself to you that my views on a matter I deem of so much importance should be properly understood. If after this Mr. Rhett should be selected the Editor of the paper ["I should"(?) *canceled*] in case we can get it up—I stand ready to give it all the support I can. I shall be turned aside by no objection to one man or predilection for another—but go for the one great object we all have in view. My most anxious desire, is to put in requisition the best & most proper men & means to accomplish that object. Hence the free & what may perhaps ["may" *canceled*] be considered the strong expression I have made of my views touching Mr. Rhett.

The Gentlemen you named or most of them have had one or two meetings but done nothing as yet to the purpose. It is not advisable for you to trust too much to us as now constituted here. You must point out & direct what is to be done & when & how. As regards myself I will do all & every thing I can to carry them out as promptly & as effectively as I know how & will do what I am able to put & keep others in motion.

Gen[era]l [Zachary] Taylor is fast gaining ground amongst the people here & if it be fairly shewn, as it is suspected by some, that he has been proscribed by the administration & attempted to be underminded [*sic*; undermined] by Gen[era]l [Winfield] Scott, it will be difficult to stop his progress, tho but little is yet known of Gen[era]l Taylor[']s political principles, or civil capacity. It is so much easier to sail with the current than against it that it may be necessary to caution some of your friends here against yielding to the pressure.

Mr. [Daniel] Webster is here & has & will be civilly rec[eive]d— no more. Y[ou]rs &c very truly, H.W. Conner.

ALS in ScCleA; PC in Boucher and Brooks, eds., *Correspondence*, pp. 374–375.

From EDWIN W. SEIBELS, JAMES FARROW, and W[ILLIA]M B. TELFORD

S.C. College
Columbia, May 7th 1847

Sir: At a regular meeting of the Clariosophic Society held some twelve months since, a Committee was appointed to address you on the subject, of having your portrait taken & suspended in our Hall, as a testimony of the very high regard this Society cherishes for Carolina's favorite statesman; & after obtaining your consent, they employed Mr. William Barkley [*sic*; Barclay], a native artist of this Town, to perform this work, but having failed to do so, we are again solicitous to know if you will comply with our wishes & inform us when it would suit your convenience to sit for your portrait, as there is now in this place an eminent artist (a Mr. [William H.] Scarborough) who executes likenesses with the most life like fidelity & whose servises we contemplate engaging for this special purpose, as soon as we can hear from you. With great respect, We have the honor to be Your Ob[edien]t Servants, Edwin W. Seibels, James Farrow, Wm. B. Telford, Com[mittee,] Clar[iosophic] Soc[iety].

LS (with letter and signatures in one handwriting) in ScCleA. NOTE: An AEU by Calhoun reads "Committee. To Set for my portrait."

From LEWIS E. HARVIE

Elk Hill, Amelia Co[unty] Va., May 8th 1847
Dear Sir, Our elections in Virginia are over with the result that you have seen & which ought to have been anticipated as a necessary consequence of the conduct of the Hunker portion of our party in our last Legislature. They succeeded in achieving an apparent victory over us at the expense of their own ascendancy in the State. I am now nearly alone in the Legislature, and feel anxious to know your views as to our future action. The Democratic party cannot exist in our State without us and they know it. Whenever they are reduced to extremity they court our favor and vociferate our principles, but such is their lust for place & power that they never fail to sacrifice them & us whenever they get in ["to" *canceled*] the ascendant.

The Whigs with more of talent but even less of principle & with an equal thirst for office are worse than the Democrats. They are our antipodes in political principle, utterly unscrupulous in their professions, & trammelled by no restraints, constitutional or other. There is no affinity between them and us. What policy then shall we pursue? The line indicated by you in a letter which has been recently published, seems to me to be the wisest as well as the most patriotic: ie[,] to pursue a course disconnected from & independent of both parties as now organised, but I think it should be strictly so particularly as regards the whigs. There should not be even an appearance of union or concert with them: if so we lose all of our moral force, & in the public estimation will be viewed as mere Swiss. There can be nothing in common between us & them. We are as wide asunder as the poles. If we were with them we could have no influence over them, for they know us & also know that we know them. I am equally clear that we should not suffer ourselves to become identified with this administration, but that we should avoid any open breach with it. I cannot but think that events are ripening[?] to a conclusion, that will make it indispensable for the South ["to rouse to whi" *canceled and* "awake" *interlined*] to her true situation. Both parties

351

will bid for northern support in the national convention by a surrender of her rights. In all probability we shall have two Wilmot proviso candidates for the presidency. If not the candidates will both be against the acquisition of Southern slave holding territory. Then will be our time for action & it seems to me that we should not unnecessarily offend our present allies, false as they have proved themselves to be to us, but that we should give our decided support to the domestic policy of the administration & as far as possible to its foreign policy so as to prevent their total demolition by the Whig party. I have hastily sketched these views more with the purpose of eliciting yours, than in the hope [*partial word missing*] what you may consider wise. [I am?] sure you will pardon the freedom with which I write, and ascribe it to the deep interest that I feel in the advancement of the great principles, which you have advocated with such untiring energy & devotion. If you can favor me with your views as to our present condition & future course, you may rely with confidence ["in" *altered to* "on"] my prudence in the use of them & will very much oblige me. With great Respect Y[ou]r sincere friend, Lewis E. Harvie.

ALS in ScCleA.

From D[avid] O. Hawthorn

Due West Corner, Abbeville District, S.C.
May 9th 1847

Sir, After my Best Respects to you I Embrace this opportunity of informing you that I hold at this time an account on your son W[illia]m L[owndes] Calhoun Bought of D[avid] W. Hawthorn at this place Whe[n] was Doing Buisness for me. The account is small & I thought your Son Would have Settled Before this time But I Expect he has forgotten it. The amount is $18.71½.

Please send the Money Down & I will Return the account Receipted to you. Yours Respectfully &c, D.O. Hawthorn.

ALS in ScU-SC, John C. Calhoun Papers. NOTE: An AEU by Calhoun reads, "Hawthorn bill."

To Mrs. SARAH M[YTTON] MAURY,
[Liverpool]

Fort Hill, 11th May 1847

My dear Madam, I am gratified to learn, that your book has been, even in some degree, serviceable in stemming the infatuation of the abolitionists. It is abolition, which more than any other cause, tends to seperate the two countries, & create prejudice towards each other.

Nothing is more desirable, than that two countries, in advance of all others in civilization, and so intimately related in almost every particular, should understand one another fully. On it depends, not only their own peace, safety and prosperity, but that of Christendom, & the cause of progress over the world. That your "Statesman," written in a sperit so just & liberal, would exercise a beneficial influence in that respect, I was prepared to expect, and am happy to hear, that it has had that effect on your side of the Atlantick, as I doubt not it has had on this side. You may, with the consciousness of having contributed to such a result, well smile at the illeberal [*sic*] remarks of ill natured criticks.

I regard it as a most favourable omen for the future, that there are so many & such powerful causes now in operation to bring the two countries to be better acquainted with each other. Among them, free trade & the rapidity of communication, may be placed as the most prominent. Next to them, and only next, because, as I trust, more temporary, stands the awful infliction on your side by the famine of this memorable year; but which has been the occasion of ["the development of" *interlined*] so much good feelings on our side, which never would have been known to exist ["had not," *canceled*] had not the distressing occurrence call[ed] it forth.

It has done more. It has settled the question of free trade beyond the power of reaction, by teaching both countries how important it is between two countries situated as ours are; the one old, with a dense population & vast accumulation of capital; and the other new, with a sparse population & vast regions of fertile & uncultivated lands. Had the trade between them been as unshackled on ours, as it is on your ["side" *interlined*], the benefit would be still ["more beneficial" *canceled and* "greater" *interlined*] to both. It would, in that case, [have] been a mere exchange of our surplus provisions, for your surplus manufactures, instead of gold & silver. The one would have stimulated the industry of both to the highest degree, while the other, has served, but to disturb their monetary condition ["of both" *canceled*] & to that extent, to the disadvantage of both in the end.

So deep has been the impression made by free trade on our side, that it has forced silence on its opponents, & will, probably, prevent them from making opposition to it, one of the issues in the next presidential election; & thus take it out of our party politicks. That would be a great triumph. Indeed, were it not for the unfortunate Mexican War, with its accompanying heavy debt & expenses, I do not doubt, but that a great reduction would ["have" *canceled*] be made by the next Congress in our rates of duties, & that in a short time, they would be reduced to the lowest scale, which the expense of the Governm[en]t economically administ[e]red would admit. But, I fear, as it is, that free trade, in its full latitude, will be long delayed on our side. If we shall escape from it, even with that misfortune, great as it is, we shall be fortunate. I fear my worst anticipations of its effects, will be realized. Had it not occur[r]ed our future would have been without a cloud.

My cough has not entirely left me, but is much better. My general health is good.

Mrs. [Floride Colhoun] Calhoun desires to be kind[ly] remembered to you. Yours faithfully, J.C. Calhoun.

ALS in ScU-SC, John C. Calhoun Papers; microfilm of ALS in ViU, Maury Papers; variant PEx in Sarah M. Maury, *An Englishwoman in America* (London: Thomas Richardson and Son; Liverpool: Geo. Smith, Watts and Co., 1848), pp. 1–2.

From Jos[eph] J. Singleton

Dahlonega [Ga.,] 12th May 1847

My Dear Sir, I have just returned from a visit to your mines; on the Obarr mine there has only been three men at work from the beginning of spring. They have done a great deal of work, for the number of hands, principally in cleaning out old works, by which they have arrived at nothing; consiquently have abandoned them for the present, and turned in within a few days past upon new works altogether, by which, on yesterday they discovered a small new vein near the mouth of a tunnel on the south side of the ridge, which they are persuing with a tolerable degree of hope; for my own part,

I do not think it is of much value. They are now running a tunnel from the north side of the Ridge with the view of intercepting the old vein some 20 or 30 yards from where it was abandoned; striking the line perhaps some 40 feet from the surface. In all, they have gotten out something over an hundred bushels of rubbish ore; what it will yield I have no idea, as they have pounded none yet in the mill. Messrs. [Robert H.] Moore & [William G.] Lawrence are now raising, and pounding ore from a new vein on the upper lot of the two they have, with a good prospect of success, both as regards quality & quantity. Their calculation is about one dollar p[e]r bushel, derived from a fair test in their mill. Mr. Moore has returned to me up to the 8th Inst. about 80 Dwts. toll, exclusively from the deposite, and the deposite is now doing well. They have thought best, with my approbation to deposite all the vein gold in the mint on account of its doubtful value. Up to this time they have taken from the veins on the lot in which you are interested about 170 or [1]80 Dwts. according to their report. Mr. Moore will be ready to meet your demand no doubt, whenever it is made.

You mentioned in your last letter that you would make us a visit during the ensuing summer. I assure you that no visit at my House could afford more pleasure than the one promised, where I can be enabled to converse upon matters which [it] will not do to write about, (to use the language of Gov. [Wilson] Lumpkin). Should your name be proposed to the Union for their next Chief Magistrate, may your prospects be as bright as mine is for the next senatorial Representative from this District, composed of Lumpkin & Union Counties; and may your success in putting down the pernicious system of Caucuses throughout the Union ["be" *interlined*] as mine has been in this senatorial District. I attacked the system upon the broad basis of the Ballat [*sic*] Box, as the only legitimate means of a perpetuation of our inherent rights; repudiating all other attempts short of that great, glorious, and only Constitutional alternative; by which we can inforce obedience in despite of all village combinations, Cliques, or Caucus[e]s.

Should it be in your power to state within a day or two of the time you expect to visit this part of the Country, I think I can arrange it so as to have our friend [William C.] Dawson to meet you here; and our old friend Gov. Lumpkin has often promised me a visit. I will particularly invite him on the occasion; if I am not mistakened in his Southern views, embracing as they do the soundest principles of patriotism East, West, North & South, he will come. Do let me hear from you in time. I have the honor of being Your humble Servant, Jos. J. Singleton.

ALS in ScU-SC, John C. Calhoun Papers.

From T[homas] R. Cherry

Pendleton [S.C.,] 14th May 1847

Dear Sir, The within is a sketch of the route which has been adopted as the most direct one by the commissioners from Pendleton to Athens.

You will find the Route & distances marked on the same. There will be three ferries to cross which is the greatest obstacle in the way. We find the country generally well adapted for a Road beyond Tugaloo [river]. It is very level until you arrive near the [Broad] River or the Franklin Springs. Thinking you may wish to write the P[ost]M[aster] Gen[era]l [Cave Johnson] in regard to the route I send the within for your examination. I will leave home on Saturday next, but will return in a few days & can give you any further information you may wish in regard to the route. Resp[ec]t[fully] y[our]s, T.R. Cherry.

ALS with En in ScCleA. Note: Included in this letter is the drawing described by Cherry. An AEU by Calhoun reads "Mr. Cherry, Relates to the road to Athens."

To H[enry] W. Conner, [Charleston]

Fort Hill, 14th May 1847

My dear Sir, It has not been my wish, or intention to take any decided course, or express any decided opinion on the subject, who should be the editor of the paper proposed to be established at Washington. I am, & have been of the opinion, that the selection should be made by the principal contributors; & accordingly, in my letter to Mr. [Pierre] Soulé [Senator from La.], I suggested, if New Orleans should enter heartily into the measure, and raise ["of" *canceled and "an" interlined*] equal amount to that which would be raised in Charleston, that the principal contributors should in each city appoint a Committee, say of three or four, ["&" *canceled and* "which" *interlined*] jointly select the editor & make other arrangements for carrying the establishment into effect.

I infer[r]ed from Mr. [Franklin H.] Elmore's letter, that the gentlemen in Charleston, who take an interest in the subject, had compared ideas, as to who ought to be selected & that they had turned their eyes to Mr. [Isaac W.] Hayne & Mr. [Robert Barnwell] Rhett, as ["suitable" *canceled*] possessing suitable qualifications for the place of editor, if either could be had. What I wrote was a mere acquiescence, & was not intended to control the opinion of others. Indeed, it would be indelicate in me to undertake to influence the selection.

I see from indications on all sides, that General [Zachary] Taylor will probably be a prominent candidate at the next election, and I might add a successful one. Indeed, it seems now to be established, that the administration, which makes war will be turned out of power by it; if the war be successful by the successful General, and, if unsuccessful, by the opposition. Such at least seems certain will be the fate of Mr. [James K.] Polk and his administration. Let who will succeed, their defeat is certain. Perhaps, it is well, that it is so. It would seem to be the only way, that a stop can be put to the war mania of the country. If the honors of the war should accrue to the administration, which made ["it" *interlined*] & became the means of upholding it, & perpetuating its power, the country would be kept incessantly in wars. But as it is, future administrations will learn caution by the fate of this; & long hesitate, before they undertake to plunge the country in war. Had Mr. Polk & his administration [*one word canceled and* "dreamed" *interlined*] that sending Taylor to the del Norte would make him President, we would have had no war.

It seems to me, our true policy is, to stand fast on our own ground and wait events for the present. There will be great confusion & ["braking" *canceled and* "breaking" *interlined*] up of parties. Indeed, the old organization of parties is worn out. A new, & I hope, a better one, must take place. It is possible circumstances will place General Taylor in a position, where, in reference to our views, it will be our duty to support him, as little as ["I" *canceled and* "we" *interlined*] are inclined to military chiefta[i]ns. The fact, that he is a slave holder, a Southern man, a cotton planter, is one of no little importance at the present moment. Nor is it to be over looked, that his election would go far to prevent future administrations from plunging the country into a war. Let us, then, treat him kindly and wait for developements of events. It is the course, that would be the most dignified, most consistent with our character & principles, & best calculated to give us the control of events.

I regret to see an article in the Southern [Quarterly] Review, advocating the general ticket system for the appointment of [Presidential] electors. It is true, it proposes to count the votes of each district, according to its federal population; but that, in my opinion, instead of ["meeting"(?) *canceled and* "lessening" *interlined*] the great objections to a general ticket will only aggravate them. It will make the caucus system, if possible, more indispensible; while it would not the less certainly destroy the ["fed" *canceled*] due weight of the lower country in the election.

If the election must be taken from the Legislature, & given directly to the people, let it be done ["the"(?) *canceled*] the only way it can be fairly & honestly, by districts. The general ticket, where many ["is" *canceled and* "are" *interlined*] to choose many, is a humbug, however modified; and ["a" *interlined*] most dangerous one. Its introduction into our State would be fatal to the State institutions, & the morals and standing & influence of the State. I feel deeply in reference to the subject, because I see, as clear as the light of heaven, its fatal consequences. I cannot be mistaken, as to them. Who are at the bottom of the movement? From whose pen does the article come? And what is the object? Yours truly & sincerely, J.C. Calhoun.

ALS in ScC; photostat of ALS in DLC, Henry Workman Conner Papers.

To E[DMUND] S. DARGAN, [Mobile]

Fort Hill, 14th May 1847
My dear Sir, What you state, as to the apathy of the people of your State on the vital question of our domestick institutions, does not surprise me. The cause lies deep. It does not originate in indifference to its fate, for there is not a man, who is so stupid, as not to feel, that it is a question involving the fate of the South. The real cause is, that our people have been lulled into a false security by party presses & party leaders on both sides, who take a far deeper interest in the result of a presidential election, than in what relates to the interest and safety of the South. Nothing alarms them so much, as the abolition question, for fear they may be seperated ["by

it" *interlined*] from their Northern allies [in] the Presidential game; and hence the insidious attacks on ["any one" *canceled and* "all" *interlined*], who dare raise their voice to warn the South of its danger. And such have been their influence, that he ["who" *interlined*] stands up to defend the South, is regarded by a large portion of the South, as an agitator for some selfish purpose. I have long seen & understood all this; and, if I have taken a decided stand on the question at all times from its first start, it has been from a sense of duty, & not because, I hoped to gain the good will of the South. No; to gain that, the most certain way, I am ["dis" *canceled*] sorry to say, is to ["go" *canceled*] join with the unprincipled party leaders & party presses to betray her.

I apprehend nothing will or can be done about the paper. The plan you suggest is plausible; but, if I may judge from passed experience, it would not prove successful. It has never yet been found possible to obtain a majority of Southern men for the last 16 or 17 years to unite on any measure, where the South was interested, and especially in reference to abolition. The reason is obvious; too large a portion of the members, on both sides, look too much to party influence to secure their ["ele" *canceled*] reelection, or advance themselves in the federal Govern[men]t, to disturb party relations on that, or any other question, however, important.

I regret exceedingly ["that" *canceled*] to hear, that you intend to retire from Congress. We have but too few members from the South with sufficient independence to speak out and do their duty irrespective of party and individual consideration, and your retiring will make them still fewer at this critical juncture. I hope, however, your absence will be short; & that circumstances ["will" *canceled*] in a few years, will permit you again to resume your seat in either one or the other House of Congress.

Although, I hope, I hold in due contempt the temporary popularity of the day, I place a high value on the favourable opinion of the wise & good, and I assure you, that I am greatly gratified with your assurance of friendship. Yours truly & sincerely, J.C. Calhoun.

ALS in NcD, John C. Calhoun Papers; variant transcript in NcU, John Caldwell Calhoun Papers. NOTE: On the ALS there is an ALS dated at "Blakeley," Ala., on 5/5/1865 and written by L.B. McAlpin to "Friend Hinman," which reads: "This letter is one among other papers picked up after the capture of this place, I thinking perhaps it might be a pleasure for you to read such an old document." Edmund Strother Dargan (1805–1879) was a native of N.C. and a former mayor of Mobile. He was Representative from Ala. 1845–1847, declining to seek reelection, and was subsequently chief justice of Ala. and a member of the Confederate House of Representatives.

To EDWIN W. SEIBELS, JAMES FARROW, and W[ILLIA]M B. TELFORD, Committee, [Columbia, S.C.]

Fort Hill, May 14th 1847

Gentlemen, The mail before the last brought me your note of the 7th inst. In answer I have to say that I expect to be absent from home until about the 24th inst., & that it will afford me pleasure any time thereafter, to sit for my portrait for the Society.

I have no choice as to the particular time, and hope, in that respect Mr. [William H.] Scarborough will select the period, which will best suit his convenience. I expect to be at home the residue of the season. With great respect I am &c, J.C. Calhoun.

Contemporary copy in ScU-SC, University Archives, Clariosophic Society Papers, Minutes, Letterbook and Constitution, 1842–1849, p. 295.

From F[RANKLIN] H. ELMORE

Charleston, May 16, 1847

My Dear Sir, Yours of the 8th I have just read. I was in Columbia at the Greenville R. Road convention when it arrived & have just returned home.

I concur with you intirely about the article in the [Southern Quarterly] Review. I think it was not such an one as ought to have gone into it. It appears to me out of place & that our local questions when we have divisions of opinion had better be avoided. I had expressed this opinion & my views of the article frankly & freely to Mr. [J. Milton] Clapp. Strangely enough, his opinions of the measure agree with yours & mine. Last fall, when the subject was agitated he took ground in the [Charleston] Mercury decidedly against it. He, I suppose, felt it difficult to refuse the insertion of the article. The author of it is understood to be Col. [Benjamin F.] Perry of Greenville.

I have been casting about for some person to answer it. I would undertake it if I could, but my engagements are such that I cannot do it as it ought to be done. [James H.] Hammond would do it well I think, but I do not know if he can be induced to take his pen. Alex[ander] Mazyck could do it well & I heard he had been urged to do it, but with what result I have not heard. He has removed out of the City to his plantation, but will be back for the summer. I suppose I shall see him in a few days. James S. Rhett agreed to attack the article in the Mercury & said he had materials prepared. I will see him.

I have never been more distracted by my own affairs than now—they press upon me so as to disqualify me for almost all public matters. Indeed nothing but the magnitude of the stakes & the vast importance of the present crisis could for a moment draw me from my own matters. I cannot however be indifferent nor altogether idle. I do & am willing to do all I can & I only regret it is so little. I lament it just now more than I can express, in respect of the matter you wrote me on in answer to my letter. Your answer has been in the hands of our friends [Ker] Boyce, [Henry W.] Conner, [Henry] Gourdin, [Moses C.] Mordecai, & [George A.] Trenholm & [Isaac W.] Hayne. We were to meet & confer upon our ultimate course but my trip to Columbia prevented it. I had been unwell—very unwell for 10 days before, with sore throat & chest—& was unfit for any business, which had also caused delay. Gen[era]l [James] Hamilton [Jr.] was with us & goes back to Columbus [Ga.] to prepare the way there for something to be done amongst our friends.

We had thought it best perhaps to get the names of Gentlemen who are not in active life in public positions, to sign our Circular. Several have been applied to & the list is making up. When they are completed, we thought of send[ing] a Representative, who should be a Gentleman of good standing & address to see prominent men throughout the State who have means & can help our object. To propose to them to put down what they will do towards it, on condition a given sum (our proportion) can be raised in this State & the rest elsewhere. Several young Gentlemen are willing to go when the courts are over & they can leave their posts. Col. [Alfred P.] Aldrich of Barnwell will take the Savannah side & see you in his round. Young [Arthur P.] Hayne, a son of Gen[era]l [Robert Y.] H[ayne] will probably visit the East side of the State—with him young Mr. [Edward J.] Pringle son of W[illiam] B. Pringle may perhaps be associated. But when our movements will become active I cannot now say. We in some sort are waiting in hopes that you may be able to inform us what our friends elsewhere may do.

I lately, (some 20 days ago) was at Washington & saw [David Levy] Yulee & [Dixon H.] Lewis. Yulee was afraid our Circular was not *Party enough*. That it might be considered as separating from the Democracy & setting up an opposition. Lewis thought it exactly right—but I fear we would not get much pecuniary aid from either

361

Florida or Alabama. They seemed to think so. Hayne visited Alabama & was at the bottom of the action you saw at Montgomery & Lowndes & of the final action of the Gubernatorial Convention. While at Washington I saw Rob[ert M.] McLane of Baltimore & Gen[era]l [Duff] Green & others. They thought that the people of Maryland woul[d] be brought decidedly to the ground to vote under no circumstances for any man who did not avow open uncompromising opposition to the Wilmot proviso, whether the nominee of a Convention or not. McLane said he feared to press the question further than that now. Rob[ert G.] Scott at Richmond thought Va. could be easily be brought to that ground—and all of them said if Gen[era]l [Zachary] Taylor was safe on the free trade question, it would be next to impossible to resist the current in his favor.

Do you know anything of the General[']s principles or what guaranties can be given that his principles are safe? I have not seen any one, nor any thing from him that is at all satisfactory. At present there seems a fair chance for his election by both Parties or against both. I am not sure but the latter is the most probable & it would seem far the most desirable to us, if he is to be elected at all. But can we go for him & in what contingency? I can see nothing nor learn any thing that satisfies my mind in regard to his principles. It seems to me extremely probable that he in fact had no fixed political principles—that he has never studied a great Constitutional principle—but that his social ties & tendencies are with the Whigs more strongly than with us. The evident unwillingness of their leaders & organized partisans to take him up, may weaken those tendencies & lay him more open to those who would sustain him in an independent position against the party hunkers of both Whigs & Democrats. Gen[era]l Hamilton seems to think that a very controlling influence for good might be obtained over him, if it were found advisable to look to him, & if proper steps were pursued. The Gen. told me of his letter to you & showed me your reply. If he is to be trusted on free trade & will take his ground against Convention or Caucus nominations, got up as they have been heretofore or in other words against the party machinery of both, there will be much to reconcile us to his success—but I confess that while I look on his prospects ["with" *canceled and* "as" *interlined*] exceedingly strong, I can not but feel very reluctant to support him & great apprehensions from his success. To be afloat as to principles, with a successful general at the Head of the Government, without a safe & steady & strong Counsellor in his Cabinet to keep him straight, is to exchange the corruptions of party usage as at present exercised, for almost if not quite as dangerous a condition. Still there is hope that he may be regulated. Gen[era]l Hamilton seems to think there is at least Gen[era]l [Memucan] Hunt of Texas who is Gen[era]l Taylor[']s cousin & a warm Democrat & friend of your[s] & has given strong assurances to that effect. If you were at the head of his Cabinet, it might be—but what other guaranty could we rely on? I see none. If there is any I should be glad to know, for the current of popular feeling is evidently so strong towards him, that in prudence we must consider him as formidable & should in time look out for the consequences of his success.

At Columbia, the only topics were Mr. [Daniel] Webster & our Rail Roads. Of the first you have seen his reception here & at Columbia. In both places it was calm—civil—& unexcited. I felt the part that was devolved on me was a very delicate one, & endeavored in discharging it to do him all the honor due ourselves & him, at the same to show that we surrendered no ground. I hope our course has not compromised either our principles or position & that it has your approbation.

The Rail Road feeling is now stronger than I have known it for years—indeed it seems to me irrisistible. I think the State will be brought in to take a part. Four Roads are ultimately almost if not quite certain of being built.

1. The Columbia & Greenville
2.   "   & Charlotte.
3. Aiken & Greenville or Pendleton
4. A connexion of the S.C. R. Road & Wilmington—or Raleigh.

For these a powerful effort will be made to get Legislative aid. The surplus Revenue & its legitimate profits amounts to about $1,400,000. A subscription on this amt. between these roads, in 5 per cent bonds, for the payment of which the stocks subscribed, those held now in the S. Ca. R. Road & Bank, & two debts owing by the S.C. R. Road amounting to about $500,000 may be set apart as a sinking fund, has been suggested. To avoid increasing the debt of the State, in such a way as to make a general liability, it has been suggested that the Bonds be similar to those issued by Georgia to finish the Western & Atlantic. They discharge, on their face, a general liability & are to look for payment to the Road & its profits alone, which are pledged for that purpose. These Bonds sell well in our market here. The proposition to sell out our stocks in the So. Ca. R. Road has been made & at one time met favor; but I think it has not now so much consideration. To sell now, or even at par, would be to part with the stock when it is rapidly rising to a price that will reimburse by premium, the interest lost by short profit while it was building—it will glut the market—injure the stockholders—absorb large sums that would otherwise be available for subscriptions or loans & bring on an unquiet stock speculating feeling extremely adverse to steady progress. I would be very glad to have your views on this subject. The tendency of my mind is to the proposed action of the State in favor of these roads. Their completion would add immensely to its power, influence & wealth. It has been said to us by Mr. [Joel R.] Poinsett & Gen[era]l [Waddy] Thompson, that if we go to Charlotte, the road will be continued to Danville & Richmond & ultimately the trade of our own Country & of N. Ca. be carried to Baltimore. What do you think of this?

For myself I had hoped to get into western Virginia—into Botetourt [County] & that region. It has not seemed to me we should lose as much as we should gain. Our market at Charleston I thought would be more attractive than Richmond or Baltimore. I would be greatly pleased to hear your views of that connexion or line of Road, should it ever be completed—its effects & our interests in it.

You ask about Lewis. He had almost perfectly recovered when I saw him. I find a letter from him dated 10 inst. showing his mind & body at ease. I expect him in some 10 days or two weeks. I am My Dear Sir Yo[ur]s truly, F.H. Elmore.

ALS in ScCleA; PEx in Boucher and Brooks, eds., *Correspondence*, p. 376.

From F[ranklin] H. Elmore

Charleston, May 17, 1847

My dear Sir, My friend W[illia]m B. Pringle Esq. a son of Mr. John Julius Pringle & one of the most respectable Gentlemen in the State, has just asked me to procure from you, if you will oblige him & me so far, a letter or two for his son Edw[ar]d J. Pringle to some persons in Europe. Young Pringle was graduated at Cambridge [Mass.] a year or two ago with the third distinction in his class—is just admitted to the Bar, & goes at 21 years of age to travel a year or two in Europe for improvement. He is a very clever & well conducted Gentleman—and promises to be useful. In all respects he is a Gentleman & will do no discredit to Carolina. His Father w[oul]d be greatly pleased if you could give him a letter to Lord Ashburton & Mr. [Thomas G.] Clemson. You may do so with the perfect assurance that Mr. Pringle is in every sense of the word deserving. Yo[ur]s truly, F.H. Elmore.

P.S. Inclose to me—or to W[illia]m B. Pringle would be better.

ALS in ScCleA.

From JOHN HOGAN, "Private"

Utica New York, May 17th/47

My dear Sir, I hope that your return to your family has improved your health or that you have recovere[d] from the Cold under which you were labouring ["under" *canceled*] when you left Washington. On my return from Washington I stop[p]ed for some weeks in the city of New York & met many men of various political opinions. Indeed so utterly unhinged are political matters that no one can for a moment make any calculation on which he himself can place the least reliance. Commercially speaking the country is rapidly advancing & becoming rich and so too in all matters connected with the Country, (*proper*) but then we are all at fault when we look to political matters for they are all in the wind.

The Election in Virginia necessarily places the Administration in a minority in the lower house & then another question will present itself[:] what will be the Course in relation to the Mexican War. I see Col. [Thomas H.] Benton throws upon you the defeat of the Oregon bill. Foolish man. The country from one end to the other knows to[o] well the cause of his dissatisfaction toward you. No harm will arise from that source. I see by this day[']s paper the dealth [*sic*] of Senator [Jesse] Speight of Missi[ssi]ppi. I regret his death he was friendly.

Now I come to another point and indeed I do not know how to [s]peak[?] on the subject. I have been written to by three or four Gent. as to the propriety of the Whigs nominating Gen. [Zachary] Taylor for the Presidency or for our friends to bring his name forward for the presidency. I have not replied to one of the letters neither shall I give any opinion either one way or the other for the present. Let Gent. take what course they think proper. I hope *you* will not deem it necessary for me to say that I do not know of but one Candidate for that office neither do I wish unless *driven* by the most imperious necessity to know any other but the one. That Gent. is from *South Carolina*. Should that Gent. decline in toto then in that case

I have no Candidate and what is more care but little who is the Candidate or whether there is one or not. Therefore I have but little say about Candidates for the Presidency. I see from time to time that ["you are" *canceled*] your name is brought before the public as the friend of Gen. Taylor & that you bring him forward. I did suppose that Gen. [Duff] Green at Washington was the man who used your name in connection with Gen. Taylor[']s nomination. The Gen. is one of the Gent. who has written me enquiring whether Gen. Taylor would get the whole of the Whig vote of this State & a part of the Democratic vote. I have not answered his letter neither shall for the present. Now I believe that I have put you in possession of those matters or at least at a peep into them.

Your relatives in this vicinity the Miss Calhouns both make close enquiry for yourself & family. My health improves but slowly. The weather in this place has until recently been cold & wind raw which affects me unfavorably. Be kind enough to write me a line should you have leisure.

I hope Mrs. [Floride Colhoun] Calhoun & family enjoy good health & be kind enough to give to Mrs. Calhoun my best wishes & respects. I have the Honour Sir to be your ob[edien]t Ser[van]t, John Hogan.

ALS in ScCleA.

From A[sa] Whitney

New York [City,] 17 May 1847

Sir, Your esteemed favor under date of March 29th reached me in my absence where I could not give the information you desired, and expecting to return daily is the cause it has not been sooner acknowledged.

I am much indebted for the "Reports" you were so kind as to send me. I had before read your "report" with great interest. The Railroad report gave me information which I desired, and which coincided with my own opinions on that subject. It does appear to me there is no subject of greater importance to the interests of all the Atlantic coast, of that great rich basin of the Mississippi, and also to the old world, ["as" *canceled and* "than" *interlined*] the opening of the great route from the Atlantic cities to that valley, and none of which can produce so great and so immediate beneficial results and changes as the railroad from Charleston to the Ohio and to Memphis, and next to it, would be the one from Richmond to Cincinnati, which latter would shorten the route from New York to Cincinnati about 200 miles.   The two together would entirely change the travel and commerce of the Mississippi valley.   Your road would take off every thing from north of *all* Tennessee, saving the immense distance via New Orleans, dangers of navigation and destruction by climate, and then the produce of *all* the Mississippi basin north of all Tennessee could be taken to market either at Charleston or Richmond at any season of the year, and as you say "would effectually establish free trade with all its blessings."

We agree that these works cannot be accomplished by the general government, and I am ["not" *interlined*] in favor of their being done by State governments, because they would in a greater or lesser degree influence legislation, but they can be done by individuals if proper efforts are made, and I consider it a subject so important that the owners of property in your State and in Virginia might well afford to give out of their possessions enough to complete the works and be enriched by so doing.

These two routes I have always considered as being most directly connected with and most to be benefitted by the carrying out of my great project.   The Charleston road to the Ohio would then pass through the center and entire length of the great State of Illinois, and join the Pacific road at ["at" *canceled*] the Mississippi river, thus bringing to your Port a far greater amount of commerce and production, than is possible, to be centered, upon any other route, and also the first to strike the Pacific road.

Railroads are fast changing natural localities.   The climate of New Orleans is such as to cause an immense destruction of property, animal and vegitable and the rivers are not always suitable channels for transit, and so soon as railroads form other and better localities New Orleans must diminish in importance.

The gentleman whom it was my principle [*sic*] object to see in Europe has arrived here, therefore I shall not go at present, and the present situation in Europe is rather against the object I had in view, but their capital and their people will come here and build our railroads.   Were it not for this Mexican war (to which I can see no end) our prosperity would be without a parallel.   At foot is a statement of freights on the Mississippi river, and in a few days I will forward a more particular one, which I have amongst my papers but as I have been in town but one day and am called away again today, have not time to find and arrange a statement in the order that would be useful. I have taken the liberty to forward the proceedings of the Legislature of this State on my project for a railroad to the Pacific. The people are with me for this project and I think it can be carried. The whole plan is, the connecting the sale of the lands and the settlement of the country on the line with the building the road; that is, the road sells the lands and the lands build the road. I hope you will be pleased to give the subject your attention, and if it should be your pleasure to make any suggestions, they shall be considered as strictly confidential as you may desire, and I shall feel myself under great obligation. With highest considerations of respect I am Your ob[edien]t Serv[an]t, A. Whitney.

[Appended:] Freight from St. Louis and Louisville considered equal.

Flour to New Orleans		. . .	55 cts. pr. bbl.	
Corn and wheat	to d[itt]o	. . .	15 to 17 pr. bushel	
Hemp . . .	to d[itt]o	. . .	$11.00 pr. ton	
Lead . . .	to d[itt]o	. . .	25 to 30 cts. 100 lbs.	
Insurance . . .	1¼%	. . .		

The above are the lowest rates when the rivers are up.

From New Orleans to New York varies from 12½ to 15 cts. pr. foot measurement or $5 to $6 pr. ton of 40 feet. Ten bbls. estimated as a ton.

Insurance 1½%.

ALS with En in ScCleA. Note: Enclosed is a clipping from the [Albany, N.Y.] *Argus* containing a speech by Whitney in the N.Y. legislature, headed "Railroad to the Pacific."

From JOHN A[LFRED] CALHOUN

Eufaula [Ala.,] May 18th 1847

D[ea]r Uncle, My copartner Tennant [*sic*] Lomax is about to join the army in Mexico under the new call for volunteers. He will go as an officer in a company to be raised in this place. He requests me to procure for him some letters to the officers of the army, Generals [Winfield] Scott, and [Zachary] Taylor and any others to whom you may deem it proper to write. If there are no circumstances to forbid your giving Mr. Lomax letters to the officers named or any others that you may deem it proper to write, I would thank you to inclose to me introductory letters for him. Mr. Lomax is a son of your old friend William Lomax formerly of Abbeville and is a nephew of Dr. William Tennant [*sic*; Tennent] now of Abbeville. He is a young man of considerable promis[e], and I doubt not will do himself credit in the army. He is an old acquaintance of your son Patrick [Calhoun], having gon[e] to school with him in Abbeville. He has much of *the old Tennant spirit*, and is an enthusiastic Carolinian. He came to this State with me, and studied Law in my office and for the last four years has been in copartnership with me. If you can furnish me with the desired letters it will be desirable for them to be sent on immediately, as his company will be off in the course of three weeks.

I have not heard from you since your return from Washington, and would be pleased to have your views of the probable course of things in the political world. Since my location here I have studiously avoided mingling in political matters; having bestowed all my attention to my pecuniary matters. I have been [*one word canceled*] quite fortunate in my aims, and now if a fair chance should present itself I believe I would again aspire. But my situation is a peculiar one. The old States right, or Carolina portion of the Democracy are in the minority in the Democratic party of this county. This interest is much devoted to me & I think would follow me in any connection with the Whigs, which I might feel disposed to direct. Indeed we have at all times formed but a loose connection with the [*"Whigs" canceled and "Democrats" interlined*], and to sever our ties with them would cost us but lit[tle] effort, and less regret. I am, however, affraid of occupying a false position; and hence have advised my friends to stand aloof for the present. The Whigs are exceedingly anxious to unite with us. Mr. [Henry W.] Hilliard [Representative from Ala.] is the[i]r leader, and in his late visit to this place was marked in his attentions to myself, and uniformly complimentary to [*"of" canceled*] you and of your course in Congress. By uniting ourselves with the Whigs we have every thing in our hands, and I doubt not but that I can at once be placed in a strong position. Mr. Hilliard's cour[s]e in the last Congress has rendered my union with him easy, as I believe him more nearly with you than the mass of the Democracy. What advice will you give me as to the cour[s]e to be pursued in future? Write me fully on this subject; and of course all that you say shall be held in the strictest confidence. The low, and dishonest policy of the Democratic party makes it any thing but unpleasant for me to be *eternally* separated from them. Indeed I never have been able to consent to accept honors from them. They have been frequently tendered to me here but as often declined. I have always held the[i]r proscriptive policy in great contempt; and nothing but the necessity of the case has ever reconciled me to act with them. I believe now that we have got all we can can [*sic*] get out of them on the Tariff and other questions for which we have been contending.

We are all well, and would have been glad to have had you with us when you were last in the State. Should you ever visit the State again I hope you will not pass us without a call. Your nephew &c, John A. Calhoun.

ALS in ScCleA.

From F[ranklin] H. Elmore

[Charleston] 20 May 1847

My Dear Sir, I wrote you a few days ago. Since then I saw Mr. [J. Milton] Clapp & he mentions a fact which I had not before heard or if I had forgot it when I wrote to you, which is that the article on the Presidential Electors was in the hands of Mr. [Daniel K.] Whitaker when the [Southern Quarterly] Review was purchased & could not well be excluded as it had been received by Mr. W[hitaker] on the understanding that it was to go in. The Review was got out of his hands so late that articles were wanting & they had not a line to spare to fill it up.

Mr. Clapp fully accords with us. He desires an article on the other side. I saw Mr. [Alexander] Mazyck who exhibits an unwillingness to write, not from any objection to the ["task" *canceled*], matter of principle, but an indisposition to write. Mr. Clapp suggested [James H.] Hammond or Judge [William] Harper & I have at his instance & that of many others here, written to Harper an earnest request to write an article. He is at Columbia. Perhaps if you were to add your influence he might do it & if he will he can do it as well or better than anyone else. Mr. Clapp says he thinks it w[oul]d be better in the October number, as just preceding the Legislative Session. In haste You[r]s truly, F.H. Elmore.

ALS in ScCleA.

From J. Sappington Pearson

Cumberland College, Lebanon Tennessee
May 20th 1847

Dear Sir: At a late meeting of the Philomathian society of Cumberland College you were unanimously elected an honorary of that body of which I have the honor to give you the information.

A long and useful life spent in the service of his country—in advocating those truths which are for her best interests—contending and advancing those principles which are for her preservation and protection—the friends no less of literature than of independence and freedom—the literary attainments and virtuous qualifications—in fine all that is good for mankind seems concentrated in you. Free and happy America can boast of few such sons. Our society exult in enrolling that name at the mention of which suggest every thing good—patriotic—upon our list. Yours very respectfully, J. Sappington Pearson, Cor[responding] Sec[retary,] Philomathian Society.

ALS in ScCleA. NOTE: An AEU by Calhoun reads "Notice of being elected an honorary member of the Philo[mathia]n S[ociety] of Cum[ber]]land College Ten[ness]ee."

From R[OBERT] B[ARNWELL] RHETT

[Washington] May 20th 1847

My Dear Sir, On returning here, I find yours written from Fort Hill, informing me that you do not think the funds necessary to set up a Press in Washington will be obtained—consequently my residence here, with a view to it, is not necessary this Summer. My arrangements for the Summer are completed, and can not now be changed. It would be next [to] impossible to hire now a proper house in Charleston. The sacrifice whatever it may be, must now be encountered.

The events of the war, altho very brilliant thus far justify your counsels. No signs of peace, have followed our victories; and if the war is still raging when Congress meets, you will undoubtedly hold a commanding position. The Whigs, unfortunately for them, will have a majority in the House of Representatives, and will therefore be put into the position of actors: but I do not believe, they will act. They will not have the courage, to stop the war, because the Southern Portion, will be too proud to seem to back out of it, and the Northern-Tariff portion desire the war. The supplies will be voted therefore and the war go on, for them. One result seems to be inevitable, the Democratic Party is to be over thrown in the next Presidential election—and Gen[era]l [Zachary] Taylor, be the President. I write to day to Jefferson Davis to know what we are to expect from Gen[era]l Taylor on the subject of the Tariff. I suppose however the Kentucky Whigs, with [Senator John J.] Crittenden at their head, will rule the Counsels of his Administration.

The Elections in Virginia seem to have somewhat quenched the rage of Old [Thomas] Ritchie, against the Calhoun clique. He and his Masters, have in two years overthrown one of the most triumphant Parties, that ever entered upon power, with a fair prospect of defeating also all its measures and principles.

Mrs. [Elizabeth Washington Burnet] Rhett joins me in respects to Mrs. [Floride Colhoun] Calhoun and yourself and believe me Yours sincerely, R.B. Rhett.

P.S. I have not received nor seen your Speech in Charleston which you say you sent to me.

ALS in ScCleA; PEx in Boucher and Brooks, eds., *Correspondence*, pp. 376–377.

From H[enry] W. Conner

Charleston, May 21 1847

My Dear Sir, Your fav[or] of the 14th is rec[eive]d & the plan you suggest for the selection of an Editor—when we are ready for it, corresponds exactly with my views. I wish we had got on far enough to make it more proper for us to take up that part of the subject.

Gen[era]l [Winfield] Scott I should judge from appearances is like to divide the military renown with Gen[era]l [Zachary] Taylor. They may perhaps weaken one another in popular favour. Much may occur in the next 6 mo[nths] to change the prospects of things in general & those generals in particular. I cannot but believe that ["it is" *interlined*] the duty of your friends to maintain a quiet—but firm & unflinching position—& being particularly guarded against saying or doing aught to imply any disposition to yield; or to doubt your political strength ["or magnify others" *interlined*]. Great distraction is certain to prevail in the councils & conduct of both parties & factions & I have always observed when that was the case in common life men turned instinctively to the side of virtue & wisdom—confided in by all parties & all men & of admitted superiority to all present aspirants[;] it appears to me it would be attended with little effort for the people to concentrate upon you for the next presidency[,] the more especially that it is known you do not seek the office & besides I trust the power of politicians & their contrivances are fast declining. Next to yourself I am quite sure ["Gen(era)l Taylor" *interlined*] is the man for us—unless some new developments are made.

Major [Benjamin F.] Perry of Greenville is the author I understand of the article you refer to in the last [Southern Quarterly] review. It was prepared before Mr. [J. Milton] Clapp took charge of the review, as I learn & could not prevent its insertion tho opposed to it. What is the present object of it other than to gain popular favour I know not. There is some expectation that it may be answered by Chancellor [William] Harper—his health permitting. Last summer the movement ["here" *interlined*] came from the demagogues & had reference only to office & perquisites I think. I am apt to think a very decided move will be made here at a proper time against the project of changing the mode of elections. Very Truly y[ou]rs &C, H.W. Conner.

ALS in ScCleA.

From J[OSIAH] C. NOTT

Mobile, 21st May 1847, Friday

Dear Sir, Your son Andrew [Pickens Calhoun] came down to Mobile a week ago on business, & brought William [Lowndes Calhoun] with him thinking the trip might be of service to his health, but more especially with the view of having some work done on his teeth which had been giving him a great deal of pain.

The poor fellow had been suffering so dreadfully with pain in his teeth, that his nervous system became completely upset. The dentist extracted two of his teeth after which (on Wednesday last) he had a chill followed by a high fever. For the last two days he has been up & well enough to ride out, though still rather disposed to be feverish.

Andrew was very much pressed for time & I persuaded him to return home & leave William with me, which he has done. He has given me discretionary powers to ["do what" *canceled*] advise what

373

I think best with regard to his future movements. His general health seems to be quite delicate & I was anxious to have him under my eye for a week or so hoping I might give some advice as to the best plan of treatment.

I do not see any Organic disease about him, & his nervous system seems to be more at fault than any thing else, but he is at an age now when the constitution should be ripening & I am sure you had better not think of confining him to school this summer—it had better be devoted to his health. I think it probable that a couple of months at the white Sulphur [Springs, Va.], where the change of climate would be complete, would do him more good than any thing else, but of this you can think when he gets home.

Mr. [Charles] Auzé talks of going down to a watering place on the Coast (Pascagoula) [Miss.] where the sea air & bathing are very fine, & if so W[illia]m will probably go down & stay a few days. I do not think it prudent for him to start home, until he is some days entirely clear of fever, & regains a little strength & appetite. If he goes to Pascagoula he will probably leave here for Pendleton in 10 days—if he does not I shall probably advise him to leave for Marengo again in 5 or 6 days & Andrew will then direct his movements.

I am now giving him Quinine, & I think after his fever leaves entirely he may be very much benefitted by some preparation of Iron. This is the form of tonic which usually answers best in giving tone to the nervous system.

He seems to be very well satisfied where he is & we are very much pleased with him—he is a perfect child of nature, with an honesty & simplicity of character which the world can never corrupt. With best respects for Mrs. [Floride Colhoun] Calhoun I remain dear Sir very respectfully & truly yours, J.C. Nott.

ALS in ScCleA.

From W[illiam] Gilmore Simms

New York [City]: May 21 [1847]
Dear Sir, Your kind & comprehensive letter [*not found*] reached me but a little while before my leaving Carolina for the North, and while I was busy in preparing & packing for the journey, to say nothing of the task of bestowing the last strokes & touches upon a biography of the Chevalier [Pierre Terrail] Bayard, the knight *sans peur*

sans reproche, upon whom I have been engaged all the winter. My purpose now is not so much to answer as to acknowledge your Letter, and to express the hope that I shall have an opportunity of seeing you at home this summer, and conversing with you in proper person, in regard to those great topics of national & local concern, upon which nobody can so properly or ably discourse as yourself. My visit to the North is some six weeks earlier this season than usual, in order that I may get back to Carolina in due time to give my family the benefit of a summer jaunt among our own mountains. Putting them down in quiet in some healthy neighbourhood, I shall probably ramble into yours, and contemplate a free & frequent conversation with you as one of the rewards of my wanderings. My purpose will be to pick up as much historical material as possible in relation to the events of the revolution in the interior, so that I may make my History of the State more complete, and more satisfactory to the upper country. My publishers Harper & Brothers, have just addressed you a Letter [*not found*] in regard to the speeches which you have ["recently" *interlined*] delivered & which they desire to incorporate with the volume already published. I percieve [*sic*] that you are spoken of as engaged upon an ["ab" *altered to* "analysis"] of the subject of Government and the Constitution. Such a work would be, indeed, ["the" *canceled*] at once the proper base & apex of your fame. In publishing your speeches, it will be well to class them according to their periods; and their applicability & value would be greatly increased to the younger generation, & those yet to follow, if a brief history of ["the" *interlined*] events by which they were provoked, could be made to ["separate" *canceled*] accompany & illustrate them. I throw out the suggestion with great deference, and simply as one accustomed to the manufacture of books, and not wholly ignorant of the many helps and appliances which our *hurrying* people require, in the attainment & appreciation of their histories. I suppose that General [Zachary] Taylor, unless he experiences some unlooked for disaster, will be elected by acclamation. The successes of [Winfield] Scott, at Vera Cruz, and his victory at Cerro Gordo, have, in a measure, restored him to a front place among the whigs; which, without securing their nomination of him, will prompt them to halt too long in regard to Taylor, with whom they have been coquetting. But they are very much bewildered. With great respect, Y[ou]r ob[edien]t serv[an]t &c, W. Gilmore Simms.

ALS in ScCleA; PC in Oliphant, Odell, and Eaves, eds., *The Letters of William Gilmore Simms,* 2:318–319.

W[ILLIAM] L. M[ARCY] to J[ohn] C. Calhoun, Jr.

War Department, May 22d 1847

Sir, I have received your letter of the 7th instant asking permission to raise a company of Volunteers under the recent call of the Department for additional troops. In answer I regret to inform you that your letter was not received until after requisitions had been made for the whole amount of force contemplated to be received into service, and as it is not at present designed to increase the number called for in those requisitions, the Department is constrained to decline the acceptance of your patriotic offer. Your letter will be placed on file, and should additional troops be required from your State your application shall receive due consideration. I have the honor to be, Very respectfully, Your Ob[edien]t Serv[ant], W.L. Marcy, Secretary of War.

FC in DNA, RG 107 (Secretary of War), Letters Sent by the Secretary of War relating to Military Affairs, 1800–1889, 27:344–345 (M-6:27); CC in DNA, RG 107 (Secretary of War), Letters Received by the Secretary of War (Main Series), 1801–1870, C-132 (M-221:139).

From R[OBERT] B[ARNWELL] RHETT

[Washington] May 22d 1847

My Dear Sir, I found your Speech, (Mrs. [Elizabeth Washington Burnet] Rhett having put it away) and to Day went with it to the [Washington] National Intelligencer, which had just published [Thomas H.] Benton[']s Speech at St. Louis, in which you are furiously assailed. On this account, in a short introduction, I claimed[?] that your speech should be published ["also" *interlined*]. It will come out accordingly Day after tomorrow. I waited also on the [Washington] Union, but found both of the Editors [Thomas Ritchie and John P. Heiss] out. I have no doubt I shall have it published in the Union also.

You remember you urged me to write an Article on the Wilmot Proviso, at the close of the last Congress for the Southern [Quarterly] Review. I told you that I did not think it possible for me to do it within the time required: and that if done within that time, it would probably do but little credit to the author. Upon reflection however, I thought that any kind of article of a proper tone, might be of more use, than a far abler one at a later Day. I therefore undertook to do it, and in the mornings of six Days, wrote the Article you will see in the Southern Review on the Wilmot proviso, and sent it off as I wrote it, to Charleston. I suppose it must be pretty poor, since I see no notice taken of it in any of the Southern Papers.

Mrs. Rhett joins me in kind remembrance to Mrs. [Floride Colhoun] Calhoun & yourself and Believe me Yours sincerely, R.B. Rhett.

ALS in ScCleA. NOTE: The article referred to was "The Wilmot Proviso," *Southern Quarterly Review*, vol. 11 (April, 1847), pp. 377–406.

From R[OBERT] BEALE, [Sergeant-at-Arms of the Senate]

Document Room of the Senate, May 23d 1847

My Dear Sir, In looking over my draw[er] of papers[,] letters[,] &c &c I find a news paper which I put by for you and which I thought I had either sent or handed to you. I send it by the same mail that takes this—it contains in a letter from this place from the correspondent of the ["N.Y." *interlined*] Herald a few words which are as true & just as they are merited—it has had pretty extensive circulation in the papers in Va. & Md. & I have no doubt it may have fallen under your notice. I nevertheless send it that you may see that your friends were alive to your feelings & interest upon that occasion.

The whigs are in a dilem[m]a—they prefer [Winfield] Scott to [Zachary] Taylor & the [Washington] Union ["has" *canceled and* "is" *interlined*] joining in his praise—their great fear is that the democrats will take up Taylor—there ["are" *interlined*] however a very large portion of Mr. Clay[']s friends who are opposed to a military man, particularly when fresh from the battle field. *All* the friends of Mr. Mclain [*sic*; John McLean] of Ohio are equally opposed to a military man & they are sounding the country from one end to the other by private correspondence to see what force they can collect to make successful resistance to the claims of military men. If they find a military man is to be taken they are for Taylor to a man.

I would say many things I here [*sic*] of you from the intel[l]igent & thinking men of the country but it would appear to you probably too flattering.

377

I intended when I sat down to tell you all I hear in the shape of news but I have just been sent for by Mr. [Dixon H.] Lewis who is still here & I must go. I can not omit to say however that even the whigs begin to think that *Free Trade* is about to cover the earth as the waters cover the sea. Freights, Revenue, Manufa[c]tures, Agriculture every thing that appertains to government seems to flourish in every part of the earth where a single beam of the sun of Free Trade [h]as shed its light—to use the phrase of Mr. Sacer [*sic*; possibly John Sarchet] (a great friend of yours) it[']s the *natural* & common sense policy of the world. I directed Mr. [Robert P.] Anderson to be particular in attending to sending off your boxes, books, papers[,] documents &c &c. Do let me hear from you if all has gon[e] right.

My kindest regards to Mrs. [Floride Colhoun] Calhoun—wishing ["*you*" *interlined*] the best of fates I have the honor to be your friend & servant, R. Beale.

ALS in ScCleA.

From ELLWOOD FISHER

Cincinnati, 5 mo[nth] 25, 1847

Dear Friend, I received duly the paper containing thy speech in Charleston with the note accompanying it. The strongest evidence of its truth, is the silence which has been observed here by the papers on both sides concerning it—and the attempt which [Thomas H.] Benton is making to misrepresent the whole controversy. The Whig and Democratic papers published Benton[']s St. Louis speech—none have published thine at Charleston. Determined not to permit this course to be adopted with impunity I wrote several days since a reply at some length to Benton[']s speech for the Louisville Journal, the Editor [George D. Prentice] agreeing to publish. But he has not yet fulfilled his promise. At the time I was in Louisville ["and" *canceled*; Senator John J.] Crittenden also was there and I think it probable that ["the" *canceled*] Prentice has some how or other changed his views, and may not think it expedient either that Benton should be attacked in his paper, or that the controversy between the South and North should be discussed. I suspect that Benton anticipates the success of [Zachary] Taylor—possibly desires it, as an alternative, and may have an understanding with Crittenden on the subject.

Benton[']s speech has not been published here by the Democratic paper, which indeed is less hostile to us than it has been. And the Wilmot proviso here has lost ground, and would be voted down now if proposed in a meeting of the party. The [Columbus, Ohio] "Statesman" however has published Benton—and to day I sent it also, a reply in which all the points are discussed.

We are determined here to have a paper and that shortly. Meanwhile to let no attacks pass unanswered. But there ought to be one first established at Washington—and why is it still neglected by the South?

The [Henry] Clay Whigs are for Taylor: as was clearly evinced in the meeting recently held to nominate him in Louisville. And there is doubtless a considerable portion of the Democratic party leaders and followers in this State and Kentucky who will go for him also. In fact the Editors generally of Demo[cratic] papers in this State are already non committal. But the successes of [Winfield] Scott have had the effect of producing a pause in the Whig demonstrations for Taylor. As yet however [Thomas] Corwin is the strongest man in this State and next to him [John] McLean. In conversation with the latter not long ago, he said that he was in favour of an immediate declaration by the next Congress against any acquisition of Mexican territory—and if the President [James K. Polk] did not immediately offer Peace on that basis—then to stop the supplies. And I find that becoming more and more the favourite ground with the Whig papers here. I think this arises from fear of the consequences of pressing the Wilmot proviso.

[Robert J.] Walker it seems is getting very sick, and may be compelled to retire from the Treasury. In that event Benton might become Dictator of the Administration. Meanwhile however some circumstances have occurred which render it not very improbable that the policy will be adopted of attempting to conquer and hold all Mexico. Nothing probably but difficulties not now calculated on in the progress of our army will prevent the serious prosecution of this purpose. I was told the other day by a catholic of this place that a special messenger had just passed through here for Washington with despatches from Scott, and who stated while here to the Catholic bishop [John B. Purcell] that numerous overtures had been made to Scott by eminent Catholic clergy of Mexico in favour of the annexation of the whole country to this—on the ground that their property would be safe in that event instead of being exposed as now to ["the" *canceled*] native military exactions. And the messenger said that Scott was in favour of the proposition. It is not unlikely that Walker

379

also would be in favour of such a scheme, as he has always been for large acquisition. And I see that eastern democratic papers are taking similar grounds. If peace cannot now be made in accordance with Walker[']s views, and I see no probability of it, he will ["very probably" *canceled*] prefer to aim at the whole rather than to adopt thy counsel for a defensive line—and if Scott is really in favour of taking all, it is not probable that the Whigs can unite on the proposition of McLean. So that instead of having to discuss the controversy between the north and South, a subject ["of" *canceled*] sufficiently portentous of public calamity[,] we may be called on seriously to consider whether we shall not relinquish our very identity ["as a people" *interlined*], social, political, religious and geographical—for such I think would be the ["question" *canceled and* "result" *interlined*] if the conquest of Mexico were accomplished, or seriously under taken.

Meanwhile the present abundance of money here and its increasing scarcity ["of it" *canceled*] in England promises us a financial revulsion before long to demoralize and disorganize us still more. With great regard thy friend, Ellwood Fisher.

P.S. I have just seen a gentleman from the South, a very shrewd observer, and extensively acquainted there, thought [*sic*] not a supporter of thine—who says that with a reasonable prospect of success thee would get the votes of both Louisiana and Mississippi.

ALS in ScCleA; PEx in Boucher and Brooks, eds., *Correspondence*, pp. 377–378.

From [Brig. Gen.] N[ATHAN] TOWSON

Washington, May 27th [18]47

Dear Sir, I received two packages from you for Mr. H[enry A.] Wise. In the letter accompanying the first, you request it to be delivered as soon as he returns. The Secretary of the Navy [John Y. Mason] told me some time since that Mr. Wise would not return [from Brazil] before September. What shall be done with the packages?

Important military events have transpired since we last saw each other. These have not changed, but confirmed my opinion as to the course that should have been adopted to bring the war to a speedy and happy termination. It is now, I apprehend, too late. This nation is infatuated with victory and conquest, anxious to advance, but will not listen to withdrawal. The Mexicans are getting up gu[e]rilla

bands that will soon be beyond the control of that feeble government, and making a trade of war, will be able to continue it so long
as the produce of the country and the plunder of their enemy, can
subsist and pay them. Of all descriptions of force this is ["the" *canceled*] best calculated to develope military talent and to attract it.
Here then are the elements of a long war that, I believe, can *now*
only be terminated by annexing the whole country. Looking to this
as a probable event, the question of slavery must be settled; and perhaps the sooner the better; and, I think, I can see how it will be done.

The great mass of the people of the U. States are cultivators of
the soil, and when enlightened on political subjects in which they
have an interest will enforce that policy which best promotes the
interest of the country, despite political gamblers, demagouges and
fanaticks. The agitation and discussion of the question, under circumstances that must compel all to reflect seriously upon it, cannot
fail to enlighten the mass, and I feel confident that the northern as
["well as" *interlined*] the southern States will see that it is the interest
of the Union that slavery should be authorized within the ["latti-
tudes" *changed to* "latitudes"] where ["the" *canceled*] blacks alone
can cultivate the earth.

The great staples of cotton, rice and sugar are as necessary to the
non slaveholding States as to Europe: the white man cannot labor in
the open air where these are produced, the ["black" *canceled*] negro
can, but will not, unless compelled; hence slavery must be tolerated,
or the cultivation of those important staples within the U.S. abandoned. Who does not see that the alternative will be disasterous to
every section of this Union?

It is those staples that have made the U.S. the most flourishing
nation on earth and the greatest power on this continent. Abolish
slavery where it is necessary for their cultivation ["within the U.S."
interlined] and we transfer all the advantages we have derived from
them to Brasile. Capital and commerce will immediately follow and
Brasile will occupy the position, as to wealth and power that the U.S.
now do. I cannot think the people of the non slave holding States
when they see the inevitable consequences of abolition will permit
it. Slavery is gradually receding South, for the simple reason that
it is not profitable north of the cotton region and the time is not
distant when all States, where cotton is not a staple, will voluntarily
abolish it. There is one thing that the free States will insist upon in
settling the question and that is that the slave population of any new
States that may hereafter be created shall not be represented in the
federal government; but as the great increase of States will be south

of Mason's and Dixon's line, I do not see any serious objection to your granting it after the north understands that ["the" *interlined*] preservation of slavery for cultivating ["of" *canceled*] the staples named will be for the interest of the whole Union.

This view of the subject has relieved my mind of much anxiety in contemplating the consequences likely to grow out of the war with Mexico, which, I apprehend, will end in annexing the whole country. With great respect your Ob[edien]t Ser[van]t, N. Towson.

ALS in ScCleA; PEx in Boucher and Brooks, eds., *Correspondence*, pp. 379–380. NOTE: An AEU by Calhoun reads, "Gen[era]l Towson."

From J E F F [E R S O] N D A V I S

Brazos Sant Jago [Texas,] 28th May 1847
My dear Sir, Your esteemed favor of the 30th March after unusual delay has reached me, nothing could add to my willingness to serve the young gentleman [Samuel Warren White] who was the subject of your communication. His gallantry in battle and soldierly conduct on all occasions has attracted my notice and received my highest commendation. I had very little power to serve the deserving, my reccommendations have in no instance been noticed and the Regimental appointments within the power of a Colonel are limited to the non com[missioned] Reg[imen]t[a]l staff. Before the battle of Buena Vista, I appointed our your [*sic*] young friend Quarter Master Sergeant. On the day of the battle he shouldered his rifle and took his place in the ranks of his old company. His conduct as at Monterey was worthy of the highest praise, and had the better fortune to escape from wound. He has entirely recovered from the effects of the wound he received at Monterey and if there be any way in which I can promote his views be assured that it will always be with the greatest pleasure my exertions will be made in his behalf.

He is now with the rear detachment of the Reg[imen]t but will join us probably in the early days of June at New Orleans, at which place our Rgt. will be mustered out of service.

Please accept my best wishes and most cordial assurances of Regard. As ever y[ou]r friend, Jeffn. Davis.

ALS in ScCleA; PC in James T. McIntosh and others, eds., *The Papers of Jefferson Davis*, 3:180. NOTE: Davis was, of course, at this time Colonel of the 1st Mississippi Volunteers. He had been wounded at Buena Vista on 2/23; had on

5/17 declined an appointment as brigadier general on Constitutional grounds; and at the time of this letter was with his regiment on Brazos Island a few miles north of the mouth of the Rio Grande waiting to sail for home.

From DUFF GREEN

Washington, 28th May 1847

My Dear Sir, I have returned from New York where I have been for some weeks. I find that a controversy is springing up betwe[e]n the partisans of [Zachary] Taylor and [Winfield] Scott. The *Whig* Politicians are for Scott, and the mass in *both* parties inclined to go for Taylor, not because they are attached to Taylor but because they are opposed to Scott and because the democrats feel that they have no *party* man who can defeat Scott.

In this state of feeling there is a kind feeling growing up for you, and I have heard it frequently said that the democratic party could elect you but no one else as a democratic candidate, but, there is a common *sentiment*, (I use this word, as stronger than belief or opinion) that you are unmindful and regardless of your friends. It is charged that you voted for [confirmation of Marcus] Morton and others known to be hostile to you & who had proscribed your friends, *because they were your friends*, and hence there is not only lukewarmness, but a shrinking back—The patience and meekness! with which you and your friends in the south have received [Thomas H.] Benton[']s attacks deters many who would rally to your support in case of an active conflict.

I mention these *facts*, knowing that it is always unprofitable for an humble, friend to bring truth to the ears of great men, but I do it because I am your friend and I feel that it is necessary that you should act, and act immediately. The question[s] of the bank and the Tariff have passed away. The results of the last year, have given a new impulse and [*blank space*] force to the question of internal improvement. The convention of Memphis was the parent of the convention to be held at Chicago; great efforts are making to send a large and influential delegation to Chicago on the 5th July. That convention if rightly directed will do much to control the question. If wrongly directed it will give birth to much mischeif. I have often urged you to travel in the North and West, and I would now urge you to go ["to" *interlined*] the Chicago convention and thence visit New York and the East. I have urged Mr. [Isaac E.] Holmes who is now here to get up a meeting in Charleston and send you with a strong delegation.

The Civilians of both parties see that the election of Scott or Taylor will necessarily create a class of Military claimants for all the honors and emoluments of office for [the] next generation and tend to foster a mischievous military mania for a long time to come and the reaction has already commenced. The best, the safest and the only means of control[l]ing this military enthusiasm is by creating an excitement which by appealing more directly to the interest of the people [*sic*]. There is no other mode of touching the pocket nerve so efficiently as the system of Internal Improvement, and it is with you now to say what direction that question shall take. By going to Chicago you can do much to control it. If you do not go there is great cause to fear that it will go [w]rong very [w]rong. I have put parties in motion in New York and will induce the p[r]ess there and elsewhere to call upon the South to send Delegat[e]s to Chicago. Yours truly, Duff Green.

P.S. Upon the subject of a press I fear that my time will be so much occupied that I cannot become the Editor but as my arrangements are progressing favorably I will contribute if your friends determine to establish a paper. I send you an extract.

FC in NcU, Duff Green Papers, vol. 12, pp. 25–27 (published microfilm, roll 25, frames 58–59).

From JOSIAH C. NOTT

Mobile, 29th May [18]47

Dear Sir, I am very happy to make you a good report about William [Lowndes Calhoun]. One of my Children requiring some change of air I went down to the Sea Coast two or three days after writing you & took William with me & he has improved so much that I think there is every reason to believe his health will very soon be fully restored. He ["is" *canceled*] has in reality had no disease about him since the extraction of his teeth. His occasional fevers, Neuralgia & general nervous derangement seem to be all attributable to the neglected teeth, & the cause being removed I hope all will soon be right—in fact no one would take him for an invalid now.

He goes up to Marengo [County] this evening & I presume

Andrew [Pickens Calhoun] will forward him on without delay. Very respectfully & truly yours, Josiah C. Nott.

ALS in ScCleA.

To R[ICHARD] RUSH, [U.S. Minister to France, Paris]

Fort Hill, 29th May 1847

My dear Sir, I take pleasure in making you acquainted with Edward J. Pringle E[s]q[ui]r[e] of Charleston, who will deliver you this.

He belongs to one of our oldest and most respectable families, & possesses talents and acquirements calculated to sustain its high standing.

He has just finished his legal studies & been admitted to the bar, & visits Europe with the intention of spending a year or two there in travelling for improvement.

Your attention to him will place me under personal obligation. Yours truly, J.C. Calhoun.

ALS in NjP, Rush Family Papers (published microfilm of The Letters and Papers of Richard Rush, reel 20, item 11076).

To NANCY CALHOUN, [Cornwall, Conn.?]

Fort Hill, 30th May 1847

I received last winter through Mr. Haswell the genealogical information which you were so kind as to transmit to me and for which I am obliged to you. It was new to me and I read it with much interest. Although a Republican I am far from being indifferent to the character and reputation of those from whom I am descended. I am happy to find them so highly respectable through so many generations.

My family emigrated from Donegal, Ireland, in the year 1733 to Pennsylvania when my father was a child. His name was Patrick and his father James. The spelling of the name from Colquhoun to Calhoun was changed about the time of the emigration. My grandmother on my father's side was a Montgomery [Catherine Montgomery Calhoun] and related as I understand to Gen[era]l [Rich-

385

ard] Montgomery who fell in our revolutionary war. I have no doubt but that our families are related, and I mention these facts as they may contribute to trace the degree in which they are. There was another branch of the family in this State, the head of which was Hugh Calhoun. I recollect him when he was a very old man, in my boyhood. I have heard my father say they were related. I have delayed acknowledging your communication until this time in consequence of its detention by a relative who desired to read it and only returned it a few days since. (Signed) J.C. Calhoun.

Transcript owned by Lilian Gold; variant transcript owned by Mrs. J.F. Chisholm. NOTE: The grandfather to whom Calhoun referred was named Patrick Calhoun, although that ancestor has often been called James.

From DUFF GREEN

Washington, 31st May 1847

My dear Sir, I enclose you copies of letters to Mr. [Franklin] Ellmore [*sic*; Elmore] & Mr. [Richard K.] Cralle. You will understand why I write to them thus. If you act on the suggestions here given and proper measures be taken to sustain you all may yet go well. You can not but see that a few influential friends meeting you at Chicago will enable you to control the measures of that body and that by the tour I propose you can organise your friends in the northern states to sustain you. You will be assailed by [Thomas] Ritchie and a few dependant presses but you will have powerful allies to defend you, and his attack will in that do us great service because all that we want is to create an issue that will rise over the present imperfect political impressions. Let me hear from you. Your sincere friend, Duff Green.

[Enclosure]

D[uff] Green to "Col." F[ranklin] H. Elmore, Charleston

Washington, 29th May 1847

Dear Sir, I have been sometime in New York and have seen and conversed with many persons of intelligence and influence upon the present aspect of public affairs.

In Pennsylvania & New Jersey, both parties are nominating Gen[era]l [Zachary] Taylor, and in New York, [William H.] Seward and his ultra abolition wing of the Whigs are declaring themselves for him. The Albany Ev[ening] Journal is their organ. The regular organised Whig leaders are for [Winfield] Scott, or [Henry] Clay &

many persons in both parties are becoming alarmed at the progress of the military. They see that the Election of Scott or Taylor will bring forward persons claiming all the offices from Constable to President, because they have been to the "wars." A reaction has commenced and excitement will take another direction, at least great efforts will be made to control the military mania by a direct appeal to the "pocket nerve" of the people. The elements of counter-action are the "Wilmot Proviso" and "Internal Improvement."

I need not enlarge on the first, but the purpose of this letter is to make a few suggestions relative to the latter. You must be aware that the western members of Congress were much displeased by Mr. [James K.] Polk[']s vetoes of the Harbour & Internal Improvement bills and that they suggested a call of a convention to be held at Chicago Illinois on the 5th of July next. The northern and western States are sending full and able delegations, and my opinion is that the deliberations of that body will do much to control the future destiny of this country.

You cannot convince the farmer who resides on the [*one word canceled*] shores of the great lakes dividing us from Her Brittanic Majesty's Canadian possessions that it is constitutional to expend money on the shores of the Atlantic to protect and promote commerce between England & the United States and unconstitutional to expend money to protect and promote his commerce with the Colonies, or if you please with the mother Country—He does not admit the constitution makes such distinction between fresh and salt water.

If I am correct in this you must see that if the South oppose all appropriations for Harbors and Internal Improvements, the Great West will unite with the East, and carry the measures against the South. In that case Abolition and Internal Improvements go together & strengthen each other. On the other hand if the South unite with the West *now* and by entering into this convention moderate and regulate the System, they may command the West as allies and secure their aid in denouncing and suppressing abolition.

In a word, it is no longer a question as to power, for it is impossible to arrest the progress of "Internal Improvement." It may be modified, and restrained but cannot be defeated—by opposing the South will magnify the Evils of a corrupt system, by Cooperation, they may regulate, and secure a healthy and vigorous system. My opinion is now is your time for action, & I would act in this wise. Charleston should send a delegation of your ablest men and Mr. Calhoun of the number. You should leave home without parade or noise, and the first thing the public should know of your movements should be Mr. Calhoun's arrival at Knoxville on his way to Chicago by way of Nashville, St. Louis[,] Alton, & Springfield to Chicago. Thence he should go by Detroit across Michigan, and thence by way of the Madison[?] R. Road on through Indiana to Cincinnatti & then by Pittsburg[h] & Harrisburg to Phil[adelphi]a, Trenton, Newark[,] Patterson to New York. Then I would go by way of the Hudson to Albany & Saratoga, to Buffalo, thence to Montreal & thence through Vermont & New Hampshire to Boston & then return through R. Island to New Haven to Wash[in]gton.

Such a trip may bring forth great results. If undertaken for the purpose and he be accompanied by proper associates it will be a death blow to Abolition and do much very much to give a right direction to the Government for a long time to come.

Please to let me hear from you. Yours truly, D. Green.

[Enclosure]

D[uff] Green to R[ichard] K. Crallé, Lynchburg, Va.

Washington, 30th May 1847

Dear Sir, I have spent some weeks at the North and find that altho both parties are committing themselves by proceedings in primary assemblies for [Zachary] Taylor neither are much in earnest. What has been done is more the effect of disaffection towards the party organisation & party leaders than of a strong and fixed preference for Gen[era]l Taylor. The Democratic party feeling that they have no candidate are claiming Taylor as a good enough Democrat! more to annoy the whigs than to commit themselves.

In short, Both parties are precisely in that condition when the inward feeling is not indicated by the outward show, and which is best suited, to a new developement. The party leaders of both parties have their own preferenses [*sic*], and both see that the election of a mere military chieftain will give a popular sanction to military services which will create applicants for all the offices for years to come to their entire exclusion.

In this dilemma there is a strong desire, especially in the Democratic party to unite on some candidate who can be elected, and all see that the candidate to be selected must be carried forward by some question whose strength shall counteract the Military mania which constitutes Taylor[']s merit.

You must be aware that the western members were much dissatisfied at [James K.] Polk[']s vetoes of the Road & Harbour bills, and have called a convention to be held at Chicago on the 5th July. The Northern & Western [States] are sending full and able deligations, and I am disposed to think that the action of that body will do much to control the future destany of this country.

You cannot convince those who reside on the western lakes that it is constitutional to expend money on the harbours of the Atlantic and Unconstitutional to expend it on the Harbors of lakes. They do not believe that the Constitution has one power on salt and another on fresh water. They have taoted [*sic*] the benefits of *foreign* trade and if the South oppose ["these" *canceled*] appropriations, they will unite with the ["North &" *canceled*] East and obtain them. It is no longer a question of whether these appropriations are to be made. It is a question of whether the South by opposing them shall Compell the West to form an alliance offensive and defensive with the East. It is a question between the South and Abolition. If the West are ["desireous" *canceled and* "driven" *interlined*] to ally with the East then Internal Improvement & abolition act together and strengthen each other. If on the other hand the south will for once take council [*sic*] from the past and act with a little practical good sense you will send your ablest men as delegates to this convention. You will modify & regulate its proceedings. You will aid to build up a wholesome, well defined and vigorous system, instead of creating by your opposition a corrupt and dangerous politica[l] local party.

I beg you my dear Sir to think of this matter & if you agree with me write to Col. [Franklin H.] Elmore of Charleston & to Mr. Calhoun urging them to send an able delegation, and ["write" *interlined*] also to such other persons in the south as you can rely upon. If Mr. Calhoun goes he should be well sustained. All depends upon prompt and wise action.

Let me hear from you. Yours truly, D. Green.

ALS with the first En in ScCleA; FC's of the letter and two Ens in NcU, Duff Green Papers, vol. 12, pp. 27–32 (published microfilm, roll 25, frames 59–62).

From C.H. Sutton, [Clarkesville, Ga., *ca.* 5/31]. He requests that Calhoun remit $5 payment for a subscription to the Clarkesville *Aegis* from 8/1846 through 3/1847. The newspaper having changed ownership in 4/1847, it is desirable to collect all sums due. Calhoun's AEU indicates that he remitted the $5, requesting a receipt and that the paper be discontinued. ALS owned by Bruce W. Ball.

From Ashbel Green, "Sec[retar]y," Princeton, N.J., 5/——. Green invites Calhoun to attend a meeting of the American Whig Society on Commencement Day, 6/30, "being the day appointed for the Centennial Anniversary of the College of New Jersey." AEU's by Green read "Elected Hon[orar]y Member 1835" and "An answer is respectfully requested." An AEU by Calhoun reads "Invitation to attend the centen[n]ial Celebration of the Whig Society of Princeton." PDS in ScCleA.

To ——

Fort Hill, June 1847

Dear Sir, In answer to your note of the 8th May, which came in my absence from home, I have to state, that I wish you to retain the books, to which it refers, until my return to Washington next winter. With great respect I am & &, J.C. Calhoun.

ALS in ScU-SC, John C. Calhoun Papers.

From E. & J.W. Agnew, Due West Corner, Abbeville District, S.C., 6/5. Having "discontinued business at this place," this firm seeks payment of an appended "acc[oun]t made by your son [William Lowndes Calhoun] while at College." The account itemizes about 50 purchases made during 11/7/1845–3/24/1846 and totals $192.52. Four other unsettled accounts that were "handed to" them bring the total owed to $271.16. An AEU by Calhoun at the close of the bill reads, "See Elam Sharp[']s bill for Tayloring, $14." An AES by Calhoun reads, "William[']s bill at Due West. $271.18. 25th of March 1848. Remitted to E. & J.W. Agnew a check drawn by Corcoran & Riggs of Washington for $271.18 on the Bank of America New York, No. 1743. J.C. Calhoun. The check covers their Bill & the sums due to Mr. [David W.] Hawthorn, Mr. [William] Norton, Mr. [R.C.] Sharp & Mr. [Thomas] Robinson annexed to this." LS in ScU-SC, John C. Calhoun Papers.

From F[itz] W[illiam] Byrdsall

New York [City,] June 6th 1847

Dear Sir, I enclose you an Editorial article from the N.Y. Courier & Enquirer upon the subject of the modern British Crusade of Abolitionism, not because I have any imagining that it will give you a single new idea, but simply that ["as" *interlined*] a proper American feeling is beginning to spring up in this section of the Union, I like to send you an evidence of it.

Amongst the working masses here unconnected with membership in churches, there is but little sympathy for the modern crusade. Christian sects since the era of the Reformation, crusaded against each other untill the pharasees discovered that the contests were tending to the depreciation of the belligerents, hence we have the "Evangelical Union" movement, evidently growing out of the idea, "United we stand, divided we fall." But as mere priestianity must have always something to make a crusade against, the priests are busy with the subject of Southern slavery to the manifest neglect of the most sacred duties of Gospel christianity, that spiritual religion which is always degraded & defiled when intruded into the arena of political or municipal Institutions.

But I have a strong belief that the people will come to a right comprehension of the subject. Indeed we have enough and more than enough of domestic consumption for ten times the real philanthropy ["and" *canceled and* "or" *interlined*] Christian benevolence that exists in this part of the United States. I do wonder how any really good man can trouble himself about the evils of Southern Slavery when he can see around him the alms houses and prisons full of poverty and of crime ["mainly" *interlined*] resulting from poverty and destitution; when he can see our streets thronged with beautiful females driven to prostitution from want of employment. So true is the last sentence that Bishop [John J.] Hughes of the Catholic Church is now busily engaged as I am informed in what he states to be an object to which he is willing to devote his life, to establish an Institution to preserve destitute females from prostitution.

The crusade against slavery has scared the most of those who in 1837 were "Northern men with Southern principles" into being now Northern men with Abolition principles. This reminds me of a newspaper war lately between the N.Y. Globe and the Evening Post respecting Silas Wright and the Wilmot Proviso. The Globe assured its readers that Mr. W[right] was opposed to it. The Post stated that he was decidedly in favor of it. The former in reply had it from high authority that Mr. W[right] was not as represented by the Post, and the Post knew it from the highest authority that Mr. W[right] was in favor of the Proviso. Neither paper gave up—both were possitive.

Singularly enough to most men, it now appears that both papers were right & Wright—Here it is—He was *opposed* to the Wilmot

Proviso being brought forward in Congress—but being introduced he was *in favor* of its being sustained. A parallel case to that of *speaking against* the Tariff of '42 and *voting for* it. Such a man in the estimation of some, may be held as a *safe* and not a bold or rash political Leader. In my opinion the days of the political wisdom of Kinderhook are gone by any thing to the contrary notwithstanding.

I think the prospect is that the Democratic party will have a majority of States in the next House of Rep[resentatives] even though the Whigs might have a majority of members. If we have a majority of States I shall oppose a National nominating Convention because I would under present circumstances, prefer the Election going to the House.* But if the Whigs have a majority of States, it appears to me that we had better go for General [Zachary] Taylor. I am Dear Sir with the highest respect yours &c &c &c, F.W. Byrdsall.

* I would rather trust the Election of President to the House of Rep[resentatives] in 1848 than to the nomination of a National Convention or to the popular impulses that now prevail. The last Baltimore Convention had many members of Congress in it, and it is well known that the members of that convention came in for a large share of the Executive patronage directly ["for themselves" *interlined*] or indirectly for their friends. There has been much said about the corrupting tendencies of an Election going to the House, but if National Conventions contain many members of Congress and if Executive Patronage follows in favor of those most active in nominating the candidate for the Presidency, where lies the difference as respects these evil tendencies? After all it may be, that sometimes it may be best to have a National Convention—sometimes an Election by the House and sometimes a nomination & Election by the people independently of ["the" *canceled*] national Conventions—i.e. by the States separately.

ALS in ScCleA.

From H[ENRY] H. TOWNES and Others

Calhoun's Mills S.C., June 7th 1847

Dear Sir; At a late meeting of the regular & honorary members of the Abbeville Artillery Company, they resolved to celebrate the 4th of July by a public dinner to be given at Calhoun's Mills on Saturday the 3rd proximo. We were appointed a joint committee of arrangements & instructed to give you a cordial invitation to the dinner.

It gives the committee individually much pleasure to make known to you the wishes of the company, & we sincerely hope it may be convenient for you to accept our invitation.

It is well known to you the dinner will be given in the immediate vicinity of your birth place. Some of the members of the company have known you from your boyhood, many were once your constituents & others have grown to men[']s estate since you left the district. Old & young wish to see you, & to have an opportunity to manifest some of the gratitude which they feel for the great & brilliant services which you have rendered the whole country, & above all for your devotion & unwavering fidelity to the rights & interests & peculiar institutions of the south. Very Truly & Sincerely Your friends, H.H. Townes, H. Duracotte [*sic*; Herbert Darracott], W[illiam] T. Dren[n]an, W[illiam] Taggart, H[ugh] G. Middleton, B[enjamin] E. Gibert, J[ohn] S. Reid, W[illiam] C. Ware, E. Noble, W[illiam] H. Parker, D[ionicious] M. Rogers, W[illiam] H. McCaw.

LS in ScCleA. NOTE: The names signed to this letter were all written in the same hand. An AEU by Calhoun reads "Invitation to Barbacue in the Calhoun settlement."

From JAMES CARNAHAN, SAM[UE]L MILLER, M[ATTHEW] NEWKIRK, and JA[ME]S S. GREEN

Princeton, June 10 1847

Sir, The Trustees of the College of New Jersey, having resolved to celebrate the Hundredth anniversary of that Institution, on the 29th & 30th days of the present month, would most respectfully request you to honour us with your company on that occasion.

The Centenary Discourse, by the Reverend Dr. James W. Alexander, will be delivered on the 29th instant, at 4 o'clock P.M. & the Hundredth Commencement will be attended on the 30th. [President] James Carnahan, Saml. Miller, M. Newkirk, Jas. S. Green.

LS (in Miller's hand) in ScCleA. NOTE: An AEU in Calhoun's hand reads "Invitation to attend the 100th An[niversar]y of Princeton College."

To A[NNA] M[ARIA CALHOUN] CLEMSON, [Brussels]

Fort Hill, 10th June 1847

My dear Anna, If I have not written you more frequently, it is because [Martha] Cornelia [Calhoun] and your Mother [Floride Colhoun Calhoun] write you constantly, & that for the last several
packets, it has been necessary for me to write to Mr. [Thomas G.]
Clemson, in reply to his letters and on business. It happens, for the
first for a considerable period, that there was no subject, which required I should write to him, and that your letter to me, was the
only one received from Brussels ["by the packet before the last" *interlined*]. The last steamer which sailed took no letter from us to
either of you, as we were absent in Abbeville in attendance on Kate
Townes['s] Wedding. I think she has done well; but as Cornelia
sends a long letter to you, in company with this, I take it for granted,
she will be very full in her narrative about the wedding & all that
relates to our visit to Abbeville, so I shall pass ["it" *canceled and*
"them" *interlined*] over.

I am happy to hear, you are all so well, and that the children
[John Calhoun Clemson and Floride Elizabeth Clemson] are making
such progress; not in what is called learning only, but what is ["of"
canceled] vastly more important at their age; in good sense & habits.
I hear such favourable accounts of them, that I am extremely desireous of seeing them again, as well as yourself & Mr. Clemson; and
sincerely hope, the time is not distant, when he shall think it for his
interest to return to the U. States. If cotton should ever rise to 8 or
9 cents, steadily, as I hope it will, now that the immense stock, which
had accumulated will be reduced to nothing by the end of the year.
The present ["crop" *interlined*], thus far, is by no means promising.
It is generally very backward, small and not a good stand. Besides,
that planted on the Mississippi bottom has been in a great measure
ruined by the Fresh. I saw not more than two tolerable crops on
my visit to Abbeville, and neither of them much, if any more forward,
than mine. With their exception, mine is the best by far I have seen
this season. The weather has been unfavourable, and insects have
abounded. We have not had since the 1st Week in April a single
day, that could be called warm, and are yet sleeping under a blanket,
and 'till lately under two. We have rains now, but it is still too
["cold" *canceled and* "cool" *interlined*] to give any great impulse to
the growth of cotton.

I met in Abbeville [James H.] Hammond at [George] McDuffie's,

& spent a night with him there. He gives the same account of the crop, as low down as his residence [in Barnwell District], and I do not doubt, it is much the case over the whole cotton region. He speaks very favorably of his experiment in marling & ["the use of" *interlined*] plaster of Paris; & enthusiastickly of the results of his efforts in reclaiming the Swamp land on his tract. From what he states, they must be equal to the best lands in the Union, while the expense, is far less than it was supposed it would be at first. Should Mr. Clemson return, it would ["be" *interlined*] worth while to look at the lands adjacent to him. The ["situation" *interlined*] has great advantage in climate & position.

I am not at all surprised, that the state of things in Belgium & Europe, generally, should excite the feelings & sentiments you have so strongly expressed; and, yet, bad as is, the state of things there, it must, with the exception of this year of famine, be vastly superior to what it is on any other part of the old continent. We are for the present far better off; but it may be doubted whether we are not tre[a]ding in the path, that will lead in the end to a similar or worse state. Certain it is, that the preservation of our institutions & liberty occupy but little of the attention of our Governm[en]t, Federal, or State, or ["that of" *interlined*] the people. Wealth & power engross the attention of all. We act, as if good institutions & liberty belong to us of right, & that neither neglect nor folly can deprive us of their blessing. I almost stand alone, in taking a different view, and soon I fear shall be entirely out of fashion.

We have ["a" *interlined*] most uncertain future before us. It began with the Mexican war. It has reached a critical point. I see nothing that can prevent us from taking the city, but what is to be the end of that, no one can tell. The present indication is, that we shall go on & subject, & hold in subjection, if we can the whole country; & who can tell to what that may lead? The only thing that seems probable is, that the Army & Navy are to become the controlling influence in the country, at least for another Generation.

I am looking on calm[l]y, but with deep interest, with the fixed resolve to do *my duty*, regardless of all consequences. The next session must be one of the most important, that has yet taken place. It will lead to many developments, & give us a glimpse of what is to come. My position is one of entire independence of party, & of great command; but it will require much firmness, prudence & foresight to meet its duties, & responsibilities. I hope I will not prove unequal to the task it may impose.

We are all well, & all join their love to you & Mr. Clemson & the children. Kiss them for their Grandfather & tell them how glad I am to hear they are so well, & behave so well.

Willie [William Lowndes Calhoun] has not yet returned, but we expect him next week. Your affectionate father, J.C. Calhoun.

ALS in ScCleA; variant PC in Jameson, ed., *Correspondence*, pp. 729–731.

To Duff Green

Fort Hill, 10th June 1847

My dear Sir, I received your two last letters, the one written at New York and the other after your return from Washington, in which you urge me to attend the [Northwestern Harbor and River] Convention to be held in Chicago on the 4th July.

After giving the subject the most deliberat[e] consideration, I cannot concur with you in opinion as to the expediency or propriety of my attending.

My opinions in reference to internal improvement, both in reference to the [Great] Lakes and the Mississippi, have been fully expressed in my remarks at Memphis and the report on the proceedings of the Memphis convention. I have seen no reason since to change, or modify my opinion on any point. If I were to go to the Chicago convention, it would only be to repeat them, and to expose myself to the attack of those, who may be disposed to go farther than I can go, with my views of the Constitution, aided and backed by all, who may be politically opposed to me; while I would expose myself to the imputation of the very motive you assign for my going, and would lose more weight with the South, than I could possibly gain in the West.

Such are the objections, which occur to me, regarding the subject in the light you do, in reference to myself and my political advancement. But political advancement has ceased to be for a long time any object to me, personally. I would accept the Presidency on no condition but to reform the Government and carry out the principles and policy with which I am identified; and I have no idea that it will ever be tendered me for that purpose. All that remains for me is, to finish my course with consistency and propriety, and that I can only do, by an honest and manful discharge of my duty, while I remain in publick life. I am thankful to my friends for the interest they take in my elevation to power. One of the strong motives I would have to accept should it come to me, in a manner I could accept, would be to serve those, who have stood by me through so many trying scenes. Their attachment to me, has been the result of a community of sentiment in reference to the principles and policy of the Government; and, as such, I have ever regarded it, as alike honorable to them and me. Many of them, you among the others, overestimate the chance of my elevation, by not taking the proper view of the nature of the difficulty in my way. It may all be summed up in one, that I am not in favour of the spoil's policy. They who seek them are for the present masters of the country; and so long, as they continue to be so, ever will resist successfully my elevation. Nothing but a reaction, which shall rouse the country to a sense of its danger, which may not occur, until too late, can ever elevate me to power. That such should be the case, I have no reason to complain. I selected my course with a full knowledge, that such would be the case; and so far from regretting it, I would do it over again, if it was in my option to choose. I am not disappointed, and have none of the feelings belonging to the disappointed. But, I must say, that I am occasionally mortified, at seeing how little I am understood by some of my oldest and most faithful friends, and you among them, as I infer from some of your remarks in your letter from N. York. It is a grave charge to say, a man is unmindful of his friends. If I know myself, I would rather injure myself than a friend; and have ever been more unmindful of myself, than of them. It is I, who head without hesitation, or dread of consequences every assault on our common principles, and, if I have been careless of them, I have been much more so of myself. It would be a much truer estimate of my character to say, when duty is concerned, I am not only regardless of friendship or enmity but of myself. As to the case of [the confirmation of Marcus] Morton, my impression is, that I neither took part, nor voted. When I saw how badly the democratick party was acting on the Wilmot proviso, I saw little choice between one, or another of the party, or between a democrat, or a Whig. Besides [Lemuel] Williams [Jr.], whom he turned out [as Collector of Customs at Boston], gave a statement in his favour; and yet, it seems, this miserable affair, is the proof that I am not mindful of my friends. It had nothing to do with any friend. If he had been rejected it would have only made room for some other, equally objectionable.

PC in Jameson, ed., *Correspondence*, pp. 731–733.

From WALKER & BRADFORD

Hamburg [S.C.,] June 11th 1847

Sir, We regret to have occasion to address you concerning a draft drawn by us on you in favor [of] Mr. J[ohn] S. Lorton for amount of your a/c. The considerations for which the draft was given bear date from the fall of 1844, and the cash in every instance has long since been paid by us & our predecessor, for every article included in the a/c e[x]cept, the items of commission. Our means are limited, and consequently we are unable to give protracted indulgence. We dislike to press for payment; but we labor in this instance under the weight of necessity. If you can, with any degree of convenience, favor us with the money, it would be thankfully received; or even a part of it, in case you can not at this time spare the whole. Yours Respectfully, Walker & Bradford.

LS in NcD, John C. Calhoun Papers.

To T[HOMAS] G. CLEMSON, [Brussels]

Fort Hill, 15th June 1847

My dear Sir, The last steamer brought me yours of the 29th April, & I am happy to hear you are all so well.

Your desire to consolidate the debt due you by Andrew [Pickens Calhoun] & myself in the more permanent form of a bond is altogether reasonable; and I have since the receipt of yours, requested Mr. [John Ewing] Bonneau to furnish me with a statement of our account with you up to the 1st January last. The only point, I object to in your suggestions, is that of giving a mortgage. If there could be the least hazard it would be proper; but where that is not the case, it is undesirable on several accounts, which I need not suggest, as they will occur to you on reflection, except, that it always has the appearance, more or less, of some doubt as to solvency, where it takes place among those intimately acquainted, or supposed to be so, with each other['s] affairs. Among strangers, or those ["or those" *canceled*] who cannot be supposed to be so intimately acquainted, it is considered, but as a just precaution. I have never yet given one. There is not a dollar of incumberance on our estates, which ["is" *canceled and* "are" *interlined*] worth many times our indebtedness;

398

& which ["even" *canceled*] is productive & becoming yearly more so, for its amount, estimating cotton even as low as 6 or 7 cents the pound. Cuba is paid for, with the exception of the last annual instalment, & we now plant, including this & the Alabama place, not less this year, probably, than 1000 acres of cotton. Our crop of last year, cut short in Alabama as it was, fully ⅔, will, if we should sell at 11 cents, ["will" *canceled*] give a net profit, dededucting [*sic*] all out lays, of nearly $7,000. We are waiting for the next steamer to sell.

I have not since I wrote you last heard any thing from your place. It has been a delightful season for the last month for the crops, except rather cool for cotton. The rains have been very gentle & abundant, but there has ["not" *interlined*] been one day, that could be called hot, & not a night, that a blanket has not been agreeable, since the first week in April. My cotton, nevertheless, looks well. The stand passable, and the growth about equal to what is usual at this season. I hear the stand and appearance are bad in the Districts below this. The corn looks well; but the stand on the whole bad, in many places very much so, in consequence of worms & insects. The small ["crop" *canceled*] grain crop is fair. Our Alabama crop exceedingly good, never more so at the season.

Your views in reference to our political condition & affairs is so good, that I have little to add. I regard my position the best that it could be, in the present state of our affairs. By having done my duty fully in reference to the Mexican war, as it relates both to its origin & the mode it ought to have been conducted, I stand free of all responsibility, & independent of both parties, & their entanglement. It is difficult to say, which is most so in reference to the war; the administration & its party, as its authors, or the whigs for the folly & weakness of having voted for a war, which they had in discussion proved to be unconstitutional & unprovoked.

I regard every thing in reference to the war & its consequences as still uncertain. Whether victorious, or defeated our situation is bad. If the former, it would seem impossible almost to stop short of the Conquest of the country; and then comes the question, what shall we do with it? To annex it would be to overthrow ["the" *canceled and* "our" *interlined*] Govern[men]t &, to hold it as a Province, to corrupt & destroy it. The farther we advance, the more appearant the folly & wanton[n]ess ["of" *interlined*] the war; & the more fully will the wisdom & patriotism of my course be vindicated. Indeed, already have the assaults on me terminated, except from the Would be Lieut[enant] General [Thomas H. Benton]. But his ravings prove not only his wounded pride, & his spite, but that he regards my position as strong.

We are all well. Willie [William Lowndes Calhoun] is not yet returned from Alabama, but we expect him by every stage. James [Edward Calhoun] will be home the last of the month to spend vacation. Patrick [Calhoun] is in New York. He was well when last heard from a few days since. All join their love to you, Anna [Maria Calhoun Clemson] & the children [John Calhoun Clemson and Floride Elizabeth Clemson]. Your affectionate father, J.C. Calhoun.

ALS in ScCleA; PEx in Jameson, ed., *Correspondence*, pp. 733–734.

From JOSEPH GOODMAN

Columbus, Miss., June 15 1847

D[ear] Sir, I have assumed to myself the liberty of addressing ["mys" *canceled*] you to solicit your views ["on the" *canceled and* "and" *interlined*] opinion on the subject of the discharged volunteers Bounty in the present war. The object of this enquiry is predicated on the enclosed notice from the Pension Office (J[ames] L. Edwards to the Adj. Gen[era]l U.S. Army [Roger Jones]). I find a great many is discharged on a/c of sickness, and with a Broken Constitution. On that point I feel a deep Interest. Our only two sons went out as Volunteers in the lines of the 2 Miss. Reg[imen]t. The Eldest was discharged at Monterey on a/c of Rheumatism. Amediately on his return with others—this notice came out to our view. As there is different opinions entertained here what will be the rights after being discharg[e]d before their term of service expires—induced me to address you on the subject. Being Fountain Head, and one who[se] opinion I hold above all others—after I make myself known to you— I am flatter[e]d to believe you will notice me with a reply. My name I presume you have some recollection of in Newberry District. My Father['s] name was Joseph Goodman lived on Saluda [river]. I am the only child out 16 now living. My Wife is the daughter of Capt. Peter Ray who lived on the Public ["road" *interlined*] leading down near Santee canal. In your younger days he Capt. Ray kept a Public House where you have often Tar[r]ied[?] all night. Mrs. G[ood-man] was the Eldest of the children. She recollects you & Mrs.

[Floride Colhoun] C[alhoun] well. I mer[e]ly mak[e] this citation of myself & family to let you know who it is has assumed the liberty of writing you. For any further details of myself I refer you to James Gillam your relative who was my school mate. If I had a disposition ["to" *canceled*] for flattery, I should feel myself incapable to ["ap"(?) *canceled*] attempt ["it" *interlined*] to wards you when I say I have been a strong admire[r] of your course ever Since your Speech on the War of 1812, then in [18]16 on the Bank & Tariff and on to your speech in Charleston 1847. If you have ever changed I confess I have not had sense enough to detect the change and still I am an uncomprimising *Calhoun* Politician. *That is my Creed.* I am not the only one ["in" *interlined*] this Town who profess the same Creed. Doct[o]r Lipscombe [*sic*; David Lipscomb] my family Physician ["is" *interlined*] uncomprimising with many others who I could name. Our time for this life is rapidly passing away but still I have hopes I may yet live to see ["my" *interlined*] desire reallized that ["th" *canceled*] your Hon[ora]ble Self ["be" *interlined*] Elevated to the Chair of the Chief Magistrate of the U.S. You will excuse the honest expression of my feelings. I am Sir yours with respect, Joseph Goodman.

ALS with En in ScCleA. NOTE: In the enclosed newspaper clipping Edwards states that no "soldier discharged before the expiration of his term of enlistment, on his own application and for his special benefit, is entitled to land or scrip" under the act of 2/11/1847.

From F[RANCIS] LIEBER

Columbia S.C., 15th June 1847

Dear Sir, Do you not think with me that if any country or community ought to be represented at the ["proposed" *interlined*] international Free Trade Convention, to be held at Brussels in the month of September, it is ours and ourselves? I ["think" *canceled and* "believe" *interlined*] it would be much to be regretted if delegates from all nations of our civilized race were to meet there, except from our country. Yet I own, I do not know, precisely, how some united action ["could" *canceled and* "can" *interlined*] be had so as to settle upon a fit person who combines sound principles, detailed knowledge and long observation. It is for this purpose that I take the liberty of addressing you and inviting your attention to a brief article which will ["be" *canceled and* "appear" *interlined*] in the [South-]Carolinian of this town on Tuesday next, that is on the 22d of this month. You will be able to see whether anything can be done, and if so, what ["is to" *canceled and* "had best" *interlined*] be done, while I make bold to suppose that you agree with me on the advisableness and, even, importance of sending one or more delegates to that Convention. I dare say Mr. [Richard] Cobden will be there, and possibly wind up his civic triumphal tour through Europe, by presiding over an assembly which will show and "symbolize," in a very remarkable degree the trite truth "Magna est Veritas"—trite, because ["so" *interlined*] true and noble, and ["also" *interlined*] the rapidity with which Truth now-a-days ["may" *interlined and* "works" *changed to* "work"] out her victories. For, is it not but yester-day that Adam Smith ["ventured" *interlined*] to gainsay old habits of ["thoughts" *changed to* "thought"], supposed ["general" *interlined*] interest, deep-rooted national vanities, and the most plausable illusions? And is it not the most signal victory which Truth has ever obtained in practical and government matters, unaided by all ["official" *interlined*] power, by all éclat or romantic hue, *against* powerful and privileged classes and against the deluded masses ["themselves" *interlined*]? I think ["that" *interlined*], on ["this point," *interlined*] Adam Smith's influence may be compared to that of Hugo Grotius.

We had here last night a Concert for the relief of the famished in Germany. It was very crowded and I shall get as much money as I had any right to expect. I wish the Germans in your upper country would make collections, and send me the money. The suffering in Germany is immense, and has been fearfully increased by our lately passed Emigration Law. Thousands of poor wretches sold their all, realizing just money enough to travel to the sea port and to pay the passage according to the accustomed rate; but when they had arrived ["at the sea town" *interlined*] our law struck them ["like" *interlined*] a thunder clap. The passage money was too high; their scanty sums were soon consumed, and they are now dying, in huddled squallidness, of hunger and typhus, in spite of all the exertions that are making by the benevolent near them; for the potato has failed; grain is excessively high, and food of all sort scanty, dear or ["not failing"(?) *canceled*] altogether unattainable. If there be some cluster of Germans or German descendants near you I wish they could be informed of the dread extent of suffering in the old country. I am with the very highest regard Your most obed[ien]t, F. Lieber.

ALS in ScCleA.

To H[ENRY] H. TOWNES and Others,
[Abbeville District, S.C.]

Fort Hill, June 15, 1847

Gentlemen:—I am in the receipt of your note of the 7th instant, inviting me, in the name of the members of the Abbeville Artillery Company, to attend a dinner, to be given by them at Calhoun's Mills, on the 3d of next month, in celebration of the Anniversary of our Independence.

I regret exceedingly, that I am compelled, in consequence of my engagements, to decline an invitation, coming from those I have so many reasons to respect, and tendered in a manner so kind and acceptable.

No public man ever has had stronger reasons to be attached to his native District, and devoted to the State, of which he is a citizen, than I have; for no one, who has passed through so many and such trying scenes, and been on the stage of action for so long a period, has ever been more uniformly and warmly sustained by his early friends and supporters, and the citizens of his State at large, than I have been. I have cause to be proud of the support I have received. It was won, not by management, trick, party combination, or party reaching, patronage, flattery, subserviency, or deception, but by the observance of a simple rule; to endeavor on all occasions to understand what duty demanded, and when my mind was made up, to discharge my duty fearlessly—the only way, in my opinion, it can be won with honor, both to those, who bestow, and him, who receives.

In adopting this plain and simple rule for my guide, I had entire confidence in the intelligence and patriotism of those I represented. I believed, that nothing more was necessary to obtain and retain their support, but to deserve it. I have not been deceived. It has been my fortune to take a prominent part on many and trying occasions in the long period since I first entered public life. I have in many of them been obliged to act in advance of public opinion, and, in some, in opposition to it. I never hesitated to act in conformity to my rule. I never doubted but you would give me a fair and impartial hearing; and that you would sustain me, if I assigned satisfactory reasons for the course I pursued; and I have never been disappointed in a single instance.

For a support so honorable, I would be a monster not to be deeply grateful to the State, and especially to my native District, whose confidence and preference first brought me to the notice of the State and the Union, in whose service much the greater portion of my life has been spent. That the Union, with our institutions and liberty, may be long preserved; that our beloved State may ever be one of the brightest stars in this glorious constellation of States; and Abbeville, one of its most prosperous and flourishing Districts, will ever be my ardent prayer; and this I offer you as my sentiment on the occasion of your celebration. With great respect, I am, &c. &c., J.C. CALHOUN.

PC in the Abbeville, S.C., *Banner,* July 7, 1847, p. 2; PC in the Charleston, S.C., *Evening News,* July 12, 1847, p. 2; PC in the Charleston, S.C., *Mercury,* July 13, 1847, p. 2; PC in the Charleston, S.C., *Courier,* July 13, 1847, p. 2; PC in the Georgetown, S.C., *Winyah Observer,* July 14, 1847, p. 2; PC in the Greenville, S.C., *Mountaineer,* July 16, 1847, p. 1; PC in the New Orleans, La., *Daily Picayune,* July 20, 1847, p. 2; PC in the Edgefield, S.C., *Advertiser,* July 21, 1847, p. 3; PC in the Pendleton, S.C., *Messenger,* July 23, 1847, p. 1. NOTE: Because of a mutilation in the Abbeville *Banner* containing this letter, the first two paragraphs were transcribed from the Charleston *Mercury.* In addition to Townes, Committee members included H. Daracotte [*sic;* Herbert Darracott], W[illiam] T. Dren[n]an, W[illiam] Taggart, H[ugh] G. Middleton, B[enjamin] E. Gibert, J[ohn] S. Reid, W[illiam] C. Ware, E. Noble, W[illiam] H. Parker, D[ionicious] M. Rogers, and W[illiam] H. McCaw.

From H[ENRY] W. CONNER

Charleston, June 16, 1847

My Dear Sir, I am very happy to be able to say to you, that from recent communications had with prominent planters & others that there is a decided disposition in the State to contribute liberally to the establishment of a paper at Washington to vindicate their rights & interest. The feeling is deeper & stronger than I supposed until I was brought in contact with it. As evidence of what I say I may mention that Mr. Nat[haniel] Heyward authorises any am[oun]t to be subscribed for him that may be required.

R[obert] F.W. Al[l]ston puts down—$1000.

Joshua J. Ward—[$]1,000.

P[eter] W. Fraser $500—[William H.] Trapier $500.

Dr. [John D.] Magill—[$]200 &c &c &c.

Mr. R.F.W. Al[l]ston writes that their vicinity [Georgetown District] is good for $5000 & appears to take a deep interest in the matter.

From what I see I consider it no difficult matter to raise any reasonable amount of money for the papers contemplated—all that is wanting I believe for the purpose is active energy. We shall now proceed I hope with some spirit—in our duties here.

It must not be a "Carolina paper," however—other States must be merged in the enterprise. This you can arrange.

The property holders of this State will give their money cheerfully for a paper to be conducted with firmness & honesty of purpose—but seem to have a very natural repugnance to its getting into selfish hands.

I rec[eive]d a very kind letter from you some weeks since & have had the pleasure of seeing a late letter from you to Col. [Franklin H.] Elmore. Very Truly y[ou]rs &C, H.W. Conner.

ALS in ScCleA. NOTE: Among the Georgetown District contributors mentioned by Conner was William Heyward Trapier who had reportedly in 1845 taught the students of Oxford University how to make mint juleps.

From SAM[UE]L A. WALES

Eatonton Georgia, 17th June 1847

Dear Sir, At a recent meeting of the Whig party of this (Putnam) County, for the purpose of selecting Delegates to represent the County, in the approaching Convention to nominate a Candidate for Governor, the resolutions herein enclosed were passed with entire unanimity.

By another resolution of the meeting, it was made my duty, as its chairman, to transmit them to you.

In the hope that they will not be wholly unacceptable I perform the duty with pleasure.

The indications, are many that the subject of slavery, will shortly become the great party question. To the people of the Southern States, it will be of vital interest. It is to you Sir, that, that people look, as their leader, & champion, in the Contest, not doubting, that all which can be done in their behalf will be done. With great respect I am Y[ou]r Ob[edien]t Ser[van]t, Saml. A. Wales.

[Enclosed newspaper clipping:]

There is another subject upon which it becomes our duty to express our opinion; and it is that in reference to the institution of slavery. Mr. [James K.] Polk had scarcely entered upon the duties of his office, before the South were given distinctly to understand, by the appointment of conspicious abolitionists to office, that that clan of fanatics were to be respected. Several were appointed by him to high and lucrative offices. When Congress met, the rule prohibiting the reception of abolition petitions, and which had stood unchanged amidst all the changes of party, was promptly repealed—thus the feelings of the whole South were disregarded, and those of the abolitionists regarded.

A proposition was then adopted by the House of Representatives, declaring that no territory to be acquired from Mexico should admit of slave labor; and when a Southern Senator submitted resolutions declaratory of our rights on this subject, his act was denounced by a Senator from a slaveholding State, and a member of the dominant party, as a "fire brand." After all these demonstrations, Southern Democrats were found voting for the establishment of the territorial government of Oregon, prohibiting the existence of slavery there. All these facts show us conclusively, that such is the madness of party faction, that to attain its triumphs, the institution of slavery is ready to be sacrificed. It is time for the South to take care of herself.

Resolved, therefore, That as the North has demanded the exclusion of slave-labor from any territory to be acquired from Mexico, we demand that such territory as may be acquired shall be appropriated to the use of slave labor.

Resolved, We cordially approve the resolutions of the Hon. John C. Calhoun on this subject, in the United States Senate, and we hereby tender to him the homage of our gratitude for his patriotic stand in behalf of our rights; and we can but express our deep regret, that the malevolence of party faction, and the blindness of political ambition, should have so infatuated any portion of the people of the slave-holding States, as to lead them to weaken the influence or destroy the standing of one so highly patriotic and talented, and whose whole energies are given to the support and defence of *our* institutions. We can but admire his lofty patriotism, which prompts him to rise superior to party shackles, and to advocate the true interests of the country, even at the hazard of denunciation from mere party followers.

The Hon. James A. Meriwether then submitted the following resolution, which was concurred in by acclamation, to wit:

Resolved, That so much of the foregoing resolutions as allude to the course of the Hon. J.C. Calhoun upon the subject of slavery, be transmitted to him by the Chairman of this meeting.

During the progress of which, his Honor, Judge Meriwether, made a few very pertinent remarks in defence of Southern policy.

ALS with En in ScCleA; PC with En in Boucher and Brooks, eds., *Correspondence*, pp. 382–383. NOTE: An AEU by Calhoun reads, "Mr. Wales covering the Eatonton Resolutions in reference to myself."

From JOHN C. MORRILL

Memphis, Tenn., June 18, 1847

Sir: You will be surprised, perhaps, at receiving a letter from one who is entirely a stranger, and may consider such a letter a liberty. My motives for writing it, however, are those of regard to yourself as a public man only. I have no personal interest to attain by it.

I am the editor of the *"Memphis Evening Monitor,"* and have taken the liberty of enclosing to your address several of its recent numbers, and shall give a similar direction to several more. My object in this is not to solicit your patronage, but to inform you of the sentiments of the paper. My reason for addressing you this letter are some circumstances touching your intercourse with a certain gentleman of this city, which have come to my knowledge, and which from his former brief connexion with the *"Monitor,"* I feel it proper I should apprise you of; and my admiration of your public course generally, induces me to give you a frank statement as to the state of public sentiment here, with regard to you, that you may not be *imposed upon*.

Col. [John W.A.] Pettit, now of this city, the gentleman who acted as Chairman of the Reception Committee on the occasion of your visit to this city, in attendance on the Internal Improvement Convention—a native of Georgia—whom you may recollect, and who is a sincere friend of yours, has just authorised me to use his name in referring to this subject. Col. P[ettit] has been shown a letter from you (which I also have seen,) to a gentleman of this city. From the terms of that letter, Col. P[ettit], and myself infer that it is in reply to one, which professes great personal good will to yourself and further gives the assurance that the public sentiment of this community is much in your favor. As to the first—I am authorised by Col. P[ettit], to say to you that your correspondent is in the habit of speaking of you publicly and without reserve, in terms of the most unqualified reprobation. As to the second—I feel under the circumstances, I ought to apprise you that the sentiments of the politicians of this community is unfavorable to you at this time. Public sentiment has been deeply tinctured by the bitter proceedings adopted against you of late, at head quarters. I think it is becoming mollified and hope that a returning sense of justice will ere long give it a most favorable cast. But in order to facilitate this result I feel that some caution is to be adopted. I have determined in my own mind that the most feasible mode of effecting it is first to write down your main reviler—Tho[ma]s H. Benton—and at the same time to hold Mr. [Thomas] Ritchie in check by shewing the loseing effect of his unjust attack upon you. With this view were penned the articles on the "Virginia Elections," and those, in notice of Mr. Benton. I am the editor of the *"Monitor,"* and being responsible for all that appears in it—but, the fact, that this suspicious correspondent of yours, was some time since connected somewhat with me, makes it proper that I should say to you that no such connection now exists. I have the regular assistance of Ja[me]s B. Thornton, Esq., lately of Virginia, who has had a slight personal acquaintance with you. Mr. Thornton represented several years since the Caroline Senatorial District, in the Virginia Legislature—is an intimate acquaintance of [Robert M.T.] Hunter, [James A.] Seddon, Bayley [*sic*; Thomas H. Bayly] and others, members of Congress from that State; and also of the Hon. Jno. Y. Mason, and by consulting either of these gentlemen you may obtain a full knowledge of him. He is the *only* individual now connected with me in conducting ["the" *canceled*] my paper and gives the chief direction to the editorial department. His political sentiments are well known, and from the gentlemen above named, especially Messrs. Seddon and Hunter, you will learn that, as regards yourself, they have been uniform.

If I err in writing you this letter, it springs from no design to do injustice to any one—but from the just motive of placing you on your guard in reference to matters which it is not reasonable to suppose you can learn in any other mode. I would further remark, in allusion to Mr. Thornton that he is a Lawyer, recently located with us, and as some evidence of his respectability in his profession enclose you the publisher's circular of a work he has lately published. Very Respectfully, &c, John C. Morrill.

ALS in ScCleA. NOTE: An AEU by Calhoun reads "Mr. Morell[,] Editor of the Monitor."

From J[ohn] W. A. Pettit

Memphis, June 18, 1847

Dear Sir, I take the liberty to send you this letter and may perhaps others, and will neither ask, expect, or desire any reply now or here-after. The only personal acquaintance you ever had with me was during your visit to the convention here when I met you as a committeeman and introduced you to the Mayor at the Gayoso Hotel. But I had some years ago a little correspondence with you while I served in Georgia my native State—in one instance to enquire at the request of party friends as to any interfereance of yours with the election of [Wilson] Lumpkin & [Joel] Crawford which you answered satisfactorily, the other to enquire if Hon. William Smith spoken of in the life & letters of [Thomas] Jefferson was Judge Smith afterwards of Huntsville Ala.[,] which you also answered & both of which letters I still keep. The only other times you have ever heard of me was through Gen[era]l [Daniel] Newnan & T[homas] F. Foster Esq. [former Representatives] of Georgia who informed you of my being the author of certain nullification articles in a country newspaper in Georgia—of which you approved.

One object of this letter is to say as a friend which I profess to be, that it would be well for you to be a little cautious in writing to a certain man here who is no friend of yours. I perceive by a reply you made him lately that you were guarded. The Editor of the "Monitor" will write you on this point. This paper published here will come out in the right *time* & *way* for you. Mr. J[ames] B. Thornton late of Virginia, and a friend & acquaintance of [James A.] Seddon[']s is known to a few of us to be now the real editor & I have a constant confidential communication. I know the views you profess in relation to the Presidency—so far as your being a candidate is concerned—& I was in hopes that a fair & unobstructed way was about to be opened to you & the South; opened, I say, by the northern men through the Wilmot Proviso & other means whether we were ready for it or not.

But this hope we fear is for the present blasted by the determination of the South to run Gen[era]l [Zachary] Taylor for President. I have some how or other felt a desire to mention this candidacy of Gen[era]l Taylor to you & to suggest that notwithstanding his being a military man, raised in the army, it may still be a fortunate thing for the country that he is or will be a candidate *as he can be elected* over Mr. [Thomas H.] Benton[']s non-slaveholding man (whoever he may be) and any of the rest of our statesmen, yourself among the rest might fail in the contest.

I incline to think that Taylor will do—and I am told by the volunteers who have returned here that he is regarded in the army by the politicians there, as being opposed to the U.S. Bank & in favour of the present tariff.

I am fully persuaded that there will be a northern & Southern candidate for President. Gen[era]l Taylor will run I have no doubt & the next Term the northern & Southern lines will be still more distinctly drawn & then some other Southern man who may not be doubted on the slavery question will be still more loudly called for. Would it not be wise to let this Taylor feeling go ahead & even to encourage it if you know enough about him to depend on his political views.

Something must be done to head Mr. Benton—he is regarded here today by Democrats as a dangerous & bad man. His letter which you have doubtless seen, is a disgrace to him. I allude to the letter he wrote to decline a nomination for President in which he goes for a candidate from the non-slaveholding States. It is believed by a great many that his personal feeling against you dictated that letter. And that letter & that opinion has greatly exalted you in this section of the country and will have the same effect all over the South. He is a great rascal and must be stopped some how from succeeding with his contemplated alliance with the north.

Just think of the wickedness of starting a candidate at the north expressly on the ground of his antislavery feelings or views—and of the vile hypocrysy & deceit of pretending in that letter as he does that the north *is defending itself* against the South.

That letter contains more guile than did the Serpent who approached our first parents in the garden. We must take a stand against it. I must stop at present. With high respect, J.W.A. Pettit.

ALS in ScCleA; PEx in Boucher and Brooks, eds., *Correspondence*, pp. 383–384. Note: Benton's letter referred to was written to a committee of Howard County, Missouri, Democrats who had nominated him for President. He declined on the grounds that he thought that Northern candidates had been too much ignored by the party and that a Northern nominee would be safer for the Democratic party and the Union. (See the Washington, D.C., *Daily National Intelligencer*, June 9, 1847, p. 3.) Pettit (*ca.* 1800–1850) was a native of Ga. He had served in both the Ga. and Ala. legislatures and been an unsuccessful Whig candidate for U.S. Representative in the latter State. He had removed his law practice to Memphis in 1843.

From J. M[ILTON] CLAPP

Charleston, June 21, 1847

Dear Sir, I have very much desired to secure for the Southern [Quarterly] Review a series of articles from men who should understand what they say, on the industrial resources—the power of self preservation and of growth, of our Southern country. In the list of subjects, none seems to me more important than Rail-roads—and what is especially necessary on this, is that a broad foundation should be laid in the outset—that the discussion should be of matters of universal application and interest. Such an article would serve as a starting point and foundation, for discussions of local character. I conversed with Col. [Franklin H.] Elmore—told him what I wanted, and asked him to name the right man. He thought you would be willing to undertake—judging from the great interest you have ever taken in the subject. I had not dared to hope it, till after this conversation. I now propose it to you however—feeling too, that unless you will undertake it, the article such as it ought to be, will not be written. I send you the Edinburgh Review for October which contains at page 248, the most compendious view of the Railway system of Europe that has yet appeared. The information there will cover nearly the whole subject—except on such points as are peculiar to the South. I cannot well explain how anxious I feel that you should prepare the article, and trusting to receive a favorable answer, I beg you to let me know your decision as soon as convenient.

Chancellor [William] Harper has agreed to write an article on election of Presidential Electors. I have no sympathy with the opinions expressed in the April number [of the Southern Quarterly Review]—but the article was written in consequence of conversations between the author [Benjamin F. Perry] and the late Editor [Daniel K. Whitaker], and was received before I came into office. I had scarcely a right to interpose—but I think the question a great one and the proposed change full of evil. I am therefore greatly rejoiced that so able, calm and good-tempered a reasoner as Judge Harper is willing to undertake the vindication of what I think the right side. With Great Respect Your Ob[edien]t Ser[van]t, J.M. Clapp.

ALS in ScCleA.

From R[OBERT] B[ARNWELL] RHETT

[Washington] June 21[s]t 1847

My Dear Sir, I have very little communication here with the Cabinet Ministers: but I have found by relatives, and conferences with the President [James K. Polk] himself, and without giving you authority, I will tell you what I suppose to be the present probability as to future events.

In the first place, they are still full of the idea of conquering a peace: That will not be dispelled, until the City of Mexico is taken, and no peace preceeds or follows its capture. Should however, the administration be disappointed, in conquering a peace with the means at their command, I do not think they will come to Congress, to ask another loan. They will adopt a policy, consistent with the ordinary means of the Government, and that policy must be, the one you suggested and advised at the last Congress: It will be a bitter pill to many of them, but it will be swallowed rather than meet worse consequences. Altho' as you suggest there is a large Party growing up in the United States, who are for taking the whole of Mexico, the President I do not think will support it. Old [Thomas] Ritchie would if for no other reason, because you are opposed to it. [Thomas H.] Benton and Silas Wright altho now not prepared for it, might rally on this ground, believing it, a popular one; and as a good set-off to the Wilmot Proviso blunder. [Secretary of the Treasury Robert J.] Walker[,] [Secretary of the Navy John Y.] Mason & [Attorney General Nathan] Clifford in the Cabinet, will be opposed to it. Cave Johnson [Postmaster General] will do as Polk says; and he will not I am satisfied go for any such policy. I think then, matters will stand thus. If we get a peace, then the Wilmot Proviso must come up in the Senate, and the treaty be rejected, unless the South is false to itself. ["If we s" *canceled*.] This will break up the Democratic Party, and disgrace the administration. If on the contrary, no peace is obtained—then, the administration is compelled to adopt your policy—worse to them, so far as their desires are concerned, than such a disgrace. In either event, the war-makers have little to gain, by the progress of things.

I enclose you a letter I have rec[eive]d, from Lewis [*sic*] McLane, to show you his opinion as to our supporting [Zachary] Taylor. As soon as I hear from Gen[era]l [Jefferson] Davis I will communicate with you, but Gov[erno]r [Albert G.] Brown from Mississippi told me a week or so ago, that Gen[era]l Davis said that Taylor is as sound on the Tariff Question as you are. He is also said to be opposed to a U.S. Bank. We may be driven to support Taylor: but I fear the Whigs will render it impossible by nominating him, as their candidate, by a National Convention. Thinking they can elect Taylor any-how, they will insist on making the election a Whig affair. [Winfield] Scott is in furious Dudgeon, at [Nicholas P.] Trist[']s mission, whilst the administration, hate both him & Taylor. It is a hard case, that after all, as the consummation of their policy, they may be compelled to make these men or to make you; perhaps both. Some of them may grow grey or crazy, under such intolerable retributions.

You seem to suppose, that ["in declin(?)" *canceled and* "I am not" *interlined*] to be a member of the ensuing Congress. I have not *"resigned"* as you say: but only decline a reelection in 1848. By this time I suppose, the present troubled aspect of public affairs will be settled—either for our relief, or permanent endurance. Believe me Yours very sincerely, R.B. Rhett.

[Enclosure]
Louis McLane to R[obert] B[arnwell] Rhett

Baltimore, June 19, 1847

My dear Sir, I have to make you my thanks for your letter and copy of the Review which I duly received, but which from a pressure of engagements I have not sooner been able to attend to. To one of your experience and acknowledged capacity it would be a poor compliment to pronounce the "article," to which you allude, both able and instructive; It is more, however; it is, in some respects and in some of its views, original, and in all, as I think, presents just & sound views of the constitution. The compromises of the constitution are all that upon the ground of right could be insisted upon, and no form of legislation or compact whatever can in my opinion diminish the right of a State of any privilege whatever authorized by the constitution. No one supposed the Missouri compromise could be obligatory beyond the territorial condition, and that arrangement appeared to be the result of an anxious desire on all hands to compose an existing strife, and to reconcile opinions in other sections to the institutions of the South & South West.

I am not among those who dread the growing popularity of Old Rough & Ready [Zachary Taylor]. He has qualities which would reconcile me to a preference which in some aspects might not be considered altogether salutary. But I should see almost insuperable objections to cooperate in his elevation if he is to bear the flag of the Whig Party, as a Whig leader & nothing else: and I think you men of the South ought to be careful how you rashly run away from yourselves. You have done that before, as I think I hinted on a former occasion.

Why don't you run up to Baltimore occasionally and see me, and speculate more freely than we can do in a letter, upon the future?

Believe me, My dear sir with the utmost respect sincerely yours, Louis McLane.

ALS with En in ScCleA; PC in Jameson, ed., *Correspondence*, pp. 1119–1121.

From HILLIARD M. JUDGE

Eutaw, Greene C[oun]ty, Ala., 23rd June 1847
Dear Sir, I have long intended writing to you, for the purpose of ascertaining the course, you desire your friends to take, in the contests now agitating the Country. And in the outset I desire to say, that I do not write for the purpose of drawing you out on delicate questions, upon which you may choose to be silent; and that your answer, whatever it may be, will be understood and appreciated by me.

Your sentiments on the Mexican war, and the questions growing out of it, are well known throughout the whole Country, and are also well known, to be at variance with those of the Administration, and its supporters. Yet, notwithstanding the publicity of your opinions, your friends from prudential considerations, are co-operating with a party, that repudiates those opinions, and are heaping every sort of calumny upon their author, thus lending their influence to your overthrow.

I have had my feelings of indignation excited, by hearing resolutions proposed, asserting the justice and unavoidable necessity of the present war with Mexico, and denouncing those who entertain a contrary opinion, as traitors to their Country. Yet, those very resolutions of implied censure, are voted for by your friends, or are silently acquiesced in, lest opposition should hazard the integrity of the democratic party. I do not profess to understand this calculating and timid policy, yet I am told by your oldest friends, that to make an issue with them, would not meet your approval. Senator [Thomas H.] Benton, is assailing you, with the most vindictive bitterness, whenever an opportunity to do so presents itself, and in my opinion, with the full knowledge and consent of the administration. He has recently declared himself in favor of a northern Candidate for the presidency, tainted, as we know all their leading men to be, with opposition to the further extension of slavery.

It seems to me, the time has now arrived, when a definite course of action should be taken by your friends. Your anticipations of the prolongation of the war, and the consequent expenditure of life and treasure are about to be realised, by the adoption of the Guerilla system of warfare by the Mexicans. But even if your predictions should fail, and peace be concluded, a more momentous question arises.

Territory must necessarily be taken in payment of the expenses incur'd during the war. Then, and in that event, the eyes of the whole South will be turned to you for Council and advice. The far-seeing sagacity, you have ever manifested, in all the high posts you have occupied for the last thirty years, and the vigilance in seeing and warding off danger, point you out, as the man among men, for the crisis.

The free States will insist on the Wilmot proviso, in any treaties that may be made for the Cession of territory. This will necessarily unite the whole South in determined opposition. Already have the whigs of the South, in anticipation of the approaching storm, commenced using with tremendous effect, your two speeches in reply to [Hopkins L.] Turney and Benton, together with your Senate resolutions, and Charleston speech. Many of their leading men, endorse your opinions out and out, saying, "that the old party issues are all dead"—and "that they are now in favor of a revenue tarif[f]." That these opinions are daily increasing among the people, & I have not a doubt will soon generally prevail among them. The only question left, is that growing out of the acquisition of territory. I desire to ["through" *changed to* "throw"] out a suggestion, which the press accuse you of entertaining, and that is, whether it is not the policy of the South, to support Gen[era]l [Zachary] Taylor for the presidency? He is a large slave holder; coincides with you on the proper mode of conducting the Mexican war; and is said to be in favor of free trade. In a recent letter to a friend, he says, he is in favor of a strict construction of the Constitution, around which clusters all of your political opinions. My judgement approves of him, because I think he will have the power, through his popularity, to crush the growing spirit of fanaticism, and will organise a new party upon purer principles, than those that now prevail.

The abominable intrigue on foot, to place a Northern man in the presidential chair, must be crushed, and the sooner we commence organised opposition, the greater will be our chance of success. A word from you will set the ball in motion. And should Gen[era]l Taylor be elected, I sincerely believe, at the expiration of his term your principles, will be so completely in the ascendant, that notwithstanding my knowledge of your indifference to office, you will be called upon by the people with unexampled unanimity, to fill that high and responsible station. Believe me now, as I have ever been, Your sincere friend, Hilliard M. Judge.

ALS in ScCleA.

To James Carnahan, Sam[ue]l Miller, M[atthew] Newkirk, and Ja[me]s S. Green, [Princeton, N.J.]

Fort Hill, 24th June 1847

Gentlemen, Owing to some delay in receiving your note of the 10th Inst., it did not reach me in time to attend the celebration of the Hundredth Anniversary of the College of New Jersey agreeably to the request of the Trustees, had my engagements permitted.

For this mark of respect, I will thank you to present to the Trustees my grateful acknowledgement, with the assurance, that I take a deep interest in the success of the Venerable Institution, of which they have the charge. The Whole Union and, especially the South, is greatly indebted to it, for the aid it has given the great cause of education, and the services, which her Alumni ["have rendered" *interlined*] in building up our free Institutions & establishing the liberty of the Country. With great respect I am & &, J.C. Calhoun.

ALS in NjP, General Manuscripts.

From Charles G. Came

Yale College, June 25, 1847

Dear Sir, I do not know how I could overcome that awe which, I frankly avow, I feel at the idea of addressing you, did I not hope that my subject would momentarily interest you and dispose you to lend an indulgent ear to my request. To speak at once and openly— There has for a long time been a dispute here as to which of the rival Literary Societies you consider yourself as having belonged.

So zealous and fruitless has been the discussion that, now, when at the annual "Statement of facts" your name is mentioned, while the larger portion give all attention as if expecting some decisive information, the remainder raise a jeering shout at what they call "the standing joke." Conversations reported to have been held with you have been instanced, letters from different individuals have been produced, and the logic of many college generations has taken the matter in hand, and yet it affords the fiercest debate and your name is on both catalogues. Often have I asked myself the question—cannot this difficulty be settled? Hence have I written you.

I am a Linonian; but most willingly would I hear from you directly that you consider yourself a graduated member of the Brothers in Unity, for then the dispute would be at an end. But we have on *our* records what is said to be your autograph, and no consideration, except the discovery that we are in the wrong, shall induce us to take your name from our Catalogue. Will you not, then, Sir, by a word or two, dispense with all this bickering and strife and promote peace in our little community? If you consider this matter unworthy your attention, I beg of you to cast back, if you can, a glance over long years of Senatorial cares and duties to the period of your college hours, and you may, then, perhaps, *feel* its importance. Do not meet our urgent representations with *"what's in a name,"* for be assured, it is the *"magic of a name"* which compels us to address you. Hoping that you will condescend to indulge me with a reply, I remain Yours, &C, Charles G. Came.

ALS in ScCleA. NOTE: An AEU by Calhoun reads "Mr. Came of the Linonian Society of Yale College."

TO JESSE K. STONE, JAMES GAULT, and WILLIAM COX, [Greenville District, S.C.]

FORT HILL, June 25, 1847

Gentlemen: It would afford me a great deal of pleasure to accept the invitation, which you have so kindly tendered, in the name of the Lafayette Troop, to attend their celebration of the Anniversary of our Independence on the 3d of July next, but my engagements will prevent me.

I heartily approve of the celebration of the day, from which we date our Independence and liberty, and am pleased to see how well

417

it is kept up in our State. When it ceases to be celebrated, the spirit which led to the Declaration of Independence will have expired.

I avail myself of the occasion to offer the following sentiment:

The Lafayette Troop—The zeal with which they are preparing to celebrate the approaching Anniversary of Independence, shows that the ardent and indomitable spirit of liberty, which impelled our patriotic ancestors to declare it, still burns in their bosom. With great respect, I am, &c., J.C. CALHOUN.

PC in the Greenville, S.C., *Mountaineer*, July 16, 1847, p. 2. NOTE: The Lafayette Troop of Cavalry met at Cox's Old Field to commemorate Independence Day and to honor Robert A. Joyce and Henry Cook, killed in the Mexican War. Calhoun received a toast: "Carolina's noble and talented son. A just appreciation of his patriotic devotion to the welfare of the nation, will place him in the next Presidential chair."

From N[ATHANIEL] P. TALLMADGE, [former Senator from N.Y.], "Private"

Milwaukie [Wisc. Territory], June 26th 1847

My dear Sir, I have understood from different sources, that you are in favor of Gen[era]l [Zachary] Taylor for President in 1848. After your patriotic course on the Oregon question, and in relation to our Mexican affairs, I was in hopes that your name might be successfully brought forward for that high station. I assure you it would have given me great pleasure to give you my support. But, I have for a long time felt that Gen[era]l Taylor would be likely to command the popular vote, and from the high qualities he has exhibited, I am free to say I deem him a suitable candidate for the place, and believe he would give us an Administration which would redound to the honor of the country. Being at this place on business, I suggested to some of Gen[era]l Taylor's friends the propriety of making a public demonstration on that subject. A meeting was called, and I agreed to address it. I send you the proceedings with my remarks on the occasion. The People are right. The Politicians dare not oppose, but are not yet prepared to fall in, until they get farther light from high sources. Some wish farther information about Gen[era]l Taylor's principles—whether they are the same, as [John] Randolph said of [Thomas] Ritchie's, *"five loaves and two fishes."* I go for Gen[era]l Taylor, that the country may be freed from such principles, and of a party that is only "held together by the cohesive power of public plunder." I am tired and disgusted with this mere *spoils* system, and I think the opportunity is now presented of reforming it. Wisconsin will adopt a constitution, and come into the Union in time to give a Presidential vote—and you may rely upon it, that her four votes can be given for Gen[era]l Taylor. I have information from many old friends in New York from which I believe, with proper attention, the vote of the Empire State can be given him. I have no doubt of his success, if properly attended to throughout the Union. But, it requires the co-operation of those who think alike on this subject, and the information and suggestions they may be able to give each other. I have written you thus frankly my views, and should be glad to hear yours in return. Please address me on the receipt of this, at *Fond du Lac, Wisconsin Territory*. Very truly yours, N.P. Tallmadge.

ALS in ScCleA; PEx in Boucher and Brooks, eds., *Correspondence*, pp. 384–385. NOTE: Tallmadge had been Senator from N.Y. during 1833–1844 and governor of Wisc. Territory 1844–1845.

From ANNA [MARIA CALHOUN] CLEMSON

Brussels, June 27th 1847

My dear father, You see by the date of this, that we are quietly in Brussels, & probably, the children & myself will not quit it this summer. Mr. [Thomas G.] Clemson has just returned from a visit of a week to Paris, but it costs more than we have to spare, to move the family. This is a little tiresome to one who loves the country as I do, but there are inconveniences in every position, & as long as we are all well & happy in our home, it is after all but a trifling sacrifice. What I regret most is, that we have no garden, & the country just around Brussels is entirely without trees so that the children are much exposed to the sun, (when there is any,) before they reach a shade. Fortunately, however, the sun of Brussels is never the sun of Carolina, & this summer we have none at all. There have not been two really warm days, & the greater part of the time it is dis-agreeably cold, so that what I have often said is proved to be truer every day, that there is no season certain in Belgium, but the winter. I have never been warmed through since I have been in the country. To persons accustomed to bright blue skies, & a brilliant sunshine, there is something very depressing, in these eternal iron grey skies, &

watery looking sunbeams, & the necessity of always carrying an umbrella, or if you do not, being wetted through, deprives out of door exercise of all pleasure, so much so that it requires a great effort on my part to get out of the house especially as the bad pavements & the dust nearly ruin the feet. Even [John] Calhoun [Clemson] complains of his feet tho' I take the greatest pains that both should have their shoes large & easy. These are all however *little miseries* & my making so much of them is a proof that we have no great to complain of. We are all very well & the children continue to be all I could wish them in every respect. I don[']t mean they learn very fast but that is partly my fault for I do not desire to press them, setting health & cheerfulness above everything else. We get along, however, slowly, & I hope all they learn will remain, for I take pains to make them understand as they go. All the Americans who see Calhoun, are struck by his likeness to you, but I do not think him like you. The shape of the head & the hair, (except that his is lighter,) are precisely like yours, but the face is very different. His chin is sharp, & his mouth rather small than otherwise, & his eyes tho' the colour of mine, are very different in form, & expression. I think Floride [Elizabeth Clemson] resembles more our family, indeed she is said to be very like me, tho' her mouth is also much smaller, than mine. I wish you could see them to judge for yourself, in this important matter.

Brussels is as quiet & deserted as possible, every one who can, being in the country, at the watering places, or at the sea side. One half the houses in our quarter are shut up, which looks rather solitary, & there are not many more persons in the streets than in those of Pendleton.

The King [Leopold I] as usual is absent, having gone to pay a visit to his niece Victoria, to forget for a while I suppose, the troubles of reigning, for things don[']t go, just at present, in the way he would wish them. In the first place, the country has been, & is still suffering much for want of bread, which has caused, as you have doubtless seen, troubles in almost every town in the kingdom, some of them for the time quite serious, & what is worse, there seems every probability that in the Flanders, especially, things will rather get worse than better, from the want of work in the poorer classes, which makes of those provinces, a hive of beggars to over run the rest of Belgium. Then the elections, which have just taken place, have resulted in the defeat of the Catholic party, & of course of the King, who has had the folly to unite his interests entirely with theirs, by showing in every way possible his preference for them, so that his being forced, as he has been, to give up his Catholic ministry, & choose a Liberal, is looked upon by himself, & every one else, as a personal defeat on his part, & of course has had an unfavourable effect on his popularity. For that I suppose he don[']t care. He knows that Belgium is forced, by her position among the other powers of Europe, to have a king, & does not care to change "king Log[,]" for fear of getting "King Stork," so he lets things take their course, & says I suppose, his children may take care of themselves, as he has done before them. He has been quite sick, & they had a report, at one time, his mind was affected, & people began to occupy themselves about the regency, but it turned out a false rumour. I don[']t suppose you care much about all this, but I know you like to see me try to understand what is going on around me.

Our war with Mexico seems to be going on prosperously, but the doubt is, whether success is not our worst enemy, in this case. Be that as it may, if you were in Europe, you would feel gratified that victory attends our arms, & the moral effect on public opinion here, has been very favourable to us. If you could read french, I would send you a paper published here every week, by the "young liberals," who are of course the most liberal, & which paper publishes every week, what it calls American Studies, which give the only true account in Europe, I believe, of things passing our side of the water. The articles are well written, & will do good I suppose in time, but every effort is made by the monarchies of Europe, to prevent knowledge of our institutions, & prosperity, from being spread abroad.

We did not hear from you by the last steamer, nor by the Washington, which was a great disappointment, but I hope all are well, & as it is almost time for another steamer to come in, am anxiously looking for letters.

Tell mother my trunk has not yet arrived, & I wish she would write to ask cousin [James] Edward [Boisseau], if it has been shipped for Antwerp, & & [*sic*] by what ship, that I may have it inquired for when the vessel arrives.

We or rather I, for Mr. C[lemson] was at Paris, received your letter of introduction, by Mr. [St. George T.] Campbell, to whom I gave Mr. C[lemson]'s address in Paris, but he tells me he did not see him. I suppose Mr. Campbell did not arrive, till after Mr. Clemson left. There were with him a Mr. Rogers, & Judge [Edward] King of Phil[adelphi]a, who also brought us letters.

Mr. Clemson joins me in much love to you, mother, & sister

[Martha Cornelia Calhoun], & the children send many kisses. Your devoted & dutiful daughter, Anna Clemson.

ALS in ScCleA.

To Prof[esso]r F[RANCIS] LIEBER, [South Carolina College, Columbia]

Fort Hill, 27th June 1847

Dear Sir, I agree with you, that it is highly desirable, that this State should be represented at the international Free trade Convention to be held at Brussels in September next. No Community has a right to take precedence of us, in reference to that great question; no not England herself. We gave the first impulse. She but consummated what we began.

The only difficulty is, to obtain the attendance of a suitable delegation. I fear Mr. [George] McDuffie is too feeble. Judge [William] Harper's duties I suppose would ["not" *interlined*] prevent him. I see the two Senators are named in a communication in the Carolinian. It will not be in my power to go. My engagements will keep me at home this summer. If circumstances permitted, I would willingly attend, should it be the desire of my fellow citizens; but they do not. Should a delegation be appointed, Mr. [Thomas G.] Clemson, our Charge [d'Affaires] there, would, I feel assured, feel honored to be named as one. He is thoroughly free trade.

I am distressed to learn from Mr. Clemson, as well as through you, that Germany has suffered so much from the famine. Such an year has never been before known, as far as Europe is concerned.

We have few Germans among us, which I regret. I would be glad to see the tide of Emigration from there turned this way. I know of but one family in all the region hereabouts, and he [*sic*] is in very moderate circumstances. He came a few years since very poor, but is very thriving, and much esteemed for his industry & good behavior. With great respect yours truly, J.C. Calhoun.

ALS in CSmH, Francis Lieber Papers.

To Samuel A. Wales, [Eatonton, Ga.]

Fort Hill, 27th June, 1847

Dear Sir: I am in receipt of your note of the 17th inst., covering the resolution adopted by a meeting of the Whig party of Putnam county, approving the resolutions introduced by me in the Senate of the United States during the last session, in opposition to the Wilmot Proviso, and tendering the thanks of the meeting for the stand I took in behalf of our rights.

I am happy that my resolutions and stand have met with the approbation of your meeting; not so much on my own account, as acceptable as is the approbation of my fellow-citizens to me, but for a reason far more important. Coming from a quarter of the State so respectable and influential, I hail it as an omen that the Whigs of Georgia are prepared to do their duty in reference to the vital question involved in the resolutions I introduced.

I hope it is the precursor to the union of all parties with us to repel an outrageous and unprovoked assault on us—one that involves our safety and that of the Union. We have the Constitution clearly with us. My resolutions have been assailed and denounced, but the truth of the principles they assert remains uncontested and incontestible. In defending them, we not only defend ourselves, but the Constitution; and in defending it, the Union itself, of which it is the basis.

We must not be deceived. The time has come when the question must be met. It can no longer be avoided—nor, if it could, is it desirable. The longer it is postponed, the more inveterate and dangerous will become the hostile feelings between the slaveholding and non-slaveholding States. With union among ourselves we have nothing to fear—but without it, everything. The question is far above the party questions of the day. He who is not for us is against us.

For your kind expression of feelings towards me, in communicating the resolution, accept my sincere acknowledgment. With great respect, I am, &c., &c., J.C. Calhoun.

PC (from the Milledgeville, Ga., *Recorder* of 7/13) in the Charleston, S.C., *Mercury,* July 15, 1847, p. 2; PC in the Charleston, S.C., *Evening News,* July 15, 1847, p. 2; PC in the Camden, S.C., *Journal,* July 21, 1847, pp. 2–3; PC in the New York, N.Y., *Evening Post,* July 22, 1847, p. 2; PC in the Pendleton, S.C., *Messenger,* July 23, 1847, p. 2; PC in the New York, N.Y., *Journal of Commerce,* July 24, 1847, p. 2; PC's in *Niles' National Register,* vol. LXXII, no. 21 (July 24, 1847), p. 323, and no. 25 (August 21, 1847), p. 389; PC in the New York, N.Y., *National Anti-Slavery Standard,* July 29, 1847, p. 2; PC in *The*

Liberator, July 30, 1847, p. 122; PC in the Nashville, Tenn., *Whig,* August 5, 1847, p. 2; PC in the Philadelphia, Pa., *Pennsylvania Freeman,* August 5, 1847, p. 1; PC in the Tallahassee, Fla., *Southern Journal,* August 9, 1847, p. 3; PC (addressed to Samuel S. Wells) in the Huntsville, Ala., *Democrat,* August 18, 1847, p. 4.

From F[RANKLIN] H. ELMORE

Charleston, June 29 1847

My Dear Sir, In the pressure of business of almost every sort which can absorb & embarrass a man, I have a few moments to report progress in our newspaper affair. We have lately held repeated conferences & compared notes. The responses have not been general nor in all cases satisfactory. Out of So. Carolina I never hoped for much & it seems to be as I feared it would be. In this State we may do some thing. There seems hope of it & we determine to make the effort & throw the responsibility of failure off our shoulders should there be a failure. Mr. [Henry W.] Conner wrote you how matters stood some time ago. Since then we have not had much. [James H.] Hammond is cold. [Francis W.] Pickens has not answered. We hear nothing from [Armistead] Burt & under all circumstances we think of sending Mr. [Alfred P.] Aldrich to see the upper & middle country men face to face & know beyond doubt what is to be expected.

I was directed to draw up the form of caption for a subscription, which I did & submitted it this afternoon. It was approved & is sent to you to have your opinion of it & any alterations you may suggest. When it is received from you it will be immediately tested by presentation to each Gentleman who may be decided on in the State. We go for at least $30,000 & hope to get $50,000.

Pray exercise your judgement ful[l]y on the prospectus for subscription. Cut out or add to it as our object is to make it as perfect for the purpose as possible.

We will sound N. Orleans through our friends there. Would it not be as well for you to say something to Mr. [Pierre] Soule, by which he will at least be prepared to confer with my Brother [William A. Elmore] & others? Or what do you advise in regard to him? What line of action shall we adopt as to him for the future?

It has struck us that Gen[era]l [James] Hamilton [Jr.] might go to N. Orleans & be of service in combining a support. Could you write to him & see what he would do?

In your letter to Mr. [Henry W.] Conner you speak of an Editor in the West—one in Virginia & one in N. York. Have you any objections to inform us who they are & what is the probability of getting them. This is a point on which we feel most anxiety. If we had the right man, more money could be raised. A fear that our man may be seduced & bought off is in our way.

I think a letter from you to Hammond would be of service. He answers us in Chills. Has a terror of issues on this question—as if it were avoidable—as if we seek them.

I write in great haste & must ask your indulgence for my letter.

Direct your answer to H.W. Conner & H[enry] Gourdin as well as myself as I may be absent.

Your business letter I rec[eive]d today & it will be attended to as you desire. Yours truly, F.H. Elmore.

ALS in ScCleA. NOTE: The enclosed "caption for a subscription" has not been found. However, it was doubtless a draft of the printed circular which appears below as an En with Henry W. Conner's letter to Calhoun of 8/8/1847.

From H[ENRY] W. CONNER

Charleston, June 30 1847

My Dear Sir, We have rec[eive]d yours of the 25th. I feel now for the first time—a full confidence in our being able with proper industry & energy to raise a sufficiency of funds to establish the paper & I think we are about to put both industry & energy into play on the subject.

Col. [Franklin H.] Elmore will enclose you this morning—the caption proposed for the subscription lists. Please send it back as soon as you have examined it with such alterations or improvements as you wish. We will then proceed apace with the work.

Col. Elmore will see or write the [Wade] Hampton influence & does not doubt their cooperation. We are approaching Leading whigs ["here &" *interlined*] in other quarters besides with whatever we can get along with ourselves. We had better to do so & call upon you for your name & influence only where we cannot get along without it. If ["found" *interlined*] necessary for you to write the gentlemen your name we will apprise you but I expect Elmore can secure their influence.

We can operate through merchants in N. Orleans & through them upon the planters. Would it not be as well for you to advise Mr. [Pierre] Soule that this Committee are progressing with the work—& are or will be pushing their object in his State & invite his countenance & cooperation. It would prevent any possible collission—if it did not procure concert. I have written letters to N. Orleans that will procure for us a view of the ground upon which we ["may" *canceled and* "are to" *interlined*] move. Col. Elmore has done the same.

We can do nothing with the politicians I think any where but march with the people & to my mind there should be ["the" *canceled*] our efforts directed.

The paper cannot be put in motion before the meeting of Congress. It is impossible to do so. I think we can & must however have the subscriptions complete & in your hands or any other you may designate at that time. Until then it appears ["to me" *interlined*] the Editorship should be kept out of view. This is a matter however that will & should be deferred to your Judgment & wishes.

We are organising for a few talented gentlemen to write a series of articles in the Mercury in the mean time & if written with ability— & in a proper spirit may do much to keep alive the proper spirit until our paper be ready to take ground.

It is very desirable that you would give us your directions & suggestions frequently. ["Some of us" *canceled.*] One or two of us have agreed that as soon as measures are agreed on that the executory part of the business shall be promptly carried out—a very necessary part of the business I believe in public matters. Very Truly Y[ou]rs, H.W. Conner.

ALS in ScCleA.

JULY 1–AUGUST 31, 1847

◫

Farmer Calhoun seemed to fare better than most. He wrote his son from Fort Hill on July 8: "I have some of the best corn I ever saw. My cotton crop is also good . . . ." This despite an unusually cool and moist summer and the ravages of cotton pests through adjacent regions.

Calhoun the public man continued to answer correspondence on "the most vital of all questions" to the South. The question was assuming even grimmer and more immediate aspects. Charles J. Faulkner of Virginia wrote Calhoun at length about the recent murder of a Maryland slaveholder trying to recover his property at Carlisle, Pennsylvania. Of the behavior of the Pennsylvania authorities in that instance, Calhoun wrote in reply: "There is not on record a more deliberate and undisguised breach of faith" than allowing a clear provision of the Constitution to be trampled on and a citizen to be murdered in attempting to secure his rights. Should the South acquiesce, "we shall really deserve the fate, that will most assuredly await us."

Wilson Lumpkin, an old friend, formerly Governor and Senator from Georgia, agreed, writing Calhoun on August 27: "Eventually we shall be forced to decisive & direct resistance, or we must yield every thing . . . ." So did many others agree, including the citizens of Eufaula, Ala., where a public meeting at the end of August resolved: "That we agree with the Hon. John C. Calhoun in his construction of the Constitution upon the subject of the power of Congress to exclude slavery from the territory belonging to the United States; and that he deserves the gratitude of the South for the powerful and fearless manner in which on all occasions he has defended her peculiar institution." (Greenville, S.C., Mountaineer, September 3, 1847.)

◫

To Mrs. P[LACIDIA MAYRANT] ADAMS, [Pendleton]

[Pendleton, *ca.* 7/1847?]
Dear Madam, I enclose a draft on Mr. [John S.] Lorton for $150 agreeably to your request. I will thank you to add it to the other credits and also add $10.72[,] the amount of 13 bushels of wheat at 62½ [cents] per bushel & 5 of Rye at 50 cents. I desire it to be added simply to keep our accounts square. With respect yours & &, J.C. Calhoun.

ALS owned by Mr. Holbrook Campbell. NOTE: This undated document has been assigned a tentative possible date.

Deed executed by John C. Calhoun, [*ca.* 7?/]1847. By this document, which is dated only by the year, Calhoun conveys 103 acres of land in Pickens District, S.C., to Mrs. Placidia Adams for $309. James H. Rion and Willis Burket witnessed the deed. Appended is a notarized renunciation of dower rights to the land by Floride [Colhoun] Calhoun, dated 11/23/1848. The deed was recorded by the Clerk of Court of Anderson District on 2/28/1850. DS owned by Mr. Holbrook Campbell; recorded copy in Sc-Ar, Anderson County Deeds, A-2:113–114.

From WILLIAM G. BARTELL

Providence, R.I., July 1st 1847
Dear Sir, Pardon me for thus obtruding myself upon your notice. The only apology I have to offer is that I claim to be an *American citizen*. As such, I am proud to know that my country can boast of such noble spirits, & such exalted statesmen, as him whom I now address. I am proud to know that the great men of our republic, are not merely the *rulers* of her citizens but are also her fountains of political wisdom.

In view of this, I have taken the liberty to solicit from you an answer to the following questions;

First; Can the execution of Charles I, be justified either by right or by State necessity?

Secondly, Ought Literature, under any circumstances, ever to be connected with legislation?

Entertaining for you sentiments of profound admiration, I have the honor to be, Your obedient servant, William G. Bartell.

ALS in ScCleA.

To "Col." JA[ME]S ED[WARD] COLHOUN, [Abbeville District, S.C.]

Fort Hill, 1st July 1847

My dear James, There begins to be a good deal of feelings in this quarter, in reference to the navigation of Savannah River, and Mr. [William] Sloan has been appointed by the farmers society to attend the barbacue in Calhoun's Settlement on the 3d Inst. to represent the views & feelings of the people hereabouts, as it is expected the subject will be agitated on the occasion. His opinion at present ["is" *interlined*] rather adverse to the practicability of rendering the river capable of steam navigation, except at an enormous cost. In this, I think, he is mistaken, and I am sure he would be very happy to find he is.

I have conversed with him freely, as to what would, in my opinion, be the proper mode of proceedings ["to" *canceled*] on the part of the meeting to bring the subject fairly before the Legislatures of our State & Georgia. The subject is one of great importance & I hope will be prosecuted with vigour. Truly, J.C. Calhoun.

ALS in ScCleA; PC in Jameson, ed., *Correspondence*, pp. 734–735.

From JOHN H. STEELE

Milledgeville [Ga.], July 2d 1847

Sir, I take the liberty, as one of the Secretaries of the Whig Convention, held in this place on yesterday, of enclosing to you a printed Copy of the Proceedings, in which will be found a resolution referring to yourself, and which will be heartily responded to, it is hoped, not only by the Whigs of Georgia, but by every patriotic heart within the bounds of our State.

Wishing you, my dear Sir, health and happiness, with long life to serve, what it would please me much to term, a *united and grateful people* for the sake of the *South* and the *Union.* I have the honor to be Very Respectfully, Y[ou]r Ob[edien]t Serv[an]t, John H. Steele.

ALS in ScCleA. NOTE: An AEU reads, "The proceedings of the Whig Convention of Georgia." The En has not been found, but according to newspaper reports the convention passed resolutions nominating Zachary Taylor for President and Duncan L. Clinch for Governor, as well as the following in regard to Calhoun: "*Resolved,* That the Hon. John C. Calhoun is entitled to the thanks of the people of Georgia for his independent and patriotic course in the Senate of the United States in reference to our recently disturbed foreign relations." (Tuscaloosa, Ala., *Independent Monitor,* August 3, 1847, p. 3.)

To BEN[JAMIN] E. GREEN, Washington

Fort Hill, 3d March [*sic*; July] 1847

Dear Sir, If it were in my power, I would gladly aid you to obtain the Consulship at Havre. I consider you every way to be well qualified for the place; but I feel assured from experience, that any recommendation from me instead of aiding you, would be the certain means of defeating. In no instance have any I made had the least influence. In consequence, I have abstained, for some time back, from considerations of self respect from making any. Yours truly, J.C. Calhoun.

ALS in NcU, Duff Green Papers (published microfilm, roll 6, frames 884–885). NOTE: This letter was postmarked in Pendleton, S.C., on 7/5. Green's EU reads, "3 July 1847. J.C. Calhoun to B.E. Green."

From JOS[EPH] W. LESESNE

Mobile, July 4th 1847

My Dear Sir, I designed long since to have replied to your kind and interesting letter of the 26th March last, and particularly to that portion relating to the establishment of an independent press here. From present appearances the current of public opinion is moving with a strength and in a direction that I fear it would be useless to offer resistance. We may guide it, but can not resist it. In what light the new movement is to be regarded is a question about which men may differ, but that difference will scarcely manifest itself in action. You will of course understand me as speaking of the movement in favor of Gen[era]l [Zachary] Taylor for the Presidency.

I enclose you a paper containing an abstract of a Speech delivered at a Taylor meeting recently held here, by our friend [John A.] Campbell. I must say that even the qualified sanction he gives to the recommendation in my opinion is premature. I can not obtain the approbation of my own mind to the idea of electing to the Presidency a man who apart from his *opinions* of which we know nothing, has never given the slightest evidence of civil ["virtues" *canceled*] talents. That a good Soldier should make a good Statesman is the rarest occurrence—and I have no idea that Gen[era]l Taylor possesses the requisite qualifications. If not illiterate, he is certainly not well informed; and the idea that what people call *good common sense,* combined with the excellent virtues of moderation, modesty and prudence, are all-sufficient for an Office, unquestionably the most difficult on earth—is a grave and mischievous mistake. A man may possess all the qualifications ascribed to Taylor, and still fall into the hands and under the influence of the worst men in the Country. Such was the fate of Gen[era]l [Andrew] Jackson, a much stronger man. Such will be the fate of every other military chieftain taken from a sphere of duty so utterly unlike that to which he is called at the head of a nation like this—ignorant of the foreign relations of the country—ignorant of the principles of legislation, ignorant of the details of civil business, ignorant of the men who should be his instruments, ["and" *written over* "but"] who thus ["necessarily" *interlined*] become his masters. Who can not realize the perplexity of a man thus situated:—the first and uppermost feeling is that of utter confusion and ["perplexity" *canceled and* "and distress" *interlined*] of mind—for he finds himself "a novice in a Labarynth," in which darkness terminates every path which he attempts. With whatever determination he may enter, at last he must call for a guide—some one to relieve a state of mind that would end in insanity if it continued. This I apprehend is the secret of the ascendency of practiced politicians over even superior minds who attempt an employment of which they know nothing. The consequences ["to the country" *interlined*] of electing such men ["to the Country" *canceled*] depend wholly upon character of the persons who are fortunate enough to obtain the controll of the novice. But generally speaking, the worst men in the country have the best chance of obtaining it. They who have no opinions, no principles, no conscience to sacrifice or compromise—who flatter and faun and play the sycophants—these are the men, who generally obtain the ascendency when the government is in the hands of one who must from the necessity of his case be guided by *somebody.*

But apart from this, can the project of electing Gen[era]l Taylor be reconciled with that self respect and jealousy of their institutions which any poeple having a capacity for self Government ought to feel. ["And will the Stat true Statesmen of our Country" *canceled.*] Is it not apparent that if it succeed the idea will become a fixed one in every part of the Country that military achievements alone open the avenue to the Presidency—and that thus that Military virtues and Military talents will acquire a permanent ascendency among us. Whenever this deplorable state of things is brought about, we may bid adieu to peace and the trophies which it has spread and is spreading over the whole earth. So far from affording an example we shall become the terror and the scourge of mankind, and provoke a war in which the whole civilized world will combine, and properly, to crush the terrific power that threatens ["the repose of the" *canceled*] its repose. Who does not see that hereafter our difficulties with foreign nations will be more difficult to adjust than heretofore—that we have already given a large portion of our poeple the taste of blood merely for the sake of blood—A war of defence, a great and necessary war does little mischief in a moral point of view, and has its en[n]obling effects—but not so with such a war as as [*sic*; "the" *changed to* "this"; "miscreants at Washington have got us into" *canceled and* "one in which we are now engaged" *interlined*]. Its effects will be to brutalize only. It has ["been" *interlined*] attractive chiefly ["of" *canceled and* "to" *interlined*] bad passions ["only" *canceled*], and when it is over ["and done with those passions in Mexico" *interlined*] it will turn them back and let them loose to prey upon us in every form of evil. It will build up a permanent war party, which if we succeed in putting down and keeping down, we shall owe our good fortune to Providence and not to ourselves. It is a bad beginning of this necessary work to take a hero from this war for ["the" *interlined*] Presidency, to commit our destinies to one who must necessarily ["by" *canceled*] in his own personal elevation make that abhorred war conspicuous, and build up claims to favor and reward for all who have served in it.

In short, it appears to me that we have at length got fully upon the great Republican highway to destruction—the great military road that terminates ["through all past history" *interlined*] amidst the buried constitutions and ruined temples of freedom.

I sincerely trust that I may be needlessly concerned on this subject. But it appears to me so evident that there is an inherent vice in the popular mind on the subject of military glory—that ["where" *canceled*] there is such a mass of ignorant lawless population upon which this vice is operative, that I see nothing in the future but cause for apprehension and alarm.

If the good effects anticipated by Mr. Campbell and others result from the election of Gen[era]l Taylor I shall be heartily rejoiced— but I doubt it. If it break one faction it will I fear build up another, more commanding and more difficult to controll and hence much more dangerous.

But what if we should have two heroes in the field. Gen[era]l [Winfield] Scott[']s claims will certainly not be overlooked by *himself*—nor by any party or faction however despicable ["who" *canceled*] if he can attract their attention. It would not surprise me to see him the northern and abolition candidate in opposition to Taylor. That party will take up any man with whom they can make head against the extension of Slave territory: and if I remember correctly Gen[era]l Scott has already more than intimated a willingness to serve them on this point.

Our friends here are deeply anxious to learn your views on the question of taking up Taylor. None of them however have my strong feelings against the measure.

Judge [Edmund S.] Dargan withdraws from the canvass. The contest is between [John] Gayle (ex Gov[ernor]) and a young man John T. Taylor—of hunker tendencies, but honest, and when at Washington I think will take the true direction in all Southern questions. Very truly your f[rien]d &c, Jos. W. Lesesne.

ALS in ScCleA. NOTE: John Gayle succeeded Dargan as Representative from Ala.

Toast sent to a 4th of July celebration at the College of William and Mary, [Williamsburg, Va., 7/4]. "William and Mary College: Whatever may be the boast of other institutions, she justly claims superiority over all others in the illustrious part her sons acted in declaring Independence, and in asserting and maintaining the great principles of Liberty, which led to that ever-to-be-remembered event." PC in the Richmond, Va., *Whig and Public Advertiser* (semi-weekly), July 13, 1847, p. 2.

From SAM[UEL] J. RAY

Georgia Telegraph office
Macon, July 6 [1847?]

My Dear Sir, I am greatly at a loss as to the grounds your friends should occupy in the present state of part[i]es and at the suggestion of my friend Maj. E[dward] J. Black [former Representative from Ga.], take the liberty to address you this brief note. If you can find a leisure moment from your other engagements I would be most happy as well as greatly aided by a freer communication of opinions ["with" *written over* "from"] you. The strictest confidence will be observed with respect to any communications you may make. With sentiments of high respect I am very Truly Y[ou]r ob[edien]t s[ervan]t, Sam. J. Ray.

ALS in ScCleA.

To "Col." A[NDREW] P[ICKENS] CALHOUN, [Marengo County, Ala.]

Fort Hill, 8th July 1847

My dear Andrew, Since I wrote you, I received from Mr. [John Ewing] Bonneau, an account of the Sales of my cotton. He sold at 12 cents round, with the exception of one bale, for which he got 10. I hope if you have sold, you have done as well; but as I apprehend that would not be the case, I trust you still have your cotton on hand. If so, hold on. The prospect of a rise is fair. All accounts represent the prospect of the harvest in Europe as fine.

The weather ["here" *interlined*] continues cool & moist. It is now raining. I never saw so little of the sun in any summer before. My corn crop is excellent, wherever the stand is good. I have some of the best corn I ever saw. My cotton crop is also good; ⅔ very good, & the residue, with some exception, not bad. It is, I understand, by far the best in the vicinity, but that is not saying much, for I am told it is almost failure hereabouts. Mr. [William] Sloan, who has just returned from a visit to Abbeville, & who walked through mine yesterday, says it is ["the" *canceled*] better than any he saw between here & there, except one in Abbeville. The lice has been more prevalent, & the indication of the worm greater, than I ever saw. I found some of my squares already penetrated by them, in my walk through the cotton yesterday.

Mr. [Thomas G.] Clemson in his letter to me by the last steamer, writes me, that a German chymist of the name of Biches [*sic;* Francois Henri Bickes; "who" *canceled*] has discovered the art of preparing seed, so as to add greatly to its vegitative powers & production, & that the process is cheap. He disclosed the secret to him, in confidence; and ["says" *interlined*] that he has full confidence in it. It has, it seems, been tried with success in many places. He also writes me, that if I would have a few bushels of cotton seed sent to him, Mr. Biches would prepare it for me. I wrote Mr. Clemson, that I would write to you to forward from Mobile 2 bushels of Petitt Gulf seed, and a half gallon, of indian corn & like quantity of Cow peas ["to send" *canceled*] to Mr. [James Edward] Boisseau of New York [City], to be forwarded ["by him" *interlined*] to the care of our Consul at Antwerp for him. I wish you, accordingly, the first time you go down this season, should you go again, or if not, to write to your factor in Mobile, to forward them accordingly. I wish the cotton seed to be of the finest & best Petitt Gulf, to be put up in a close barrel, well hooped, with the quantity of corn & Cow pease stated, in seperate bags, in the same barrel; to be addressed to James Edward Boisseau, of the House of Ingoldsby & Boisseau, New York, with instructions to be forwarded to the care of ["the" *interlined*] American Consul at Antwerp Belgium, & to be forwarded by him to Tho[mas] G. Clemson Brussels.

I wish you to attend to the subject immediately, so that the prepared seed may reach here before I leave for Washington, in November. I wish to have a fair experiment made of the effect of the preperation, and to give direction in reference to it before I leave.

William [Lowndes Calhoun] is not yet returned, nor have we heard from him for 10 days passed. I hope he has suffered no relapse.

I hope the place continues healthy, & the prospect of the crop good. I shall expect to hear from you shortly. Write me fully.

We are all well & all join in love to you. Your affectionate father, J.C. Calhoun.

[P.S.] I would be glad to learn as soon as the seeds are sent, so that I may write to Mr. Boisseau & Mr. Clemson in reference to it.

P.S. I wrote to Mr. Bonneau, to ascertain, what payment had been made to Arthur Simkins ["through him" *interlined*] on account of the debt Mr. Clemson owed him for the ["bond" *or* "land"; "through him" *canceled*] & what Papers Mr. Clemson had left in his hands of ours. In his answer he says but one instalment of $3000, with $70 of interest had been made, & that Mr. Clemson left with him two notes on us for $8,500 each & a due bill for $7144; and adds that, "as no payments have been made on either directly to me, the notes & due bill remain as he left them." I had been of the impression, that the money he advanced to us, had been applied to the ["taking up the" *canceled*] due bill, and that a small balance only remained ["on" *canceled*] to be paid on it; & had also supposed ["it" *canceled and* "the amount paid" *interlined*] had been credited on it. What is your recollection of the facts, & of the amount still due on the due bill, if any still remains to be paid? Have we paid any thing since that transaction, but the one instalment on Mr. Clemson['s] account to A. Simkins?

Mr. Clemson, as I believe I stated to you in one of his letters, had expressed a desire, that our debt to him should ["be" *interlined*] consolidated in a bond, secured by Mortgage; and my object in writing to Mr. Bonneau was to ascertain how much we did owe him. I answered him, (Mr. C[lemson]) that there could be no objection to giving our joint bond in lieu of the notes, but that I objected to the mortgage as unnecessary & calculated to impair our credit. I have not yet had time to hear from him. I will write you when I do. J.C.C.

ALS in NcD, John C. Calhoun Papers.

To A[nna] M[aria Calhoun] Clemson, [Brussels]

Fort Hill, 8th July 1847

My dear daughter, The opinions you express, on the subject of your note, accord very much with those, to which I had come, as you will, I suppose, infer from my letter to you, written about the same time. The difficulty is, what shall he [that is, Thomas G. Clemson] do with his negroes? The three alternatives are, to sell; to hire, or purchase & establish another place. The former is the most simple, & that which can best be done in his absence, but it seems to me, that it would not be advisable for him to sell, until he has fixed on his future course. He cannot calculate permanently on his office, or employment abroad. If it were even eligible of itself, the fluctuation of parties & the prevalence of the spoils principle, would make ["it" *interlined*] uncertain. Nor can he well ["*calc*" *canceled*] determine on his future course, while abroad. The country even in his short absence, has greatly changed. It is growing & thriving, and improving. Nothing now is talked ["about" *interlined*] almost, but railroads & the like. We, even in this remote region, begin to talk seriously of making Savannah River navigable ["for steam" *interlined*] to Anderson Ville [S.C.], or even near to Portmon [*sic*; Portman's] Shoals on the Seneca, within 12 miles of this. Many suppose it can be done at a moderate cost.

If Mr. Clemson should think of returning, I doubt much, whether there ever will be a more favourable period to do so, whether he looks to the disposition of his property, or determining permanently on his future course than this fall will be.

James [Edward Calhoun] has returned from College, and is much imimproved [*sic*]. We expect William [Lowndes Calhoun] daily, & I hope Andrew [Pickens Calhoun] will make us a visit with his family this summer or fall, so that, if we had you with us, we should all once more meet.

We are all well. The season has been delightful, & continues to be so.

All join their love to you, Mr. Clemson & the children [John Calhoun Clemson and Floride Elizabeth Clemson]. Tell them that their Grandfather is glad to hear that they are so well and improving so fast, & that he would be very glad to see them. Your affectionate father, J.C. Calhoun.

ALS in ScCleA.

To T[homas] G. Clemson, [Brussels]

Fort Hill, 8th July 1847

My dear Sir, The last Steamer brought me yours of the 28th May, with Anna's note enclosed; and I am happy to hear, that you are all well.

On the subject of selling your place [in Edgefield District], I had made up my mind, in a great measure, before I received your letter, that it would be advisable. I still think it a place very capable of improvement, and that might be made very profitable under the eyes of an experienced owner residing on it. But it will take much labour to put it in good order & to make it highly productive. It is, besides, remote & has no society, & in very wet years uncertain. I fear this year has been entirely too wet for it. We have had a great deal of rain, with a very small portion of sun shine, and without example cool. We have not had one real hot summer like day, since the first week in April. Winter clothing is still comfortable.

If you should determine on selling, I think it would be advisable to write to Col. [Francis W.] Pickens early in reference to it, with authority to dispose of it on the best terms he can, fixing a minimum. I would authorise long credit, taking care to secure the debt by mortgage on the place with a bond. It would, perhaps, be well to fix a cash & credit price, making a pretty marked difference in the amount. By selling early, it will give you time to look out, and ["making" *changed to* "make"] other arrangement for next year. I wrote Anna, from what [James H.] Hammond told me, I thought his vicinity [in Barnwell District] had many advantages. I would advise ag[ai]nst selling the negroes, as I think them a good gang. If you could get a real good cotton plantation, favorably situated for manuring & improving, I do not doubt in the least you could make planting profitable, or, if it would better suit your taste and habits, manufacturing cotton. There cannot be the least doubt, we can, all things considered, manufacture cotton goods cheaper than ["any" *interlined*] people in the world. Mr. [William] Gregg, our most experienced manufacturer, told me, that he could manufacture a pound of cotton into Osnaburgh, 3 yards to the pound, boxed for market, for 2½ cents ["per pound" *canceled*]; an expense but little more, than that of sending it to Liverpool & selling it there. Cotton manufactures are rapidly spring[ing] up in the South.

What you state in reference to Mr. Biches [*sic*; Francois Henri Bickes] discovery is very interesting, particularly in reference to a region so remote from Lime & p[l]aster & marle. I shall be very glad to have an opportunity to make a trial of his prepared seed; and will write to Andrew [Pickens Calhoun] to forward from Mobile 2 bushels of the best pettit Gulf seed to Mr. [James Edward] Boisseau to forward to the care of our Consul at Antwerp for you; and to enclose with it, a half gallon of indian corn & the same quantity of our cow pea. I wish the experiment to be made with our finest & best cotton seed, & on the three discriptions of agricultural products, which we, in this quarter, are the most interested ["in" *interlined*]. I would write to Col. Pickens as you suggest, but I wish the experiment to be made under my own eyes. It will be far more satisfactory to me. I shall take care before I leave to give such directions, in reference to the seed, as will ensure a fair trial. I hope ["the" *can-*

celed] it will be received here before I leave for Washington in the last week of November. If the experiment should succeed well, I do not doubt a large subscription could be had to purchase ["it" *canceled and* "the secret" *interlined*]. I shall take the deepest interest in the subject, & am, therefore, very solicitious to be in possession of the prepared seed before I leave.

My crop of corn & cotton, especially the former, where the insects & worms in the spring have not injured the stand, ["is" *canceled and* "are" *interlined*] very fine. I have in cotton the whole of Speed's field, to which I have added about 13 acres of cleared land since you saw it, in Cotton. It is a field of 125 acres, two thirds of which has a fine growth of cotton, & a large portion of the residue not bad. Mine, as far as I can learn, is the only good crop, in the vicinity, of cotton. It is a plant much effected by the culture. Mr. W[illiam] Sloan has just returned from Abbeville, and walked through mine yesterday. He says he saw but one crop of cotton equal to it.

There is not much to be added about politicks to what I wrote you last. The difference between North & South is daily increasing, in reference to the slave question. It is hard to say to what it is destined to come. From every appearance, it will at least break up the old party organization. The indication is daily becoming stronger, in favour of General [Zachary] Taylor. The administration is evidently greatly alarmed at his popularity. Their fate is, however, sealed, whatever may become of the General.

The prevailing opinion seems to be, that there will be peace ere long. I regard it, as doubtful. I have no doubt, but the administration is most anxious for it, & that Mexicans desire it, but when they come to fix on terms, there will be great difficulty in agreeing. The former must insist, after so much blood & treasury, on a large cession of territory, & the latter will feel great repugnance to such cession. But be the terms what they may, our difficulty *within*, will commence with the termination of those with Mexico. Your affectionate father, J.C. Calhoun.

ALS in ScCleA; PEx in Jameson, ed., *Correspondence*, p. 735.

To P[IERRE] SOULÉ, New Orleans

Fort Hill, 8th July 1847
My dear Sir, It greives me to see, the state of profound to[r]por, into which Louisiana & the other States in the lower section of the Valley

of the Mississippi have sunk into, in reference to the most vital of all questions to them. Of all the Southern States, they have by far the most vital interests in the subject of slavery; and yet they witness appearantly, with the most imperturbable ["composure" *interlined*] its approach, step by step, and the more so the near it comes. It is to me amazing, that a people so segacious in other respects, do not see, that such a course must in the end prove fatal, not only to the Country & its liberties, but to party organization and association. The means necessary to preserve the former, are equally so to preserve the latter. Nothing can arrest the aggression of the North on this subject, or prevent it from pushing the issue to its final result, when political & party associations between the two sections will terminate in deadly hostilities, or our utter degradation & subjugation, but prompt, & efficient resistance on our part. Let it be once understood at the North, that either side may court the abolitionists, without losing thier political associates at the South, & that we, rather than seperate from our Northern allies, are ready to vote for a northern man, although unfaithful to the Constitution & the South on this vital ["question" *interlined*], and the result will soon be such as I have stated. But why should I dwell on consequences, in writing one, whose segacity has long since foreseen them?

If I supposed the object of the paper was to countenance the formation of a third party, it would not receive mine. It has been my unpleasant duty, on many and important occasions, to resist the popular ["party" *interlined*] in some of its most important movements, with the view, not to destroy, but save them; among which the two two [*sic*] measures, which seperate the parties most strongly from its opponents, & which constitute almost its only strength; I refer to free trade & the subtreasury, are striking instances. My object now is the same as it was then, when I stood up in favour of both of them, against General [Andrew] Jackson & his administration. I hope, I may be as successful now in bring[ing] the party to my views, as I was then; but candour compels me to say, that the character of the present question is of a nature so vital to our safety, as well as that of the Union, that I hold it paramount to all others, & above all party consideration. I cannot, & will not assent to see ["it" *interlined*] placed subordinate to the Presidential. The highest & most solemn ["consideration" *canceled and* "obligations" *interlined*] of duty forbid.

I trust our democratick friends of Louisiana will take the same view. If they do not, & are supported by any considerable portion of the party South, the doom of the party will be sealed. The question cannot be tampered with safely. The true course to save the party, as well as ourselves & country is, to let our northern associates understand, they cannot unite our votes and that of the abolitionists. That once understood, will speedily seperate them from the latter, & restore our old relations, when all will be well.

I am sure you will excuse me for the candour with which I ["speak" *canceled and* "write" *interlined*], on a question, involving such weighty consequences.

My immediate object in writing you now, in addition to acknowledging the receipt of your kind letter, is to state, that I learn from some of our prominent friends in Charleston, who beleive, that it is indispensable, that the South should have an organ at the Seat of Govern[men]t at this time, that they are resolved, notwithstanding the discouraging to[r]por, which seems to prevail the South at this ["time" *interlined*], to continue their efforts to raise funds, necessary for the purpose; & that they hope, that farther reflection & the daily demonstration at the North of both parties to sustain the Wilmot proviso, will open the eyes of the South, and induce a general cooperation to effect so indispensable an object. They still rely, in particular, on the aid & co[o]peration of Louisiana. They wish ["it" *canceled and* "the paper" *interlined*] to [be] the Organ of the whole South, & to be confined exclusively to the avowed object, for which it is proposed to establish it. They will probably write to some of their friends in ["the" *canceled and* "your" *interlined*] city, and I am sure, they would be very happy to have your countenance & support.

As to myself, I am much obliged to my friends in New Orleans for the confidence they repose in me, on this great question. It shall never be betrayed; but they must remember how feeble the efforts of any one ["must prove" *interlined*] if not ardently sustained by those, in whose behalf they are made. To me, it is [a] question of duty. I have too small a remnant of my life left, [to; "induce me" *interlined*] to go through the toils & sacrifice; the misrepresentation of my motives and assaults on my character, incident to my station in the Senate, but duty. With great respect I am yours truly, J.C. Calhoun.

ALS in private possession. NOTE: Soulé had been and would be again Senator from La. as well as Mayor of New Orleans at the time of its occupation in 1862.

From Jos[eph] Macmanus

Bellefonte, 13th July 1847
Centre County, Penn[sylvani]a

Dear Sir, In the years of 1833–34 I had the pleasure of receiving several letters from you at a time when the late Col. Andrew Gregg of this place, selected me, then a youth, to transmitt some of his correspondence to you, and your answers were returned through the same mode of conveyance. Since that time, I have occationally taken part in the political contests of the day; and believing the next Presidential Election of the utmost importance to the Democratic party, and the Country, I have thus taken the liberty of intruding myself upon you, for the purpose of obtaining some information, if consistant upon that subject. I do so because I have ever had the highest opinion of your Patriotism and political honesty. The past is rich with instruction, and the last session of Congress in some of its acts, is well calculated to cause alarm in the breast of every friend of the Union. The vote on the "Wilmot Proviso" evidently shows a disposition on the part of certain Northern and Western politicians, to go even beyond the fanaticism of the Abolitionists, and in my opinion of a much more dangerous tendency; the permanency of the Union is lossed [*sic*] sight of, in a dishonest and criminal design to sever that Union, by hypocritical professions of philanthropy. But I do assure you a majority of the people in this section are intelligent, and can see the object of this political Ruse. The Northern Whigs and their allies in the zeal to find an available candidate for the Presidency, have committed themselves, if they can be committed by nominating Gen. [Zachary] Taylor as their candidate ["for the Presidency" *canceled*]—a portion of the Democratic party are doing the same. And it is for the purpose of knowing something about Gen. Taylor and his political principles that I now trouble you. The information is sought for *myself confidentially*. All that I know about him is that he is a successful General—a Planter and owner of a number of *slaves*—and this of itself would put the *veto* upon the Wilmot *Provisso*. But what are his principles with regard to a U.S. Bank—Tariff—distribution of the proceeds of the public Lands—assumption of State debts—Internal improvements by the General Government, and is he not only in favour of a strict construction of the Constitution, but also for a *strict observance* of its plain letter and spirit. If he is the South should go for him at this time, as the Whig party of the North and portion of the democrats are already committed for this "Millitary Chieftain." If he is not, then I do hope

442

non[e] will be elected but who will be a democrate in principle—recognizing the Virginia & Kentucky resolutions of [17]98 as his text book and who will adhere to the Constitution as it is.

I send you [*not found*] some remarks delivered by myself in the Penn[sylvani]a Legislature 1842. You will find I was not afraid to defend the South—and you will also see my views upon other subjects.

I reside in the same place with Gen. [James] Irvin the Whig candidate for Governor—called the Iron district. The Whig party endeavoured to defeat me for this free trade—Southern Speach—but my constituents sustained me handsomely at the next Election by giving me a large majority of the votes—which is some evidence that they are not unfriendly to their Southern friends and believe in their democracy. There are many omissions &c in the printed remarks which you will perceive on its perusal. I should be happy to hear from you at your leasure. Respectfully yours, Jos. Macmanus.

ALS in ScCleA. NOTE: An AEU by Calhoun reads "Dr. Macmanus."

From Cha[rle]s Ja[me]s Faulkner

Martinsburg, Berkeley County Virginia
July the 15th 1847

Dear Sir, The active and patriotic ["interest" *canceled*] zeal, which you have always exhibited in every thing that affects the great & vital interests of this country and the special & particular position which you occupy as the most prominent defender of the institutions of the South, have emboldened me, notwithstanding our personal acquaintance is but limited, to advise and consult with you upon a matter which now intensely absorbs the attention of the slave holders of the State of Maryland & of that portion of the State of Virginia in which I reside.

I herewith enclose to you a copy of a law passed by the General Assembly of Pennsylvania in March 1847, also the proceedings of a public meeting recently held in Hagarstown Maryland exhibiting one of the consequences & results of that law.

I have been appealed to by many of my fellow citizens here to invoke the attention of the legislature of Virginia to this atrocious & perfidious legislation of a neighbouring State & to suggest, if possible some remedy that may mitigate, countervail and defend us from the grievance under which we now labor.

The subject is full of difficulty and embarrassment & I should like to be fortified by the views & suggestions of one of your matured experience & comprehensive mind.

The Law of Pennsylvania referred to, has rendered our slave property throughout Maryland & a large portion of Virginia, utterly insecure & will, if it continues in force a few years longer destroy any further interest that we may feel in that domestic institution.

The law is manifestly prepared by a man of some shrewdness & legal ability, & is without exception, the most deliberate & perfidious violation of all the guarantees of the Constitution which the fanaticism & wickedness of the abolitionists have resorted to & the most serious & dangerous attack yet made on the institution of slavery.

It denies as you will perceive, to the master, all *legal remedies* for the recovery of his slaves; treats him as as [*sic*] a tresspasser & a felon, & subjects him to ["the" *canceled*] harassing prosecutions for kidnapping & breach of the peace if he attempts to recapture them under the rights secured to him by the Constitution of the United States.

I pray you Sir, read this law carefully & deliberately, if your patience as a Southern man will allow you to do so; it is adapted to every exigency; suited to every change of circumstances & covers the slave with an invincible shield of protection in every emergency in which he may be placed in a contest with his master.

Since the passage of this law slaves are absconding from Maryland & this portion of Virginia in gangs of tens & twenties & the moment they reach the Pennsylvania line, all hopes of their recapture are abandoned.

The existence of such a law on the Statute Book of any State is not only a flagrant violation of the spirit of the Federal Constitution & indeed of its *express provisions*, but is a deliberate *insult* to the whole Southern people, which will not & ought not to be submitted to & would amongst nations wholly independent & disconnected by Federal relations be a *just cause of war.* It is a solemn, public legislative invitation to our slaves to abscond from their masters, with a promise of an asylum & protection in the territory of Pennsylvania.

Have we any remedy & what is it?

Can the legislation of Congress reach the evil here indicated? & if it can, have we any just grounds for hoping, that the Act of 1793 will be so amended & enlarged in its provisions as to afford us adequate protection?

Is there any countervailing legislation within the power of the

Southern States—or shall we be driven to the expense of establishing a cordon of sentinels along our entire Northern border[?]

Can it be hoped that Pennsylvania will repeal this law upon proper representations of its tendencies & effects by ["a" *canceled*] Commissioners appointed by Maryland & Virginia, or could any advantage be derived, from a Convention of the slave holding States of the Union?

No proposition can be plainer than that the slave holding interest of this Country is every where, one & the same. An attack upon it *here* is an attack upon it in South Carolina & Alabama. Whatever weakens & impairs it *here*, weakens & impairs it *there*. The fanaticism of Europe & of Northern America is embarked in a crusade against it. We must stand or fall together.

I pray you Sir revolve this subject in your mind. It is one of vital & absorbing interest to every Southern man. The time has come when we must maintain our ground with firmness or yield to an over-[r]uling destiny; and favor me with ["your" *canceled*] the result of your best reflexions to guide us in our present emergency. I am very truly yours, Chas: Jas: Faulkner.

[Enclosed clipping]

SECT. 1. BE IT ENACTED BY THE SENATE AND HOUSE OF REPRESENTATIVES OF THE GENERAL ASSEMBLY OF PENNSYLVANIA, That if any person or persons shall, from and after the passage of this Act, by force or violence, *take and carry away, or cause to be taken and carried away*, and shall by fraud or false pretence entice, or caused to be enticed* or shall *attempt so to take, carry or entice any free negro or* mulatto, from any part or parts of this Commonwealth, to any place or places whatsoever out of this Commonwealth, with a design and intention of selling and disposing of, or causing to be sold or disposed of, or of keeping and detaining, or of causing to be kept or detained, any free negro or mulatto as a servant or slave for life or for any term whatever, every such person and persons, his or their aiders and abetters, shall be deemed guilty of a high misdemeanor, and on conviction thereof in any court of quarter sessions of this Commonwealth, having competent jurisdiction, shall be sentenced to pay, at the discretion of the court passing the sentence, any sum not less than *five hundred nor more than two thousand dollars*; one half whereof shall be paid to the person or persons prosecuting the same and the other half to the Commonwealth; and moreover, shall be sentenced to undergo a punishment *in the proper penitentiary, for a period not less than five nor exceeding twelve* years; and on conviction of the second offence of the kind, the person so offending, shall be sentenced to pay a like fine, and undergo punishment, *by solitary confinement in the penitentiary for twenty-one years.*

Sect. 2.   That if any person or persons shall hereafter knowingly sell, transfer or assign, or shall knowingly purchase, take a transfer or assignment of any free negro or mulatto for the purpose of fraudulently removing, exporting, or carrying such free negro or mulatto out of this State, with the design or intent by fraud or false pretences, of making him or her a slave for life, or for any term whatsoever, every person so offending shall be deemed guilty of a high misdemeanor, &c. (penalty as in section 1st.)

Sect. 3.   *That no Judge of any of the Courts of this Commonwealth, nor any Alderman or Justice of the Peace of said Commonwealth, shall have jurisdiction, or take cognizance of the case of any fugitive from labor, from any of the United States or Territories, under a certain Act of Congress, passed on the 12th day of February,* 1793, entitled "An Act respecting fugitives from justice and persons escaping from the service of their masters"; nor shall any such Judge, Alderman, or Justice of the Peace *issue or grant any certificate or warrant of removal of any fugitive from labor, under the said act of Congress, or under any other law, authority or act of the Congress of the United States,* and if any Alderman or Justice of the Peace of this Commonwealth, shall take cognizance or jurisdiction of the case of any such fugitive, or shall grant or issue any certificate or warrant of removal as aforesaid, then, and in either case he shall be deemed guilty of a misdemeanor in office, and shall, on conviction thereof, be sentenced to pay, at the discretion of the Court, any sum not less than five hundred, not exceeding one thousand dollars, &c.

Sect. 4.   That if any person or persons claiming any negro or mulatto, as fugitive from service or labor, shall violently or tumultuously, under any pretence whatsoever, *seize upon and carry away to any place, or attempt to seize upon and carry* * *away in a violent, riotous or tumultuous manner, and so as to endanger the public peace, any negro or mulatto* within this Commonwealth, *either with or without the intention of taking such negro or mulatto before any district or circuit judge,* the person or persons so offending against the peace of this Commonwealth, shall be deemed guilty of a misdemeanor, and on conviction thereof, before any court of quarter sessions of this Commonwealth, shall be sentenced by such court to pay a fine of not less than *one hundred dollars,* nor *more than one thousand dollars,* with costs of prosecution; and further, to be *con-*

fined in the county jail, for any period at the discretion of the court not exceeding three months.

Sect. 5. That nothing in this act shall be construed to take away, what is hereby declared to be invested in the Judges of this Commonwealth, the right, power and authority, at all times on application made, to issue the writ of *habeas corpus,* and to inquire into the cause and legality of the arrest and imprisonment of any human being within this Commonwealth.**

Sect. 6. It shall not be lawful *to use any jail of this Commonwealth for the detention of any person claimed as a fugitive from servitude or labor,* except in cases when jurisdiction may be lawfully taken under this act, by any judge; and any jailor or keeper of any prison, or other person, who shall offend against the provisions of this section, shall, on conviction thereof, pay a fine of five hundred dollars; one-half thereof to the use of the Commonwealth, and the other half to the person who prosecutes; and shall, moreover, thenceforth be removed from office, &c.

Sect. 7. That so much of the Act of the General Assembly, entitled "An Act for the gradual abolition of Slavery," passed the first day of March, 1780 as authorizes the masters or owners of slaves to bring and retain such slaves within this Commonwealth for the period of six months, in involuntary servitude, or for any period of time whatever, and so much of said Act *as prevents a slave from giving testimony against any person whatsoever, be and the same is hereby repealed.*

Sect. 8. That the Act passed March 25, 1826, and all laws of this Commonwealth, which are hereby altered, be and the same are hereby repealed.

JAMES COOPER,
Speaker of the Ho. of Rep's.
CH. GIBBONS,
Speaker of the Senate.
Approved Mar. 3, 1847. F.R. SHUNK.

*It is to be noted that any slave who may reach the borders of Pennsylvania is by her law regarded as a *free negro.*

**The design of this section, is evidently, to insist upon the *right* of a Judge to bring any slave captured by his owners, before him, that under the provisions of this law he may escape.

[Enclosed clipping]

Proceedings *Of the meeting, held on Saturday last, in the Town Hall, for the purpose of expressing the sense of this community, in relation*

447

to the recent outrage committed upon Citizens of Hagerstown by a mob at Carlisle, Pa., and the consequent death of one of our most esteemed and valuable Citizens.

On motion of Edwin Bell, Gen. O.H. WILLIAMS was called to the Chair. Wm. B. Clarke, moved the appointment of JERVIS SPENCER, and Jos. I. Merrick, that of T.E. BUCHANAN, as Assistant Chairmen; and on motion of Jos. I. Merrick, *Geo. W. Smith* and *Edwin Bell*, were appointed Secretaries.

The object of the meeting having been stated by the Chair, in a few pertinent remarks, on motion of Jos. I. Merrick, Esq., the following gentlemen were appointed by the Chair a committee to draft a report and resolutions, expressive of the sense of the meeting:

Jos. I. Merrick, Wm. B. Clarke, Fred'k. Humrickouse, Jacob Swope, and Wm. F. Brannan, Esq'rs.

The Committee having retired, made the following report, which was unanimously adopted:

The People of Washington County, Maryland having recently, with mingled emotions of astonishment and sorrow, received from the State of Pennsylvania the mangled corpse of their fellow citizen, JAMES H. KENNEDY, most foully done to death within her borders; and having mingled their sympathetic tears with those of his widow and helpless orphans, as they laid his remains in the scarcely closed tomb of his venerated father, are spontaneously assembled this day, in the Town Hall of Hagerstown, to think of him, and of the circumstances of his death—and to give utterance to such feelings, and to direct such future action, as they may deem necessary and becoming.

JAMES H. KENNEDY was born and has spent his days among us. Most of the members of this meeting readily recall the yet recent days of his bright, and kind, and playful and happy, and cherished boyhood, when

"None knew him but to love him,
None named him but to praise."

According to the promise of those halcyon days, was the unfolding and the progress of his manhood. A dutiful son, a tender husband, a fond father, generous and devoted as a brother and friend, kind and gentle as a master, faithful and true as a citizen; such and no less was the universally recognized character, of him whose untimely death we deplore and who died as he had lived, without an enemy upon earth; the deep damnation of his taking off, must rest with crushing weight, some where within the shadow of the flag, and under the cognizance of the laws of our sister State of Pennsylvania.

Mr. KENNEDY was a Maryland Slave-holder. Several of his domestics had escaped into Pennsylvania, and having read in the third clause of the second section of the 4th Article of the Constitution of the United States, the following words: "No person held to service or labour in one State under the laws thereof, escaping into another shall in consequence of any law or regulation therein, be discharged from such service or labour; but shall be delivered up on the claim of the party to whom such service or labour may be due," he thought he might rely upon that solemn compact, to which, as all know, Pennsylvania was a willing and a leading party.

He was also well aware that by the second section of the sixth Article of the same Con[stitu]tion, it was agreed and declared that "This Constitution and the laws of the United States which shall be made in pursuance thereof—shall be the supreme law of the land, and the judges in every State shall be bound thereby, any thing in the Constitution and laws of any State to the contrary notwithstanding."

He had also full knowledge of the act of Congress of Feb. 12, 1792, sections 3 and 4, which are in the following words:

"Sec. 3. *And be it also enacted,* That when a person held to labour in any of the United States, or in either of the territories on the north-west or south of the river Ohio, under the laws thereof, shall escape into any other of the said States or territory, the person to whom such labour or service may be due, his agent or attorney, is hereby empowered to seize or arrest such fugitive from labour, and to take him or her before any judge of the circuit or district courts of the United States, residing or being within the State, or before any magistrate of a county, city or town corporate, wherein such seizure or arrest shall be made, and upon proof to the satisfaction of such judge or magistrate, either by oral testimony or affidavit taken before and certified by a magistrate of any such State or territory, that the person so seized and arrested, doth, under the laws of the State or territory from which he or she fled, owe service or labour to the person claiming him or her, it shall be the duty of such judge or magistrate to give a certificate to such claimant, his agent or attorney, which shall be sufficient warrant for removing the said fugitive from labour, to the State or territory from which he or she fled.

Sec. 4. *And be it further enacted,* That any person who shall knowingly and willingly obstruct or hinder such claimant, his agent or attorney in so seizing or arresting such fugitive from labour, or shall rescue such fugitive from such claimant, his agent or attorney when so arrested pursuant to the authority herein given or declared; or shall harbour or conceal such person after notice that he or she was a fugitive from labour, as aforesaid, shall, for either of the said offences, forfeit and pay the sum of five hundred dollars."

He knew and felt and was educated to believe that the Constitution of the United States, solemnly adopted by the authorized representatives of the several States (the honored name of Benjamin Franklin being at the head of the delegation of Pennsylvania:) afterwards solemnly ratified by all the State Legislatures, and finally accepted and hailed with great joy by the universal voice of the nation, was binding and inviolable, if any thing could be devised to bind the consciences of true and loyal men:

Binding upon all posterity, and upon every man as much as if he had individually subscribed and sworn to support it.

He was moreover aware that by the third section of the sixth article, it is declared that "the members of the several State legislatures and all executive and judicial officers both of the United States and of the several States shall be bound by oath or affirmation to support this Constitution."

And he might well have deemed it wholly incredible that legislators or other high functionaries, thus pledged and bound, could ever have been tempted to enact or to sanction any law or proceeding calculated or intended to nullify the express letter and spirit of the Constitution; to forbid obedience to it, to undermine, and by indirect means render unattainable, the rights so guaranteed, and which they were enjoined and bound and sworn to support and secure.

Mr. KENNEDY relied upon his rights and upon the constitution and laws of the land, and pursued his property which he found and caused to be arrested in the Borough of Carlisle, on the 2d day of June. A writ of habeas corpus being served upon him, he appeared and answered it, and by plain, direct, undeniable proof satisfied the eminent judge who heard the cause, that the persons arrested by him did, by the laws of Maryland from which they fled, owe service and labor to him, and the Judge therefore ordered the slaves to be delivered to Mr. KENNEDY to be taken back to Maryland. A tumult immediately ensued, even in the hall of Justice, but reached its full proportions shortly afterwards near the door, where heavy missiles and ponderous bludgeons were used by a riotous assembly, chiefly of negroes; the slaves of Mr. KENNEDY were rescued and borne off by masterful violence: and himself cast to the earth bruised, crushed and senseless.

It being understood that these transactions are in the hands to which they properly belong, the legal authorities of Pennsylvania, many circumstances and names are here purposely omitted; but we should hold ourselves utterly inexcusable not to state that many citizens of Carlisle manifested a horror and repugnance for these proceedings, and an astonishment at the high-handed outrage, such as amply proved their loyalty as citizens and as gentlemen.

Mr. KENNEDY reduced to helplessness was placed in the hands of eminent physicians of Carlisle, who exhausted in his behalf, all that science could suggest and kind and skilful hands perform; but in vain.

JAMES KENNEDY was in his 30th year—His health was unbroken from childhood—His habits and mode of life were prudent and regular. He possessed decided courage and a spirit habitually cheerful. After languishing in his bed 23 days his case was perceived to take a fatal turn and on the 25th of June he died, in consequence of injuries inflicted upon his person in the riot which has been mentioned.

His blood has sunk into the soil of Pennsylvania, and Heaven will require it.

But who was his slayer?

Was it the ignorant and infuriated African Automaton whose hands wielded the club or hurled the stone?

Or was it some active instigator of higher intellect, exciting and stimulating into deadly energy the brute force at hand?

Or alas! when the Legislature of Pennsylvania, by their act of the last session, prohibited her judges, magistrates and other officers from exercising the powers which Congress by the Act of 1793 *made it their duty* to exercise;

When they forbade under penalties, any person claiming a negro, to *violently* seize and carry him away (seizure necessarily implying *violence*, especially when Judges and Magistrates were prohibited from action conservative of peace and order;)—when they forbade the owner not only to disturb, but even to *endanger* the peace, by seizing or taking the negro claimed;

When they declared such seizure equally criminal or penal, whether with or without the intention of taking the negro before any district or circuit Judge;

When they prohibited their jailors from receiving such slaves; what did the Legislature of Pennsylvania, in fact, say or imply—and what was the necessary tendency of that language?

They said, virtually, although the Constitution declares that a slave escaping to Pennsylvania *shall not be discharged from service*,

but *shall be delivered up on the claim of the party*—HE SHALL NOT
BE DELIVERED UP—THE CLAIM SHALL NOT BE HEARD—HIS ESCAPE SHALL
AVAIL AS HIS DISCHARGE FROM SERVICE as far as our authority and power
can make it so.

Although the law of Congress, in conformity with the Constitution, empowered the owner to seize and arrest his slave and to take
him before a Circuit or District Judge of the U.S. within the State,
"or before any *magistrate* of a county, city or town corporate, wherein such seizure or arrest shall be made, and that it shall be the duty
of such judge or magistrate to give a certificate to such claimant his
agent or attorney, which shall be sufficient warrant for removing the
said fugitive"—Pennsylvania by her act said, further, impliedly:

No—None of these things shall be done. WE NULLIFY THIS LAW
(although the right to pass it is undeniable)—he shall not seize or
arrest (for that would be *violence*)—he may take the slave to Philadelphia or to Pittsburg, but to no other place, and then only if the
slave *be willing* (otherwise there will be *violence*)—no magistrate
or judge or other officer of this State shall interfere, (*unless invited
by the slave.*) Further, *We repeal all laws* heretofore passed in aid
of the constitutional rights of the master; we will not *hear* him, we
deny him the shelter even of our prisons. He shall only go with his
slave and then *without violence*, to Pittsburg or to Philadelphia,
hundreds of miles through hordes of runaway negroes and hostile
fanatics, and then if he get his slave away, it will not be because we
have not afforded countenance and occasion for every mode of
violence and resistance, nor because we have not sought to disarm
and to outlaw the man who claims his property, with his proof of
ownership in one hand and the constitution of his country in the
other.

And this notwithstanding our solemn and reiterated obligations,
compacts and oaths! ! !

Behold as the natural result of fanatical and lawless legislation,
THE SLAUGHTER OF JAMES HUGH KENNEDY.

But we forbear. Not Pennsylvania, but some enemy who has
crept unawares among her counsellors, while they slept, hath done
this thing!

Pennsylvania is a gallant State—one of the noblest of the old
thirteen. She cannot *intend* disloyalty to the Constitution. She will
be faithful, and will rebuke the fanatics who may for a season have
misled her.

If it were proper to add a word relating to expediency, after suggestions of Constitutional duty, we should desire to consider briefly

the object and aim as well as the practical results which have sprung from the reckless spirit by which the constitution and rights of Maryland have been assailed and hemmed in.

To the venal tribe who, for base lucre, make a trade of incendiary publications, or the equally contemptible body, who have attained a bad eminence under the name of political abolitionists we should disdain an appeal; but we know that there are, here and there, to the North of us, virtuous men, animated by real and generous enthusiasm, with a zeal not according to knowledge, clamouring for the immediate emancipation of slaves every where; demanding instant conformity to *their* views of right, though the Heavens fall. The aim of their mistaken zeal, is to benefit the slave, to lift up a downtrodden and oppressed race to the full equality of citizenship, and to hasten the obliteration of the blot of slavery from the escutcheon of America. Could sincere enthusiasts of that character, know that every such lawless and unauthorized effort, *increased* the evils which they would diminish, their own principles and good feelings would compel them to desist and be still.

This present meeting is probably a fair portrait of the population of Maryland. A majority of the persons composing it are not slaveholders and the number is not small of those who are non-slaveholders on principle; but yet there is not one who will violate, or patiently see violated, the chartered rights of his fellow citizens.

The black race as free people and as slaves are here all about us. It is fair to suppose, that with like intelligence, our opportunities must have given us fuller and more exact knowledge, of the subject of negro slavery, than have those who from their distant abodes, cry aloud and spare not, of matters in no wise concerning them and which they do not see, and cannot understand.

The State of Maryland, in proof of her active benevolence to the blacks, might refer to the fact that the loudest lover of that race has not gone before her in solid efforts to colonize them in that land, in which alone they can hope to rise to the proper level of man.

The census also shews that compared with her white population, no State has ever contained so large a proportion of emancipated negroes—all emancipated within her own limits.

It is notorious that from year to year the course of our Legislature had tended to improve and liberalize the condition of the free people of colour, while the growth of spontaneous benevolence had caused all the most painful features of slavery to disappear, and almost every day brought new instances of voluntary liberation. Such was the case some twenty years since.

Nor did Maryland stand alone in these things which made it plain that the day was not distant when a way might appear, in which without violating a simple right and by common consent, the cloud of slavery would be rolled away.

But vilified, threatened, assailed! the men of the South are not of the blood which will quail before injury, or hearken to the voice of insolvent dictation.

It is here well known that every cry of abolition; but especially that every assault in Legislative bodies upon our rights, has produced and made necessary stringent laws to restrain or regulate emancipation; that the privileges and comforts and hopes of those already freed have been abridged, by the necessity of more rigid surveillance. Nor is this all.

Chiefly by reason of the proceedings of Pennsylvania, negro property has become insecure in Maryland, and its value greatly diminished here, while in other regions it is increasing.

Do the lovers of the blacks in Pennsylvania think they act favorably to them when they make it necessary that they should be sent away from the mild discipline of Maryland to the far south?

Yet such has been and is the fact; and thousands and tens of thousands from the cotton and rice fields there, might justly accuse of their fate, the false and misguided philanthropy of their too busy friends.

Nay, were it possible for Pennsylvania to take away entirely the domestic value of our slaves; what would it avail? It would destroy utterly every hope of freedom for generations to come; rivet the chains and add weight to the shackles of slavery.

Fact might be piled upon fact and argument and illustration multiplied, to shew the absurdity, in addition to the wickedness, of those who are intent upon the mote in their neighbour's eye, forgetting the beam in their own; but the time and the occasion are not suitable for the further prosecution of the subject. Other seasons will not be wanting, it is time that it should be ascertained whether the pledges and guarantees of the constitution are to be considered valid and effectual, or empty words *without* meaning.

We therefore resolve, unanimously that we deeply sympathize with the bereaved family and relatives of our lamented citizen, JAMES H. KENNEDY.

Resolved, That in the sympathy and active kindness manifested towards our deceased friend, by many citizens of Carlisle, and in the soundness of views by them expressed on his constitutional rights and their readiness to support them, we recognize what was to be expected from sons and compatriots, undegenerate, of revolutionary sires, and of the framers of the Constitution.

Resolved, That a Committee of five be appointed by the chair, whose duty it shall be in behalf of the people of this County, to remonstrate with the authorities of Pennsylvania against the injuries to which we have been exposed and are yet liable to undergo, in asserting our rights as citizens under the 4th Article of the Constitution.

(*Committee*—Joseph I. Merrick, J. Dixon Roman, George W. Smith, Andrew Kershner, John O. Wharton.)

Resolved, That a like committee be appointed to lay the complaints of the meeting before the Legislature of Maryland and to invite appropriate remedies.

(*Committee*—Jervis Spencer, James Biays, Thos. E. Buchanan, Col. Wm. H. Fitzhugh, Hezekiah Boteler.)

Resolved, That a like committee be appointed, to present a memorial to the next Congress to ask the enactment of such laws, as have become necessary to carry out the purpose of the 4th article of the Constitution.

(*Committee*—Judge Thomas Buchanan, William B. Clarke, John T. Mason, Daniel Weisel, Robert Wason.)

On motion of Col. S. Carmack, it was resolved, that the proceedings be signed by the officers and published in the several papers of the County.

On motion the meeting adjourned.

> O.H. WILLIAMS, Chairman,
>
> JERVIS SPENCER,
> THOS. E. BUCHANAN, } Asst. Ch'n.
>
> *Geo. W. Smith,*
> *Edwin Bell,* } Secretaries.

ALS with Ens in ScCleA; PC in Boucher and Brooks, eds., *Correspondence,* pp. 385–387. NOTE: An AEU by Calhoun reads "Mr. Faulkner[,] relates to the case of Mr. Kennedy." Faulkner (1806–1884) was Representative from Va. 1847–1859; U.S. Minister to France 1859–1861; an officer in the Confederate army; and Representative from West Va. 1875–1877.

From JOHN H. BRINTON

West Chester, Penn[sylvani]a, 16 July 1847

Dear Sir, It is within your power to secure the ascendancy of the Democratic party in 1848, and to perpetuate, certainly strenghten [*sic*], the liberal principles brought into existence since 1844. *Five lines* from Gen: [Zachary] Taylor to yourself, published in the [Charleston] Mercury, announcing that he is opposed to a National Bank, and to Distribution, and in favor of the Constitutional Treasury and the Tariff of 1846, will secure an overwhelming support to him from the North in the National Convention. Local justice gives us the candidate at this time, but how cheerfully would our patriotic yeomanry adjourn["ed" *canceled*] any claim till 1852, in favor of Taylor. They are anxious to support him. They like him and would feel assured of success.

Not one word need be said about the slave limit of 36° 30'. I am persuaded the Democracy would agree to ["that" *interlined*] line. Yet this [Wilmot] Proviso is a complete humbug—for the Pacific States when organized and admitted into the Union, would have the matter of slavery completely under their control. Otherwise some States would be less sovereign than others. Without doubt, Ohio could establish slavery to morrow, despite the ordinance of 1787. Taylor's consenting to the Missouri line, or saying nothing about ["it" *interlined*], would make no difficulty in conducting our campaign before the people. The misconception which clouds this question could be easily cleared away.

Why not then, have this matter attended to? Taylor must be sick of Whiggery, and so must the Army. Their deeds have been praised but the justice of the War denounced—a very equivocal method of eulogy. The Whigs here have relaxed their hold of him. Just let a letter from him to you be given to the public, calling him neither Democrat or Whig, but announcing his political principles as specified, and he will be supported with enthusiasm by the North.

I am and always have been a distinctive party man of the Democratic School. Your career I am well acquainted with. You have not always been with us, in every movement, but to your purity, as a public character, I have always borne testimony. With high regard truly yours, John H. Brinton.

ALS in ScCleA; PC in Boucher and Brooks, eds., *Correspondence*, pp. 387–388.

From F[itz] w[illiam] Byrdsall, "Private"

New York [City], July 19th 1847
Dear Sir, You expressed yourself in the Senate of the U.S. to the purport that the Mexican war was the commencement of a new

career in our political history, which precluded your View into the future. I was much impressed with the force and beauty of the declaration at the time you uttered it, and since then, the idea your words conveyed, has remained indelibly traced upon my memory.

This war has given additional excitement to the fanaticism of Abolition, and has already divided the republican party of the North within itself, as well as almost placed it antagonistically towards the Southern portion. The battlefields of Mexico have also introduced Gen[era]l [Zachary] Taylor to the people of the United States, as the most prominent candidate for the presidency in 1848, and how many more candidates for that high office, are to come from the same source in future times, who can tell? It is remarkable too, in this era of anti war societies, evangelical unions, anti slavery conventions, mutual guarantee associations and propagandism of philanthropy that a war chief should stand high in the estimation of these modern crusaders, and that the partizans of every kind of movement, are much taken with the notion of a no party candidate, i.e. ["the" *altered to* "no"] movement at all. But with all this eclat about a no party, or all parties Candidate, it is very evident that Gen[era]l Taylor is not the first choice of those who have hitherto controlled the action of the two great political parties. There are other public men that the politicians would greatly prefer to him, but they will yield to the popular will, when they cannot with safety to their selfishness do otherwise. Now, although I do not consider the elevation of a military commander to the highest office in the Republic, as a desirable object as respects republican Institutions like ours, yet under existing circumstances, with Wilmot provisoes, vicious organizations of political parties &c &c, it may be that Gen[era]l Taylor is the best man to break up those long standing corrupt organizations, which have ["been" *canceled*] exercised more despotism over the citizen than ever existed under any other Constitutional Government. If Gen[era]l Taylor is disposed to exert the influence and patronage of the Executive department to this end, he would deserve the gratitude of every friend of freedom of suffrage, and I would prefer him to all other men that I know of, save one.

The recent batch of political manifestoes of the great I am Thomas H. Benton, together with the billing and cooings between the Wilmot proviso Democrats and the abolitionists, have greatly invigorated the hopes and desires of ["the" *interlined*; Martin] Van Buren myrmidons as respects a restoration of the Albany Regency Bourbons in the person of Silas Wright. They speak confidently of his being the candidate of the party in 1848, that with him the State

457

of New York can be carried, and, "as goes the State goes the Union." They allege that the loss by the [Albany] Argus faction, will be more than made up in other quarters; and besides, there is some prospect of a reconcilliation. There is evidently an under current movement on foot amongst the managers, and no effort will be left untried to regain ascendancy, or to triumph in working a defeat.

Party organizations, as managed, are the curse of the Union. Their operation is calculated to afford demonstration to the world, that the beautiful theory of representative Government is Utopian. The least Virtuous of our politicians in secret cliques and combinations, contrive, by packing the conventions, to controll the nominations, while there is at all times, a concert of action amongst them to keep the most high minded and capable men in the back ground. For many years you, and all your unflinching friends in this part of the Union, have been jealously guarded against, for there has grown up, nurtured by the partizans of Van Buren, Benton, Wright & Co. a hostile feeling towards you in the minds of many otherwise well meaning men, which amounts at this day to a fixed prejudice, with which no facts or reasonings can prevail. Have you not ["for years" *interlined*] been opposed by the organized presses of these politicians? Has not every measure you advocated been resisted to the uttermost, without regard to the principles avowed by the party? How many men in the Senate have risked encountering you ["as a means" *interlined*] to recommend themselves to favor or popularity, or to make themselves great, like as in the fable of the frog and the Ox? Without going fa[r]ther back than the last session of Congress, if Benton, [Lewis] Cass, [Hopkins L.] Turney, or any of your antagonists had prevailed against you the presses of the organization would have fulminated a yell of triumph throughout the land, the echoes of which would not have ceased during your life time; for in one sentence, you are the object of the malignity of three of the worst passions of human nature, namely, the *selfish ambition* of your political foes, the *avarice* of the protectionists and the *fanaticism* of the abolitionists? But it is greatly to your credit that you nobly sustained yourself through every trial; it is greatly to the honor of the State you represent that she has stood by you while opposed by all sorts of organizations ["of political and" *interlined and* "and" *canceled*] selfish interests, and which would have probably overwhelmed any other man of any other State. Nevertheless, the most wonderful feature of your career is, that notwithstanding all the above adverse circumstances, and even more, you have fixed upon the American mind, your views of Constitutional powers, your ideas of Republican Government, your principles of political economy, more extensively than all your competitors or Cotemporaries. Yet this is not all, there are thousands of politicians who in these days, are in favor of the constitutional expositions they formerly condemned, while they still retain the animosity towards the exponent, which his course *then* excited. For myself, I avow the fact that to no man of the dead or the living do I feel that I am so much indebted for a proper comprehension of our system of Government, as yourself.

Your recent speech, which you delivered in Charleston, is of timely import to the Southern States. It presents to them their true position in the confederacy, and the dangers to which they are exposed. No division should be *there* on the old party grounds about the presidency, but all should unite for the one great object of placing the veto power of the Constitution in the hands of a faithful Southern man. Let me tell you here, that the anti Southern Democrats in this part of the Union, are looking forward to the death of the defender of the Constitution, and calculating upon their future success after that event. "After him" say they, "there never will be another John C. Calhoun to stand boldly up in the defence of Southern slavery." "The wish is father to the thought," and that it exists in high quarters, I give you proof by naming W[illia]m F. Havemeyer the ex mayor of New York, as one of those who has uttered those words. There is truth in them too.

Some time ago, I was in hopes that the Republican party would have a majority of States in the next House of Rep[resentatives] but with Florida since lost, Georgia and N. Hampshire equally divided, I doubt the policy of sending the election of president to that body in 1848. If the Republican party should have a majority of States, and were you one of three candidates before the House, I cannot doubt the result, for with the intelligent members who are friendly to you (no other public man standing so high in the estimation of the virtuous and intelligent men of our party,) and the Whigs, who certainly prefer you to any of the opposing candidates of their party, your success would be almost inevitable. For many years, you have been my first choice for that office. I know of no other man who deserves it so well of the whole country, but a crisis has arrived which enjoins us to take no step in that direction, unless we have light upon our path, unless we have a candidate with the popular prestige of success. It appears to me that the path you have indicated for the South, would lead to General Taylor for the next presidency. I think we can elect him by the popular vote. In that event,

God grant for the safety of the Union that he may prove to be all that the true hearts of the Republic anxiously and patriotically desire.

The Hon. Dixon H. Lewis of Alabama has had a short sojourn in the city of New York. It is not my wont to call on public men when they are en route in this section of country. I never did so when [Andrew] Jackson, Van Buren, [John] Tyler, [James K.] Polk and others of distinction were here, but Mr. Lewis merits from me grateful consideration and I visited him twice with much gratification to myself. I regret that circumstances prevented me from evincing those attentions to him which would have afforded pleasing recollections to me. His frankness and kind heartedness are so evident as to ensure him a passport to the best feelings of every body. He went about our city and its environs considerably. I do not recollect an instance of a public man that left more favorable impressions upon those who came in contact with him than he has. At a meeting of the farmer's club, he descanted upon his own agricultural experience and observation, in a way that pleased many of the ["spectators" *canceled and* "auditors" *interlined*] some of whom have since highly commended the original yet common sense character of the views he expressed. The Tammany Society learning that he was not an ordinary minded man, but one attracting popularity and notice, not only from the citizens, but also from its rival body the Texas and Oregon association, sent a deputation to him ["with an invitation" *interlined*] to become a brother of the Columbian order, which he acceded to, and was regularly initiated into that Society, the over twenty Sachems of which, are nearly all of the Van Buren & Wright Kidney. Strange as it may seem, the rival factions united temporarily on him to a certain extent, and he became for a time, a sort of Lion to the two sets of Democrats; one set in favor of nominating him for the vice presidency with Silas Wright for the presidency, the other set for him the same office with Gen[era]l Cass; both sets calculating that a vice presidential candidate from the State of Alabama, would be from the right section of the Union to run with their man, especially as Mr. Lewis is well known as a friend of Mr. Calhoun, *of course*, his nomination would draw all the friends of the Carolinian. As to the motives of either set, I confess my want of faith in N.Y. politicians, and could more readily believe that enmity to Mr. Calhoun is at the bottom of these matters, that to work upon the self love of Mr. Lewis, a common feature of all men, is not the most difficult method of accomplishing an alienation between friends.

In connection with these remarks, it may be well to examine the political characters of those whose names are attached to the letter inviting him to a public dinner. The list comprises some of the best names amongst our merchants, but them I shall pass over to get at the politicians; and first I shall give you the *Van Buren men of the anti Southern stamp.* Viz. J.J. Coddington—Elijah F. Purdy—W[illia]m F. Havemeyer—Cha[rle]s A. Secor—James Conner—A[aron or Augustus?] Vanderpoel—B[ernard] J. Messerole—Andrew Carrigan—Niel Gray—Tho[ma]s B. Tappan—W[illia]m C. Bryant—F[rancis] W. Edmonds—Nathaniel Jarvis—J[ames] McCullough—Theodore Sedgewick—D[avid] D[udley] Field—J[ohn] J. Cisco—J.J. Westervelt—A[ndrew] H. Mickle—W[illia]m A. Walker—Robert H. Ludlow—Edward Sandford—Thomas C. Fields—Henry Nicoll—Cha[rle]s P. Brown.

Next I shall present before you the men of the Gen[era]l Cass stamp—Viz—E[dward] K. Collins—John McKeon—F[rancis] B. Cutting—Cha[rle]s McVean—Prosper M. Wetmore—J[oseph] S. Bosworth—W[illia]m C. Bouck—H[enry] H. Byrne—D[avid] C. Broderick.

I shall now give you a list of the active but convenient politicians whose names are to the letter—the men who profess democratic principles, but care more for ascendancy in the party—*The always administration men.* Viz—James C. Stowall—R[ichard] T. Compton—Oliver Charlock—L[orenzo] B. Sheppard—Rob[er]t H. Morris—T. Jefferson Smith—Cha[rle]s Webb—D[avid] S. Jackson—A.J. Bergen—Sam[ue]l Osgood—C[ornelius] S. Bogardus—John B. Haskins—S[amuel] J. Willis—Geo[rge] F. Thompson—A. MaClay—G[eorge] H. Purser—George E. Baldwin—Abijah Ingraham—Eccles Gillender—M[oses] G. Leonard—George Montgomery.

Finally the Calhoun signers, steadfast and true are—John Le Conte—A[braham] D. Wilson—Henry D. Cruger—Geo[rge] B. Butler—John D. Van Buren—E[manuel] B. Hart—James T. Brady—John Commerford.

The reply of Mr. Lewis to the Gentlemen who invited him to a public dinner is admirable in its style, temper, and patriotic sentiments, and still more so in the enlarged scope which ["he" *interlined*] attributes to free trade principles, and the mighty results they are calculated to produce as regards personal freedom, political economy and general civilization. I have seldom seen more sound doctrine, clearer argument, or better philanthropy expressed in as few words, in short, it is a happy compendium of the whole. It gives great satisfaction and many persons have complained to me because I did not put their names to the letter of invitation.

I sat down my dear Sir, to write you a letter about generalities and I find I have written a longer one than I intended. I trust however to your indulgent consideration of my motives if I trespass too much upon your time; for as this is not intended either for public display of myself—or for private gain, and is written to a man I have never seen, ["if" *canceled*] I may reasonably hope you will receive it with considerations similar to those, which have self-evidently dictated it. I am Dear Sir, with the highest Respect Your Ob[edien]t Ser[van]t, F.W. Byrdsall.

[P.S.] The annexation of Texas with its cotton soil and Anglo American population was a measure of absolute necessity to the United States—not ["so" *interlined*] the annexation of Mexico with the population she has. It *was* our interest to preserve her republican nationality equally from ourselves & from Europe. But *now* we must take her, in order to keep her from the hands of others, and ["we" *interlined*] will become deteriorated by such a junction morally, while politically the Union of the States will not be strengthened.

However we may *want* the lands, we surely do not *need* the incorporation with us of such a people of inferior mixture as the Mexican. We have started upon the course of conquest, we cannot now recede if we would, our success will create circumstances to impel us onward in that direction, whether we are willing or not.

With the accession of several millions of Mexicans at one swoop— with the vast increase of Emigration from all parts of Europe, the question presents itself, can this extensive territory and people ultimately escape the fate all Monarchal and Republican Empires have fallen under? namely dismemberment.

ALS in ScCleA; PC in Jameson, ed., *Correspondence*, pp. 1121–1127.

To JOSEPH W. LESESNE, [Mobile]

Fort Hill, 19th July 1847

My dear Sir, I am obliged to you for the opportunity you afforded me to read Mr. [John A.] Camp[b]ell's address, & for your views on the subject to which it refers.

Regarded in the abstract, there is not an opinion expressed by you, in which I do not concur; and yet, under circumstances, I am not prepared to say, that our friend Campbell was premature in addressing the meeting, or expressing the Sentiments he did. He has taken his ground very ably & cautiously.

It does really seem extraordinary, that mere soldiership should be regarded by the great body of the American people, as furnishing the best proof of statesmanship—& It is certainly a very unfavourable omen, as to the duration of our institutions. I go farther and admit, that the election of the successfull General is calculated to impress more deeply on the publick mind, the idea that soldiership is the only certain road to the highest civil honors, & to increase, in the same degree, the military sperit of the country, which is already too high for its institutions & liberty.

But I am disposed to believe, as paradoxical as it may appear on the first glance, that the only certain way left us to remedy the evil, is to elect the successful General [Zachary Taylor], in this case. It will make clear to all, who may hereafter be entrusted with the administration, what ought to have been known without it, that the certain effect of making war is the defeat of the party in power; if the war be successful, by the successful General; &, if unsuccessful, by the opposition. Let this once be clearly seen, and we shall have no more wars, when it is possible to avoid them. The party in power will be too much averse to paying the penality [*sic*] to rush head long into war; and instead of using every art to force the opposition into war, the opposition will be scarcely able to force them into it. Had Mr. [James K.] Polk & his administration dreamed, that the war with Mexico would make a man so little known, as General Taylor was then, President, we never would [have] had the war. He never would have been ordered to the del Norte. Scores of constitutional objections would have occurred to them against it. On the contrary, they ordered him, because they believed war would be popular; that its popularity would accrue to them, & that instead of turning them out of power, it would be the certain way to retain & perpetuate power in their hands. If the result should prove, that it will have that effect, as the election of Mr. Polk or the election of any one of its supports would prove it to have, we shall never again be free from war. No; those in power must be taught, that the almost certain retribution for making war is the loss of power; & that nothing but the clearest justice & the most urgent necessity for making it, can prevent the retribution.

Again, I am disposed to believe, that there is not the slightest chance for reforming the government & pressing [*sic*; preserving] our fine & popular institutions, through either of the existing parties. The leaders on both sides are thoroughly rotten—incorri[gi]bly [*or* "unconscionably"] so—mere spoils men, and hollow hearted hypocrit[e]s, without a particle of regard for principles, & perfectly indifferent to country. I am also disposed to believe, that the only chance for reformation is to break up the present party organization; that, that can only be done, by breaking up party machinery, & especially the Baltimore convention; & that, that can only be done by running as the people[']s candidate, one of wide spread popularity, like General Taylor. I also am inclined to believe, that it is the only way, in which the South can be united, and thereby avert the calamity, impending over it.

These are certainly are [*sic*] weighty considerations—so much so, as to make it our duty not to put ourselves for the present against him. It may be, that no other alternative will be left us, but to support him, & strong as are the objections you state, regarded apart from the circumstances under which we are placed.

My own course is made up. I wait for farther developements with a fixed determination to take the course most consistent with my passed course; best calculated to promote the success of the principles & policy, for which I have so long contended, & to avert impending dangers to the South & the institutions of the country. But I see many reasons, why, with these views, I *may* in the end find it my duty to support General Taylor; but I can see none, which can possibly induce me to support a caucus candidate; an old hunker of the [Martin] Van Buren, [Silas] Wright & [Thomas H.] Benton school, or one who runs on the existing party grounds, which whatever may be profession on either side, means nothing but the spoils. [Winfield] Scott I do not think, I could support in any case. I think him hollow hearted & unsound in reference to the South. I write you freely & in confidence; but if you desire, you may show this to Camp[b]ell or any other friend, in whose good sense & fidelity, you can put entire confidence. Truly, J.C. Calhoun.

Transcript in NcU, Joseph W. Lesesne Papers.

From R[ICHARD] K. CRALLÉ

Lynchburg, July 20th 1847

My dear Sir: Owing to my absence in Kanawha [County] I did not, until recently, receive your favour of the 6th of May last. The views you express entirely accord with those which I expected you entertained; for though the Papers had stated with much positiveness that letters had been received from you warranting their statements, I did not well see how they could be true. We all felt surprise, as it was not in your usual line of action. The facts, so far as I am able to form an opinion, obviously indicate a decided movement in favour of [Zachary] Taylor in certain sections of the country; but it is equally certain that it is by no means agreeable to the political Leaders, *at least*, in others. The course of [Thomas H.] Benton shews very clearly that the Hunkers are by no means satisfied; and I have no doubt the late letters of Taylor, which exhibit such decided opposition to the machinery of the Party, will bring upon his head the full measure of their wrath. This will also, to a considerable extent, be the effect on the Whig side of the House; for the aspirants of this faction are as much interested in keeping up this machinery as the Hunkers themselves. What will be the ultimate resolution of Parties in this state of things, time alone can show. I am utterly unable to foresee the end, farther than this, that it may force the election into the House. This must be if the Whigs and Hunkers adhere to their old system. Perhaps the former, *in the South* and *South west* may surrender the Convention and unite on Taylor; but considering the abolition question as destined to exercise a powerful influence in the ["question" *canceled and* "election" *interlined*], I very much doubt whether the North and North west, will follow the example. I think they will not. And as to the Hunkers I am persuaded they will never yield up the weapons of their trade. Benton and [Silas] Wright, and [Thomas] Ritchie and the rest will take care to have a candidate of their own. I have received some letters from the North which declare the movements in favour of Taylor in that section are entirely superficial, and that the leaders are exerting themselves to the utmost to arrest it. These exertions, I understand, are not confined to one but extend to both Parties.

Suppo[s]ing that they succeed in rallying the north and northwest against an independent candidate what would be the effect so far as the State Rights Party are concerned? It would undoubtedly tend to unite the South on two of the most important questions of the day—Abolition and the Convention—and in doing this great additional strength must be given to our principles. This, it is true, may not tell in the ensuing Presidential Election, especially if your name be withdrawn from the list of candidates, but it will certainly have a powerful influence hereafter in the final triumph of your principles. As to Taylor himself I have lived too long to trust implicitly to professions, couched in generalities. Yet something may be gained in an issue so distinctly made against the two corrupt dynasties of the past, and their corrupting machinery. The history of Jacksonism, however, contains admonitions I can never forget, and it seems to me dangerous for us to desert, at present, the position of *"masterly inactivity."* If the Hunkers discover they cannot get into power *against* him, they will not hesitate to do so *with* him. You elected [Andrew] Jackson in 1828 against the efforts of Hunkerism, and he immediately repaid the service by throwing himself in their arms. Taylor may do the same; and, estimating the seductive arts of the Albany and Richmond Juntos by the history of the past, I confess I am far from being certain he will not. Your proper course, therefore, (excuse my freedom) appears to me to stand aloof and wait events. Public sentiment must shortly become more settled one way or the other, and circumstances will determine the line of duty and patriotism.

Your last letter was written before the final result of our spring elections was known. This has greatly galled the Hunkers—and had our friends firmly maintained themselves the vile faction might have been extirpated. As it is, they have felt the strength of the State Rights Party, scattered as it was—and will learn hereafter to rely less on their own. I do not think they can ever recover; for those of your friends who shamefully deserted and went over to the enemy, have gained only the contempt of all, and lost the reward for which they basely sold themselves. [Thomas S.] Bocock [Representative from Va.] will lose his seat—Treadway [*sic*; William M. Tredway], the two Leakes [that is, Shelton F. Leake and Walter D. Leake], and [Augustus A.] Chapman have been driven ignobly into retirement, and R[ichard] K. Meade, (an old friend) has been taken up in preference to [Richard H.] Baptist the protojee of Ritchie. On the whole I think the lesson will deter others hereafter from following their example.

I regret I did not reach home in time to forward you a letter from Washington suggesting the propriety of sending a delegation from South Carolina to the late Convention at Chichago, with its reasons. You have written, however, as I learn from the Papers; so that your views are known. I wait to see what Ritchie and his followers will now say in reference to the views expressed by you at Memphis. Benton & Wright have, I understand, fully sanctioned them. Such is one of the political necessities of the times; and the Mexican affair, if I mistake not, will furnish another at no distant day.

By the sudden death of an old and esteemed friend, I have been compelled to assume very many urgent duties, which, combined with others, will keep me so engaged that I shall have little leisure to devote to political matters; but I shall not fail to keep you informed of such matters here and elsewhere as may come to my knowledge.

My family will go to Meadowgrove, our summer residence, in the course of next week, where they will remain until November. They unite with me in affectionate regards to yourself, Mrs. [Floride Colhoun] C[alhoun] and Miss [Martha] Cornelia [Calhoun]. We have endeavoured in vain to ascertain whether Patrick [Calhoun] has gone to Mexico. I see the name of Capt. Calhoun mentioned, but have not ascertained whether it be him. Where is he? If John [C. Calhoun, Jr.] and James [Edward Calhoun] be with you, please present my best respects, and say if they visit the Virginia Springs this season, they must not fail to visit and stay a part of their time with us at Meadowgrove. With the highest regard & esteem I am, dear Sir, truly yours, R.K. Crallé.

ALS in ScCleA.

From ROBERT N. GOURDIN

Charleston, 23d July 1847

My dear Sir, I venture to trespass upon your time to remind you of your promise to send me from Pendleton two Copies of your speeches, the one having your autograph simply, and the other to be inscribed to Mr. Richard Cobden as sent from yourself. I had the pleasure to spend several hours with Mr. Cobden last summer, and much of his Conversation turned upon the influence of your principles upon the destinies of the great Commercial Communities of the old as well as the new Wor[l]d. He has never seen your speeches as published, and the very high estimation in which he holds you will make a Copy from yourself especially valuable. As your fellow Citizen of our little State I will be gratified in being permitted to take it to him. I will sail for Europe in the steamer of the 1st prox[im]o but should you forward the books immediately they will be sent to me by a ship to sail from Charleston in the next ten days. With kind regards to Mrs. [Floride Colhoun] Calhoun. I am dear Sir with high respect, Robert N. Gourdin.

ALS in ScCleA.

From FERNANDO WOOD

New York [City,] July 23 1847
Dear Sir, I have read your letter to the Putnam [County, Ga.] Whig meeting dated 27th June 1847 with much pleasure—and concur entirely in its sentiments.

You may be assured that the whole north do not hold opposite opinions to you on this subject.

Many of my friends and myself have long ago determined that if this narrow spirit of fan[a]ticism continues at the North, and produces disunion, *our homes* will be found south of the Potomac, where true freedom, chivalry and honour characterise the people. We are heartily sick and disgusted with the conduct of many of our immediate citizens on this question. Very Truly Yours, Fernando Wood.

ALS in ScCleA; PC in Jameson, ed., *Correspondence*, pp. 1127–1128.

To THO[MAS] G. CLEMSON, [Brussels]

Fort Hill, 24th July 1847
My dear Sir, I am happy to learn by yours of the 14th June, that you are all so well. We are, also, in the enjoyment of good health, ["except" *interlined*] Mrs. [Floride Colhoun] Calhoun, who has had some slight symptoms of the return of the nerveous affection, to which she has for some time back been more or less affected at this period of the year. I do not ["think" *interlined*] she has any just cause to expect any thing more than a very slight affection of the kind; but she is so easily alarmed, that she proposes to take a short excursion to Glenn's Springs. William [Lowndes Calhoun], who returned a week or ten days since from Alabama, in fine health & much increased in size, will accompany her. He gives a very florid discription of our corn & cotton crop. He says the neighbours think the corn [will yield] from 70 to upwards [of] 100 bushels per acre, and that the cotton was on an average head high, & looked as fine as it can do. My own crop both of corn & cotton looks as well as I have had ever at this season. Were it not for a defective stand in places, and a few acres injured from excess of rain, it really would ["be" *interlined*] the best corn crop I ever saw. Some of it must go to 60 bushels per acre. About ⅔ of my cotton is very fine, and most of the rest pretty fair. We have in 920 acres in cotton in Alabama, & 125 here, making

1045 acres, which, if there should be no accident ["must make" *inter-lined*] upwards of 350,000 pounds of clean cotton.

It is now entirely free from insects and worms, but I dread, (not here) but in Alabama, the worms. It has ever since I last wrote you been very cool & wet. It rains every day, & often many times in the day, & some times very hard; & the prospect of its continuance is as good, as it was three weeks ago. It is the right weather to produce the worms. The cotton crop generally over this State & Georgia is said to be very indifferent.

I wrote, as I think I wrote to you I would, to Andrew [Pickens Calhoun] to forward from Mobile 2 bushels of cotton seed, and a half gallon each of corn & peas, to be prepared for planting. If the experiment should succeed with them, it will give us all we could wish for successful agriculture. I am still improving my place; & shall begin, as soon as the crop is laid by, that is in the course of a week, to prepare for a regular system of manuring. My ditches effectually protect my land from washing.

I fear the rain has been in excess for your place. It has been heavier below, than with us.

We have had little of publick interest of late. The Mexican war has been at a stand. There is ever now & then a movement in favour of General [Zachary] Taylor. The indication still is, that he will be the popular candidate, in opposition to the caucus nominees. I think with you, that my position is the most eligible of all the publick men of our country. It is the only independent one; and I can see symptoms, that it begins to be felt.

I do not in the least doubt, but that you are right, as to the European terminus of our steam boat line; or as to the means, by which it was selected. It was done as every thing with us is done, through favouritism.

It is appearent ["daily" *canceled*], that the conflict between North & South is every day becoming more pointed and determined. If nothing else should be in the way it, of itself, will do much to break up the old party organizations.

All join in love to you & Anna [Maria Calhoun Clemson] & the children [John Calhoun Clemson and Floride Elizabeth Clemson]. Tell them how happy Grandfather is to hear that they are so well, & are such good children. Your affectionate father, J.C. Calhoun.

ALS in ScCleA; PEx in Jameson, ed., *Correspondence*, pp. 735–736.

Floride [Colhoun] Calhoun, Fort Hill, to Mrs. A[nna] M[aria Calhoun] Clemson, [Brussels], 7/25. She writes of her recent nervous indisposition, milder than that of a few years ago, and her proposed visit to Glenn Springs. The boys at home are all studying and preparing for school; the remainder of the family is well. [George] McDuffie is very ill and not expected to live. Cudy [Martha Maria Colhoun] and her father [John Ewing Colhoun] are both ill, and it is expected that his illness also may prove fatal. Floride hopes that [Thomas G.] Clemson may be able to sell his S.C. place and procure another more to his liking. ALS in ScCleA, Thomas Green Clemson Papers.

From H[ENRY] W. CONNER

Charleston, July 27, 1847

My Dear Sir, Your letters to me of the 8th & to Col. [Franklin H.] Elmore[,] myself & others of same date was duly rec[eive]d & I delayed saying any thing in reply until I could say something to the point.

After some—to me—unpleasant delay we have reached a starting point—& the ballance of the work will be pushed on with energy.

We have adopted your caption for the subscription list—with very slight alterations & have procured almost 30 names—amongst the most influential planters & men of substance (not a politician amongst them) in the State as signers to the circular prepared sometime since under your approval & have them now in the press printing—& in the course of this week will set about directing them. We will ["suggest" *canceled and* "adopt" *interlined*] the plan you suggest of sending different lists for different amounts. The distribution & correspondence will be mainly with I[saac] W. Hayne & myself ["in behalf of the Committee" *interlined*]—& we will be obliged if you will designate to us parties in Virginia[,] North Carolina—Georgia[,] Mississippi & any where else to whom we might address ourselves. Also where necessary to say any thing beyond what is contained in the general circular & subscription list. Please give us the key or if you prefer to say any thing yourself give us your directions. We will send you a number of the circulars & lists in a few days. Our desire is while we wish not to overdo—at the same time intend to leave nothing undone to entitle us to succeed in the undertaking. Every thing I have seen since my last confirms me in the belief that we can raise a large sum of money immediately in this State. I have been in fact agreeably surprised to find our planters &

men of substance so prompt to respond—without exception whenever they have been approached.

From other States—I receive also gratifying replys—not in money—but shewing that the right feeling exists *amongst the people* & only requires a proper occasion or proper means to bring it into action. I enclose you now a copy of a letter rec[eive]d from an active & efficient young man in New Orleans—formerly of this city. It is I am confident a true exhibit of the state of things here. Other friends write me in the same tone, but all ["of them" *interlined*] are ready to act with us & for us. They are preparing me a list of planters & other proper persons, in Louisiana & Mississippi.

The signers of the circular embrace some prominent whigs.

Dixon H. Lewis [Senator from Ala.] was here last week. He had a letter from Jef[ferson] Davis to himself & I believe Col. Elmore dated Monterey in May I think. It was in reply to their inquiries touching Gen[era]l [Zachary] Taylor[']s (Davis[']s] Fatherinlaw[']s]) politicks & a more cautious—guarded & [William Henry] Harrison ["letter" *canceled*] like letter I never saw.

Mr. Lewis is of opinion you ought to go to New York or the Springs & see & hear *the people*. He says Silas Wright[']s] prospects are hopeless, & [Lewis] Cass not much better. Taylor he says is the man of the people.

We will report progress as we go & beg your advice & directions as often as possible. Very Truly y[ou]rs, H.W. Conner.

[P.S.] We (as far as we are concerned) desire to keep the Editor out of view[?], until we have first the money.

[Enclosure]

E. Warren Moise to [H.W. Conner, Charleston]

New Orleans, July 18, [18]47

Dear Sir, Your letter of the 1st instant came duly to hand, its contents I note with pleasure. The necessity of a thorough union of the slave interests is apparent, and yet a remarkable anomaly is shown in the fact that those who have an interest absolutely identical in the preservation of the same property and same institutions are divided among themselves. The cause of this is obvious. The Presidency is the first consideration and therefore the slave question must not be touched or rather the slave interest must not be defended. This is the policy of the Central Press at Washington. The [Washington] Union dare not speak out[;] it would distract the party! Its duty—which in this respect it performs to a miracle, is to conceal, apologise—and deceive on the one hand while on the other it must denounce all who would enlighten. The party press follows

471

in the wake of the Union and the consequence is that few seem to ["care and" *canceled*] know and none to care for the anti slavery movements at the Capitol last winter. The remedy of course is to be found in the establishment of a proper paper at Washington to be extensively circulated at the South. In Louisiana little can be done until public attention is thoroughly aroused to the importance of the issues. We have but one democratic paper in New Orleans and its sympathies are with the Northern portion of the party. The Whig papers like the Democratic are afraid of alienating the North. The press is in the hands of the politicians. Circulate a proper newspaper among the people and things will go right.

I am forced in candor to say that all political movements originating in S. Carolina are regarded here with a great deal of suspicion. It is a lamentable truth that the indepen[den]ce of South Carolina of party trammels lies at the bottom of the feeling that prevails here. This independence provokes the politicians—the politicians denounce her and the public mind is thoroughly misled. Every thing beginning in South Carolina is charged upon Mr. Calhoun and the whole is wound up with Mr. C[alhoun]'s ambition to be President. You & I know better than this yet it is true and all suggestions coming from So. Carolina are regarded with doubt and distrust.

So far as in me lies, I will do all in my power to carry out the views expressed by you[;] my theatre however is a very narrow one as I have no idea of seriously entering upon public life. I am too poor to think of much beyond my profession. I should be pleased to hear more definitely from you. If you wish me to make inquiries as to the practicability of raising funds here for the establishment of a press in Washington as indicated in your circular I will do so. I do not think however much can be done here[,] Nor do I believe the scheme practicable to raise by a *general* subscription the necessary funds and I am clear that efforts to raise money for the purpose should be limited to that class of persons who entertain the same views upon national affairs—without reference to the particular object, the defense of the slave question. All political topics somehow run into one another and I consider it impossible in the *present state of the public mind* to create a party to rest on one idea. If the slave owners were once awakened to the subject it could be done—but the press must be established and the paper circulated before you can get them out of their profound slumber.

Mr. [Henry] Gourdin of your City forwarded me some packages of Mr. Calhoun[']s speeches and the proceedings of a public meeting in Charleston for distribution. I was sorry they did not arrive during the session of the Legislature as I could then have had them sent all over the State. Be good enough to mention this to Mr. Gourdin. As it is I intend distributing them next month so as to let them bear if practicable on the Fall elections. I shall be very happy to hear from you and give you any information in my power touching the politics of this State. Very Respectfully Yours, (Signed) E. Warren Moise.

ALS with En in ScCleA. NOTE: Edwin Warren Moise (1811–1868) was born in Charleston but settled in New Orleans in 1840. He was an attorney, a member of the La. legislature, and Attorney General of that State, 1856–1860.

From R[OBERT] F. W. ALLSTON

Waccamaw Beach [Georgetown District, S.C.] 28th July 1847
Dear Sir, I beg leave, tho' tardy, to acknowledge yours of the 18th Ap[ri]l which came to me under cover from a Committee in Charleston post marked June 2d. After attending without delay to what seemed to be most needful, ascertaining the sentiments of my neighbors, I laid the Communications aside under the immediate pressure of domestic afflictions and many consequent claims upon time which every man will acknowledge who has at heart the wholesome entertainment, as well as the business of his family. And now I have little to say and you perhaps less time to read a letter. Still I feel impel'd, on taking up this package, to inform you that within 10 days after its receipt, I had written to the Committee to advise they might draw upon us as soon as the new crop comes in for $2810 (+ $30 annual subscription). Our small society here entirely approved of the object as expressed and if our people were all at home the sum could have been doubled easily.

Absenteeism is the curse and will be, unless diminish'd, the ruin of the low country—inasmuch as its tendency is to disorganization. It diminishes the value of Estates, abridges the revenue of the planter—and the comforts of the negroe, except in the case of smart progressing[?] fellows, because they (and there are a number of this kind) manage to convert to their ["own" *interlined*] use and profit a portion of their time & labor which should properly go to swell the income of the owner and so far contribute to the comfortable supply of the whole plantation.

It breaks in upon (has broken in several instances) that tie between master, master's family and slave of which you know the force, and which depends so much upon mutual intimate acquaintance, and occasional, nameless, kindnesses shown.

I had occasion to address my constituents on the 5th inst., who were much startled by the plain manner in which I spoke of the "Wilmot Proviso" the reasons for it, and of our conduct in regard to it. (I fear our representative [Alexander D.] Sims, train'd by his late relative [and former Representative from Va.] Gen[era]l [George C.] Dromgoole, is too much bound to "the party.") On this occasion I refer'd (the first time any one has had the temerity to refer to it publicly) to absenteeism & traced its influence on pauperism: and in enumerating as well as I could from memory the Rice plantation settlements of Georgetown District I discover'd that of 108 settlements, the proprietors (& in case of Estates the Executors) of *46* only are bona fide *residents*. The Proprietors of *50* are, at this moment, absent, and are habitually absent, without the limits of the district from the latter part of May till the beginning of November. The proprietors of *12* are absentees the year round—having permanent residence of family elsewhere, and coming up occasionally in winter to look after their individual interest. As you may well suppose the mass of wealth is own'd by the *62* absentees. The *46* however are creeping up, as they make more of their property and it is among these that you will find the best discipline. With my best wishes for the success of the proposed experiment, I am Yours Respectfully, R.F.W. Allston.

ALS in ScCleA; PEx in Boucher and Brooks, eds., *Correspondence*, pp. 388–389.

From F[ITZ]W[ILLIAM] BYRDSALL

New York [City,] July 29th 1847

Dear Sir, I enclose you a portion of yesterday[']s [New York] Globe for the sake of a well written article from the Worcester Palladium, as well as the Globe editorial. The Wilmot Proviso movement both in its origin and object is becoming better understood.

I learn that the calculation here is, that the abolition voters in this State are about twenty thousand, at least so say the partizans of [Martin] Van Buren & [Silas] Wright, and that with this assistance, they can carry the State of New York. I believe Van Buren, Wright, [Samuel?] Young, [Azariah C.] Flagg, [Michael] Hoffman & Co. are going body and soul for the Wilmot Proviso. There is no doubt about it. I regretted the confirmation of Hoffman by the Senate, for now, he requites the favor as I knew he would; he is one of strongest of the conspirators against the Constitution. It is openly declared by their partizan that no man can be elected president who is not favorable to the principle of the Wilmot proviso.

It appears to me that these men by proper caution and skill on our part, can be put in their proper position of antagonism to the Republican party of the Union. Strong ground should be taken at once by the South and the whole ["question" *interlined*] be met firmly but calmly—the longer this is deferred, the worse will it be hereafter.

I hope the next Session of Congress will present men and things in a full and unmistakeable light to the whole people of the Union. I hope there will be a sifting; no matter if parties are broken in pieces, so the Union be preserved.

Gen[era]l [Zachary] Taylor's chance of a nomination by the Democratic party of the North is lessening. In consequence of cliques, the tide is setting in in favor of a national convention and if we shall have one, as usual, it will be packed but not for the General.

I should like that every county in the Southern States ["would" *interlined*] hold public meetings against the Wilmot proviso project. Such an expression of public opinion is needed. With all Respect I am Dear Sir Your ob[edien]t Ser[van]t, F.W. Byrdsall.

[P.S.] The quiet manner in which the Palladium ["rubs" *canceled and* "touches" *interlined*] Mr. [James K.] Polk for his magnanimity towards [Thomas H.] Benton & Co. to whom he was under so little obligation for his elevation to the Presidency, is equal to ["the" *interlined*] severest blows that could be struck. He who penned the introductory paragraphs intended to cut deeply and therefore used the smoothest edge.

ALS in ScCleA; PEx in Boucher and Brooks, eds., *Correspondence*, p. 389.

To HENRY GOURDIN, [Charleston]

Fort Hill, 29th July 1841 [*sic*; 1847]
My dear Sir, I received a note [dated 7/23] from your brother Robert [N. Gourdin] by the last mail, reminding me of my promise to send him two copies of my speeches, one for himself & the other for Mr. [Richard] Cobden. He stated that he would sail by the steamer the

first of next month, and as this cannot reach him before he leaves I address to you.

He says in his note that a vessel will sail for Liverpool in about ten days & that if the volumes should be sent immediately they will be in time to go by her. As there is no immediate private opportunity I have concluded to send them by ["mail" *canceled*] the stage & rail road. Truly, J.C. Calhoun.

ALS in GEU, Robert Newman Gourdin Papers. NOTE: Robert Newman Gourdin (1812–1894) and Henry Gourdin (1803–1879) were prominent Charlestonians who contributed substantially to the posthumous payment of Calhoun's debts and were involved, during the Civil War, in the concealment of Calhoun's body from federal troops.

From H[ENRY] W. PERONNEAU

Charleston, July 29/47

Dear Sir, Mr. N[athaniel] Heyward called upon me some weeks ago and requested me to acknowledge to you the receipt of your letter to him on the Subject of the Paper to be established at Washington, to thank you for it, and to say that he would most willingly aid in this effort. Mr. H[eyward] also requested me to call upon him, whenever we should require funds—and he would then do whatever I should advise him as proper to be done by him.

I have the satisfaction to inform you that I have never known a movement of this kind more *warmly* received by our friends, or more liberally responded to by subscriptions of money, so far as we have yet made applications. On the score of ["the" *canceled*] *funds* we shall have no difficulty. I believe that we can raise $40,000 or $50,000 in this State. Would that I could hope ["to" *canceled and* "we should" *interlined*] have as little difficulty in finding the proper man for the Editorial department.

It has been suggested as important that we should make the effort soon to prepare some of our friends in each of the Southern Legislatures to get those bodies, at their ensuing Sessions, to follow the Virginia lead, by adopting her *Resolutions*. I presume, to effect this would not be attended with much difficulty, and I think a movement in this direction might with advantage be made *simultaneously* with our efforts for the newspaper. The one probably would aid the other. Very Respectfully & truly, H.W. Peronneau.

ALS in ScCleA.

To RICHARD RUSH, [U.S. Minister to France, Paris]

Fort Hill, 29th July 1847

My dear Sir, I take much pleasure, in introducing to you, Edward R. Laurens, who will deliver you this.

He is a grand son of Henry Laurens, & Nephew of Col. John Laurens, both of whom bore such distinguished parts in our revolutionary struggle, the one in council and the other in the field. He himself is a highly respected and esteemed citizen.

His Lady [Margaret Horry Laurens] accompanies him. She is in bad health, & he visits Europe with the view to its restoration.

Your attention to them, will place me under particular obligation. With great respect Yours truly, J.C. Calhoun.

ALS in NjP, Rush Family Papers (published microfilm of The Letters and Papers of Richard Rush, reel 21, item 11123).

From SARAH MYTTON MAURY

[Liverpool, England, *ca.* August 1847]

My dear Mr. Calhoun, Your letter of the 11th of May is now at Alton Towers the seat of [John Talbot,] the Earl of Shrewsbury in the hands of his Chaplain, a Mr. Conolly an American from Wilmington in Delaware. The Speech which you sent me is also in the same custody, and the "slavery" question *there* is gaining somewhat. I have also recently seen a vehement Abolitionist who has just returned from Paris where he met some very intelligent Americans, and his views are considerably modified; he now acknowledges that he would be far less precipitate than he formerly should have been; and he listened with great patience to my argument as to what would become of Old England & New England if cotton should fail them.

I hear from several private friends that you have now won golden opinions for your opposition to the Mexican War.

Our election has terminated in favour of the Free ["Trade" *interlined*] Candidates—of course the contest everywhere is ridiculous against that *now recognised measure.*

For reasons which you would approve both on his account, and on account of his competitors, I gave my voice in favour of Lord

477

John Manners—he could not injure Free Trade, and on all other accounts I consider him to have been the most eligible candidate. "The Lady's Address to the Electors of Liverpool" has been highly approved by the adverse party as well as by our own—and I should like to have your opinion of its constitutional doctrine.

Partly through the aid of Lord John Manners I have made great progress with the "Emigrant Surgeon's" Affair, as you will see by a Liverpool Albion [newspaper] which I send you.

The "Statesmen" are travelling into Ireland—and meet with much praise—indeed the Dublin Review has commended me most heartily.

I trust you are well. While you are possessed of health and strength America is safe.

Pray do not let Mrs. [Floride Colhoun] Calhoun forget me—indeed I think she will not.

From what I hear Mr. [George] Bancroft sustains the position of [U.S.] Minister [to Great Britain] creditably. Mr. [Richard] Pakenham passed through Liverpool but he was quite incog[nito]. Always, my dear Mr. Calhoun, your very sincere friend, Sarah Mytton Maury.

[P.S.] The "Address" was written partly to contradict a report that I have been endeavouring to introduce American politics into England—this of course would be an absurdity though there is much in your system the adoption of which would greatly improve ours.

[Enclosed broadside]

TO THE ELECTORS OF LIVERPOOL.

Among the various reflections suggested by an inquiry into the several qualifications possessed by the four Candidates for this most important Representation, there is one not yet commented upon. As it is a point, however, connected rather with a Constitutional than with a Political view, it very possibly may not be regarded as one of vital importance by those who regard the Members of the House of Commons solely as the individual organs by which certain existing and present and immediate measures are to be effected; forgetful that they are also the permanent, united, consolidated representation of the third estate of this country. The Commons of England, as a body, have an existence in the past and in the future, as well as in the present. They have possessed this existence since the year 1266, there being still extant writs of that date to summon Knights, Citizens and Burgesses to attend Parliament; and the inheritance of the Commons is as direct, lineal and inalienable as that of the Lords. The Members are not *merely* the instruments by which such and such measures either recommended by the Government or the People are to be effected. Viewing the subject in this light, it may be observed that LORD JOHN MANNERS is the only Candidate for the Town of Liverpool connected with the Aristocracy of the Land. To support his claims upon grounds so slight as these would, indeed, be an absurdity *primo fronte*, but Hallam says that "the general harmony between the two Houses of Parliament is mainly owing to the "happy graduation of ranks which renders the elder and the younger sons of our nobility two links in the unsevered chain of society;" that the presence in the House of Commons of the sons of Peers "keeps alive the sympathy for public and popular rights or *sensus communis*" in the English nobility.* [*Footnote*: " *Hallam. Constitutional History of England. Vol. II. Page 22."] The democratic tendencies of this people are daily more and more clearly and more rapidly developed; and, indeed, it is the unavoidable influence of the genius of a constitutional Government combined with an enlightened population. But there is a point beyond which even Englishmen may not go without endangering those very liberties which they seek to expand.

The Peers of England stand between the People and the Throne, as well as between the Throne and the People; they are the shield of the subject as well as the bulwark of the Crown! The Barons of the vilest of Kings converted, by their noble efforts, his weakness and his vice into the most inestimable of blessings. The Magna Charta is yet the model of free governments—the boast of this nation—and was the achievement of her Nobles. During the long ages of England's History, we have reasons sometimes to deplore the separation between the Peers and the People, sometimes to admire their union. While this country retains her existing form of government, *and dark will her doom be if ever she change it*; the connexion between the first and middle classes should be increased by every possible tie. The younger son of an illustrious race may not himself become a Member of the House of Peers, but the opinions and feelings of one branch of a family influence the rest, and from the constant intercourse between the representative and his constituents, kindly relations spring up, mutual respect and esteem are increased, each becomes more thoroughly versed in the respective duties of the Peer and of the People, and of their mutual relationship in society. The Peer becomes one of the People, and the People find that in the hands of their noble representative their rights, their liberties, and their happiness are held as sacred as if their guardianship had been entrusted to one of their own immediate body.

Liverpool was never more faithfully, more efficiently represented than by Lord Sandon; and it may be anticipated with confidence that the youthful scion of the House of Rutland will give ample proof, not only that he inherits from his ancestry love of country and loyalty to the Sovereign and the Church, but that the interests of Commerce and Manufactures and the prosperity of the people are essential points in his political creed, and that they will be watched over and guarded with fidelity, with zeal, and with devotion.

It is in every respect desirable that the most powerful commercial constituency in England should be brought into immediate and close communication with the Aristocracy; and the success of LORD JOHN MANNERS is earnestly to be desired on these *constitutional and enduring* grounds, as well as on those of social, political, and religious expediency.   [Signed:] A LADY.

ALS with En in ScCleA.   NOTE: The printed enclosure is initialed "S.M.M." below the closing.   Maury's *An Englishwoman in America* . . . (London: Thomas Richardson and Son, 1848), contained a detailed investigation of health conditions on ships carrying immigrants to America and a plea that laws be enacted in England and the U.S. to require physicians on all immigrant vessels.   The London *Times* of July 28 and 31, 1847, p. 2, states that polling in the British elections began on 7/29 and the official return from Liverpool was declared on July 30, which has allowed an approximate dating of this undated letter.

To Cha[rle]s Ja[me]s Faulkner,
    [Martinsburg, Va.]

Fort Hill, 1st August 1847

My dear Sir, I regard the occurrence, which led to the meeting and the proceedings of the citizens of Hagerstown [Md.], a copy of an account of which accompanied your letter, as one, which claims the solemn attention of every man, who loves his country and desires to perpetuate its institutions.

I have read your letter, and the proceedings of the meeting & the act of the Legislature of Pennsylvania, which lead to the tragical event, with grief & indignation.   With grief, not only for the fate of a worthy citizen [James H. Kennedy], but for the consequences, to which it is calculated to lead; and with indignation, at the deliberate and undisguised violation of the Constitutional compact by the State of Pennsylvania.   There is not on record a more deliberate and undisguised breach of faith and the solemn obligation of Oath.   If we of the slave holding States should permit one, to us, of the most important provisions of the Constitution, to be thus trampled ["on"

interlined] with scorn & contempt, & one of their worthiest citizens
to be murdered in his attempt to secure the rights guaranteed to him
by it to pass with impunity, we shall richly deserve the fate, that will
most assuredly await us. It will not end with emancipation, as bad
as that would be. That would be but the begin[n]ing. I see clearly
the whole train of calamities, which would befall us. I cannot trace
them in a letter; but they will be greater than ever befel a people.
The condition of Ireland would be a state of bliss to ours. But let
me say, neither Virginia, or Maryland can escape them. As soon as
abolition becomes apparent, the States to the South of you, will prevent the purchase, or the im[m]igration of ["their" *canceled and*
"your" *interlined*] negroes, free, or Slave, ["&" *canceled and* "while"
interlined] those North & west of you ["will" *interlined*] prevent
their egress in either direction. You will be penned in with your
black population, as every other slave State will be, while the non
slave holding States will never cease their agitation until ["they"
canceled and "blacks" *interlined*] are placed in all respects on an
equality, politically ["& socially" *interlined*] with their ["mast" *canceled*] former masters; when they would govern us and our posterity
through our former slaves, and their posterity. Think not, I look too
far ahead, or that I am deceived. I see the future thus far, if we do
not meet & repel the attack, as clearly, as I do the rising of the sun
tomorrow.

You ask me my opinion, as to the remedy; & in the first place,
whether the Legislation of Congress can reach the disease? I do not
see how it can. The act of Pennsylvania is in open defiance & contempt both of the Constitution & Congress; and cannot be reached,
of course, but by subjecting the courts of the State & its officers to
["the" *interlined*] jurisdiction of the courts of the United States in
the performance of their official duties; which, in my opinion, we
have no right to do. But, if we had, it would be impossible to pass
such an act.

You next ask, is there any countervailing Legislation, within the
power of the Southern States. I answer yes; and the most effectual;
but to make it so, it would require their united action. The peace,
security & the internal police of the States are clearly among their
reserved powers, and are acknowledged so to be, in reference to
["their" *interlined*] security, as far as health is concerned; as the
passage of quarantine laws by most of the States prove. The same
principle applies to intercourse of every discription, which may endanger the, peace, security, or the domestick institutions of a State.
Its application ["of it" *canceled*] to all commercial intercourse, sea-

wise or by river, would at once bring the non slave holding States, to their senses. It would execute itself. It would give to the South direct trade, and make our commercial capitals, what their's now ["is" *canceled and* "are" *interlined*]; and would transfer their shipping & manufactures from their cold & barren region to our more genial & fertile. It would, in particular ["make" *interlined*] Baltimore, Norfolk & Richmond, what New York, Philadelphia & Boston now are. The very menace, that we were prepared to take such a step, unless the guarantees of the Constitution, should be respected by Penn[sylvani]a, & the other non slave holding States, would bring them at once to terms. You will find the principle fully illustrated & established, in a report & speeches made ["by me" *interlined*] on the circulation of incendiary publication[s] through the mail. They are contained in a volume of my reports, speeches & & & published, some years since, by Harper & brothers of New York, and may no doubt be had from them.

You next ask, whether there is any hope, that Pen[nsylvani]a would repeal its act, on proper representation? I doubt it; and doubt, whether it would in the end do any good. Now, if ever, in my opinion, is the time to bring the question to issue. The longer it is delayed, the worse in the end, both for us & the Union. I have always so believed. But, if it should be thought otherwise, I would by all means recommend, not to beg, or expostulate, but deman[d] the repeal, on the high ground of right & constitutional obligation, assuming it at once, without argument, that the act is an open & flagrant breach of faith & constitutional obligation. Entreaty would be degrading, & ["would" *interlined*] but aggrevate the evil. The higher & bolder the tone, the better. The commissioners, if ["it" *interlined*] should be deemed advisable for Maryland & Virginia to appoint them, should be men of high & decided character, & not party hacks, & ["should be" *interlined*] instructed to make a peremptory demand, in the most decided language, ["in order" *interlined*] to bring the question to issue. If proper men be appointed, & take the course indicated, good may come of it, but, if not, it will do mischief, especially, if party hacks, should be appointed.

Your next question is, as to the advantage of calling a convention of the slave holding States? I regard the step as indispensable, to a thorough and effectual cure of the evil, and that the call ought to come from Maryland & Virginia; and the meeting ["to" *canceled*] be ["held" *interlined*] in Richmond, or Baltimore. It may be ["made" *interlined*] by ["your" *canceled and* "their" *interlined*] Legislatures, or informally by their members; & ought to be done speedily. The sooner the better. If both parties should unite, & agree to make the defence of our rights the paramount question—overriding the Presidential & all others, a speedy end would be put to our difficulties. But, without that, there is, for us & the whole Union, slave holding & not slave holding, a gloomy future. It is hard to say, on which the heaviest calamity will fall; unless we manfully, & at once meet the danger. If such should be our course, let what may come, we shall be a great & prosperous people, in the Union, if our course should save it; and out of it, if it should not. They, & not we, have been throughout the aggressors; and it belongs to the great law of retribution, that where the party aggressed ["on" *interlined*] has the sperit to meet & repel the aggressor, ["the" *interlined*] meditated evil recoils on him, while the rich blessings, which always accompany the successful resistance to wrong, will fall to the lot of his intended victim.

I have from the first, and throughout this whole question, been actuated by one feeling; to save the Union & our free institutions, if possible; but, if not, to save our selves, at all event. The great difficulty, I have had to encounter has been, from the prevalence, on all sides, of the spoils principle. The desire to participate in the spoils has been so prevalent, for more [than] 16 years, and the ["desire" *interlined*] of keeping the parties together, in order to be able to participate, that the great business of most of the leaders has been, to merge all questions in the Presidential election, in order to avoid party distraction; and that, I fear, will prove an insuperable difficulty, in taking the high & decisive stand, which only can arrest the evil, that threatens to engulf all. The Union of a few manly sperits on both sides, in your Legislat[ur]e, would go far to overcome it, in your State & the whole South. People begin to think, & to see the real extent of the danger, and in the present state of their feelings, should a convention be called, the States South of Virginia would send forth to meet you all their ablest & most patriotick citizens. Yours very truly, J.C. Calhoun.

[P.S.] I think it important that the Legislatures of Maryland & Virginia should, through their members of Congress bring the subject before that body with all the facts & circumstances, including the Hagerstown proceedings.

ALS in CSmH, Huntington Mss.; PEx in P[atrick] F. Madigan, *A Catalogue of Autograph Letters, Historical Documents and Manuscripts Offered for Sale* (New York, 1914), p. 18.

From Elizabeth A. R. Linn

Boon[e]ville [Mo.,] August 1, 1847

My Dear & *Truly great* Cousin, I cannot resist, the pleasure, of sending you, every now, & then, a News Paper from this State to let you see, that the Political Days of the *Tyrant*, & great calumniator, Col. [Thomas H.] Benton, are numbered, in Missouri. The noble People, of this State *now* know him, in all the *black deformity*, of his long *concealed* Character, & they will make him feel, the weight, of their just indignation. Senator [David R.] Atchison, & the Hon[orab]l[e James S.] Green, of this State, have just called to see me, & assured me, that Benton could quite as soon, be Elected, Pope of Rome, as ever again, to [be] sent from Missouri, to the U.S. Senate.

With the most fervent wishes, that you, & your family are enjoying good health, I remain with the highest Esteem, & warmest Respect Your sincere Friend, Elizabeth A.R. Linn.

ALS in ScCleA.

From Young D. Allen

Baton Rouge, La., August the 2, 1847

Dear Sir, You will I trust not think me acting the part of an intruder When I take the liberty of asking you a few simple questions. Will you vote for Gen. Z[achary] Ta[y]lor if put in nomination for the presidency in 1848, & at the same time in youre answer to this please give me youre views relative to the Mexican War. I take the liberty of thus addressing you as I have bin & am now youre Warmist supporter, & Though not personally [k]nown to you I presume you are acquainted With my relatives in Abbeville Dist[rict]. Charles B. Foshee of Abbeville is my uncle, & old Jack Foshee late of Abbeville that mar[r]ied a sister of the Honorable Joel Smith of Abbeville is allso my Mouther's oldest Brother, & in the mean time allow me to give you the names of my Foure surviving children. My oldest son I call after yourself Augustus Calhoun[;] my Two Twins I call after the Honorable George Mcduffie & Robert Y. Hayne. My Daughter I call Cornellia S. Allen. My little son Adolphus Colquitt died at the Arkansas Springs in 1845, & in conclution let me refer you to the Honorable Walter T. Colquitt & Col. John H. Lumpkin of Georgia in referance to me. Trusting you may find it conviniant to answer this as early as conviniant & that you & yours may continue to enjoy all the good health & Hap[p]iness on earth & be prepar[e]d for a blessed immortality beyond the grave, I subscribe myself youre & the Nulafyers Friend, Young D. Allen.

ALS in ScCleA. NOTE: An AEU by Calhoun reads "Mr. Allen. Not answered."

From LEWIS S. CORYELL

New Hope [Pa.,] 2n[d] Aug. 1847
My dear Sir, The newspapers are full of daily prognostics, and no part of the community are more misled by them than the Adm[ini]s-[tration] who are hourly looking for a serpent to rise for them to look upon, and free them from difficulty. There is a rumor of Peace in yesterday[']s [Philadelphia] Ledger, which may or may not be the case. If true it would give us the Election in Penn[sylvani]a, which is now doubtfull, but for the last 2 months [Governor Francis R.] Shunk has been gaining on account of the universal prosperity in our State and particularly among the coal & Iron men.

I saw Major [John P.] Heiss in Phil[adelphi]a. He tells me that Buck [James Buchanan] & [Thomas] Ritchie are at war[?], and that he is for [Zachary] Taylor & means to sell his ½ [of the Washington, D.C., *Union*] as soon as he finds a purchaser & will take $15,000 for his ½ buildings[,] presses[,] fixtures &C &Ct. The impression prevails that [Thomas H.] Benton will attack the adm[ini]s[tration] as [Charles J.?] Ingersol[l] has already, at the next session—and strange as it may be, that in the even tenor of your way you may have to defend the adm[ini]s[tration] from their venom and malice. [Lewis] Cass has lost cast entirely by his foolish letter to Chicago for the Improvement men were his men, but the working of the Tariff has so demonstrated for the country that no anti Improvement man can be upheld[.] [Daniel] Webster has taken bold ground, and I am glad that you so judiciously developed your views at Memphis. I am sorry I have nothing interesting to write you. I hear, that it is supposed that Buck & [William R.] King are against the reelection of Dixon H. [Lewis, Senator from Ala.]. Y[ou]r fr[ien]d truly, Lewis S. Coryell.

[P.S. Robert J.] *Walker* [Secretary of the Treasury] *is for Taylor.* [Simon] Cameron [Senator from Pa.] is playing for V[ice-]P[resident]. [George M.] Dallas [Vice-President] is between the stools.

ALS in ScCleA.

From MIKE WALSH

New York [City,] August 5th 1847

Dear Sir, Permit me to introduce to you the bearer Mr. [Ulysses] Ely who is about to settle perminently in Charleston, where he intends engaging extensively in mercantile business. Mr. Ely is a gentleman of fine talents, extensive information, and stands very high in the estimation of all who enjoy the pleasure of his acquaintance. He has travelled extensively in both hemispheres—has resided for some years in the West india Islands—and has profited much by the advantages and experience thus afforded. Though not a Southern man by birth—he is, in the fullest sense of the phrase, one in feeling, and is indeed personal[l]y endowed with that lofty and unbending integrity, and manly frankness which form such a glorious and refreshing distinction between the hightoned Southern gentleman, and the crafty, deceitful, time serving *mere* politician of the North[.] With sentiments of the most profound respect and adherence, I remain dear Sir, both personal[l]y and political[l]y Your devoted and disinterested friend, Mike Walsh.

ALS in ScCleA. NOTE: Michael Walsh was the former editor of the New York, N.Y., *Subterranean*, a newspaper that espoused working-men's rights and free trade principles. He was a member of the N.Y. State Assembly in 1846 and 1848 and was a Representative from N.Y. from 1853 to 1855. Calhoun was at Fort Hill at this time and Ely may have visited him there. In filing this letter Calhoun wrote an AEU that reads "["Mr. Walsh" *canceled*] Mike Walsh."

From R. B. LEWIS

Dahlonega Ga., August 6, 1847

Dear Sir, Yours of the 3d inst. was rec[eive]d yesterday and on that day, I was handed by Dr. [Joseph J.] Singleton your note of the 10th July sent by Mr. [William] Sloan[,] the only letters I have rec[eive]d from you since your return from Washington City.

Mr. E[dward] J.C. Milner was here a few days ago[.] I call'd on him for the rent Gold due you from the OBar lot; his reply was that he left home with his Books prepared to make a final settlement but broke his Buggy and was obliged to leave his Books &c. on the way; he promised to send me a copy of the amount of gold dug and the amount of rent due together with the money so soon as he got home[;] he has had sufficient time I think & have not heard from him since[.] Benjamin Milner's address is Barnesville, Pike County, Ga. No one is operating on 817 at this time nor has since February. I have on hand one hundred dollars 26 cents rent from lot 817[,] also Eight dollars 51 cents from the OBarr lot rent paid me by a Mr. James Moore and old Tom Howell, two men Milner leased to a short time before he left. I have no information of your lot in the *Big Bend,* 817 that would be of interest to you. Messrs. Bedford & Reese speak of working a portion of 817, so soon as they finish a place on the other half[.] I have not tried to lease to any one else as it is so uncertain about getting the rent. Very respectfully yours, R.B. Lewis.

[P.S.] I sent you last winter $39.61 by Mr. Sloan rent from 817.

ALS in ScU-SC, John C. Calhoun Papers. NOTE: An AEU by Calhoun indicates that on 8/22 he wrote to B.M. Milner "in reference to the toll due me."

To Mrs. PLACID[I]A [MAYRANT] ADAMS, Pendleton

Fort Hill, 7th August 1847

Dear Madam, On looking over my papers I find three other letters in reference to your Michigan land, which possibly be of some use to you. They contain some politicks, but nothing of a confidential character. With great respect I am & &, J.C. Calhoun.

ALS owned by Mr. Holbrook Campbell.

From H[ENRY] W. CONNER

Charleston, August 8 1847

My Dear Sir, I wrote you a fortnight since & have now to report further progress. Our circulars & subscription are out—2000 of them & pretty well distributed all over the slave States. A package of them went to Mr. [Pierre] Soulé at New Orleans & Mr. [Henry S.] Foote [Senator] of Miss.

The series of essays I mentioned some time since will commence to appear in the [Charleston] Mercury of tomorrow or next day. They will appear as editorial. We shall have extra's issued for the best articles & distribute them likewise over the Southern States. We shall endeavour also to have some of them republished elsewhere or induce similar articles to be written.

I feel more & more satisfied from the intercourse I have latterly had with various sections & persons that there is amongst *the people* a strong & decided feeling on the subject at issue that will ["soon" *interlined*] speak out & act out too. The enclosed copy of a letter from N. Orleans is to the point in one case & the [printed] subscription list with its signers is evidence of the other. The same prompt & liberal spirit I have every reason to believe prevails amongst the planters generally & we will endeavour to use proper means to bring it into play.

About the 20 or 25th I expect to go to New York, where there is always a great Concourse of Southerners at this season. Others of our colleagues are also there, & we shall endeavour to make the most of our opportunities ["while" *interlined*] there. It is very apparent to me however, that after we have provided for & established the paper, we are still far short of our object. We want an organization & an effective & well regulated one of some kind. The Southern people are indolent & dilatory—*distressingly so* & the fact from what I see of it furnishes more cause of alarm than the whole abolition movement put together. To counteract this & to make the whole strength of the South available on a given point & at a given time, it appears to me it is indispensable to have formed a Southern assosciation—with its head at Washington or perhaps Richmond—with subordinate assosciations in every State & at every prominent point in every State in the South & S. West. The difficulty in bringing this about I can well imagine, at least for the present & the past but my impression is, that on the first move of the Wilmot proviso men in Congress that the excitement produced by it with the sense of impending danger will prepare the people for it so that if it be determined the Southern members by a prompt & decided movement may procure an assosciation to be formed in each district throughout the South. We could soon get up any thing we wanted here—but this is not the place for the movement to commence.

This is what occurs to my mind & I submit it with great deference.

The State Legislatures that meet this fall & winter I suppose will take some decided action on the Wilmot proviso? Very truly yours &C, H.W. Conner.

[Enclosure]

G[ustavus] Schmidt to P[eter] Conrey, Jr.

[New Orleans, *ca.* July 1847]

Dear Sir, I have read Mr. [Henry W.] Conner's letter, the Charleston Circular and Resolutions, as well as Mr. Peter's opinion with much [*ms. torn*]ation, and I will in accordance with your request, frankly make known my views and opinions on the very interesting questions they embrace.

I think it not only demonstrable, but clear beyond the possibility of dispute, that there exists a party in the United States, whose avowed aim is to abolish Slavery throughout the Union. That this party, fostered in many instances by foreign influence, has attained such a degree of importance that it has been ultimately courted by the two great political parties which divide the country; that it is gradually gaining strength and influence not only in Congress, but throughout the non slaveholding States, to such an extent, that it threatens to abort all other party distinctions; That confident in its power it now attempts, in spite of the Missouri Compromise, to exclude Slavery not only from Texas, but from such territory as the U.S. may hereafter acquire from Mexico.

This being the state of the case, submitted to the consideration of the Slaveholding States, the question is simply whether they shall permit the abolitionists to carry into effect their schemes, or whether they shall by timely and firm resistance prevent their execution!

This question appears to me susceptible of only one answer, to wit that their attempts to encroach on southern rights must be resisted to the utmost.

1st. Because, if the abolitionist succeed in excluding Slavery from all States, hereafter to be admitted into the Union, they virtually change the Constitution of the United States by altering the provision that Congress may admit new States, by superadding ["a" *interlined*] stipulation, that Congress shall not admit any where Slavery exists; This is evidently a violation of the Const[itutio]n since it effects a change in its provisions in a manner different from that prescribed by the instrument itself, and without the sanction of three fourths of the Legislatures of the different States composing the Union.

2d. Because, if such a change should be tolerated, there can be no reasonable doubt, that in the course of a few years, Congress would, either usurp the power, or by the admission of New States effect such a change in the Const[itutio]n of the U.S. as would enable it to abolish Slavery in all the States where it is now tolerated.

3d. Because, such a measure would permit Congress to interfere in the private organization of the individual States, and their domestic arrangements, which is in point of fact equivalent, to a surrender of all sovereignty on the part of the States, and must eventually lead to the centralization of all power in the hands of Congress.

That the above reasons are sufficient to stimulate the Southern States to a prompt and energetic resistance will hardly be doubted, and that every consideration of duty to themselves and their posterity ought to rouse them to immediate action is equally clear.

The danger is imminent, the interests which the South have to defend, involve the future prosperity of themselves, their descendants and their Country, and if these causes be not sufficient to inspire them with Zeal, we can hardly imagine any other of sufficient potency to beget the requisite courage to meet the approaching crisis.

The interests which the South defend are not ideal abstractions as Mr. T. supposes, but real, tangible and vital interests which no man either should or would abandon without Justly subjecting himself to the charge of being a recreant to his duty, and possessing a craven heart.

The mode and manner of defence becomes the next subject of consideration.

The importance of the interests at stake, & the emminency of the danger forbid delay, and justly resistance in almost every form. Yet, reason requires, and prudence commands, that every means of conciliation should be resorted to and exhausted ere violence of any Kind is even threatened, and such is the good Sense of the American community, and such their innate respect for what is right and just, when not blinded by passion or fanaticism, that there is not reasonable ground to doubt, that a clear, calm, dignified & firm exposition of our rights would cause them to be respected & avert the impending danger.

The plan proposed, to establish a Newspaper at the City of Washington, devoted exclusively to the vindication of Southern rights & Southern interests, appears to me one of the most efficient means to accomplish the objects in view, and ought to be carried into effect immediately. That such application would meet with the hearty cooperation and support of the wealthy planters of Louisiana, I am perfectly assured, and with the editorial department in proper hands, as I am convinced it will be, it will be of immense advantage to the South.

It is not, as I understand it, required, that the supporters of the proposed plan should abandon their former predilections & associations, be they what they may. All that is expected of them is that they should cooperate heartily in defending themselves against a more imminent danger, than ever yet threatened the South, and when that is averted let them return their attention to the defence of minor interests. The South now requires all her sons, whether democrats or whigs, to unite in the defence of the integrity of her institutions, and not by imitating the bear & the wolf of the fable, to allow the fox to carry off the spoils, while they are fighting about the manner of its division.

For my own part I concur fully and heartily in the plan proposed by Mr. Conner, and will cooperate to the utmost of my ability to carry it into effect. Your friend, Signed, G. Schmidt.

[Note by Conner:] This gentleman is no political or public man, but a sound lawyer & upright fearless & independent man. H.W.C.

[Enclosed circular]

The undersigned, profoundly impressed with the conviction that imminent dangers are impending over our constitutional rights as regards the institution of Slavery, which can only be averted by prompt, energetic and united action among the citizens of the Slaveholding States, and believing that the measure first to be adopted, as indispensable to this end, is the establishment of a paper at the city of Washington, to warn and rally those whose all is at stake, have associated themselves together, and do hereby agree to subscribe, for this purpose, the sums respectively affixed to their names.

It is clearly understood that the following are fundamental and controlling principles in the undertaking; that the paper shall not be connected with either of the great political parties, or with sustaining or opposing any administration, as such, or with personal or party politics in any way; that all its energies shall be directed to the defence of the constitutional rights, and the maintenance of the political, moral and social equality of the Slaveholding States, as paramount and controlling objects, to which all others shall be subsidiary; that it shall neither solicit nor receive the patronage of the government or any of its departments, and shall stand independent of its influence; that its aims being purely conservative, it shall confine itself to that line of conduct by which these can be best accomplished, and which appropriately belong to a newspaper press; that while it shall freely discuss measures and opinions in their bearings on the paramount objects of its establishment, it shall carefully abstain from all personalities, when they can possibly be avoided, in performance of the great purpose of its establishment; and finally, that all proper safeguards and provisions shall be made to insure a faithful and honest application of the funds to be hereby raised, and to confine the paper strictly to an adherence to the foregoing fundamental principles.

It is further understood, that as the intention of the enterprise is to aid in securing permanent quiet in the enjoyment of our ancient and constitutional rights, and to preserve that perfect equality which belongs to all the members of the Union, and which cannot be surrendered without debasement and degradation, the duration of the paper is to be commensurate with the continuance of the dangers against which it is intended to guard; and that to prevent an abortive effort, it is agreed as a condition, that no subscription made shall be binding until the sum of thirty thousand dollars has been subscribed, and we pledge ourselves to use every exertion to procure that sum for the purpose proposed.

It is agreed that the amount subscribed, shall be paid, when required, to Isaac W. Hayne, or his order, to be held by him in trust for the purposes above specified.

Nath[anie]l Heyward	$1000	W[illia]m Aiken	$1000
R[obert] F.W. Allston	1000	J[oshua] J. Ward	1000
D[aniel] E. Huger	500	J[ohn] L. Manning	500
P[eter] W. Fraser	500	W[illiam] H. Trapier	500
D[aniel] Heyward	500	M[oses] C. Mordecai	500

[Note by Henry W. Conner:] *we have only just commenced presenting our list for subscriptions.

ALS with Ens in ScCleA. NOTE: An AEU by Calhoun on the first enclosure reads, "Copy of Letter sent by Mr. Conner." Gustavus Schmidt (1795–1877) was a prominent Louisiana attorney. Peter Conrey, Jr., was a New Orleans banker. The second enclosure, a printed circular, has all names and subscription amounts written by hand. Another copy of this circular, in the same collection, has the following appended:

"John D. Magill	$200	John La Bruce	$50
Fr[ancis] Weston (pr. annum)	20	J[oshua] W. La Bruce	50"
Hugh From "	10		
W. P[ercival] Vaux "	10		

A series of *ca.* nine editorials in the Charleston *Mercury* between August 11 and August 30, 1847 discuss various effects of the operation of the Wilmot Proviso on Southern States and society and decry the growing support for abolition in the North.

From JAMES L. ORR

Anderson [S.C.], 9th August 1847

My Dear Sir, My brother Jehu A. Orr left here today for Princeton N.J. where he intends taking his collegiate course and I was unable to give him letters to any members of the faculty, inasmuch as all their number are strangers to me. He is accompanied by young Mr. [Ibzan J.] Rice of our village[,] an orphan but of very respectable parentage. Now the purpose of addressing you this communication is to ask of you the favour to address any member of the faculty who has the honor of your acquaintance in the form of a letter of introduction enclosed to my brother. Your name will be of infinite avail to them and give them position with the faculty; it will be a kindness which they will gratefully appreciate.

I have very recently returned from Mississippi and have the pleasure to inform you that Dr. W. Henry Calhoun & family are enjoying excellent health and that the Dr. has made a most admirable selection for his planting interest—in what I conceive to be the choice region of North Miss.—he is well pleased with his move. The health of my father [Christopher Orr] and family was good, & he had many kind inquiries to make after yourself and family.

The Miss. Democracy are ultra in their support of the administration and [Thomas] Ritchie[']s hobby (expulsion) affords an admirable theme there for the demagogue to round his periods with. Even the Democratic State Convention a body of some intelligence passed a Resolution *unanimously* setting forth the expulsion of Ritchie as an infringement of the liberty of the press. My observations in their midst led me to the conclusion that Miss. Democracy generally knew no higher duty to themselves or their country, than absolute and unwavering allegiance to *party*.

In my rambles through Georgia, Ala., Miss. & Tenn. I found but *few* individuals, their number certainly not exceeding one dozen, opposed to Gen[era]l [Zachary] Taylor, for the Presidency, and I am not sure that he is not the man for the South in the present crisis. I should be glad to hear your opinion on the subject but I suppose it would hardly be prudent for you to commit it to paper. I hope however I shall have the honor to see ["you" *interlined*] at Pendleton the day of the Rail Road meeting at that place, when I may learn something on the subject. Very respectfully Your Ob[edien]t S[er]v[an]t, James L. Orr.

ALS in ScCleA; PEx in Boucher and Brooks, eds., *Correspondence*, pp. 389–390. NOTE: Jehu Amaziah Orr (1828–1921), after attending the College of New Jersey, became a lawyer in Miss. where he held a number of public offices. He was a colonel in the Confederate army and a member of the Provisional and Second Confederate Congresses. William Henry Calhoun (1813–1869), a son of James Calhoun and Sarah Caldwell Martin Calhoun, was married to Jane Stewart Orr, James L. Orr's sister; he left Abbeville District in the early 1840's to establish a plantation in northern Mississippi.

To A[nna] M[aria Calhoun] Clemson, [Brussels]

Fort Hill, 13th Aug[us]t 1847

My dear Anna, As your sister [Martha Cornelia Calhoun] wrote you by the last steamer, I delayed answering yours, until the present sailed as I concluded she would give you all the news.

The continued good health of yourself & Mr. [Thomas G.] Clemson & of the children [John Calhoun Clemson and Floride Elizabeth Clemson], & the favourable account you give of them, are to me great sources of happiness—next to having you all about me. Since Cornelia wrote you, Andrew [Pickens Calhoun] and his family arrived on a visit; and I hope Patrick [Calhoun] will make us a visit before they leave on their return home, which will be early in October; so that, if you & Mr. Clemson & the children could be here at the same time, we should all again be assembled once more under the same roof, at Fort Hill. It would complete my happiness.

Andrew & Margaret [Green Calhoun] are the pictures of health, and the children are really remarkably good looking, & well behaved. John C[aldwell Calhoun] is, in particular, a very striking looking boy, & very intelligent. His head and eyes are remarkably fine.

If you had been with us this summer, you would have supposed yourself, as far as the season is concerned, still in Belgium. We have seen little of the sun and have not had one really warm day and night since the first week in April. It has been very wet & cloudy, since the last of April, & there has not been a night, but that a sheet, cotton blanket & counterpain have been agreeable before morning. Notwithstanding the cold season and the great quantity of rain that has fallen, my crop of corn & cotton, and pease & potatoes, is very good & has been entirely exempt from damage by the rise of the river. The corn is made and the cotton begins to mature; & if the rain should now cease, with occasional showers, will be very fine. Much of it, is breast & head high even on upland. Andrew gives also a fine account of his, but dreads the effect of continued wet weather on cotton. From what he says his corn cannot fall much short of 100 bushels to the acre. I have had no account from Mr. Clemson's crop for some time. I hope Col. [Francis W.] Pickens keeps him well informed in reference to it.

Your mother [Floride Colhoun Calhoun] & William [Lowndes Calhoun] have not yet returned from Glenn's Springs; but we are in daily expectation of their arrival. She gives very favourable accounts of the effects of the water on her health.

I am not at all surprised, that the [*partial word canceled*] victories our arms have atcheived [*sic*] in Mexico should make so deep an impression in Europe. They had greatly underestimated our strength & military skill; but I fear their development will have more prenecious [*sic*] influence at home, than beneficial abroad. I fear my forebodings will be realised to the fullest extent. The bitter is yet to come. I look forward to the next session of Congress, as one pregnant of events of the most momenteous character. We shall, before it terminates, begin to realise the train of events, to which the Mexican war was destined to lead. I shall go prepared to speak the truth freely & boldly, and to do my duty regardless of responsibility. The next news from Mexico will probably bring information of the occupation of the capital by [Winfield] Scott & his Army.

All join their love to you & Mr. Clemson & the children. Kiss them for their Grandfather, & tell them I wish to see them much. Your affectionate father, J.C. Calhoun.

ALS in ScCleA; PEx in Jameson, ed., *Correspondence,* p. 736.

To [CHARLES J.] INGERSOLL, [Representative from Pa.]

Fort Hill, 14th Aug[us]t 1847
My dear Sir, I have just heard that you were in our Village [Pendleton], and have sent my son James [Edward Calhoun] who will deliver you this to convey you to my residence, which, I will expect you to make your home, while you sojourn in our vicinity. You must not pass without calling on me, & spending with me, what time you can. I will take no excuse. Yours truly, J.C. Calhoun.

ALS in ScU-SC, John C. Calhoun Papers.

From ARMISTEAD BURT

Calhoun['s Mills, S.C.,] 17 Aug[us]t [1847]
My dear Sir, I had received a few weeks ago, a letter from H[enry] W. Connor of Charleston on the subject of a paper at Washington. A meeting will be held on Sale day at the [Abbeville] Court House and I will make an address.

As a means of uniting the South and preparing it for resistance, I am disposed to think a paper at Washington will be useful and important. But argument on the subject of slavery, except at home, is no longer useful. Resistance is our policy as well as our duty. I should have been much gratified if I could have gone up with Martha [Calhoun Burt]. I would be pleased to see you and your family, also Andrew [Pickens Calhoun] & his wife [Margaret Green Calhoun].

The Mexican War presents at this moment a phase of deep and exciting interest and topics for much conversation. I would like to talk them over with you, but some engagements forbid it.

I am pleased to hear that your crop is good. Mine was very fine until the first of August but has been materially injured by the excessive rains. I have never known such torrents to fall from the clouds. The branches and dry ravines were filled to the height of five and seven feet. The rain was constant until ten days ago. The worm (boll) has done a good deal of damage to many crops in Abbeville. I have seen but few in mine.

My love to all. Yours sincerely, Armistead Burt.

ALS in ScCleA.

From EDW[ARD] D. ELLIS and ISAAC S. SMITH

Detroit, (Michigan,) Aug. 18, 1847

Sir—Although having no personal acquaintance with yourself, yet in behalf of a committee appointed by a respectable number of our fellow citizens in primary meeting assembled, and representing, as is believed, the views of numerous Citizens of the North-West, we take the liberty of addressing you.

We are, sir, among the number (by no means few) of the citizens of the North-West, who condemn the useless and mischievous agitation of questions calculated to disturb the peace and tranquility of other portions of the Union; and, in view of the probable attempted formation of a political party in these Northern States, having for its motto and its objects, a warfare, as we conceive in derogation of the principles of the Constitution and the terms of the National compact, upon the peculiar institutions of our sister States—we are disposed to co-operate with our fellow-citizens elsewhere in supporting, as the *Peoples'* candidate for the Presidency, Gen. Zachary Taylor, of Louisiana. For the second office within our gift, William Wood-bridge, an old and distinguished Citizen of Michigan ["of Mi" *can-celed*] and of the North-West, and late a member of the Senate of the United States, seems to be the choice of a large proportion of our citizens. We think we have a just right to claim the selection of the Vice President from this section of the Union, and we invite the co-operation of our friends South in forwarding the measure. A union of the South and West, upon the principles of the Constitution, would not only settle the Presidential question, but check and silence those ebullitions of partisan and sectional zeal, which are rapidly bringing into disrepute the honor, the fame, and in fact the *institutions* of our common country.

We have said thus much, without at all desiring to elicit a reply on your part—trusting, however, that you will give to our brief suggestions all the weight they may seem to deserve. We have the honor to be, Respectfully, Your's, &C, Edw. D. Ellis, Chairman, Isaac S. Smith, Secretary.

ALS (in Ellis's handwriting) in ScCleA. Note: Edward D. Ellis (1801–1848) had been a member of the Mich. constitutional convention of 1835 and a state senator 1835–1837.

From Fred[erick] P. Stanton

Memphis [Tenn.,] 18 Aug[us]t 1847
Dear Sir, Although I have not always agreed with you in sentiment, I have been an enthusiastic admirer of your genius and character. I know your frankness and boldness, and hence I take the liberty of asking your opinions upon the subjects mentioned below. My sole object is my own individual satisfaction. I have been reelected to Congress, (by a small majority), and desire to reflect upon the questions which will probably engage our deliberations for the ensuing two years. I have no intention to publish, or make known your reply, unless you should be indifferent to such a publication.

Can peace be made ["without" *altered to* "with"] Mexico, without indemnity for spoliations and for the expenses of the war?

Is not indemnity in territory desirable?

Is it not advisable to go into a National convention, with a determination of the Southern Delegates to withdraw, unless the

"Wilmot proviso" should be abandoned by a distinct pledge to that effect?

What possible injury could result from such a course on the part of the South? Would it not show her disposition to conciliation, and throw the consequences of a rupture upon the North?

Has England any desire to acquire California?

Is the late movement on the subject of the State debts, connected with Mexican affairs in any way, and does it indicate any disposition on the part of the English government to interfere in our quarrel with Mexico?

What think you of the projected canal across the isthmus of Tehuantepec? Does not your late report upon internal improvements assume grounds, which would give to our government the power to construct such a work?

I would be much gratified to know your views upon the subjects mentioned, and I know of nothing which can prevent you from giving them if you have the leisure to do so. Brief words will be sufficient, and will be understood by Your friend and ob[edien]t S[er]v[an]t, Fred. P. Stanton.

ALS in ScCleA. NOTE: Stanton was Representative from Tenn. during 1845–1855 and governor of Kansas Territory from 1858 to 1861.

From EUSTIS PRESCOTT

Harrodsburg Springs Ky., Aug[us]t 20th 1847

My Dear Sir, Having spent the summer at the Blue Licks and these springs for the restoration of my health—which has been much impaired during the last year—I have had an opportunity of meeting many of the western and southern politicians and of scanning political movements.

I have arrived at the conclusion that the Whigs have only been using the military popularity of Gen[era]l [Zachary] Taylor with the hope of carrying the autumnal elections both State and Congressional, and that Mr. [Henry] Clay will again be the candidate of the Whig convention. The Whig party of the South, and a portion of the West would prefer Gen[era]l Taylor, but the North & East will never give up their *protective* candidate. I saw him at Lexington, his health is good, and he is now on a tour to the eastern States.

The Administration will be in a minority this winter. Tennessee has declared most emphatically against it, Col[o]n[el Thomas H.]

Benton will fulminate his opposition, he expressed it very decidedly—as I am informed in this State, and I gathered it from Mrs. Freemont [*sic*; Jessie Benton Fremont]—who spent several days here & with whom I frequently conversed.

I hope the little band of State rights and Free trade, will remain united and firm. They will hold in the Senate—at least, the balance of ["th" *canceled*] power, and this may enable you again to save the country from the experiments of *small* men.

The war with Mexico at its commencement was popular, in most of the western and southern States, it has rendered the Administration very unpopular—from the inefficient manner in which it has been conducted, and the appointment of Officers to a high rank, many of whom had no other recommendation than political subserviency.

The volunteers who have returned complain most bitterly of the discomforts and risks to which they have been subjected in consequence of insufficient supplies, and paucity of men, and however the [Washington] *Union* may scold and attribute it [to] the want of action in Congress, they impute it to a want of decision and energy on the part of the Administration.

Believing most sincerely myself that Gen[era]l Taylor will not be a candidate for the Presidential chair, I have urged all other friends—whom I have met with, to abstain from a committal, and await the events of next winter, which will I believe indicate *our* position for the next presidency. I do not yet despair of seeing the people enlightened as to their true interests, and the unequivocal recognition—by a large majority, of those principles for which we have for so long contended.

Not having heard of you for several months, I have felt anxious to learn if you have got rid of that troublesome cough contracted at Memphis. Should you have a moment's leisure, a line will find me at Louisville until 15 or 20 Sept[embe]r and afford much gratification to your old and sincere friend, Eustis Prescott.

ALS in ScCleA; PEx in Boucher and Brooks, eds., *Correspondence*, pp. 390–391.

From JOS[EPH] W. LESESNE

Mobile, Aug. 21st 1847

My dear Sir, I thank you for your kind and interesting letter [of 7/-19], which I designed answering before, but for the receipt of the

Circular from Col. [Isaac W.] Hayne of Charleston relative to the paper proposed to be published at Washington.

I recognize the strength of your veiws with regard to the necessity of breaking to pieces the present corrupt party combinations, and with increasing repugnance to and distrust of Gen[era]l [Zachary] Taylor[']s fitness for the Presidency I would vote for him or any one else to attain this paramount object. Every day however convinces me that at present our wiser course is to wait developements at the next Congress, and not to precipitate matters. Our section of the party must if possible avoid the appearance of leading, altho' it is clear we shall have in fact to lead. I doubt if any thing is to be gained by forming a third party—our friends here think it can not be done, and that by prudent management we can bring over the democratic party of the South who are every day loosing [*sic*] confidence in their Hunker allies North and South. If these miserable miscreants had not the controll of the press we should have no difficulty—but it is mellancholly to reflect that except in South Carolina the South has no voice—no speech. To read the papers in this region one would suppose that we were never more secure. The "Wilmot proviso" never ["makes" *canceled*] attracts an allusion, and is in fact shunned with a cowardice, utterly unaccountable ["unless" *canceled*] except from the fact that the enemies of our institutions alone speak to us through the press. For my own part I freely confess that my feeling on the subject is almost that of flat despair. But I hope that our poeple [*sic*] are only asleep and that the fearful torper we witness all around us arises from the base fear and baser treachery of those who pretend to act as our centinels and guides. I believe that unless at the next session of Congress the Southern members unite the contest will be over, and we may surrender at discretion. It will afterwards be useless to continue a contest which tends only as heretofore to develope our weakness. If the laws, resolutions, and mobs ["at the" *canceled*] in the north which have for years past nullified the constitution and the act of Congress passed to enforce our rights of property, have not heretofore produced Union among us, I know not what outrage will. In the present emergency we want political Apostles, who renouncing all selfish ends, all hope or expectation or desire of federal office, will travel from State to State, from County to County and house to house to rouse up and sound the fire bell of alarm. Through the Press our poeple will learn nothing—that organ of public information corrupter than the politicians is muzzled by ignorance ["and" *canceled and* "in some cases, in some by" *interlined*] sympathy and others by interest. If we are really in danger, it is time that those who see and feel it should know this truth and act upon it. Except ["in" *interlined*] our poor brave little State of South Carolina, we have not a single News paper that speaks out, and what she says falls lifeless because in the Southern press there ["has" *canceled*; is] no echo.

I have had a great deal of conversation with our friends in relation to the paper proposed to be started at Washington. They think that the Session is now so near at hand and that so much will depend upon the veiws and temper of the next Congress that the enterprise ought for the present to be suspended. Our friend [Edmund S.] Dargan is also of this opinion, and Mr. [Pierre] Soulé of New Orleans, whom I met here the other day thinks that we had better wait the opening of Congress and be governed in regard to this project by what we find to be the state of things then existing.

Should the whig party concur with us that for the sake of peace on this question we will take no more territory we may escape the danger that threatens us. But if you are decidedly of opinion that the paper had better be got at once under way if you will write and say so, we will do what we can for it. But in regard to the amount subscribed you must expect disappointment. The causes referred to in the first part of this letter (the prevalent apathy on the subject of our danger) together with the *season* will operate against any efficient action both here and in New Orleans. Allow me to say also in ["great" *interlined*] confidence that the belief that Gen[era]l [Duff] Green is to be the Editor does not ["meet" *canceled*] gives [*sic*] the enterprise no additional favor; not that our own peculiar friends would be dissatisfied with him, but they think that his name would not command for the paper a favorable first impression. His course they think has been somewhat fickle and capricious, and he has been too much identified with Washington politics and news paper tactics to give to such an organ as we desire that lofty and disinterested tone indispensable to its influence. His connection with yourself too they fear would be used as a handle by our opponents who will avail themselves of every pretext to give the enterprise in the public estimation a personal and selfish character. These ["considerations" *canceled and* "veiws" *interlined*] are certainly entitled to great consideration.

I think Soule is a little shy—but still he is a warm friend of our cause. Very truly your f[rien]d &c, Jos. W. Lesesne.

ALS in ScCleA; PC in Boucher and Brooks, eds., *Correspondence*, pp. 391–393.

From ELLWOOD FISHER

Cincinnati, 8 mo[nth] 22, 1847

Dear Friend, Much absence from home and the obscure aspect of public opinion in this quarter have prevented me from making an earlier response to thy last favour. The elections of several Western States have now occurred and have surprized almost every body. It was previously thought that the position of parties would be but little affected by them, and that if any change occurred it would be in favour of the Administration. The contrary has happened in Indiana and Tennessee and but for some local dispute would have taken place in Kentucky.

In all these States the War was the principal topic—the whigs making no attack on free trade. Opposition to the War and the mode of prosecuting it were the main subjects. The result will be to bring the whigs forward at next session again in opposition to all acquisition of Territory—by which they expect not only to put an end to the War but prevent the agitation of the Wilmot proviso. This is certainly the plan of [John] McLean who is I think now in the ascendant of his party in the West and North. I had a conversation with him on the subject a day or two since—in which he repeated the views formerly expressed to me, of the propriety of passing a resolution at once repudiating accessions of territory—and then if the President [James K. Polk] did not offer peace to Mexico on that basis to stop the supplies. I remarked to him that such a policy would be much dependent on intervening events. That Congress might on assembling find a treaty made by which Territory was to be acquired. Or the War might have assumed a new complexion. I observed also that I thought something more would be demanded by the South: which would insist since the North had raised the question of the territorial rights of the two sections—that it should be settled now, when the relative strength of the South was greater probably than it would be hereafter. For that although territorial extension might be declined now as the fruit of conquest, it would probably in future be sought as heretofore by purchase. And I remarked that if Congress would pass a joint resolution next session recognizing the right of the people of every territory to determine for themselves the character of their institutions it would be as satisfactory as it was just—and would put an end for the present to the controversy. He seemed to think the South had better not press that point too far.

I observe that the Southern papers of both parties are becoming more and more impressed with the magnitude of the Wilmot proviso question—and that they are united. In the North both Whig and Democratic parties have two classes of politicians, one in favour of waiving the question, the other of making it. I saw Gov[erno]r [Thomas] Corwin [of Ohio] the other day who attended the Chicago convention and saw many of the northern politicians of both parties. He says that those of New York are both warmly in favour of the Wilmot proviso, and that rather for the purpose of beating each other in that State than any thing else. The Silas Wright men insist also on acquisition of territory to augment the strength of the non-slaveholding States. The older and abler whigs who desire to preserve the strength of their party in the South are in favour of avoiding or evading the issue of the Wilmot proviso.

Here the Democratic party is perplexed on the subject and it is doubtful how it will act this fall in reference to it.

General [Zachary] Taylor is losing ground rapidly—and I think his last letter[,] that to [Edward] Delany will put an end to his availability as a Candidate. I think also that the whigs are again turning ["to" *canceled*] their eyes to [Henry] Clay who has put himself in motion eastward. If the Wilmot controversy runs high will not the Whigs make that a pretence for calling in Clay to make another Missouri compromise?

I saw Senator [David Levy] Yulee [of Fla.] here the other day for a few ["days" *canceled*] minutes on his way with his wife to Kentucky. Having seen occasional notices in the papers of some correspondence between Dixon H. Lewis [Senator from Ala.] and the friends of General Taylor, I asked Yulee about it. He said that the answers had been unsatisfactory even on the Tariff. Yulee says he is himself in favour of preserving the States rights party unconnected with the Taylor movement. And he thinks that the no-party sentiment[,] so far as it is just[,] on which the friends of Taylor desire to take ground[,] belongs more justly to thyself.

The Chicago convention has made no impression here. Pretending to be more practical than that of Memphis, the recent convention did not dare to designate the works it would advocate. Their number was too great to be enrolled.

General [Lewis] Cass has gone hopelessly down.

The North it seems to me is now divided for the present irreconcilably on the Wilmot proviso and on the Tariff questions. On these two the South is united. If she could be united on a Candidate her success would be certain—and how she can hesitate, when not only [*partial word canceled*] safety but triumph are [on] one side and on the other ruin and degradation, is as derogatory to her honor as to her sagacity. With great regard thine truly, Ellwood Fisher.

P.S. I send a copy of the [Columbus, *Ohio State?*] Journal in which thee will recognize my hand. I have taken some pains that the War question should be properly ["prop" *canceled*] presented to the country—and have not permitted Democrats to denounce with impunity those opposed to the War.

ALS in ScCleA; PC in Boucher and Brooks, eds., *Correspondence*, pp. 393–395. NOTE: A great River and Harbor Convention had convened in Chicago on 7/5 in which mainly Northern States were represented. Thomas Corwin had given one of the main addresses and the convention had resolved that internal waterways had been neglected in federal appropriations and this should be corrected. Zachary Taylor's letter to Edward Delany, dated June 9, 1847, had been made public. Taylor declined to answer questions in regard to his opinions on the Mexican war, the national bank, and the tariff. Further, he stated that if he was "considered a candidate for the presidency, it has been by no agency of mine in the matter; and if the good people think my services important in that station, and elect me, I will feel bound to serve them . . . ." *Niles' National Register*, vol. LXXII, no. 25 (August 21, 1847), p. 389.

From H[ENRY] W. CONNER

Charleston, August 23 1847

Dear Sir, Your favour of the 8th was duly rec[eive]d and before leaving for the North to day I propose to give you an outline of what we have done here since my last.

We have distributed in the slave States 2000 circulars & 1000 subscription lists & have sent about 5000 copies of the Mercury (an Extra) of the 11th containing—an Editorial (written by [Franklin H.] Elmore) accompanied by the Wilmot proviso & the resolves of 10 of the Northern States in its favour—with the Virginia & our resolutions &c on the other side. So far as we have yet learned these documents have awakened the people & been most favourably received.

A few days since we got together some 15 or 20 gentlemen—as a sort of preliminary step to a larger meeting. They all subscribed to a man—& brought our subscriptions up to near $13000.

Tomorrow—a larger meeting is to be held (by special invitation— not public) & I have no doubt the am[oun]t will be much increased. A short time hence—a still larger meeting—to be called in the same way is proposed. In the meantime committees of correspondence are being formed—to operate on the different sections of this State & upon all the slave States. It is the intention also to send round—amongst the wealthy planters of this State a special agent to collect.

While at the North It is proposed that I shall press the matter amongst the Southerners on [*sic*] there from all quarters—& particularly in reference to a Southern association or other organization which I will endeavour to do to the best of my ability. My address—will be to the care of L.M. Wiley & Co. New York—if you should desire to advise me. From what I see I believe we can raise in this State an am[oun]t sufficient to establish the paper—say 30 to $50000. Some talk of $100000. In fact there is but one view in this quarter. *I do believe* too that the feeling is becoming deep & widely extended all through the South & that with a proper degree of tact & energy that it may be embodied into a compact form & given the right direction. I believe if Maryland or Virginia would begin by establishing an association to be called "an antiabolition association for the defence of slavery & of the rights of the slave holding States & their Citizens" that it would be taken up by the whole South & similar associations be every where formed. With this organization all other parties & influences on the South would sink before its power & we could come up to the conflict with our whole strength brought to bear.

To my apprehension the two greatest dangers we have to encounter—is our own apathy & indolence (which it is distressing to behold) in the first place & the danger of compr[om]ise when we have got into the conflict. It is unnecessary however for me to fatigue you with subjects you understand so much better than we do.

A reference to the Missouri Compromise in one of our articles in the Mercury as the aim of our efforts—was thought impolitic by some of us & the force of the remark modified some ["in the original draft" *interlined*]—but another article contending that the violation of the Compromise [*one word canceled and* "threw" *interlined*] us back upon our original Constitutional ground counteracted it in some sort.

I have heard the names of Jno. A. Campbell of Mobile, R[obert] W. Barnwell, W[illiam] F. Colcock, & [William L.] Yancey of Montgomery [Ala.] spoken of for Editors. Yancey I think would be willing for it. The others—probably not, tho I do not know. The time has not yet come to discuss it. Very Truly y[ou]rs &C, H.W. Conner.

ALS in ScCleA; PC in Jameson, ed., *Correspondence*, pp. 1128–1129. Note: The "circular" mentioned by Conner was the document dated 8/2/1847 which appears below as an En with Calhoun's letter of 9/5/1847 to Eustis Prescott.

From W. S. CASSEDY

Meadville Miss[issipp]i, Aug. 24 1847

Dear Sir, I have been for some time past and am now engaged in ["writing" *canceled*] collecting materials for the purpose of writing a History of the present Administration, the object I have in view being somewhat public in its nature will excuse to you I hope the liberty I take in addressing you on the subject.

From the eminent position you occupy as well as from your personal influence I was induced to believe you could furnish me with documents of a public nature which would more essentially aid me (than any other) in the design I have in view which is in the work.

1st. To discuss the state of parties on the accession of Gen[era]l [William H.] Harrison and as far as possible the Causes which led to that result.

2d. The State of Parties, of the Country (and as far as may be possible) of the departments of government when John Tyler went out of office.

3d. The Administration of James K. Polk in which I shall discuss in detail the prominent measures effected during his administration—The tariff—the war[;] the Oregon Question[;] the Sub treasury; and in addition the Annexation of Texas in which more particularly you performed such valuable service to the Republic.

The object I have in view in writing the work is to give a History of the politics of the Country from the Administration of Mr. Van Buren down to the present and endeavor to show the beneficial influence democratic politics have had on the welfare of the country in contrast with Whig. I intend it to serve as a *manual* of Statistical facts and as far as may be of political truths to assist the *Democratic Party* in the Canvass of 1848, and shall endeavour to make the work by its size, style[,] price and arrangement such an one as may be useful among the people.

Any documents you will be kind enough to furnish me in aid of this undertaking, convenient to yourself would be thankfully received and appreciated by Your Ob[e]d[ien]t Serv[an]t, W.S. Cassedy.

ALS in ScCleA.

From E. D R A Y T O N E A R L E and Others

Greenville C[ourt] H[ouse, S.C.,] 24th Aug. 1847
Sir, At a meeting to day of Citizens of this place favorable to the Completion of the Greenville & Columbia Rail Road The undersigned were appointed a Committee to invite from abroad Gentlemen known to be friendly to the enterprise to partake at this place of a Barbecue on Wednesday 8th Sept. next. Your attendance therefore on that occasion is most respectfully Solicited. E. Drayton Earle, E[rwin] P. Jones, R.B. Duncan, W[illiam] B. Thompson, Com[mittee].

LS (in Earle's handwriting) in ScCleA. NOTE: An AEU by Calhoun reads "Invitation to attend Barbecue In Green Ville."

From J o s [e p h] W. L e s e s n e

Mobile, Aug. 24th 1847
My Dear Sir, Since writing you last some of our friends have requested me to obtain your veiws, in ["view" *canceled and* "anticipation" *interlined*] of some action contemplated in our next Legislature, relative to the ground which ought to be taken against the "Wilmot proviso." There is a growing disposition among our friends to come out boldly against the further acquisition of Territory as the only practicable mode of saving the south against the danger that threatens from this alarming question. It is a fact not to be disguised, that at present there is at the South a large party in favor of the acquisition of territory. An insane thirst after land is the great American disease, and divested of other considerations the party that holds out the prospect of Territory would unquestionably have the advantage. Nor would the *means* of its acquisition, in a moral point of veiw make much difference. To take ground therefore against the acquisition of Territory even among the poeple [*sic*] of the slave holding States successfully, they must be convinced that there is no other mode of preventing their defeat on the question under consideration.

It is certain then, or highly probable that if the war results in the increase of our territory, the Wilmot proviso will become a law. If so our poeple can not be too soon convinced of the fact—nor can we too soon take measures to force the president to a course which will

507

save us from ruin. It will be too late to act after the territory is acquired and the question of its free or slave character determined by Law. Under such circumstances I should not have the least hope that our poeple could or would take measures to deliver themselves from the distant ruin that would certainly await them. Indeed it is not easy to conceive what mode of effectual redress could be adopted. It would be a wrong beyond the reach of State interposition joint or separate. We could secede from the Union, but would that help us? Would it change or in any manner affect the territory over which Federal Laws had been already extended ["and" *canceled*] with federal officers to enforce within the jurisdiction of those laws the opinions and the objects of the victorious party.

I regret to see in the [Charleston] Mercury an article, from the pen I presume of Col. [Isaac W.] Hayne the tendency of which is to create the impression that the interdict of Slavary in the Territory would be harmless—because unconstitutional and void. The writer did not probably intend this. He does not seem to have considered that whatever, in an abstract point of veiw, the rights of the Southern States may be, the exercise by Congress of jurisdiction over newly acquired territory by the ["passage" *canceled and* "enactment" *interlined*] of Laws and the appointment of Judges[,] Marshalls &c would have the effect of releasing every slave carried there, on a writ of Habeas Corpus—just as much so as in the State of Pennsylvania where the Constitution of the U.S. has been practically nullified.

I do not think that even in South Carolina all ["the" *interlined*] bearings of this alarming subject are fully seen and comprehended. The articles in the Mercury are very unequal to the occasion. I have seen nothing that approaches it properly since the adjournment of Congress except the arti[cle] in Bro[w]nson[']s Review, which I am endeavoring to get republished for distribution in this State with the Laws and Resolutions of the other States—["recently republished in the Mercury" *interlined*]. I would like to hear from you before this is done.

I have again met Mr. [Pierre] Soulé, who repeated what fell from him in our last interveiw and added again that "no public man ever occupied so high commanding and difficult position as yourself—that if by the meeting of the next Congress the war was not terminated the elevation and peculiarity of that position would be still further augmented, and that he thought that both parties would be compelled to look to you as a counsellor and guide," and in conclusion that "all that he desired was that neither in word or act you would show yourself in the least degree a partizan." I answered that on that point he might make himself easy. He has great confidence in you, but is more reserved and cautious than when he first reached home. Very truly your f[rien]d &C, Jos. W. Lesesne.

ALS in ScCleA; PC in Jameson, ed., *Correspondence*, pp. 1130–1131. NOTE: The article referred to was apparently "Slavery and the Mexican War," *Brownson's Quarterly Review*, new series, vol. 1, no. 3 (July, 1847), pp. 334–367. It said, in part, that abolitionists are "the worst enemies of the country, and the worst enemies, too, of the slave. They are a band of mad fanatics, and we have no language strong enough to express our abhorrence of their principles and proceedings."

To [HENRY W.] CONNER, [Charleston]

Fort Hill, 25th Aug[us]t 1847

My dear Sir, I have been delayed by various occurrences, from acknowledging your letter of the 8th Inst. until this time. I am happy to see, the subscription commence with so much sperit, and hope it had continued to progress well. I made, what seemed to me, the best distribution of the papers sent to me. Should the subscription warrent it, the paper, if possible, should be under way by the meeting of Congress, or shortly after. Should the amount not be sufficiently large to authorise the establishment of a press, the object in view might, probably be effected equally advantageously for a limited period, by having the paper printed by contract at some one of the many printing establishments at Washington. Indeed, it may be doubt[ed], whether that would not be the most advisable mode, be it small or large. It would save a vast deal of trouble, and go more promptly into operation, & be, perhaps, in the long run, the most economical. The amount raised might be ["put" *canceled*] vested in some safe stock, or put out at interest, and drawn on as wanted.

I am glad to see you in such good sperits. I concur with you, that a better tone begins to exhibit itself in the South. The articles in the Mercury will, I hope, contribute to raise it higher and make it more universal. Indeed, every thing depends on Charleston, & you & our other friends there. It is politically the head of the South, as I hope she will, one day, or another be, commercially.

I entirely concur in your suggestions as to forming associations in the South, in defence of our rights & institutions. This fall during the sessions of the Southern Legislatures, will be the proper time to organize them. I hope steps will be taken beforehand among, our Charleston friends, for the purpose. You must take the lead. If we do not move no other State will, & we can take the lead only through your city. The great point is to rouse the South, and to unite it. If that can be done all will be safe.

In this connection, and as the means of uniting the South, as well as to give to Charleston the greatest commercial prosperity, I regard the completion of the railroad to NashVille of the Utmost importance. For that purpose, we must meet the efforts of that ["State" *canceled and* "city" *interlined*] & the State of Tennessee to the full. It will be nothing for the three States immediately concerned, S.C.: Ga.: & Tennessee to complete it at once. Indeed, I regard it so important every way, that I am decidedly of the opinion, that it is a matter claiming the attention of our Legislature. I have not a doubt of the Stock being worth more than par, from the day of its completion; and am of the opinion, the Legislature might, with perfect safety, guarantee a loan towards its completion. It is destined to be one of the most important and profitable roads in the Union. If its advantages were fairly exhibited, either in the North, or in Europe, it would, in my opinion, command any amount of stock necessary for its completion. Would it not be well for you, while in the north, to call the attention of some of the capitalists to it[?]

Its completion would unite commercially, socially, & politically the slave holding States; so as to combine ["our" *canceled and* "their" *interlined*] influence in the Union, if it is destined to last; & to connect them strongly together, in one bound [*sic*] of Union, should it not be. If I had leisure, I would prepare a memoir on the subject.

I will direct this to Charleston, so as to reach you there, if you have not sailed for the north. If you have, I take it for granted, it will follow you. Should you be there, I shall be glad to hear from you. Yours truly & sincerely, J.C. Calhoun.

ALS in ScC; photostat of ALS in DLC, Henry Workman Conner Papers.

From F[RANKLIN] H. ELMORE

Charleston [S.C.], 25 Aug. 1847

My Dear Sir, A letter ["This" *canceled*] will be handed to you by Col. A[lfred] P. Aldrich who goes as the rep[resentative] of the Ex[ecutive] Com[mittee] from Charles[ton] to see our friends personally in the country. He can report to you more fully than I can state what we have done. My occupation is so incessant that I cannot write to you as I would desire—or I would keep you advised more fully. So far the prospect seems fair for filling up our am[oun]t of $30,000—and many are looking to a much wider base, say $100,000. [James] Hamilton [Jr.] has just written us to that effect & thinks the funds can be got. We have here one of the Mississippi Planters[,] Mr. And[rew] Turnbull (son of Brutus [Robert J. Turnbull]) who is very warm & goes shortly to the Va. Springs where he expects to meet many Mississippi, Louis[ian]a & other Southern planters to whom he will put our plans with all his vigor.

Judge [Daniel E.] Huger, [Richard I.] Manning & [John P.] Richardson are there now & have been addressed & constituted a committee. A Special Delegate from this City has gone on to see & put them in action. [Henry W.] Conner has gone to N.Y. [City] to stay a month & he is a committee with Cart blanche & unlimited zeal for that point. He takes a list of Southern men now there & is to organize an efficient working Committee while there to get them into action.

Hamilton writes that he will move in Georgia[,] Ala.[,] Lou[isian]a & Mississippi & Texas as soon as he can.

The idea of Hamilton has our intire sanction here, but we have thought it best, not to propose so wide a base at first, but to urge the sub & get all we can & if so much, then to graft the extension on the present basis.

As to Editor—What do you think of J[ohn] A. Campbell of Mobile? If you think he would do would you have any objection to sound him[?] Of Mr. [William L.] Yancey we think well in all respects but one & that is his prudence. The position is one that requires the highest cast of intellect, judgement, firmness & discretion. Where is it to be found?

Mr. Aldrich will show you his instructions & we would be glad to have your views in regard to any thing that would require remark in them.

We would like to know more of Mr. [Muscoe R.H.] Garnett of whom you spoke in one of your letters.

Would it not be well for you to see [Armistead] Burt before Mr. Aldrich visits you & Abbeville & concert[?] with him, [Richard F.] Simpson & others for Aldrich's movements. He must see Mr. [George] McDuffie. I give him a chart in part, but not for all. He goes up to Edgefield, to be there next Sale day—thence to Abbeville—

thence to your House & thence as you may direct. He is to see all whom it is thought worth while to visit & to try & organize in each District for subscriptions.

When I began this letter I intended it to be taken by Col. Aldrich, but perhaps it will be best to send it to you at once that you may be thinking as to the best arrangements before he comes up. I will give him a letter of introduction. I suppose he will be with you by the 12 or 15 Sep[tember].

The subs[criptio]n here now amounts to some $15 to 18,000 & we have many more who are certain of liberal subscriptions. Most men of property subscribe ["from" *canceled*] $500. I think if it is properly responded to in the Country we can get $40,000 in this State. If $100,000 could be got & an office be put up on the basis that the Methodists have their press & book concern at N.Y. it would be permanent & a powerful auxiliary.

We are opening correspondences in N[ew] O[rleans,] Mobile & Montgomery—to induce similar organization there to ours in Charleston. If you could write to Hon. Ed[mund] S. Dargan, David Chandler, [Philip] Phillips, Ja[me]s S. Deas, J.A. Campbell, Jos[eph] W. Lesesne & any others as a committee in Mobile—to Gov[ernor] Ben[jamin] Fitzpatrick[,] W.L. Yancey[,] Peachy R. Gilmer[,] J[ohn] A. Elmore, Tho[mas] S. Mays, Tho[mas] Williams [Jr.] & N[imrod] E. Benson[,] Tho[mas] M. Barnett[,] Jesse P. Taylor[,] Abner McGehee, Sam[uel C.] Oliver, Dr. R[obert] J. Ware, J[ames] E. Belser & Col. Alex Carter in Montgomery, and to Mr. [Pierre] Soule, W[illiam] A. Elmore and any others you may think of in N[ew] O[rleans] suggesting the like movement it will do well. Let us know who you have addressed—or what perhaps would be better, send us your letters & we will write & send them on.

If anyone in Mississippi could in like manner be reached, we would be glad to have the like means of reaching that State.

I have written you in great haste & disconnectedly—& fear you will consider me a very unsatisfactory reporter.

[Andrew P.] Butler [Senator from S.C.] came down to attend a consultation yesterday—he returned today & is full of the measure. He arranged with Aldrich to meet him at Edgefield Sale day.

He tells me that Col. [Francis W.] Pickens is out & out opposed to the movement—denouncing it as a scheme for personal objects. I hope he is mistaken & that if Pickens has been adverse, that his views have been on misapprehensions which may be removed. If you can aid in doing so it would be well to do it early.

Col. Ja[me]s Ed[ward] Colhoun was down a few days ago. I

hope you have seen him. He expressed a warm concurrence with us. Can you stimulate him?

The effort that is being made here, demands an adequate cooperation from the Country. Burt sh[oul]d aid us. He did nothing when we all strained so hard to establish the Constitution & some of his warm friends here have complained very much of it.

We arranged some time ago to keep up a run of Editorials in the Mercury on this [Wilmot] Proviso. The first was written by [Andrew G.] McGrath. It was not intended to have been the first, but one I was to prepare was not ready & he occupied the first column. Then followed one I had prepared with the Resolutions of the several States for the Proviso, your resolutions, Virginia Alabama's [*word illegible*] & Georgia[']s—the law of 1793 & Pennsylvania[']s nullification of it. McGrath followed for one or two numbers, then came [George A.] Trenholm, who ended [*one or two words canceled*] yesterday the fourth I think of his series. Mr. Nelson Mitchell follows next. [Isaac W.] Hayne & [John Milton] Clapp & some others are to succeed, & so we intend keeping up the fire. What do you think of the course of the arguments? Ben[jamin F.] Hunt wrote the two communications signed H. Ione [*sic*; Jacob Bond I'On] also wrote an Editorial preceding McGrath[']s a few days.

I fear cotton crops are to suffer from worms as well as wet. The market here is firm under the Cambria[']s news—and I will not give way, but advance.

Our health is perfectly good in the city & country. Very truly Yours, F.H. Elmore.

[P.S.] If you think of anyone Conner could see to advantage in N. York, could you not write to him there?

P.S. Mr. Gilmer of Montgomery Ala. has this moment come in from N. York & reports the cotton market as firm. He sold some at an advance.

ALS in ScCleA. NOTE: In the list of names of persons to whom he wished Calhoun to write in Ala., Elmore made by symbols a differentiation between Democrats and Whigs, which has been impossible to reproduce in this printing.

From THOMAS G. KEY

Hamburg [S.C.], Aug. 26th 1847

My Dear Sir, Trusting that you will pardon the liberty that a stranger and an humble individual like myself has taken in addressing you, I proceed at once to state my object for doing so.

I have thought that I would hoist the name of Gen[era]l [Zachary] Taylor at the head of my columns as my Candidate for the Presidency in 1848—and as mine will be the first press in the State to make this movement I desire first to obtain your opinion, and solicit your advice in the matter.

I regard the growing popularity and increasing prospects of the Gen[era]l for that office as peculiarly fortunate for the South in this crisis; and should they end in his triumphant election, I think we may consider *her safe* from the attacks of her enemies.

It is, perhaps, not unknown to you, that I would much prefer you to any other man for that office; and would not, therefore, make the movement if it would be in any manner injurious to your prospects, or against the welfare and interest of the South—hence the necessity I have felt in addressing you.

You may rest assured that I will make such a disposition of your reply as you may direct. I do not desire, ["it" *canceled*] of course, to publish it. Very respectfully, Your Ob[edien]t Servant, Thomas G. Key, Editor "Hamburg Journal."

ALS in ScCleA. NOTE: An AEU by Calhoun reads "Editor of the Hamburgh Journal."

From W[illia]m W. Lea

Trenton Tenn., Aug. 27th 1847

D[ea]r Sir, Believing that you feel a deep interest in the welfare and prosperity of the Southern and western portions of our happy confederacy and particularly in the great enterprise of connecting the Atlantic ports, Charleston and Savannah, with the Mississippi River; by way of renewing an acquaintance formed in Washington City some years since, I send you a copy of a memorial, which will be presented to the Legislature of Tennessee at its next session, for the purpose of obtaining a charter for the last link in the great undertaking above referred to. I may hereafter send you something more on this subject. I shall devote my time and energies to the accomplishment of this great enterprise and hope for success. I have the honor to be, with great respect and consideration your ob[edien]t serv[an]t, Wm. W. Lea.

[Printed Enclosure]
CENTRAL RAIL ROAD.
To the Honorable the General Assembly convened at Nashville, the

undersigned citizens of Tennesse[e] respectfully beg leave to represent that:

Ten years ago the Legislature of Tennessee made an appropriation of fifteen thousand dollars to defray the expenses of a preliminary survey of the Central Rail Road commencing at the Mississippi River and extending through West and Middle Tennessee to the base of the Cumberland Mountain, to be connected with a Turnpike Road, continuing thence across the mountain and through East Tennessee to the Virginia line. This was a noble enterprise, worthy of the State, and had it been carried out faithfully, on the plan proposed, the State paying one half and individuals the other, the benefits, to the State at large, would have been much greater than those which have resulted, from the sub-division of the funds thus raised and appropriated to various local and sectional objects. It is true that Nashville and its immediate vicinity have been greatly benefited, that section having secured nearly all of the advantages of creating a State debt of more than two millions of dollars for internal improvements, and many abuses were practised, which have rendered the system unpopular. The time moreover was not auspicious for carrying on a great work of the kind, and although the report of the engineers of the reconnoisance and survey of the route for the Central Rail Road was extremely favorable, the undertaking was temporarily abandoned.

The time has now arrived for prosecuting the work under more favorable auspices. The multiplication and extension of Rail Roads, in other sections of our widely extended country and the invariable success, which has attended their judicious location and economical construction, have created confidence in such enterprises and a disposition on the part of capitalists to seek such investments, as affording greater security and larger profits than Bank Stocks, State Stocks and other securities. Great improvements have been made in the construction and working of roads and locomotives, and the management of them, when in operation, which have diminished largely the original cost as well as the subsequent expenses of all such public works and rendered them much more profitable and popular. The increased power of traction given locomotives, is alone sufficient to reduce the cost of grading in uneaven localities, fully one half, which is often the heaviest part of the expense of constructing rail roads. There are, however, fewer difficulties, of this kind, to be encountered in the route of the Central Rail Road than in any other work of the same extent that has yet been undertaken, in any portion of our country. West of Tennessee River the road may be made almost perfectly level at a very small cost for grading, and in Middle Tennessee, with the exception of a few miles near the mouth of Duck River, but little difficulty will be found in obtaining a good route with easy grades throughout. The rapid progress of the Georgia works and the certainty of their being speedily extended to Chat[t]anooga, imperiously require that Tennessee should rouse up from her slumber, shake off her apathy, and stand boldly forward, in carrying out the great national object of connecting the Atlantic and Mississippi by rail road. An important link in this line, the Nashville and Chat[t]anooga Rail Road, was chartered by the Legislature of the State at its last session, and is about to be commenced, under very favorable auspices. The Central Rail Road intersecting the Nashville and Chat[t]anooga Road, will complete the connection between Charleston and Savannah on the Atlantic sea board and the Mississippi river, and, when finished, will double the business and profits on the whole line. It will become the great thorough-fare of travel between the north and the south and the profits from this source and from the transportation of the products of the soil, of mines, of forests and of all kinds of merchandize, will make it the most profitable of all the great lines of rail-road communication, now in progress or in contemplation between the Atlantic and the great Valley of the West. No region abounds more in natural wealth and resources; in fertile soil, in variety and abundance of agricultural fruits, in rich minerals, in abundant products of the forests and in the necessity and advantages of mutual interchanges of commodities. The travelling and transportation on this route must, therefore, be immense and the profits correspondingly great. Rail Roads always create business for themselves and, as in other cases, the amount on this great line will speedily be multiplied four fold, with a like increase of profits.

In a political view, also, the benefits of this rail road will be incalculable. The remote sections of our common country will be drawn and held together by iron bands, community of interests will strengthen the union and, in case of invasion or insurrection, relief can fly from one section to another on the wings of the wind. The State of Tennessee, which, by geographical devisions, has somewhat diversified interests, will become more united, and by the Hiwassee, the Nashville and Chat[t]anooga, and the Central Rail Road, be drawn together as one people, having a common interest. So great and general being the objects to be subserved and the interests to be promoted by the construction of the Central Rail Road, no difficulty is apprehended in obtaining a charter from the Legislature, with most favorable provisions and a subscription, by the State, for stock to the amount of the remainder of the proceeds of the sales of the lands, south and west of the Congressional Reservation Line, ceded by Congress to the State for purposes of education and Internal Improvement.

It is also hoped that an enlightened policy and enlarged views of true political economy and of the best interests of the State, will suggest to your honorable body the propriety and expediency of authorizing a much larger subscription on behalf of the Central Rail Road. To the consideration of all which, your memorialists beg your favorable attention.

ALS with En in ScCleA.

From WILSON LUMPKIN,
   [former Senator from Ga.]

Athens [Ga.,] Aug[us]t 27th 1847
My dear Sir, I am pleased to acknowledge the receipt of your favor of the 22d Inst. with its enclosures. I had some time ago rec[ei]v[e]d, the printed papers which you have forwarded, (from Charleston I presume.) My views, opinions & feelings coincide, with those who have called my attention, to the subjects embraced in your letter & the papers refer[r]ed to.

And I have not been altogether an idle spectator of passing events, for the last six or eight months. But to effect any thing in Georgia on this subject, & at this time—I can assure you, is quite an uphill business. The interest of Georgia & South Carolina, on the slave question, is *identical*, but the political state of the public mind, is very different indeed, owing to various causes, which would require too much space to explain in this letter.

The only news paper in Georgia, which speaks out upon this subject, freely & independently is the *"Macon Tellegraph."* The Editor [James R. Gardner] of the Augusta Constitutionalist, is right in principle, & possesses an Independant spirit—but with a view to expediency, or to the pending Elections, or something Else—has of late rather modifyed, his high tone on the Slave question. In fact our Georgia papers, are all too closely identifyed, *with party*, & *party leaders*. The principles upon which it is proposed to establish the new paper at Washington, meets my entire approbation, for I am

517

entirely disgusted, with most of the leading papers of both parties—
as well as with most of the leading men of both parties, as they now
stand organized.

Unless we could have a party, that would rally on the Constitution—& maintain the principles of the Va. resolutions of '98, It is all
folly, to demagogue the people, with professions of Democracy, &
love of Equal rights. All I want is the Equal rights, secured to me
in the Constitution.

But the spirit of most of the leaders of both parties, at the present
day—is to lay aside the Constitution—and cry out let the majority of
the people govern—and thus change our system of Constitu[ti]onal
govt. into one great consolidated Despotic, Democracy. A many
headed monster, which would speedily crush our section of the
Union. Our Constitution was designed to guard the rights of
minorities.

Upon the slave question, I firmly believe, that the apathy of the
South, is rapidly hastening trouble & danger. The conduct of our
adversaries should before now, have been met, with decision & firmness. So long as we rely upon yielding and compromising any part
of our rights on this subject, we are but nourishing & inviting further
aggressions. Eventually we shall be forced to decisive & direct resistance, or we must yield every thing, & become more degraded,
than any people on earth, who have enjoyed the advantages & blessings which we now possess. If we yield our rights on this subject,
the slow unwavering finger of scorn, will point to us, by the present
generation, & in all time to come.

I know the temperament of our opponents. We can effect nothing by argument & discussion. But when we of the South use imperative language, & say, we will yield nothing on this subject, The
case will be settled. They will cease to trouble us.

Decisive action, without delay, is all that is necessary.

The Slave States United, would be impregnable on the Slave
question. But alas! what is the condition of our Southern people,
at this moment? A large majority of the Southern politicians, are
like clay in the hands of the potter, ready to be moulded into any
form, that may best suit the aspirations of party leaders. And like
Sampson we are thus I fear, to be shorn of our strength, until we
hear a sudden cry. Our Enemies are upon us. With but very few
exceptions, our people in Georgia, are whol[l]y unprepared to yield
up, their old party attachments. The constant & unceasing Efforts
of the press, has been to dis[s]ipate all their apprehensions on the
slave question. And they have been so long accustomed to the cry

of danger upon this subject, that they would scarcely believe, even one sent from the dead. Those who entertain the opinions, which is set forth in the paper before me, can & do exercise a great & salutary influence, in their present disorganized condition, & they can & do act, regardless of the interest of present party organizations, & become a balance of power, conservative party, which has done much good for the Country.

But the moment the contemplated organization shall be effected, it becomes to all intents & purposes, an organized political party— and nothing but the purest patriotism, prudence, & great wisdom, can prevent it from partaking of some of the evils of the existing parties. The design of this organization, like that of the abolitionist seems to be confined to a single object. That of resisting aggressions upon our rights as slave-holders.

And if the slave States, whose vital interest are in jeopardy upon this question, could be united, we should at once be in an attitude to defy all assaults from every quarter. Moreover, we should soon become, the glory and admiration of the whole earth—provided always, that God[']s blessings are continued to us, as heretofore to our progenitors. But to come to the particular point, to which you have called my attention. My heart is with So. Carolina on this subject.

What little influence I now exercise, has & will be directed, to the promotion of the cause & objects contemplated. But my influence is very limited, to what it once was in Georgia. In politics I have run my race. I have finished my course. I am an old man. Age & experience, does not govern the country as it once did. The disposition to muster old men, out of the public service, is rapidly encreasing. Moreover, if public trust be desirable, I have had an ample share. Much more, than I could have claimed. If office be a burthen & sacrifice to the incumbent, I have borne my full share.

I have voluntarily withdrawn from public life. I enjoy my retirement more & more—and am blessed with perfect health & quietude. I can & will cooperate with others, in the great struggle which awaits us, on the subject under consideration. I shall do it, openly, fearlessly & independantly.

But cannot attempt, any thing like, leadership, even in a subordinate position. We have many patriotic, enlightened men in Georgia, who feel as we do, on this subject. But too large a portion of these noble spirits, have not yet abandoned former party predilections.

In Georgia, it will still require further developements, to produce the conviction which rests upon my mind, of the utter corruption of both the great parties of the Country. It is true, that on most subjects, the Democratic party, profess the principles by which I am governed—but it is equally true, that they hold the truth in unrighteousness, their practices are in many things, corrupt, selfish, & based upon the single object of engrossing the offices of the Country. The extent of corruption is so great, that the best men of both parties, are unpopular with their political associates.

Our Democratic candidate for Gov[ernor] Mr. [George W.B.] Towns, in his letter of acceptance has come out in a manly tone, & the convention which nominated him, was forced into a declaration, that they would support no man for the Presidency, who was not openly opposed to the Wilmot policy. They however go for continuing the Mis[s]ouri Compromise. I claim some credit & took some trouble, to gain this much. I hope we shall adhere to the ground thus assumed.

The Canvass now going on in Georgia, begins to excite unusual zeal—and the Excitement will increase. Connected with the Election of Gov[erno]r is that of the Legislature, & the Legislature has to elect two Senators to Congress & all the State house officers &C &C— so you perc[e]ive the office seekers have much at stake—and a very large portion of the people, will not at this time stop to enter upon a due consideration, of the vital importance of the slave question. Moreover, many begin to doubt, whether any acquisition of Territory will be obtained from Mexico, which will bring on an immediate collision between the North & the South on the slave question.

The suspended state of opperations in Mexico, indicates difficulties of no ordinary character. The result of the recent elections, in a number of the States, must be conclusive with every reflecting man, that a want of confidence in the administration pervades the country, to a very great extent. The administration at this time, is most certainly in a minority, with the people.

The responsibility of your position, official & otherwise—your extensive range of thought & information—the weight & influence of your character—all combine, to give importance to any opinion which you express.

The closing sentence in your letter, excites more than ordinary solicitude in my bosom, & inclines me to extend my contemplations to the future. What are the momentous events, connected with the action of the next Congress? What are the calamities to be averted?

I have discontinued Mr. [Thomas] Ri[t]chie[']s paper [the Washington *Union*], some time since, and will most cheerfully support, as far as I can, such a paper as the one proposed to be edited at Washington. But am not prepared at this time to pledge any sum for the

establishment of such a paper. I have neither the means nor the position to lead in such an enterprize. I am D[ea]r Sir Very Sincerely
Y[ou]rs, Wilson Lumpkin.

ALS in ScCleA; variant PC in Boucher and Brooks, eds., *Correspondence*, pp.
395–398.

From F. G. Thomas, T[homas] R. Gary, and P[aul] W. Connor

Cokesbury [Abbeville District, S.C.] Aug. 28th 1847
Dear Sir, At a public meeting recently held in our District a series
of Rail-Road meetings were appointed, commencing at Abbeville
C[ourt] H[ouse] on sale-day next. Having been appointed by that
meeting a Committee of invitation, and believing that you are a
friend to the great Rail-road Enterprise in contemplation, and that
you are favorable to the rout[e] through Abbeville & Anderson Districts, we solicit your aid, specially, at the meeting at Abbeville
C[ourt] H[ouse] on sale-day. Knowing that you possess an influence
in our District that no other man does, we think it is only necessary
that you should express an opinion in favor of this great measure to
unite the District warmly in its support. We regard this, almost, as a
case of life or death with the people of Abbeville. According to an
estimate made by Messrs. [Joel R.] Poinsett, [Alexander] Black &
[Franklin H.] Elmore, the benefits of this road to Abbeville District
would be some seven or eight millions of dollars. Take off one half
for an over estimate yet it amounts to millions. We believe that no
estimate has ever yet been made too high.

We beg leave to suggest for your consideration the following
view of this subject. A Rail-road being completed from Columbia
to Newberry C[ourt] H[ouse], thence across Saluda river striking
the ridge that divides the waters of that river from those of the Savan[n]ah, near the village of Greenwood, thence along that ridge
through Abbeville and Anderson Districts either to Anderson C[ourt]
H[ouse] or some point near Old Pickensville, thence to Greenville
C[ourt] H[ouse], there will be a distance of only thirty or thirty five
miles from the place where it strikes this dividing ridge to Edgefield
C[ourt] H[ouse] to which place a Rail-road is to be built from
Aiken. We therefore think that these two roads will be united by a
connecting link, furnishing a direct line of communication to Aiken,

and affording great facilities for all passengers and freight going west.

Again. The road will run through Abbeville District within twenty five miles of the Savanna[h] River: and we think it is very probable that a branch will be built from the main trunk by Abbeville C[ourt] H[ouse] to that river. It will be to the interest of our citizens, on the Savan[n]ah side of the District, to three or four counties of Georgia and especially to Charleston to have that branch built. With all these important interests in favor of an enterprise of that kind, and especially where the obstacles to be overcome are so few, it does seem to us that no man can doubt that it will ultimately ["be" *interlined*] accomplished. This we think should be a strong inducement for our friends on the Savan[n]ah side of the District to unite with us in favor of this great enterprise. It is very decidedly our opinion that if you can spare the time, which we hope you will do, in consideration of the very great importance of this matter to your native District and will favor us with your presence on next sale-day at Abbeville C[ourt] H[ouse], that the success of our efforts to get the contemplated road through our District will be certain. We remain Dear Sir with the highest respect Your humble servants, F.G. Thomas, T.R. Gary, P.W. Connor, Com[mitte]e.

LS in ScCleA. NOTE: An AEU by Calhoun reads, "Invitation to attend the railroad meeting at Abbeville."

From WILLIAM B. JOHNSTON

Camden So. Ca., August 31, 1847

Dear Sir: You will please pardon the liberty I take in addressing you, but knowing that your long experience in affairs of public interest, and your devotion to the South, eminently qualify you to give an opinion, on the subject about which I now address you, which must to a great degree, influence the action of the people of the South, I beg leave to request an answer to this note, if perfectly Convenient.

I have suggested in the Camden Journal, a newspaper which I conduct here, that the people of the South should hold primary meetings for the purpose of electing delegates to a General Southern Convention, the object of whose deliberations should be to adopt some preventive measures against the aggressions of Northern politicians. The calm and deliberate action of such a body would I think have more effect upon the *people* of the North, than any other means we might use to stop their folly—hence it is I have made the suggestion, which has been well received by most of the presses I have seen, and only one expressed a dissent—a *Whig* paper in Savannah. Would the meeting of such a Convention, before the sitting of Congress, be premature or not? I would be much pleased to have your opinion, either as a private communication, to guide me, or for publication, as you may suggest. Very respectfully, William B. Johnston, Ed[itor, Camden] Journal.

ALS in ScCleA. NOTE: An AEU by Calhoun reads, "Editor of the Camden Journal."

SEPTEMBER 1–30, 1847

◫

"I hope your health has improved," wrote Calhoun on September 5 to Eustis Prescott, a New Orleans and New York City cotton broker who had been an ally for the past several years. "Mine is good, but I still, at intervals, am subject to a cough. It is about my throat, and is of long standing."

Agriculture, his Georgia gold mine, railroads, improvement of navigation on the Savannah river, unrest in Europe, party maneuverings for next year's election, and many other matters filled Calhoun's correspondence, but the most important topic was the South's response to the Wilmot Proviso. He wrote the Greenville editor Benjamin F. Perry on September 20: "Indeed, I would regard a compromise offered by us & carried by our votes, with bearly [sic] a sufficient number of votes from the North to pass it, as the most unfortunate result possible for us. It would be binding only on us, & would but procrastinate the evil day & make it tenfold worse. Indeed, a compromise, at best, is but a surrender on our part. We concede every thing, & they nothing."

As an American, as a republican, and as a father, Calhoun must have been pleased by the sentiments addressed to him on September 13 by his beloved daughter, Anna Maria Calhoun Clemson. She wrote from Europe, where she had been for more than two years now: "I must acknowledge to you, to whom I confess every thing, a little vanity. I am really proud to find how little effect all the splendour, & falsehood of the life around me, has on my mind, & I believe I may safely say, I shall return to America & [sic] simple, unsophisticated, & American in my habits, thoughts, & feelings, as tho' I had never left a plantation, perhaps even more so, for I have now had an opportunity of seeing, & judging near, of many things, which at a distance seem very wonderful, & tempting. You say you fear our country is following on the footsteps of Europe. Much indeed do I regret to hear she has even turned into the same road, but you have

524

no idea of the immense distance she has to pass over, before she arrives at the glittering rotten[n]ess, of social & political life here...."

⫼

From W. C. FERRELL

Charleston So. Ca., 1 Sep[tember] 1847

Dear Sir, When I received your favor of 14th July indisposition prevented an immediate reply. Some time in August I received by the Ship H. Allen through Mr. J[ohn] E[wing] Bonneau the six varieties of the Tea Plant. But Mr. B[onneau] could not inform me whether there were any expenses beyond the freight from New York. This induced me to delay acknowledging the receipt of the plants untill I could learn if there were any further expenses not knowing but the bill might have been sent to you & if so we presumed you would return it to Mr. B[onneau] but as yet none has come to hand. If any has been presented to you—you have the goodness to forward it immediately to Mr. B[onneau]. Permit me Dear Sir to acknowledge my obligation to you for your kindness in procuring the Plants for me. At the same time I have to regret that they were all dead at the time I received. They had evidently not been taken care of on the voyage. You can immagine my disappointment. Still my obligation to you is the same as if I had received them alive. I hope however to have better luck with the seed which Mr. [Alexander H.] Everett said he would send on [from China]. Y[ou]r ob[edien]t Servant, W.C. Ferrell.

ALS in ScCleA.

From JAMES C. JONES,
[former Governor of Tenn.]

Nashville, Sept. 1st 1847

Dear Sir, Ere this reaches you, you will have received a communication from the Board of Commissioners for the Nashville and Chattanoog[a] Rail Road inviting you to visit this place. My object in trespassing on your attention at this time is to join them in most earnest solicitude that you will comply with their invitation. I need not assure you that your visit would be hailed with joy and delight by all irrespective of party[;] true many of us differ with you on some of the great questions that divide the two great parties of the Country yet be assured that these differences of opinion do not make us insensible of the great and invaluable services you have rendered your Country; nor do they at all lessen the obligations we owe you as the great vindicator of Southern rights from the userpations of the most wicked fanaticism. Then come among us[;] we are prepared to receive you with all the warmth and cordiality of bretheren having a common interest and all bound to a common destiny.

I regard your visit at this time as very auspicious. We have no political excitement and consequently no improper motives could be imputed and in addition to this we are now makeing an effort to secure and carry out that great enterprise (a connexion between Charleston and Nashville) in which I know you feel a deep and abiding interest. You can render us great and essential service in promoting this object and be assured this is a critical moment in the history of this undertaking. Our people have no experience in Rail Roads and consequently we have much prejudice to incounter[?]. I know of no one so well calculated to remove this prejudice as yourself. In the name then of the Union between South Carolina and Tennessee I entreat you to come. Our Legislature convenes on the 1st Monday in Oct. We shall have a large concourse of people from ev[e]ry portion of the State here at that time and I should regard that as a most favourable time for your visit. I am aware that a later period might suit your convenience better. You might prefer to take this in your rout[e] to Washington. I am satisfied that a visit on the first of Oct. would be more gratifying to you and vastly more beneficial to us. If however you cannot come at that time let your visit be as soon thereafter as possible. But little has as yet been done in forwarding the Rail Road project. I have determined to devote myself to the work and hope to effect some good. The publick mind has first to be informed before much can be done in the way of getting Stock. I set out in a few days on a tour of speech makeing. What success may attend it I know not. I shall confidently expect a favourable response to this entreaty. Very Respectfully your friend, James C. Jones.

ALS in ScCleA. NOTE: An AEU by Calhoun reads "Gov[ernor] Jones."

From Jos[EPH] J. SINGLETON

Dahlonega [Ga.,] 2d Sept. 1847

My Dear Sir, I certainly owe you an appology for this delay in writing to you. If you knew, the time I am absent from home, and the company I have to entertain, I am persuaided it would be a sufficient excuse for me.

The Rubbish taken from the old places of operation on your **Obarr** Mine which I spoke of in a former letter, has yielded by being operated upon in your old mill about 600 Dwts., your portion of which will be ready no doubt upon application. There is but little doing on your other lots, since the last remittance by Mr. [William] Sloan. I trust that I shall have the pleasure of seeing you shortly after our October Elections. My prospects of success [in election to the legislature] are about the same as has been during the year. I have often been publicly attacked as a Calhoun Candidate, and have as often yielded to the accusation, by asking in reply if you were before the people, hoping that there were no serious apprehensions in such an event, but none can I find. Things are going on finely in this part of the Political Horizon. I have a great deal in reserve for personal communication, should I have the pleasure of an opportunity afforded me; hence I would be happy to know as near as human calculation will permit, what time you contemplate visiting this section, and I repeat, I hope it will be shortly after the 1st Monday in October proximo. Very sincerely I have the hon[or] &C, Jos. J. Singleton.

ALS in ScU-SC, John C. Calhoun Papers. NOTE: An AEU by Calhoun reads, "Dr. Singleton reports $600 dwt. [*sic*] made ["at Dahol(?)" *canceled*] by my lessees on the Obar."

To Prof[esso]r [JOSEPH] HENRY, [Princeton, N.J.?]

Fort Hill, 3d Sep[tembe]r 1847

Dear Sir, I take the liberty, as slight as is our personal acquaintance, to introduce to you, Jehu A. Orr, & I[bzan] J. Rice, two young Gentlemen from this vicinity, whose object in visiting Princeton, is to become members of your College.

They are both respectably connected, and, as I understand from a re[li]able source, ["are" *interlined*] young men of good character

527

& much worth; and as such, I recommend them to your attention. With great respect I am & &, J.C. Calhoun.

ALS owned by John S. Mayfield. NOTE: Henry had recently been appointed the first director of the Smithsonian Institution.

From LEWIS S. CORYELL

New York [City,] 5th Sep[tember] [18]47

My dear Sir, It seems perfect supererogation for me to write you on any subject, as the papers and other correspondents will give you all that I could were I to attempt a detail of matters & things—and whatever I write will be an infliction upon your daily duties of reading that which others have given or your own sagacity long understood. The signs of the times are strange & by no means in my opinion shaped into certainty. The northern visit of [Henry] Clay has afforded more cause of speculation than you of the South may ["have" *interlined*] given to it. My opinion now is, that if possible the Whigs of the North will cleave to Clay as their only hope. [Zachary] Taylor will not answer *their* views, and I am by no means sure that Taylor will be a reliable man for *us*—& more he may prove the mere auxilery of Clay by which & thro' whome they (whigs) expect to obtain power! Besides the death of Silas Wright has thrown all the [Thomas H.] Benton, [Martin] Van Buren & Co. schemes into ghastly wo[e]. There has been a congregation of those spirits here. I have seen old [James I.] McKay of Ways & Means, [Ransom H.] Gillet[,] [Augustus R.] Soll[er]s[,] [Ogden] Hoffman[,] [Smith M.] Purdy, [William] Paulding[,] &Ct. together, but what will grow out of it none yet can tell. Suppose they unite on [Levi] Woodbury, would he be their man or would he be ½ horse ½ alegator. Buck [James Buchanan] is out of the question even in Penn[sylvani]a. His letter is of no account when in opposition to the Senators & mem[bers] of Congress. Then & not now was the time for such ["a" *interlined*] letter. I tell you I am affraid that Taylor aspires only to make Clay Pres[ident]. I have become very sceptical & that I see less certainty in the Political index, than most who I meet & confer with. The condition of the country ["&" *interlined*] operation of the Tariff has worked most admirably for the Adm[ini]s[tration]. A single turn of adversity would convulse us to the very centre, but you know all about this matter. [Simon] Cameron [Senator from Pa.] is evidently playing his game in favor of Taylor to be V[ice-]Pr[e]s[ident] on his ticket! Now what is best, for the country that if *we* cannot—shall Taylor[,] Clay or a northern man be next Pres[iden]t[?]

I am going to New Hope [Pa.] tomorrow and if you write me, direct there, but don[']t write much those times. Y[ou]r fr[ien]d truly, Lewis S. Coryell.

ALS in ScCleA. NOTE: Buchanan's letter referred to was addressed to citizens of Berks County, Pa. on 8/25. In it he deplored abolitionism and favored the Missouri Compromise line, suggesting that as a practical matter there would be no significant extension of slavery into any of the new territory even if permitted. This position prompted Buchanan's rival, Lewis Cass, to declare in favor of the alternative policy of "popular sovereignty" in regard to slavery in the territories.

To EUSTIS PRESCOTT

Fort Hill, 5th Sep[tembe]r 1847

My dear Sir, I hasten to answer your note received by the mail of yesterday.

The true policy of our little band is, undoubtedly, the one you suggest, to stand fast and wait developements. There is much in the wheel of time. Our position is commanding; and, if properly used, may save the country and its institutions. The old party organization is deeply disordered, and the authority of a caucus to make a President, greatly weakened.

This State is wide awake. We never were more united, or better prepared for coming events. We are now engaged in raising funds to establish an independent organ for the defense of Southern rights & interests, at Washington. All parties have united for the purpose, & the ["contribution" *altered to* "subscription"] is going on well. It is desirable, that the amount raised should be large; certainly not less than $50,000, in order to command the highest talents, to take charge of it. Great care will be taken in selecting an editor, both as it regards competency of qualification, and fidelity to the cause. We hope our friends every where, will rally to its support.

I enclose you a copy of the address and a paper containing the conditions on which the press is to be established. The address is signed by the most respectable men in the State, of both parties. Our late Senator, Mr. [Daniel E.] Huger, stands at ["its" *canceled*] head of the list. The papers have been largely circulated throughout the

South. Some have been sent to N. Orleans, and I hope you may be able to do something to aid, ["among" *canceled*] in the circle of your friends, when you return to the City. I regard the establish[men]t of such a paper, at this time, at the seat [of] Government, as indispensable. If we desire to save the Union & our admirable system of Government, it is the most efficient step that can be taken. If the abolition question is not arrested, it will certainly destroy both.

I hope your health has improved. Mine is good, but I still, at intervals, am subject to a cough. It is about my throat, and is of long standing. I shall be glad to learn, what is the prospect of the cotton crop when you return to the city [of New Orleans], & to hear from you at all times. Very truly, J.C. Calhoun.

[Enclosed circular]

CHARLESTON, August 2d, 1847

Sir—We trust that we shall not be considered as taking an unwarrantable liberty in addressing to yourself, and some others, in whose discretion we rely, the following communication. We make an appeal to you, irrespective of Party Politics, as one having a common interest with ourselves, upon a matter, as we conceive, of momentous concern to every Southern man.

You cannot but have observed the rapid progress of the Anti-Slavery spirit, for some time past, and the alarming influence it has exercised on the politics of the country, as exhibited at Washington, and throughout the non-slaveholding States of the Union.

The inundation of Congress with petitions for the abolition of slavery in the District of Columbia, though the act of petitioning for such a purpose assumes an inferiority in the Slaveholding States, and the language of the petitions is replete with vituperation and insult, has been persevered in until it has almost ceased to arrest attention. The application in the United States, of the principle of the English case of Somerset decided by Lord Mansfield, by which it is declared that the relation of master and slave ceases as soon as the parties pass the jurisdiction of the local laws which authorize slavery—a principle which isolates and degrades the slaveholder, has been more than half acquiesced in. We have seen State after State legislating with a view to avoid the act of Congress in regard to fugitive slaves, and prevent its interference with the above principle, until we are so familiarized with such legislation, that the public are scarce aware that the Pennsylvania Legislature has recently nullified this act of Congress, and affixed a heavy punishment to the attempt to enforce it within the limits of the State.

The missions of [Samuel] Hoar and his compeer [Henry Hubbard] to South-Carolina and Louisiana, by which Massachusetts undertook, on the very soil of these States, by agents resident in Charleston and New-Orleans, to obstruct the execution of the local laws in regard to the introduction of free colored persons, though met promptly by the States respectively, to whom particularly the insult was offered, excited in the South but a passing interest, and is now almost forgotten.

Apathy on our part, has been followed by increased and still increasing activity on the part of the enemies of our institutions.

The introduction at the close of the session of Congress before the last, of the *Wilmot Proviso*, and its passage then in the House of Representatives, by a vote of 85 to 80; the provision, at the last Session, against Slavery, in the bill, organizing a Government for Oregon; and the repudiation of the principles of the Missouri Compromise evinced by the rejection of Mr. [Armistead] BURT's amendment; the renewal of the Wilmot proposition by Mr. PRESTON KING, the vote on this; and the adoption finally of the Proviso, as shaped by Mr. HANNIBAL HAMLIN, of Maine, in the House of Representatives, by a large majority, are facts, which leave no shadow of doubt as to the utter disregard of Southern rights in that body. The defeat of the obnoxious measure in the Senate, give us no security in the future. Senators, in their places, openly proclaimed their approval of the principle it contained, and placed their opposition, distinctly, on the ground, that, though right in itself, the "time and occasion" rendered its adoption inexpedient. The Legislatures of eleven States have, with singular unanimity, urged a renewal of these efforts. Delaware, Pennsylvania, New-Jersey, New-York, Rhode Island, Vermont, New-Hampshire, Massachusetts, Ohio, Michigan, and more recently Maine, have all, through their Legislatures, spoken still more explicitly than by their Representatives in Congress.

The tone of the press, Whig and Democratic, Agrarian and Religious, in every non-slaveholding State, manifests a foregone conclusion, that the Abolitionists are to be conceded to, at least so far as to forbid the extension of slavery in the United States beyond its present boundaries.

While clouds thus gather, what preparation do we make for the impending storm? Are our people even aware of its approach?

How have the Abolitionists, so inconsiderable in numbers, and themselves without official station, effected so much? The answer is obvious. They have *adhered to principle*. They have made it paramount to party organization, and temporary policy, and they have thus held the *balance of power* between the two great parties.

They have on this account been courted alternately, and together, by Whig and Democrat, until it has come about that no politician on either side, is considered as *"available,"* who cannot enlist in his behalf this necessary vote; and they are actually at this moment controlling the destinies of this great Confederacy? Shall we not profit by their example?

The Abolitionists have throughout the non-slaveholding States presses zealously, ably and efficiently enforcing their views, and presenting *their* paramount principle—and they have lately established an organ in the City of Washington.

We have, in the South, papers of both parties worthy of all confidence, but these are but little read elsewhere, and there is no one of them of very general circulation, even in the Southern States; and we have not one paper in a non-slaveholding State, and none in the City of Washington, which, in this emergency, has proved a fast and fearless friend; not one which habitually reflects *the public sentiment of the* SOUTH on this question. The Intelligencer blinks the question; the Union rebukes equally the spirit of Abolition, and the spirit which resists its aggressions; and with ALL, except the Abolitionists themselves, *party success*, with its triumph and its spoils, is the absorbing, if not the sole consideration.

The object of this communication is to obtain your aid, and active co-operation, in establishing, at WASHINGTON, a paper which shall represent Southern views on the subject of SLAVERY—Southern views of Southern Rights and Interests, growing out of, and connected with this institution.

We want a paper whose polar star shall be the sentiment, "that danger to our Institutions can only be averted by jealously watching our rights under the Constitution; by insisting upon the proportionate influence intended to be secured to us by the compromises of that compact; and, above all, by maintaining, at all times, and at all hazards, our equality full and complete with whatever other communities we hold connection." We wish a paper which we can *trust*, firm and fearless, which cannot be bribed, cajoled, flattered, or frightened, into furling, for an instant, the Banner of SOUTHERN EQUALITY.

To effect this, we must render the press free from party influences, and unite in its support others besides politicians. We would therefore desire to engage in the undertaking men in every way INDEPENDENT; and whose means and positions are such as free them from all temptations of profit or place.

If you concur in our views, please confer with us, as soon as practicable; and inform us what amount in money you are willing, yourself, to contribute to effect this object, and how much you think can be raised in your immediate neighborhood.

Enclosed you will find a subscription list with a heading, setting forth the principles on which it is proposed to establish the paper. If you approve of it, please obtain such signatures as you can and return the list by mail to this place.

Address your communication to ISAAC W. HAYNE, Esqr., No. 3 State-street, who has consented, until the proposed association is fully organized, to act as Secretary and Treasurer. Respectfully, your obedient servants,

DANIEL E. HUGER,	ROBT. W. BARNWELL,
NATHANIEL HEYWARD,	JOHN S. PRESTON,
WADE HAMPTON,	ANDREW TURNBULL,
R.F.W. ALLSTON,	WM. BULL PRINGLE,
JACOB BOND I'ON,	JNO. L. MANNING,
JNO. P. RICHARDSON,	M[OSES] C. MORDECAI,
JOSHUA J. WARD,	WILLIAM F. DAVIE,
J. HARLESTON READ,	WHITEMARSH B. SEABROOK,
WILLIAM POPE,	GEO. W. DARGAN,
JOHN S . ASHE,	W[ILLIAM] H. TRAPIER,
H[ENRY] W. PERONNEAU,	JOHN R. MATHEWES,
HENRY BAILEY,	P[ETER] W. FRASER,
DANIEL HEYWARD,	ALEX. ROBERTSON,
W[ILLIAM] W. HARLLEE,	N[ATHANIEL] R. MIDDLETON,
W[ILLIAM] F. DeSAUSSURE,	JAMES H. ADAMS,
HENRY GOURDIN,	WM. A. CARSON,
JAMES GADSDEN,	GEO. A. TRENHOLM,
CHARLES T. LOWNDES,	JAMES ROSE,
JOHN RUTLEDGE.	

ALS with Ens in ScU-SC, John C. Calhoun Papers. NOTE: Calhoun addressed this letter to Eustis Prescott "of New Orleans, Louisville, Kentucky." An AEU by Prescott reads "Answ[ere]d 9 Nov[embe]r."

From V[ERNON] K. STEVENSON

Nashville Tenn[esse]e, Sep[tembe]r 5th 1847

Dear Sir, When at Washington last March was a year ago you was kind enough to say to me that when you could be of use in get[t]ing the stock taken to extend the S.C. & Ga. R.R. improvements to Nashville that you ["would" *interlined*] come at any time except at the sit[t]ing of Congress & I stated this to our board of Commissioners of whoom I am one & they ordered there Secretary A.O.P. Nicholson (former Senator from Tenn[esse]e) to invite you to pay us a visit this fall at such time as will best ["you" *canceled*] suit you but if equally agreeable it will be better for us that you should come about the first of October say abo[u]t the ["6th" *altered to* "4th"] to the 10th at that time our legislature meets when there is allways a great number of ["personsons" *altered to* "persons"] that congregate with the members at Nashville & in this way we can be able I hope to send out a good feeling from Nashville that will facilitate us in get[t]ing subscriptions. Ex Governor [James C.] Jones & myself have been appointed to procure stock & to manage the raising of money to build the Road & we have procured ["the" *canceled*] subscriptions to the amount of near seven hundred thousand dollars & are get[t]ing more every day & are gaining upon the better part of our community but as our charter expires the first of January next unless there is a million of dollars taken our board are verry anxious to have all the aid in ther reach & therefore as you have so often expressed an anxiety about ["the success of" *interlined*] this road & a willingness to help us by a visit we hope that we will not be disappointed for I can assure you that we are making large calculations upon your help. Our members to the Memphis Convention were so favorably impressed with your speech at Memphis &C that they feel assured that your presence & countenance would give character & greatly aid the subscriptions & final construction of this Great work which will bind the South & West togather more firmly than all the oaths & pledges that can be given.

I shall be most happy to learn that you will pay us a visit which you could do on your way to Washington & Gov[erno]r Jones & myself will meet you ["in" *canceled*] on the line say at Chatenooga, if you will let us know when you could be there, & accompany you to Nashville.

Please give my kindest regards to Mrs. Calhoun[,] Miss Calhoun & Mr. & Mrs. [Armistead] Burt & receive for your self the best wishes of a devoted friend. Most Truly, V.K. Stevenson.

ALS in ScCleA.

To T[homas] G. Clemson, [Brussels]

Fort Hill, 6th Sep[tembe]r 1847

My dear Sir, I am not at all surprised, that you should be discouraged, with the results of your planting operations. I still think the place [in Edgefield District] might be made a valuable one, but it requires skill in its management. The land is strong, but a large portion is unkind, at least for cotton, and a great part requires ditches, drains ["& manure" *interlined*] to bring it into successful operation. It is not a place to be cultivated with success, in the absence of the owner, by overseers. In addition, you have had bad seasons, & low prices, & been unfortunate in overseers. One year out of the four was unprecedented for its drought, & two, for the superabundance of its rains. On your place, the latter were more adverse to good crops, than the former. The rain of this year has exceeded even the last. We have had continued wet weather since the last of April, & I see no prospect of its clearing. It has been raining for two days, & is still cloudy. The great excess of rain has made it very difficult to cultivate the crops; yet my crop is fine; corn, cotton, Rye, wheat, potatoes & pease are all good. My cotton is ["maturing" *canceled and* "doing" *interlined*] well. The weed is large, the bolling good, & the plant well matured. If we should have a dry fall to open the bolls, it will be the heaviest per acre I ever made. I should think it a safe calculation, in that case, ["that" *canceled and* "to say" *interlined*] I will make 30,000 pounds of pick cotton from 125 acres; & that on Speed's field, which you know is my oldest ["& worst" *interlined*] land. I attribute much to hill side drain[in]g, & sub ploughing. I feel confident, that all we want is good cultivation & and [*sic*] ready access to market to make cotton planting profitable here.

The extreme wet weather is like again to reproduce the worm, to be followed by another short crop. We are comparatively safe here, but there are greater numbers even with us, than usual; & it is possible, should the wet weather continue, we may suffer by them.

But to return to your place. I fear the extreme wet of the year will greatly injure you, from the want of drains & ditches, & the unabsorbent character of a large portion of the place. As to what disposition you ought to make of your property, I am clearly of the opinion, that, if you are to continue an absentee, you ought to dispose of it, if you can get a fair price, & vest it safely in bonds or stocks; & that you ought to return next ["year" *canceled and* "fall" *interlined*], at farthest, in order to determine on your future course. I cannot doubt leave would be granted you on application. You ought to be

535

here early in the fall, so as to have time to look round & determine deliberately what you ought to do. Your property and a proper application of your talents, ought to be sufficient to [*one word canceled and* "maintain" *interlined*] you & your family well, in any pursuit, you might choose. As to an overseer, there is ["no" *canceled and* "little" *interlined*] chance of getting a good one here. There are few in this section skilled in the cultivation of cotton, or accustomed to managing gangs of negroes as large as yours. The prospect of getting a good overseer in Edgefield, Abbeville, or Newberry is far greater. I will, however, make inquiry. Mere accident may throw one in my way.

You are entirely right in desiring to place your affairs with us on such grounds, as will be perfectly satisfactory to you, and that will prevent the possibility of misunderstanding here after. The enclosed [*not found*] is a statement drawn up by Andrew [Pickens Calhoun] & myself of our joint affairs. We wish you to examine it, & if there be any error to correct it, and, if not, approve of it, & return it, when we shall give our joint bond for the amount. He will leave his name in blank for the purpose. When signed it will be deposited with Mr. [John Ewing] Bonneau, or whomever you may designate, on your giving ["an" *interlined*] order to him to deliver up the evidences of our indebtedness to you in his possession. We wish the bond to be so conditioned, that we shall have the right to pay & you to demand payment, on giving six months notice.

I agree with you, that the political condition of all western Europe is very unsettled, and especially France. Nor are we much better off. Our future is very uncertain. The old parties are disorganized. The administration weak; & the termination of the Mexican war, and what will grow out of it, uncertain. We must wait for the developments of the next 12 months to know where we are. In the meane time, [Henry] Clay & his friends are making a great effort to bring him out again, as a candidate, and will probably succeed. [Zachary] Taylor has lost ground greatly, & will probably be ruled off. He has written too many letters, and some of them very illy advised. [Silas] Wright has died, a severe blow to the Hunkers; and [Thomas H.] Benton is denouncing the administration, whether to break with them, or control them is uncertain; probably the latter. We (the State rights party) are making an effort to establish an independent press at Washington, as the organ of the South. A large amount has already been subscribed, and it is hoped, it will be in operation by the meeting of Congress.

On the whole, I regard my position as a strong one. It is independent of all parties; and yet calculated to give much control. Whatever it does, shall be used for the good of the country.

Mrs. [Floride Colhoun] Calhoun returned yesterday from Glenn's Springs. I do not think they have been of any benefit, but her health is not bad.

All join their love to you, Anna [Maria Calhoun Clemson] & the children [John Calhoun Clemson and Floride Elizabeth Clemson]. Kiss them for their Grandfather & tell them how much I desire to see them. Your affectionate father, J.C. Calhoun.

ALS in ScCleA; PEx in Jameson, ed., *Correspondence*, pp. 736–737.

From R O B [E R] T M O N R O E H A R R I S O N

Consulate of the United States
Kingston Jamaica, 6th Sept. 1847
Sir, With great deference and respect, I take the liberty to invoke your aid and assistance with General [Lewis] Cass to induce Congress to pay the amount of a bond for which I am liable to the British Government in consequence of my becoming security that an American citizen (falsely accused of the abduction of two negroes from this Island, and of selling them in the U. States), should remain here and stand his trial for the same.

The Honorable Secretary of State [James Buchanan] who has nobly stood forward and done all he could to relieve me, will furnish you with particulars which have already been laid before the Senate by General Cass, whose kindness I shall never forget.

The Honorable Mr. [George] Bancroft, our Minister in London, has informed me that the Colonial Minister had sent all the papers which were forwarded to him in proof of Mr. Frisbie's innocence, (the person charged with the offence in question), to the Governor, and his legal advisers, whom he admonishes to *receive with great caution any documents coming from the U. States, as the parties granting the same are all interested:* although these in the present instance are actually furnished for the most part, on the authority of the Governors of Ohio and Louisiana, and have the Seals of those States attached to the same.

By this you will perceive that this thing is still hanging over my head; for although I did not commit my official position by personally giving bond to the British Government I am bound to the worthy individual who did so at my suggestion, by which, as he is in business here, he has been seriously injured as the Banks will not discount his papers while the affair is in suspense.

Our talented Minister in London seems to think that the authorities will let the matter drop; but he is not aware of the hostility of the Attorney-General—the Governor's constitutional adviser, nor is he aware of the prejudice by which, with few exceptions, all classes here are influenced against our countrymen.

Mr. D[ouglas] Vass of the General Post-Office Department will have the honor to deliver this, and I can with truth declare, that there is no greater admirer of your worth and transcendant abilities than this gentleman. To him, I have likewise confided a memorandum [*not found*] of my wishes on other subjects, to effect which, I entreat you also to use your friendly interest.

Trusting that you will make indulgent allowances for an old and faithful servant, who has served his country for many years, I have the honor to be Sir Your very humble serv[an]t, Robt. Monroe Harrison.

LS in ScCleA.

From H[ENRY] W. CONNER

New York [City,] Sept[embe]r 7, 1847
My Dear Sir, I have just rec[eive]d your fav[o]r of the 25th [August] sent to me from Charleston.

I have been so much interested in the efforts to raise the money—that my attention has not been directed much to the plan of the paper. Your suggestions appear to me however to be applicable to the case & I would go further & say that if we can compass the funds for it that we ought to have the use of a paper here (the Herald for instance) & in Virginia—Kentucky or Tennessee & Mobile or New Orleans. These things will all however come up in their proper time & place.

I notice what you say of the Nashville [rail]road. That road is every thing to Charleston & the corporation should without doubt advance its credit to its use whether the State does or not. I should be glad to see both—but doubt the latter. We have felt the delicacy of taking the initiative in Charleston & done so only from necessity—but I do not find amongst the great number of Southerners whom I see & take the opportunity of talking with—the objection to it that I expected. I find more from Virginians than others but we are taking the proper means to remove the impression. The people I meet from the slave States almost without ["the" *canceled*] exception are decided in their determination to resist the Wilmot proviso. The only difference is as to time & extent & I am sorry to say I perceive too great a disposition to postpone the issue as long as possible. The move on the Wilmot proviso I find is considered here a political blunder & great address will be used to evade the issue & give it the go bye until after the presidential election. They appreciate the power of the South when united upon principle & by a common interest far beyond our conceptions of it & it is the ["apprehended" *interlined*] organization of the slave States that has produced the reaction on the Wilmot proviso. It is perceived that no great party measure can be carried or a president elected without the concurrence of the South—if united & acting as one man. Hence we see the prompt & palpable ["evidences"(?) *canceled and* "efforts" *interlined*] of the friends of [Henry] Clay, Buckhannan [*sic*; James Buchanan, Zachary] Taylor & [Lewis] Cass to conciliate & court the South. I am witness to this daily amongst the friends of the different parties—but the truth is so far as my knowledge extends there never was so much confusion & uncertainty in both parties as at the present time.

My great fears have been that the issue (the most favourable for us that could be offered) on the Wilmot proviso—may be permitted to be evaded or if Joined—may go off on another compromise. If we are united (& we are inevitably lost if we are not) & firm however—we are beyond all question safe. I understand Virginia is filling up very much with northern people who sell to emigrants their own lands hereabouts & to the Eastward at high prices & remove to Virginia with all their peculiar notions & are gradually undermining the State.

Something has been said to me here about the formation of Free trade associations—which I will look into on my return from Boston.

The subscriptions to the paper I learn are still progressing in Charleston. I am almost afraid however that the meeting of Congress will find us not quite ready.

I shall return about 1 Oct[obe]r. Very Truly y[ou]rs &c., H.W. Conner.

[P.S.] Mr. Clay I think will be withdrawn. His *best friends* are op[p]osed to ["it" *canceled and* "his being a candidate" *interlined*] on ac[count] of his age. His mind it is thought now shews evidence of being impaired.

ALS in ScCleA.

From H. M. WARE

Columbus Ohio, Sept. 7th 1847

Dear Sir: The liberty I take Sir in thus addressing you will I trust from the nature and importance of the subject be considered sufficiently apologetic.

Though I am myself entirely unknown to you I am not unfamiliar with your public character—having looked with admiration and the deepest interest upon the course which as an independent public servant you have so long and successfully and so consistently pursued.

I have sir in conjunction with thousands of my fellow citizens looked forward to the period when we should be afforded the highest gratification of our lives in aiding by our influence and votes in electing to the Chief Magistrate[']s Chair one so distinguished and worthy—so incorruptible as yourself.

Having progressed thus far a single step will lead me to the immediate object of this communication.

The unexpected and prolonged continuance of *this* Mexican War will undoubtedly eventuate in the lasting fame of those military chiefta[i]ns most conspicuous in its prosecution. Already does the nation ring with loud and ceaseless peans to the name of *Zachery Taylor,* and it requires in the estimation of your humble admirer no uncommon foresight to discern with prophetic verity the final termination of the popular feeling in his behalf—*una voce he* can be carried on and aloft sweeping by the irresistible power of his magical name every ["impedient" *changed to* "impediment"] to his triumphant progress. The question here arises—Have you declined allowing your name to be used in connection with the Presidential Office? And is it the determination of yourself and friends to *merge* that noble band of *State Rights men* (in which class I have always numbered myself) with that of General Taylor? I am thus *explicitely presumptive* my dear Sir for the following reason: I am anxious to establish a Democratic Republican newspaper during the coming winter and if by your consent permission could be obtained to employ your name as the first and worthiest object of our approval in the coming contest the entire energy of my nature would be directed to the successful prosecution of the undertaking.

Party men are afraid of Taylor—the *people* without apprehension or fear of any kind shout aloud *every where* in his behalf.

The untimely agitation of the slave question by the wild fanatics of some of the free States can produce no good *any where* it seems to me, while its continued discussion is fraught with consequences serious in every aspect of contemplation. The interest of all must be protected—the "peculiar institutions" of the south will *by the nation* be upheld in right—free and unpolluted by the ruthless touch of reckless demagogues.

I cannot close this letter without a single allusion to my own character.

I am a *Virginian* by birth—a southern man in feeling though an adopted son of Ohio, & have long desired to visit the South with a view of permanently settling but circumstances will not permit. John G. Miller Esq. of this City and brother in law of the late President John Tyler is my uncle—either to whom or Dr. N.M. Miller also of Columbus I refer you in regard to any information in reference to myself.

I trust that the candor and freedom with which I have written will be rightly construed and conclude by saying that an early reply would be most highly gratifying. I have the Honor to be very Respectfully Y[ou]r Ob[edien]t Serv[an]t, H.M. Ware.

ALS in ScCleA.

From R[OBERT] B[ARNWELL] RHETT

[Washington] Sept. 8t[h] 1847
My Dear Sir, You requested me, as soon as I heard from Gen[era]l [Jefferson] Davis as to Gen[era]l [Zachary] Taylor[']s opinions, that I would inform you. I rec[eive]d a few Days [since] from Gen[era]l Davis a Letter marked *private*, which hinders me of course from sending it to you. It is of little consequence however, for it contains nothing distinct as to his opinions—very like what you have seen in the Papers.

Things are looking bleaker in Mexico. If [Winfield] Scott triumphs handsomely however, I am still of opinion, that if no peace is obtained by the opening of Congress, the Administration will fall back ["substantially" *interlined*] to your policy. If there is any reverse however, which may give such a movement the aspect of compulsion, they will not do it: In either event, as peace now seems out of the question, your warnings and counsel must give you a very lofty position. On the subject of the Wilmot Proviso, the Administration is doing all it can, to settle the matter on the Missouri Compromise line. You see in this morning[']s Paper [James] Buchanan[']s Letter

541

on the subject. A friend of Silas Wright, informed me to Day, that he, had he lived, would shortly have taken the same ground. If so, it is to be lamented that he died so soon. [Levi] Woodbury is open-mouthed against the Wilmot Proviso—[Lewis] Cass following suit. I think therefore, after all ["we" *canceled and* "it is not improbable we" *interlined*] will make them back out on this great point. At all events it is dividing and weakening the North, and if we of the South can only act unitedly, our triumph is certain. The Anti Slavery Democrats, [Benjamin F.] Butler of New York, [Hannibal] Hamlin [former Representative from Me.] &c.—must be driven off to the Whigs. Certainly since the foundation of the Government, there never has been in politics so silly a move as that of the Northern Democrats on this subject. Their leaders see it, but so many are committed, as to render a return to the right policy very difficult.

On the point of closing the war, should it not be closed by peace by the meeting of Congress, nothing will be done by the Whigs. [John M.] Clayton[,] [Senator from Del., Robert C.] Winthrop [Representative from Mass.,] ["& (Joseph R.?) Ingersoll" *interlined*] & others, who look on the war as by no means much of an evil, since it will create a Debt, by which high duties will be maintained, in [*one word canceled and* "support" *interlined*] of their Tariff policy, will not withhold the supplies. They with the Democrats generally, if the Administration determines to go on with the war, will secure the supplies. With this conviction I am doing all I can to induce the Administration to take the proper course—and propose a course themselves to close the war—and I hope not without success. If they do this, and can settle the Wilmot proviso matter, the Democratic Party may carry the next Presidential Election. Woodbury will most probably be their candidate. Buchanan[']s course as Secr[etar]y of State, and Tariff affinities will I think put him aside. Cass wants the confidence of the South. But if the war, and the Slavery question are not settled ["by" *canceled and* "during" *interlined*] the next session of Congress, the Democratic Party will be defeated, and new organizations of Party will arise.

Mrs. [Elizabeth Washington Burnet] Rhett joins in remembrance to Mrs. [Floride Colhoun] Calhoun and believe me Dear Sir Yours sincerely, R.B. Rhett.

ALS in ScCleA; variant PC in Jameson, ed., *Correspondence*, pp. 1132–1133.

From Ja[me]s B. Thornton

Memphis, September 8th 1847

Dear Sir, Circumstances which have recently transpired here induce me to address you this letter. Your letter of the 14th July to J[ohn] C. Morril[l] Esq. has been shewn me, and I was privy to that to which it was an answer. Since the receipt of your letter the [Memphis *Evening*] *Monitor* has so changed its relations (indeed it has been merged) as to induce me to contemplate an independent effort (independent of Newspaper agency) for effecting the object I hoped to attain through its columner. That object you were apprised of through Mr. M[orrill]'s letter. Mr. Morrill is, I think, a man of the most reliable honor but not of enlarged education or views, and defective in information. He is exceedingly industrious, but is pressed for means. He established a paper here under many disadvantages & which for some time was badly conducted. For six months past however it ["was" *canceled*] had assumed a consistancy as a political ["journal" *interlined*] which much increased its circulation, and upon ["the" *interlined*] principles which it developed connected with its rapid increase of patronage excited the alarm of the politicians of this section. They combined and offered such inducements as made it to his interests in a pecuniary point of view to unite his paper with the Appeal of this City. The Editorial department of which is ostensibly with Mr. [Richard H.?] Stanton, brother to the Hon. F[rederick] P. Stanton M[ember of] C[ongress] from this district. It is believed however that it is virtually to be under the direction and control of Levy D. Slamm, late of N. York, now Purser in the Navy Yard here and Mr. Curren, a lawyer of some talents but of very contracted party politics. However this may be I have satisfied myself that the paper will be strictly and vigilently guarded against the admission in any shape of any views taking the southern ground with regard to the Slavery question (Wilmot proviso) & the National Convention. Mr. Morrill takes the publishing department exclusively.

Under these circumstances I propose addressing the Southern people and especially ["of" *interlined*] Tennessee, in pamphlet form, to be immediately prepared some considerations upon these questions. With that view however I need much material. In moving, I lost your letter touching the proper manner of constituting a national convention written shortly preceeding the last Presidential Election. I have not within my reach at this time, the discussion in the Senate on the Resolutions offered by yourself last winter on the Wilmot principle. Can you conveniently furnish me with these documents? or do you approve of the course? I think there is one view which may be illustrated to great advantage. It is that the establishment of the Wilmot proviso by Congress will be a change in itself of the articles of our Union. It will be proposing new termes for our acceptance, and the further connection between the different sections of the confederation will depend upon the assent of the people to be subsequently procured. In the event of its being insisted upon therefore it will ["*not*" *interlined*] be for us to dissolve the Union, but to say whether we will enter into a new Union on the termes proposed.

The next Congress I believe will be Whig, but voting by States, I think, it would be otherwise. You see to what this leads. There would be no danger of the election of a whig in the event of the Election's going to the House. But there is more reason to apprehend the election of a Whig by the people. Electing a Whig Congress they would reasonably be expected to elect a Whig President. On the other hand the Whig States would vote against the regular democratic nominee, if by so doing they elected an independent candidate. I will not write more fully on this point, but would be glad to hear your views touching the whole subject.

I have none of your speeches of the last cession except the one [of 2/9/1847] on the three million bill. Any that you can send will be thankfully received and to the best of my judgment properly used. Any views you may deem it prudent to address me will be strictly confidential. Your letter to Mr. Morrill is now in my keeping & I expect to retain it. I remain Sir, with great respect & sincere good will, your &c &c, Jas. B. Thornton.

ALS in ScCleA. NOTE: Found among Calhoun's papers in ScCleA is a 2-pp. printed prospectus announcing the publication in Philadelphia in 1847 of *A Digest of the Conveyancing, Testamentary, and Registry Laws of All the States of the Union* by James B. Thornton, "Late of Virginia, Now of Memphis, Tennessee, Attorney at Law."

From JOHN D. WATKINS

Spring Hill
Elbert County [Ga.,] Sept. 8, 1847

My Dear Sir, There is considerable talk in this county & the County below [Lincoln?] on the Savannah river in regard to improving the navigation of that stream. I learn that you take great interest in the subject of ["that" *interlined*] improvement & many ideas are advanced here & in the adjoining district of Abbeville in S.C. which are attributed to you & thereby have acquired much weight. In this connection I allude particularly to the small sum said to be requisite to render the Savannah river navigable for Steamers to Andersonville [S.C.]. Permit me to beg of you the expression of your views on this subject in such form as may be read to any meeting that I may attend where the matter may be under discussion. Can the Savannah river be made navigable for small Steamers & at what cost & what would be the best plan? Would the work be a joint undertaking of the two States of Geo[rgia] & S.C. or would private contributions have to be resorted to to help along the reluctant & small contributions ["appropriations" *interlined*] of the States.

A Rail Road enterprise is about to be undertaken from the village of Washington in Wilkes County Geo[rgia] via Double Wells on the Geo[rgia] R. Road, Sparta & to join the Central R.R. about 130 miles from Savannah. $500,000 have been subscribed for this enterprise which is the sum wanted to construct the Road 60 miles long. This company will apply for a charter at the next meeting of our legislature & will immediately commence work. Some of our citizens think that if this road is built, it would be preferable to bring it on through Elbert County in the direction of the Rabun Gap or towards Andersonville if the Carrolinians would take an interest in it ["to clearing out the river" *interlined*]. Is not this the most practicable project for upper Geo[rgia] & the Districts bordering on the Savannah. Freights could take either the Geo[rgia] R.R. to Augusta & Charleston or go on to the Central R.R. to Savannah. Distance from Washington [Ga.] to Savannah by the Junction R.R. 190 miles—by Junction R. Road to Double Wells 18 miles[,] by Geo[rgia] R.R. to Augusta 52—to Charleston 136 = 206 miles from Washington to Charleston. Now from Washington to Ruckersville [Ga.] in the direction of Andersonville is 34 miles[;] it is but a short distance from Ruckersville to Andersonville but I know not what it is. From there, that is Andersonville, could not a road be taken to Greenville cheaper & pay better & subserve all purposes though a little round about than by carrying a road against conflicting interests from Columbia to Greenville? This latter distance I do not know.

In making Rail Roads for the accom[m]odation of those sections of country remote from [*one word changed to* "markets"] I think it wiser policy to run the shortest & most practicable rout[e]s to roads already in existance ["that" *changed to* "than"] to undertake gigantic improvements; though more direct, they might be less apt to pay.

The general impression is that it would take 500,000$ to run small steamers from Augusta to Andersonville; & to do that, canal & locks around the shoals when a slack water dam would not subserve the purpose would have to be made. It is thought that $30,000 judiciously expended would so improve the navigation of the river from Hamburg up as to nearly enlarge the capacity of our boats to double what they now carry; thereby diminishing the cost of transportation nearly one half. Would S.C. appropriate a like am[oun]t with Geo[rgia] & each appoint her commissioners to expend her appropriations?

What is the best plan for interchanging ideas & efforts on the part of the inhabitants of the two States on this subject?

Please give us your ideas in regard to the best mode of improving the navigation of the Savannah river—whether for Pole or Steam Boats—the probable cost, &c &c & whether any Rail Road could be constructed (at less cost than the improvement of the river), that would answer the same & even a more enlarged use, whether said road were constructed along the valley of the Savannah in Carolina from Hamburg up, or from Washington through Elbert in a direction to your upper Districts. If the Edgefield R.R. could be begun at Hamburg & go up the valley of the Savannah & our talked of road from Washington be combined with it—It would bring the Road up as far as Vienna [Ga.]—where the upper districts could take it & carry it on. Yours with sentiments of the highest respect, Jno. D. Watkins.

ALS in ScCleA.

From J[ohn] Raven Mathewes

at Home [Habersham County, Ga.,] 10 Sept[embe]r [18]47
My Dear Sir, I have been anxiously up to the present moment waiting for a cessation of unprecedented wet weather to pay you a visit on my way to Greenville So. Ca. but I fear that it is now too late. I wish[e]d to have seen you in addition to my personal gratification to have convers'd upon some important points which are shortly to rouse our Southern public rights & Interests into action. I think Silas Wright (wrong) Gen[era]l [William Henry] Harrison & the Wilmot proviso are in the Tomb of the Capulets deploring their absence & failure in ruining this great and envied section of the Union.

We are here over[r]unning with electioneering; during my absence in Charleston last July both parties put me up for the Legislature but I hope that [*one word changed to* "my"] itinerant & more active & anxious opponents will keep me out as I have in the low country "other fish to fry" but if elected I will serve as in the Jury or any other public Box, to the best of my poor judgement & skill. Next week there is to be a Regimental Review at Clark[e]sville (17th Inst.) when & where the Gubernatorial Rival Candidates will display their pretensions—as usual this State is yet in the Hands of the Politicians & the people are at Sea. This section ["is" *canceled*] for the want of opposition & exposition is insensibly dovetailed into the ["Silas Wright" *canceled*] Tom Benton northern Wilmot Pro[vis]o faction—that is their leader [Howell Cobb?] is so, but the people are not aware of it [*Interpolation*: "immediately on hearing the death of Silas he has gone on to New York."] I am anxious to see you on R[ai]l Road concerns[;] an important ["era" *interlined*] for the up country of both States is now before us. The Valley of the Savannah certainly is your position. Your rich Districts bordering on the River offering to the opposite ["dis"(?) *canceled*] counties on this side &c &c &c all & every thing conspire, towards the line of Savannah. Remember that from Andersonville to the mouth of Panther creek in this State is navigable for Steam boats & has long since been clear[e]d out by this State. A nearly level road from the Toogaloo can be made to Clark[e]sville 14 miles—to the Rabun Road 9 miles. I have many of the magnets of Geo[rgi]a to dine with me on Tuesday next. If you could drop in in the midst of such an affair I am certain it would afford great pleasure to all parties. In my humble opinion your presence more frequently in this State would tend to a more general acquaintance (desired) and the promotion of Public good. I have much to say about the dangerous fanatical position of Charleston—The Washington newspaper &c &c &c. I had much conversation with Planters whilst I was there. This State I think is getting true to herself, that is the mass. Rail Roads ["is" *canceled and* "are" *interlined*] absorbing Presidential & Loaves & fishes Questions. Do not let the Valley of the Savannah ["of" *canceled*] sleep. It is more important & will be more successful to both States than most persons are aware of. I remain as ever my Dear Sir with great respect & esteem y[ou]rs, J. Raven Mathewes.

[P.S.] Sunday [9/12.] I have tried to get this over in time, by private conveyance but have fail[e]d to do so.

ALS in ScCleA.

From S[TEPHEN] MOYLAN FOX

Yorkville [S.C.,] Sept[embe]r 12th 1847

Sir, Understanding that his excellency the Governor of South Carolina [David Johnson] had some intentions of making examinations of the Broad river to ascertain its capabilities for inland navigation, I, at the request of the Hon. F[ranklin] H. Elmore, have written to him offering my services to conduct this investigation—and taken the liberty of referring him to you for my standing.

I made application for the office of engineer to the Charlotte & Columbia Railroad but have reason to suppose that I will not get the appointment; while upon this subject I think it my duty to state to you that at a meeting held at Winnsboro upon this subject in August last, the Hon. J[ames] A. Black of Columbia, after reading the letter I had the honour to receive from you, to the meeting stated that he believed me fully qualified for the station but that he was afraid your letter would injure me.

I state this merely for your information not that I believe that it had any but good influence upon the question. With the greatest respect I have the honor to be Your Ob[edien]t Serv[an]t, S. Moylan Fox.

ALS in ScCleA.

From JOS[EPH] W. LESESNE

Mobile, Sept[embe]r 12th 1847

My Dear Sir, I can scarcely tell whether I was more pained or pleased at your letter of the 4th ult. which only reached me two days ago. After having read it over several times deeply impressed by the truth and justice of all that you say, I felt the most painful misgivings lest by the freedom I used I may have given you cause for offence. If so I beg to assure you it arose from that entire frankness and unlimited confidence which I conceived due to all intercourse with you— ["from" *canceled*] towards whom I have no other feeling than that of a son towards a father, if I may make bold to use a descriptive metaphor of such character. Such I believe is the universal feeling with the friends here in whom you confide. You but do them justice in the confidence you express towards them and that ["confidence" *canceled and* "which" *interlined*] you bestow. They are worthy of

548

it. You have none in South Carolina who love you better or revere you more. Indeed if the organ of Reverence performed its functions there as well as it does here—as truely and lovingly—I think that our little Macedonian Phalanx would be even harder to break than it is.

Let me assure you that we shall be guided entirely by your counsels in the matter of the paper. I have never doubted for a moment its importance. What I wrote you was in the way of suggestion and consultation, and nothing more, in regard to *time*, ["a consideration" *interlined*] to which others attached more importance than I did. Your letter has now removed all objections; for you must remember that it is the first time we have heard personally from you on the subject. We will now go forward as far as we can, which ["I fear" *interlined*] will not be far at present. There are few persons left in the City, now being ravaged by yellow fever, which deprived us to day of a most estimable man who promised to do much for the character of the place—the Rev[eren]d Fr[ancis] P. Lee late of Camden S. Ca.—recently ["appo" *canceled*] called to the Pastorship of the 1st Episcopal Church here. Our friends [John A.] Campbell and [Percy] Walker are both absent at the North. We will nevertheless send on as many names as we can collect. I wrote to Col. [Isaac W.] Hayne that ["there"(?) *canceled*] the interior of the State, Montgomery, Marengo [County,] Lowndes [County] &c must be attended to, and that it would be necessary in order to ensure any efficient action, especially to entrust particular persons with the duty of collecting the names of subscribers. I hope this will be attended to. Col. Hayne sent me the Copy of a letter addressed by him to [Pierre] Soulé, which I trust will have the desired effect in removing his scruples. I have myself never supposed that the idea of forming a third party had any connection in reality with the enterprise, but our friends desired to avoid any demonstration which might provoke this old outcry anew, and hence what I said on this point. In Gen[era]l [Duff] Green there is no lack of confidence on our part; ["and" *canceled*] on the other hand so far as I can understand ["here" *canceled*] our friends here would not object—but looking to other quarters they thought the idea which some how had become general, originating possibly with Mr. Soulé, was not a good one. I sincerely hope you have not misinterpretted me on ["th" *canceled*] either of these points. I fully agree with you that the fund provided ought to be large enough to ensure the best talent in the Country, and I shall share all your mortification if we fail to accomplish this object. I think it would be well even to pay contributors ["for miss" *canceled*] on miscellaneous subjects. The paper ought to be interesting to the general, as well as the political, reader. This is the only way to give a paper a wide circulation and a commanding influence. ["The interest of" *canceled*] Politics die out ["of interest" *interlined*] with the transitions of the temporary causes that that [*sic*] make them attractive. Besides, the man who feels pleased or edified on one subject is prepared to be similarly affected on all others that are as well handled ["for him" *interlined*]. The avenue to the head is through the heart. When that is gained the door ["is" *canceled and* "to reason" *interlined*] opens of its own accord.

The papers of this State are beginning to pluck up courage. I gave them all a sound scourging for their cowardice and truckling through a neutral agricultural paper, (the Alabama Planter) and I am glad to see that it had its effect—first upon the [Mobile] "Register" which, for the first time, a few days after my first article, manifested signs of vitality on the subject so decided as to astonish every one. Several papers, two at Montgomery and one in Tuscaloosa, have since responded—the latter (the "Monitor," a whig paper) in decidedly the best and boldest spirit I have seen from any quarter in this State. I sat down and wrote at once to the Editor [Thomas O. Burke] and offered him (an old acquaintance[") the ri" *canceled*] and once a Nullifier) the right hand of Southern fellowship. The blast sounded by the [Charleston] Mercury startled the slumbers of the poeple [*sic*] throughout the South notwithstanding the "opiates" administered to them, and alarmed beyond measure the execrable quacks that stood about the beds of the sleepers. The Condition of the Press at the South is a ["cons" *canceled*] a [*sic*] subject of constant thought and mortification to me—controlled like our schools by narrow minded and grovelling yankees—Recurring to the proposed paper—would not two Editors be preferable to one. Col. Hayne mentioned among others the name of our friend Campbell, but I have no idea that he could be induced to abandon his large and lucrative practice—his family being large, and his private fortune inconsiderable.

I trust that the Southern Review will not be the less esteemed and supported in consequence of the important movement now on foot.

I send you an Alabama Planter with an article of mine. One of the v[i]ews it contains appears to me to deserve a greater expansion than I could give it in such limited space.

The veiw you present on the subject of territory are conclusive with me. They are so simply because I confide in your estimate of the ability of the South to defend herself. Our friend [Edmund S.]

Dargan thinks otherwise but I had a long conversation with him this afternoon. He will acquiesce in whatever course you deem best on the subject. But should it be ascertained generally that these are your veiws I should not be at all surprised to see the Administration take directly the opposite Course—for it appears to be an anti-Calhoun Administration and nothing else. I sincerely hope that your confidence in the South may not be disappointed but I have great fears on the subject. It will require the utmost prudence and circumspection to unite them at the next Congress. The delegation from our State is a very inferior one. In conclusion I will only add that you may say ["very tr(?)" *canceled*] to our friends in Carolina that they may look with confidence to ["Mobile to do" *canceled*] their friends in Mobile for support. Those upon whom you particularly rely here ["will" *canceled*] have the most unbounded confidence in your judgement. They will suffer any martyrdom for you if necessary. When you draw the sword and say *follow* no hope ["could" *canceled and* "will" *interlined*] be so forlorn that you ["would" *canceled*] will be found alone in the attempt to carry it. Very truely your f[rien]d &c, Jos. W. Lesesne.

[P.S.] Your letter of the 5th reached me since writing the above. It gives us full possession of your veiws, and is as opportune as it will be useful. I regret that Campbell is not here: for I fear that his visit to the North will only tend to confirm veiws directly at variance with those you express on the subject of Territory. I hope that his interveiw, with [Franklin H.] Elmore in Charleston, which he promised me he would have, may have given another direction to his opinions, in which he is at times prone to be very impracticable. Unity of sentiment on this subject is indispensable. I will show him your letters when he returns—but I regret that a correspondence had not been established between you. There is ["no" *interlined*] fear of trusting him to any extent—and I do not doubt that he would be flattered by your confidence.

I concur most cordially in every word that you say as to the ["retaliatory" *interlined*] course the South ought to take to bring the Northern States to their senses. Their conduct has been most attrocious. No language is strong enough to denounce it. The shameless impudence with which they have trampled the Constitution under their feet—and their mean and despicable contrivances to deprive us of our slave property ought to be held up to the scorn of the whole Union. Not half has been said on this subject that ought to be. The Pennsylvania Law is bad enough, but most of the other States have accomplished the same end only by ["a(?) more" *canceled and* "more" *interlined*] cowardly and contemptible contrivances. The Laws providing a trial by jury for fugitive slaves are the most barefaced invasions of the Constitution ever committed. It is none other than a deliberate attempt ["by" *canceled*] to manumit our slaves by with[h]olding the question of property from ["the jurisdiction of" *interlined*] our own courts of justice. And a grosser insult could not be offerred to a friendly State, for it assumes that justice will not be administered in ["the Southern States" *canceled and* "these" *interlined*] to a man claiming to be free ["to one of its own citizens" *interlined*]. I consider the South completely absolved from the slightest obligation to observe any faith to these poeple. And I do most earnestly wish that we had sperit enough to vindicate our dignity and rights in the manner you reccommend. Your observations on this point for the first time ["present" *canceled*] from any quarter, reflect my own sentiments entertained for years past. We are at this moment as deeply disgraced as any poeple can be by our tame submission to the wicked and perfidious course of legislation to which you allude. I do hope that if the Wilmot Proviso is discussed next winter in Congress, this other grievance will be unfolded and its iniquities painted in their true colours. Had any nation in Europe violated ["a" *canceled and* "the faith of" *interlined*] treaties in the same manner and as often as the Northern States have the ["Consti sol" *canceled*] more solemn pledges and obligations of the Constitution, it would have been spurned from the pale of all Christian fellowship with other communities.

You speak of the advantages derived by the North from the Union. My dear Sir, no man at the South dreams of the extent of those advantages. He who would set down without the detail to prove it, ["what" *canceled*] the annual cost entailed upon us by the Union would be pronounced a madman or a fool. Our whole commerce except a small fraction is in the hands of Northern men. Take Mobile as an example—⅞ of our Bank Stock is owned by Northern men—as large a portion of the Insurance Stock of the Companies chartered by our ["own" *interlined*] Legislature; besides 7 or 8 foreign Companies who do their business by agencies. Half our real estate is owned by non residents of the same section. Our whole sale and retail business—every thing in short worth mentioning is in the hands of men who invest their profits at the North. The commercial privileges extended by the Constitution to these poeple has wholly deprived us of a mercantile class—and thus deprives us, (I think) of the most certain means for the accumulation of wealth. Instead of the condition of Ireland being that which we may *expect hereafter*, it is in fact that which we now suffer. *This little town* ["looses" *canceled and* "pays" *interlined*] *2 Millions annually for the reflected glories of the Union.* I speak advisedly and from figures. If a swarm of Locusts should every 4th year settle upon our fields of corn[,] cotton and rice and lay them waste we should loose [*sic*] less than we do from the causes I have enumerated—causes not peculiar to this place, but in active operation from N. Orleans to the smallest village at the South. Financially we are more enslaved than our negroes. But I ["must be" *canceled*] am abusing your patience. ["But really" *canceled*] When I get on this subject I know not when to stop.

Should any difficulty ["occur" *canceled*] arise as to a concurrence in your veiws on the part of our friends here, I will not fail to advise you of it. It is important to keep us posted up with the current of events. J.W.L.

[P.S.] The article in the Paper to which I particularly refer is on the last page. There is also a short one on the first.

ALS in ScCleA; PEx in Jameson, ed., *Correspondence*, pp. 1133–1135.

From ANNA [MARIA CALHOUN CLEMSON]

Brussels, Sept. 13th 1847

My dear father, This quiet Sunday, which I am passing alone, cannot be more agreeably employed, than in writing to you. Last steamer brought me letters from mother [Floride Colhoun Calhoun], sister [Martha Cornelia Calhoun], & yourself, but really our life is too quiet to afford material for more than one letter, at a time, without repeating the same thing; & you know, tho' a great talker, I am not fond of repetitions, so as it is your turn, I will only write to you, & take the others the next steamer.

I say I am alone. The children [John Calhoun Clemson and Floride Elizabeth Clemson] are only out to take exercise, but Mr. [Thomas G.] C[lemson] went, by invitation, to dine, & spend the night, at Mariemont, the centre of [the] coal region, with Mr. Waroquiere [*sic*; Warocqué], one of the wealthiest *coal miners*, in Belgium, & from there he goes, also by invitation, to pass a few days with the Vi[s]comte Desmanet de Biesme, at his chateau near Namur. M. Desmanet has also one of the overgrown fortunes of this country, so he will have the opportunity of seeing country life in all its perfection, in two different phases, for M. Waroquiere has made his own fortune, while the other belongs to the aristocracy. I am curious to know the different manner of exhibiting their wealth, in these two cases. I was also invited, but it is too much trouble & expense, for me to leave home with the children, so I determined to be reasonable & remain, tho' I must confess, I should like to get out of town a little while, as I have now been more than a year, without leaving it, & you know, no one is more impressed than myself with the feeling, that "God made the country & man the town." I would like very well to spend the three winter months in the town, but for the other nine, give me the country, & I don[']t care how retired. But fortunately happiness depends neither on town nor country, so I manage to get along very well with the town. I must acknowledge to you, to whom I confess every thing, a little vanity. I am really proud to find how little effect all the splendour, & falsehood of the life around me, has on my mind, & I believe I may safely say, I shall return to America & [*sic*] simple, unsophisticated, & *American* in my habits, thoughts, & feelings, as tho' I had never left a plantation, perhaps even more so, for I have now had an opportunity of seeing, & judging *near*, of many things, which at a distance seem very wonderful, & tempting. You say you fear our country is following on the footsteps of Europe. Much indeed do I regret to hear she has even turned into the same road, but you have no idea of the immense distance she has to pass over, before she arrives at the glittering rotten[n]ess, of social & political life here, especially in France. You have doubtless read the accounts of the late trials in that country, of its ministers for corruption, & of ["the head of" *interlined*] one of the highest families, for the murder of his wife, (the Duke de Praslin,) & those trials, if you followed them at all carefully, must have made your blood run cold, from the cold blooded, & heartless contempt, of every thing like social, or political, sentiment, feeling, or even decency, which they developed. I do verily believe France, & the french, from Louis Phillippe [*sic*] down, to be the most utterly depraved, & corrupt nation, which exists, or ever did exist. As to Spain, Portugal, & Italy, they are no nations at all. England, this country, & Germany, appear by contrast with the others, immaculate, but even they are most wo[e]fully defficient in public & private morals. No doubt we have many & great faults, & much do I lament them, but I must confess, I have confidence in the freshness of our country, just as there would be more hope, in a dangerous illness, to save a young & vigorous man, than one worn out by a long life of dissipation, & bad habits.

I have written you all this nonsense, because really, when I have told you that we are all well, & as happy as we can be, (myself at least,) so far from all of you, I have nothing more to say. To repeat the, not "twice-told," but an hundred times repeated, tale of the *manifold perfections* of my dear little children, would tire even you in the end, & besides "perfection is perfection, & can[']t be perfected" as some one says, so there is no more to be said on that subject. With all their perfections however, I begin to fear they will never learn to read. They are full of life, & hate their books, & I am inexperienced, & much interrupted by my many avocations, so the progress is slow, I might even say imperceptible, but with patience I suppose it will come one of these days. They both became very thin towards the end of last month, & lost their appetites, & I was a little uneasy about them, but at present they eat like cormorants, & are beginning to pick up a little.

Mr. C[lemson']s health continues wonderfully good for him, & as for myself I have as great a double chin as Mrs. Ezekiel Pickens, who used to live at Cherry Hill, so you see as far as health is concerned we cannot complain.

I am sorry to hear mother was again complaining but hope, [*ms. torn; word missing*] her attack was slight this time, her favourite Glenn [Springs], will soon set her up again. Sister writes me you are looking uncommonly well, which delights me. Oh! if I could only see you all if it was only for an hour!

Pat's [Patrick Calhoun's] match with Miss Tibbatts is again broken of[f] sister says. What does he mean by behaving in such a way? I am ashamed to see him act, to say the least, so lightly. His reputation must be far from an enviable one by this time. I am pleased to hear such good accounts of all the rest of the family, & hope James' [James Edward Calhoun's] studious habits may continue. His separation from [William] Ransom [Colhoun] is an excellent thing.

Love to mother, sister, & any of the family who may be with you. The children send many kisses. Do have a good miniature of yourself about the size of mother's taken for me. Your devoted daughter, Anna.

ALS in ScCleA.

From Rufus A. French

Giles C[ourt] H[ouse Va.,] Sept[embe]r the 13th 1847
My Dear Sir, Circumstances connected with my history require that
I shall make a speedy trip to one of the Northern States, and it is
important that I should have a letter of introduction from some one
of my friends who enjoys a National reputation. You have known
me by reputation since my boyhood and in our short personal intercourse would be enabled to form a pretty correct estimate of my
character & capacity.

Will you be so kind my dear Sir to transmit as soon as you can
conveniently such testimonial as you may deem from your knowledge of me personally or otherwise I merit. I ask no more.

Tender my kindest salutations to Mrs. [Floride Colhoun] Calhoun
and your daughter [Martha Cornelia Calhoun] & believe me as ever,
Your friend, Truly & sincerely, Rufus A. French.

ALS in ScCleA.

From J[ames] M. Legaré

Aiken S.C., Sept. 14th 1847
Sir, When I call to mind that so far from possessing any claim upon
your consideration, I have not so much as the honor of your acquaintance, I am almost discouraged, and would at once abandon
the design with which I began of preferring a request, did I not hope
that you who have already attained to fame and fortune, will bear
patiently with one who (young and unsupported) is as yet only solicitous of the one, and ambitious of the other.

Before, however, venturing to ask that which I purpose, I will say
a few words in regard to myself, Sir, which the circumstances under
which I write appear to me sufficiently to warrant. Allow me then
(as briefly as possible) to narrate, that at [Charleston] college I was
so fortunate as to obtain the first honor, but so unfortunate as to
obtain it at the expense of my health. Immediately after, much
moved by the sudden death of an eminent kinsman [Hugh S. Legaré]
in whose house I was staying in Washington, I returned home ambitious of nothing so much as of acheiving [*sic*] a reputation—a design which was unhappily frustrated after a year's *violent* and in-
judicious study in Mr. [James L.] Petigru's [law] office, by a succession of hemmorrhages from the lungs.

It is true I did not at once yield, but renewed my studies when sufficiently recovered again and again; but since the fourth failure, I I [*sic*] have utterly abandoned all hope in that quarter, because, involved with my Father [John D. Legaré] in pecuniary difficulties (rather, disaster) I am unable to acquire that *slowly*, which would be essential for purposes of present maintenance. Thus it happens, I cannot but regard the last year ["of" *canceled*] as one wasted in my life, since during that period I have awaited (not *idly*, indeed) the fulfilment of promises made by friends, as yet without result.

At length I have resolved (comite fortuna, as [Augustinus] Steuchus writes on his title page) to do for myself—and in what manner, the Prospectus enclosed, will, Sir, inform you.

Indeed I can no longer hide from myself that only in an enterprise of this nature can I expect success, since from all laborious study my health effectually debars me: and it is in the earnest hope that you will not consider this undertaking, in which I have embarked what trifling means I possess and all my energies, unworthy of your favorable notice, that I have (after some consideration) determined to solicit the weight of your wide influence. With these views, Sir, I enclose also a copy of the heading to the list of subscribers used in Georgia, and to which several of my personal friends in Augusta, who have interested themselves warmly in the matter, have attached their names.

I have *too much* at stake, from any false ideas of delicacy, to leave that to a hireling which to prove successful should be assumed only by myself, and thus in person I design obtaining subscribers—["and" *canceled and* "an" *interlined*] end ["the attainment of" *interlined*] which will be materially assisted by the recommendations of those to whom we (Carolinians) are accustomed to look up with respect, or, as to you Sir, with honest pride, trust, and (yes, I for one speak from my heart), affection, thus reversing the bearing of Cicero's nam laudem adolescentis propinqui existimo &c &c.

Do I then ask too much for a stranger, Sir, when I beg that you will, if you approve of my enterprise, write in your own hand the heading I have referred to, (*with what more it may please you to add*) on the blank page of my subscription book, enclosed—and first enroll yourself among the subscribers in Carolina? Truly, Sir, I cannot think that you will hesitate, when at so small an expense of trouble you can give such importance in the eyes of your fellow citizens to this undertaking in which God knows how earnestly I have embarked my future.

As you will observe in the prospectus I have stated that for half the amount, the subscriber will receive a work quite similar to Littell's Living Age; This is not strictly true, since the Living Age is published twice as often as the Journal will be; but the deception was unintentional and did not appear to me in the light in which it occurs in those circulars until they were all out of press. It is my design next year, however, should the number of subscribers at all warrant (as I trust it will) the outlay, to double the size of each number, thus placing them in regard to bulk, on an equality with the numbers of Lyttell's [*sic*] Age. Even as it *is*, however, there are many who would readily subscribe the half when they would hesitate at the whole. What I desired to have understood from the prospectus was, that although the work would in fact be only half the size of Mr. Littell's, yet the amount of of [*sic*] strictly *literary* matter would be the same, since it is part of my design to exclude all mere extracts from American newspapers, with which Mr. Littell fills his pages, and which are generally stale to everyone having access to the daily Journals.

I purpose next year, also, to greatly extend the field whence the contents of my work will be derived, and to draw more largely on the literature of Germany, France and Spain, as I believe I can read the languages of these three countries with sufficient ease to turn them to good account.

In conclusion, Sir, I again earnestly beg you favorably to consider my request, and even (if it pleases you) to influence those in your neighborhood in support of my venture; for in your immediate portion of our State, I have few or no personal friends. With the highest respect, I have the honor to remain your ob[edien]t Servant, J.M. Legaré.

[P.S.] Pray remember me, Sir, to your niece (Miss Martha [Maria Colhoun]) when you see her, whose pleasant acquaintance I have by no means forgotten.

ALS with Ens in ScCleA. NOTE: The text of Legaré's enclosed prospectus for the "Journal of Literature: European and American" is published in Curtis C. Davis, *That Ambitious Mr. Legaré, The Life of James M. Legaré of South Carolina, Including a Collected Edition of His Verse* (Columbia, S.C.: University of South Carolina Press, 1971), pp. 42–43. Apparently enclosed also was a "list of subscribers used in Georgia" with the names of Henry H. Cumming, W[illia]m Cumming, Charles J. Jenkins, J[ohn] W. Wilde, Richard H. Wilde, J[ohn] P. King and W[illiam] T. Gould. In the margins of the list Legaré wrote "It is true, Sir, that *all* of these gentlemen are well acquainted with me, and four of them are the warmest personal friends I have anywhere, and that I am an utter stranger to you, yet I trust for this reason after all I have narrated, you will not refuse my request."

From I[SAAC] W. HAYNE

Charleston, Sept. 15th 1847

Dear Sir, I send you a copy of our subscription list thus far. We have just taken steps for a more *general* subscription & shall, so far as St. Philip's & St. Michael's is concerned, have every voter applied to.

I get, occasionally, letters from Florida, Alabama, Louisianna, Mississippi, North Carolina and even *Missouri*. The *politicians* speak *doubtingly*, but those *not in the current of politics* hail the project with enthusiasm.

The objections *out of So. Ca.* are altogether political, connected with supposed prejudices to *yourself*, and what they term the "Chivalry."

I enclose [*not found*] two letters from Columbia & Camden that you may be aware of the objections within the State. I have received several such. Very Respectfully Y[ou]r Ob[edien]t Serv[an]t, I.W. Hayne.

ALS with En in ScCleA. NOTE: Enclosed is the circular presented above with Henry W. Conner's letter of August 8, 1847, to Calhoun, with the following subscribers and amounts pledged: Nath[aniel] Heyward, W[illia]m Aiken, R[obert] F.W. Allston, and J[oshua] J. Ward, $1,000 each; M[oses] C. Mordecai, C[harles] T. Lowndes, J[ames] Rose, F[ranklin] H. Elmore, W[illiam] B. Pringle, A[lexander] Robertson, J[ohn] L. Manning, W[illiam] H. Trapier, P[eter] W. Fraser, G[eorge] A. Trenholm, James Gadsden, Andrew Turnbull, H[enry] Bailey, O[tis] Mills, J. Harleston Read, W[illia]m Lucas, W[illia]m Dubose, J[ohn] L. Nowell, Dan[ie]l Heyward, and D[aniel] E. Huger, $500 each; John H. Alston and Robert Smith, $300 each; H[enry] W. Conner, Edd. S. Dargan, and Jacob Bond I'On, $250 each; Jno. D. Magill, J.M. DeSaussure, Gabriel Manigault, Sam[ue]l Porcher, and John Exum, $200 each; W[illiam] B.S. Horry, R.S. Ball, D[aniel] H. Hamilton, Rice Dulin, W. Henry Heyward, James B. Heyward, I[saac] E. Holmes, E. Horry Deas, James S. Rhett, J.J. Pringle Smith, W[illia]m Mason Smith, Ed. Tho[ma]s Heriot, Tho[ma]s G. Simons, Maunsel White, T. Leger Hutchinson, Alfred Huger, F[rancis] Y. Porcher, A[braham] Tobias, Jno. Rutledge, Tho[ma]s E. Prioleau, Joel Adams, Sr., J. H. Adams, and W[illia]m Weston, $100 each; Edward Barnwell, Jr., F.J. Withers, John Labruce, J[oshua] W. Labruce, Robert Adams, Ja[me]s R. Sparkham, W.S. Whaley, and Solomon Legaré, $50 each; J.A. Fripp, $40; Stephen Ford, $30; Jos[eph] A. Black, C.R. Bryce, J[ohn] P. Ford, T.C. Ford, J. Rees Ford, A.P. Vinson, Joel R. Adams, Ja[me]s U[?]. Adams, and R.J. Adams, $25 each; F[rancis] Weston, M[icajah] J. Roper, Tho[ma]s S. Curtis, Jno. B. Whaley, Tho[ma]s Legare, Jno. Rivers, E[phraim] M. Clark, W[hite]m[arsh] B. Seabrook, $20 each; James Adams, $15; Hugh Fraser, W. P[ercival] Vaux, F[rancis] W. Heriot, W[illia]m Mathews, J.B. Hinson, $10 each; E.P. Coachman, J.C. Porter, B[enjamin] A. Coachman, A.J. McLellan, J.E. Nelson, T.R. Sessi[o]ns, Tho[ma]s Wilson, T.W. Ford, S[amuel] T. Atkinson, $5 each;

R[obert] E. Fraser and G. Durant, $3 each; W.F. Small, Elias Thomson, and B. Soloman, $2 each.

From R. B. LEWIS

Dahlonega Ga., 15th Sept. 1847

Dear Sir, Yours of the 13th instant came to hand last evening[.] Mr. William G. Lawrence showed me a letter a few days past, from Mr. E[dward] J.C. Milner, directing him to pay me 17 dwts. of Gold, rent due you[.] He further said if I would give a receipt in full, to pay me thirty dwts. which I suppose from his statement is all that is due. Will you please write me what I shall do in the matter. Very respectfully Yours, R.B. Lewis.

ALS in ScU-SC, John C. Calhoun Papers. NOTE: An AEU by Calhoun reads "R.B. Lewis[,] requested him to receive the 30 dwt. & to give a receipt in full."

From B[ENJAMIN] F. PERRY

Greenville S.C., Sept. 15th 1847

My Dear Sir, I hope you will excuse the liberty I take, in writing to you, on a subject of deep interest to yourself, as well as the whole Southern Country.

The restrictions attempted to be imposed, by Congress, on the extension of slavery, demand an expression of public opinion throughout the Southern States. It is proposed to have a meeting at this place on sale day in October, for the purpose of expressing our views in relation to the Wilmot Proviso, and the establishment of a Paper in Washington to defend our constitutional rights & the equality, of the Southern States with other members of the Union.

Would it be asking too much, to request you to prepare for us, an address and resolutions? You are so familiar with the subject in all its bearings, & know so well the proper course to pursue, that the preparation of such a Paper would scarcely cost you an effort.

There is an other subject, which I hope you will pardon me for mentioning to you. The signs of the times indicate that the next election of President will devolve on the House of Representatives. General [Zachary] Taylor will not receive the nomination of the Whigs. They are determined to fight an other battle on the Tariff,

as is manifested by [John M.] Clayton[']s recent Letter. The Democratic party will not unite on any Northern candidate. If you will
permit your name to be used in the canvas, so as to carry you into
the House of Representatives from the Electoral Colleges, your
election may be secured in a vote by States.

It is not likely that either party will have a majority in the House
voting by States. At present there are eleven on each side, three
divided & four yet to elect members of Congress.

I feel assured there never was a time when your elevation to the
Presidency would have been of more service to the country than it
would be at present. It is therefore important that your friends
should place you in a position, where it would be possible to unite
on you. A movement to effect this might be made, during the next
sitting of our Legislature, in Columbia.

I make these suggestions for your consideration, & hope they may
meet your approbation, as I have reasons to believe they would that
of your friends. I am with great respect yours truly, B.F. Perry.

ALS in ScCleA; variant retained copy in A-Ar, Benjamin F. Perry Papers.

To J[AMES] M. LEGARÉ, [Aiken, S.C.]

Fort Hill, 18th Sep[tembe]r 1847

Dear Sir, I return the subscri[p]tion with my name, as you request.

I regret to learn, that you have been forced to abandon the pursuit of your studies, in consequence of your ill health; and wish you
the greatest success in your undertaking. In my opinion, a work of
the kind, under the selection of citizens of the Southern States of
adequate qualifications, deser[v]es the patronage of the entire South.
We want, above all other things, a Southern literature, from school
books up to works of the highest order. With great respect I am & &,
J.C. Calhoun.

ALS in ScU-SC, John C. Calhoun Papers.

To V[ERNON] K. STEVENSON, [Nashville]

Fort Hill, Sept. 18, 1847

My Dear Sir: I hasten to answer yours of the 5th inst., received by
mail yesterday.

It is with unfeigned regret that I am compelled to decline the invitation of yourself and Ex-Gov. [James C.] Jones, to visit Nashville at this time, in consequence of an engagement which I cannot well dispense with, and which will engross all my disposable time until I leave home for Washington. Had it been in my power to accept, I assure you it would not only have afforded me much gratification personally to visit your city, but I would have felt it to be my duty to do so, in connection with the highly important object towards effecting which you suppose my presence would contribute.

There are few objects which I have more at heart than the construction of the road from Nashville to Chattanooga, where it will meet the Georgia road, and through it form a continuous connection with the Southern Atlantic ports, and, in time, with those of the Gulf of Mexico. In whichever light it is viewed, whether in reference to the prosperity of Nashville, Savannah, Charleston, and other cities connected; or still more broadly, that of the Southern Atlantic, and the Southwestern, Western and Northwestern States; or broader still, the whole Union, in its commercial, political and social relations, I regard it the most important of all the railroads to be constructed— as time will show, when it is completed; especially if the Cumberland river can be made as navigable, at all seasons, from Nashville to its mouth, as the Ohio is from that point to its mouth. This is no new opinion of mine. I have long entertained it. Indeed, I may say, I believe with truth, that I was the first to point it out, as the best route between the centre of the valley of the Mississippi and the Atlantic, and, through its ports with the rest of the world. That it was not originally adopted, instead of the one that is direct from Charleston to Cincinnati, was no fault of mine.

That the stock will be very profitable to its holders, if it should be judiciously and economically constructed, I feel confident, from the ability and business habits of those who have taken it in hand. Such is my perfect confidence in the road, that if I had at my disposal a half million, I would not hesitate to invest it. I would regard it as the safest and best investment that could be made. It will not only be vastly profitable hereafter with the growth of the country, but will pay from the first legal interest, and make Nashville one of the first cities in the great valley of the West. So strong is my conviction, that I would regard it as a matter of just pride to have my name associated with the noble work.

Entertaining these impressions I shall feel it my duty to give any aid and encouragement in my power to the work. I am decidedly of the opinion that Georgia and this State should both lend their aid in its construction; and feel confident it may be done without the least hazard, while they will be every way benefitted by its completion. The amount of subscription necessary to secure the charter must, by all means, be secured. I would be glad to know what progress you are making from time to time in that respect.

I received your letter shortly after my return from Washington, giving much valuable information as to the relative cost of transportation from New Orleans, and from New York, and other points on the Atlantic to Nashville, compared with the probable cost from Charleston and Savannah by the projected road, when completed. It is very favorable to the road; and I have been prevented from preparing a memoir in reference to it, agreeably to my promise, only in consequence of the extent of my engagements since my return from Washington, and the unfavorable state of the money market for such works in this country from the Mexican war, and in Europe from the scarcity of provisions.

I have not heard from Mr. [A.O.P.] Nicholson. Yours truly, J.C. Calhoun.

PC in the Charleston, S.C., *Mercury*, October 16, 1847, p. 2; PC (from the Nashville, Tenn., *Union*) in the Charleston, S.C., *Evening News*, October 16, 1847, p. 2; PC (from the Nashville, Tenn., *Union*) in the Edgefield, S.C., *Advertiser*, October 20, 1847, p. 2; PC in the Pendleton, S.C., *Messenger*, October 29, 1847, p. 4.

To J[OHN] R[AVEN] MATHEW[E]S, [Clarkesville, Ga.]

Fort Hill, 19th Sep[tembe]r 1847

My dear Sir, I would be exceedingly glad to see & converse with you on many subjects, & do hope you will yet have an opportunity to make me a visit. I am glad to learn, that both parties have united to solicit you to be a candidate. It is a good sign, that party ties & the cohesion of plunder, are giving away. It is time that the madness of the many for the benefit of a few should cease. If it should, the South will be safe.

I am not surprised, that your section is so benighted on political subjects; for I am of the opinion, that there is not a baser hunker paper in the Union, than the [Athens, Ga.,] Banner, or ["one" *interlined*] better ca[l]culated to delude an unthinking people.

I place a high importance on improving the navigation of Savannah river, so as [to] fit it for steam boats. I visited a short time since Anderson Ville [S.C.], where I met most of the experienced & skilful Pilots of the River. I obtained from them a very full & I have no doubt correct statement of all the impediments from Hamburgh [S.C.] to that place. It seems, that the most formidable of the whole is Trotty's [Trotter's] Shoal, just below the mouth of the ["Rocky" *interlined*] River [S.C.]. I have since addressed a letter to an Engineer at Gadsden in this State, and requested him, if he could make it convenient to visit me in order to examine it & give his opinion as to the practicability of improving it & the cost. From that an estimate may be made of the whole. I have not had time to hear from him. Should he come, he will de[s]cend in a boat from Anderson Ville to Trotty's Shoal, which will give him a good conception of the Stream. Truly, J.C. Calhoun.

ALS in DLC, John C. Calhoun Papers.

To B[ENJAMIN] F. PERRY, [Greenville, S.C.]

Fort Hill, 20 Sep[tembe]r 1847

My dear Sir, I would with pleasure comply with your request to prepare a report & resolutions on the very important subjects to which you refer; but I am so engrossed with other subjects, as hardly to have sufficient leisure to reply to the numerous communications made to me on a variety of subjects. If you would permit me to make any suggestions, as to the character of the report & resolutions, I would say, the more pointed and emphatick the better. I think, nothing ought to be said about compromise. It is one thing to offer a compromise, with a pistol at our breast, and another to acquiesce in one offered to us, for the sake of peace. Indeed, I would regard a compromise offered by us & carried by our votes, with bearly [*sic*] a sufficient number of votes from the North to pass it, as the most unfortunate result possible for us. It would be binding only on us, & would but procrastinate the evil day & make it tenfold worse. Indeed, a compromise, at best, is but a surrender on our part. We concede every thing, & they nothing. I might even [*ms. torn;* go] farther, and say, it is but changing the terms of [*ms. torn;* the] compact for the worse ["for us" *canceled*], on the most [*ms. torn;* vi]tal of all subjects to us. I am not prepared to [*ms. torn; word missing*] that I would ["not" *interlined*] acquiesce in the extension [*ms. torn;*

words missing; com]promise, if offered by the [*ms. torn; words missing*] of peace; but I do not [*ms. torn; words missing*] induced to vote for it, with my views of the Constitution. My impression is, that the sooner the subject is met, & put an end to, the better for all; North, East, South & West. We ought to *settle it now, & forever, & put an end to all future agigation* [*sic*; agitation]. It is in the power of the South to do so, if united. If backed by the United South, I would underwrite the result.

In reference to the other subject to which you allude, I am perfectly passive. I do not desire the office, and would ["*not*" *interlined*] accept ["*of*" *canceled*] it, but as a burthen, should it be offered to me. My cheif [*sic*] desire is, to have the disposition & control of the residue of my time. But, if it should be thought by the people of this State, and any respectable portion of the Union, that I could render any essential service in that, or any other office, I would not decline the burthen, so long as I may have the strength to perform its duties. But you must permit me to say that I do not think it likely, that I could reach that high office either by the votes of the electoral College, or the House [of Representatives]. The election is in the hands of the Spoilers & long has been; and I am the very last man in the Union, that they would wish to see in the control of the power & patronage of the Government; but I leave others [to; "*form their opinions*" *interlined*; and] to act according to their judgment.

ALU (signature cut out) in A-Ar, Benjamin F. Perry Papers.

From A[LFRED] P. ALDRICH

Barnwell C[ourt] H[ouse, S.C.] 21 Sept[embe]r 1847
My dear Sir, With this I send you a draft [*not found*] of a report and resolutions which I propose to offer to the meeting to be held here on the 1 Monday in October. Be pleased to look over them & see if they meet your approval & if I have taken your ideas. Any suggestions or alterations which you may make will be kindly received & carefully attended to. If possible return them in time for the meeting. V[er]y respectfully & truly yours, A.P. Aldrich.
[Enclosure]
Proceedings of a Meeting
of the Citizens of Barnwell District, on the subject of the
Wilmot Proviso.

The citizens of the District met at the Court House in a numerous assembly. The Hon. Angus Patterson was called to the Chair, and Messrs. W[illiam] H. Thomson and John E. Tobin were requested to act as Secretaries.

The chairman having announced the object of the meeting in a concise and sensible address, explaining the nature and giving the history of the Wilmot Proviso, expressed himself ready to entertain any proposition which might be made respecting the action to be taken by the people of the district in the matter.

Maj. A.P. Aldrich then moved that a Committee of twenty-five be appointed to consider and report upon the matter.

While the Committee had retired and were engaged in their deliberations, Col. W[illiam] A. Owens was called upon by several citizens to entertain the audience with his views. He responded in an off-hand and manly address, which displayed the ready orator and the warm patriot. There was a boldness and fire in his style which was greeted by the audience with repeated applause.

The Committee having returned, through their Chairman, Maj. Aldrich, submitted the following Report:

The Committee of twenty-five, to whom it was referred to prepare a Report and Resolutions for the consideration of the meeting, beg leave to

REPORT:

The Wilmot Proviso and the recent act of the Legislature of the State of Pennsylvania, and of other non-slaveholding States, of like object and character, force on the people of these States, and especially the slaveholding, questions of the most solemn import that have ever been presented to them. The former would degrade the slaveholding States, by divesting them of the equality secured by the Constitution to all the members of the Union, while the latter openly and without semblance of pretext or attempt at justification, not only sets aside the express stipulation of the Constitution, which makes it a duty of the non-slaveholding States to deliver up fugitive slaves found within their limits, and the act of Congress passed to carry it into effect, but even makes it highly penal to enforce them. Already the act of Pennsylvania has led to the murder of a highly respectable citizen of Maryland, who, under the solemn stipulation of the Constitution, and the authority of the act of Congress, attempted to reclaim his slaves.

Our perfect equality under the Constitution, and the rights secured under this express stipulation, are questions not to be discussed. It only remains to repel attacks on them, and the only question open for discussion is, how that can best be done? Fortunately, we have a great choice of means. The utter disregard of Pennsylvania, and most of the non-slaveholding States, of the only stipulation of the Constitution of any moment to us, and their attempt to degrade us, with the bad faith which they have for years evinced towards us, would justify us before the world and the forum of conscience to retaliate, by setting aside all the numerous and important stipulations of the Constitution in favor of the non-slaveholding States; and, among others, that which secures to them free access for their ships and commerce into our ports. To adopt at once this decisive measure would be the proper course, and should be done, if a cherished regard for the Union, and the hope of applying milder remedies successfully in the first instance, did not interpose to prevent. Of that description of measures, the least exceptionable in their character, and the most likely, at the same time, to prove effectual, may be ranked those that calculated to unite the slaveholding States in determined resistance to the outrageous and unprovoked assaults which have been made upon them. If they could be once so united, there can be little doubt it would be effectual for that purpose. Should they prove true to themselves, they will not fail to have numerous allies in the non-slaveholding States. We have truth and the stipulations of the Constitution in our favor. They cannot but have a powerful influence with the intelligent and patriotic in the non-slaveholding States, which will become apparent, so soon as it is seen we are resolved at all and every hazard to maintain our perfect equality, and to enforce the constitutional stipulations in our favor.

But the important question is how, and by what means, can the slaveholding States be made to unite? The first step is to remove the impediments in the way; and among them the greatest is the ascendency of party considerations, especially as connected with the Presidential question, which takes precedence over all others, including the honor and the safety of the slaveholding States, and the Constitution and liberty of the country. Although there are but few in those States who profit by party struggles, compared to the whole, they exercise great control, being generally influential party leaders, with the control of the party organs in their hands; and require to be carefully watched, to prevent them from bartering away our honor and safety for the patronage and offices of the *Federal Government*. For that purpose, and to keep the slaveholding States thoroughly informed of all movements against them, it is indispensable that they should have an able and trustworthy organ at the seat of government, pledged never to look for support or patronage but to those whose honor and safety it was established to defend.

To this must be added the most watchful jealousy of the dictation of party caucus, or convention, held to make a President. It is not sufficient to reconcile us to acquiescence in its act to declare that no one shall receive the nomination who is not opposed [to] the Wilmot Proviso. Our honor and safety require that we should take higher ground, and refuse to go into a caucus or convention (the name is nothing) where we would be associated and would have to fraternize with its advocates, the Hannibal Hamlins, the Preston Kings, [David] Wilmot, the author of the Proviso himself, and the like, who are as deadly foes to us, and as rabid abolitionists at bottom, as [Joshua R.] Giddings or [William Lloyd] Garrison. Such association would degrade and debase us. Just pride and proper indignation forbid it, and sound policy warns us against it. To meet as political associates and brothers *such men*, in order to elect by joint efforts a President, and to divide with them the honors and emoluments of the Government, would sink us to the lowest level of infamy, and would most certainly prepare the way for our final overthrow and ruin. It is ominous that the first named of these deadly foes, Hannibal Hamlin himself, was the first man delegated to the next Baltimore convention.

Another means for effecting the union of the slaveholding States still rema[i]ns, which, in our opinion, should have long since been adopted: we refer to the Convention of these States. Their meeting in Convention could not fail to have the most happy effect towards uniting them, and thereby averting, by gentle means, the danger impending over us and the country at large.

But we recommend these milder measures for no other reason than that already assigned. If they should fail, we are prepared to retaliate, by adopting the high measure of excluding their ships and commerce, and that with the certain conviction that it would bring the intelligent and patriotic of the non-slaveholding States to unite with us to put down forever these unjustifiable assaults on our rights, honor and safety; but if in that we should be deceived, we are prepared to throw the responsibility on our assailants, and take the final remedy into our own hands, without the least fear that we shall be the greatest sufferers.

Resolved, That the Wilmot Proviso is a violation of the Constitution and in derogation of the equality of the slaveholding States as members of our Federal Union.

Resolved, That the act of the Legislature of Pennsylvania, passed at its last session, and other acts with like object and character, passed by non-slaveholding States, to prevent the reclaiming of fugitive slaves, are in express violation of the most important of all the stipulations of the Constitution in our favor, and would justify us, before the world and the forum of conscience, in retaliating, by setting aside like stipulations in their favor, and among them free access of their ships and commerce to our ports.

Resolved, That in not recommending so decided a step at the present time, and proposing milder measures, we are not actuated by any fear of the consequences to which it may lead, but by our cherished regard for the *Union,* and the peace and harmony of these States.

Resolved, That among milder measures, we regard the union of the slaveholding States on this vital question (in order to resist this unprovoked and outrageous assault on their rights and honor) as the most efficacious; and feel assured that, if it can be accomplished, it would be successful.

Resolved, That with a view to unite and rally the South in the defence of their constitutional rights, we approve the plan to establish, at the City of Washington, an organ independent of *party,* *President-making,* and *Government patronage,* having for its main design the defence of those guaranties which the Constitution secures to the slaveholding States of this Confederacy.

Resolved, That we are decidedly opposed, not only to the Southern States agreeing to run any man as a candidate who is not openly and thoroughly opposed to the Wilmot Proviso, but also to their uniting or fraternizing in caucus or convention with those who are in its favor—as derogatory to our character, wounding to the feelings of just pride, and calculated to lead to the most dangerous consequences.

Resolved, That if milder means should fail to repel these assaults on us, we stand prepared to adopt the higher, suggested in the report; and if that should fail, we stand prepared to throw the responsibility on our assailants, and to take the final remedy into our own hands, without fear that we in the end will be the greatest sufferers.

Resolved, That we are of the opinion that now is the time to compel the non-slaveholding States to respect our rights and honor, and to observe the stipulations of the Constitution, and that the longer it is delayed, the worse it will be for us and them.

Resolved, That we regard the act of Pennsylvania, and other acts of like character passed by other non-slaveholding States, as at least as palpable violations of the Constitution, and as dangerous in their consequences, as the Wilmot Proviso; and that we should regard any compromise or settlement of the latter, without effectually putting down the former, by expunging them from the statute books, as among the most unsafe and dangerous termination of the question to the Slaveholding States; as its effect would be to lull us into repose, without extirpating or diminishing the real cause of danger.

A. P. ALDRICH, Chairman.

Major A[ldrich] having read the Report, sustained it with an argument of decided ability. His speech indicated great familiarity with the secret springs of the Abolition movement, and with the methods by which that rabid fanaticism has attained to its present overshadowing influence in the Northern States. He disclosed to the people some startling facts, which of themselves went a great way to show the advantages which would result from adopting the suggestion made in the Report.

Maj. S.M. [*sic*; Lewis M.] Ayer then arose, and briefly expressed his views of the attack now being made on the institutions of the South. His views were clear and his sentiments patriotic. The handsome style of his delivery made a very favorable impression on the audience, which was signified by their applause.

The Hon. S[amuel] W. Trotti offered the following additional resolutions, to be appended to the proceedings:

Resolved, That it be recommended to the Legislature of this State, at its next Session, to instruct and request the Senators and Representatives of this State in the Congress of the United States, in the event the Wilmot Proviso, or any other proposition affirming the same or similar principles, should pass that body, to retire forthwith from their seats, and return to their constituents, to consult on the measures proper to be adopted for the protection of the slaveholding States; and

Resolved, further, As the interest and honor of the Slave States, in this important crisis, in some measure depend on unity of action on their part, that our fellow-citizens of the South be respectfully invited to take the subject of the preceding resolution into consideration, and give a prompt, plain, and fearless expression of their views.

These Resolutions being unanimously adopted, along with the Report of the Committee, Mr. Edmund Bellinger was called for, and responded in his usual happy style. The late hour of the proceedings induced him to decline making a lengthy speech. He proceeded, however, to make some brief, though pertinent, remarks on the history of the Wilmot Proviso, which were characterized by the taste and beauty of elocution for which he is distinguished. He offered the following additional resolution, which he said he had extracted from the Journals of the Legislature, (which he considered as worthy of repetition.)

"*Resolved,* That the people of this State have cause to congratulate themselves that the party feuds which formerly weakened the vigor of her counsels have happily ceased, and that South Carolina now presents to the enemies of her policy and her peace an undivided front, and is prepared (as she is resolved) to repel, by all proper means, every aggression upon her rights, as a Sovereign Republic, the instant that aggression is attempted."

On motion of Col. N[athaniel] G.W. Walker, it was

Resolved, That the proceedings be published in the Charleston and Columbia papers.

On motion of Mr. Bellinger, it was further

Resolved, That copies of the Resolutions offered by Col. Trotti, and adopted by this meeting, be forwarded to our State Senator and Representatives, with a request that they present the same to our Legislature at its next session.

ANGUS PATTERSON, President.

JOHN E. TOBIN, ⎫
             ⎬ Secretaries.
W.H. THOMSON, ⎭

Barnwell C.H. Oct. 4, 1847.

ALS in ScCleA; En in the Charleston, S.C., *Mercury,* October 9, 1847, p. 2.

To A[RMISTEAD] BURT, [Abbeville, S.C.]

Fort Hill, 21st Sep[tembe]r 1847

My dear Sir, I concur with you as to argument on the subject of slavery; & I feel confident, that it constitutes no part of the object of the proposed paper. As I understand it, it is for the South & not the North it is proposed to establish it—to keep the former thoroughly informed of all that is transpiring in reference to her, to warn her of ["its" *canceled and* "her" *interlined*] danger, to sustain those, who support her and expose those, who for party or any other consideration, would betray her. Such a paper, at this time, for such purposes, I deem indispensible. Now, in my opinion, is the time to settle the question finally, & put an end to all agitation on the subject. It is high time it should cease. It is time we should know where we are to stand in the Union, if we are to continue in it; but without a faithful sentinel at the seat of the Federal Govern[men]t, the South

571

will be kept deluded ["& divided" *interlined*] until ruin & destruction come on her.

I regret that you could not come up with Martha [Calhoun Burt]. There are many subjects, on which I would have been glad to exchange views with you. The next session will be one of profound interest. We shall soon know, what is to grow out of our late victories; but whether it shall be peace, or the prolongation of the war, it will bring trouble with it. We are entangled in Mexican affairs inextricably.

I am sorry to hear your crop has been so much injuried [*sic*] by the rain. I am glad to learn, that you are about to make a movement on the improvement of Savan[n]ah river for steam boat navigation. It is a subject, in which I take a deep interest. I made a visit, not long since, to AndersonVille [S.C.], where I met half a dozen intelligent patroons of boats, and got my full account of the impediments, which obstruct its navigation. They are numerous & some what formidable; but, I doubt not, may be overcome, at an expense much less than the construction of a rail road. Trottey's [*sic*] Shoal is the most formidable of all. I ["have" *canceled*] wrote to Mr. [Stephen Moylan] Fox[,] an Engineer of much experience in the Pennsylvania works, & who is now at Gadsden in this State, to make me a visit, if he can make it convenient, in order to look at the river, & examine that shoal. Should he come, he will de[s]cend the river from AndersonVille that far. I have not had time to hear from him yet.

It is true, that we on this side of the State, should look to our interest. The State as yet, has done nothing for us, while it has expend[ed] millions in other quarters. I am opposed to her interfering at all, except it can be done by an advance of her credit on some safe security; but, if she interferes at ["all" *canceled*] all, we ought to insist on an equal share in proportion to our just claims. Would it not be well to take ground in your resolutions to that effect? It [should] stop all interference or give us our ["share" *interlined*].

All join their love to you. Truly, J.C. Calhoun.

ALS in NcD, John C. Calhoun Papers.

From G[EORGE] F. TOWNES

Greenville C[ourt] H[ouse, S.C.] Sept. 21 1847
D[ea]r Sir, I enclose to you a receipt [*not found*] of Mr. [John C.] Zimmerman of Glenn Springs for Eighty Eight dollars which Mrs.

[Floride Colhoun] Calhoun placed in my hands to forward to him.

I avail myself of this opportunity to express to you the satisfaction I received from a private conversation with Col. [Richard F.] Simpson [Representative from S.C.] on his late visit to Greenville, in which he confirmed my own previous opinion, that you would not lend your name and influence to espouse the claims of any particular candidate for Congress. Knowing the harmony of sentiment which now prevails in this State, and particularly amongst the Democratic party of this Congressional district on all the vital questions of the day likely to be agitated at Washington, and the full confidence and respect with which you are ["politically and" *interlined and then canceled*] personally regarded by my friend Major [Benjamin F.] Perry, as well as by his friends generally, I confess I have felt some solicitude lest an unnecessary excitement and divisions should be artfully fomented ["by those (quondam whigs)" *interlined*] who are, to say the least, not ["*political*" *canceled*] friends of either yourself or ["of" *interlined*] the party to which you belong. And I use the word *party* in its highest and most honorable sense of distinguishing the Southern Republican or Democratic from the Federalism of the Whigs, and the agrarianism of a portion of those calling themselves Democrats in the North. As matters now seem we shall certainly have a reliable successor to Col. Simpson, whether a Greenville or Pendleton candidate succeeds, and *my own opinion* is that Major Perry will unless so much division arises as may bring out a whig, and you know it is unfortunately the case with the influential portion of that party that all their feelings and prejudices are deeply, and, I fear, incurably hostile to all those in this State, to whose *influence* they attribute the meagre minority in which they stand.

Do you not think Mr. [James] Buchannan[']s letter and the apprehension of a general union of the Southern States, and the necessary disruption of party ["lines" *canceled*] ties which the Wilmot proviso is obliged to produce, *especially the latter consideration,* is already producing good effects in the North?

Mrs. [Elizabeth Sloan] Townes unites with me in respects to Mrs. [Floride Colhoun] Calhoun & the family. Most Respectfully and sincerely yours &c, G.F. Townes.

P.S. On looking over the foregoing since I wrote it I think proper to say that in my conversation with Col. Simpson he did not profess to have heard you speak on the subject alluded ["to" *interlined*] but was influenced like myself in his opinions by reasons predicated on a proper estimate of your ["intelligence and" *canceled*] sense of propriety &c &c. I need not assure you that there is no other public man ["in the U" *canceled*] living upon whose reputation and usefulness at home and abroad I fix so high an estimate, and therefore hope you will excluse [*sic*] my allusion to a subject in this letter, in regard to which the seeming *caution* I have ventured to suggest might appear presumptuous. G.F.T.

ALS in ScCleA.

From HENRY W. PERONNEAU

Charleston, Sep[tember] 25th 1847

Sir, The Executive Committee of the Citizens of Charleston who have associated to resist aggressions upon the property & rights of the Slave holding States invite your attendance at a meeting of the Citizens of Charleston to be held on Wednesday Evening 13th October next at 7 o[']clock P.M. for consultation with regard to organizing an association throughout the southern States & for the adoption of such other measures as may be deemed necessary for their safety. Respectfully, Y[ou]r Obed[ien]t serv[an]t, Henry W. Peronneau, Chairman.

[Enclosed printed circular]

CHARLESTON, AUGUST, 2D, 1847

Sir—We trust that we shall not be considered as taking an unwarrantable liberty in addressing to yourself, and some others, in whose discretion we rely, the following communication. We make an appeal to you, irrespective of Party Politics, as one having a common interest with ourselves, upon a matter, as we conceive, of momentous concern to every Southern man.

You cannot but have observed the rapid progress of the Anti-Slavery spirit, for some time past, and the alarming influence it has exercised on the politics of the country, as exhibited at Washington, and throughout the non-slaveholding States of the Union.

The inundation of Congress with petitions for the abolition of slavery in the District of Columbia, though the act of petitioning for such a purpose assumes an inferiority in the Slaveholding States, and the language of the petitions is replete with vituperation and insult, has been persevered in until it has almost ceased to arrest attention. The application in the United States, of the principle of the English case of Somerset decided by Lord Mansfield, by which it is declared that the relation of master and slave ceases as soon as the parties pass the jurisdiction of the local laws which authorize slavery—a principle which isolates and degrades the slaveholder, has been more than half acquiesced in. We have seen State after State legislating with a view to avoid the act of Congress in regard to fugitive slaves, and prevent its interference with the above principle, until we are so familiarized with such legislation, that the public are scarce aware that the Pennsylvania Legislature has recently nullified this act of Congress, and affixed a heavy punishment to the attempt to enforce it within the limits of the State.

The missions of [Samuel] Hoar and his compeer [Henry Hubbard] to South-Carolina and Louisiana, by which Massachusetts undertook, on the very soil of these States, by agents resident in Charleston and New-Orleans, to obstruct the execution of the local laws in regard to the introduction of free colored persons, though met promptly by the States respectively, to whom particularly the insult was offered, excited in the South but a passing interest, and is now almost forgotten.

Apathy on our part, has been followed by increased and still increasing activity on the part of the enemies of our institutions.

The introduction at the close of the session of Congress before the last, of the *Wilmot Proviso*, and its passage then in the House of Representatives, by a vote of 85 to 80; the provision, at the last Session, against Slavery, in the bill, organizing a Government for Oregon; and the repudiation of the principles of the Missouri Compromise evinced by the rejection of Mr. [Armistead] BURT's amendment; the renewal of the Wilmot proposition by Mr. PRESTON KING, the vote on this; and the adoption finally of the Proviso, as shaped by Mr. HANNIBAL HAMLIN of Maine, in the House of Representatives, by a large majority, are facts, which leave no shadow of doubt as to the utter disregard of Southern rights in that body. The defeat of the obnoxious measure in the Senate, give us no security in the future. Senators, in their places, openly proclaimed their approval of the principle it contained, and placed their opposition, distinctly, on the ground, that, though right in itself, the "time and occasion" rendered its adoption inexpedient. The Legislatures of eleven States have, with singular unanimity, urged a renewal of these efforts. Delaware, Pennsylvania, New-Jersey, New-York, Rhode Island, Vermont, New-Hampshire, Massachusetts, Ohio, Michigan, and more recently Maine, have all, through their Legislatures, spoken still more explicitly than by their Representatives in Congress.

The tone of the Press, Whig and Democratic, Agrarian and Religious, in every non-slaveholding State, manifests a foregone conclusion, that the Abolitionists are to be conceded to, at least so far as to forbid the extension of slavery in the United States beyond its present boundaries.

While clouds thus gather, what preparation do we make for the impending storm? Are our people even aware of its approach?

How have the Abolitionists, so inconsiderable in numbers, and themselves without official station, effected so much? The answer is obvious. They have *adhered to principle.* They have made it paramount to party organization, and temporary policy, and they have thus held the *balance* of *power* between the two great parties. They have on this account been courted alternately, and together, by Whig and Democrat, until it has come about that no politician on either side, is considered as "*available,*" who cannot enlist in his behalf this necessary vote; and they are actually at this moment controlling the destinies of this great Confederacy? Shall we not profit by their example?

The Abolitionists have throughout the non-slaveholding States presses zealously, ably and efficiently enforcing their views, and presenting *their* paramount principle—and they have lately established an organ in the City of Washington.

We have, in the South, papers of both parties worthy of all confidence, but these are but little read elsewhere, and there is no one of them of very general circulation, even in the Southern States; and we have not one paper in a non-slaveholding State, and none in the City of Washington, which, in this emergency, has proved a fast and fearless friend; not one which habitually reflects *the public sentiment of the* SOUTH on this question. The Intelligencer blinks the question; the Union rebukes equally the spirit of Abolition, and the spirit which resists its aggressions; and with ALL, except the Abolitionists themselves, *party success*, with its triumph and its spoils, is the absorbing, if not the sole consideration.

The object of this communication is to obtain your aid, and active co-operation, in establishing, at WASHINGTON, a paper which shall represent Southern views on the subject of SLAVERY—Southern views of Southern Rights and Interests, growing out of, and connected with this institution.

We want a paper whose polar star shall be the sentiment, "that danger to our Institutions can only be averted by jealously watching our rights under the Constitution; by insisting upon the proportionate influence intended to be secured to us by the compromises of that compact; and, above all, by maintaining, at all times, and at all hazards, our equality full and complete with whatever other communities we hold connection." We wish a paper which we can *trust*, firm and fearless, which cannot be bribed, cajoled, flattered, or frightened, into furling, for an instant, the Banner of SOUTHERN EQUALITY.

To effect this, we must render the press free from party influences, and unite in its support others besides politicians. We would therefore desire to engage in the undertaking men in every way INDEPENDENT; and whose means and positions are such as free them from all temptations of profit or place.

If you concur in our views, please confer with us, as soon as practicable; and inform us what amount in money you are willing, yourself, to contribute to effect this object, and how much you think can be raised in your immediate neighborhood.

Enclosed you will find a subscription list with a heading, setting forth the principles on which it is proposed to establish the paper. If you approve of it, please obtain such signatures as you can and return the list by mail to this place.

Address your communications to ISAAC W. HAYNE, Esqr., No. 3 State-street, who has consented, until the proposed association is fully organized, to act as Secretary and Treasurer. Respectfully, your obedient servants, Daniel E. Huger, Nathaniel Heyward, Wade Hampton, R[obert] F.W. Allston, Jacob Bond I'On, Jno. P. Richardson, Joshua J. Ward, J. Harleston Read, William Pope, John S. Ashe, H[enry] W. Peronneau, Henry Bailey, Daniel Heyward, W[illiam] W. Harllee, W[illiam] F. DeSaussure, Henry Gourdin, James Gadsden, Charles T. Lowndes, John Rutledge, Robt. W. Barnwell, John S. Preston, Andrew Turnbull, Wm. Bull Pringle, Jno. L. Manning, M[oses] C. Mordecai, William F. Davie, Whitemarsh B. Seabrook, Geo. W. Dargan, W[illiam] H. Trapier, John R. Mathewes, P[eter] W. Fraser, Alex. Robertson, N[athaniel] R. Middleton, James H. Adams, Wm. A. Carson, Geo. A. Trenholm, James Rose.

ALS with En in ScCleA; PC with En in Boucher and Brooks, eds., *Correspondence*, pp. 398–402.

From S[AMUEL] C. DONALDSON

Baltimore, Sept. 28th 1847

Dear Sir, Herewith I send you a copy of Mr. J[ohn] L. Carey's pamphlet, & also a Review of the same in last week's [Baltimore] "Western Continent." The latter was written by my brother, Mr. John Donaldson, who undertook the task because no one else offered to do it—& as thinking it not well that such a *manifesto* should go un-answered, lest its arguments should be deemed unanswerable. I think you will at least commend the article as sound in constitutional doctrine, & as enforcing the right view respecting the position & in-terests of the South.

You will be amused at the manner in which your *Resolutions* are introduced by the Pamphleteer. Not being able to disprove your propositions, he has chosen the easier way of dismissing them with a sneer. But for the introduction of your name so prominently, I should not have thought it worth while to trouble you with the pamphlet or with this letter.

Our State Election will be held in nine days from this date. Not-withstanding the fatuity & feebleness of this Administration in bring-ing on the war & in the conduct of it—which has greatly injured the party—the Democrats are in good spirits, & talk of electing the Gov-ernor. We have greatly the advantage of the whigs in our candidate. Col. [Philip Francis] Thomas is an able man, & an adroit public speaker: while Mr. [William T.] Goldsborough is feeble in every respect. I am not so sanguine as many of our friends, & do not expect victory, although I think it probable we shall run our opponents close. *Three* of our five Congressional candidates are said to be [Zachary] Taylor men—a circumstance that may aid us not a little. If the party all over the State had followed Mr. [Thomas] Ritchie's dictation, we sh[oul]d not be able to carry *one* district.

The project for establishing a purely *Southern* paper at the farthest Northern point in the Slave States seems to me admirable, & indeed indispensable in the present condition of things. Yet I cannot but regret that Baltimore had ["not" *interlined*] been chosen as the location, instead of Washington. Here there is every advan-tage that belongs to Washington—centrality of situation, accessibility &c; besides others which the Capital does not possess. With a popu-lation of nearly 120,000, we have but five daily papers—an inade-quate supply for our wants. Even these are generally allowed to be very deficient compared with the well-conducted establishments in New York, Boston &c. The *commercial* print ("The *American*," of which *Carey* is Editor) advocates high-tariff principles! A press sup-porting true commercial doctrines, especially if unconnected with party, & well-edited, could not fail of succeeding. Its advertising alone would make it a profitable concern. This we know to be the case now with the "*American*." In Washington, the new paper w[oul]d have to encounter the opposition of "Houston's Reporter" as well as of the two party prints, for a very small advertising patronage. Thus thrown upon its subscriptions alone for support, it would require a vast subscription barely to keep it up—probably would even necessitate large *contributions* for that purpose merely, with scarcely a hope that the money advanced c[oul]d ever be refunded. Its existence under such circumstances would in the nature of things be exceedingly precarious. Excuse my troubling you with these remarks upon a subject in the decision of wh[ich] I am not aware that you have much interested yourself. My concern for the object must be my apology.

Next to yourself, I w[oul]d like best to see Gen. Taylor President. I congratulate you upon the prospect of having at the head of the government an honest Southern man, untrammeled by party pledges, & elected in defiance of caucus influence.

With best wishes for your health, & a long continuance of your public services to the Confederacy, I am, with high respect, Your obliged servant, S.C. Donaldson.

ALS in ScCleA. NOTE: Carey's pamphlet was *Slavery and the Wilmot Proviso; with Some Suggestions for a Compromise* (Baltimore: J.N. Lewis, 1847).

To [HENRY W. PERONNEAU, Charleston]

Fort Hill, Sept. 28, 1847

Dear Sir: I regret exceedingly that it will not possibly be in my power to meet the wishes of the executive committee, which has associated to resist aggressions upon the property and rights of the slaveholding States, by attending the meeting of the citizens of Charleston, to be held on the 13th October next, for consultation to organize an association throughout the southern States, and the adoption of such other measures as may be deemed necessary for their safety. My numerous engagements will fully engross every moment of leisure in the short interval between this and my departure for Washington.

I take the profoundest interest in the object of the meeting. I am under a deep and solemn conviction that the time has arrived when we must meet and put down the abolition movements at the North, or prepare for the most calamitous events that ever befell a people. It has been too long delayed. The movement ought to have been met from the first with a fixed determination to put them down, at all and every hazard. Our perfect equality and right in our property ought never to be permitted to be questioned or disturbed. The

579

constitution which guaranties them guaranties their quiet and undisturbed possession. Such has ever been my opinion, and if my counsel had been followed the evil would have been arrested at the start. But the past is past; and the question is, What shall we now do? It is a solemn question. My impression is deep, if we do not now meet and put down abolition effectually, the opportunity will be lost, never to return. It is not sufficient to defeat the Wilmot proviso. As insulting and bad as that is, it is by no means the worst and most insulting. I regard the late act of the legislature of Pennsylvania relative to fugitive slaves, and those of the other non-slaveholding States of similar character, a more palpable, if possible, violation of the constitution, and dangerous in its effects, than even the Wilmot proviso. I go further, and regard the establishment of societies and presses in the non-slaveholding States, with the express intention of questioning and disturbing our right in property over which the federal government has no control, and which is expressly guarantied to us by the constitutional compact, as a direct breach of faith and violation of the terms of the compact[.] To defeat the Wilmot proviso, and to leave these acts, and the spirit in which they originate, unresisted and in full operation, would, in my opinion, be a victory more fatal than a defeat—especially if its defeat should be by a mere compromise, proposed by ourselves, and carried mainly through Congress by our votes. Such a result would be the most disastrous of all. It would put us off our guard, without removing or even diverting the danger.

The next question is this: Shall we meet and put it down? Nothing would be more easy, if the slaveholding States should agree to forget their wretched party strifes, and to unite for the purpose. The mere union itself, in my opinion, would enable us to dictate terms, or, if not, would put into our hands ample means to compel the non-slaveholding States to respect our rights to the full, and to fulfil the stipulations of the constitution in our favor. The mere right of retaliation, if they refused, would be effectual. There are more stipulations in their favor, and of vastly greater importance, than in our favor. Union among ourselves would enable us to resort to retaliation, if, after due notice, they should refuse to respect those in our favor. But I have no idea, if we were once united in fixed resolve to put an end to these assaults on our rights, that it would be necessary to resort to higher measures. The power of resorting to them, and the certainty they would be resorted to if the assaults were not desisted from, and the measures adopted for the purpose of making them abandoned.

The great question, then is: How can we be best united? I regard the proposed association, which the meeting is to be convened to consult about, as a great and indispensable step. I hope it will be approved by the meeting, and that measures will be adopted to extend it throughout the entire slaveholding States. That, and the establishment of an able and trustworthy press at the seat of the federal government to watch over our interests and rights, and to warn against approaching dangers, with the determination to sink party considerations below what relates to our rights and honor, would do much—very much—to bring about the desired union. That done, I will underwrite the rest. With great respect I am yours, J.C. Calhoun.

PC in the Washington, D.C., *Daily Union*, May 8, 1851.

To A[NDREW] J. DONELSON,
   [Minister to Prussia]

Fort Hill, 29th Sept. 1847
My dear Sir, I take much pleasure in making you acquainted with my young friend, Edward Wyatt Geddings, who will deliver you this.

He is the son of Dr. Eli Geddings of Charleston of this State, who may be justly said to stand, as high in his profession, as any other member of the profession in the United States. His father sends him to Berlin to obtain his education in its University.

I take great interest in his success, as a native of the State, and the son of a highly esteemed friend, and recommend him to your kind attention. He [*sic*; You] will place myself, as well as his parents, under lasting obligation. With great respect Yours truly, J.C. Calhoun.

Transcript in DLC, Carnegie Institution of Washington Transcript Collection.

From CHA[RLE]S GOULD

New York [City,] September 29th 1847
My dear Sir, It is a long time since I have had the pleasure of either addressing or hearing from you. The leisure hours of one prominent as yourself must be few.

It has for years been my desire to cultivate your acquaintance: and had not constant engagements prevented my leaving home, I should have ventured to intrude upon your busy hours at Washington, or throw myself upon Southern hospitality at Fort Hill.

New York, at this season of the year has a delightful climate. The clear, cool, bracing air gives new life and new enjoyment to every hour. My residence is in one of the most pleasant parts of the city—No. 10 West 14th Street—And my house large enough to accommodate my family & friends.

Mrs. Gould and myself would be exceedingly gratified could you be induced, with any part of your family, to come to our city—to enjoy our autumn weather, and fruits—to see whatever may be of interest—to mingle, either as a public man whom men of all parties honor, or as an individual in so much of our society as may be agreeable—and, during your stay to make our house your home, and yourselves part of our family circle. Will you not be persuaded to accept the invitation? and inform us when to expect you.

I beg you distinctly to understand that no idea of influence, or politics has the slightest connection with the desire long entertained by Mrs. Gould and myself, and above expressed. I have no desire for any attainable office: nor for influence among the great men of our country—farther than that we love to be esteemed by pure and high-minded men of every station.

It seems to me that a visit here, quiet, and unannounced, would be found by you agreeable and interesting: and I know that to us it would afford more real pleasure than can well be expressed. Believe me, my dear Sir, Your friend and Servant, Chas. Gould.

ALS in ScCleA.

From H[ENRY] W. PERONNEAU

Charleston, Sep[tember] 29th 1847

Sir, Being induced to believe, from information just rec[eive]d, that a decided & energetic movement on the subject of the growing aggressions upon the rights of Slave holders may be expected from the Citizens of Louisiana as soon as the health of New Orleans will permit a safe access to that city, we are induced to believe it politic that the public meeting in Charleston [proposed for 10/13] should be postponed for the present. We think it far better that the impulse should appear to come from that quarter.

In the mean time every private effort will be made to increase the subscription to the proposed paper. Respectfully Y[ou]r Ob[edien]t serv[an]t, H.W. Peronneau, Ch[airman,] Ex[ecutive] comm[itt]ee.

ALS in ScCleA.

OCTOBER 1-31,
1847

⪓

Family and plantation occupied most of Calhoun's attention while at home at Fort Hill in the fall, but he could not help but respond to the many who wrote him about public matters. To the governor of South Carolina, who had asked for advice in regard to the upcoming session of the General Assembly, Calhoun wrote, among other things, on October 8: "I am decidedly of the opinion, that the time has come when we and the other States holding slaves should insist on a final settlement of the question, and a termination of its agitation. The longer it is delayed the worse it will be for us & the whole Union. If not arrested shortly, disunion, or our utter distruction [sic] will be the result."

His most considered and elaborated comment on the question was made in a letter of October 23 to Mobile where there was an active group seeking guidance. In that letter Calhoun outlined what he felt needed to be done to save both the South and the Union. This letter would be made public eight years later, when Calhoun was long gone from the scene but the issues he had addressed were still very much alive.

⪓

From EDWARD J. BLACK, [former Representative from Ga.]

Scriven County, *Jacksonboro Georgia* [*ca.* Oct. 1847]
My dear Sir—Your last letter, received a few days since, gave me great gratification. I appreciate it very highly as a testimonial of your approbation; than which nothing is more grateful to me. I send you herewith that No. of the [Augusta] Constitutionalist which contained Mr. [James R.] Gardner's erroneous report of the speech

I made in your behalf in the Dem[ocratic] Convention last June. I send it to you that you may be aware of the occasion which elicited my letter to him. He is mistaken, however, when he says that a defence of yourself is not the high road to favour with the Democracy of Georgia. You have many, & warm friends in this State, who look to you as the only safe and competent exponent of their principles.

Pray send me Gardner's paper back again, as it is the only copy I have, and I am compelled to keep it by me for future reference, if I should find it necessary to write to him again.

I am, & have been, wholly with you in the proposition you make of *retaliation*. It is The True Course, & the *only* one, because it will attack their pecuniary interests. That is the only point in which they are vulnerable. But how is it to be effected? I confess the attitude and evident inclinations of the Dem[ocratic] Party of this State, as I found them in Convention in June last, were any thing but satisfactory to me. I found the great mass of the Party inclining strongly to their old ways of temporizing with principles, and postponing necessary, and ultimately, inevitable issues. They were disposed to cover up, and plaister [*sic*] over things, and while they acknowledged facts they could not deny, they were not disposed to look them full in the face. This state of feeling & position is not altogether attributable to the masses of the party, but may be traced to a few leading men who are eminently selfish, and are manoevering for federal offices. I found great difficulty in restraining them from going the full length & breadth of hunkerism. It was not until after a spirited remonstrance that [Howell] Cobb and his friends, gave up their resolution of "Confidence in our bretheren of the No[r]thern Democracy." The Legislature which is about to convene, if Democratic, of which I am not yet aware, may be of dif[f]erent material from the Convention. We have succeeded in electing Mr. [Alexander R.] Lawton, native of S. Carolina, & a Democrat, from this Senatorial District. He professes to be your friend. I have conversed with him upon the subject of retaliating on "our No[r]thern bretheren" if within a given time, they refuse to do us Justice. He believes it is right, and promises to introduce a *prospective resolution* into the Senate upon the subject—that, if within a given time our rights are not respected & conceded, the ships & ["comerce" *canceled*] commerce of those States which have invaded, and are invading, our rights of property ought to be expelled from our Ports by an act of the Legislature. In this shape it would stand a better chance in the Geo[rgia] Legislature than if it were immediate & peremptory. If you think so, & can find time to draft a set a [*sic*] resolutions for me, with a suscinct preamble, setting forth the States that have assailed us, & the nature, manner, & time of the assault—I will keep the original strictly to myself, and send a Copy by Lawton to our friends at Milledgeville. If the health of myself and family will permit I hope to be at Milledgeville during the session for some days and will do all I can to organize and encourage our friends. The idea here is that [Senator Walter T.] Colquitt is anxious to be run for the V[ice-]Presidency on [Lewis] Cass'[s] ticket, and that Cobb is maneuvering for the Speakership. If it is true—neither of them will give us any aid. But I think if the Preamble is full, and strongly sets forth the attacks that have been made on us, the Resolutions, if *prospective*, will command a strong support. At all events it will be a good ral[l]ying point. If you send me any thing let me have it shortly—& I will keep the original strictly to myself. I would draw them up myself, but I know I cannot do it as you can. I would have written you before, but I have been ill since the spring with a troublesome cough; I think I am getting better. If I could conveniently, I would go for a time to some more genial climate—with the hope that travel, a change of scene, & occupation would permanently restore me; but my limited means, and the demands of a large family keep me at home. I hope however, with care to recover my usual health. I cannot close this letter without saying that every position you have assumed, and every vote you have given on the questions growing out of the Mexican war has met my entire approbation. Although it is not so reported by Mr. Gardner, I spoke of it in the Convention, and maintained it to the best of my poor ability. I was happy too to have, upon that occasion, an opportunity to speak of [Thomas H.] Benton precisely as I have long thought of him. There is no other prominent man in the Country for whom I have so utter an aversion as I have for that personage.

By the way Mr. *Sam[ue]l J. Ray* of the Macon Telegraph is warmly and truly your friend. He is altogether with us in principle and in feeling. His paper, far more than any other in Georgia, has on all occasions vindicated & maintained you. He was with me in the Convention and sustained me in every position I took. I doubt not but that he would be highly gratified to receive from you some mark of recognition—documents—perhaps a letter, if a proper occasion for one should present itself. I mention him because I suppose you may not know him personally, or receive his paper. If you could see the Telegraph you would find that he is neither afraid, nor unable, to defend you. Other than him, I know of no ["other" *canceled*] Editor in Geo[rgia] at present, who dares say his Soul is his own.

If I can serve you, in any way, personally or politically, pray let me know it, and at your leisure give me such information of the movements, intentions, and prospects of your friends as it may be proper to commit to a letter—So that, being advised, I may take no step to Thwart their plans.

I fear I tire you with this long letter.

With ardent hopes for your success Very Truly Your friend, *Edward J. Black.*

ALS in ScCleA; PEx in Boucher and Brooks, eds., *Correspondence*, pp. 380–382. NOTE: This undated letter has been ascribed a very approximate date from the content.

From Jos[eph] Graham

Buenos Ayres, 1st October 1847

Sir, I know you will excuse the liberty I take in writing to you, when I tell you, that my object is to correct a misrepresentation, refer[r]ing to yourself, which appears in the New York Herald of the 29th May last, in what *purports* to be a copy of a private letter, "from the U.S. Consul at Buenos Ayres" to a friend in New York, and signed with my initials. That letter is in relation to my trip to Paraguay and makes ["me" *interlined*] to say in its conclusion—"Tell me who is to be the next President. Mr. [James K.] Polk I suppose will not run again—and the great Southern statesman, *to whom I owe my appointment,* is in my humble opinion, too great a man to stand any chance." Nothing of this kind or any-thing like it, was ever said or written by me to any friend in New York or anywhere else.

There is no man in the United States of whose friendship, & regard I would be more proud, than yours, but the presumption of *claiming* them, never entered my head. I feel it the more necessary to make this statement because I saw before that some officious friend, in attempting to shield me from removal by President Polk, stated in his correspondence with the Herald, that I was appointed by you—your protegé—and that to remove me would be to *insult* ["your" *altered to* "you"], or something to this effect.

My appointment it is true was made whilst you were Secretary of State, but I know full well as I presume you do, that it was not of my seeking, and that it was given to me, by Mr. [John] Tyler in lieu of a very different kind of appointment, which he had promised, and which he could not, under the Circumstances, give me.

I have always felt obliged to you for concurring in my appointment, but I never claimed any right to be considered your especial friend or favourite, proud as I would be of such a distinction.

I did write a private & careless letter to an intimate friend & former schoolmate, in *Cincinnati*, giving some account of a trip to Paraguay, and in the letter published in New York, I had the mortification of seeing many things I said to him, made publick, in fact the greater part is copied from that letter. I have written to him to explain to you, if he can, how it happened, that I am made to claim your especial & particular regard. The paragraph I have quoted was added by somebody.

I was extremely annoyed by seeing any part of that private letter published. My great effort and study in Paraguay and on my trip, was to promote a friendly feeling towards our Government, & I flattered myself, that my efforts were not without effect, especially in Paraguay, where I encountered a very bitter feeling towards us, because we had not recognised their independence, and because they considered us the friends of Gov. [Juan Manuel] Rosas.

If my *private* letter as published should ever reach Paraguay, which I hope may not occur, it would destroy all the good I attempted to accomplish. I may be *boring* you about a matter which you have never seen or heard of, but I feel that justice to myself demands this explanation, both as it regards the impropriety of what I did say being published, as well as to deny that which some one has written over my name.

The extracts from my unguardedly written private letter, make me to appear very indiscreet, to say the least of them; I would therefore be glad if you would read at the State department, the report of Young Mr. [George L.] Brent & myself to Mr. [William A.] Harris, and my report to the Sec[retar]y of State, that you may see why ["we" *interlined*] went to Paraguay and what we did in the mission.

There have been so many appointments of Consul for this place, in the last two & a half years that, although you signed my commission, I doubt not, you will have to turn to the signature to this note, to learn who is filling the place now.

I had not been two weeks on my voyage here before the office was given to another, notwithstanding I had called on President Polk and Secretary [of State James] Buchanan, before leaving Washington & told them of my destination, that, if they intended to displace me, they might inform me of it before I sailed.

For the last two years this port has been blockaded. I have continued serving the Govt. to the best of my ability & paying my expences as I best could. Having accepted the appointment, I conceived it my duty to remain, till I was superceded, or till I obtained permission to leave. The frequent appointments have kept me in constant expectation of the arrival of my successor. You can judge whether my situation has been a pleasant or a profitable one.

I do not mention these facts to excite your sympathy, but simply as an additional evidence of the necessity, of reform in our Consular system.

Please give my respects to Mr. [Thomas] Corwin [Senator] of Ohio, and if you please you may shew him this letter. I am his *constituent* and as far as that goes, at least, have more right to *bore* him than yourself. Very Respectfully Your Obedient Servant, Jos. Graham.

ALS in ScCleA. NOTE: An AEU by Calhoun reads "Mr. Graham[,] Buenos Ayres."

From L[AURENCE] M. KEITT

Orangeburgh C[ourt] H[ouse, S.C.,] 1st Oct. 1847
Dear Sir, I trust the magnitude of the Subject upon which I address you, will excuse the liberty I take. The momentous controversy now pending between the North and South, and ["now" *canceled*] threatnening—unless speedily and pregnantly arrested—to terminate in a portentous catastrophe to the South, forces her to gird herself in every way to meet the nescessities of the Conflict. The Local Legislation of the North has been of such an aggressive character as to sap and impair the Institution of Slavery unless met by corresponding Legislation at the South of a vital and retributive nature. The confiscation of our property at the North, justifies us in adopting a similar policy. We are in the position of distinct and conflicting communities. Piracy justifies Letters of Reprisal, and forays, ["such" *canceled*] of such an insolent and rapacious kind as have been perpetrated upon us by the North should not pass unnoticed and unredressed. I propose then, at the next Session of the Legislature, to introduce a Bill, prohibiting under proper penalties, the Courts of this State, from extending any aid in the collection of debts, due to the Citizens of any State which has made it penal for similar tri-

bunals within her jurisdiction, to aid in the recapture and restoration of fugitive slaves. I should be very glad if you have any documents ["th" *canceled*] touching the Subject if you would communicate them to me. Any information or advice you have leisure to give me in this matter I shall be very glad to receive. I regret very much there are rumors here that in consequence of failing health you design resigning your seat in the U.S. Senate. The State will ["g" *canceled*] regard it as a great calamity and we hope it is a mistake. Very Respectfully your Ob[e]d[ien]t Serv[an]t, L.M. Keitt.

ALS in ScCleA; PC in Boucher and Brooks, eds., *Correspondence*, p. 402. NOTE: Keitt (1824–1864) was Representative from S.C. 1853–1860 and died of wounds received in Confederate service.

From S[TEPHEN] MOYLAN FOX

Columbia, October 3d 1847

Dear Sir, I received, this morning, a letter from you dated the 9th of last month[;] it has been lying in the Post Office at Gadsden since that time and my absence prevented me from receiving it. Since that date I wrote to you from York.

It has been a matter of much surprise to me, that while railways have been extending themselves all over the South, that the improvement of the rivers has been so much neglected. Their value is of so much more importance here, from the absence of obstruction during the winter months; and the facilities of improvement are much greater than the northern rivers from having no ice to contend with— the great sledge hammer of our northern rivers which in the end breaks up all barriers we can oppose to it.

The great mistake which is usually made in the early improvements of a river is that they are not of a sufficiently comprehensive character. Water is an element with which there is no compromise, it must be either servant or master.

I doubt much if it be the policy of the South to adopt the improvement for steam navigation; it will incur a much greater expenditure at first and the trade must be very considerable to support the after expenses. It is my impression that the canal boat system would be better as enabling the planter to transport his own crop with his own force at seasons of the year when they cannot be used for other purposes. The expense of transportation by this mode is very small.

I will give you an estimate; A boat carrying seventy five tons will cost $800 and will last 1000 days. It will require to transport it;

Two mules & drivers and if working 12 hours per day—3 men. The boat travels 2 miles per hour; one mule tows at a time while the other is stabled in the bow of the boat; they are changed every six hours. The cost, then, to transport 75 tons 24 miles would be—

for Boat	80 cents	
Two mules & track rope	1.90	"
2 drivers; boys @ $6 per month	40	"
3 Men @ $12 " "	1.20	"
Total	$4.30	

equivalent to ¼ of a cent per ton per mile; if the boat returns empty this will be increased to say ½ cent per ton per mile. Or it would cost to transport a bale of cotton 350 lbs. from the mouth of the Seneca river to Hamburg 92 miles 7 cents.

The charge by steamboat from Columbia to Charleston was 95 cts. for 180 miles equal to for 92 miles 48½ cents.

The charge by steamboat from Columbia to Charleston was 95 is 75 cents—equal to for 92 miles 53 cents.

The actual freight on coal transported on the Lehigh & Delaware Canals for the years 1843 & 42 was 6½ mills per ton per mile including all charges & transporters ["proffit" *altered to* "profit"].

This subject has led me into a much longer letter than I anticipated for which I must beg your indulgence.

It will give me great pleasure to visit you, which I will undoubtedly do, as soon as I have an interview with Col. [James] Gadsden, with whom I have some professional business. As I have a pretty large family and depend altogether upon my profession for support, I am obliged to let it take precedence of other considerations. I have already lost many months waiting in expectation of an appointment upon the Charlotte Rail road, led into the ["erroneous" *interlined*] belief that I should receive the place by representations made by many of the men who are now directors.

I will write so soon as I can fix upon any time that I can come to see you.

My direction is now Columbia and not Gadsden. With great respect I remain Your Ob[edien]t Serv[an]t, S. Moylan Fox.

ALS in ScCleA.

From G[EORGE] L. L. DAVIS

Baltimore, Oct. 4, 1847

My dear Sir: Mr. [John L.] Carey, who is the Editor of the [Baltimore] American, and the author of several books, upon the subject of Slavery, has recently published, in this city, an Essay entitled "Slavery, and the Wilmot Proviso, with some suggestions for a Compromise."

I do not know, whether you have seen this Essay; though I understand, a copy of it has been transmitted to you, through the Post. In the opinion of persons residing here, and capable of forming a judgement, it is marked with all the ability, for which Mr. Carey is distinguished. But I do not agree with him, in any of his leading propositions. And it is my intention, in the course of the present fall, to publish an Essay, in opposition to the views advanced by him.

My main proposition will involve a denial of the power of Congress to legislate, in any form, upon the subject of slavery. And, upon the assumption of the theory, which I hold to be true, that the Constitution is an emanation from the States, as distinct political communities, it will be easy to maintain this proposition. But, in a community holding a different theory of the Constitution, I deem it advisable to maintain it, upon other grounds. You will be good enough to suggest to me any points, which may occur to you, as falling within the scheme of my proposed argument. You will be good enough also to send me a copy of your late Address to the people of Charleston; together with a copy of your remarks, in the U.S. Senate, upon the same subject, during the late session.

Looking to you, as the expounder of the Constitution, and of the true doctrine, with regard to the rights, and obligations of the States, as well as with reference to all the relations, both social, constitutional, and philosophical, which belong to a right understanding of the question of Slavery—I am sure you will pardon me for the liberty, I take, in addressing you this Communication.

You will also oblige me, by sending me a copy of your *Letter to Mr.* [William R.] *King.* With assurances of the highest consideration and regard: I have the honour to be, My dear Sir, Y[ou]r Ob[edien]t Serv[an]t, G.L.L. Davis.

ALS in ScCleA. NOTE: An AEU by Calhoun reads "J.L.L. Davis."

From Ulysses Ely

New York [City], Oct. 5th 1847

Sir! I am indebted to the Hon. Mike Walsh ["for the enclosed" *canceled*] for the enclosed letter of introduction to yourself [dated 8/5/-1847], by which you will perceive that I contemplated going to Charleston to reside, since the date of that letter however, I have changed my plans, and instead of going to Charleston I shall leave here in 2 or 3 weeks for Vera Cruz, Mexico, which will be my future place of residence.

Tho' perfectly acquainted with the language, I shall be in Mexico comparitiv[ely] a stranger. If you will have the kindness to send to me here, letters to any friends you may have in that country you will confer a favour.

Tho' my business is of a mercantile character, still, it will afford me pleasure to know such countrymen of ours there, as you are acquainted with. As General [Juan N.] Almonte was in Washington about the time you were in the Cabinet, you will confer a favour, if you can with propriety, give me a letter to him, tho' I may not under the present exciting state of affairs there, have an opp[ortuni]ty of presenting it for some time to come. With sentiments of great respect permit me to subscribe myself D[ea]r Sir Very Respectfully Your Ob[edien]t S[er]v[an]t, Ulysses Ely.

ALS in ScCleA.

From H[enry] W. Conner

Charleston, Wednesday, Oct[obe]r 6, 1847

My dear Sir, I have just returned from the North & hasten to say a word or two in reference to the state of things there as well as here which may be not unacceptable to you.

At the North the disposition to escape from the Wilmot proviso is becoming general—among the politicians & people—not the abolitionists or Eastern folks for they are as rabid as ever.

The desire to escape from the Proviso originates in no conception, of its wrong—as to principle or its practice but because it is ascertained to be a false move—in fact a political blunder for it has given us the advantage of position—& all the argument on our side—but what exerts the most decided influence in effecting the change is the apprehension of a *union of the South.* Our papers & documents have been widely extended (I distributed 5000 of our Circulars with copies of the [Charleston] Mercury of the 11th August to every part of the U.S. myself) & their effects have been far beyond my expectations. The movement has been considered as evidence of a determination to unite & the power of such a union—based as it is upon a principle & a feeling—the strongest known to man—that of interest & self preservation, I am sorry to say is far better understood & appreciated by the people of the North than by ourselves. They see at once that if united we are the controuling power & must ever be so & it is the dread of it that has produced the change In the condition of things that must always exist at the North & even at the West where they combine as the free booters used to do to descend upon & pillage the coast of Mexico & as the plunder was secured fell to pieces & had again to be reorganized for every voyage. The South united upon a principle & kept united by the constant outward pressure from the abolitionist—they readily perceive must be the lever to regulate the whole machine. This we seem to understand but imperfectly. To prevent this union—& to make up a better issue for themselves is now ["I find" *canceled*] the motive for postponing the action on the Wilmot proviso until after the next presidential election. In a word—united—the South is discovered to be a stronger power than that of the abolitionists—hence the court paid to the South as you perceive by all the aspirants to the Presidency. Such are in part the results of my observations as to the condition of things at the North.

As to the South—I saw many[,] very many people in New York—Boston[,] Phila[delphia]—Baltimore & Washington from every slave holding State in the Union—& I found but one sentiment to prevail & that was opposition to the Wilmot proviso & all other similar aggressions—but while that was found to be the universal sentiment I readily perceived it varied greatly in degree. Some considered the danger imminent—others as remote. Some were for immediate & decisive action—some wanted to wait & others thought they would fight very hard when the abolitionist come to take the negroes out of the field—but none of them had any fixed or well defined plan of action but agreed that some organ[iz]ation ought to take place & appeared willing to come into [any] arrangement that might be proposed. Mississippians appeared to me to be the most decided & most aroused. So were many in Louisiana but they look at the danger as prospective. Alabama appeared to be pretty well up to the mark—Florida quite so. I saw fewer Virginians—but what I did so they were right—& the whigs as much so as the democrats.

There is to my mind two great difficulties we have to contend with all over the South. The first & greatest is our *own indolence & procrastination.* This to me is the ["South" *canceled*] source of extreme mortification & pain. The next is the difficulty of effecting organization or association of any kind in the Southern States in the abscence of quick & easy communication between different parts—in a word the want of rail Roads. Yet with proper efforts I feel great confidence in these difficulties being overcome, for the feeling & interest of the whole South is one & the same & with labour & address may be brought into action.

The cause here I regret to say has languis[he]d[?]. A new & larger committee was appointed soon after my abscence. They placed my name at its head but I was not there to perform its duties. A meeting had been called for the 15th but it was reconsidered & abandoned. I called the Committee together last night—(many were absent[ )]—& organized the ["best" *interlined*] measures ["we could" *interlined*] for proceeding right a head in collecting subscriptions & all that can be done shall be done & as speedily as possible.

My opinion *is decided* that we ought to have *a paper* in operation at the opening of next Congress—& I think it may be done. For instance let a paper be printed by contract under a different under any [*sic*] name we please & to be edited temporarily by an association of gentlemen about Washington—until we can bring in the main paper itself. [John] H[e]art now of the Mercury or some other proper person might be got to conduct it for a time—the paper to be distributed gratis all over the country if necessary. This is a hasty sketch of my idea. Pray write me your views & wishes immediately.

There is a report this moment rec[eive]d that President [James K.] Polk is dead. He was quite sick I know on Thursday last. The passengers this morning say there was a telegraphic despatch at Richmond as they came along to that effect. I hope it is not true & trust it may turn out that he is only very ill.

The ac[count]s from England are bad & many large failures announced as Reid[,] Irving &C. (Reid was late Governor of the Bank of England)[,] [A.A.] Gower & nephews (a director in Bank of England[ )], Sanderson & Bros.[?] & others. In great haste. Yours, H.W. Conner.

ALS in ScCleA; variant PEx in Boucher and Brooks, eds., *Correspondence*, pp. 402–404. NOTE: The 8/11/1847 issue of the Charleston *Mercury* mentioned in Conner's third paragraph contained a four-and-a-half column resumé of the Wilmot Proviso controversy, reprinting many relevant documents including the Proviso itself, Calhoun's resolutions of 2/19/1847, the pro-Wilmot resolutions of ten Northern State legislatures, and the anti-Wilmot proceedings of one legislature and two Democratic State conventions in the South.

To S[AMUEL] C. DONALDSON, [Baltimore]

Fort Hill, 6th Oct[obe]r 1847

Dear Sir, I am obliged to you for a copy of Mr. [John L.] Carey's phamplet [*sic*], although I had previously received one, & for the Review of it in the Western Continent. I have read the Review with pleasure. It conclusively refutes the position taken by Mr. Carey. Indeed, it is surprising, that a gentleman of his intelligence should entertain opinions in reference to the federal Constitution & Government, so utterly irreconcilable with recorded facts, & the plain and incontestestible [*sic*] intention of the instrument. The article does credit to your brother [John Donaldson].

I am glad to see so sound a paper as the Western Continent established in Baltimore. It is doing much good, and I hope it will be well supported. I am also glad to learn, that your prospect is so good in the State in reference to the approaching election. All that the Republican party requires to ensure its permanent success is, to adhere regidely [*sic*] to its principles & to place able & honest men in its lead. It is the attempt at dictation by Mr. [Thomas] Ritchie and the like, who in their eagerness to get & hold the patronage of Government forget principles & country, that has well near ruined the party & country.

Baltimore certainly possesses many advantages for the establishment of the paper to which you refer; but, I presume, those, who have the control, are induced to give a preference to the seat of Government, on the beleif [*sic*] that its circulation would be greater and more general throughout the Union, if established at the seat of Government. With great respect yours truly, J.C. Calhoun.

ALS in NcD, John C. Calhoun Papers.

To T[HOMAS] G. CLEMSON, [Brussels]

Fort Hill, 7th Oct[obe]r 1847

My dear Sir, The last Steamer brought me your's of the 30th Aug[us]t.

I agree with you, that you will not have time to return this fall without throwing your return into the winter months, which would not be advisable; but, I hope, you will not fail to return next year on many accounts. First in reference to your affairs. I do not think it would be advisable to act on your letter, and to make sales of your property [in Edgefield District] this year in conformity with your request. I do not see how it can well be done. It would require the exclusive attention of some one on the spot. With every possible disposition on my part to aid, in the execution of your wishes, I will not have the time. It is now less than two months to the time I must take my departure for Washington, nearly the whole of which will be engrossed with my own affairs, preparatory to my departure. Col. [Francis W.] Pickens, I would infer, is not disposed to act in the business. I got a letter from your overseer [—— Mobley] by the last mail, in which he says that he had applied to him to order up some necessary supplies, and that he replied, that he had nothing more to do with the place, & that he must apply to me. Under these circumstances, I have concluded, that nothing should be done for the present, and that the only alternative was to make another crop. I have written, accordingly, to Gen[era]l Gilliam [*sic*; James Gillam] to look out for a real good overseer for you, & if he can find one to make a conditional engagement with him. In the meane time, I shall look out here, although there is little prospect to get one in this quarter.

But if this course was not under circumstances absolutely necessary, I should think it the most advisable. There is at present a pressure in the money market, which would prevent the property from selling as well as it ought. You might possibly sell your place on the terms you propose; but that is doubtful, as the cotton crop is, from what your overseer writes, quite inferior, which would injuriously affect its sale. But there would be, I think, no prospect of selling your ["hands" *canceled and* "negroes" *interlined*] at $500 round, at this time. That at least is the result to which I have come after making inquiries as to the price of negroes.

But I hope, the fine crop in Europe will soon put the money market on a good footing there, which would ease it here, & give an upward tendency to prices; especially, if the wretched Mexican war should come to a close. Whether it will or not, we shall at least soon know. While it continues it must act as a great disturbing cause on the money market. I hope also, that a good overseer, if one can be had, would do much to put your place in good order, & raise its reputation by making a good crop. For these reasons, I have decided not to act on your request. Indeed, I think your presence is almost indispensible to a satisfactory & successful sale of your property. In addition, your visit would enable you, before your return, should you conclude to do so, to ascertain the result of the Presidential election, and what prospect you would have to retain your place. It would also afford the mutual pleasure of meeting again, & seeing each other with the childrenen [*sic*; John Calhoun Clemson and Floride Elizabeth Clemson]. It would, indeed, have been very agreeable at this time, had it been practicable, as Andrew [Pickens Calhoun] & his family, & Patrick [Calhoun] are now here. It would have brought the whole family once more together.

I do hope, when you do return, you will be be [*sic*] able to find some position, which would suit you; but, I think, that will be difficult; the crowd of partisans are so numerous & so pressing. Nothing certainly would suit you better than the mint at Philadelphia, but unless you can obtain the cooperation of [James] Buchanan, or [George M.] Dallas or [Robert J.] Walker you can have no hope of getting it. I stand in that relation with the powers that be, that I can do nothing. But there is one, & to my opinion great objection, to any position under the Government; the uncertain tenure by which all are held under the wretched spoils principle. I would prefer any private pursuit, even with far less emolument. I hope you may yet find some one, that will ["be agreeable to you" *interlined*]. Mr. [John Raven] Mathew[e]s spent a night with me recently. He is making a great efforts [*sic*] to get a rail road to Clark[e]sVille [Ga.]; & thinks the iron works would in that case, give good profit. Patrick, also, informs me, that the copper mines [*marginal note*: "The ore is the pyrites & ("black" *canceled*) brown oxid(e) of copper and the vein, large & rich."] to the South of lake Huron on the British side, are of a very different character from those on Lake Superior, & are promising remarkably well. They have been discovered recently. He, with two Englishmen & another American, have taken up 36 square miles on the direction[?] of the vein for a small sum. The iron business is every where doing well; so, I think, there is a fair prospect, that you will find some occupation suitable to your talents & acquirements, which will give good profit.

My crop of every discription is good. The only danger is a wet fall, & early hard frost, as the cotton is more backward than usual.

Should Mr. Biches [*sic*; Francois Henri Bickes] preperation of the seeds be successful & the price of preparing be moderate, this, I doubt not, can be made a good cotton country. Indeed, without it, but with a good system of manuring, I do not dispair of making it so. I am commencing in good earnest the trial. I am just finishing a fine cow House, as connected with it, of 106 feet long & 35 wide, with a rack running through the center to receive the food from the loft. I am also putting my stables in a good condition to make manure, and have adopted [George] Bommer's artificial system ["to" *canceled and "for" interlined*] making manure, which I think promises well. I hope to manure the the [*sic*] whole of my cotton crop this year, and to increase its product 150 or 200 pounds to the acre. I am also making arrangement with two of my neighbours, to purchase a lime quarry not more than 25 miles from me, to aid my manuring process. Should we succeed, in getting a rail road on this side of Saluda, of which there is reasonably good prospect, I have no fear of making this a profitable planting region.

We are all well & all join in love to you, Anna [Maria Calhoun Clemson] & the Children. Kiss them for their Grandfather. Your affectionate father, J.C. Calhoun.

ALS in ScCleA.

From W[ILLIAM] R. HILL

Canton Mississippi, Oct. 7, 1847

Dear Sir, Mr. Robert Anderson at present the principal of the Female Academy of this place being compelled by circumstances to resign his situation, has placed before the Board of Trustees the name of Mr. [J.F.] Gould of Pendleton Village as his successor, at the same time reccommending Mr. Gould in the highest terms, and referring among others to you for his character and qualifications as a teacher. I am directed by the trustees to address you on this Subject, and have to request a reply at your earliest convenience, in which you will please give your opinion of the general character of Mr. Gould, and of his fitness and capacity for the station he applies for.

Years have rolled by since I left my native State and probably my name has been forgotten by you. I cannot however forego the occasion to say, that as I was in So. Carolina among the earliest advocates of *State interposition*, I am still the admirer and political friend of its most distinguished champion. Very Respectfully, W.R. Hill.

ALS in ScCleA. NOTE: William Randolph Hill (died 1866) was, like Calhoun, a graduate of the Litchfield Law School. He had served in the S.C. General Assembly from York District 1828–1833, and had moved to Mississippi some time after 1837.

To Governor [D A V I D] J O H N S O N

Fort Hill, 8th Oct[obe]r 1847

My dear Sir, I would been happy to have an opportunity of conversing with you fully & freely on our affairs connected with the federal
relations of the State, before the meeting of our Legislature. But as
it is not probable I will have ["the opportunity" *interlined*], I have
taken the liberty of addressing you on the subject. There are, in my
opinion, two subjects, in that connection, claiming the most deliberate attention; the one is the propose[d] change in the mode of
appointing electors, & the other the abolition question. In reference
to the first, I have pretty fully expressed my opinion, in a letter addressed last year to the Representatives from this District, in the
Legislature, which I presume you have read. Reflection has confirmed ["me" *interlined*] more & more in the views it takes. I cannot
be mistaken in the effects, which I attribute to to [*sic*] a general
ticket, should that fraudulent mode of appointing electors be adopted
by the Legislature. It will assuredly destroy the balance of our
State Constitution, and introduce universal conflict & corruption, to
be followed by the debasement of the State & loss of influence in the
Union, as it is adopted. I will not enlarge on this point, as my views
are fully expressed in my letter in reference to it. But as there must
be some change, in consequence of the act of Congress, the question
which claims attention is; what ought to be done? My opinion is
decided, that the best course is to retain the present mode. It has
long been acted on, without inconvenience, or any serious objection.
The only one, indeed, made, entitled to be seriously considered is,
that it is not Constitutional; that the Legislature has the right of deciding, who shall appoint electors, but has not the right of appointing
them themselves. Fortunately, this cannot be considered an open
question, depending on the ingenuity of verbal construction, by
which doubts might possibly be raised. The language is borrowed
from the old Articles of Confederation, in reference to the appointment of members to the old Congress; and it is notorious, that almost
every State appointed its members, under its provision by its Legislature, as we do electors under the same language in our present Constitution. It was well known to its framers to have been the practice
under the Confederation; and, of course, in adopting the language,
they ["did" *canceled*] intended to leave it at the option of the Legislatures of the States to make the appointment of electors themselves,
or to designate some other mode by which it should be done. We
find, accordingly, most of the States at first appointed them by their

Legislature, & that the change to a general ticket, was not the result of any doubt, as to the constitutionality of the mode, but of party contests.

But the retention of the present mode would involve an earlier meeting of our Legislature every four years, and the question ["is" *interlined*] how that is to be effected? I have not examined our State Constitution, and am not prepared to say, whether it can be done by an act of the Legislature, or whether it would require an admendment of the Constitution. No one is better able to decide that question than yourself. If it can be done by the former, there would be no difficulty, as the act could be passed, and the Legislature convened the next year, in time, to appoint electors. But such would not be the case, if it must be done by the latter, as it takes two consequetive Legislatures to alter the Constitution. In that case, the question would arise can the Governor convene the Legislature to meet in time to appoint the electors, under the provision, "he may on extraordinary occasions convene the General assembly." Here again, no one is more competent to decide than yourself, as to the true meaning of the provision; but if I may be permitted to offer an opinion, I would say without hesitation, that the Governor would have the right to convene ["it" *interlined*] in the case in question. The case would be an extraordinary & not an ordinary one, whether the necessity should result, from the impossibility of effecting the change of the Constitution in time, or from the impossibility of the two Houses agreeing, as to what should be done. I would regard any emergency, be the cause ["at" *canceled and* "what" *interlined*] it may, or whether it the cause [*sic*] occurred before, or after the adjournment of the Legislature, which made the convening of the General Assembly necessary to the performance of any important duty, such as this, as an extraordinary occasion, within the meaning of the Constitution.

But, if the sense of the Legislature should be decidedly against retaining the power to appoint electors, I do hope, the district, instead of the General ticket system may be adopted. It is at least honest & fair; and it is better, the voice of the State should be divided, than that the people of the State should be cheated, debased & corrupted.

I come now to the other question, the most vital of all to us & the other slave holding States, & I may add the whole Union.

I am decidedly of the opinion, that the time has come when we and the other States holding slaves should insist on a final settlement of the question, and a termination of its agitation. The longer it is delayed the worse it will be for us & the whole Union. If not arrested shortly, disunion, or our utter distruction will be the result. I have looked on long and attentively, and have not expressed myself too strongly. The aggression on us and our institutions will, if not stopt by decisive measures, go on until there will be no alternative left, but to dis[s]olve all political connection, if indeed, sufficient strength should be left us to take so decided a step, or to be subject to calamities greater than ever befel a people. The evil already has made great progress, of which the Wilmot proviso is not the only proof. As bad & insulting as that is, it is by no means the worst of the aggressions. I regard the act of Pennsylvania, passed since the rising of Congress, which override & sets aside the Act of Congress & the express provisions of the Constitution relative to the delivering up of fugitive slaves as far worse & more dangerous. It is an open violation of law & Constitution, without pretex[t], or excuse, or even an attempt at justification. Other States have passed similar acts, intended to prevent the reclamation of our slaves. To make another compromise in reference to the Wilmot proviso, and leave these and the other aggressions on our rights & security unredressed, would be, in my opinion, the most unfortunate of results. It would lull ["us" *interlined*] asleep again, without diminishing the danger, while the non slave holding States will be growing daily more strong, & we more weak. But what can be done to prevent it, & put an end to these aggressions & the agitation of the question of slavery? We have ample ["power" *canceled and* "means" *interlined*], if we have the sperit & unanimity to use them, to bring them to our terms. What they are I will now briefly explain.

The federal Constitution, in addition to forming a Government and clothing it with power & subjecting it to certain restrictions & limitations, contain stipulations between the States, in the nature of treaty stipulations, requiring them to perform certain duties towards each other, and which are more sacred, than the most solemn treaty stipulations, because they constitute part of our Constitutional compact. Among these some are in our favour & others in favour of the non slave holding States. Among the former, & far the most prominent and important to us, is the provision to deliver up our fugitive slaves; a stipulation of the nature of an extradition treaty to give up fugitives from justice, which requires the active cooperation of the government ["to give them up" *canceled*] where they are found. This provision every non slave holding State has either evaded, or set aside, and even made it highly penal to enforce, like Pennsylvania. There is but one way by which ["a" *canceled*] States so faithless, can be made to observe the sacred stipulations, into which they entered, in ratifying the Constitution, and that is, by retaliation, by refusing to fulfill the stipulations in their favour, which we have the unquestionable right to do, if they, after due notice, shall presist [*sic*] in refusing to respect those in our favour. Fortunately, those in their favour are far more numerous & important to them, than those in ours, to us. Among them are those, which permits their ships & commerce to enter our ports freely. To retaliate by with[h]olding this priviledge ["would" *canceled*] from all sea going vessels of the non slave holding States, would soon bring them to their senses, if the South could be brought to act in concert. Even to give notice, that it would be done, unless the stipulations in our favour should be faithfully observed, of itself would be sufficient, if done by concert. If they yielded, then all would be effected, that we desired; &, if not, it would turn the whole commerce of the country in our favour.

I know the South is not yet prepared for ["so" *interlined*] decided a step; but what I would suggest for your consideration is, would it not be advisable in your message, to state the remedy & to hold a warning voice, if they presisted in their measures of aggression, & the non fulfilment of the stipulations of the Constitution in our favour, we shall be compelled on our part to retaliate by the non fulfilment of those in favour of the Northern States. It would, I think, do much good by attracting the attention of the country both South & North to the only effectual remedy for the evil, short of disunion.

I am sure you will appreciate the motive I have, in addressing you on these vital questions. With great respect yours truly, J.C. Calhoun.

ALS in ScU-SC, John C. Calhoun Papers.

From R[ICHARD] K. CRALLÉ

Elwah Cottage [Lynchburg, Va.], Oct. 10th 1847
My dear Sir: Your last letter reached me some weeks since on my return from Meadowgrove (our mountain home,) and I delayed answering it until after the meeting of our Rail Road Convention when I expected to meet and converse with many of our friends from various parts of the State. The attendance was not as large as was anticipated, yet quite respectable in number and talents. Since its adjournment I have had to visit the County of Hanover, whence I have just returned. Could I possibly go to Cincinnati and Louisville,

603

whither I am deputed by the Common Council of this place, in order to promote the interests of the Road, or could I *certainly* go to Richmond, as one of six Delegates for the same purpose, I would yet further delay this answer; as I might hope to collect something worth communicating. But my engagements will not allow me to accept of either appointment, and I sit down rather to acknowledge the receipt of yours, than to fill a page with any local intelligence of interest.

As far as my information extends public sentiment is very much at a *stand still*. Party feelings seem, in a great degree, extinguished, and the operations of the army in Mexico seem, alone, to excite interest. It is too early to say what may be the direction of the popular feelings and opinions, since the failure of the negotiation. Yet I can hardly doubt but that the result will tend much to strengthen the war feeling, and by indirection, the administration. I have heard men of soberness and influence who have heretofore censured the war, speak in different tones since the intelligence reached us of the course pursued by the Mexican authorities. The Resolutions of the late Massachusetts Convention, will find no echo, I think, amongst the Southern wing of the Party. I mean the Resolutions in regard to the war. The same remark will apply yet more forcibly to those which relate to the Wilmot proviso, and to Mr. [Daniel] Webster. I have not seen his speech, but Mr. [William M.] Blackford, the Editor of the [Lynchburg] Virginian tells me this morning that it is highly complimentary of you.

This movement, combined with the results of the late Syracuse Convention in N. York are, in my opinion, very significant. They show that the two great Parties are on the eve of disruption. The Whigs cannot be brought to rally on Mr. Webster, nor the Democrats on any one of the old dynasty. The death of Mr. [Silas] Wright leaves the most powerful division of the Party without a leader; for [Thomas H.] Benton is too obnoxious to public sentiment every where out of Missouri to entertain a reasonable hope even if the machinery of a national Convention can be repaired and put in operation. In this latter event, [Robert J.] Walker and [George M.] Dallas and [James] Buchanan will be too powerful for him. The two former will be, I suppose, the Chief Managers, for the latter is too timid ever to be a leader. He will have to succumb; but what will the Missourian do? He will never yield to Walker, for his hate is as deadly towards him as to you. Indeed, I should not be surprised to find him sustaining you even, if he can find no other means of crushing the two Secretaries and the Vice-President. Unless he can *rule* the Party he will certainly *ruin* it if he can.

I have not seen the proceedings of the Syracuse Convention; but hear from Blackford, (who by the way, has the highest respect and admiration for you,) that the [Martin] Van Buren division of the Party has been signally defeated, and that your views as respects the organization of a National Convention, have received the decided approval of a large majority of the body. This is far better than I expected; though I have lately received two letters from New York in which I am assured, not only that the Van Buren Party was dead in the State—not only that the movement in favour of [Zachary] Taylor was altogether superficial—but that your strength in the State was great and rapidly increasing. Through one of these letters I received a message from Mike Walsh, desiring that I should write a series of numbers for his Paper [the New York, N.Y., *Subterranean*] placing your name prominently before the Country as a Candidate— and that he would cooperate to the full extent of his ability. Always suspicious of the *honour* as well as *honesty* of of [*sic*] the School of New York, and being somewhat out of the current of politics, I excused myself for the present on the ground of pressing private engagements; intending to communicate with you on the subject. I would have yielded to his request, but coming from me, I could not assure myself that he might not, if he saw his interest in it, use the matter to your injury. I have thought maturely on the subject since, and do not regret my course. In a full conversation with Mr. [James A.] Seddon [former Representative from Va.], a few days ago, I am strengthened in the opinion that it is best to allow the aspirants, Benton, Walker, Dallas &C to *commence their war against each other*, before any movement is made by your friends. Seddon is very sanguine in his anticipation of great changes during the next Session of Congress, and I concur with him in opinion that some very *decisive* results may be confidently anticipated. Things cannot long remain as they are. Public sentiment is becoming more healthy every where, and I cannot but flatter myself with the hope that the dawn of a better day is not distant.

Mr. [Henry] Clay I did not see while in the mountains. He reached the White Sulphur the evening before I left it. His relative, and your warm friend ["(Gnl. [Odin Green] Clay)" *interlined*] went to see him—and had a long conversation with him. He tells me that he is much changed in his appearance and deportment—that he spoke with deep feeling of his domestic afflictions, and seemed to be, in truth, a new man at heart. Politics he eschewed—tho' I can hardly believe, that he considers himself as off the arena. His friends in this State have certainly not given him up—and the late movement of Mr. Webster's friends is received with no very cordial feelings.

The friends of Taylor are about to issue a tri-weekly Paper in this Town, which is likely to lead to a complete rupture of the Whig Party in this Section; and, (if, as I suppose will be the case, a similar movement be made in Richmond,) throughout the State. The Editors are popular, and possess ability. One of them, Joseph K. Irving, is of the old State Rights Party, and left us in 1838. The other is a decided and influential Whig. The Paper will be issued in a few weeks. I should not be surprised if it drive, Blackford the Editor of the Virginian, into the State Rights Party. He is—being a gentleman, strongly disposed that way.

I learn from the conversation of the members of the late Convention here, that no very general or deep feelings are entertained towards Taylor. His friends need the customary *imprimatur* of a *Party* nomination. So long accustomed to act under the dictation of ["a" *interlined*] Convention the masses seem to await its voice before they can be stimulated into action. He has, however, many warm friends, and will be, undoubtedly, strong enough to break up the Whig Party in this State. The other, the Democratic, will have a more powerful principle of cohesion—but I very much doubt, if they can ever recover ["the" *canceled*] from the blow they have received. As far as I can see into the future it seems to me inevitable that there must be a reorganization of Parties. You will, of course, call up your [slavery] Resolutions of the last Session, at an early period of the next. They will compel, if you can get a vote on them, the leaders to show their hands. Buchanan, and Dallas have already anticipated the fire of the battery, and have got [*ms. torn*] think, behind the breech, instead ["of in front" *canceled*] of before the muzzle. But their professions are looked upon with suspicious eyes. Will Polk or Van Buren be again on the arena? Benton has but little hope, except from the one or the other. He will not, I think, assail the administration, as your correspondent from N. York expects. His position, since the death of Wright, is weak indeed, should he adopt this course. With all his vanity, I doubt whether he has not too much sagacity to attempt to stand alone.

But these views are thrown out with but very imperfect means by which to form a correct opinion. Not having heard from you since Mr. Wright's death, and the letter of Buchanan and speech of Dallas, I wish, if you can readily command the leisure, you would answer this soon, and give me your views as to the probable influence of these events on the future. The time is drawing near when, if your friends are to act ["at" *interlined*] all, they should be comparing opinions with one another.

Mrs. [Elizabeth Morris] Cralle and Mary beg me to remember them most affectionately to yourself and Mrs. [Floride Colhoun] Calhoun, and to Miss [Martha] Cornelia [Calhoun] if she be with you, to whom also I ask to offer my heart-cherished remembrances. Very truly and affectionately yours, R.K. Cralle.

ALS in ScCleA. NOTE: In his speech at the Massachusetts Whig convention on 9/30/1847 Webster endorsed the Wilmot Proviso and denounced the Mexican War as unjustifiable, stating that Calhoun was correct on the latter point.

From J o s[eph] J. Singleton

Dahlonega [Ga.,] 10th Oct[obe]r 1847

My Dear Sir, Our Elections are over, and to the astonishment of the better disposed part of the Natives, I am permitted to remain at home, where my immediate interest constantly demands my presence. The Democracy of this Region came to a very recent conclusion that the principle of nominations by our pernissious system of caucusing should not be defeated, hence their nominee should succeed at every hazard of reputation, office salaries &c. &c. The man at the head of our Br[anch] Mint [James F. Cooper] was the principal mover of my defeat, which is assertained by an early declaration of his, "that I should be beat—if it cost him all he was worth." So much for Executive patronage. In the days of Mr. [Thomas] Jefferson's administration it would have been good cause of removal from office. Well may we dread such interferances, tolerated as they are at present. I had no other motive in offering than the belief that my success would better enable me to promote your views with regard to the interest of the whole Union, and especially that of its Southern portion. Although I am unapprized of your present aspirations, be them what they may, my feeble efforts are yet at your command. I will here mention one fact which perhaps you may not have been apprized of, which is, In our late convention for the nomination of a ["Democratic" *interlined*] Candidate for Governor—out of a Committee of 21 of the most intel[l]igent part of that Convention 16 were your particular friends, anxious for your nomination for the next President, and but for our Mr. [Howell]

Cobb, assisted by our Superintendent of the Br[anch] Mint at this place, it is certain you would have been their nominee. On the return of the lat[t]er Gentleman to this place, he remarked that he never was more alarmed than he was on discovering the complexion of that Committee, and that Cobb[']s speech saved Georgia &C. or words to the same purport. I merely mention this to inform you of the state of feelings which existed in that Convention.

As regards your mining interest, under my agency, the most I have to say is that there has been no increase of operations upon your Obar lot since my last letter to you. The am[oun]t of Toll in my hands from that lot is one hundred & twenty five dollars. I have not had any recent settlement with the Lessees of your other interest in the two lots upon Cane Creek, but will shortly have.

I shall of course be glad to see you in this country. Should it not be in your power to come, do let me hear from you. I have the hon[or] Sir of being yours very sincerely, Jos. J. Singleton.

ALS in ScU-SC, John C. Calhoun Papers.

From PERCY WALKER

Mobile, October 10th 1847

Dear Sir, For sometime past I have thought of addressing you upon a subject of vital moment to the South, and one that has been to you, full of painful interest, but my unwillingness to trespass upon your time and the fear of being considered obtrusive have thus far deterred me. I have, however determined to run the hazard, & trust to your kindness.

Unless I am wholly forgotten by you, I need not assure you of the weight your opinions have with me, and the almost reverential regard I have for your person and character. In common with all, who value Southern rights and institutions, I look to you as the only safe guide & counsellor amid the perils that threaten all we hold most dear—State power & dignity, & individual right.

Northern fanaticism has acquired fearful strength within the last year or two, and the manifestations it has made of its strength & energy within that period are well calculated to awaken alarm, or rather rouse us to action. The Mexican War has been used by our Northern & Eastern enemies as a means by which they hope to rob us of all constitutional guaranties—subvert institutions most, essential to our peace & prosperity—strip us of the insignia of sovereignty—pass a sentence of social degradation upon us, and effect our complete and total ruin. The "Wilmot Proviso" and it's substitute of "No Territory" are schemes designed solely for the purpose of destroying that equality of political power to which the Southern States are entitled under the Constitution. The danger they threaten to us is imminent, and forces upon us, the question, how is this danger to be met and overcome? The assault has been kept up, for years, but under the false assurances, that the great majority of the non-slaveholding people were not parties to it, we have remained idle and inactive, untill our enemies have become powerful enough to control the Legislatures of *Ten* Sovereign States, which in the most solemn forms of Law, have declared against us. In this emergency, I again ask, what are we to do? Submit to this emasculation of State power, and it's consequent social and political degradation! God forbid, that any Southern man should be sunk so low, as to utter the craven cry of Amen! Perish rather our whole Governmental fabric. In it's fall we may go down, but we will be saved the bitter reflection of having lost our dignity & self respect.

But it will not do, to content ourselves with empty declamation, and Resolves, that look fierce, upon paper. Our action should be calm, determined, and above all united. We must endeavour to make the Southern States think & feel and act alike, upon this subject. How is this to be done? And to you my dear sir, I apply for an answer. I am determined to do all in my power to bring Alabama, "up to the mark." I have been elected a Representative from Mobile in the Legislature, and am anxious to get that body to take a decided stand in support of Southern institutions. I have thought very seriously of introducing resolutions, as soon as the session opens, instructing our Senators & requesting our Representatives in Congress, to abandon their seats & return home to their constituents, in the event of the passage of the Wilmot Proviso, or any similar law.

What think you of this? Again—How would it do, formally to request the disaffected States to withdraw from the Union, if they cannot tolerate the Constitution? I think that we had better "*show fight*." We have lost much by silence & being tender-hearted towards our "northern *allies*." It is time to be in earnest about this matter.

Will you my dear Sir, favor me with your advice & counsel. I earnestly solicit them, and trust that my motives for doing so, will sufficiently apologize for this intrusion.

Trusting to hear from you, at length & without reserve, I remain, Your's truly, Percy Walker.

P.S. Just as I was about to seal my letter, our friend Mr. [Joseph W.] Lesesne paid me a visit, and kindly placed in my hands, your letters of the 4th & ["22" *canceled*] August & 5th ["& 22d" *interlined*] Sept[embe]r last. The freedom with which you have written to him & the desire you express to learn the views of your Mobile friends, have dissipated all the doubts I had entertained of the propriety of my addressing you.

My absence from the State for more than two months, has kept me unapprized of your correspondence with Lesesne and of the contemplated establishment of a Southern organ at Washington. I rejoice that a step so essential to the preservation of our rights and dignity is about to be taken. I cannot doubt of the success of the enterprise if proper efforts are made to impress it's importance upon the Southern mind. Mr. Lesesne informs me that owing to the absence of most of our friends, but little has been done, in obtaining subscriptions here, but we trust to being able to raise a respectable sum.

During the session of our Legislature, I will endeavour, to gain friends for the enterprise in that body, and with the aid of [William L.] Yancey, [James E.] Belser, [John A.] Elmore & others who will be at Montgomery, I hope that not a little may be effected. I hope therefore that you will contrive to send me some of the Circulars, & Headings for the subscriptions.

I am pleased to see that you disapprove of the idea broached some time since, & which to my surprise, was inclined to be favored by some of our friends here. I mean that of taking no territory, at the end of the war. As you justly remark, this would be only postponing the dangers with which we are threatened by the Wilmot Proviso, & would be a degrading surrender of our rights. The issue should not be avoided or *staved* off. It should be met boldly and at once. We should not only meet it, but *court* it. The first thing to be done, it seems to me, is to break off all alliance with either of the parties at the north. They are both untrue to us, and court our association, only to effect their own aggrandizement. They will use us, as they have already done, as aids in Presidential elections, while they are traitors upon all questions involving Southern interests. If we can once satisfy the South of this, and break the spell of *party*, we are safe. The chief agent in effecting this enlight[en]ment would be such a Press, as you describe to be located at Washington. Let us hope that this can be done.

In one of your letters to Lesesne, in reference to the actions to be had, you suggest the enactment of laws, by which commercial

relations with the hostile States could be suspended untill they repealed their obnoxious Statutes in relation to our slaves, and adopted
effective measures to put down Abolition within their borders. I
heartily concur in this, and as a member of our Legislature would
not hesitate to introduce and advocate such a law if I saw clearly
how it could be enforced without a conflict with the Revenue laws
of the Country. Would not a Statute excluding the vessels from
Pennsylvania for instance, lead to a controversy with the Revenue
officers?

I put this enquiry, for information, for I confess the idea is new
to me & I have had no time to reflect upon it. Am I troubling you
too much to ask your views at length upon this point & also as to the
frame-work of such a law as you indicate?

I am anxious that Alabama should meet the issues presented by
our enemies, with spirit and decision. She cannot, in my opinion
go too far—and the suggestion of a bold measure in her Legislature,
will I think do much towards breaking up the party associations by
which she has been so long blinded to her true interests.

I fear Sir, that I have already trespassed too long upon your time,
but the anxiety I feel upon the matters discussed must plead my
apology. With the highest regard I am, very truly, Your's, Percy
Walker.

ALS in ScCleA; PEx in Boucher and Brooks, eds., *Correspondence*, pp. 404–406.
NOTE: An AEU by Calhoun reads "["Mr. Lesesne" *canceled*] P. Walker."

From WILLIAM WHEELER

at home, Oct[obe]r 12, 1847
Colemans X rodes, Edgefield District, S.C.
dear Sir, I under stood you wanted a over seer on your plantation on
Saluda and if you hav[e] not engauged one I would like to engage
with you for the next year at a fare price and if you will write to me
when you will be down I will come and see you[.] You can direct
your letter to Colemans X rodes Edgefield District, S.C. As we are
not acqua[i]nted I will refer you to Col. [Francis W.] Pickens as I
suppose he is all the Gentlman in my acquaintens you are acquainted
with an[d] I Remain your[s] with due Respe[c]ts[.] I want you to
write me as ["you" *changed to* "soon" *and* "as you" *interlined*] re-
c[e]ive this note. Oct. 12th 1847. William Wheeler.

611

ALS in ScCleA. NOTE: This letter was addressed to Calhoun at "Pendletonvill." An AEU by Calhoun reads "W. Wheleer [*sic*,] applies to be overseer."

From [THOMAS G. CLEMSON]

Brussels, Oct. 14th 1847

My dear Sir, I have received your letter of the 16th Sept. 1847 [*sic*; 9/6] & with it the statement prepared by you & Andrew [Pickens Calhoun] of which you desire my approval. As I find ["in" *canceled*] it ["incomplete & I think it contains," *interlined*] several errors, it will be impossible for me to sign it & as I have already said it appears to me equally impossible to draw up such a document ["satisfactorily to both parties" *interlined*] without all the premises before one & this is the reason why I requested you to desire Mr. [John Ewing] Bonneau to draw up a statement from the papers in his hands which you would examine & sign & then send it to me for my approval & signature. This you could easily do by writing him that you desire him to prepare such an account to be ready on your passage through Charleston for Washington when you can examine it together. I write him by this steamer to prepare such an account for me & if you will write him immediately he will not have the same trouble twice.

In the meantime I will mention the principal errors of the account you send. As to the questions of interests &c it is not necessary to discuss them since the bases being changed they become null. To begin

The first item in the account sent (of which I suppose you kept a copy) states that at the date of our settlement (Oct. 1st 1843) the sum due me was $24,114 which was to have been paid by a due bill for $7,114 & 2 notes of hand. Here is the first & great error. There were ["3" *canceled and* "4" *interlined*] notes of hand ["one for $7,114 & three others each for $8,500" *interlined*] which makes the sum due at that date $32,614 instead of $24,114. This fact once substantiated which can ["instantly" *canceled*] be done by reference to the original notes in the hands of Mr. J.E. Bonneau (with whom I deposited them when I left Charleston) renders all further discussion of the memorandum you sent unnecessary & proves the absolute necessity of the statement I mention from Mr. Bonneau to bring into accord so wide a difference in our basis. I shall therefore only mention one other statement which seems to me to desire correction. In the Cr[edit] part of the memorandum you send is this item "By payment on the due bill ($7,193.18) per J.E. Bonneau's account rendered to J.C.C. over paid $79.15." This I think must be a mistake. I have Mr. Bonneau's accounts to June 3d 1844 which give as drawn on the account of A.P. & J.C. Calhoun for me $6,937.65 ["leaving a surplus" *canceled*] leaving a balance *in my favour* of $176.35 & if you will remember I stated to you before leaving the U.S. verbally & I think by letter that there was a balance due me on the bill of $7,114 which Mr. Bonneau refused to pay alleging at the same time that he had already advanced as much money as he could afford & that the advances he had made me were made on the promise of A.P.C.'s shipping his cotton to him (J.E.B.) ["in Charleston" *canceled*] which he had failed to do. But this like the first statement can ["be" *interlined*] easily arranged by John Bonneau's ["certified" *canceled*] accounts without which let me say for the third & last time the first step cannot be made in the proper settlement of our affairs. I therefore earnestly urge you not to delay in procuring such a statement & bringing this disagreeable business to a satisfactory close to all parties.

As I see no mention is made of the carriage & horses I sold you in the memorandum I suppose you prefer making that a separate account between ourselves & if it be convenient for you to pay me the amount ["due" *canceled*] for which I sold them to you $600—without interest I should be obliged to you.

Retained copy in ScCleA, Thomas Green Clemson Papers. NOTE: An EU reads, "Copy of letter to Mr. Calhoun[,] Oct. 14th 1847." This ms. is written in Anna Maria Calhoun Clemson's hand except for the final 2½ lines which were written by Thomas G. Clemson.

From R. B. LEWIS

Dahlonega Ga., Oct. 14th 1847
Dear Sir, By Mr. Pike I send you $108.86—the amount of tole re-[ceive]d as per statement sent you some weeks ago. Mr. [Edward J.C.] Milner[']s friend has not paid me the thirty pennyweights of gold yet. No one is operating on 817. Messrs. Reese & Bedford say they want to do so after awhile. So soon as Mr. Milner[']s friend pays me the thirty penny weights of Gold, I will hand it to your friend Dr. [Joseph J.] Singleton. Very respectfully yours, R.B. Lewis.

ALS in ScU-SC, John C. Calhoun Papers.

From F[RANCIS] LIEBER,
[South Carolina College]

Columbia S.C., 14th October 1847

My dear Sir, Your son [James Edward Calhoun] gave me yester-day the copy of your Life and Speeches in which you have inscribed your name. I thank you most sincerely for the work as well as for your enhancing the value of this copy by placing in it your distinguished name as a sign of good will toward me. That I shall peruse it and thus reperuse many of your eminent speeches with close attention I need not say. It will occupy me many an hour when you, probably, will be engaged in adding to this stock of patriotism and information, for, if I am not much mistaken, the next session of Congress will be one of the most spirited.

What will become of the war, if the Mexicans have but the least grain of wisdom left? I suppose thousands and millions are asking with me this anxious question? Our soldiers will always ["prove" *interlined*] the Buena Vista and Churubusco pluck—but our Cabinet? I am with the greatest regard My dear Sir Your obliged, F. Lieber.

ALS in ScCleA.

From P[ATRICK] C. CALDWELL and Others

Newberry C[ourt] H[ouse, S.C.,] Oct. 15th 1847

Sir, At a meeting of the Stockholders in "the Greenville and Columbia Rail Road Company" in Newberry District, it was resolved to furnish a Barbecue at this place, on Friday the 19th November next, to be given to the Stockholders in said Company.

The undersigned, a committee appointed for the purpose, invite you to be present with us on that occasion. Respectfully yours, P.C. Caldwell, T[homas] H. Pope, S[imeon] Fair, J[ohn] S. Carwile, L[ambert] J. Jones, D[rayton] Nance, Henry Summer, Committee.

LS in ScCleA. NOTE: An AEU by Calhoun reads "Invitation to attend a barbacure at Newberry Court House at[?] the meeting of the Greenville & Columbia railroad."

To "J.D." [*sic*; James M.] Legaré, [Aiken, S.C.], 10/21. Calhoun wrote regarding a recommendation of Legaré's proposed work by Col. Henry H. Cumming and others, saying that he assured Legaré of his interest in the success of the work and that he had answered a former note promptly enclosing a strong endorsement and subscriptions of himself and of his son. Abs of 2-page ALS offered for sale as item 19 in List 127 [1929] of Adeline Roberts of New York City.

From WADDY THOMPSON, [JR.]

Greenville [S.C.,] Oct. 22, 1847

My Dear Sir, Our present relations both personal & political as well as a general coincidence in our views as to this most disastrous war will I hope justify me in what I am about to say. I do not desire any expression of your own opinions although if you needed an assurance that such confidence would be safe I will take this occa[s]ion to say to you that when our relations were changed in 1838 I burned all your letters which I had preserved. This war must stop and it becomes your position & character and the noble stand which you took on the Oregon question to say so. I know your accurate habits of thought and investigation too well to doubt that you think as I do that we had no pretense of title to the country beyond the Nueces—and I agree with you that but for the march to the Rio Grande there would have been no war. That was the cause of the war and it is false to say that any thing else was. We were then in the wrong in commencement of the war & have no right to retain any thing acquired by it. If the premise is true the conclusion must be or we set at naught those principles of truth and justice without which society cannot be held together. The administration ought to have acceded to the Mexican offer of cession. The wilderness as a boundary beyond the Nueces was just as good for the next fifty years as the cession of the country—and considering the slave population of Texas, much better—for that would be a barrier to their escape into Mexico—so of California the cession proposed or a little more is all of California which is of any value. But if it were otherwise who doubts that when that is settled by our people that as much more as we needed would be at our command not by conquest of arms—but the surer conquest of superior race, power and civilization. As to the fact that we sh[oul]d have got nothing below 36 30—no sane man can suppose that a slave State will ever be formed there 3000[?] miles from any other such State and surrounded by free States on one side & non slave holding Mexico on all others. Would it be wise to annex all Mexico? All will answer no. The same reasons apply in proportionate degree to annexing any portion of it. We shall get no public domain, but a worthless, idle & insubordinate Catholic population. Mr. [Joel R.] Poinset[t] agrees with me in all these views & undoubtingly [*sic*] in the opinion that no slave State will ever exist beyond the Rio Grande.

The only outlet for our slaves is in that direction. If we allow events to take their course that outlet is open to us. For the Mexicans must recede before us as certainly as that such has been and will be the fate of our own Indians. But if we get the country and a cordon of free States is established there that outlet is dammed up.

The only view on the other side is that it will bring up at once the slavery issue—and it may be the sooner that comes the better. I am one of those who look for little help on that issue. Look at the profound sleep—the torpor on that subject throughout the entire South. Except here Except [*sic*] in the wild & essentially warlike West the people every where are [*one word or partial word canceled*] tired of this war and sick of carnage & slaughter and fruitless victories—and daily becoming more so. You will find as I long ago predicted that now that our Army is in the City of Mexico—our troubles are just commencing. Let inadequate force remain there six months and you will see the cost of maintaining and the derangement of our currency from the drain of specie.

I find that I have nearly filled my sheet and fear that even this much will tire you. I could fill a volume on the subject. My forebodings are I confess of the gloomiest kind. With great Respect y[ou]r ob[edien]t Ser[vant,] Waddy Thompson.

[P.S.] I find I have commenced writing on the wrong corner of the sheets.

ALS in ScCleA. NOTE: Both Thompson and Poinsett were former U.S. Ministers to Mexico.

To PERCY WALKER, *Mobile*

Fort Hill, Oct. 23, 1847

My Dear Sir: . . . . But to come to the subject of your letter. I am much gratified with its tone and views, and concur entirely in the opinion you express, that instead of shunning, we ought to court the issue with the North on the slavery question. I would even go one step further, and add that it is our duty—due to ourselves, to the Union, and our political institutions, to *force* the issue on the North.

We are now stronger relatively than we shall be hereafter, politically and morally. Unless we bring on the issue, delay to us will be dangerous indeed. It is the true policy of these enemies who seek our destruction. Its effects are and have been, and will be, to weaken us politically and morally, and to strengthen them. Such has been my opinion from the first. Had the South, or even my own State backed me, I would have forced the issue on the North in 1835, when the spirit of Abolition first developed itself to any considerable extent. It is a true maxim, to meet danger on the frontier, in politics as well as war. Thus thinking, I am of the impression, that if the South act as it ought, the Wilmot Proviso, instead of proving to be the means of successfully assailing us and our peculiar institution, may be made the occassion of successfully asserting our equality and rights, by enabling us to force the issue on the North. Something of the kind was indispensable to rouse and unite the South. On the contrary, if we should not meet it as we ought, I fear, greatly fear, the doom will be fixed. It would prove that we either have not the sense or spirit to defend ourselves and our institutions.

But in making up the issue, we must look far beyond the proviso. It is but one of the many acts of aggression, and in my opinion, by no means the most dangerous or degrading, though more striking and palpable.

I regard the recent act of Pennsylvania, and laws of that description, passed by other States, intended to prevent or embarrass the reclamation of fugitive slaves, or to liberate our domestics when travelling with them in non-slaveholding States, as unconstitutional. Insulting as it is, it is even more dangerous. I go further, and hold that if we have a right to hold our slaves, we have the right to hold them in peace and quiet, and that the toleration, in the non-slaveholding States of the establishment of Societies and presses, and the delivery of lectures, with the express intention of calling in question our right to our slaves, and of seducing and abducting them from the service of their masters, and finally overthrowing the institution itself, as not only a violation of international laws, but also the Federal compact. I hold also, that we cannot acquiesce in such wrongs, without the certain destruction of the relation of master and slave, and without the ruin of the South.

With this impression, I would regard any compromise, or adjustment of the proviso, or even its defeat, without meeting the danger in its whole length and breadth, as very unfortunate for us. It would lull us to sleep again, without removing the danger, or materially diminishing it.

This brings up the question, how can it be so met, without resorting to the dissolution of the Union. I say without its dissolution, for in my opinion a high and sacred regard for the Constitution, as well as the dictates of wisdom, make it our duty, in this case as well as all others, not to resort to or even to look to that extreme remedy, until all others have failed, and then only in defence of our liberty and safety.

There is, in my opinion, but one way in which it can be so met; and that is the one related in my letter to Mr. —— [Joseph W. Lesesne] and to which you allude in yours to me, viz: by retaliation.

Why I think so, I shall now proceed to explain.

The Constitution of the United States is a complex instrument, consisting of many and different parts. It created a government, and designated the functionaries for carrying it into effect. It granted powers and imposed limitations to prevent abuse and oppression; and finally it prohibited the States from doing certain acts, and made it their duty to perform certain stipulations towards each other, into which they entered in ratifying the constitution, and thereby solemnly pledged themselves to perform faithfully. Of these stipulations, some are favorable to the slave States, and others to the non-slaveholding States, or more briefly, some to the Southern, and the others to the Northern.

Of the former, the most striking is that which stipulates the delivery up by the other of fugitive slaves, and which clearly implies the principle that the non-slaveholding States should adopt no measure to seduce our slaves or to abstract them from their masters, or to weaken or destroy our right in them. The legislation of those States for the last twenty years, has either directly or indirectly, by act or omission, been in violation of this leading stipulation in our favor; and the recent act of Pennsylvania has put it aside openly, without pretext or attempt at justification; trampling at the same time, under foot the act of Congress to carry it into effect.

To understand the full force and effect of the stipulation in our favor, it must be borne in mind that it has the character of what is called extradition treaties, that is, treaties to deliver up fugitives from justice, which in good faith requires, not only that the party where the fugitive is found shall place no impediment in the way of his reclamation, or even to stand neutral, but that he shall take active measures to seize and deliver him up.

Against this flagrant breach of faith, more sacred than any treaty stipulation, by this act of Pennsylvania and similar acts of other States, the constitution affords no effective remedy. The appeal to the Federal Court is a mere farce. The expense, the delay, and the means it affords for the escape of the slave, make it no remedy at all, while our principles and safety will not permit us to resort, for remedy, to the principles of the Force Bill, passed to compel the obedience of this State.

There is and can be but one remedy short of disunion, and that is to retaliate on our part by refusing to fulfil the stipulations in their favor, or such as we may select, as the most efficient. Among these, the right of their ships and commerce to enter and depart from our port is the most effectual and can be enforced.

That the refusal on their part would justify us to refuse to fulfil on our part, those in their favor, is too clear to admit of argument. That it would be effectual in compelling them to fulfil those in our favor can hardly be doubted, when the immense profit they make by trade and navigation out of us is regarded, and also the advantages we would derive from the direct trade it would establish between the rest of the world and our ports. My impression is, that it should be restricted to *sea-going* vessels, which would leave open the trade of the valley of the Mississippi to New Orleans by river, and to the other Southern cities by Railroad; and tend thereby to detach the North-western from the North-eastern States.

Nor is there any impediment from the power of Congress to regulate commerce among the States. The right of the States to adopt laws to protect their health, their internal policy and peace and safety, is paramount to the right of Congress to regulate commerce. You will find the subject fully argued in my report [of 2/4/1836] on the subject of circulating incendiary publications through mail, and the speech [of 4/12/1836] made on the occasion. Several of the States have acted on it in reference to the subject of Abolition, and especially this State and Virginia.

There is but one practical difficulty in the way: and that is, to give it force, it will require the cooperation of all the Slaveholding States lying on the Atlantic [and] Gulf. Without that, it would be ineffective. To get that is the great point, and for that purpose a convention of the Southern States is indispensable.

Let that be called, and let it adopt measures to bring about the co-operation, and I would underwrite the rest. The non-slaveholding States would be compelled to observe the stipulations of the constitution in our favor, or abandon their trade with us, or to take measures to co-erce us, which would throw on them the responsibility of dissolving the Union. Which they would choose, I do not think doubtful. Their unbounded avarice would in the end control them.

Let a convention be called—let it recommend to the slaveholding States to take the course advised, giving say one year's notice before the acts of the several States should go into effect, and the issue would fairly be made up and our safety and triumph certain.

I have written fully, freely, hurriedly and in the midst of the pressure of my engagements; but I hope with sufficient clearness to be fully understood. I aimed at nothing higher. I shall be happy to hear from you during the session of your Legislature and all times when you find it convenient to write. Yours truly, J.C. CALHOUN.

PC in the Montgomery, Ala., *Southern Times*, April 14, 1855, p. 4; PC in the Richmond, Va., *Enquirer*, May 1, 1855, p. 4; PC in the Charleston, S.C., *Mercury*, June 13, 1855; PC in the Washington, D.C., *Daily National Intelligencer*, June 22, 1855, and August 9, 1855; PC in the Sumterville, S.C., *Watchman*, July 11, 1855; PEx's in Thomas H. Benton, *Thirty Years' View*, 2:698–700; PEx's in John W. DuBose, *The Life and Times of William L. Yancey*, pp. 200–201. NOTE: Charles M. Wiltse, who had available only undated PEx's addressed to "an Alabama legislator," was in error in naming Joseph W. Lesesne as the recipient of this letter. (Wiltse, *John C. Calhoun*, 3:532, note 22.)

To T[HOMAS] G. CLEMSON, [Brussels]

Fort Hill, 24th Oct[obe]r 1847

My dear Sir, The last Steamer but one, brought me your letter of the 12th Sep[tembe]r, but too late to acknowledge it in the regular course. Indeed, I had anticipated by my last or preceeding letter, the necessity of an immediate answer, by giving my views of the course, which I think it advisable for you to take in reference to your property in Edgefield. I hope you have received it.

I agree, you ought to dispose of it, and that it is too late this fall for you to come out and attend to it, for the reasons which you have assigned in your last; but I am of the opinion, that you ought to get leave to return early next fall in order to be present to dispose of it yourself. To dispose of it to the best advantage, & in a manner to be satisfactory, would require the exclusive attention for months of him, who might undertake it. I would attend to it with pleasure; but have not the time. Nor do I suppose that Col. [Francis W.] Pickens has; nor do I know of any one who has, who could be properly trusted with it. Under this impression, I saw no other alternative, but the one I adopted; ["but *canceled*] to continue operations on the place for another year under a good overseer, if one can be had, and wrote you accordingly to that effect. Such continues to be my opinion. I am sure, that any other course, under circumstances, would involve a greater sacrafice, than the one I adopted. I have, however, taken the precaution, not to conclude definitively the employment of an overseer until I have time to have an answer to my former letter; so that, if you, should take different views, you are left free to act.

To be a little more particular, as to the course, I think, you ought to take. You ought to make your arrangement to be here the latter part of the summer, or early in the fall, & to bring your family with you. By that time it may be fairly anticipated, how the presidential election will terminate, & whether it would be probably favourable to your continuance in your present post, or not. In the meane time, you could be engaged in making arrangement to dispose of your property, conditionally, if you thought proper, ["to" *canceled and* "until" *interlined*] the fate of the election should be known, and to look out for other employment, in case it should be unfavourable to your continuance. Your presence here might have a salutary effect in that respect. Should it be unfavourable, you could return ["alone" *interlined*] and at the proper time ask ["leave" *canceled*] to be recalled, and leave your family with us; but, if not, you could return with your family in the spring. In either case your pay will be going on, and in addition to other recommendations, it would be the most economical, as your pay would exceed the expense of going & returning. I would also suggest, as you might not return, that you should pass through England & take shipping at Liverpool, so as to give Anna [Maria Calhoun Clemson] & your self an opportunity of seeing it before you left Europe. I feel satisfied that ["it" *canceled and* "this" *interlined*] would be your best course, all things considered.

You will have seen by the papers, that the City of Mexico is in possession of our army, & that the prospect of conquering peace is as remote as ever, as I suggested it might be in that case. Thus far, not an anticipation of the administration has been realised; and yet, if we may judge from indications, they are resolved to go though[t]-less[ly] forward, when it is clear, whether defeated or successful, the result will be unfortunate to the country. If we should succeed in conquering the whole what shall we do with it, or what can do with it without ruin to our institutions? If we fail where shall we be?

We are all well. My crop of corn, cotton, potatoes, & pease is yielding well. My low grounds, I think, will ["yield" *interlined*] 40 bushels round; and my cotton 700 in the seed and that on the poorest field I have.

All join in love to you, Anna & the children [John Calhoun Clemson and Floride Elizabeth Clemson]. Kiss them for their Grandfather. Your affectionate father, J.C. Calhoun.

ALS in ScCleA; PEx in Jameson, ed., *Correspondence*, p. 737.

From [Governor] DAVID JOHNSON

Lime Stone Springs [S.C.,] 26th Oct[obe]r 1847
My D[ea]r Sir, I am much indebted to you for your favour of the 8th inst. and regret that my absence on a visit to my plantation in Union from whence I returned only two days ago has prevented my sooner ["replying to it" *interlined*] and I equally regret that I have not had it in my power to confer with you personally on the only important matters to which it refers—["and" *canceled*] but for physical disability the result of an accident I should have done myself the honor of making you and my friend Judge [Langdon] Cheves a visit in the course of the summer.

Both of the subjects embraced in your favour have been matters of anxious consideration with me and I shall feel it my duty to present them both to the consideration of the Legislature at its next sessions. In regard to the first, the election of Electors of President & Vice President, It will be for the Legislature to determine whether they will by Law provide for their election by the people and if so whether by general ticket or District. Now you know from my general habits of though[t] that neither of these would meet with my approbation. Pure democracy is beautiful; in theory but observation & reflection has taught me and the whole ["word" *canceled*] world that under this guise is hidden the most despicable tyranny and I have some times thought that some thing like inspiration entered into the organization particularly of our State constitution in which the elements of the various forms of government are so happily blended as to have secured us for the most part perfect harmony and order, and I should deprecate any changes which might endanger ["it" *interlined*]. If we are obliged to submit to the one or the other of these alternatives I should greatly prefer the District System as in some sort preserving that balance of power so necessary to the healthful operation of the system. I remember to have read your address to the delegation of Pendleton on this subject when it was published but it has slipped through my hands and I can[']t obtain it here. I shall therefore be much obliged if you have a copy that you would send it to me as early as may be convenient as I know I shall derive instruction from it. If either alternative is adopted the matter will be at rest. If not the question will arise, in what manner is the election to be provided for. On this question I have some thing like a sett[l]ed opinion. I take it for granted that the Legislature will not pass it over wholly unnoticed and will have to decide whether they will adjourn to the time appointed for the election or provide for the assembling of the newly elected members. You will recollect that under the administration of Gen[era]l [James] Hamilton [Jr.] the newly elected members were convened by proclamation before the time appointed by the Constitution to pass the Act of Nullification. Before he took this step he asked the advice of the Judges of the Court of Appeals as to its constitutionality. The Court then consisted of Judges [William] Harper, ONealle [*sic*; John Belton O'Neall] and myself and without concert we all came to the conclusion and so advised the Governor that ["that" *canceled*] the new members constituted the Legislature— & then gave it full consideration and believe that the conclusion met with the approbation of the profession of the law and the community. The question would then arise whether the out going Legislature could provide for the assemb[l]ing of the incoming. I think not authoritatively. One Legislature can[']t provide for the meeting or adjournment of another or prescribe rules for its government, and in that event I should regard it as one of those "extraordinary occasions" which would authorise the Executive to convene them and regarding it as a duty I should not hesitate about it. But I can[']t suppose that the Legislature will adjourn without some action on it. They will certainly not suffer the State to go unrepresented on an occasion of so much importance or will determine to reassemble themselves or advise the Executive to convene the incoming members.

The other subject, abolition to which you refer is one of infinitely more importance. That too I shall feel it my duty however reluctantly, to bring to the view of the Legislature. The Virginia resolutions on the subject of the Wilmot proviso and of several of the non slave holding States in support of the proviso have been forwarded to me with directions to submit them to the Legislature and however willing I may be to avoid the excitement which it may create I feel that the occasion and the subject leave me no right to exercise any discretion. I agree with you that in itself the Proviso is unimportant compared with the other movements of the Abolitionist. The flagrant violation of the Constitution of the U. States in the act of the

Legislature of Pen[n]sylvania punishing all who may aid the owner in the reclamation of a fugitive slave and the general habit of the citizens of the non slave holding States to oppose by force even without the sanction of [us"law" *canceled*] local Law all attemp[t]s to reclaim our runaway slaves are evils which stricke at the very root of our peculiar institutions, and must if it cannot be corrected break up the very foundations of our once happy and prosperous Union. The case contemplated by the Wilmot proviso may never arise. If unhappily it should, for I should deprecate the acquisi[ti]on of territ[or]y from Mexico by conquest, the new States will probably come to our aid—but when the abolitionists invite our slaves to run away from us an[d] acting upon it[?] the north[?] promise them security and protection—It is time we should inquire whether the guaranties of the Constitution is sufficient to protect us and if not to vindicate our rights in the best way we can. An occasion has recently presented itself to show how far Pen[n]sylvania is prepared to go. In the course of the last summer a man by the name of Eaton a native of that State but for some time an inhabitant of Columbia stole two slaves there and carried them to Phyladelphia. At the last Court held in Columbia the Grand Jury found true bills against him for these offences and I have sent in a formal demand on the Governor of that State for his arrest and delivery and have authorised the agent to offer a reward of two thousand dollars for his delivery here in the hope of bribing him to do right. Sufficient time has not yet elapsed to know the result and it remains to be seen whether the Governor will have courage enough to oppose himself [*one word canceled*] to their legislative enactments. I hope he has and have indirectly some authority to suppose that he will—but if it proves otherwise that of itself would require that I should bring it before the Legislature. But I have dwelt already too much on this incident. The evil practicably exist[s] and the question is as to the remedy and the time of action.

I had thought of this matter before without being able to form any satisfactory judgment and I am exceedingly obliged by your suggestions on the subject. Our only means of retaliating is through their Commerce and knowing that this was by the Constitution of the United States under the protection of the General Government, my habitual respect for the law and the Constitution induced me to hesitate about the adoption of this remedy, but more reflection has satisfied me that it is admissible on the soundest principles of morality and justice. The precise case is provided for by the Constitution and if disregarding this a sister State invades our rights and the arm of the Federal Government is unable to protect us we are thrown back upon our natural rights and must depend on ourselves. This ["may bring down on us" *canceled*] may well be said to be in violation of the Constitution of the U. States and an usurpation of the powers of the Federal Government. Be it so. I hold it fair to defend ourselves with the same weapon that our adversary uses to assail ["us" *interlined*] and if the Federal Government employs force to put us right let her begin at the root of the evil and do ["us right" *canceled*] justice.

I agree with you that there ought to be concert between the States similarly situated with us both as to the time and remedy. How is this to be brought about? But two modes have suggested themselves to my mind. Let some one of the States lead off in a manner sufficiently strong to indicate a course and a decided purpose to pursue it without acting definitively untill the purpose of the others are sufficiently developed. The other is a conference of the members of congress of those States recommending some decisive course & simul-[t]aneous action by the several States—and I agree with you that definitive action ought ["to" *canceled*] not to be delayed for the obvious reason that the enemy is daily acquiring strength and every accession to it diminishes our own. How far it would be prudent in me to press this matter on the Legislature at the present time is a question about which I must beg your opinion and advise. I would not willingly do any think [*sic*] calculated to widen the breach between the States but I have neither motive or inclination to shrink from any duty demanded by the occasion.

There is another subject about which I very much desire your advise. This war with Mexico—the ostensible object of its commencement was the protection of what was assumed and I suppose rightfully our territory against the intrusion of Mexico, that was attained in the battles of Palo Alto and Resica de la Palma & the reduction of Matamoras—To "conquer a peace" the avowed object of carrying it into Mexico. Let the Seminole war tell how visionary such a project was. Having failed in that the indications of the public Journals point to the conquest and permanent occupation of the Country. If that be the object of the Government I protest against it from the bottom of my heart as unwise and unjust. I have already troubled you too much with these undigested lucubrations to attempt any argument in support of this conclusion but I will go further. The acquisition of the territory on the rout[e] of a communication between our North Western territory and the Gulph of California and an indemnity for the expenses of the war is ["to" *canceled*] made the pretense for seizing on this territory by force. I can not reconcile this course to my notions of moral right. To make offensive war upon an enemy ["for the sake of" *canceled*] as a justification for seizing on his territory as an indemnity for the expenses admits of no pal[l]iation. Supposing the war rightfully waged, is not the wrong of the enemy already sufficiently ["avenged" *canceled and* "punished" *interlined*] & the honor of the U.S. sustained in what has already been done and may we not ["fall" *canceled*] without dishonor fall back upon our own rights and depend on the occupation ["of the" *canceled*] and blockade of the enemys sea ports as the means of bringing her to a sense of justice.

I am disposed to look ["on" *canceled*] with indulgence on the commencement of the war. It was probably the necessary consequence of the acquisition of Texas. Mexico ["sems" *canceled*] seems to have acquiesced in ["th"(?) *canceled*] our right to the Nueces but disputed our claim to the Country lying between that and the Rio Grande and having driven her out of that—might it not have been reasonably concluded that she never would again have intruded upon us. In her fe[e]bleness she had yielded much more to Texas standing alone and it is unreasonable to suppose that she would have again invaded the territory of the U.S. What under these circumstances ought to be done? Of necessity I must allude to the subject in my message to the Legislature and I beg you will advise me how far I ought to go, for I feel, that it is one of much delicacy & what in your judgment ought to be the action of the Legislature. May I ask your early attention to it in the spirit of kindness which has characterised our intercourse through a long acquaintance ["of" *canceled*] certainly on my part and as far as I know on yours. I am with sincere regard and esteem very respectfully your Ob[e]d[ien]t Serv[an]t, David Johnson.

ALS in ScCleA; variant contemporary copy in ScU-SC, John C. Calhoun Papers; variant PEx in Boucher and Brooks, eds., *Correspondence*, pp. 406–408. NOTE: The Virginia resolutions against the Wilmot Proviso are summarized above in the note to Calhoun's speech of 3/9/1847.

From J[AMES] M. LEGARÉ

Aiken, S.C., Oct. 26th [1847]

Dear Sir, Within a few moments I have received and read your *second* letter, and cannot postpone the gratification of thanking you for that so kindly intended. In good truth however, your *first* letter [of 9/18] and recommendation having been duly received, I could not conjecture whence the recommendation of Col. [Henry H.] Cumming and the rest could have been derived, until I called to mind that in the same envelope I had enclosed a copy of that written and signed by those friends with a view of acquainting you with my desire and design, with the least expense of words: This slip of paper must have fallen out of the envelope, and only caught your attention more recently—believe me, dear Sir, I am *sincerely grateful* to you ["for the consideration you" *interlined*] have been pleased to show me, in this matter from first to last. I confess I should not have delayed to acknowledge the receipt of, and thank you for, the former favour—and so in truth I would, had not my time latterly been most fully occupied, and my respect for you prevented me from writing (as I am now compelled to do) in haste. With this I will enclose a copy of a brief prospectus [*not found*] (or rather heading of subscription lists) which I have already made use of to the greatest and most flattering advantage in a couple of places of Carolina: The names subscribed to the right are designed merely to influence the Georgians—if that be possible!

Col. William Cumming's name was the only one I hesitated to use for that especial purpose (ie. in print &c) without his especial sanction, ["by reason of his eccentrick habits of retirement" *interlined*] and accordingly when the proof only had been struck off I showed it to him, not without a smile at his expected reluctance to find his name (a proposed Major General in the invading army!) united *with those of so many others* to constitute a balance of (recommending) power, when occurring in the same page with yours. The Col. however did not object in so many words to an arrangement founded less on expediency perhaps, than upon my honest belief, but contented himself with asking, half seriously, whether I *really* thought all *their* names combined sufficient to compete with your own. I was much amused, as the real drift of the question was easy to be detected, but parried it by assuring the Colonel with a smile and inclination of the head, that surely had I desired merely *an equipoise* I would not have chosen more than *one!* (this, be it said, to the prejudice of my conscience!) "Well, well"—he replied laughing—"you are quite welcome to use my name as you choose"—and so I have.

In illustration, dear Sir, of the *real* benefit *your* name will bestow, I will mention (among many) one amusing little incident. A leading lawyer at —— (in Carolina) became a few days ago so interested in the enterprise, that he requested me to let him canvass for me, and accordingly together we went to, among the first, the Sheriff of the District. I did not foresee much ["promise of" *interlined*] success in the Sheriff's countenance, and indeed when Mr. —— had concluded a famous exordium on foreign literature in general and that of Carolina in particular, hesitation was plainly portrayed in the manner of the former gentleman. "Come" cried Mr. —— in a happy moment—"you were a warm 'Nullifier'—were you not, eh?" "Yes to be sure," returned the Sheriff, his countenance lighting up in a moment—"that I *was*!" "Very well," returned my friend—["]let me read you what Mr. Calhoun has written here." The Sheriff listened with gratified ears, took up his pen on the instant and signed his name, a firm convert to the cause of Southern Literature, while Mr. —— caught my eye and smiled! As I said, this is only *one* instance of the service you have rendered: and now I recall another incident connected therewith which can [not] fail to please you. As an axiom it may be taken that none are so jealous of our State and it's institutions, as our neighbours the Georgians. Conceive then, dear Sir, the weight of your influence, when a young lady (*very dear to me*) from that State, wrote in reply to my statement of your kindly worded letter, that henceforward she "would regard Carolina as *her* native State, and Mr. Calhoun's politics forever should be her's! ! !"

I fear however I have quite exhausted your patience with these trifling narrations, and yet I am aware for the first time that in writing at such length I have paid ["to" *interlined*] you an *involuntary* compliment, for surely I would never have presumed (even thus unintentionally) to so encroach on your time and endurance, had I not felt a secret conviction that the ["size" *canceled and* "greatness" *interlined*] of your heart is surely not less than ["that of" *interlined*] your reputation. With all respect, and very gratefully I have the honour to remain your humble servant &c, J.M. Legaré.

[P.S.] Allow me, dear Sir, to beg your acceptance beforehand of a little vol. of poems the Ticknors (of Boston) have now in press, as it will be much more easily conveyed to you, at my direction, while you are in Washington from Boston than from this place. J.M.L.

ALS in ScCleA. NOTE: Legaré's only published volume was *Orta-Undis, and Other Poems* (Boston: William D. Ticknor, 1848).

From B[ASIL] MANLY

University of Ala. [Tuscaloosa,] Oct. 26, 1847

My Dear Sir, I ask leave to trespass on your time so far as to say that the members of the two Literary Societies in this University have joined, with great unanimity & cordiality, in the request that you will consent to deliver their Anniversary address, on the second monday in July 1848.

If, in any case, you could be induced to undertake a service of that kind, allow me to unite my own earnest solicitation to that of the Young Gentlemen. Our Institution is struggling for existence. Its large & munificent endowment, the gift of the general government, is sunk & lost in the failure of our State banks; and its fate is now hung upon the contingency of the popular voice; whether the State by taxation, will honestly comply with the conditions of the sacred trust, or not.

Your presence & efforts, on an occasion like that which our Young Gentlemen present to you might, & probably would, secure an object so vital to the interests of all coming generations in Alabama.

It has been the distinguished honor of your life to have touched & illustrated a very large number of subjects involving the honor of your country and the happiness of man. Hitherto, if I mistake not, you have not made any set effort in behalf of the promotion of high letters in our Colleges. It is the dictate, at once, of admiration & of friendship for you, & of regard to the welfare of the rising generation in Alabama, which is to be the home of part of your own family, to express the hope, that an effort in behalf of the liberal training of the young may be recorded among the later & maturer contributions of your life to the welfare of the country.

Allow me to present to you a copy of the address, delivered before the two Societies who have now addressed you, at their late anniversary; which I send by the mail that bears this. With the highest consideration & respect, I am, dear Sir, most truly yours, B. Manly.

ALS in ScCleA. Note: An AEU by Calhoun reads "Re[veren]d Dr. Manly." Basil Manly, the elder, (1798–1868) was a native of N.C., a graduate of South Carolina College, a noted Baptist minister, and president of the University of Ala. 1837–1855.

From CHA[RLE]S A. PEGUES and EDW[AR]D L. JONES

University of Alabama, Oct. 26, 1847

Dear Sir, Our object in addressing you this communication is to inform you, that at a meeting held today by the two literary Societies of this University you were unanimously elected to address them on the second monday in July 1848, their next Anniversary occasion.

Our Institution is in a very critical situation. Its splendid and ample endowment has been greatly diminished by the failure of our banks and it is a problem yet to be solved whether the University will stand or fall. Obviously some powerful exertion must be made in our behalf or the sad fate which has been so long expected and so greatly feared will certainly befall us. The two Societies knowing your influence throughout the country, have without a dissenting voice chosen you as the Instrument by which we may conciliate the favor of the people and place our beloved Institution, once more upon a permanent basis. We are selfish enough to hope that you can so arrange your affairs as to comply with our urgent solicitation. Your Ob[e]d[ien]t S[er]v[an]ts, Chas. A. Pegues & Edw[ar]d L. Jones, Cor[respon]d[in]g Sec[retarie]s.

LS in ScCleA. NOTE: An AEU by Calhoun reads "Relates to the University of Alabama." On the same day E.G. Baptist and A.C. Davidson, evidently students at the University of Ala., wrote to Andrew Pickens Calhoun asking his assistance in persuading John C. Calhoun to deliver the anniversary address. (LS in ScU-SC, John C. Calhoun Papers.)

From DUFF GREEN

Washington, 27th Oct. 1847

My dear Sir, I have just returned from Pen[nsylvani]a where I saw Gen[era]l [Simon] Cameron [Senator from Pa.] and at his request I wish to say that he desires to make up a mess to be composed in part of yourself, Mr. [Robert M.T.] Hunter [Senator from Va.,] Mr. [David R.] Atchison [Senator from Mo.,] and Mr. [Edward A.] Hannegan [Senator from Ind.,] believing that such a mess can exercise much influence on the measures of the next session, and he desires to act on your advice and under your lead. I promised to write to you and Mr. Hunter and he is to write to Mess. A[t]chison & Hannegan.

I had a conversation a few days since with Mr. [Robert J.] Walker [Secretary of the Treasury] who seemed very anxious to know what your course would be. I told him that I did not believe that you oppose the acquisition of territory on the ground assumed by Mr. [John M.] Berrien and Mr. Waddy Thompson and that I believed much opposed to war as you had been at the outset I believed you would unite in requiring some indemnity from Mexico.

In fine I told him that proscribed and persecuted as you & your friends had been you required nothing to secure your support for the measures of the administration but that those measures should ["be" interlined] such as will in your opinion best advance the honor and interests of the country and advised that he and Judge [John Y.] Mason [Secretary of the Navy] should write and consult with you. He said that he would see Judge Mason on the subject. Since I had that conversation the Pen[nsylvani]a elections have doubtless given them new hopes, and they are now less disposed to conciliate you. I do not expect them or either of them to write to you, unless they become fearful that [James] Buchanan [Secretary of State] may become a formidable candidate[;] in that ["case" interlined] one & perhaps both of them would desire his defeat and may endeavor to conciliate you as a means of doing it.

I am assured that the result in Pen[nsylvani]a was brought about by no feeling of friendship for Mr. Buchanan or the administration. It was owing chiefly to the folly of the whigs in the manner in which they opposed an *unpopular* war & to the belief that if the whig candidate was elected the whigs would nominate Mr. [Henry] Clay. This induced the friends of Gen[era]l [Zachary] Taylor of both parties to unite on [Francis R.] Shunk [for governor].

I learn from a well informed source that a leading whig will immediately after the meeting of Congress move a resolution declaring that the whole of Mexico is ours by right of conquest and as far as I can learn the chief difficulty with the administration is where they shall fix the line of seperation.

[David Levy] Yulee [Senator from Fla.] has been here, and rumor says that he has labored hard to make his peace with Mr. [Thomas] Ritchie and the Heads of Departments. [Robert Barnwell] Rhett [Representative from S.C.] is here also, ready if reports be true to barter all the South for a foreign mission.

What think you of Buchanan's compromise line[?] I told Ritchie today—that I for one looked upon it as the most impudent and insulting proposition, sustained as it had been by his press that ever had been made to the South, impudent because it was a fraud upon its face, and insulting because the Union seemed to take it for granted that there was not ["vir" *canceled*] intelligence in the South to see it, or public virtue or public spirit to denounce it. But enough. What shall I say to Mr. Cameron[?] Yours truly, Duff Green.

ALS in ScCleA.

From H[ENRY] W. CONNER

Charleston, Oct[obe]r 28, 1847

My Dear Sir, I wrote you soon after my return from New York [City] & now beg to add—that we last night held a pretty large private meeting of our friends & have increased our subscriptions for the paper up to 24 to $25,000.

We are in communication with the country besides & suppose we may receive thence with what further sums we may get here a sum get nothing further from other States I feel satisfied a paper with the sufficient to make the Total am[oun]t $30,000 & with that—even if we very extensive subscriptions which with half exertions may be obtained can be started & made [to] sustain itself with full effect.

The Editor & organization preliminary to its commencement are now matters I think of pressing importance. Very Truly y[ou]rs &c, H.W. Conner.

[Enclosed printed circular]

OFFICE OF EXECUTIVE COMMITTEE
Charleston, Oct. 22, 1847

Sir: THE imminent dangers which beset the institution of Slavery and the rights of the States in which it exists, from the Wilmot movement, so far from diminishing, are believed in reality to be greater NOW, than at any period of its progress. The partial reaction in some of the Northern States is caused in no small degree by our preparations, and is predicated on support expected from the Slave States. The advantage we have gained, if we fail to show a prompt and united front for its support, will be soon lost. In truth, our security must depend mainly on our own action, and it is very clear that the friends of the Constitution, and above all, of the Slave institutions, must provide for future safety NOW, by a course of firm, united and concerted measures, or they will, in all human probability, experience the most deplorable consequences from their apathy. The movements of Abolition must be met and defeated at this time, by efficacious and peaceful measures on our part, or we may expect, in future, every species of aggression on our property and rights, and every degree of degrading insult on our feelings and character.

As a South-Carolinian, having a proper sense of your privileges, and a due sensibility for the honor and rights of your State, and as a citizen of the United-States, attached to the integrity and observance of the compact of Union, we invite you to meet at the City Hall, at 5, P.M., on Wednesday next, the 27th inst., to consult and unite on such measures as are best adapted to maintain our rights, protect our institutions and preserve the blessings of our Constitution and Union to ourselves and our posterity.

By order of the Committee, H.W. CONNER, *Chairman.*
[Enclosed printed circular]

CHARLESTON, S.C., OCT. 22, 1847

Sir: A SHORT time since you were addressed on the subject of a Press at Washington, to combat the Wilmot movement, and to warn and unite the Slave States for their safety and preservation. The dangers then adverted to as impending over the Slave interest, are far from being abated. It is true, we have the evidences of some reaction, and the avowals by distinguished men of opinions more conformable to our rights, but these must be supported by the united Slave interest, or they will be sacrificed; and *their strength* and efficiency depend entirely on the support we shall bring them. The fact is, that this reaction, limited as it is, results more from the measures we have started to unite the Slave States by a central Press, than from any other cause, and in it we should see the importance of pressing on in our enterprize. If we falter, we sacrifice the best opportunity and prospects we shall ever again have. We shall lose the friends who have stood up for us in the Free States, and we shall most probably never again recover the advantage.

Under these circumstances, we are of opinion that there is a call for energetic action. The crisis is one of fearful import. The preservation of our dearest rights and privileges are in no small degree hanging on our conduct. Here we are alive to the peril, and are doing our duty. May we look to you for co-operation?

It is highly important that we be informed as to what has already been done, at as early a day as will suit your convenience. We therefore beg you will write and inform us, by the 5th day of November, how much has been subscribed for the paper, to the Subscription List of which you have charge, and also how much more you think you can obtain by the meeting of the Legislature—at which time we hope you will be prepared to report more fully and satis-factorily.

I write at the joint request of the signers of the "Circular" which you have received, and of the "Executive Committee" of this District, having in charge the matter of the aggressions of the North on Southern institutions.

ISAAC W. HAYNE, *Secretary.*

ALS with Ens in ScCleA.

From G[EORGE] L. L. DAVIS

Baltimore, Oct. 29, 1847

My dear Sir: I am much indebted to you, for the pamphlet contain-ing your reply to Mr. [Hopkins L.] Turney, together with your re-marks upon the Resolutions introduced by you, into the Senate. I am also much indebted to you, for the views and suggestions in your letter of the 13th inst. The volume, to which you refer, has long been in my possession. And when I assure you, that I have been a fond student of your political philosophy, I am in hopes, you will not doubt, that I attach the highest importance to that principle, which forms the *very basis* of the whole system.

As I intimated to you, in my former note, I shall lay down the broad proposition, *that Congress has no power whatever to make a law, with reference to the Institution of Slavery.* And, in maintaining this proposition, I shall argue:

1. From the *nature of the Institution itself.* And:
2. From the *fundamental* principle of constitutional Law.

I propose also to go into a close analysis of the historical relations involved in an examination of the Virginia Deed of Cession, and of the Louisiana, & Florida Purchases. And I propose also to examine, with great care, the history of the [Northwest] Ordinance of '87, and that of the "Missouri Compromise."

It has occurred to me, that I would adopt the above mode, for the following reason. However conclusive a constitutional or legal argument may be to a logical mind, the masses of a community are much more easily convinced by a statement of historical facts and illustrations. But I hope, I shall be able, in harmony with your wise suggestion, to assign the highest possible place to the principle, which *lies at the foundation of our political system.*

In the historical branch of the argument, my main difficulty arises from an examination of the facts connected with the "Missouri Compromise." But my object is not to write a letter, but to thank you for your kindness, in replying to my former note, and sending me a copy of your Speech. I have the honour to be, Y[ou]r ob[edien]t Serv[an]t, G.L.L. Davis.

ALS in ScCleA. NOTE: George Lynn Lachlan Davis (1813–1869) later published books on the growth of religious toleration in Maryland (1855), the U.S. Japanese expedition (1857), and the history of Maryland (1860). The publication contemplated in this letter has not been identified.

REPORT ON A PLOWING MATCH

[Pendleton, *ca.* October 29, 1847]

The Committee of the Pendleton Farmers Society, on the sub-soil plowing match between Dr. O[zey] R. Broyles and R[obert] A. Maxwell Esqs., submit the following *report and observations.*

The plow used by Dr. Broyles was one of exceeding cheapness and simplicity of construction, and invented by himself. Mr. Maxwell used the celebrated one horse plow of Ruggles, Nours[e], and Mason from New York.

The ground selected by the Committee, was, a level lot in the Village of Pendleton, composed of a shallow grey soil, with a firm red clay subsoil, which had been used as a grass lot, exposed to the hoof, and not having been lately cultivated, was about as firm and compact as the ordinary old fields of similar composition, a few years after being turned out.

To enable the Committee, to come as nearly as possible at the relative amount of draught, it was agreed that the same breast of horses should be used in both cases.

The New York plow was first introduced, with the following result on a fair trial.

Ultimate depth at full draught	12 to 13 ins.	
do at ordinary "	8 9	"
Furrow slice	12	"

Dr. Broyles' plow was next introduced, and resulted as follows:

Ultimate depth at full draught	17 to 18 ins.	
do at ordinary "	12 13	"
Furrow slice	12	"

Neither of the plows were preceded by any other.

The only remaining question, *pulverization* was next tested by cautiously scraping away the earth, which was found thoroughly broken to the depth the plows had penetrated in both cases.

The result of the whole experiment may be summed up as follows:

1st. *As to depth*, the most material point—Dr. Broyles' plow, penetrated with the same apparent draught, about *five* inches *deeper* than the New York plow. A fact which must be considered the more remarkable, when it is recollected that this excess was in the lower, and consequently, more tenacious and resisting part of the land.

2nd. *As to pulverization*, the performance was considered equal and perfect in both cases.

3d. *Width of furrow slice*, the same—twelve inches, no wider space having been tried, because not desirable.

4th. *Cost of construction*, the difference in this respect is truly astonishing, and is as follows:

Dr. Broyles' plow cost,

To 12 lbs. bar iron ⅜ by 2 inches at 5 c.		60
" Smith's bill for making, and clives	1	25
" A plain Coulter stock,		75
Rough and without paint.	$2	60

Ruggles & Co.'s plow cost,

In Charleston,	6	50
Freight to Pendleton,	1	50
	$8	00

5th. *Adaptation.*—In this respect Dr. B[royles]'s plow cannot, or has [not] to the knowledge of your Committee—been surpassed; consisting of a single bar which passes downward through a beam, in the manner of the old fashioned coulter. It is obvious that nothing more is required to make it a one, two, or even four horse plow, if desired, than simply to extend the bar further through the beam, and by the same means, it is obvious that it may be regulated so as to attain any desirable depth in weed, or grass land, which would present an insuparable obstacle to successful results with the New York plow when not preceded by a turning plow.

The Committee, in conclusion, feel no hesitation in awarding to Dr. Broyles, the *honour* of a complete triumph over his competitors.

The superior performance of his plow is evidently owing to its having been constructed in conformity to scientific principles, which, impart to it the power of such astonishing performance, at such comparatively small expense of horse power.

And considering the *very great* advantages likely to result from sub-soil plowing in our future efforts to reclaim & improve our lands we regard this plow as a very valuable acquisition to the interests of Agriculture.   Respectfully submitted, J.C. Calhoun, R[obert] A. Maxwell, Geo[rge] Seaborn, Com[mittee].

P.S.   Notice having been given previous to trial that the field would be open to full competition a third competitor appeared in the field on the day in the person of Mr. Fredericks, the overseer of the Hon. J.C. Calhoun.

He brought a plow, the model of which had been taken from Dr. Broyles, being his first conception and the original invention which he afterwards matured and perfected.   This plow from the fact of the superior set in the stock and perhaps the length of the beam, (for Dr. B[royles]'s plow when transferred to this stock done equally as good work,) and being in the hands of a skilful & practical plowman, in the opinion of the Committee did the best execution but the credit and honor of the invention is due and is hereby awarded to Dr. Broyles.

PC in the Pendleton, S.C., *Messenger*, October 29, 1847, p. 4; PC in *The Southern Cultivator*, vol. VI, no. 2 (February, 1848), pp. 21–22; PC in the Tallahassee, Fla., *Southern Journal*, February 14, 1848, p. 1.

To W[ADDY] THOMPSON, [JR., Greenville, S.C.]

Fort Hill, 29th Oct[obe]r 1847

Dear Sir, I have read your letter with attention, and will answer it in the same sperit of candour and freedom, with which it is written.

We do not disagree, as to the cause of the war, nor as to its certain disasterous consequences in the end, let it terminate as it will. We al[s]o agree in the opinion, that the war ought to terminate, and that my position requires me to use my best efforts to bring it to an end.   But the great practical question is: How can that be done?

In deciding that question, it must not be overlooked, that both parties by large majorities stand committed by their recorded votes, not only to the war, but that the war is a war of aggression on the part of the Republick of Mexico, aggression by invation [*sic*] and spilling American blood on American soil, and thus committed also to the Rio Grande being the Western boundary of the State of Texas. It is true, that very few of either party believed, that there was any just cause of war, or that the Rio Grande was the Western boundary of Texas, or that the Republick of Mexico had made war on us by the invasion of our territory, or any other way; but it is equally true, that by an act of unexampled weakness, to use the mildest terms, both stand by admission on record to the very opposite of their belief. And what is worse, they have by this act of unpar[all]elled weakness, committed large portions of both parties out of Congress to the war, as just and unavoidable on our part.

The effect of all this, with brilliant atchievements [*sic*] of our arms, have been greatly to weaken the opposition and to strengthen the party in power, and to make it impossible, in my opinion, to terminate the war in the manner you propose. I go further, to attempt it, would only tend, under circumstances, to weaken those, who make it, and give a new impulse to what is called the vigorous prosecution of the war, instead of bringing it to a termination. I thought so at the last session, and so informed Mr. [John M.] Berrien [Senator from Ga.] and the other Whig members, when he presented his amendment, and such in my opinion has been the effect, and will continue to be its effect, if it should be renewed at the next session. The course I adopted then, or rather suggested, was the only one that had the least prospect of bring[ing] the war to an end. I stood prepared to carry it out, if I had been supported; and, if I had been, the carnage and expenses of this campaign, would have been avoided. I shall take my seat prepared to do all in my power to bring it to an end, consistently with the state of things, in which I may find the country; but I fear with as little support, as I had in opposition to the war, or in my attempt to terminate it, at the last session. The fatal error of the Whigs, in voting for the war, has rendered them impotent, as a party, in opposition to it; and let me add, that while I agree with them in the policy of preserving the peace of the country, as long as it can be consistently with honor, I fear their timidity, as a party, on all questions, including peace and war, is so great, as to render their policy of preserving peace of little avail. It is not only in this instance, that it has disclosed itself. Even on the Oregon question, they gave away, before my arrival at Washington, on [Lewis] Cass's resolution, and rendered it very difficult to re[co]ver what was then lost. To go farther back; they made but feeble efforts to preserve peace during [Andrew] Jackson and [Martin] Van Buren's time on the Maine boundary question, and permitted me to stand alone in open opposition to Gen[era]l Jackson's course, in reference to the French indemnity, backed by the report of the Committee of Foreign relations in the Senate, which, had it not been for the mediation of England, would have ended in War. I rose in my place in the Senate, after the report was read, and exposed and denounced the whole affair, without a voice raised in my support. It is this timidity, when they are right, in questions connected with our foreign relations, and their errors, in reference to those appertaining to our domestick relations, which keeps them out of power, notwithstanding their individual respectability, and prevents them from performing, with effect, the important duties of an opposition. I am sure you will excuse this free expression of my opinion, in relation to a party, with which you rank yourself. With great respect I am &c., J.C. Calhoun.

PC in "Letter of John C. Calhoun, 1847," in the *American Historical Review*, vol. I (1895–1896), pp. 314–315; PC in Jameson, ed., *Correspondence*, pp. 737–739. NOTE: No ms. has been found. Both printed versions were derived from a ms. in the possession of the historian Lyon G. Tyler.

NOVEMBER 1–DECEMBER 5, 1847

⫸

On November 3 Calhoun wrote advice to his next-to-youngest son who was a student at South Carolina College. And two days later he advised the governor of South Carolina about matters of more public interest.

It was necessary to begin to think in earnest about the session of Congress which would convene on December 6. "I foresee a session of great distraction and confusion," Calhoun wrote Duff Green. "The old party organization cannot much longer hold together. The want of sincerity and honesty on the part of both parties has confounded the country and the Government, and caused a state of things, from which it will be difficult to extricate ourselves. . . . If our institutions are destined to be overthrown, I am resolved, that no share of the responsibility shall rest on me."

On November 26, Calhoun left home, his first stop being son-in-law Clemson's plantation near Edgefield, to which he had promised to give some attention. He arrived in Charleston on December 1 and left there on the Wilmington boat on December 3, bound for the convening of the 30th Congress.

⫸

From SARAH MYTTON MAURY

Liverpool, Nov[embe]r 1st 1847

My dear Mr. Calhoun, Will you kindly accept this book from me as a slight tribute of esteem and affection?

I am watching with exceeding interest the gradual progress of political events in America, and with the highest admiration am observing that they tend to the fulfilment of your predictions.

The Chicago Convention are *blindly* adopting your views also in regard to the Mississippi, for their Lakes.

640

I do not think that this time you are delivered over to the Whigs, though the majorities are strangely averaged—but I believe that in regard to Mexico, and Free trade, *you* will rule Congress.

If the Whigs side with Mr. [Daniel] Webster against the supplies, *you* will still have your own way, and it seems to me that the War Question has ruled the Elections.

Does not the present position of Switzerland interest you strongly? The Sonderbund are surely proving the inherent truth of your principle of Nullification.

We suppose that Austria will interfere however to prevent bloodshed.

Pray present me to Mrs. [Floride Colhoun] Calhoun most kindly. I hope she remembers me—and believe me always with every grateful feeling of friendship, yours most faithfully, Sarah Mytton Maury.

ALS in ScCleA.

From DUFF GREEN

Washington, 2nd Nov[embe]r 1847

My dear Sir, I have made arrangements for the publication of a weekly paper and my prospectus will appear in a few days. I pay much less than it would cost me to print it, as my arrangements are made with the Editor of the [Richmond?] Whig, who gives me the first page of his day paper, and transfer's [*sic*] my articles to a weekly paper and prints it for about one half of the actual cost if I had an office of my own. I have thus the advantage of a daily paper without the cost, and diminish the cost of publishing my weekly nearly one half.

Parties are so nearly divided that much may be done to control events if your friends act together in the organisation of the House and the Committees of *both* Houses. I will begin the paper in time that they may feel that they have an organ able and ready to sustain them before the country. I hope that you will be here at the commencement of the session as we have for several years lost much by your absence.

Let me hear whether you will be here.

Remember me kindly to Mrs. [Floride Colhoun] Calhoun & [Martha] Cornealia [*sic*; Calhoun]. Yours truly, Duff Green.

ALS in ScCleA.

To James E[dward] Calhoun, Jun[io]r, [Columbia, S.C.]

Fort Hill, 3d Nov[embe]r 1847

My dear son, I have read your letter with pleasure. It is well written, both as to composition and penmanship, and, what is still more important, is in good tone. I am glad to learn, that the [South Carolina] College is so flourishing, & to perceive, that you are animated with the proper sperit. It is a great point to belong to so good a class; and, I trust, that you will not content yourself to occupy a position of mere mediocrity. You have ample talents to stand high, and I have great confidence, from the tone of your letter, you will be found in the front rank. Now is your time.

I am glad to inform you, that Willie [William Lowndes Calhoun] has become quite studious, and has set in on lattin in good earnest. He got upward of 50 lines in Virgil last evening well. I go over his lesson every evening with him. If I could remain at home this winter, it would do much to brush up my knowledge of latin. You must write to him and encourage him. It will have a good effect.

The weather is fine and my crop is yielding well; but I fear cotton, from the deranged condition of the currency in England, will fall in price. If it should, it will throw quite a pressure on me this year, which will, with the expense of yours & John's and Willie's education, be heavy. I shall expect you all to be economical as possible.

We are all well, & all join their love to you, and kind regards to James Rion. You showed great judgment & prudence in getting him his place; & I am sure he will prove that he deserved it. Your affectionate father, J.C. Calhoun.

ALS in ScU-SC, John C. Calhoun Papers.

To Gov[erno]r D[avid] Johnson

Lime stone Springs [S.C.,] 5th Nov[embe]r 1847

My dear Sir, I am much gratified to find that there is such accord between us in reference to the subjects, touched on in my letter, to which your's is an answer. The probability is, that the Legislature will not have time to do any thing in reference to ["the" *canceled*] appointing [Presidential] electors, & that it will devolve on you to call the new members in time to meet to appoint them. I have but one copy left of my letter, to which you refer; but have applied to our editor for a number of his paper, in which it was published. If he has a spare number, I will forward it to you, as soon as received.

The veiws [*sic*] you take in reference to our right to retaliate are incontestably correct. If the non-slave holding States shall presist [*sic*] in setting aside ["the" *interlined*] stipulations of the Constitution in our favour, or adopt, or permit their citizens to adopt measures to render them nugatory; and, if the Government of the United States, theirs ["and our" *interlined*] common representative & agent, either cannot, or will not enforce their observance, we not only have the right, but it ["our" *canceled and* "will be a" *interlined*] duty to ourselves, & to the Constitution itself, to retaliate, as the only means of protecting ourselves, and to preserve the Constitution, by causing its provisions to be respected. In my opinion, the States, which permit ["its" *canceled*] stipulations to be violated in their persons, if I may use the expression, when they can prevent it, are not much less guilty, than those, who violate them. By taking the course indicated, we can save both ourselves & the Constitution. Any other will, in the end, terminate in the distruction of both. The only question is; Have we the sperit and the unanimity to adopt it? I have no doubt, as to the former. The difficulty is as to the latter. To make retaliation ["proper" *canceled and* "efficient" *interlined*], concert of action among the slave holding States is indispensible; and for that purpose, I hold a Convention to be equally so. I do trust one will be called to meet, at some convenient central point, next summer or fall; and that, if no other State should move, our's will take measures for the purpose. The meeting of such a body would bring the non slave holding States to their senses. They insult & threaten us, because they deem us too tame & distracted to take any effectual measure to resist their aggression.

How far you ought to go in your Message is a question of great delicacy. Prudence requires, that you should not go too far in advance of the sentiment of the State, and the State too far in advance of the other slave holding States. What is the actual state of the sentiment of the State at this time, you can better judge than I can, as I have been very little among the people since my return from Washington; but my impression is, that there is great unanimity as to our wrongs, but not much thought or reflection, as to the remedy. My ["suggestion" *canceled and* "advice" *interlined*] is, to dwell fully & strongly, on our wrongs, especially the act of Pennsyl[vani]a & similar acts and doings of other non slave holding States; and in more general terms, as to the remedy, but sufficiently explicit to be understood. You might take the ground, I should think, safely, that, if Pennsyl[vani]a & other States will presist in disregarding the stipulations of the Constitution in our favour, & the Govern[men]t of the United States either cannot, or will not cause them to be respected, the States agreived [*sic*] will be forced in self defence to retaliate, as the only remedy left them to protect themselves & to enforce their observance. I think you might add, that in that case, concert of action among the States interested, in enforcing ["obedience to" *interlined*] them, would become indispensible to make the ["retali" *canceled*] remedy effectual; but doubt, whether you could, with propriety go farther, in alluding to a convention. Thus far, I think you may safely go; but you can best judge. The Legislature might go farther, but that is for them to judge.

The other subject, on which you ask my opinion, is of mom[en]tious interest; I refer to the Mexican war. The two have, to a considerable extent, become blended. I will give it freely—the more so, because I do not concur altogether in the view you present. I doubt, indeed, if you touch on it at all, whether you should go farther, than to do justice to our gallant Army, & especially our own regiment, which has so nobly done its duty; and to express, in General terms, your regret at the continuance of the war, & a hope for its speedy termination. The question of peace & war belongs, under our system, ["of Governt" *canceled*] exclusively to the federal Government. While I admit, that, even on such questions, the seperate Governments of the States have a right freely to express their opinion, where they may think the power has been abused, I am of the opinion, that it ought to be done with a certain degree of caution and reserve in all such cases. In this, there are special reasons, as applied to our State, why it ought. The whole delegation, excepting myself, voted for the war; and have thus far ["so far" *canceled*] acquiesced in the mode of conducting it, as not to object to the avowed object to acquire territory. In addition, there are reasons for doubt, whether the State would sustain you in taking ground against the acquisition of all territory; and whether the taking it, ["would" *canceled and then interlined*] not tend to devide & weaken the State; a thing which would be deplorable, when Union among ourselves is ["so" *interlined*] desirable, in reference to the other great subject.

In giving this opinion, I retain, to the full, my objections to the war. I believe that all our differences with Mexico might have been easily settled, without a resort to it, after the settlement of the Oregon question. Nor can I admit, that it was in any degree caused by the annexation of Texas. It is true, without it, there might have been no war, just as there would certainly have been none, if the Continent had never been discovered. The real cause was, the unauthorised & unconstitutional order to Gen[era]l [Zachary] Taylor to March to the Del Norte; & take possession of a disputed territory. That itself was an act of war. Nor have I changed my opinion, as to the disasterous consequences, which must grow out of it; terminate when & how it may. I am also decidedly opposed to conquoring [*sic*] the country, and holding it either as a Province, or incorporating it in our Union. Either would be distructive. I am, also, decidedly in favour of bringing the war to a speedy termination, and see no reason to change, on that point, the opinion I expressed at the last sessession [*sic*].

I avail myself in conclusion, to reciprocate the expression of kind feelings. I have ever entertained them for you, since our first meeting in Columbia; and I assure you, that you have no friend, who more sincerely desires ["any" *canceled and* "you great" *interlined*] success & honor in the discharge of the duties of your high station. Yours truly, J.C. Calhoun.

ALS in ScU-SC, John C. Calhoun Papers; variant typescript in NcD, John Clopton Papers.

From J[OHN] B. JONES

Phil[adelphia], Nov. 5th 1847
Dear Sir—Be pleased to accept ["of" *canceled*] the first series of my new publication (in four numbers) which I send by this mail. I hope the course I have taken may merit your approbation, as I have uttered nothing but what was the result of conscientious conviction.

By the notice on the ["fourth" *canceled and* "last" *interlined*] page of the fourth number, you will see that I have modified my plan of issuing the work every week. This was not because the receipts were disproportionate to the expenditures—but rather because there were not readers, ["and partly because of the" *canceled and* "owing in part," *interlined*] perhaps, to the ominous silence of the Southern press. Not one of the editors South of Richmond Va., to whom the Compact has been sent, has vouchsafed to send me a paper in exchange, much less copied my prospectus. Among those to whom my paper was sent was the ["editor of the" *interlined*] Charleston Mercury.

I have ample means of my own to continue the paper, if it were only generally circulated. Hoping, nevertheless, that your just views—and they are all just—may ultimately prevail, I am Respectfully yours &C, J.B. Jones.

ALS with En in ScCleA. NOTE: Jones enclosed a prospectus for *The Compact,* "devoted to discussions of the nature and principles of the Federal Government" and other political topics. Jones was former editor of the Washington, D.C., *Madisonian,* organ of the John Tyler administration. He was a prolific author, best remembered for his mean-spirited record of Confederate experiences, *A Rebel War Clerk's Diary.*

From A. G. ROSE, "Cash[ie]r"

Bank of Charleston S.C.
5th Nov[embe]r 1847

Dear Sir, As requested, I now hand you the enclosed Copy of your check for $311 71/100 referred to in ["your" *canceled*] our Statement of your Bank a/c. Very respectfully Y[ou]r Ob[edient] S[er]v[an]t, A.G. Rose, Cash[ie]r.

ALS with En in ScCleA. NOTE: Enclosed with this letter was a copy of a check for $311.71 drawn on 7/30/1847 upon the Bank of Charleston and made out by Calhoun to "Messrs. Walker & Bradford." An AEU by Calhoun reads, "Pay-[men]t to Walker & Co.[,] factors[,] Hamburgh."

From CHA[RLE]S H. ALLEN

Abbeville C[ourt] H[ouse, S.C.] Nov. 6th 1847

Dear Sir, excuse the liberty I take in addressing this brief epistle to you. I am collecting all the information I can of the history and early settlement of Abbeville District, with a view of making a short publication, and in my researches I find mention of your father Patrick Calhoun, as one among the first settlers in 1756 in this district. Please let me know, if you have the date, the year and the section of the district he settled in, and who were his neighbors—and any other information that you may possess of the early history of the district— I regret that no one has left on record, any concise history of Abbeville[.] The old men of the land who might have given me much information have passed away, and the only resources left are a few imperfect records.

Please let me know also in what year you commenced the practice of Law at this place—was not the first speach you delivered made under the oaks in front of the residence of Mr. Ja[me]s Wardlaw? I have hesitated some time to write you upon this subject for fear of trespassing on your time—should you have leisure, your attention to the above will greatly oblige, Yours very Respectfully, Chas. H. Allen.

ALS in ScCleA. NOTE: James Wardlaw, father of David L. Wardlaw, was Clerk of Court for Abbeville District. His home, Quay House, was located near Abbeville Court House. Allen was editor of the Abbeville *Banner*.

From JAMES B. DAVIS

Constantinople, Nov. 6th 1847

My D[ea]r Sir, Permit me to introduce to you my friend Baron Notebeck[?] of Russia.

The Baron goes to America for the purpose of observing our cotton factories[,] agriculture &c &c.

Any assistance you can give him in Washington, by putting him in contact with Machinists, Manufacturers[,] Cotton & Tobacco Planters will be most gratefully remembered by your ob[edien]t S[ervan]t, James B. Davis.

ALS in ScCleA. NOTE: An AEU by Calhoun reads, "Mr. Davis Introducing Baron Nottbeck." James Bolton Davis (b. 1809) was a Fairfield District, S.C., planter who had been sent by President James K. Polk to study cotton agriculture in Turkey. He is said to have brought back the first two Brahman cows imported into the U.S.

From W[ADDY] THOMPSON, [JR.]

Greenville [S.C.,] Nov. 6, 1847

My Dear Sir, I have received your letter in reply to mine and I honor both the wisdom and the feelings which direct your course. One occupying the position which you do can not even with propriety speak out as fully as a private man like myself. It is not proper that he should unless he could speak in a whisper which would not be heard by our enemy or the world. I have felt the difficulty of even doing so myself. I agree with you fully as to the timidity of the whig party. Indeed the chief recommendation of that party is its conservative character—which is akin to timidity—and the destructive character of the opposite party. But I say to you in all candor that in view of the present & prospective issues before us I do not think that any Southern man who is really a patriot can say that he belongs now to either of the great parties. The whig party true to the timid character of which you speak has for years been conciliating the abolitionists and it must now be manifest to all that we have nothing to hope from the Democratic party. We really had no friends at the Syracuse Convention [of N.Y. Democrats]. It was only a question as to time and party policy. They did not vote down the Wilmot proviso but laid it on the table. The greatest of all our dangers in my poor judgment is from the west. They are essentially a warlike people and the only people on the face of the earth to whom war is an unmixed blessing. They suffer none of its calamities and are furnished with a market for all their *live stock* from pigs to men.

I confess that I am appalled at the annexation of ten or twelve new States and all of them of absolute necessity free States with or without a Wilmot proviso. If I am not mistaken that is becoming the prevailing sentiment of the South. With great Respect Y[ou]rs truly, W. Thompson.

ALS in ScCleA.

From Eustis Prescott

Memphis, 8th Nov[embe]r 1847

My Dear Sir, I have to thank you for your note of 5th Sept[embe]r and accompanying documents. I concur fully in the sentiments they embody, and hope that our friends in Louis[ian]a will have ere this come forward with their full quota of money in aid of the undertaking. I now hope to reach New Orleans in about a week, and shall use all the influence I can exert in furtherance of the cause.

I deem Kentucky and Tennessee sound on the great question, and if ever brought to a vote I doubt whether the "Wilmot Proviso" will receive a single affirmative vote in either State. They may submit to the "Missouri compromise" but it strikes me that at last is but an expedient, and that any compromise of the constitution should be resisted.

If we must receive territory it should be open to the citizens of every State with their property, if such territory ever applies to become a member of the Union, the people will decide whether she shall, or shall not prohibit slavery within her borders.

The [Martin] Van Buren section of the Democracy have—as I anticipated, taken their stand for the "proviso" and parties must now divide—for or against & this will be an important feature in the next presidential election. Gen[era]l [Zachary] Taylor has about served the purposes of the Whigs in the State elections and will now be permitted to rest [as a] Major Gen[era]l.

You ask me of the Cotton crop. At this point it is said the receipts will be larger than ever before known—indeed I cannot now learn of a short crop any where in the Miss: valley. Estimates 2,250,000 up to 2[.]5 [million bales]. I am inclined to lean toward the latter as Texas makes a very heavy crop. Estimated receipts at N[ew] O[rleans] [$]1,200,000. Price now here 6 cts. [per pound].

My health is still feeble and I must endeavour to visit Europe in April or May. A voyage rapidly builds me up.

I hope your cough will have been removed ere this—if not, permit me to recommend to you a *gargle* which I have found very beneficial[:] half pint sage tea well sweetened with honey[;] when cold add one teaspoonful of Sp[iri]ts Esth: Sulph: and 2 teaspoonfuls Tinct[ure] Myrhh [*sic*]. I remain Dear Sir Very sincerely yours, Eustis Prescott.

ALS in ScCleA; PEx in Boucher and Brooks, eds., *Correspondence*, p. 409.

To Duff Green

Fort Hill, 9th Nov[embe]r 1847

Dear Sir, I received by the last mail your note, with the Message from Mr. [Simon] Cameron; and will thank you to say to him, that I am obliged to him for his proposed arrangement, but that I had previously made another arrangement for the session.

I foresee a session of great distraction and confusion. The old party organization cannot much longer hold together. The want of sincerity and honesty on the part of both parties has confounded the country and the Government, and caused a state of things, from which it will be difficult to extricate ourselves. I confess, I do not see the end. My own course is clear and easy; to do my duty, without regard to consequences personal to myself. If our institutions are

destined to be overthrown, I am resolved, that no share of the responsibility shall rest on me.

PC in Jameson, ed., *Correspondence*, pp. 739–740.

From JAMES GADSDEN

Charleston So. C., Nov. 11, 1847
Dear Sir, Our Friend Sam[uel L.] Gouverneur is a Candidate for
Clerk of the House of Representatives, and as I am advised with
good prospects of success. He is among the Few New York[er]s
who has not been politically tainted with the poison of the policies
or democracy of that State. Could he [have] been as pliable as
[John A.] Dix [Senator from N.Y.] he could have occupied his place
& with far more ability in my estimation. However this has no connection with the subject in which I feel an interest. His success, as
a worthy man of great honesty of character, and a near relative of
our truly great Friend President [James] Monroe. Can you aid him
in any way[?] The W[h]ig vote which he can to a great extent control with the vote of those Democrats who are not servile & bound to
party, will secure success. But more probably you have been already
communicated with, and must feel an interest for Gouverneur[']s
success.

I have not heard much from or much of you of late. I should be
pleased to hear your views on the exciting state of things. The unexpected protraction of the Mexican war and the revulsion in England I fear will operate unfavourably on the progress of our Rail
Road schemes. The temper in Tennessee was most favourable, and
our own citizens were working up to a fever; which we could no
doubt temper down and direct into proper channels. But I fear the
monetary embarrassments in England with the decline on cotton,
will cool the ardor of our citizens and indispose them to do much at
home & still less abroad. What think you of the English news? Will
there not be a reaction, and permanent good to trade come out of the
breaking up of those Old & monopolizing houses, which have been
rotten ever since 1836 & struggling to recover under the efforts to
retain & monopolize. Trade sh[oul]d be more distributed, made to
depend on Individual energies, and integrity. An overgrown Commercial House is as injurious to the freedom of commerce as is a
mammoth Bank.

Have you been able to form any estimate of the Cotton Crop[?] What has been the influence of the late dry fall with you in Alabama[?]

In some quarters it has only afforded greater facilities for picking without any promise of increase of production. Ought not our Planters to stand firm & hold on, untill this Tornado at least passes by[?] I shrudely [*sic*] suspect England has designs on depressing cotton. But she is no longer the controling power. The consumption of the Continent & of the U.S. is more than one half of this year[']s crop—& we can now begin to make her respect the ordinary & wholesome currents of trade, without those revulsions which she has hitherto produced at will. Yours respectfully, James Gadsden.

ALS in ScCleA.

From JOS[EPH] J. SINGLETON

Dahlonega [Ga.,] 11th Nov. 1847

My Dear Sir, Yours of the 4th Inst. has just been handed me by a servant. I called immediately to see Mr. David Sloan, but as yet have not seen him. I will endeavor to see him in the morning. I am sorry that I have no toll to send you this time; Mr. [R.B.] Lewis has paid me nothing for you, he is now from home, hence I have no opportunity of making the desired enquiry of of [*sic*] him. I have just called on Messrs. [Robert H.] Moore & [William G.] Lawrence, both of whom informed me that they had no toll worth speaking of, and Mr. Moore says he expects to abandon the lots shortly. They are doing but little on the Obarr lot, consiquently have made no deposite lately. So soon as Mr. Lewis returns I will see him and write you the result at Washington, and whatever other information I may have in relation to your business. I presume you also received the hundred dollars I sent you by Mr. Sloan some time ago, making in all I have sent you, two hundred & twenty five dollars.

I notice with much interest your remarks upon the absorbing political interest of the day, and fully concur with you in your opinions generally. Most unquestionably, the crisis is fast approaching when the South will be necessarily compelled to see to her own interest regardless of our present political divisions. The Constitution must, and will become our watchword, and without a strict observance of its provisions I would not give a fig for the government.

651

On the defeat of my friend [William C.] Dawson before the Whig convention, when they nominated their Candidate for Governor I immediately urged upon ["him" *interlined*] the propriety of availing himself of the opportunity of giving full vent to his often declared principles, and to come out like a man, for Southern rights upon the broad platform of orriginal principles, as the only "surge repelling rock" upon which ["we" *interlined*] will have to stand upon, sooner or later, and I believe the sooner we take the stand the better. But Mr. Dawson like too many other polititians now a days, believes it to be an unpardonable sin not to adhere strictly to the dictates of his party, and he is now fishing for a seat in the Senate of the U.S. And it is thought he will succeed, his party has the power if they will exe[r]cise it in his behalf. Should he fail in this, I will try him again, I think.

As I mentioned to you on a former occasion, I still think that all things are working together for the best. The South must concentrate for its own safety, if it does, upon whom, and upon whose principles will it ["take"(?) *canceled*] adopt more readily than those which have been the most congenial to her interest for the last forty years, it appears to me too obvious to admit of a doubt. Merit will be rewarded, and nothing but the time allotted to man will prevent it here, but will he not be rewarded hereafter, though it may be too late for his Countries good[?] Yet will it ["not" *interlined*] be a great source of consolation to be received with a "well done thou good and faithful servant &C.["?] I have the hon[or] of Yours as usual, Jos. J. Singleton.

N.B. My wife [Mary Ann Terrell Singleton] leaves in a day or two for LaGrange [Ga.] to see our Daughter, in a critical situation, or I would make a trip to Milledgeville, [the capital,] for the sole purpose of promoting Southern rights, in accordance to your views. J.J.S.

ALS in ScU-SC, John C. Calhoun Papers. NOTE: This letter was addressed to Calhoun in Pendleton and as if it was to be carried by "Mr. Sloan."

From F[ITZ]W[ILLIAM] BYRDSALL

New York [City,] Nov[embe]r 12th 1847

Dear Sir, I enclose you the [New York] Herald's full Report of the vaunted speech of John Van Buren at the Herkimer mass Convention. The Editorial remarks in relation to the ["speech" *interlined*] are neat, appropriate, and give several admirable hits as regards the "Sage of Lindenwald."

Our State Election is over and the enemies of what they term the "Southern influence,["] have destroyed their own influence and placed the matter of the next presidency in the hands of the South. They have placed New York in a position disgraceful to her as a State, and disadvantageous to her amongst her sister States, for none can make any safe calculation upon her in the contest of 1848. Her politicians with all their cunning, have shewn their want of true wisdom to be as deficient as their lack of steadfast principle. "The dough faces" are also dough brained.

New York politicians have "headed" themselves. While they had the great personal popularity of Andrew Jackson as their support, they were invulnerable, but since he left public life, they have been going down hill and will soon be at bottom. It is a laughable fact, that in the recent Election three Victories were achieved; the Whigs gained a victory by carrying the State, the Barnburners gained a victory by defeating what they call the old Hunker State ticket, and the old Hunkers gained a victory by laying [Azariah C.] Flagg and his co adjutors of the Central Regency on the shelf.

As to the Wilmot proviso, it was only assumed as a cover under which to do battle against the old Hunkers and the administration at Washington. The Barn Burners of this State have never been reconciled to the defeat of Mr. [Martin] Van Buren's nomination in 1844. In their eyes it was a fraud and a usurpation over him that brought in Mr. [James K.] Polk and they dislike him as a usurper. But the great body of the people care little about the Wilmot Proviso at this time. It would soon die a natural death if the politicians & papers would let it depart in peace. Politically it is a monstrosity, for if Congress has power to *prohibit* slavery in the territory of the U. States, then it has power to *establish* it in the territory of the U. States. Here we have the idea of the Old federalist party of forming a supreme National Government. As regards the extension of slave territory, those who want to abolish slavery should go for diffusion instead of concentration, for they would ["find" *interlined*] a natural law in their favor if the Institution be an evil. Morally considered, I am satisfied that the Southern patriarchal system is the best condition for the African race, so long at least as it remains in the United States. There is far less suffering & crime in the millions of the slaves than in the thousands of the free negroes.

The Republican party will have a majority of States in the next House of Rep[resentatives] viz:

653

Dem.	Arkansas	Missouri	Whig—Connecticut	New York
"	Alabama	Tennessee	" Delaware	No. Carolina
"	Illinois	Texas	" Florida	Ohio
"	Indianna	Virginia	" Kentucky	Pen[n]sylvania
"	Iowa	So. Carolina	" Massachusetts	Vermont
"	Maine	Mississippi	" New Jersey	Maryland
"	Michigan	Louisiana = 14 Dem.		12 Whig.

Here we have 14 States to 12 Whig States. We should have to get two more States to give us a majority of all the States and I think out of the three States tied Georgia, N. Hampshire and Rhode Island, and Wisconsin yet to come in, we would get two, with a strong chance for Florida, besides. It strikes me that the Southern States should "bide their time," and not go into any National Convention with the Northern political parties to nominate candidates for the Presidency. They have bowed down to Abolitionism and cannot be relied upon only when the lower propensities of man, selfishness & love of gain are to be subserved. Let it be remembered that the spoils of States Government will always be sufficient to keep up two parties of some sort in the Northern States and this being probable, the Southern States by "biding their time," can respond to a nomination of the right sort, and if there be none such, they could then nominate their own candidate, go for him strongly and send the Election to the House which would ensure the election of a Southern man. The moral effect of such a result would be mighty for good. It would force one of the Northern parties to unite itself with the Southern through the next half century.

Matters may change—parties may adopt a different course from present appearances. Mr. [Henry] Clay's coming speech may afford some light upon the future. We have only to "bide our time" a few months to know what we should do.

Gen[era]l [Zachary] Taylor is not now spoken of by the non politicians and little by any order of men. Yours with profound Respect, F.W. Byrdsall.

ALS with En in ScCleA; PEx in Boucher and Brooks, eds., *Correspondence*, pp. 409–410. NOTE: The enclosed page from the New York, N.Y., *Herald* of 10/29/-1847, contained John Van Buren's address to the Barnburners at Herkimer, in which he strongly endorsed the Wilmot Proviso. On 11/13/1847 Clay, now a private citizen, made a speech in Lexington, Ky., in which he dwelled on the horrors of the Mexican War, ascribed it to executive usurpation, opposed annexation of Mexican territory, and condemned the acquisition of territory for the purpose of extending slavery. Thus the Whig party's presumptive leader and Presidential nominee set the platform for next year's election.

To DUFF GREEN, [Washington]

Fort Hill, 13th Nov[embe]r 1847

My dear Sir, I have received your last [dated 11/2]. It is my intention to be at Washington by the commencement of the session [on 12/6].

The position of the country is very critical. Great caution and great firmness combined are necessary to extricate it from its present difficulties; and you will have to exercise them in an eminent degree to make your paper effective and successful. With them it may do much. Look to the country exclusively, avoid as much as possible personalities, either of praise or censure, and limit yourself to statements of facts, and calm and impartial discussion. I hope you have not taken a step, which will involve you in any pecuniary difficulties.

PC in Jameson, ed., *Correspondence*, p. 740.

From T[HOMAS] L. SMITH

New York [City], November 13th 1847

My dear Sir, Many things conspire to make the approaching Session of Congress the most important & eventful in the history of our Government. Our foreign & domestic relations are disturbed with gloomy forebodings. War with its countless evils is pressing hard upon us, and our commercial and financial channels are threatened with gre[at] revulsions. The war with Mexico presents many phases, & some of the[m of] alarming magnitude. It seems to be the policy of the administrati[on to] look to the entire subjugation of that country, in reference to a[*mutilation*]tion. In my poor judgment this is the most stupendous conception [*mutilation*] error or ambition that ever threatened the harmony & permanency [*mutilation*] institutions. To add to such an extent of territory, such a popula[tion; *mutilation*] such a religion to our own, so dissimilar in all the elements of char-[*mutilation*] is frightful to think of. The policy to be pursued in disposing [of and] regulating this appendage, would be fraught with difficulties & dan[gers] that no foresight can reach. We could look only to the worst [*mutilation*]. To look to indemnity for debts due our citizens & the expenses of [the] war is hopeless if we demand dollars & cents—if it is to be paid [*mutilation*] territory, then how much, where, & within what boundaries will be the question. When obtained, how to be disposed of, & how to be governed, must be studied as a momentous consequence of possession. Then if our policy is to be changed in reference to the prosecution of the war, what shall be that policy. Here various & conflicting views may be expected. Thus in relation to this one subject, our war with Mexico, we have a vexed question, environed with the most serious difficulties. This is but one of the important subjects that will come before Congress. An alarming revulsion has taken place in England in her monetary & commercial affairs, which is shaking her whole fabric, & has in its consequences, reached us already. So comp[le]tely is English & indeed European credit destroyed, that our merchants have ceased to draw bills, & to meet the demands of commerce, we are now shipping specie for all engagements. The effect of this measure, which is at all times to touch a very sensitive point in our fiscal matters, is rendered peculiarly so now, in view of the causes. The banks begin to act upon the principle of self preservation, & they are narrowing their discounts. Capatalists are stringent, looking forward to coming troubles when money will be in demand to catch sacrifices. The foreign markets hold no inducements for the shipment of our exports, & our domestic buyers withdraw, not only from the admonitions from abroad, but from [re]duced monied facilities at home. These are so many premonitions [*mutilation*]t lead to the last & fatal point—a panic. From all that we have [to] guide us in speculating upon the condition of England, her [dif]ficulties have not reached their climax, & with her best exertions, [*mutilation*] recovery will be protracted & distant. Such is England's central[iz]ing power, over the fiscal & commercial relations of the world, [tha]t whatever calamity stagnates her resources, will produce changes [and] embarrassments every where else. In all the relations of money & [tra]de, we are so closely in contact with England, that she has not [a] pulsation, more or less, that we do not feel. If hers be a malady [it] does not follow that it becomes contagious with us, but we feel [the] want of her healthful atmosphere, & our sympathies cause [de]spondency. In view of all this, & as links in the same chain, we are sending millions of specie to Mexico to defray the expenses of the war; which if the war continues, the drain will continue. The Sub Treasury is operating to produce its share of embarras[s]ment. This great current, fed by so many tributaries, & rushing on in one direction sweeping before it all obstacles, must be calamitous, unless the potential arm of wise legislation guide its course, & limit its power.

We must have a large loan to meet the demands upon Government—from thirty, to fifty millions. If, from the derangements of commerce & financial embarrassments, money is scarce with us, & will command from the ordinary channels of business ten, twelve, or fifteen per cent per annum. If the monetary affairs in Europe be in ruinous derangement, may we not expect great difficulty in obtaining a loan, & if it be obtained at all, may it not be at a large bonus? At such times there is but little sympathy with Government, & for a loan to meet the expenses of an unpopular war, capatalists would stand at a greater distance, & say to our Exchequer "we have nothing for you." In company with these engrossing subjects will be found many important preliminary movements connected with the approaching Presidential election. Wholly extraneous as this subject will be in connexion with the legitimate objects & demands of legislation, it will nevertheless, be a presiding monitor, & will guide events to bear upon the campaign of 1848. This is only calculated to multiply difficulties, & cloud our hopes. In view of this extraordinary state of things, [the] country will call for the highest exertions of her statesmen, & sh[*mutilation*] will demand the tribute of an honest patriotism. Are there enou[gh men] equal to the task, who will rise superior to the trammels of pa[rty and] the subornation of unworthy influences? The times, the character [of] the men in power, the objects of base ambition, the influences that [*mutilation*] a large portion of popular opinion, & the fatal change that has [taken] place in the constitutional administration of the Government by pros[*mutilation*] all its available power to the corrupt errors of Executive tyranny, & [*mutilation*] Supremacy are inauspicious to encouraging hope. But my dear Sir, [in the] trials & struggles of the approaching Session, your friends, & I may [say the] country will look to *you* with abiding solicitude. It will not only [require] all your experience, & the vast ressources of your great mind, but [will] call for a degree of Roman fortitude to grapple with dangers th[at] may involve political martyrdom. I have seen you face dangers [w]hen you could have avoided them, & when there was a less demand upon your patriotism than now. This is known to be your character, & this gives you preeminence above all your compeers. These things have doubtless threaded your mind, but I have ventured to call your attention to them in my own way, that I might remind you what your friends expect, & what I have heard many northern men say of you within the last few weeks. I hope to see you at the beginning of the Session, & to hear your views upon some of these points. Believe me most truly your friend & obedient Servant, T.L. Smith.

ALS in ScCleA. NOTE: Thomas L. Smith had formerly been Register of the U.S. Treasury. In newspaper advertisements appearing in mid-1847, he, in partnership with A.T. Smith, former Chief Clerk of the Navy Department, offered services as agents or attorneys in business before the federal government. They listed as references a number of prominent people, including Calhoun, Daniel Webster, James Buchanan, Thomas H. Benton, and Generals Winfield Scott, Zachary Taylor, and John E. Wool. (See the New Orleans, La., *Daily Picayune*, July 29, 1847, p. 1, and subsequent issues.)

From S[TEPHEN] MOYLAN FOX

Office of the South Carolina R.R. Co.
Charleston, 15th Nov[embe]r 1847

D[ea]r Sir, I regret that it will be out of my power to pay you a visit this fall and more especially as I will not be able to make a personal acquaintance with you. I do not think that my merely passing through the valley of the Savannah river would be of any importance. I am already pretty well acquainted with the character of the river and every thing else cannot be known without an instrumental examination.

It appears to me that a communication by canal & Rail road with the Tennessee river & thence by canals to steamboat Navigation is of much more importance to the Cities of Savannah & Charleston than the railways now projected. Observe how rapidly the increase is upon the Canals of N. York & Penn[sylvani]a. The tolls of the Penn[sylvani]a Canal in 1833 the year in which it was finished amounted to $151,400—in 1847—a period of only 14 years it has increased to upwards of $2,000,000. The tolls of the N. York Canal in 1820 was $5,437—in 1847[,] $3,200,000. When it [is] recollected that the cost of transportation on the Southern rail roads is three times as great as upon these canals some idea may be formed of their great usefulness. There may be causes ["in" *interlined*] operation which I do not perceive which prevents Charleston from becoming the Shipping port for the whole south west—but I believe that the only thing necessary is a *cheap mode* of communication between them. I would like to see this subject properly investigated; the unfortunate expenditure of the sums formerly appropriated for the improvement of the rivers has caused an erroneous but popular terror on the subject which it will be hard to combat.

I will try and see you as you pass through this place. I remain very respectfully Your Ob[edien]t Serv[an]t, S. Moylan Fox.

ALS in ScCleA.

From J[oseph] A. Binda

Paris, November 16th 1847

Dear Sir, Some days ago I took the liberty of sending to you at Washington some secret papers on Canada. They are unpublished, printed only for the strictly confidential service of the english cabinet. In your hands they may perhaps be of some use and importance: and I beg you will receive them as a demonstration of my devotedness to you, and of my strong desire of serving you and the country of my adoption.

Private affairs very essential to my small fortune have obliged me to make a rapid excursion to England, and I am now on my way to return to my Consulate at Leghorn. I was in danger of a heavy loss in one of the bankruptcies, that have lately rendered the english pecuniary affairs so difficult, and to save my property I went to London. I hope this short absence will not be the cause of any dissatisfaction at the State Department: a very competent consular agent has fulfilled the duties of my office during my journey; and otherwise I have the conscience of having done my duty. I recommend myself to your protection, and to the kind assistance and favour you have always honoured the Sumters and myself with. I know there have been and there are attempts to take the place from me, but if you continue to protect me, I am in hope now and for the future all the efforts of pretenders or enemies will be in vain.

The affairs of Europe continue on very precarious ground. England is declining every day in her commerce and her navigation. The immense capital sunk in railways; the bad harvest of 1846; and the subsidies to Ireland are amongst the principal causes of the actual distress. A great change I have found in the spirit of the abolitionists. Their follies in the West Indies bear the fruits your high prevision foresaw. Lord John Russell's administration is very weak, but it is so very ["difficulty" *altered to* "difficult"] to find successors

659

to the present ministers, that they will go on for some time. However the new Parliament cannot be calculated upon by any party. In France Mr. [F.P.G.] Guizot is considered safe for the next session of the Chambers; but there is little sympathy between the nation and the Government. The affairs of Switzerland and of Italy preoccupy the attention of Europe for the present. There is still some hope of seeing the civil war averted in Switzerland; the chances are in favour of the radical Cantons; and today it is said that Fribourg and Lucerne have made some steps for an amicable arrangement. In Italy the chances of liberty and independence are improving every day. Austria is frightened and decrepit.

If I could be of any service, of any use to you, Sir, and to your friends, I would consider it as a very great happiness. Your command, your letters, if you honour me with any, are to be ad[d]ressed to Leghorn. My high admiration for you, my affectionate profound respect, and my warm sincere gratitude are feelings inseparable from me, and with them I have the honour to be Your devoted, obliged Servant, J.A. Binda.

ALS in ScCleA.

From A[NDREW] P. BUTLER,
[Senator from S.C.]

Stonelands [Edgefield District, S.C.,] Nov[embe]r 16th 1847
My dear Sir, It was my wish and design to have paid you a visit this autumn whilst on a visit to see my friends in Greenville. Events have occurred to deprive me of that pleasure ["and" *canceled*]. Since Sept., I have scarcely had time to look at, or think of any matters beyond family concerns.

I am compelled to leave here tomorrow or next day for Columbia to attend to some arrangements connected with my late brother[']s [Pierce M. Butler's] affairs; and I am afraid that I shall not be at home about the time you will be going thro this part of the Country for Washington. I hope, however, that my absence will not prevent your calling at my house. You will find my mother [Behethland Foote Moore Butler] at home, with some of my nieces—and I am sure that you are a gentleman who has retained enough of the Simplicity of former times, to feel yourself at ease *and at home*, under such circumstances.

Some of my friends tell me they are very well satisfied, some times, not to find me at home; as they can better be entertained by my mother.

I look with some anxiety to the developement of future events but with very little patience or forbearance, on some of the signs of the times.

However, as I have not leisure to say more on politics, I shall desist from further remarks, but shall always be glad to have free conferences with you.

I think I shall be detained in Columbia for a week; & shall go thence to Charleston, where I may be detained for a day or two before I depart for Washington. In truth I subscribe myself with great respect & regard your obe[dien]t Ser[van]t, A.P. Butler.

ALS in ScCleA. NOTE: Col. Pierce M. Butler had been killed at the battle of Churubusco on August 20, 1847.

From J[AMES] D. B. DE BOW

New Orleans, November 17, 1847

My dear Sir, I take the liberty of troubling you once again. I send you by today[']s mail a copy of the Commercial Review for November in which you will find an article by Dr. [Josiah C.] Nott of Mobile on the statistics etc[.] of our negro population. His facts so far as they go are striking, but we have been collecting many more and hope to publish soon.

I have some idea that you will find this paper or these papers of use to you this winter in the Senate in meeting those men on the Wilmot Proviso. I would I had much more to furnish you. It would afford me great pleasure if you could refer to them *as from the Review* and I have no doubt it would be a substantial advantage to the work in extending its subscription ["& influence" *interlined*]. You see by inspection that I am making it eminently a *Southern work*.

Among the planters here the Wilmot Proviso attracts lively interest & I believe a great deal has been collected for the paper at Washington. I do not think the politicians here take much concern about it[.]

In New York last summer I conversed with Mess[rs.] Harper & Brothers about the volume of your speeches. The Edition is exhausted and they are anxious to publish another. I need not say how many hundreds & thousands desire a complete copy of these speeches & I would to heaven they could be had.

I have once or twice troubled you about writing me an article for the Review but this I admit is going too far with one whose time & attention must be so uninter[r]uptedly occupied with concerns of weightiest moment. With continued wishes for your health[,] long life & happiness I am Your friend & fellow Citizen, J.D.B. De Bow.

ALS in ScCleA. NOTE: Nott's article was entitled "Statistics of Southern Slave Population, with Especial Reference to Life Insurance."

From WILSON LUMPKIN

Athens [Ga.,] Nov. 18th 1847

My dear Sir, With feelings of deep interest & sober consideration, I have read your favor of the 7th Inst. Your letter presents a correct, but breif [*sic*] view, of the external & internal relations of the Country at the present time—and you are right in your conclusion, That the questions now before the Country, are pregnant with the most vital and important consequencies—["& the result" *interlined*] beyond the Ken of mortal man. What ought to be done, in regard to our present relations with Mexico, I am not prepared to say. I am however, prepared to say, that our national character demands, an increased vigor in the prosecution of the War, to that point which may be necessary, to humble the pride of the Priesthood & military Chieftains of Mexico. Then the question will arise, what is to be the next step?

The Annarchal Rulers of Mexico, being prostrated, the people will desire peace. But the whole letter & spirit of our government, stands opposed, to ["our having conquered" *canceled and* "conquering" *interlined*] provinces to govern, or to that of conquering a Country, for the purpose of annexation to our Union. Circumstances might justify, our wresting territory from an hostile enemy, & holding it, peopleing it, & annexing it to our Union. But a Territory already peopled, with materials unfit, to enter into the spirit of our institutions, & become good Citizens, should never be annexed to our Union.

On the subject of our internal relations, you present the case, as I conc[e]ive of it, *justly*. The long, constant, & increasing disposition, of the people generally, of the non Slaveholding States, to intermeddle, ["with," *interlined*] & finally destroy & overturn our Constitutional rights, connected with negroe Slavery, must be resisted efficiently & speedily, or our Federal Union will be dissolved.

Our forbearance on this subject, has to my mind, already become intollerable.

The Wilmot proviso, is but one, of a long list of our grievances on this subject. And we ought to make one general & consolidated issue, of the whole subject. Our great & only difficulty is, to unite & consolidate the action of the Slave holding States. Attempts made by States single-handed, must fail. If we cannot produce Unity & concert of action on this subject—Then we may make up our minds, to meet the most gloomy anticipations, which your letter presents. And strange as it may appear to you, yet I assure you—That the people of no one of the Southern States, except South-Carolina—are prepared for such action at this time, as you & myself, deem to be, not only necessary, but indispensible to the security of the Southern States. Upon this subject, our people have been most wickedly & awfully misled, by office holders & office seekers, aided by a Subservient press. One party, *the Whigs*, have deemed it, their party interest, to preserve a calm quiet silence, least a division might spring up between them & their Northern associates, & thereby prevent the success of their party, at the next Presidential election.

On the other hand, The Democrats, have labored, long & hard, to convince their Southern partizens—That the [Martin] Van Burens, [Silas] Wrights, [Lewis] Casses, &C &C was their shield & hiding place from the coming storm. It is true, that daily developements are strip[p]ing off this flimsy Vail of deception. But the minds of the large masses of the people, are inveloped in thick & gross darkness on this subject.

I trust I am not wanting in courage or Patriotism, to do my duty on this subject. I have most faithfully endeavored to use the humble means, at my Command—To sustain those who are battling for the Country. We have many difficulties, connected with the Slave question—which are rapidly pressing upon us. To meet them as we ought, I concur with you, that concert of action is the first object to be obtained, & I can see no way of effecting this object, but by a convention of the States interested. And if a plan can be devised & prosecuted to success, which will approach to a general feeling on the part of the States interested, I should indulge strong faith, that the heart burnings & strifes, on this Slave question, would ultimately be settled, & the Union preserved. But our enemies will never cease in their warfare upon our Constitutional rights—so long as we keep up our party divisions at home, so as to manifest to the world, that we have more thrist [*sic*] for office, and selfish party ascendancy—than for the Constitutional rights of the States, & the true interest & liberty of the people.

As they now stand, I am thoroughly disgusted with both the great political parties of the Country. Both are under the influence & controul, of a cunning selfish combination of corrupt office seekers.

They are ready to barter the most vital & sacred ["rights" *canceled*] Constitutional rights of the people, for place & power. To be sure, there are many good men & true, attached to both parties, but the influence of such are paralized, by the overwhelming numbers of a different character. Nothing short of a thorough reorganization of parties, can save our glorious Republic from destruction. If the Country is so far depraved—That it cannot afford material, for the leaders of an honest, patriotic party—then indeed, will our days, soon be numbered—and like Greece & Rome, It will be written, The United States *WAS*.

I would not hesitate a moment, but move in the matter which you suggest without delay—if I could be as sanguine as you seem to be, that good would result from the effort. Our State elections being over, indicates the present as a favorable time for such a movement, it is so. Nevertheless, when I look over the material[s] which compose the Legislature of Georgia, & consider the influences under which they are governed, I assure you, they are the last body of men in the State, that I would ["look" *interlined*] to, for a patriotic movement, at this momentous crisis. Look at our Congress men, of both parties from Georgia, & you have a good specimen of the leaders, who at this time hold the reigns in ["Georgia" *canceled and* "this State" *interlined*].

Our best men in Georgia, are now in private life, pretty generally disgusted with political life. Those however, who concur with my views, are evidently gaining strength rapidly, & I entertain no doubt will ere long become the dominant party in Georgia. I venture the opinion, that the actings & doings of the present Legislature, will greatly tend to strengthen the ranks of the Faithful & honest portion of the State. And if the Wilmot proviso, (as you anticipate) should rec[e]ive the sanction of Congress, it will strongly tend to favor the views which we entertain. Indeed, the passage of the Wilmot resolutions by Congress, I believe will be one of those wicked Acts, which will be over-ruled for great good. It will ["enlarge" *with the* "r" *interlined*] the platform, on which we stand.

Should the Wilmot resolutions, or something like them, pass both houses of Congress, I suppose as a matter of course, the President will *vetoe* them. If he does not, few friends as he now has, the number will be greatly diminished.

You are not apprized of all that I have done, for a year past, or you would not suspect me of supineness, in regard to the subjects which now agitate the Country. I am not idle, although no aspirant for notariety. As far as ["my" *interlined*] circle extends, I have been very successful in exerciseing a salutary influence in Georgia. My position in relation to public affairs, is universally known in this State. When the proper time shall arrive, I will shrink from no position which may be assigned me, in an attempt to get up a Southern Convention, for the purposes suggested in your letter. The Slave holding States, have only to Unite in council & proper action, on the Slave question—and our opponents would be crushed at once. Union amongst ourselves, would give us strength, to face a frowning world.

Your views may be sound upon the subject of retaliatory measures, as suggested in your letter, but my first impressions are not favorable, in regard to their expediency, or practicability.

I at this time strongly incline to the opinion, that the high ground, imperitively taken—that we will no longer submit, to the Variegated Violations of our rights, connected with our Slave property, or domestic institutions, by the non-Slave holding States, would be the most wise & expedient measure for the South. And after due notice, upon the pledge of our sacred honor & our lives—maintain the ground assumed.

No man loves or attaches more importance to the Union of these States, than he who now holds this pen. But I desire the continuance of no Union, which degrades me. If a new State would be ejected from the Union, On account of recognizeing the institution of Affrican Slavery, Then the Slave holding States ought no longer continue in such a Confederacy of States. The repeated assaults upon our Constitutional Compact, has greatly mar[r]ed its beauty & sym[m]etry, & to my mind, it is most clear, that if the General Government cannot be brought back to the Constitution, this generation will not pass away, before the glory of our Confederacy, will have departed. Write soon & write freely. As ever your friend, Wilson Lumpkin.

ALS in ScCleA; variant PC in Jameson, ed., *Correspondence*, pp. 1135–1139.

From JOHN A. CAMPBELL

Mobile, 20 Nov[embe]r 1847

Dear Sir, I have but lately returned from a summer[']s excursion, taken with the view of improving ["the" *canceled*] my own health & as a part of the education of my daughter. I designed writing to you as soon as I could find the necessary time after my return but my health & other causes combined have prevented.

In the first place allow me now to express to you how warmly and cordially I sympathised in your opinions & feelings in all the measures ["of" *canceled*] connected with the declaration of war upon Mexico. The folly of that proceeding ["is" *altered to* "was"] so stupendous that one has hardly an opportunity to contemplate its wickedness. You must now ["feel" *canceled and* "derive" *interlined*] in the approbation of all right minded men in the country ["that" *canceled*] a compensation for the scurrilous abuse to which you were subjected.

It is clear to us, that the difficulties on the subject of slavery, in so far as the action of parties & politicians have occasioned difficulty are rapidly approaching the degree, that a settlement will be [*partial word canceled*] required of them. Things cannot remain as they now are. The Wilmot Proviso is that which naturally excites most interest. I regard the subject of the acquisition of new Territory mainly as it may affect the *balance* of power in the federal government. What will be the effect of any large acquisition? Will it be to preserve the balance of power as it now exists? The territory is wholly unfit for a ["slave" *canceled*] negro population. The republic of Mexico contains a smaller number of blacks than any of the ["old" *interlined*] colonies of Spain & tho' this is not conclusive yet it is a persuasive argument that negro labor was not found to be profitable.

Mr. [James] Buchanan informs his friends in Berks [County, Pa.] that the territory ["proposed to be acquired" *interlined*] will never be used by slave holders & Gen[era]l [Waddy] Thompson tells us that the territory is wholly unfit for that population. These Gentlemen do not have with me a great deal of influence but I suppose in this case that they are not far from the truth. If this is the case all acquisitions of Mexican territory results in an increase of ["the" *interlined*] strength of the nonslaveholding States and a corresponding diminution of our own.

I have purposely left out of view the more general question whether a further extension of our limits is desirable. I suppose that if such an extension would result in a serious disturbance of the present action of the government of the U.S. that it is to be deprecated.

The first consideration then for Southern men to ["consider" *canceled and* "take" *interlined*] is, could it be used by a slaveholding community or would it be filled by a ["pop" *canceled*] mixed population of masters & slaves? My impression is that its population would be in a great measure of the free class.

Let us suppose that I am in error & that the territory acquired might be used by a slaveholding community. Still, the largest share would fall to the nonslaveholding States. I take it that the line of slavery is gradually being removed southwardly & that the largest portions of the occupied lands ["below" *canceled and* "above" *interlined*] the 35° & ["below" *interlined*] 36° 30′ of north latitude will be cultivated exclusively by ["white &" *canceled and* "a" *interlined*] free population—and still the line ["abve" *canceled and* "above" *interlined*] which slaves cannot be used to advantage will be found to be as low as the 34° of north latitude. If Mr. Polk should obtain the line that he proposed under the Missouri compromise the nonslaveholding States would be the largest beneficiaries. Looking then at the question of the acquirement of new territory as it affects the balance of power between the North & South I cannot see any ground for a hope that we shall receive an equal share of advantage.

Regarding the question of acquisition in a more general & comprehensive view I still have been adverse to the acquisition.

This war was not brought on by any act and I may say any fault of Mexico. Our President invaded a territory claimed by that Republic & over which its laws prevailed. Our armies met the armies of Mexico & assailed & defeated them. Our Congress before any notice of the fact of an encounter & upon the loosest information makes a proclamation of war. 1. We have maintained a very triumphant contest and have seized their capital. I confess that I do not find in any facts that have been presented a just ground for dismembering their territories.

2. I have very great ["doubts of" *canceled and* "fears" *interlined*; "the" *altered to* "that"] the existing territories of the United States will prove too much for our government. The wild & turbulent conduct of the western members upon the Oregon question & their rapacity & greediness in all matters connected with the appropriation of the revenues induce great doubt of the propriety of introducing new States in the Union so fast as we do. The connexion of the whig party with the Abolitionists ["have" *altered to* "has"] never disturbed me a great deal for the reason that the whig party is *governed* by its leading & reflecting men. The tone of the party is derived from

men of property & character & they are in a measure held to respect property guaranteed by the Constitution & laws of the country. The union of the democratic party with the abolitionists I have regarded as far more dangerous because they are held by fewer restraints and are ready to go farther lengths to carry their ends. I have a similar feeling in regard to legislators from the Western States. Their notions are freer[,] their impulses stronger[,] their wills less restrained. I do not wish to increase the number till the new States already admitted to the Union become civilized.

My opinions lead me to refuse territory. Suppose the point to be settled that territory shall be admitted I wish it received on no other terms than those of strict equality. I wish a counter proviso to the Wilmot Proviso to the effect of the first of your resolutions and with a definition of property viz. what the laws of the State from which a ["slave"(?) *canceled and* "citizen" *interlined*] may remove may define as property—and that this condition shall so remain until the people ["of the territory" *interlined*] shall form a State & be admitted to the Union and this I would like to see a part of the Treaty of peace.

The Wilmot Proviso I take it, will not be pressed upon Congress at its next session, unless it comes in the shape of instructions to the President in regulating his conduct in making a treaty. I do not believe that the President will be disposed to encounter that question. He will place upon Congress the responsibility of determining the war & the propositions of Santa Anna will be the basis. The question will then be evaded by the act of the whig party & the northern democrats. I have always suspected that the administration would not ask for a line to the South of the 36° 30′ of north latitude and whether he asked it or not, I have always supposed that this war would terminate by securing no larger portion of Mexican territory than is found north of that line. I have done the President injustice by my suspicion. I am satisfied that the Northern people would willingly yield the land betwe[e]n the Nueces & Rio Grande & take ["the" *canceled*] California—at least such would be the inclination of their politicians.

It appears to me viewing all these things together that the true course to pursue is to resume as well as we can our positions before the war commenced. The matters of boundary & of debt have to be adjusted and we must consider the expenses of the war and the losses sustained in our armies as ["the" *interlined*] penalties—the dreadful penalties of having selected an incompetent man to be our President. Do you think we will be taught any thing by it?

We shall be asked to vote for Buchanan or [George M.] Dallas in less than 12 months. I have read over with the most earnest care your letters to Messrs. Lessesne [*sic*; Joseph W. Lesesne] & [Percy] Walker. I agree with you that unless we at the South, have made up our minds that the ["question" *canceled*] solutions of slavery should be controlled by our enemies that the agitation on this subject should terminate.

It is a very great error it appears to me, to suppose that we have any party at the north, or that we shall ever have one. The politicians do not guide public opinion on this subject. They follow after in obedience to it. I believe that no where in the north would a Candidate maintaining Southern opinions on this subject be sustained for any great length of time. The sermons of the clergy—the prayers of the lay members at the church meetings contain deprecations of slavery as a sin. The literary class now becoming large & influential in the cities fill their writings with tirades against it. The Northern Press almost without an exception is opposed to us—and above all the colleges & schools are tinctured with the stain of Abolitionism. I do not use the term in the sense that it is applied to [William Lloyd] Garrison & [Wendell] Phillips, but in a sense that embraces a very large proportion of the population. Garrison & Phillips say that the Constitution of the U.S. is a pro slavery contract—containing powerful & stringent securities for the slave holder. Phillips has written quite an able pamphlet to prove this—a pamphlet we might circulate to great advantage excluding a few paragraphs. They have collected all the debates together of those concerned in making or ratifying the Constitution to prove the same truth. Their remedy is to make a *revolution*. Now all this is better to me than ["that other" *canceled and* "the" *interlined*] course ["which" *canceled and* "of those other men who" *interlined*; "denies" *altered to* "deny"] your rights or ["which disregards" *altered to* "who disregard"] them while claiming to be the friends of the Constitution. A very interesting statement of the condition[,] prospects[,] philosophy & intentions of the abolitionists you will find in the report of the Massachusetts Society at their 15 anniversary. I made it a point to go over the different offices of publication of the Society & to examine their publications. I should say that their Press was not very active. The office in New York is a poor affair. Their publications are of a low order making appeals to the credulity of the community by tales of cruelty and oppression of masters exercised over their slaves. There were two books of some pretension one by Dr. [Albert] Barnes & the other by Dr. [Leonard] Bacon & these were the only ones worth speaking of in their collection. Their list was composed of about 15 publications of a low price. The Boston office contained books of a higher order and in greater numbers. The whole collection however was insignificant. I suppose that $500 or certainly $1000 would have purchased all in the office. You hear but little of *this sect*. They do not enter ["much" *interlined*] into the general movements of Society. The things which ["does" *altered to* "do"] affect the thoughts of men & consequently the movements of Society ["is" *altered to* "are"] the various & continuous condemnations that this institution receives. The legislatures—anniversary orators & Poets—ministers of the Gospel—teachers—all combine in impressing a fixed sentiment in the people—that slavery is a sin & a folly—that it injures the country[,] the master[,] the slave. I fully agree with you that we should have no share in a convention ["to make a President" *interlined*] tho I find I am almost alone. The outbreak of the Barnburners in Newyork has given our people ["a hope" *interlined*] that the party organisation will fall into our hands & we can make the President. They wish to profit by it. I confess a profound indifferance to the election of any Democrat north of the Potomac. Mr. [Levi] Woodbury even if he could receive a nomination would have no chance of an election & I think *his* election is not so desirable as to make us bend a principle to attain it. The Whigs must be infatuated if they fail to elect the next President. I shall be passive henceforth unless you have some counsel that can move me from that condition. I have done so much work in the way of *disorganisation* that ["now" *canceled and* "I" *interlined*] feel reluctant to enter upon a new one & this ["one" *interlined*] is thought to be wholly unjustifiable. I joined a [Zachary] Taylor meeting last summer. My object was to put before the public the principles that I approved on this subject & to prepare for a war on Messrs. [Silas] Wright or Buchanan in case of the nomination of either. I see no motive for desiring the present organisation of the party & I wish to see the issue of events now before us before making a new one.

I also concur with you in the opinion that we should put an end to this constant warfare upon slavery. Already it has impoverished our credit and it daily weakens our moral power. Our States are fast losing their respectability. The tide of emigration flows past them. They are carefully avoided. Our people look to the future without confidence and our slaves are emerging above their condition not in intellect or moral culture but in feeling & temper. They ["have" *canceled*] begin to understand that society is being moved on their account. The Abolitionists profess a revolutionary purpose. They openly promulgate a design to subvert the Union. The other classes

of the Northern people perform all the acts of the Abolitionists without avowing the same purpose.

I agree too that a newspaper at Washington City would do great
good tho' I fear it will ultimately fail for the want of subscription. I
am willing to aid in the project.

I have troubled you with a long letter for which please pardon
me & believe me to be Sincerely Y[ou]r friend, John A. Campbell.

ALS in ScCleA; PC in Jameson, ed., *Correspondence*, pp. 1139–1145. Note:
First published in 1844, Wendell Phillips's *The Constitution a Pro-Slavery Compact. Or Selections from the Madison Papers, &c.* was often reprinted before
1860.

To T[HOMAS] G. CLEMSON, [Brussels]

Fort Hill, 20th Nov[embe]r 1847
My dear Sir, The mail of yesterday brought me your's of the 16th
Oct[obe]r [*sic*; 10/14?]; and in order that this may go by the next
steamer, I have concluded to answer it immediately.

In your letter of the 27th Dec[embe]r 1845 (it ought to be I suppose 1846) [*not found*] you wrote me on the subject of the debt due
you by Andrew [Pickens Calhoun] & myself, and expressed a desire,
that it should be consolidated in a joint bond; and at the same time,
expressed a desire to see Mr. [John Ewing] Bonneau[']s statement,
with one of my own. I answered your letter at the time. On my
return, I wrote to Mr. Bonneau on the subject. He stated in answer,
that you left with him *two* joint notes of Andrew & myself, each for
$8500 and a due bill for $7114, & that he had paid & taken up ["the"
canceled] your note to Arthur Simkins due the 1st January 1844, out
of funds we had supplied; and for his payments to you on our account, refer[r]ed me to his account rendered ["me" *canceled*] in
detail on the final settlement between him, Andrew & myself. On
turning to our final settlement with you, I found his statement, as to
the note and due bill, corresponding in every particular. In turning
also to your own statement, in the letter referred ["to" *interlined*], I
find you state them to be *two* notes and their amount to be $17,000,
so that you & not we, have made "the first & great error," that you
suppose existed; that there were ["were" *canceled*] four notes; one
due bill for $7114 and three notes for $8500 each. In the statement
in the same letter, you make the sum due by us to be $13,465, interest
and all, on the 1st Jan[uar]y 1846. But even in that, you have com-

671

mitted two considerable errors. You state, as the basis of your calculation, that there was due you on the first of January 1845[,] $18,388, made up of capital $17,000, and 14 months['] interest $1,388, when in fact $3000 had been paid on the 1st instalment on your land, that fell due after the notes were given (1st Nov[embe]r 1843) on the 1st Jan[uar]y 1844; and ought, of course, ["to have" *interlined*] been deducted at the time, in calculating the interest. Again, the next instalment was paid 1st Jan[uar]y 1845, and ought to be deducted at the ["time & not at the" *interlined*] end of the year, as you have. I have assumed, that the two instalments were paid, when they fell due, although they were not for some time afterwards; but we paid the interest, which accrued on them, which made it the same to you, as if they had been paid at the time.

As to the due bill, I was ["some what surprised, I was" *canceled*] somewhat surprised to see it was over paid, ["when I turned" *canceled*] when I turned to Mr. Bonneau's account in making out our statement for you; and said to Andrew, at the time, that you had informed me, that there was a small balance due you on it. Since I received your letter, I again ["have" *canceled*] looked over it, to see if there had not been some mistake; and I conclude there has been; but cannot certainly say, until I can see our statement. Mr. B[onneau] states his account with us, in two columns; one consisting, as I had supposed, exclusively of the sums paid you in detail, and the other of interests calculated on them, until the time of our final settlement with him. But in looking over the former, I find a charge of commissions on the cotton, the same as if it had been sent to him to sell, instead, of ["selling" *canceled and* "of (*sic*) being sold" *interlined*] in Mobile, as it was. It amounts to $175, and ought, of course, been charged to us, & ["to" *interlined*] come in the interest column, instead of charged with the sums paid to you. I wish you to return our statement, as we kept no copy; supposing that you would return it, either with, or without corrections. Of course, you may take a copy, if you desire.

I hope with these facts & statements, you will find no difficulty in making out a statement satisfactory to yourself. There can be no difficulty in so simple a transaction. I did not include our seperate account, because ["you" *interlined*] did not desire it, & because, it would not be right to include it in our joint transactions.

I expect to leave on the 27th for Washington, & to take your place [in Edgefield District] in my route. You ought certainly to come out next summer or fall, as I wrote you. I trust it will be a better time to make sales than the present of your property.

The fall has been, & continues delightful. We had a sharp frost this morning, which killed for the first time the tender vegetables in the garden.

We are all well and all desire their love to you, Anna [Maria Calhoun Clemson] & the children [John Calhoun Clemson and Floride Elizabeth Clemson]. Your affectionate father, J.C. Calhoun.

ALS in ScCleA.

From L E W I S S. C O R Y E L L

New Hope [Pa.,] 20th Nov[e]m[ber] 1847

My dear Sir, Whatever solid objections has existed through the country in regard to the war with Mexico, is now yielding to the necessity of the case, and the support of our gallant soldi[e]ry now in that country. Therefore to withhold supplies w[oul]d meet with most universal disapprobation.

Your first advice to abstain from the declaration of war was *the right advice.* Next to take possession of their Ports & levy Taxes, & withdraw our troops to a reasonable line for indemnity, was the next best advice, but we have gone too far now to carry out that advice fully, and circumstances alters applicable means, only applicable at a particular stage of ["the" *interlined*] Phase.

There is a deep arrangement going on. [Henry] Clay[']s speech is a mere reecho of [Daniel] Webster[']s at Fanneuel [*sic*] Hall, ["and I" *canceled*]. I feel assured that the [Martin] V[a]n Bu[re]n men must be allowed to rule or they will any where ["or for any body go" *interlined*] for ruin, in the Presidential contest.

Had the President [James K. Polk] taken your advice & asked Congress for authority to do what [he] has ["done" *interlined*] in regard to Mexican Tariff, It would have prevented a defence for his false position in this act at least. I look with great confidence to your advice & demonstration. Tis strange but true, that you hold a mighty power, over the events & destinies of this Poeple [*sic*], and the foreground ought to be given to you at once. I am D[ea]r Sir Y[ou]r Obe[dient] Ser[vant,] Lewis S. Coryell.

[P.S.] By whose direction was the armistice, before the City of Mexico which cost us which cost us [*sic*] more than a 1000 lives[?]

ALS in ScCleA.

673

From S[IMEON] DRAPER and Others

New York [City,] Nov. 20th 1847

Dear Sir, The New England Society of the City of New York request the honour of your presence at the Dinner to be given at the Astor House on the 22nd Dec. next, in commemoration of the landing of the Pilgrims.

We the undersigned a committee appointed for the purpose are very desirous to receive your early acceptance of this invitation. With great respect Your Ob[e]d[ien]t Servants, S. Draper, Cha[rle]s A. Peabody, John Thomas, B.W. Bonney, L.B. Wyman, M[oses] H. Grinnell, President.

LS in ScCleA. Note: In its report of the dinner the New York *Herald* of 12/23/-1847, p. 1, reported that letters from Calhoun, Henry Clay, and other notables were read in reply to invitations. "All these gentlemen excused themselves in handsome terms, and sent each a toast to be read in his name." An AEU by Calhoun reads "Invitation from the New England association of N. York."

MEMORANDUM [by Lyman C. Draper]

Calhoun Settlement. Hon. J.C. Calhoun, writes Nov. 21, 1847, Fort Hill, to Ch[arle]s H. Allen [editor of the Abbeville, S.C., *Banner*]:

"My father (*Pat[ric]k Calhoun*) with his three brothers & his sister with her husband arrived in the district (Abbeville) February, 1756, & settled in a group in what is now known as Calhoun's Settlement, at the fork of the two streams of that name. The names of his brothers were *James*, the oldest, *Ezekiel*, the next, *William*, the third, my father being the youngest. The sister [Mary] had married Mr. [John] Noble, & the late Governor [Patrick] *Noble* was her grandson. My father settled on the place owned recently by a son of my brother Patrick, where a monument is raised to his memory. The elder brother settled on a place afterwards owned by my brother *James*, & now owned by Mrs. [Ellen L.?] *Parker. Ezekiel* settled on the place on which she resides. *William* in the fork of Calhoun's Creek & Little River; & Mr. *Noble* in the fork of the two creeks of the name of Calhoun.

I am not certain who accompanied them, or who immediately followed them & settled in the neighborhood. But among their very early neighbors were [Robert] *Norris*, who after the death of *Ezekiel*, married his widow [Jane Ewing Calhoun]; a family of the name of

Mercer, & one of the name of *Houston*, of which *Squire Houston* is a descendant, & probably can give you some information. Our family were, however, the pioneers, & my impression is[,] came alone. My father kept a journal of their emigration from Wythe County, as it is now called, in Virginia, but then [the] extreme limits to which the white population had advanced. I saw & read the journal before I went to College, & left it with his other papers in a desk in which they were all kept, but was unable to find it after my return, & I fear [it] has been lost forever.

There were at the time they made their settlement but two others in the District; one at White Hall, on Hard Labor Creek, settled by [Andrew] *Williamson*, a Scotch trader, in 1754, & the other at Cambridge, then called Ninety Six, settled about the same time by a man of the name *Goudy* [*sic*; Robert Goudey], also a trader. The region composing the District was in a virgin state, new & beautiful, without underwood & all the fertile portion covered by a dense canebrake, & hence the name of Long Cane. It had been recently got from the Cherokees, & the settlement was more than 16 or 17 miles from the boundary line between them & the whites. The region was full of deer & other game, & among them, the buffalo.

Our family were driven from the back part of Virginia in consequence of *Braddock's defeat* in the old French war. The hostilities of the Indians (the war continuing) extended South; & in Feb. 1760, the Cherokees made a sudden inroad on *Calhoun*, & the other settlements, that had been formed subsequently. The inhabitants fled, but were overtaken by the Indians mounted on horseback. The entire number of whites, men, women & children, amounted to about 250, of which about 55 or 60 were capable of bearing arms; but the onset was so sudden that but few, more than about 14, could get their arms out of the wagons in time to make resistance. They made a desperate struggle, but with the loss, by being killed, of one half the number; & among them *James Calhoun*, the oldest brother, who commanded the party. They were overpowered, & scattered in every direction. The killed altogether amounted to about 50, mostly women & children. The men who escaped, returned to bury the dead, pick up the stragglers, & recover what property might not be destroyed, & found 21 Indian warriors dead on the ground, & among them a principal chief. Those of the settlement who escaped, fled to Augusta. The battle was fought on the East Side of Long Cane, near where the old road from Calhoun's Settlement to Charleston, called the Ridge Road, crossed it, at a place near to where Patterson's bridge, I think it is called now, or was some time ago, crosses it.

A tombstone erected by my father to the memory of his mother [Catherine Montgomery Calhoun], who was among the killed (an old woman of seventy six years of age) marks the spot.

My father shortly after visited Charleston, & gave an account of the affair, of which I have a copy containing most of the facts stated. The rest I had from him. He was appointed Captain of Rangers, & served in that capacity on the frontiers to the end of the war without pay. After the termination of the war in 1763, the family returned & re-occupied the settlement, but the Indians continued trouble-some, & the whites to continue to be forted for some years."

DU in WHi, Draper Collection, Sumter Mss., 16:348–352; PC in "Account of the Settlement of the Calhoun Family in South Carolina," in *Gulf States Histori-cal Magazine*, vol. I, no. 6 (July, 1902), pp. 439–441; PEx in *Historical Collec-tions of the Joseph Habersham Chapter, Daughters of the American Revolution* (5 vols. Atlanta and Athens, Ga.: Charles P. Byrd, 1902–1929), 3:97–99; PEx in John H. Logan, *A History of the Upper Country of South Carolina from the Earliest Periods to the Close of the War of Independence: Biographical and Historical Extracts from the Unpublished Manuscript of Volume II* (Easley, S.C.: Southern Historical Press, 1980), pp. 97–99; typed excerpts in ViHi, Hugh Blair Grigsby Papers. NOTE: The manuscript volume in which the docu-ment presented above is found consists of materials collected by Draper during a field trip in 1871. Draper is thought to have acquired most of the material in the volume from Dr. John H. Logan, who had collected it in connection with a proposed history of the S.C. Upcountry.

From JOHN A[LFRED] CALHOUN

Eufaula [Ala.,] November 22d 1847
D[ea]r Uncle, I am about to visit Montgomery during the sitting of our Legislature, and should like to hear from you in advance, on the probable course of events, so as, to shape my course with the more discretion. I declined a seat in the Senate of this State in order to effect a certain end (the amalgamation of the old Parties with a view to the formation of a new ["one" *interlined*] under the suggestions of your last letter to me). So far my efforts have been quite as suc-cessfull as I expected. The gentleman whome I yielded to in the Senate is Mr. [Jefferson] Buford—a *Carolinian*, a *Nullifyer*, a whig. He occupies much the same ground which Mr. [Henry W.] Hilliard [Representative from Ala.] occupies. I was assured on all hands that I could have been elected—but it would have been by the aid of ultra whigs and Democrats; and it would have separated me from that portion of the whigs which I think must soon be with us. Hence

I declined, and managed so far in bringing over Mr. Buford and his friends that they are now your *loud* advocates. My reason for visiting Montgomery is to carry out these plans in our State as far as practicable. The only way to manage the Democratic party, constituted as it has been, is, to keep them in such a situation as to render our aid *necessary* for their success. Plunder is all that they seriously contend for. The tone of the old hunkers of this section of country has materially changed within the last six or eight months. Then you were a *tra[i]tor*—Now they say you were right in all your positions, but were to[o] *arrogant* in announcing them.

My particular object in writing to you at this time is to ask your opinions on certain features of political movements of the day. What do you think of the [Zachary] Taylor movement for the Presidency? What of [Levi] Woodbury, [George M.] Dallas, and [James] Buchanan's position on the "Wilmot proviso" and what course should we adopt towards them? To what extent should we (I mean the States['] right portion of the Democracy) concilliate the old hunker portion of the Democracy[?] What degree of interest do you feel in the election of [Dixon H.] Lewis over [William R.] King for the Senate? And finally I would like to have your views as to the probable course, on the Mexican war, which will be adopted by the administration. Information on these points as well as on any other you may deem proper will be thankfully received by me. It is scarcely necessary for me to add that all the information you may impart will only be *discretely used*, and will be held as strictly confidential. As I expect in future to take a more active part [in] the political transactions of my adopted State I am anxious to take a position, and hence my contemplated visit to Montgomery.

My family are all well and have been so during the last summer & fall. In great haste your nephew &c, John A. Calhoun.

ALS in ScCleA; variant PC in Boucher and Brooks, eds., *Correspondence*, pp. 410–411.

From J. L. De Su

Clinton [La.,] 22nd Nov. 1847
My Dear Sir, I have ventured to address a few lines to you on the subject of the Mexican war. In the first place I must inform you that in this part of Louisiana all eyes are turned towards you—and in the next place we are all except the old Federalists, in favor of the War.

We was in favor of the annexation of Texas And look [*one word canceled and "on" interlined*] you as the master mind that achieved it. We are just as much in favor of the present Mexican war, and expect all great Southern men will support it. And you my Dear Sir are among if not the very first in our hearts—to you we look and look with confidence as the mighty champion of Southern rights to lend it the influence of your mighty intellect. Although to you at present a stranger I have ventured to make these few suggestions. At the same time I will inform you that nine tenths of this portion of Lou[i-sian]a is settled by your particular friends many of whom are from Abbeville & Edgefield. At any rate do as you may on the all exciting subject—it will be our pride and I hope our boast that our own Calhoun has done his duty. By the way Sir I should like to hear from you occasionally and will only add—I am one of the sons of Carolina and have been one of your admirers and still am, and look to you as the only man the South has to look to.

I hope my Dear Sir you will not take this epistle ["*as*" *canceled*] a miss coming as it does from an obscure individual But at the same time one of your admirers & stedfast friend. With sentiments of Esteem I Remain yours truly, J.L. De Su.

ALS in ScCleA. NOTE: An AEU by Calhoun reads "Mr. De Sue."

By Dr. William L. Jenkins, [Pendleton], 11/27. Jenkins recorded in his daybook a medical visit to the Calhoun household: "Hon. John C. Calhoun. To visit & advice boy Isaac. [$]2.00." Another entry for the same day reads "To visit & dressing wound (boy Isaac). [$]2.50," making a total of "[$]4.50" for the day's services. Entries in ScCM, Waring Historical Library, William L. Jenkins Daybook, 1840–1848, p. 80.

From BARNARD E. BEE

Pendleton So. Ca., Nov. 28, [18]47
My dear Sir, I left home to spend the night with you on Friday—when I met Willie who informed me [you] had that morn[in]g left for Washington.

The whole Country are looking to you. Think well—as is your custom—before you break ground in the Senate. Mr. [Henry] Clay's resolutions *not bad*—meet with no response!

Unnecessary as the War was—The success that has attended our army—has produced a *feeling* in our People which tho not to be *encouraged* must be *met*—and particularly by you.

They will not be satisfied now with the Rio Grande. The "Sier[r]a Madre" [Mountains] must now be your aim. Fall back upon this line with a *Competent* force—and abandon all thought of universal conquest—and I think the *People* will be satisfied. I would assume the debt due our citizens by Mexico—(very much exag[g]erated) but there I would Stop.

The Country has lost enough in blood and treasure and would not sanction an expenditure of millions for territory already conquered. This may not be in strict justice to a feeble enemy—and that a Sister Republic—but it is entirely in accordance with the justice of Nations.

As to Slavery—I do not know that I would name it—not that I would blink it—but that the Constitution creates no distinction and Virginia has as much right to move *bag* and *baggage* to Mexico—as Pen[n]sylvania or Massachusetts.

Pardon my troubling you. I have sometimes thought you were more *excited* on that War than usual—and I want you to be perfectly yourself. As I said before—The eyes of the Country—nay of the World are upon you. I am as always Sincerely, Barnard E. Bee.

ALS in ScCleA.

From R[ICHARD] K. CRALLÉ

Lynchburg [Va.,] Dec. 1st 1847

My dear Sir: My friend, Francis B. Deane Esq. starts to Washington tomorrow morning, and furnishes me an opportunity, briefly, to acknowledge the receipt of yours of the 25th of Oct. and at the same time to introduce him, as an intelligent gentleman, to your acquaintance which he desires to make. He is a correspondent of Mr. [Franklin H.] Elmore and the most influential and energetic friend of the great Rail Road West from this place, the Charter of which we are endeavouring to secure.

It would have given me much pleasure to have met you in Richmond as you suggested, but the late destructive freshet which has swept over the Canal, leaves us no direct means of communication with Richmond except a miserable hack, and over roads nearly im-

679

passible. Besides, I am compelled to leave Town on an excursion through the Western Counties of the State, and as far as Cincinnati; having been appointed by the Citizens of the Town to reconnoiter the line of the proposed Road with the view of procuring subscriptions. This duty will require me to be absent some six weeks and in the meantime I must make some arrangements of business to authorize it.

On the subject of politics—You have doubtless seen [Henry] Clay's Speech and Resolutions. Their design is obvious. He is again in the field, & though some of his positions are less obnoxious than they might have been, others are as bad as they well can be. The idea of surrendering the whole Country can never receive the sanction of the People. His reasoning, too, on the part annexation has borne in producing the war is captious, fallacious and unjust. The object is doubtless to wound you.

I am suddenly interrupted—and must write at another moment. In haste truly yours, R.K. Crallé.

[P.S.] I have a moment to annex a postscript. I had a free though not full conversation with [William M.] Blackford before the appearance of Clay's speech; and he seemed entirely inclined to anticipate a reorganization of Parties; but the effect of this movement will, I fear, drive him back. It certainly has been felt considerably amongst the scattered forces of the Old National Party; and will probably lead to a reunion to some extent. A [Zachary] Taylor Paper, however, starts tomorrow in this place, and will lead to much bickering in the ranks. I will wait a more favorable moment to feel the pulse of Blackford. If many of the Party rally under the banner of the New Paper, as is likely, he will be compelled to look for quarters. I will write however on this and other matters more fully in a short time.

I see my name is connected with the Secretaryship of the Senate, by whom I do not know, or for what purpose. I presume, however, it is a mere attempt to re-elect Mr. [Benjamin B.] French [Clerk of the House of Representatives] by holding out threats against [Asbury] Dickins [Secretary of the Senate]. I have taken no part in the matter; and you had better take none. If the situation be voluntarily tendered I shall accept of it for several reasons both of a public & private nature. But I would not have you be concerned in the matter. Most sincerely and faithfully yours, R.K. Crallé.

ALS in ScCleA.

To "Col." A[NDREW] P[ICKENS] CALHOUN, Uniontown, Perry County, Ala.

Charleston, 3d Dec[embe]r 1847

My dear Andrew, I am this far on my way to Washington and expect to leave for there by the boat this afternoon. I have attended to our two notes in bank. They will both be [re]newed for six months. You will have to be punctual in attending to the discount on renewal. That of the bank of Charleston is ["for" *canceled and* "amounts to" *interlined*] $161.41. I do not rem[em]ber the name of the Cashier, but the check can be sent to H[enry] W. Conner the President. The amount of the other you know.

I find the prevailing opinion here is, that the crop will not exceed 2,200,000 bags, and that is my impression, as far as I can get information. That of this State is estimated at ⅔ of last year. I do not think it will exceed it. My impression is, that the market will be better in the spring, & that we had better hold on, except it should be necessary to sell a part to meet discounts & interest to [Ann Mathewes] Ioor; but I will write you again on this point when I arrive at Washington & can get fuller information.

I am quite disappointed in not having heard from you since your letter of the 6th Nov[embe]r, as I have been very anxious to hear, both as to the health of the place & what effect the long open fall has had on the production of our cotton crop. I hope it has added considerably to the amount. You must not fail to write to me on the receipt of this, & to give me your opinion, as to what will be the amount of the entire crop of the year. I would like to have it in detail, as far as your information extends.

I left all well at home. Willie [that is, William Lowndes Calhoun] was stud[y]ing quite attentively, & has made great progress in Latin, and appears to have become fond of it. The prospect is, that he will do well. James [Edward Calhoun], I understand, is doing well; and I find John [C. Calhoun, Jr.] has been devoting himself closely to his studies. I think they have all taken a new impulse.

The rail road has been located from Columbia to Anderson court House. Greenville withdrew its subscri[p]tions, & retired from the company. The prospect is, that it will be made. The Eng[ine]er offered to give bond & security to finish it in two years for [$]10,000 a mile, all complete Engines and all, & in full operation. There is enough already subscribed to finish it ⅗ of the way, so that we are like [to] have a rail road at last. It will do much for us. I have not yet heard from Mr. [George] Geddes about the plank road; but will get the information for you, when I get to Washington.

My love to Margaret [Green Calhoun] & the children. Do not fail to write often during the winter. I think you would do well to apply all your disposable [*one word canceled and "force" interlined; ms. mutilated*; to] clearing, in order to [*ms. mutilated*] to enlarge our crop, as soon as we can get hands at a fair price. I still hope, we may get Mr. [Thomas G.] Clemson's. He must return next summer to attend to his business, and as he intends to sell, if they can be had at a fair price, I think we ought to take them. Your affe[ctiona]te [father,] J.C. [Cal]houn.

ALS owned by Henry H. Welch.

By Dr. William L. Jenkins, [Pendleton], 12/3. Jenkins recorded in his daybook services rendered to the Calhoun household: "Hon. John C. Calhoun. To box salve [for] boy (Isaac). [$].25." Entry in ScCM, Waring Historical Library, William L. Jenkins Daybook, 1840–1848, p. 80.

From ELLWOOD FISHER

Cincinnati, 12 Mo[nth] 4, 1847

Dear Friend, Since I had the pleasure of receiving thy last letter, the current of events it seems to me has pursued a very salutary direction. The schism among the Caucus and spoilsmen of New York, and their overthrow, have confounded that portion of the party in this State hitherto the predominant one; and has done much throughout the West to break the spell of partyism—and its fetters. It was most just and most fit that the section and the men that gave the caucus system to the country, should be the first to witness its fall and lie beneath its ruins. The law of retribution for fraud, is as sure and as appropriate as for force. Those who live by the sword shall die by the sword. Those who spoil are spoiled.

It is well for the South that this event has occurred in time: otherwise the attempt would have made at this session and possibly with some success, to persuade the Democracy of the South to rely on the fidelity and the power of their northern allies. But now when it is seen that the Democracy of the largest State of the North are divided and destroyed merely because they were silent on the great question of plundering and insulting the South—because they did not join in the aggression—the South will see what she has to expect if she relies on any thing but herself. If however the least vestige of doubt could have remained after this development, it must vanish at the demonstration of [Henry] Clay, who by adopting the principle, although he waives the measure itself of the Wilmot proviso, has revealed the imperative demand of the North that the immolation of the South, shall be the price of the Presidency. It is true that the great mass of the people of both parties are as yet comparatively calm and even apathetic in this country on this question. They believe indeed that slavery is an evil and ought to be excluded from new territory. But they have not considered the force of the adverse opinion in the South on this question, and are not now at all disposed to run the risk of commotion and disunion to maintain these views. They may however be excited to that extremity. Much will depend on the manner in which the issue is presented—but more far far more will depend on the union and firmness of the South. If they are clearly displayed the South will have friends enough here of both parties to assert her equality. She will have the talent, the principle, the conservatism and even the partyism of this country in her favour. But if she waivers or divides she is lost. The defection of Clay has already in this respect operated unfavourably.

I was in Louisville a few days ago, and Clay was at the same Hotel. I had two long conversations with him almost without inter-[r]uption on the leading topics of the day. He is thoroughly northern in his notions of Slavery; and ["even" *canceled*] thinks it will at no distant period be abolished even in tropical regions. He is however not well versed, either in the facts or principles of the question. He was at first impressed with the notion that Slavery would be excluded from ["the" *canceled*] any territory acquired from Mexico, and this by the law of nations until Congress by positive enactment established it there. He held that inasmuch as a conquered Territory must be governed by its previous laws until new ones were imposed by the conqueror, that therefore slavery, not now existing there, must remain excluded until Congress instituted it. But I observed that whenever the acquisition was made, Congress must pass laws for its government as a territory—and must either define what should constitute property in it, and thus positively exclude or admit slavery, or give to a territorial Legislature the right generally of passing all laws not incompatible with the Constitution and laws of the United States—and thus leave the question of slavery to the people who should settle there. He maintained however that if the latter course were adopted the South would be sure of exclusion as the population already there were Mexican and opposed to Slavery. But I asked whether the Mexican population were to be allowed to vote. He thought they would be *of course*. I replied that I thought they would *not be* of course. He finally admitted that whether Congress pronounced affirmatively or remained passive on the question depended on the manner in which it was presented.

By the way—what will the Administration do on this question in its policy of armed occupation? If our army should be large enough to repress insurrection or prevent it, and our people are tempted to emigrate to Mexico, is the municipal law of Mexico to prevail—so as to exclude slavery? If so many of the Abolitionists and Proviso men will be in favour of armed occupation.

Clay[']s speech has not united his party in this State. Its leaders prefer [John] McLean—and a large portion would prefer [Thomas] Corwin. But I think Clay is now predominant. I think he will find it difficult to hold Kentucky if a proper Candidate is presented against him. His speech has enured largely to thy benefit, in that State as well as of course further South on the Slavery question, and every where on the War question. I admire the boldness with which he pronounced the preamble to the supply bill "a lie," and his rebuke of those who voted for it. As for his notion of a vigorous prosecution of the War if Mexico won't make peace on his terms, many of his warm friends dissent from it and prefer thy policy of a defensive line—amongst the rest the Louisville Journal.

I saw General [William O.] Butler before he started for Mexico and he is yet in favour of a defensive line. He would take the western base of the Sierra Madre which he thinks could be held by the regular army. And he prefers ["it" *interlined*] not because he would insist on making it the boundary but because it would afford a margin for concession in treating for peace.

I observe that the [Washington] Union is attempting to under rate the expenses of the War—as if fearful that even all its glory will not reconcile the people to the public debt and high taxes following in its train.

I expect to be in Washington some time in the session but am not now able to say when. With great regard thy friend, Ellwood Fisher.

P.S. Although Mexicans would not as matter of course be admitted to citizenship on the acquisition of their territory, yet it would be difficult to refuse a ["peace" *canceled*] treaty in which ["they" *canceled*] Mexico offered a cession of land on that condition, which is a common one. We agreed to it in the case of Louisiana and Florida and we are daily admitting citizens from all Europe. Mexico however presents the case of an Indian and a mixed race. ["Even" *canceled.*] If a line is taken and held our citizens will flock in and settle the territory we occupy—and provision would have to be made immediately for its government, when these questions would all arise. Would it not be better to take the Missouri Compromise with the modification that the North should be excluded from all South of 36, 30?

[P.S.] Thee will see the proceedings of the Peace meeting here, and recognize our Friend [William M.] Corry in the Resolutions.

ALS in ScCleA; PEx in Jameson, ed., *Correspondence*, pp. 1145–1147.

From HENRY C. CAREY

Burlington [N.J.,] Dec. 5/47

Dear Sir, In the course of the present month I shall publish a volume the object of which is to demonstrate the existence of a very beautiful law of nature heretofore unobserved—a law as simple, as universal, and as powerful as that of gravitation—*the* law that governs man in all his efforts to maintain & to improve his condition—and the one that has been required for the settlement of the various questions of food, population, tariffs, &c. about which there has been thus far so much difference of opinion.

By its aid, I have examined all these questions—& it has led me to see many things in a light that is very different from that in which I have heretofore regarded them. My reason for now writing to you is this—You have much to do this winter in regard to some questions that are discussed in this book, & to study such questions requires time of which you have, as I know, not much to spare. In the course of a day or two I shall be able to have a couple of copies of it put together for myself to look at—& if you think proper, I will send one of them to you, of which I will request your acceptance, simply requesting that you will keep it to yourself until after publication.

I have, throughout, said what I thought, and all that I thought, about men & things, whether in Europe or America—in Massachusetts or South Carolina. I have lent the sheets, as the book passed through the press, to two friends, one of whom is a Southern & the other a Northern man. Each objects to parts of what I have said in regard to slavery—not so much that they do not believe them, as because they will be unpopular. My answer to both is that what is written is true & it shall stand. It contains nothing that should offend any body. It is, as I think, a demonstration of the existence of perfect harmony of interest between the free States & those which hold slaves—between the planter & the man that labours for him—& I will not change a word to please any body, with a view to shew that there is discord where cause for discord does not exist. The law that is here shewn to exist is the standard by which all these things have to be measured, and I have never swerved right or left while engaged in the act of measurement. With great regard I remain Yours v[er]y truly, Henry C. Carey.

ALS in ScCleA. NOTE: Carey's work, *The Past, the Present, and the Future,* was published in Philadelphia and London in 1848.

SYMBOLS

◫

The following symbols have been used in this volume as abbreviations for the forms in which documents of John C. Calhoun have been found and for the repositories in which they are preserved. (Full citations to printed sources of documents can be found in the Bibliography.)

A-Ar	—Alabama Department of Archives and History, Montgomery
Abs	—abstract (a summary)
ADU	—autograph document, unsigned
AES	—autograph endorsement, signed
AEU	—autograph endorsement, unsigned
ALS	—autograph letter, signed
ALU	—autograph letter, unsigned
CC	—clerk's copy (a secondary ms. copy)
CSmH	—Huntington Library, San Marino, Cal.
DLC	—Library of Congress, Washington
DNA	—National Archives, Washington
DS	—document, signed
DU	—document, unsigned
En	—enclosure
Ens	—enclosures
EU	—endorsement, unsigned
FC	—file copy (usually a letterbook copy retained by the sender)
GEU	—Emory University, Atlanta, Ga.
GU	—University of Georgia, Athens
LS	—letter, signed
M-	—(followed by a number) published microcopy of the National Archives
NcD	—Duke University, Durham, N.C.
NcU	—Southern Historical Collection, University of North Carolina at Chapel Hill
NjP	—Princeton University, Princeton, N.J.
PC	—printed copy
PDS	—printed document, signed
PEx	—printed extract
PWbWHi	—Wyoming Historical and Geological Society, Wilkes-Barre, Pa.
RG	—Record Group in the National Archives
Sc-Ar	—South Carolina Department of Archives and History, Columbia
ScC	—Charleston Library Society, Charleston, S.C.
ScCleA	—Clemson University, Clemson, S.C.
ScCM	—Waring Historical Collection, Medical University of South Carolina, Charleston
ScU-SC	—South Caroliniana Library, University of South Carolina, Columbia

Symbols

T	—Tennessee State Library and Archives, Nashville
TNJ	—Vanderbilt University, Nashville, Tenn.
ViHi	—Virginia Historical Society, Richmond
ViU	—University of Virginia, Charlottesville
WHi	—Wisconsin Historical Society, Madison

BIBLIOGRAPHY

◫

This Bibliography is limited to sources of and previous printings of documents published in this volume.

Abbeville, S.C., *Banner*, 1844–1860.

"Account of the Settlement of the Calhoun Family in South Carolina," in *Gulf States Historical Magazine*, vol. I, no. 6 (July, 1902), pp. 439–441.

Alexandria, Va., *Gazette*, 1808–.

American Clipper: A Monthly Catalogue of American Historical and Literary Material (June, 1938).

Anderson, John M., ed., *Calhoun: Basic Documents*. State College, Pa.: Bald Eagle Press, 1952.

Athens, Ga., *Southern Banner*, 1831–?.

Before Railroads. A Contemporary View of the Agriculture Industry and Commerce of the South in the 'Forties. [Nashville:] Nashville, Chattanooga & St. Louis Railway, [1929].

Benton, Thomas H., ed., *Abridgment of the Debates of Congress.* 16 vols. New York: D. Appleton & Co., 1854–1861.

[Benton, Thomas H.,] *Thirty Years' View; or, a History of the Working of the American Government for Thirty Years, from 1820 to 1850 . . . .* 2 vols. New York: D. Appleton & Co., 1854, 1856.

Boucher, Chauncey S., and Robert P. Brooks, eds., *Correspondence Addressed to John C. Calhoun, 1837–1849,* in the *American Historical Association Annual Report* for 1929. Washington: U.S. Government Printing Office, 1930.

"Calhoun Settlement," in *Historical Collections of the Joseph Habersham Chapter, Daughters of the American Revolution.* 5 vols. Atlanta and Athens, Ga., 1902–1929, vol. III.

Camden, S.C., *Journal*, 1826–1891?.

Charleston, S.C., *Courier*, 1803–1852.

Charleston, S.C., *Evening News*, 1845–1861.

Charleston, S.C., *Mercury*, 1822–1868.

Charleston, S.C., *Southern Patriot*, 1814–1848.

Cincinnati, Ohio, *Daily Enquirer*, 1841–.

Columbia, S.C., *South-Carolinian*, 1838–1849?.

Columbia, S.C., *Southern Chronicle*, 1840–?.

Congressional Globe . . . 1833–1873 . . . . 46 vols. Washington: Blair & Rives and others, 1834–1873.

Cook, Harriet Hefner, *John C. Calhoun—The Man.* Columbia, S.C.: privately printed, 1965.

Crallé, Richard K., ed., *The Works of John C. Calhoun.* 6 vols. Columbia, S.C.: A.S. Johnston, 1851, and New York: D. Appleton & Co., 1853–1857.

Davis, Curtis C., *That Ambitious Mr. Legaré: The Life of James M. Legaré of*

South Carolina, Including a Collected Edition of His Verse. Columbia: University of South Carolina Press, 1971.

De Bow's Review. New Orleans: 1846–1880.

DuBose, John W., *The Life and Times of William Lowndes Yancey. A History of Political Parties in the United States, from 1834 to 1864; Especially as to the Origin of the Confederate States.* Birmingham, Ala.: Roberts & Son, 1892.

Edgefield, S.C., *Advertiser*, 1836–.

Georgetown, S.C., *Winyah Observer*, 1841–1852.

Greenville, S.C., *Mountaineer*, 1829–1901.

Harrisburg, Pa., *Democratic Union*, 1843–1855.

Hillsborough, N.C., *Recorder*, 1820–1879.

Huntsville, Ala., *Democrat*, 1823–1853?.

Jameson, J. Franklin, ed., *Correspondence of John C. Calhoun,* in the *American Historical Association Annual Report* for 1899, 2 vols. Washington: U.S. Government Printing Office, 1900, vol. II.

Lence, Ross M., ed., *Union and Liberty: The Political Philosophy of John C. Calhoun.* Indianapolis: Liberty Press, 1992.

"Letter of John C. Calhoun, 1847," in the *American Historical Review,* vol. I (1895–1896), pp. 314–315.

Liberator, The. Boston: 1831–1865.

Logan, John H., *A History of the Upper Country of South Carolina, from the Earliest Periods to the Close of the War of Independence: Biographical and Historical Extracts from the Unpublished Manuscript of Volume II.* Easley, S.C.: Southern Historical Press, 1980.

McIntosh, James T., et al., eds., *The Papers of Jefferson Davis.* 8 vols. to date. Baton Rouge: Louisiana State University Press, 1971–.

Madigan, P[atrick] F., *A Catalogue of Autograph Letters, Historical Documents and Manuscripts Offered for Sale.* New York: 1914.

Maury, Sarah M., *An Englishwoman in America.* London: Thomas Richardson & Son; Liverpool: Geo. Smith, Watts & Co., 1848.

Mr. Calhoun's Reply to Mr. Simmons, on His Resolutions. February 20, 1847. [Washington: 1847].

Montgomery, Ala., *Southern Times,* 1855–?.

Moore, Frederick W., ed., "Calhoun as Seen by His Political Friends: Letters of Duff Green, Dixon H. Lewis [and] Richard K. Cralle During the Period from 1831 to 1848," in *Publications of the Southern History Association,* vol. VII (1903).

[Musson, Eugène,] *Lettre à Napoleon III sur l'esclavage aux états du Sud, par un Creole de la Louisiane.* Paris: Dentu, 1862. (English language edition, London: W.S. Kirkland & Co., 1862.)

Nashville, Tenn., *Whig,* 1838–1855.

New Orleans, La., *Daily Picayune,* 1836–1914.

New York, N.Y., *Evening Post,* 1832–1920.

New York, N.Y., *Herald,* 1835–1924.

New York, N.Y., *Journal of Commerce,* 1827–1892?.

New York, N.Y., *National Anti-Slavery Standard,* 1840–1872.

Niles' Register. Baltimore: 1811–1849.

Oliphant, Mary C. Simms, Alfred Taylor Odell, and T.C. Duncan Eaves, eds.,

Letters of William Gilmore Simms. 6 vols. Columbia: University of South Carolina Press, 1952–1982.

Oregon City, Ore., *Oregon Spectator,* 1846–1850.

Pendleton, S.C., *Messenger,* 1807–?.

Petersburg, Va., *Republican,* 1843–1850.

Philadelphia, Pa., *Pennsylvania Freeman,* 1838–1854.

Remarks of Mr. Calhoun, at the Meeting of the Citizens of Charleston, Tuesday Evening, March 9, 1847. [Charleston: 1847?], an 8-pp. pamphlet.

Remarks of Mr. Calhoun, on Presenting His Resolutions on the Slave Question. February 19, 1847. [Washington: 1847].

Richmond, Va., *Enquirer,* 1804–1877.

Richmond, Va., *Whig,* 1824–1888.

Southern Cultivator. Athens, Ga.: 1843–1935.

Southern Railroad Company. Report of the Committee Appointed by the Citizens of Vicksburg to Obtain a Charter from the Legislatures of Alabama and Mississippi—Together with the Documents Accompanying the Same. [Vicksburg: 1846?].

Speech of Mr. Calhoun, of South Carolina, in Reply to Mr. Benton, of Missouri. Delivered in the Senate of the United States, February 24, 1847. Washington: printed by John T. Towers, 1847.

Speech of Mr. Calhoun, of South Carolina, in Reply to Mr. Turney, of Tennessee. Delivered in the Senate of the United States, February 12, 1847. [Washington: 1847].

Speech of Mr. Calhoun, of South Carolina, on the Bill Making Further Appropriation to Bring the Existing War with Mexico to a Speedy and Honorable Conclusion, Called the Three Million Bill. Delivered in the Senate of the United States, February 9, 1847. Washington: printed by John T. Towers, 1847.

Sumterville, S.C., *Black River Watchman,* 1850–1855.

Tallahassee, Fla., *Florida Sentinel,* 1841–1876.

Tallahassee, Fla., *Southern Journal,* 1846–1849.

U.S. Senate, *Senate Documents,* 29th Congress.

U.S. Senate, *Senate Journal,* 29th Congress.

Vicksburg, Miss., *Sentinel,* 1838–1851?.

Washington, D.C., *Daily National Intelligencer,* 1800–1870.

Washington, D.C., *Union,* 1845–1859.

Wilson, Clyde N., ed., *The Essential Calhoun. Selections from Writings, Speeches, and Letters.* New Brunswick, N.J., and London: Transaction Publishers, 1992.

INDEX

Ⅲ

Abbeville District, S.C.: 78, 272–273, 346, 348, 352, 369, 390, 392–394, 403–404, 429, 434, 439, 484, 493, 495–496, 511–512, 521–522, 536, 545, 572, 646–647, 674–676, 678.

Abbeville, S.C., *Banner*: document in, 403; mentioned, 647, 674.

Aberdeen, Lord: mentioned, 142, 189.

Abingdon, Va., *Banner*: mentioned, 90.

Abingdon, Va., *Virginian*: mentioned, 89.

Abney, Joseph: from, 95.

Abolition: 35, 49, 53, 58, 104, 137, 142–143, 155, 161, 168, 180, 189–190, 193, 201, 224, 231–232, 239–240, 252–258, 298, 300, 318, 330–331, 336, 343, 353, 358–359, 381, 386–391, 405–406, 415, 433, 440–442, 444–445, 453–454, 457–458, 465, 474, 477, 481, 488–489, 492, 505, 508, 519, 526, 529, 531–532, 540–542, 568, 570, 574, 576, 579, 593–594, 600–602, 608–609, 611, 617, 619, 623–624, 633, 654, 659, 662–664, 667–671, 684. *See also* Slavery; Wilmot Proviso.

Abridgment of Debates: documents in, 101, 115, 156, 169, 176, 195.

Abstractions: Calhoun on, 176–177.

Adams, James: mentioned, 559.

Adams, James H.: from, 530, 574; mentioned, 559.

Adams, James U.: mentioned, 559.

Adams, Joel R.: mentioned, 559.

Adams, Joel, Sr.: mentioned, 559.

Adams, John Quincy: mentioned, 199, 218, 331.

Adams-Onís Treaty: 198–200, 634, 685.

Adams, Placidia Mayrant: mentioned, 428; to, 5, 428, 487.

Adams, R.J.: mentioned, 559.

Adams, Robert: mentioned, 559.

Addington, Henry U.: mentioned, 335.

"Address of the Southern Delegates in Congress": anticipated, 241.

Agnew, E. & J.W.: from, 390.

Agriculture: in Calhoun-Clemson family, 5–9, 41, 43, 44, 73, 96–97, 103–105, 160, 166, 234, 270, 271, 272, 284, 307, 311, 312, 341, 345, 346, 394–395, 398–399, 427, 428, 434–436, 437–439, 468–469, 494, 496, 524, 535–536, 584, 597–598, 599, 611–613, 620–621, 635–637, 640, 642, 671–672, 681, 682; mentioned, 24, 38, 49, 90–91, 159, 229, 246–247, 289, 353, 387, 460, 493, 516, 525, 572, 647; Southern, 13–20, 109, 155, 175, 199, 212, 247, 251, 258, 268, 269, 290, 305, 322, 345, 381, 394, 462, 473, 474, 477, 482, 513, 524, 530, 552–553, 554, 590, 591, 637, 647, 649, 650, 651, 656, 681.

Aiken, S.C.: 22, 162, 363, 521, 556–557, 626.

Aiken, William: mentioned, 318, 342, 492, 559.

Alabama: 8–10, 18, 41, 43, 45, 67–68, 73, 94–95, 100, 103–105, 110, 160, 194, 199, 222–223, 226–227, 311–312, 315–316, 321–322, 345–346, 348, 358–359, 362, 368–370, 373–374, 384–385, 398–399, 409–410, 414–416, 427, 430–434, 438, 445, 460, 462–464, 468–469, 485, 493–494, 499–501, 503, 505, 507–509, 511–513, 536, 538, 548–553, 559, 594, 608–612, 616, 629–630, 651, 654, 661, 666, 671–672, 676–677,

Buckingham County, Va.: 77.
Buckingham, P.S.: from, 191.
Buffalo: 675.
Buffalo, N.Y.: 388.
Buford, Jefferson: mentioned, 676–677.
Bull, ——: mentioned, 261.
Burges, James S.: mentioned, 108.
Burke, Thomas O.: mentioned, 550.
Burket, Willis: mentioned, 428.
Burlington, N.J.: 685.
Burt, Armistead: from, 74, 98, 106, 495; mentioned, 43, 46, 68, 174, 212, 283, 346, 424, 511, 513, 531, 534, 575; to, 571.
Burt, Martha Calhoun: mentioned, 43, 496, 534, 572.
Bush, George: mentioned, 77.
Butler, Andrew P.: from, 74, 98, 660; mentioned, 3, 41, 104, 106, 150–151, 211–212, 260, 422, 512; to, 74.
Butler, Behethland Foote Moore: mentioned, 660–661.
Butler, Benjamin F.: mentioned, 542.
Butler, George B.: mentioned, 461.
Butler, Perry: mentioned, 106.
Butler, Pierce M.: from, 67; mentioned, 45, 95, 104–105, 660–661.
Butler, Thomas J.: from, 226.
Butler, William: mentioned, 106.
Butler, William O.: mentioned, 314, 684.
Byrdsall, Fitzwilliam: from, 154, 192, 228, 390, 456, 474, 652.
Byrne, Henry H.: mentioned, 461.

Caesar: mentioned, 49.
Caldwell, Patrick C.: from, 614.
Caledonia (ship): 8.
Calhoun, Misses —— (of N.Y.): mentioned, 12, 366.
Calhoun, Andrew Pickens: from, 103; mentioned, 8–10, 41, 43, 96, 100, 284–285, 295, 346, 373–374, 385, 398–399, 427, 437–438, 468–469, 494, 496, 536, 598, 612–613, 630, 671–672; to, 311, 434, 681.

Calhoun, Andrew Pickens, Jr.: mentioned, 43, 313, 494, **682.**
Calhoun, Benjamin A.: mentioned, 292–293.
Calhoun, Catherine Montgomery: mentioned, 385, 676.
Calhoun, Duff Green: mentioned, 43, 313, 494, 682.
Calhoun, Ezekiel (uncle): mentioned, 674–675.
Calhoun family: 12.
Calhoun, Floride Colhoun: from, 469; mentioned, 30, 39, 42, 44, 51, 73, 77, 91, 96, 148, 160, 165, 261, 269, 271–272, 294, 304–306, 308, 310, 312, 316, 329, 332, 335, 340, 348, 354, 366, 372, 374, 377–378, 394, 400–401, 421, 428, 467–468, 478, 494, 534, 537, 542, 553, 555–556, 572–573, 607, 641.
Calhoun, Hugh: mentioned, 386.
Calhoun, James (brother): mentioned, 493, 674.
Calhoun, "James" (grandfather): mentioned, 385–386.
Calhoun, James (uncle): mentioned, 674–675.
Calhoun, James Edward: mentioned, 43, 400, 437, 467, 495, 555, 614, 640, 681; to, 30, 73, 642.
Calhoun, Jane Ewing: mentioned, 674.
Calhoun, John Alfred: from, 368, 676.
Calhoun, John C., Jr.: from, 347; mentioned, 105, 160, 312, 341, 348, 467, 642, 681; to, 376.
Calhoun, John Caldwell (grandson): mentioned, 43, 313, 494, 682.
Calhoun, Margaret Green: mentioned, 285, 312–313, 494, 496, 682.
Calhoun, Margaret Maria: mentioned, 313, 494, 682.
Calhoun, Martha Cornelia: mentioned, 30, 42, 62, 70–71, 96, 304–306, 308, 312, 329, 340, 348, 394, 421–422, 467, 494, 534, 553, 555–556, 607, 641.
Calhoun, Nancy: to, 385.

Dalton, S.W.: from, 219.
Daniel, William: mentioned, 38.
Dansville, N.Y.: 229.
Danville, Va.: 364.
Dargan, Edmund S.: mentioned, 433, 501, 512, 550–551, 559; to, 358.
Dargan, George W.: from, 530, 574.
Darnall, William J.: mentioned, 292–293.
Darracott, Herbert: from, 392; to, 403.
Davidson, A.C.: mentioned, 630.
Davie, William F.: from, 530, 574.
Davis, Charles Augustus: from, 20.
Davis, George L.L.: from, 592, 634.
Davis, James B.: from, 647.
Davis, Jefferson: from, 382; mentioned, 314, 372, 412, 471, 541.
Davis, John: mentioned, 214.
Dawson, William C.: mentioned, 66, 292, 355, 652.
Dayton, William L.: mentioned, 74, 232.
Deane, Francis B.: mentioned, 679.
Deas, E. Horry: mentioned, 559.
Deas, James S.: mentioned, 512.
De Bow, James D.B.: from, 333, 661.
DeBow's Review: document in, 169; mentioned, 661–662.
Debt. *See* Public debt, U.S.; State debts and stocks.
Declaration of Independence: 177, 187, 418.
Deer: 675.
Delany, Edward: mentioned, 503–504.
Delaware: 170, 477, 531, 575, 654; Senator from (*see* Clayton, John M.).
Democratic party: ix, 3–5, 9–12, 23, 27, 30–32, 34–38, 45–46, 48–49, 52–53, 58, 61, 65–66, 69, 75–77, 87, 89–90, 93, 97, 101, 106–108, 110, 112–113, 123, 138–139, 145, 147, 149, 154–155, 160, 192–194, 202, 214–215, 220, 222–223, 228, 231–232, 235, 237–243, 245, 249, 252–257, 260–267, 273, 282–283, 285, 287, 289, 294, 296–297, 299–

301, 307–309, 315–318, 324–327, 332–333, 335–336, 343–345, 351–352, 357–359, 361, 363, 366, 369–370, 372, 377–380, 383–384, 386–388, 391–392, 397, 399, 406, 409–410, 412, 414, 433, 439–443, 455–461, 463–466, 469, 471–472, 474–475, 483, 485, 493, 497–500, 503–504, 506, 513, 518–520, 526, 528–529, 531–532, 536, 539–540, 542, 547, 561, 563, 568, 573, 575–576, 578, 585, 594, 596, 604–608, 610–611, 637–638, 640–641, 648–650, 652–654, 663–664, 668, 670, 673, 676–677, 682–683.
De Morse, Charles: mentioned, 321.
DeSaussure, J.M.: mentioned, 559.
DeSaussure, William D.: from, 95.
DeSaussure, William F.: from, 530, 574.
Desmanet, Viscomte, de Biesme: mentioned, 553–554.
De Su, J.L.: from, 677.
Detroit, Mich.: 144, 157, 388, 496–497.
Dick & Hill: mentioned, 111.
Dickins, Asbury: mentioned, 680.
Dillon, Gregory: mentioned, 59–60, 113.
Disquisition on Government: anticipated, 91, 375.
Distribution: 442, 456.
District of Columbia: 531, 574.
Dix, John A.: mentioned, 93, 114, 650.
Dixon, Edward: from, 332.
Dodge, Augustus C.: mentioned, 72.
Donaldson, John: mentioned, 577–578, 596.
Donaldson, Samuel C.: from, 577; to, 45, 596.
Donelson, Andrew J.: mentioned, 196–197; to, 581.
Dorr rebellion: 188, 229–230, 274–275.
Dorr, Robert L.: from, 229; mentioned, 234; to, 274.
Double Wells, Ga.: 545.
Dozier, Allen S.: mentioned, 7.
Draper, Lyman C.: by, 674.

703

710

(February 20, 1847); Speech at a Meeting of Citizens of Charleston (March 9, 1847).
Wilson, Abraham D.: mentioned, 461.
Wilson, Daniel A.: mentioned, 75.
Wilson, John: mentioned, 320.
Wilson, Joseph H.: to, 288, 322.
Wilson, Levy: mentioned, 97, 306–307.
Wilson, S.F.: mentioned, 194.
Wilson, Thomas: mentioned, 559.
Winchester, Va.: 245.
Winnsboro, S.C.: 548.
Winthrop, Robert C.: mentioned, 542.
Wisconsin: 170–171, 249, 417–419.
Wisconsin Historical Society: document in, 674.
Wise, Henry A.: mentioned, 380.
Witcher, Vincent: mentioned, 37–38.
Withers, F.J.: mentioned, 559.
Wofford, William B.: mentioned, 107.
Woodbridge, William: mentioned, 497.
Woodbury, Levi: mentioned, 334, 528, 542, 670, 677.
Wood, Fernando: from, 468.
Woodward, Joseph A.: from, 74, 98, 106.
Wool: 15, 38.
Wool, John E.: mentioned, 314, 658.
Worcester, Mass., *Palladium*: mentioned, 474–475.

Worth, William J.: mentioned, 314.
Wright, Hendrick B.: from, 4; to, 29.
Wright, Silas: mentioned, 10–11, 23, 75–76, 155, 231–232, 282, 391–392, 412, 457–458, 460, 464–466, 471, 474, 503, 528, 536, 542, 546–547, 604, 606, 663, 670.
Wyman, L.B.: from, 674.
Wyoming Historical and Geological Society: document in, 29.
Wytheville and Wythe County, Va.: 47, 89–90, 191–192, 675.
Wytheville, Va., *Republican*: mentioned, 89.

Yadkin River: 322.
Yale College: 168, 416–417.
Yancey, William L.: mentioned, 505, 511–512, 610.
Yankees: 32, 45, 100, 104, 251, 299, 343.
Yellow fever: 106, 127, 549.
York District, S.C.: 548, 590, 599.
Young, Richard M.: from, 292.
Young, Samuel: mentioned, 474.
Yucatan: 126.
Yulee, David Levy: mentioned, 134, 150, 361–362, 503, 631.

Zimmerman, John C.: mentioned, 572.

ers

Other books by Nancy J. Parra:

The *Morgan Brothers Romance* Series

Saving Samantha
A Wanted Man
Loving Lana

WYOMING WEDDING

•

Nancy J. Parra

AVALON BOOKS
NEW YORK

PRINTED IN THE UNITED STATES OF AMERICA
ON ACID-FREE PAPER
BY HADDON CRAFTSMEN, BLOOMSBURG, PENNSYLVANIA

This book is dedicated to Marlene and Tom Parra
for welcoming me into their family
and giving me the best of themselves.

I'm proud to put your name on every book I write.
Thanks for everything.

Prologue

"**I**'m dying," old man Edwards said. His back was turned to Shay as he looked out of his second-floor bedroom window.

"I'm sure there's a—"

Resigned, Edwards held out his hand and cut Shay Morgan off. "There's no cure. The doctors have tried everything."

"I have a friend in New York who knows one of the preeminent doctors in the field."

"I've seen too many doctors now. I don't want to see another."

Restlessly, Shay paced the blue Oriental rug adorning the polished oak floor. "What can I do? Tell me how to help." Old man Edwards had been Shay's father's best friend for years. After Shay's pa died, Edwards helped Shay with college expenses and watched over him during those wild years.

When Shay received his law degree, Edwards offered him his own firm, but Shay declined and vowed to make it on his own. The old man had been so impressed, he'd

1

sent some prominent men to Shay's firm, allowing him to build up an extensive clientele.

Shay Morgan owed the man, but more than that he loved him like a father. "There has to be something I can do besides watch you waste away."

"Well," Edwards said, and leaning heavily on his polished oak cane, turned to look Shay in the eye. "I do have one request."

"Name it. If it's in my power to do it, it'll be done."

"As you know I have a daughter."

"I'd heard a rumor to that effect."

"I want to see her before I die."

"I'll get you train tickets, just let me know."

Edwards shook his head. His snow-white hair had once been auburn. His tanned skin, now ashen. Only his gray-blue eyes still showed his level of intelligence and the strength of his will. "I want her to come here," he said evenly. "I want to show her Amesville. I want to know her a little bit before I go."

"You want me to send a cable?"

"I want you to go get her and bring her back."

"Done."

"She won't come easy," he said and blew out a long breath. "To say we're not on good terms is understating the matter."

"She'll come," Shay said with the full confidence of a man who knew how to get what he wanted. "I'll see she gets here."

Edwards sat down in a nearby wing chair. He tipped his head back against the chair and grimaced with pain. "Good," he said. "I knew I could count on you."

Chapter One

"Hey, Shay," Pete Williams hollered as Shay walked into the saloon for his nightly game of poker. It would be the last game for a while. In the morning he would be taking the stage to Denver, and then the train to a small Texas town in search of Edwards' long lost daughter.

"Pete," Shay acknowledged.

"I heard tell old man Edwards has you going after that gal of his."

"You heard right, I leave in the morning." Shay pulled up a chair and sat down with the gang. Usually he was dealt right in, but tonight was different. Tonight they stared at him like they'd never seen him before.

"You cain't be serious," Anson Lake said. "Everyone knows she refuses to see him. Heck, she even sends his money back."

"I heard tell that over the years he's sent upwards of five of his best men to git her," Pete said with an anticipatory grin. "She's sent them all packin'. Seems she hates the old man."

"Yep, I heard she swore to kill him with her bare hands if he ever showed up at her door," Beau Bradley said.

Shay didn't like the turn the conversation took. "He's dying."

"Won't make no nevermind," Anson said. "She'd just tell you good and move on."

"No one's that heartless," Shay said and grabbed the cards from Anson and dealt them. "Five card stud."

Pete picked up his cards. "She's heartless all right. I heard tell she tied the last man to a tree naked as a jaybird and defenseless as a babe. Why, if a band of Indians hadn't come by he might have died of exposure."

"Yeah, but I bet he wasn't as near as pretty as our Shay," Beau said with a bit too much enthusiasm. He threw a dollar into the kitty in the center of the table. "It would take a hard woman to tell him no."

Shay had to grin at that. Beau was right, he'd never found a woman who could resist his charms. Not even a hard woman. It was obvious he loved them all and they knew it and responded like bees to honey.

"I'll bring her back," he said and lit a cigar. The sharp smoke burst on his tongue and ringed over his head. "I promised the old man."

"Shoot, I heard she was more than hard, she was darn right vicious," Pete warned.

"Like I said," Shay said, and studied the worn slick cards in his hand: Aces and queens. "I'll bring her back."

"I knew a couple of the other guys that went after her and let me tell you, if you bring her back it will be a miracle. In fact, I bet you fifty dollars you come slinkin' back here empty-handed."

"Yeah," the rest of the table agreed in unison.

Shay studied them one by one and did some quick figuring in his head. The wooden chair under him creaked as he balanced on the back two legs. "So, what you're telling me is that when I bring Miss Edwards home, you all are going to pay me fifty dollars each."

"Naw," Pete said with a grin. "When you come crawling back into town alone, you're going to pay us fifty dollars each."

"All three of you want in on this bet?"

"Sure do," Pete said.

"I ain't seen a bet you cain't win," Beau said, and spit chaw into the spittoon near his booted foot. "But this sounds like one you can't pull off. I'm in."

"Wait," Anson said. "We need to set a limit. When are you leaving?"

"In the morning."

"Good, then you need to bring her back to Amesville in thirty days or you lose this bet."

"Thirty days?"

"Yep." They all agreed.

"Deal," Shay said with the confidence of a man who had never lost a bet where a woman was concerned. "Now pass me the kitty boys, no one can beat my hand." He laid his cards on the table. "Two pair, aces high."

The table groaned and watched as he took the pot. It was nothing new. Shay was the best poker player this side of the Mississippi. Some said he was born under a lucky star. Shay knew it was more skill than luck. He never made a bet he wasn't certain he could win.

Dr. Jenny Edwards put her head down on the table and closed her eyes. She told herself it was only for a second. She was so tired she was instantly asleep.

She dreamed of an angel with golden hair and bright blue eyes. He picked her up and held her in his arms and told her that he would take care of everything. She sighed and relaxed against his chest. It felt so good not to be responsible even if it was only for these small moments.

"Doctor?"

Jenny ignored the intrusion and snuggled deeper into the angel's arms.

"Doctor, Mrs. Hall's water broke."

The angel stroked her hair and planted a kiss on her forehead. "It's okay, Jenny," he said. "I'm here to watch over you."

"Doctor?"

Jenny felt the world shake and her angel fade. "Trust me, I'll be here for you." Jenny smiled. Unlike other men she could trust him. He was an angel.

"Doctor!"

Jenny opened her eyes to see Emily, her nurse standing over her shaking her shoulder.

"Wake up, it's Mrs. Hall."

Jenny blinked and sat up. "What time is it?"

"It's nearly nine in the evening," Emily answered. "Mrs. Hall sent her oldest when the pains got too much to bear."

"Do you have my bag?" Jenny asked, instantly awake.

"Right here," Emily said, and handed it to Jenny as she walked out of the back room and into the waiting area. The area was quiet now. Only little Patrick sat in the chairs. He was a thin boy of seven with blond hair and freckles. His clothes were worn but clean, his feet bare for the spring season.

"Emily, see that Patrick gets a good supper before he goes home."

The little boy jumped up. "But my ma—"

"Don't worry," Jenny said and rubbed his head. "I'll take care of your ma. You get yourself some nice supper. We need you to keep up your strength so you can keep helping your ma with chores."

Patrick looked torn between coming with her to make sure his ma was safe, and the thought of a real meal. The meal won out when Emily offered her hand and told him they had fried chicken in the kitchen.

Jenny grabbed her coat and slipped it on. The spring weather was warm during the day, but at night a chill wind blew across the prairie. She grabbed her bag and headed down the street.

Mrs. Hall lost her husband to consumption at Christmas, and was left alone with five children and one on the way. She made due with her work as a seamstress and washer-woman, but it was barely enough to keep food on the table. Little Patrick was proof that what they really needed was a good hot meal.

She'd have to make sure Emily brought a meal by the house at least once a day for the first week.

The Halls lived in a small house at the end of First Street. It was made of clapboard with tarpaper coating. They had wax-paper windows and Jenny knew the wind was coming in the cracks of the house. Concerned, she mentally went through the steps of what must be done once she reached the house. Banking the fire in the potbellied stove would be the most important. After that it would be a matter of keeping the children busy while their mother gave birth.

Jenny blew out a breath. It was going to be another long night. Stifling a yawn, she scurried across the dirt street, the Hall house in sight.

Jenny had vowed long ago, after her mother died, that she would never leave a woman in need. Even if it meant she had to go a couple of days without sleep.

Shay arrived in Johnstown after a restless night on the train. He glanced around at the small town. Built around a town square, it was about the size of Amesville with a main

street that was eight blocks long. He picked out three saloons among the buildings, along with a boarding house
and a real brick hotel on one corner.

He picked up his suitcase and walked toward the hotel.
The first thing he was going to do was stretch out on a bed
for a few hours. Then he would get a bath and a shave.
The barbershop was always the place to go for information
in a small town.

The way Shay figured it; he'd have met Jenny Edwards
in time to ask her to dinner. Then if he was real lucky,
he'd have her on the next train back to Amesville. He
grinned and crossed the wide dry street. The wind blew
from the south, bringing heat and stirring up the dust.

It seemed that April in Texas was a bit sharper than April
in Wyoming. The horizon wasn't hampered by the mountains in the west. As he crossed a side street he could look
out to the west and see only prairie and wide blue sky. The
prairie grass had begun to turn from the russet red and
purple of fall and winter, to the shades of springtime green.

Flowers grew along the side of the hotel. Someone had
taken great pains to try to bring a bit of the east out west
and mask the clay soil.

Shay climbed the short steps that brought him up on the
wooden walkway. It stretched out along the front of the
buildings in an attempt to urge the people to window shop,
and perhaps enter the stores with at least semi-clean shoes.

The door to the hotel jangled when he opened it. Shay
wiped his feet on the mat and took in the lay of the building. There was a small dining room to his right, a sitting
room to his left and in front was the check-in desk. The
hotel was decorated in high Victorian stuffiness from the
fancy wallpaper to the doilies to the cluttered knickknacks
covering every available surface. Shay got the feeling whoever decorated the hotel wanted it to appear upscale.

The lingering scent of lunch in the air gave Shay hope. The dark wood and fancy décor may be over the top, but it smelled like the food held promise.

A little man with a long curled mustache looked up from his paper. "You need a room?" he asked.

"Yep. One with the biggest bed you got."

The little man looked him up and down. "All our beds are the same size."

"Then I'll take what you have," Shay said. "It's been a long trip and I could use a little sleep."

"Rooms are a dollar a day, but supper is included," the man said briskly. "Paid in advance."

Shay took out $3.00 and laid the money on the counter. "I'll let you know if that changes."

The man scooped up the money and wrote in a big registration book. He reached under the desk and withdrew a key. "You're in room 310," he said and turned the book toward Shay. "There's an indoor water closet on the second floor. If you spend more than five minutes in there I'll send up the bouncer. We've got a lot of guests and they all want a turn."

"I'll remember that," Shay said and tried to hide his grin. He signed his name next to the room number the man had already inked in.

"You do that." The little man turned back to his paper.

Shay tossed the key and caught it. Then he headed up the stairs. First things first. A couple of hours of sleep should clear his mind and help him set out a plan to bring the heartless Miss Edwards home.

It was afternoon before Jenny was able to leave Mrs. Hall and the new baby. Emily had paid one of the Miller girls to come and stay the week. Jenny rubbed the back of her neck.

Everyday she thanked her lucky stars that the mysterious Widow Banks had left her such a large inheritance. Without that inheritance, Jenny would not be able to do as near as much to help the women of Johnstown.

Jenny was good with figures and had managed to invest the initial sum into a growing trust. The money kept Emily employed and the poor fed. Jenny knew they were proud, these women—they took only what they needed and paid back as best they could.

She never refused payment. To do so would insult them and they had little now except pride. She refused to take that away. So, she often had a reserve of canned vegetables or homemade pies. In fact she had a bit of a side business going with Laird's hotel.

Whenever she found herself with too much of something, they usually bought it from her wholesale. The cash that she got from the sale went straight to her expenses, leaving the bulk of the money for those who really needed it.

Jenny crossed the street. Her feet hurt and the afternoon sun was so bright it made her eyes water. The scent of flowers and dust floated passed. She glanced at the sky. It was clear as a bell and bright blue. Today would be dry. The wind had died down to a gentle breeze. There would be no rain yet again.

"Hey, Doc. How are you?"

Jenny waved at the storekeeper out sweeping the dirt off his part of the wooden walkway. "Great Chester, How's the bursitis?"

He grinned and touched his shoulder. "Better. We haven't had rain in a while."

"As soon as you start aching, you send Sammy running," she said. "That way I'll be sure to get out my rain coat and rubbers."

"I'll be sure and do that," he said. "You take care of yourself, Doc."

"I will," she said and moved on.

"Hey, Doc."

"Hey, Elmer," Jenny said as she approached the entrance to the barbershop. "Joe." The two old men were regular features outside the barbershop. "How's the game?"

"Doc, tell Elmer that chess is a game of strategy," Joe said. "He just keeps moving random pieces."

Elmer winked at her. "Got to keep the opponent confused, right Doc?"

"Hmmm," was all Jenny answered. "Elmer, how's Meg?" Meg was Elmer's daughter. She struggled alone to keep her two children fed and healthy while her husband worked with the railroad. The pay was good when it came, but that was only once a month. Right now he was reported to be in New Mexico and Meg had a respiratory infection. It did not bode well.

"Meg's a strong gal," Elmer said. "She'll pull through. Thanks for sending the little gal over to help. Don't know how we would have managed without her."

"Hey, y'all were doing me a favor," Jenny replied. "Cindy needed a week's employment to buy that ticket back to Missouri. I was pulling my hair out trying to find a way to make it happen. So, you tell Meg I said thank you, and Cindy's family thanks you as well. I heard tell she got home in time to see her grandmother before she died."

"Meg will be happy to hear that."

Jenny smiled. "Well, gentlemen, I have to get back to the office. You have a good day."

"I will," Elmer said. " 'Cause I'm gonna whoop Joe at chess."

"You wish," Joe said and moved a knight. "Check."

Jenny hid a yawn as she continued down her street. She knew her office would be full of people waiting for her to help them. She didn't have time to be tired now.

"Hey, Doc. Been up all night again?" Clay Calhoun said from his perch outside the pharmacy.

"Mrs. Hall had her baby," Jenny said.

Clay shook his head. "You do too much, Doc. If you ain't careful, you're gonna wear yourself out."

"I'll be careful," Jenny lied. She opened the door to the clinic. Inside, the chairs were all full. Sniffling children played on the floor.

Emily smiled at her from behind the receptionist desk. "How's Mrs. Hall?"

"She's doing well," Jenny said and took off her coat. She hung it on the rack beside the door and nodded at the people waiting. "Thank you for your patience," she said to the crowd. "I'll be with y'all in just a moment." Emily followed her into the back room and closed the door.

"I got a pot of black coffee on the stove," Emily said with brisk efficiency. "There's some stew on the stove too. I want you to eat."

"I'm not hungry," Jenny said, and wrapped a new bright white apron around her skirt. "But coffee sounds good."

"Sit," Emily commanded with the air of a general. "I'm not letting a single patient in here until you at least have a bowl of stew. I can't have you passing out. It would scare the children."

Jenny shook her head at the older woman. "Well, we don't want that now, do we? She sat down at the wooden desk that rested in the corner. Emily served her a bowl of piping hot stew and a cup of rich black coffee. The scent of gravy and coffee mixed, and suddenly Jenny was very hungry. "Smells wonderful," she said and spooned up a mouthful.

Emily shook her head. "You need to get some help in here."

"I was thinking about that," Jenny said. "What do you think about Mary Ambrose?"

"That little gal who just turned seventeen?"

"Sure, she's young, but she has a quick and clever mind. She worked through all her text books, but she can't afford to go to college." Jenny ate more stew. "I thought we could bring her in as an assistant during the summer and then sponsor her through med school."

"That will take years," Emily said and put her hands on her ample hips. "What about right now? You could put an advertisement in the Dallas paper."

Jenny shook her head. "No, I don't want a stranger and I don't want a man. You know how I feel about that. These women need to be listened to, and a man from Dallas isn't going to do it."

"Fine, in the meantime you're going to kill yourself."

"I'm fine, really. I just need to get a couple of days of solid sleep."

Emily looked toward the waiting room door. "That's never going to happen here, and if you expand to the outer parts of the county like you've been talking, you'll never get any rest."

"I have a plan for that," Jenny said simply. "I'm going to hire a driver."

"A driver?!"

"Sure, why not? I'll get someone who can handle the carriage. Then I can nap on the way to and from houses. It really is an ingenious solution."

Emily shook her head. "You are too smart for your own good."

"That's what you love best about me." Jenny stood and took the bowl to the small sink and gave the pump handle a few pulls until water gushed out. Then she carefully washed her hands. "Send in the worst first and the children second."

Em put her hand on the doorknob. "All right, but I'm closing the doors at four. You need to go home and get a good night's sleep or you aren't going to do anybody any good."

"Fine," Jenny said with a sigh. Em could be so persistent. It's something Jenny liked about the older woman.

"Good." She opened the door. "Mrs. Davis, you can go in now, the doctor will see you."

Shay woke from his quick nap around 2 P.M. and stretched. He glanced out the window. He was lucky it looked out over the main street and not the back alley. The street was busy with shoppers and cowboys and wagons moving back and forth. A couple walked from one walkway to another followed by a pair of young girls obviously excited about coming to town.

A movement in the street caught his eye. A tall young woman with dark auburn hair strode with purpose across the street. She wore a blue coat over a serviceable black skirt. It wasn't her astonishingly lovely profile that caught his eye. Nor was it her purposeful stride or quick smile. No, what intrigued Shay the most about the woman was the doctor's bag in her gloved hand.

What sort of young woman would dedicate herself to such a demanding profession? Shay shook his head at his own thoughts. He needed a bath and a shave and to find out about Jenny Edwards. He didn't need to be curious about pretty women carrying doctor's bags.

* * *

The barbershop was filled with some interesting characters discussing the current drought and the state of the union. Shay stepped in and took off his hat. Silence ensued.

"What can we do for you, stranger?"

"Shay," he said as way of introducing himself. He needed to get into the group fairly quickly if he were going to get them to trust him enough to give him the information he needed. "Shay Morgan."

"What can we do for ya, Shay Morgan?"

"Well, I just got off the train from Wyoming and I'm looking for a hot bath and a good shave."

"Wyoming." The barber's eyes narrowed. "You ain't from Cheyenne, are ya?"

"No," Shay said. "Why? Don't you shave men from Cheyenne?"

One of the other men took that moment to spit between the planks of the floor. "It ain't that we don't shave 'em," he said and squinted at Shay. "In fact I'd say we do shave 'em, right before we tar an' feather 'em."

One of the other men laughed. His face was weathered like leather from the sun. "Last one we shaved and tied him up naked to a tree. Elmer poured honey on him. The ants would have had a feast, too, if those darned Indians didn't come by and let him loose."

Shay climbed cautiously into the barber chair. He wasn't too worried yet, but he figured it might be a good idea not to come right out and antagonize them.

"So, what did these men from Cheyenne do to deserve such treatment?"

The barber tipped the chair back. "They came to hassle Doc," the barber said briskly. Then he slapped a very hot towel on Shay's face.

Shay tried not to flinch. "Were they bounty hunters or something?" he said through the towel.

"Nope," one of the men said. "They was men what worked for Doc's father. That evil son-of-a-gun sent them to take our doc away. Well we weren't having any of that."

Shay lifted the towel and looked at them. "So, you meddled in a feud between father and son."

The man spit again and wiped his chin with his hand. "Ain't no feud, an' Doc ain't no son. Our Doc is the most decent woman you'll ever have the pleasure not to meet, and that pa of hers won't meet her either. Not after he abandoned her and her ma."

"That's right," the Barber said and took off the towel. "Edwards lost the right to see his daughter the day he walked out on her and her ma and never looked back."

Something a tad too much like dread scooted down Shay's spine. He squirmed uncomfortable. "Edwards?" he asked. "Is your doc Jenny Edwards?"

Chapter Two

The barber looked at Shay suspiciously. He picked up his razor and deliberately tested the edge. "How do you know her name?"

Shay thought quickly. Sometimes it was best to bluff his way through a situation. He shrugged. "I've got a doctor friend in Chicago who went to school with a Jenny Edwards. I was just wondering if she was one and the same. After all, you don't see many women doctors."

"Where'd your friend go to school?"

"New York."

"Ain't the same gal—our doc went to school in Boston."

"Well, what a strange coincidence," Shay said calmly.

"Better be all it is," the barber said and brushed shaving soap lather on Shay's chin. He put the brush and cup down and sharpened the razor on the strop. "I'd hate to think you were someone we'd have to run out of town. Frankly, we're running out of creative ways to do it."

"Let's just shoot the next one," the man with the weathered face said. "Quick and easy. Then we can send Edwards his man in a body bag. He'll get the idea."

Shay was glad he had the best poker face in Wyoming or he'd have spilled his hand to this crazy bunch. As the barber leaned him back and scraped the beard off his chin, Shay realized that a change of plan was necessary.

It was clear that the town protected Doctor Jenny Edwards. That was a daunting thought. He'd have to figure out another way to get close to her. Something far more subtle.

Jenny held the door for her last patient. "Now, you be sure and take a teaspoon of that twice a day. Get some rest and drink lots of water," she ordered. "I want to see you again if you're not better in two weeks."

"Yes, ma'am," the tired mother of four said and ducked her head.

Jenny knew that rest was out of the question. Sue was barely making ends meet with the amount of washing she had taken in and she was still breastfeeding her youngest. So Jenny had prescribed an elixir with stimulants in it. If nothing else, it will keep the poor woman awake while she burned the midnight oil.

Jenny went to close the door when it was pulled back open. "We're closed except for emergencies," Jenny said. Then she looked up. Standing on the threshold of her door was the angel she had dreamed about.

Tall with wide shoulders and narrow hips, he carried himself well. The way a man did when he knew that there was nothing the world could throw at him that he couldn't handle.

He smiled at her and she was stricken with a strange déjà vu. If she believed in fate or destiny, now would be the time to admit it. Unfortunately she was a realist. She believed that nothing happened that a person didn't choose to let happen.

"I'm sorry, we're closed. You'll have to come back to-morrow."

His blond hair was long and a bit shaggy, falling over his blue eyes. He pushed it back with a hand that was wrapped in a bandage, blood seeping through it. "I think I need stitches." His voice was deep and sensual. She swallowed. Any other strange man and she would have sent him to nearby Tyler and Doc Beckman.

She took a deep breath and made a decision she knew, just knew, she would regret. She opened the door and let him in.

He stepped across the threshold and brushed passed her. He smelled of bay rum and man. It was clear he had just had a bath and a shave. Something most men waited until Saturday to do.

Jenny mentally shook herself and hurried around him. "Come on around to the patient room," she ordered as briskly as possible. "Let me take a look at it."

Em walked into the waiting area, putting on her shawl. She stopped, surprised by the sight of a man in the office, especially a handsome man. She glanced at Jenny. "I thought we were closing," she said, her tone sounding like a mother chiding her brood.

"He thinks he needs stitches," Jenny said.

The angel held up his hand to show Em the spreading stain on the makeshift bandage wrapped around his hand.

Em glanced at Jenny. Her look was uncertain.

"It's all right," Jenny said and ushered the man past Em and into the patient room. "I'm sure it won't take long."

"I hope not," the man said with an angelic smile. "I'm late for a poker game."

"You're a card shark," Em said disapprovingly as she pulled off her shawl and helped him up onto the patient table.

"I enjoy the game," he said, "but I don't make my living on it."

Jenny washed her hands and then pulled a chair up next to him. She didn't want to know anything about him. After all, he'd walk out of her office the same way he walked in; unannounced and uninvited. "Let's take a look at this," she said and took his hand in hers.

An odd shiver of awareness rushed through her palm and up her arm. His hand was big and warm and callused enough to show that he worked for a living. It was the hand of a man who wasn't afraid of a little hard labor.

She took the edge of the bandage and unwrapped his palm. The bandage hid a deep jagged gash about two inches long in the padded part of the palm under the thumb. She probed it gently. He sucked in his breath and she glanced up.

"How'd you do it?" she asked.

"Stupid," he said with a wry grin. "I tried to help an old lady across the street."

"Oh, no," Jenny said. "Not Mrs. Dewitt."

"Who's Mrs. Dewitt?"

"Crazy old lady," Em said and brought over a basin full of clean hot water. "She hates do-gooders. Tends to lay in wait. Soon as someone tries to help her she draws that wicked hatpin of hers. I swear she goes home at night and sharpens the thing." Em glanced at the nasty cut. "Looks like you just weren't quick enough."

"I've had eight men come in over the last two years," Jenny said with a shake of her head. "I'll have another talk with Sheriff Gooden. It's time they did something about Mrs. Dewitt."

"They'll have to take away more than the hat pin," Em said as she brought Jenny a needle and thread. "That old woman is crazy enough to poke a man with anything she thinks is sharp enough."

"Maybe they should just post a sign or something," the angel said. "Something like: BEWARE OF OLD WOMAN."

"What a way to be welcomed to Johnstown," Jenny said and gently washed the wound.

"It's no worse than the reception at the barbershop."

"Really, what did Albert do?" Jenny asked. She dabbed a new anesthetic on the wound, then took the threaded needle from Em.

"Told me what they did to the last guy from Wyoming."

"What'd they do?" Jenny asked casually. She didn't really care; she was busy concentrating on closing the wound as quickly and efficiently as she could. She had the urgent need to get the angel as far from her as possible.

"I guess they ran him out of town on a rail and left him tied naked to a tree. The only thing they covered him with was honey."

"With honey—why ever would they do that?" Em asked.

"It was their hope to attract ants."

"Albert just made that up," Jenny said and tied off the string. "They like to intimidate newcomers. I'm sure if you stick around you'll see that they are all bark and no real bite." She lifted his hand to check the wound in a better light. "This ought to do it for you. You'll need to keep it clean for two weeks. Then you can take the stitches out." She glanced into his angel face. He smiled at her.

"Thanks, Doc."

She stood up and moved to the sink to wash her hands. It felt better to put distance between them. "You're welcome, mister—"

"I'm sorry, Shay, Shay Morgan." He stood as well. "These stitches look right fine. What do I owe you?"

"You don't—"

"Emergency visits are two dollars," Em said, cutting Jenny off. Jenny glanced at her assistant. The older woman ignored her and held out her hand. Shay Morgan reached into his pocket and withdrew a wallet. He pulled out two silver dollars and gave them to Em.

"Small price to pay for such good care," he said. "I heard good things about your clinic."

"Really," Em said suspiciously. "From whom?"

"The gents at the barbershop. All they could talk about was Doc Jenny Edwards and the good she's done for the community."

Jenny finished washing her hands, picked up a towel and wiped her hands. She leaned against the cold sink for stability and eyed him. The man was simply gorgeous. That was not good. Men in general weren't high on her list, but smooth, fast-talking charmers were the worst.

Her father had been just like that when he'd swung into town on a cattle drive. Her mother had been swept off her feet. The courtship was a whirlwind, the marriage one of legend, until the chips were down. When a freak house fire had left her mother crippled and disfigured, her father had abandoned her and Jenny. It was a painful lesson to learn, but Jenny learned it well.

At the age of nine, she had been left with an invalid mother, no father, and no visible means of support. If Doc Beckman hadn't taken pity on her and given her steady employment after school and weekends she would never have lived the year out.

It was during her years helping the good doctor of Tyler, Texas that she saw over and over again how women put their faith in men. Men who would ultimately abandon them at the first sign of trouble or the first pretty new face to come into town.

After her mother died, Jenny had had many suitors, but she turned them away. Doc had never married. He had explained to her that he wanted to devote his life to his patients, and if he were married his family would have to come first.

Jenny knew then that that was what she wanted to do with her life. She knew she'd never trust a man enough to put her life in his hands. So instead, she went to medical school and devoted her life to her female patients.

She was happy with her life. She didn't want a dream of lying in an angel's arms. She didn't want the feeling of safety and comfort or the chance to share the heavy burden of responsibility that wove through her life.

"Doc, you all right?" Shay Morgan asked.

"Oh, yes, fine." Jenny shook out of her thoughts and hung up the towel.

"You'll have to excuse her," Em said and pushed him toward the door. "She was up all night delivering a baby. We closed a bit early so that she could go home and get some rest."

Em, bless her, knew how Jenny felt. She was often the guardian that stood between Jenny and the rest of the world. Em's daughter had been Jenny's first patient and Em was so impressed that she took on Jenny as if she were her own.

"Well," Shay said, and hat in hand stepped into the threshold of the door. "Thanks again. It was nice to meet you both."

Jenny watched as Em escorted him through the door and into the waiting room. She waited until she heard the outer door close, then she burst through the door and strode to the front windows.

Em stood looking out. Jenny moved beside her. Together they watched the handsome man cross the street and angle his way to the saloon. Neither said a word, but Jenny thought she heard Em sigh.

She never heard Em sigh like that before. She glanced at her assistant. Em shook her head. "Now there's a man who would make beautiful babies."

Jenny smiled at the thought. "Your baby-making days are over."

"But yours aren't."

"Don't even start with me," Jenny said. She took off her apron and tossed it in a basket of dirty laundry. "I'll take these and put them to soaking overnight."

"You'll do nothing of the same," Em said. "I already promised Mary Kathleen she could do it. She's got a baby at home and one on the way. She needs all the work she can get. You go home, eat something, and get some sleep."

Jenny rubbed her neck. "Fine, but just to let you know, Mrs. Harris said there were five families south of here that were sick with fever. So, tomorrow I'm going out to check on them."

"You can't go alone."

"I will if I have to, I know how to use a rifle. Mr. Wallace from the dry goods store taught me years ago and I've kept up the practice."

"I'm certain that Mr. Wallace will be happier if you have a driver. I'll put a 'HELP WANTED' sign up in the dry goods store. There's a number of nice boys who would do a good job driving you."

"Tell Mr. Wallace to have anyone interested to come by the office at eight A.M. I'll choose someone out of the group."

"Fine," Em said and tossed her shawl around her shoulders. "Now shoo on home. You have bags the size of sugar sacks under your eyes."

"That's what I love about you, Em," Jenny said. "You know how to be direct."

"That's me, Mrs. Direct herself. Now go."

"Just one more thing."

"What?"

"Make a note on that sign that I'm willing to pay good wages if they can drive and shoot."

Em shook her head and pushed Jenny out the back door. "I'll be sure and let them know. Good night, Jenny."

"Good night, Em."

Jenny stumbled her way up the back steps that led to the small apartment she kept above the clinic. Once inside, she managed to take off her buttoned half boots before she fell asleep on top of her bed.

Shay put his stockinged feet up on his windowsill and leaned the chair back on two legs. The restless wind blew cool through the windows, making the white linen curtains billow around him.

He raised a glass of whiskey and took a sip. His left hand throbbed, drawing his attention away from the smell of rain that chased the wind. It would be a cold rain when it came, but from the talk in town it was a much-needed rain.

Crazy little town. That's what he thought of Johnstown, Texas. The people here were just plain loony. First the death threats in the barbershop. Then came the slashing hatpin of an elderly lady. Shay shook his head and chuckled.

It would be a story to entertain his nephews.

It had been instinct really. The trip to the doc's office had been totally instinctual. It wasn't until he saw her standing there with the doorknob firmly in her hand that he even realized that he was face to face with the elusive Jenny Edwards.

For all the pain in his hand, he hadn't been sure she was going to let him in. That was a curious thing as far as he was concerned. Doctors were supposed to help anyone who needed it. Weren't they?

Why then did it look like Doc Jenny was going to send him away?

When her lovely assistant, the puckered-face gray-haired Em had seen him, he thought for sure she was going to run him out on a rail. Good thing he was actually hurt.

Shay took another sip of his drink. It burned on his tongue and warmed his throat and finally his stomach. It was good whiskey, the kind that tasted of peat and oak. He'd brought it with him out of Amesville. He'd been to enough small towns to know they didn't usually serve the good stuff to strangers. Even strangers with money.

Of course, they'd take his money at the poker table. There was always someone in town who thought he was the best poker player in the county. Shay liked to get in the game just to keep his own game fresh. It never hurt to see the game from another's point of view. Besides it got him a chance to hear the local gossip from more than the old men at the barbershop.

The story about the doc had been the same. Seems she's cared mostly for the widows, and children of Johnstown. Every man he spoke to had nothing but respect for the lovely doctor. So much so that there wasn't a man in town who wouldn't lay down his life for her, and they all made that very clear. This town protected Jenny Edwards.

Jenny Edwards with the wary gaze; dark hair the color of rich burgundy and eyes so blue it reminded him of the Wyoming sky on a perfect summer day. She was just the right height. Standing, she reached the crook where his arm met his shoulder, the perfect place to hold her next to him.

The first hint of a storm blew in the window, bringing the smell of damp earth. Lightning slashed across the dark sky and after a distant pause thunder followed. Then suddenly rain came down in torrents, blowing in his window, soaking his feet.

Shay tossed the rest of the glass down. Okay, he admitted to himself that he'd always loved ladies. It was no secret. Even Mrs. Em had warmed up to him in the end, smiling and letting her twinkling brown eyes race over him. But his attraction to Jenny Edwards was different.

It was something about the way she touched him. Firm, yet gently. The caring way she had unwrapped his hand and asked if her probing hurt. The concern in her gaze before she became all business and started stitching.

Or maybe it was the vulnerable way she tilted her head to see better, exposing a secret column of cream-colored skin just behind her ear. The way she smelled of soap and sugar candy.

Shoot.

Shay shook his head and pulled his soaked feet in out of the rain. He put the glass down and closed the window. There were plenty of women in his life. So many that he knew it wouldn't be fair to choose just one. So he made sure he never did.

He pulled off his socks and hung them on the back of the chair. Then he turned down the bed covers and blew out the oil lamp. Jenny Edwards was a complicated woman. He was a simple man. It would never work.

Shay put his hands behind his head and stared up at the ceiling. Lightning flashed through the window as thunder crashed around the hotel. He had to quit thinking about that. There were more important things to worry about, like how he was going to convince Doc to come back to Wyoming with him without raising the suspicions of the town. It was an interesting puzzle. One he had thirty days to figure out.

He glanced at the sign that rested on the top of the small dresser. The HELP WANTED sign had been a blessing in disguise. He managed to take it down not long after Mrs. Em put it up. With any luck he'd be the only one to show up tomorrow. If not, he was certain that he would be the best shot. She'd have to take him.

Jenny was up at dawn, bathed and dressed and working in her office. She had records to update and bills to pay. It wasn't her favorite part of the job, but she had to admit that she liked the quiet of the early morning.

A pot of sturdy coffee and a couple of leftover biscuits made a fine breakfast. Jenny put down her pen and picked up her thick mug. The coffee tasted rich with a bit of a bitter bite. Just the way she liked it. She looked out the window. Last night's storm had settled the dust and dampened the streets. The merchants opened their shops, putting out their sidewalk displays designed to entice the buyer to come inside.

Joe was already outside the barbershop setting up a new game. She glanced at the watch that was pinned to her blouse. It was nearing 7 o'clock. She wondered how many applicants she would have for the job of driver. Surely she'd have at least one. There were a lot of young men around looking for some extra income.

Jenny frowned. It was spring and most of the men would be busy working long days out in the fields planting or working the cattle as they calved.

Well, she would see who showed up today. Perhaps she

would have to change her times to accommodate the rancher's schedule. The last thing she needed was some lazy cowboy. If one applied, she'd let him down nicely but firmly. She wasn't looking for a good time, only someone she could trust enough to get her out and back in one piece.

Jenny got up and poured the last of her coffee down the sink. Then she rinsed her cup and washed her hands. She had a few minutes before the applicants came and she used it to stock her bag with essentials for the house calls.

In town, she had the luxury of working in her clinic, but she knew there were people who rarely made it into town. Those were the people she wanted to reach.

Ever since her mother had been so badly hurt, Jenny had been aware of the desperate need the ranchers had for good health care. Especially the women who were often left alone while the men moved around the country looking for enough work to buy stock or seed to keep the farm going.

She put the last wrap of bandages on top of her bag and closed it tight. The hands on her watch said it was 8:00. Em would be on her way to the clinic and Jenny's applicants should be standing outside the door.

She felt a tingle of excitement. She wanted to make housecalls for a very long time. The idea of a woman alone had prevented Em from approving. But when she had a driver, Em would have nothing to complain about.

Jenny unlocked the front door and opened it wide. Disappointment filled her. The sidewalk was empty. She glanced back at her watch. It was 8:05.

No one was coming. She couldn't believe it. Maybe Mr. Wallace hadn't put the sign up. Well, she would go over there and have a talk with him. He might not like the idea of her doing housecalls but that didn't give him the right to stop her from hiring whoever she wanted.

She turned back into the waiting room to grab a shawl.

"Morning, Doc."

Jenny glanced around. Leaning against the building was the angel himself, Shay Morgan. She clamped down the little quiver of excitement she felt. "Good morning, Mr. Morgan. If you've come to get your stitches out, I'm sorry, but they have to stay in at least ten days."

"I didn't come about the stitches," he said and smiled that deadly smile. "I came about the job."

"What job?" Jenny was stunned by the glow that surrounded him whenever he smiled. He was certainly a charmer and what was worse, he knew it. He smiled like he knew it made a woman go all weak in the knees.

That right there was a danger flag. Her father had been just as charming.

"This job," he said and held up her sign.

She gasped and grabbed the paper out of his hand. "Did you take this out of Mr. Wallace's window?"

"I don't know who Mr. Wallace is," Shay said and straightened, "but, I pulled this the moment I saw it."

"Why would you do something like that?"

"Because I'm the man for the job."

"You're the man for the job?"

"I'm the best shot in three counties back home and I know my way around a team of horses."

"But your hand."

"It's my left palm. It'll be fine. Besides you'll be with me should I injure it further."

"I'm sorry, Mr. Morgan—"

"Shay."

"You're not exactly who I had in mind when I asked Em to put this sign up." She turned back into her waiting room.

Mr. Morgan grabbed the door and let himself in behind her. She ignored him and put the paper on the reception desk. The corner was a bit bent, but it was still in good enough shape to put back up in the window.

"Who did you have in mind?" he asked. He stood before her just a bit intimidating with his arms crossed across his chest. He wore a pair of gray slacks, a clean linen shirt and fancy waistcoat. He looked like a soft card shark, but she remembered how callused his hands were. The man was definitely not soft.

She faced him and leaned back against the desk for support. "I was hoping for someone who knew the county," she said. "Since you are obviously not from Johnstown, then I doubt you would be that great of a help."

"Good point," he said. "I'll admit I don't know the countryside as well as a native would, but I have an excellent sense of direction. I can shoot both a rifle and my own pistol." He pointed to the gun slung low on his hip. He wore it as if it were a part of him. She had no doubt he knew how to use it.

"Right now it appears I'm the only choice you've got."

Chapter Three

"**Y**ou're the only one I've got because no one else had a chance to see the 'Help Wanted' sign." Jenny bristled. Anger gripped her. "Now I'll have to wait until tomorrow to hire someone."

"Why?"

"Why?" The question was absurd. "Look, just because I did some emergency stitches on your hand, does not mean I know you, Mr. Morgan."

"I know I'm new in town and I certainly don't understand all the things a local would."

"That is an understatement." She crossed her arms over her chest and leaned against the sturdy desk for balance. It was either that or she would shake the man. What was he thinking?

"I've discovered that I like Texas. I've been thinking about relocating and I thought a week or so here would give me a better idea of what Johnstown is like."

"It's like any small town, Mr. Morgan. We take care of our own."

"Well, shoot, Doc. How does a man become one of its

own? The way I figure it, the best way for me to get to know the area and its fine people is to be your driver."

He gave her such an innocent look it made her feel like some sort of shrew. "While you make a very fine argument, Mr. Morgan, you have to understand that I just can't hire you."

"Okay, I have to respect that."

"Thank you." She took in a long breath to calm herself and blew it out. At least he was willing to be reasonable.

"So, let me do it for nothing."

"What?!"

"I've heard nothing but impressive things about the good that you are doing here, Doc. I want to support that and so I volunteer to be your driver." He grinned at her with that charming angel grin.

Jenny gripped the worn oak of the desk. That grin was going to be her undoing if she wasn't careful. "You'll drive me around for free," she repeated, her tone unbelieving.

"Completely pro bono, Doc."

Jenny narrowed her eyes. "Pro Bono?"

"It means on the house."

"I know what it means," she said and tilted her head. His words were simply too educated for a card shark, his hands too callused. "Did I ever ask you what exactly you do for a living?"

"No, you didn't."

"Hmmm. Why's that?"

He grinned and leaned his hip against the desk. The motion brought him dangerously close. She could smell the soft scent of shaving soap on his skin. "I never gave you the chance," he replied.

"And why is that exactly?"

"I didn't see how it was relevant."

"I see."

"Look, Doc. I know you have families you want to help. Let me at least drive you today. I'll answer any questions you have while we're out. If you want, I'll even stop by the sheriff's office and let him know I'm driving you."

"I don't know." Indecision gripped her. Her head knew that she should say no, but her heart was set on seeing those families.

"If I were going to run off with you, would I tell the sheriff?" he argued and leaned in close. "Let me do this. I want to pay back your kindness of last night."

His eyelashes were thick black around his blue eyes. So odd for a blond man. She leaned back the moment she realized he was crowding her. It was her only defense from the clear warmth of his blue eyes and the promises her lonely body read into his charming smile. "I made a big mistake last night," she concluded.

"What was that?"

"I should have sent you to Doc Beckman."

"But you didn't," he said with a knowing look in his eyes. "So, let me help you."

Jenny thought about those five families needing care. It would be selfish to make them wait another day just because she was afraid of this man's charm.

"Before we go, I want to make one thing perfectly clear," she said and straightened away from him.

"Sure."

"I'm a professional and I expect my driver to behave in a professional manner," she stressed.

"Yes, ma'am," he said and straightened.

"That means that this is not a Sunday drive."

"Of course not."

"I don't have time for courting," she blurted out.

"Who said anything about courting?" He asked and raised an eyebrow as if he'd never considered the idea.

Jenny blushed as embarrassment creeped over her. She raised her chin in the air. "I just wanted to make that clear."

"I understand. A single woman can't be too certain."

"That's right." She looked at him. "Exactly how did you know I was single?"

"You don't wear a ring on your finger and the way I figure it, if you were married, you wouldn't need a driver."

"I wouldn't?"

"Nope, your husband would do it."

"So, the way you see it, if I were married, my husband would be in charge of the clinic."

"Yes."

"No."

"No?" He had the look of a man who didn't quite believe her.

"No, if I were to ever marry, I would expect to continue to run this clinic exactly the way I'm running it now."

"Would you?"

"Yes," she said emphatically. "If I had a husband, I would expect to be treated as an equal."

"As an equal?"

"Yes, as an equal, thereby letting me continue to manage my own affairs while I let him continue to manage his."

"So you would leave him to his own affairs."

"Yes, I would."

He made a sound that sounded distinctly like a snort.

"You don't believe me?"

"I have three sisters-in-law. Let me tell you, the first thing I noticed about so called equal marriages was the fact that there is nothing equal about them."

She shook her head. "Are you married, Mr. Morgan?"

"Nope."

"Then your whole assumption is based on what?"

"On keen observation."

"It has been my experience, Mr. Morgan, that what you see is only a small part of what really goes on. So, until you are married, I would ask you to keep an open mind."

"When you marry, Doc, you'll see that I'm right."

"Well, I certainly hope you don't wait around in Johnstown simply to prove yourself right." She decided that they had wasted enough time on conversation. So, she picked up her bag and checked the supplies one more time.

"Why's that?"

"Because, I have no plans to ever get married."

"Why?"

She knew the answer as deeply and certainly as she knew her own name, but it would make the conversation far too personal. Instead she opted for the simplest explanation. "I'm a very busy woman and I don't have the time."

"Is that supposed to be a hint?"

"Mr. Kenner owns the stables. He has loaned me a horse and buggy," she replied. "His son Jared can bring them around for you. Please let them know we will be back by supper."

"That is definitely a hint," he said and grinned. "I'll go pick them up and be around as soon as they're ready."

"I'll be watching," Jenny said and pretended to count the vials of antibiotics in her bag. From the corner of her eye she saw him tip his hat and walk out.

Through the clinic window, she watched as he crossed the street. His long lean legs strode with purpose and grace. He dressed like a gentleman, but the gun strapped to his thigh was as much a part of him as a gunslinger's.

Jenny frowned. Just who exactly was Shay Morgan and what in the world would bring him to Johnstown, Texas? The question both intrigued and disturbed her. She sighed. One thing was certain, she would eventually learn the truth whatever it was. She just hoped it wasn't something she would regret.

Shay snapped the reins and headed south out of town. Doc Jenny took him up on his word. She made him go to Sheriff Gooden and give their itinerary. He mentally shook his head. The gal was cautious.

He supposed she had reason to be. Still he hadn't planned on taking her off to Wyoming today. No, his plan was simple. To get her to trust him and then she would at least hear him out when he told her the truth. After that it would be anyone's guess how she would go.

She would go, even if he had to snatch her out of her bed in the middle of the night. Old man Edwards was dying and he deserved to see what a beauty his daughter had grown into. Shay glanced at her. She kept her eyes on the road in front of them. Her long lashes were black and curled around her lush blue eyes.

Tendrils of deep red hair escaped her bonnet and curled around smooth skin. She had a smattering of freckles on her nose. It was an imperfection that intrigued him.

"So, where to first?"

"About five miles out of town there's a couple of home-steaders' cabins. I heard that they may have come down with a fever." She glanced at him. "We may be walking into something nasty, so when we get there, I'd prefer that you stay outside."

"We'll take it as it comes," Shay said, keeping his eye on the bumpy road ahead.

"What exactly does that mean?"

He knew he was in trouble now, but what the heck. He wasn't going to lie to her. "It means that until we get there, I'm not making any promises."

She bristled beside him. "The professional thing would be for you to do what I ask. After all, I am the doctor."

"The professional thing to do would be to treat me as an equal," Shay replied and tried to stifle his grin at her reaction. "Therefore there will be no ordering about by any one."

"But—"

"I expect that as an equal, you will ask me for help when you need it."

She stewed on that a bit. He had to hand it to himself. He had her with that whole equal hooey that she was espousing back in the clinic. Truth was no one was ever really equal. To work well as a team of any kind, including a married team, the weaker had to learn to let the stronger take control or there would never be balance. As far as Shay was concerned, balance was the key to everything.

"Has anyone ever told you, you should be a lawyer?" she asked.

"Why would you say that?" A niggle of apprehension squirmed down his spine. He hadn't realized how astute she was.

"You certainly argue like a lawyer." The tone of her voice was not complimentary. In fact she sounded downright insulting.

He glanced up at the bright blue sky. The color was so clear it hurt his eyes. "I take it you've had experiences with lawyers?"

"A couple," she said vaguely.

"Were they good experiences or bad?"

"I suppose that depends on your point of view."

That didn't sound like a good answer. "I see," he said and wondered if his plan might not have been a big mistake. There was too much about Jenny Edwards he didn't know.

"Do you?" she asked. "Do you really see?"

"Well, I certainly can see that you don't think too highly of lawyers." He glanced at her. "Why's that?"

She twisted her fingers around the handle of her medical bag. It sat straight on her lap, covering her from belly to kneecap. It certainly looked like she was hiding behind the darned thing. It was odd. She didn't seem the type to hide.

"I'm somewhat jaded," she said and relaxed a bit at the admission. She looked at him from underneath her bonnet and shrugged. "The only time a lawyer is worth anything is if he is working for you. That is, if you've checked him out thoroughly before you hire him."

"Why's that?"

"Because my experience has been that a lawyer doesn't work for any purpose but money. They'll step on a client to get at it."

"Ah," he said. "That is an assumption. Just what exactly did you base this assumption on?"

She narrowed her eyes at him. "Keen observation and experience," she replied.

"Experience, huh?"

"Experience."

"So, you've met some bad lawyers."

"I've hired some bad lawyers, and I've been manipulated by some bad lawyers."

"Sounds like a story."

"I suppose it is."

The buggy rocked beneath them and he eyed the road ahead. If you could call it a road—it had narrowed down into twin tracks in the long prairie grass. The scent of dust tickled his nostrils. He waited the space of four heartbeats before asking. "Are you going to tell me?"

She glanced at him out of the corner of her eye. "I hired

a lawyer once to find my mother's family in St. Louis. He demanded I pay him two hundred dollars up front."

Shay let out a low whistle. "That's a lot of money."

"Yes it is, but I managed to gather up enough. He took it and bought a ticket to St. Louis. I received one letter in return telling me my mother's relatives had moved to Memphis and for another two hundred dollars he'd be happy to go there to find out what happened to them."

"Don't tell me you sent him more money."

"No," she said, the tone of her voice bitter. "I was very young and very poor. It took two years to work off the money I borrowed to send him to St. Louis."

"You never found out where your mother's family went?"

"I never found out." She paused. Her fingers played with the handle of her bag. "I was 12 at the time and I thought they might want to know that my mother had died."

Shay's heart squeezed in his chest at the thought of a 12-year-old Jenny alone in the world. "What about your father?"

"I have no father," she said.

That was an interesting answer. "Everyone has a father."

"Mine ran off five years before my mother died."

"Why didn't you send the lawyer to find him?"

"I didn't even consider it. My mother used to talk about her sister all the time and I thought . . ."

"You thought maybe your aunt would take you in." Shay sensed the truth. She had been a young girl alone in the world with nothing but the hope that someone out there would want her.

"It didn't matter what I thought. I didn't have the means to hire anyone else to find her, and all the letters I sent came back addressee unknown."

In essence she had been abandoned yet again. "Do you remember the name of the lawyer?"

"I'll never forget it. His name was Quincy Patterson and I went to him because he had a reputation for finding people."

"Sounds like he had a reputation for taking advantage of little girls."

"I gave him all the money my ma had when she died. That's when he told me that the only way to get my family to come to Johnstown was if I sent him after them. So, I sold our small ranch for one hundred dollars and borrowed the rest from Doc Beckman. The deal was I'd pay him back when my aunt came to get me, but of course she never came."

"So, you worked off your debt."

"Two years and I was hooked. Doc was good to me and I learned I had a passion for helping people. Especially the under-served."

"But you've never met a good lawyer."

"I've never met a good lawyer."

"There's always the chance that you will."

"I suppose that's true," she said, "but I'm not holding my breath."

"Let me introduce myself," Shay said, and held out his hand. "Shay Morgan, attorney at large."

She looked from his outstretched hand to his face. A delicious red creeped up out of her collar and rushed over her cheeks. "Good lord, you're a lawyer."

"I'm a lawyer," he said, and pulled his empty hand back. He took the reins with both hands, gripping the leather to ward off her horror at finding out his profession. "I'd like to think I'm a good one."

"No wonder they scared you half to death."

"What are you talking about?"

"The men who hang around the barbershop. They don't care much for lawyers."

Shay laughed at the idea that those windbags might actually hurt him. "They didn't scare me. I took it all in good humor."

"Well, you should be scared," she said with certainty.

"Why's that?"

"I don't know for sure." She gave a slight shrug. "There was some trouble a few years back with a lawyer out of Wyoming. No one would tell me the whole story. Finally, Bill Watts told me that the town elders had decided we didn't need lawyers in Johnstown."

"Really?"

"Oh, a few strays have come into town, but they all leave." She glanced at him again. "I suppose that's not something you really wanted to hear."

Shay flicked a grasshopper off his pants. "I figured something was going on. You don't find too many towns the size of Johnstown without at least one shingle up." He glanced at her. The sun had begun to pinken the tip of her turned up nose. "That's what had me thinking about staying. I figure there's plenty of room to grow."

It wasn't really a lie he told himself. It was a bluff. Bluffing was a way to manipulate the game to get to your ultimate goal. Shay knew how to bluff.

"Well, I hope you're not disappointed if they don't welcome you with open arms, Mr. Morgan," she said, overly brightly. "Try to remember that it's nothing personal."

He caught her gaze and pulled out his most charming grin. "I'm not worried. I figure, if my luck holds out, I can always make a living as a professional driver."

The impact of his smile was plain on her sweet face. She seemed startled at first, then swallowed and smiled smartly in return. "If you impress me, I'll be sure to give you a good reference."

"I'll have to be sure and pull out all the stops," he drawled. "Because I plan on making a very good impression."

Chapter Four

Jenny kept her worried gaze on the road ahead. She'd bet Shay Morgan could charm the birds right out of the sky if he wanted to bad enough. That was not a good thing.

The man was a lawyer. It wasn't enough that he was relentlessly charming, utterly handsome and well mannered. Now he was her worst nightmare. A lawyer. She realized that she had twisted her gloved fingers into little knots.

That was not a good thing, not a good thing at all. She glanced at him and thought about the lawyer her father had sent out to get her. He had been a thin-faced tight-lipped man with mean eyes. He had arrived at the clinic and immediately gone to work trying to close her down.

It had taken nearly all her savings to fight him. He had been under the premise that once the clinic was gone she would go running to her father. What the lawyer and her father didn't bargain for was her stubbornness.

In the end, the lawyer was run out of town and the clinic was saved. She hadn't heard from her father since. It was a relief really, she thought. She could never love the man who abandoned her mother at the first sign of trouble.

The air had warmed under the bright April sunshine. Birds swooped about fighting and singing and settling for their territory. The wind still had a bit of a bite to it and she was glad she wore her coat.

The small carriage creaked and groaned as it rolled over the uneven two-track they followed. One particular difficult bump threw her against Mr. Morgan. He was warm and solid and had put his arm around her waist to settle her. She ignored the thrill his touch sent up her spine.

"Thank you," she said and clutched her bag.

"All part of the service," he drawled and tipped his hat.

She looked away. The man was incorrigible. She needed to fill the awkward silence that followed. "What made you want to be a lawyer?"

"It was my ma, actually," he said. "I was her youngest and she had high hopes for me."

"Let me guess, your brothers are all accomplished."

"I guess they are," he said. "They weren't at the time though. When my ma died, she made my brothers Matt and Tag promise her that they would send me to college."

"So you went."

"I went, kicking and screaming, but I went."

"It must have been okay. You stayed."

"I stayed," he agreed. "I found I liked it."

"What did you like most about it?" she asked. "The literary classics? Mathematics? Logic? What?"

"I liked the variety of people who showed up on campus," Shay said. "People intrigue me."

"Ah."

"What does that mean?"

"It means I understand. You weren't there to learn, you were there for the social life."

"It wasn't all bad," he said. "I graduated with honors."

Jenny looked at him. "You graduated with honors?"

"I've never lost a bet in my life," he said.

"So, you just hit the books and graduated with honors."

"I discovered my ma was right. I had a talent for schooling."

It figured. She smoothed her dark blue wool coat over her serviceable skirt. "What would you have done if you didn't?"

"Gone back to the ranch and helped my brothers."

"You don't seem the type to work a ranch all day."

"That's what my ma said." He eyed her. "She used to worry that I would end up spending my life in saloons. The degree made sure I had a real profession."

Jenny ignored the sparkle in his gaze and concentrated on the toes of her polished black half boots. "So what brings you to Texas?"

"I came down on business, but I really like what I see here." He glanced at her and the look of warmth in his eyes made a blush threaten to creep up her neck. "So I thought I'd look into staying."

She glanced away. He was flirting with her. The realization hit her like a lightning bolt. It was exhilarating and flattering and very dangerous.

"Too bad you picked Johnstown," she said to the backside of the horse. "Like I explained earlier. There's just no place for a lawyer in town."

He didn't answer her. She glanced at him and he had his gaze on the horizon. She hoped she hadn't insulted him, but it was always best to speak the truth. No sense in anyone getting his or her hopes up for no reason.

"The first house is coming up on the right," she said, and pointed to the small wagon track that veered off the main track. Portions of the prairie had been burned. The burned parts came to life with new green growth. The parts that had not burned were thick with tall grasses and tangled leaves. The wind was lightly scented with the perfume of the daisies and chicory that bloomed among the grasses.

The tiny track dipped down into a hidden ravine. The carriage tilted from side to side, but made it down the track. Jenny hung on to her seat and watched the countryside.

A small stream trickled through the ravine and a stand of twisted poplars and Osage orange trees grew around it. Their sticky flowers drifted through the air.

Finally the trees parted, revealing a small cabin among the trees. A thin line of smoke traveled up from the chimney. Mr. Morgan stopped the carriage just outside the door and helped her out.

"I'll take care of the animals," he said. "Come get me if you need me."

She straightened her coat and gloves and took her bag from him. "I will, thank you."

"You're welcome."

No one came out to see them. No one stirred when she stepped up onto the porch. The eerie silence made it seem as if the homestead had been abandoned. Concerned, she rapped on the door. No one answered, so she grabbed the handle and opened it.

"Hello?" she called. "Is anyone home?"

A groan came from the far corner and Jenny hurried in. "Hello?" she called as her eyes adjusted to the dim light inside. As best she could tell, the cabin had one large room. A curtain separated the sleeping space from the living space. The sound had come from behind the curtain. "Hello? I'm Doctor Jenny Edwards. I heard that you might need a doctor."

"Please," croaked someone from behind the partition.

Jenny pulled the curtain back. Behind it was a large four-poster bed and a smaller trundle. A man and his wife lay on the bed with a toddler between them. In the trundle were two more children. They all looked pale as death.

Jenny pulled off her gloves and went to the trundle. She put her hand on the forehead of a little girl who looked as if she were five years old. The girl was burning up, her skin hot and dry, her lips cracked. The boy next to her was probably ten.

He, too, had fever but was well enough to open his eyes. "Water," he said. "Please."

"Of course," she said and put her bag down. She spied a basin and a dipper on the counter. It held clean water. She filled the dipper and brought it to the boy. Placing her arm around his shoulder, she helped him sit up and he drank as if he hadn't had water in days.

The father moaned on the bed. It was clear that the family had fallen ill, and if she had not come out to see them, everyone might have died. Regret filled her. She had almost stayed in town.

She managed to get at least a little water between the cracked lips of the father when Shay came into the cabin.

"Stay back," she warned sternly. "It looks like diphtheria."

He stayed near the door. "What do you need me to do?"

"They need fresh water and something to eat."

"There's a well out back, I'll bring fresh water."

"The water bucket is next to the door."

He nodded and grabbed the covered bucket and left. Jenny went straight to work. She stripped off the sheets and nightclothes. It was clear it had been days since the family had been up and about.

She wrapped the children tightly in blankets, gave them more water and medicine out of her bag.

Shay set two buckets of water just inside the door. "What are you doing?"

"I'm going to have to boil these linens. They need fresh bedding or they'll end up with bedsores or worse. In the meantime, cool baths and the medicine I gave them will help bring down the fever."

"Give me the linens; I'll wash them while you work in here."

Jenny eyed him. "Have you boiled linens before?"

"My ma was sick for six months before she died," he said, his tone gentle. "I know how to wash linens."

Something inside her melted, leaving her feeling warm and slightly exposed. He was charming, handsome and practical. "Okay," she said and put the linens inside the biggest sheet. Then she wrapped them up and handed him the ball. "There's vinegar in the cupboard. Put a cup of it in the water."

He took the linens and slung them over his shoulder as if he were Santa Claus with his pack. "Don't worry. I'll have these cleaned and dried."

"Check and see if there are any animals. It looks like they've been down for a few days."

Shay nodded. "I'll take care of it."

Jenny took a moment to watch him leave. It was strange to be able to give some of her responsibilities up. Strange and somehow relieving not to be alone.

She went back to the family and dug clean underwear out of a trunk. With Shay's help she could concentrate on the important things like the family.

Shay tossed dirty water into the dry flowerbed beside the cabin. The sun had started to sink in the west. He took a moment to absorb the clean scent of the spring wind, the quiet of the falling night. Night birds called. It was still too early for the sound of insects, but the night was more active than the absolute quiet of winter.

Texas wasn't that different from Wyoming. The seasons turned sooner, but the prairie was the same. Soft rolling hills with jagged flint and shale. A spattering of trees marking the meandering streams. He looked to the west. The only thing missing was the mountains.

Jenny stepped out onto the porch and put her hands to the small of her back. He watched her stretch. His admiration for her had grown over the day. She had known exactly what to do and had set about doing it. It didn't matter that the family was obviously too poor to pay her. Heck, they only had one milk cow and a couple of chickens.

Still, she had worked and tended until the dusty cabin was scrubbed from floor to ceiling, all the linens cleaned, the beds made around the family, and a pot of soup boiling in the fireplace. Now when you walked in, the scent of spicy soup and fresh linens filled the air, replacing the scent of impending death.

He had watched in amazement as she tended the family. Over and over again she gave them water, put balm on their cracked lips, and rubbed salve onto any sores.

He had helped where he could, doing the linens in the washpot outside the cabin, cutting firewood, shaking out blankets. He found the cow lying in a cool part of the wooded grove. Her udder had been painfully swollen. It was clear it had been at least two days since she'd been cared for. At least two days the family had lay dying in their cabin.

"You did good today, Doc," he said.

She glanced at him and smiled. The smile didn't reach the wearied worry in her eyes. "Thank you for being pushy and making sure I didn't wait another day to come out. My stubbornness would have killed this family."

Shay crossed his arms and leaned against the porch post. He had never thought of himself as pushy. Still she seemed more concerned that she had been stubborn.

"You had no idea how bad they were," he said. "What you did know is that I was a stranger. You had every right to be cautious."

"Hmmm," she said and looked out at the setting sun. "Mrs. Atchinson said there were four more families out here."

"You're going to need help."

"Yes," she said and sighed. "Yes, I'm going to need help." She glanced at him. "You've been wonderful, by the way. Thank you."

"Just hoping for a good reference," he said and grinned at her. It was his hope that his grin would help to ease the worry in her face.

It got the reaction he was looking for. She smiled. "I'll tell everyone that you're a good guy," she said.

"Thank you."

She rubbed the back of her neck. Shay moved over and drew her toward him. He put both hands on her shoulders and rubbed them. She felt tight and small under his hands.

She closed her eyes as he worked the muscles near her neck.

"How's that?"

"Wonderful," she said.

The look on her face drew him and it was all he could do to keep from kissing her. She worked so hard and she did it as if she were the only person she could count on.

It hurt him to think that she was so alone in the world. No wonder the townspeople protected her. After working with her just one day, he wanted to protect her.

Hell, if he were to be honest, he wanted to do more than protect her. He wanted to hold her and chase that weariness and worry out of her face.

He stopped touching her and stepped away before he acted on his thoughts. "What do we do now?"

She opened her eyes and worked her shoulders. "I've been thinking about that." She took a deep breath. "You need to go back to town."

"No." Stubbornness formed in his gut. He'd be darned if he was going to leave her out here alone.

"Now hear me out," she said and raised her hand to stop his protest. "It's sunset. If you don't show up in the next hour or so, the sheriff will send a posse out."

"So?" He crossed his arms across his chest. He had abandoned his waistcoat early on. The sleeves to his linen shirt were rolled to his elbows and were damp from doing the laundry.

"So, I need you to go back into town. Tell the sheriff where I am. Then I need you to get Em and tell her what's been going on. If you can, bring her with you when you come back. I've made a list of supplies I'm going to need." She handed him a folded piece of paper. "She'll be able to get them."

Reluctantly he realized she was right. He tucked the paper into his shirt pocket. "What about you?"

"I'll be all right." She nodded. "Go, and when you get to town, grab some dinner at the hotel. I have a feeling that tomorrow isn't going to be any easier."

"Do you want me to bring you some dinner?"

"I've got the soup," she said. "There's some other supplies. I'll make biscuits."

She looked so small and so tired, yet strong as steel. "I don't like leaving you," he said, clenching his fists at the lack of choices.

"I'm used to it."

He cringed at the truth in her words.

"Please," she said, and placed her hand on his chest. "It's the best thing. We can't help all the families by ourselves. We need Em and I need supplies."

Shay glanced down at her hand. He saw the logic in what she said but that didn't mean he had to like it. He reached up and took her hand, kissing the vulnerable spot at her wrist that housed her pulse. She tasted of sweetness and healing. "Don't overdo while I'm gone, okay? These families need you and you can't wear yourself out."

A look of surprise and uncertainty crossed her face. "You sound like Em." It was clear to Shay that she wasn't used to having anyone look out for her.

Shay's respect for old man Edwards dropped a few degrees. What had happened to make a man abandon his only daughter? Why hadn't he come back? Shay let go of her.

"The sooner I go, the sooner I'll be back," he said. "I'm serious about taking care of yourself. It wouldn't hurt for you to use that time to take a quick nap."

She rubbed her arms against the chill in the wind. "I'll do my best," she said.

Shay had to touch her again. She looked so small and so tired. He reached out and drew her into the heat of his body. She was soft and curved to fit perfectly against him. He knew holding her was a mistake. He didn't want to let her go.

After a moment she stopped shivering and he took a step back. "Better get inside." His voice was oddly grave. "Don't worry, I'll be back soon."

She nodded and moved to the door. "Bring Em."

"I will." He stepped off the porch but was reluctant to leave. "Go eat."

She held the door open and glanced back at him. "Yes,

sir," she said smartly. "What happened to the rule where neither of us ordered the other around?"

"I guess I broke it."

"I guess you did," she said and smiled at him. "Now you'll have to pay."

Shay watched as she went into the house. He shook his head. The gal had spirit. It was something rare and wonderful. Something he couldn't have.

Jenny sat in a rocking chair near the fire and rocked slowly. The family rested comfortably behind the curtain. Already the boy's fever had broken and he rested easy. The only real worry now was for the baby. Sometimes the littlest ones surprised her and pulled out of the direst of situations. She prayed that would happen this time.

The smell of wood smoke filled the air and Jenny poked the fire. It popped and snapped, sparks rising up the chimney. She fed it another log and it leaped into a soft blaze that warmed her face and hands. She sat back in the rocker and let her mind drift.

Shay had been so kind and so helpful all day. There wasn't a task too demeaning. He had done everything she had asked of him without question, and he had given helpful suggestions without ordering her about. Until just before he left, she smiled at the memory. He hadn't been too concerned that she caught him breaking one of his own rules.

Jenny shook her head. He was like no man she had ever met. She chewed the inside of her lip. It was true that she didn't meet too many men. She'd isolated herself on purpose, but still he was totally unexpected.

She closed her eyes and remembered how he could flash that angel grin and lift her spirits at the most important times. She was so tired. She closed her eyes for a moment. In a matter of moments, she was asleep.

She dreamed of the angel again.

This time she called him Shay and he grinned. In the dream he took her in his arms and rocked all her cares and worries away.

Chapter Five

"Diphtheria?" Em's tone was filled with concern.

"That's what she said," Shay said. Standing on Em's front porch, he twisted his felt hat in his hand. "There were five members of this family. All of them had been down for days."

"There are at least four other families out there," Em said as she bustled him into her foyer. "That means I need to round up some of the girls who do standby nursing."

"Doc gave me this list of supplies," Shay said and took the paper out of his pocket. "She said you would know where to find them."

"Thank you," Em said. "Do you need anything? Did you eat dinner?"

"I'm fine," Shay said and avoided the look Em gave him. It was the same look his mother used to give him when he wasn't being altogether truthful.

"It's going to take me a minute or two to gather up my stuff. Why don't you go into the kitchen and make yourself a sandwich. I have ham and cheese in the ice box."

"Why don't I go pick up the nurses while you pack?"

"Because they won't come," Em said and put her hands on her ample hips. "They don't know you and Doc Jenny has a strict code. So you just march yourself into the kitchen and eat." She pointed the way, and Shay felt the heat of a blush rush over his face.

Darn if she didn't treat him like a kid. No one had done that in years.

"There's milk in there too. Help yourself."

Shay shook his head and chuckled. She must have children.

Less than an hour later, Shay had exchanged the carriage for a wagon. It was filled with stacks of linens, food and medicines. Four girls in their teens rode in the back. The girls were all freshly washed and wearing crisp white aprons.

"You're well organized," Shay told Emily with admiration. She sat beside him on the buckboard medical bag in hand.

"Doc knows what she's doing. She spent five years with Doc Beckman in Tyler and then she did a four-year internship in Boston."

"She's really dedicated," Shay said, and headed the wagon into the dark.

"It's because of her mother."

The wagon rocked beneath them, kicking up dust and the damp scent of nightfall. Shay had a lantern lit and hung at the front of the wagon to help shed light on their progress.

"Doc said something about her mother dying when she was twelve. What happened?"

"When Doc was eight there was a terrible house fire. Her mother was burned over three quarters of her body. Jenny, too, was burned, but not as bad."

"How'd it happen?"

"No one knows for sure and Jenny doesn't remember." Em adjusted her shawl around her shoulder. "Her mother never recovered."

"And her father?"

"Couldn't stand to look at them. He couldn't deal with the pain and suffering so he just up and left."

"He left?"

"Yes," Em replied. Her tone was cold as ice. "After two days, Jenny pulled herself out of bed and took care of her ma."

"He just left them."

"She was only eight and badly hurt herself," Em said, her lips tight. "But she took care of her ma."

"He never came back? Never sent money or family?"

"She hoped he would. She told me once she used to make up stories in her head. She told herself he was on a quest to find a doctor who could cure her ma. She used to tell everyone that he had written that he was coming home soon."

"He didn't." Shay found himself more than a little disappointed with the man he had grown to love as a father.

"No, he didn't. She confided in me that she had made up the part about the letters."

Shay thought about his childhood. When he was eight, he had the freedom to roam the ranch, climb trees, and be carefree. It was before the winter of blizzards, before his father had lost the majority of their herd.

His own ma had been a pillar of strength then. Always laughing and smiling and giving hugs. He couldn't even begin to imagine what it was like for Jenny. It had been hard on him when his ma took ill and he was a whole lot older than eight.

Something inside him hardened. Old man Edwards had always treated him like a son. The man had been generous with both his money and his advice, and Shay idolized him. Shay shook himself mentally. This was not the man he knew. What had happened?

Shay glanced at the young girls clinging to the back of the wagon. "What's the story behind the nurses?" he asked. "They're all so young."

"It's part of Jenny's idea. These girls all come from poor families. Doc enlists them in her nurses program. Teaches them how to cook and clean and care for the basic needs of the sick. She says that it's something they can take with them no matter what they do in their life."

"Admirable."

"No," Em said. "The idea came out of anger."

"Anger?"

"No one was there to teach Jenny these skills and she's certain it's what ultimately killed her mother. She blames her father, of course."

"Of course."

"Instead of becoming bitter, she used her anger to motivate her into seeing this program through. She sees it as her ultimate revenge. The more girls she can employ, the more girls she can teach these skills to, the more she wins her internal battle." Em shook her bonnet-covered head. "A battle with a father she doesn't even remember."

"She hates him."

Em paused. The darkness surrounded them. Stars stuck out like hard diamonds in the coal-black sky. "No," Em said. "No, she doesn't hate him. Not really. Sometimes when she talks about the family they were before the accident she gets this wistful look in her eyes."

"So, she misses him?" Shay didn't know what to feel—sorrow, anger, or hope.

"I think she wonders about him," Em said.

Shay nodded. Maybe there was hope that he could convince her to see her dying father. "She told me that she hired a lawyer once to find her mother's family."

"Horrid man. If I ever find him I think I'd need a lawyer."

"You do realize it was the man and not the profession that was bad." Shay ran the rough leather reins through his gloved hands.

Em snorted. "I think it's the profession. Truth is I'd rather deal with slick gamblers than nasty lawyers."

"Good thing I'm a slick gambler," Shay said. He'd be darned if he was going to shatter her idea of him. It was bad enough seeing the horror on Jenny's face.

"See, that's what I mean." Em smiled at him. "I'd much rather work with you than a lawyer any day."

"Thank you."

"You're welcome."

They rode in the thin darkness. The wagon lantern waved over the rough track, throwing light here and there. Shay shrugged off the cold night wind that inched down his collar. He wanted to get back to Doc. She needed him and from the sound of things she'd been let down by more than one man. He vowed that as far as he could help it, he wouldn't follow in their footsteps.

"Do you think Doc would ever want to find her father?" he asked, breaking the silence.

"A few years back I would have thought so," Em said. "Not now."

"Why not?"

"I think I've said enough about Doc's personal life," Em said. "Why such an interest?"

"She intrigues me."

"She is something, isn't she?"

"Yeah, she's something."

* * *

The angel with Shay's face brushed the hair out of her face and kissed her on the forehead. "Wake up, darling," he whispered. "They're back."

"Do I have to?"

"I'm afraid so." This time the voice was far more concrete.

Startled, Jenny opened her eyes. She looked straight into her angel's eyes and blinked. "It's you."

"I told you I'd be back before you knew it," Shay said with a grin.

Jenny blinked again and the dream dissolved, leaving her empty and confused. "Mr. Morgan?"

"Shay. After today, please call me Shay."

She glanced around. "Did you get Em?"

"Right here," Em said as she walked through the door. She carried a sack of canned goods. "I thought this would be a good assignment for Arlene."

Jenny stood. It brought her closer to Shay and she had the oddest urge to step back into the comfort of his arms. She shook off the feeling. "Good, yes, Arlene is a perfect choice."

"We've got three other nurses in the wagon," Shay said. "It's near ten o'clock. So we need to either stay here for the night or go."

"I say we need to go," Jenny said, aware that Shay stood so close. But if she moved away it would be awkward. "This family was near death. We need to check on the others."

"I agree," Em chimed in.

"I'll water the horses and let the other girls know we're going to keep on going." Shay squeezed his way through the women. Jenny watched him walk out. An embarrassing chorus of sighs floated through the still cabin. Jenny eyed

Arlene and Em. It seemed she wasn't the only one charmed by strong arms and an angel face.

"You have to keep the fire going," Jenny instructed as she slipped into her professional mode. It was far more comfortable than the silly schoolgirl that came out of her whenever she looked at Shay Morgan. "Mr. Morgan stacked plenty of wood and drew two buckets of good water. Make sure they drink water at least once an hour and give them the powder I left on the sink when the sun comes up."

"Yes, ma'am."

"Either Em or I will be back sometime tomorrow to check on the family and answer any questions you might have. If you feel like there is anything you can't handle you know what to do."

"Yes, ma'am. I'll walk down to the main road and tie a white scarf to the fence post."

"Right, The McPhersons live out this way. I expect one of them will get the message and send someone out right away to help you."

"Okay. I know Steve McPherson."

"There's a loaded pistol in the bag. Use it only in emergencies."

"Yes, ma'am."

"Any questions?"

"No. I've done this before. After the Dreissers I think this will be easier."

Jenny patted the young girl's shoulder. "Good. You have some wonderful confidence."

"You can count on me."

Jenny and Em walked out into the night. She had no reservations about leaving Arlene. Shay had been a big help and the brunt of the work had been done. There was nothing left for the nurse but maintenance, and Arlene was well trained.

"Arlene told me she's saved up enough to move back east."

Surprised, Jenny turned and eyed Em. "Doesn't she have an aunt in Philadelphia?"

"Yes, and she told me with our references she plans on working as a companion to a friend of her aunt."

"Good, good for her," Jenny said.

"Your nurses program is making a difference."

"It's hard to feel good about it tonight," Jenny said. "The thought of other families out there needing medical attention, well, it's almost too much to bear."

Shay came around the side of the wagon. "Are we ready to go?"

"Ready."

"Let me help you up and we'll be on our way."

Jenny pulled her gloves on and then put her hand in Shay's outstretched one. His warmth bled through her gloves. It startled her. She glanced at him and the unguarded look in his eyes drew her. Before she could act, he helped her up on the buckboard and stepped back.

With similar efficiency, Shay helped Em up beside her and Jenny wondered if she imagined the whole thing. After all, it was very dark.

They reached the next family only to find a similar situation. A cold chill of apprehension went down Jenny's back. What would have happened if she hadn't heard rumors that they were sick? What if she had ignored the rumors? Like a never-ending nightmare, they moved along the river. Cabin after cabin held the sick and dying. Exhausted, Jenny did what she had to do and set about tending the sick.

* * *

"How are you holding up?"

Jenny blinked at the odd question. Em had been the only other person her whole life who ever asked her that. "I'm okay," Jenny said. "Just taking a break."

Shay put two new buckets of fresh water on the porch and straightened his shoulders. He looked better than he should considering they had been working for nearly three days straight.

"How about you? This has got to be more than you bargained for when you volunteered to drive me."

"I'm fine. I got some sleep last night which is more than you can say."

"This is my profession," she said with a mixture of pride and quiet understanding. "I knew what I was getting into when I started the clinic. You, on the other hand, are only being kind."

"I wouldn't call it kind. The way I figure it, this is the best way to get to know the area and the people."

"By cutting wood, hauling water, and washing linens?

"That's minor," he said and sat on the worn porch step. "Sit." He patted the step. "I bet your feet are killing you."

Jenny sat. The steps were wide planks, but Shay was big enough that her skirts brushed his thigh. She tried to ignore that fact, put her elbows on her knees and her chin on her palms.

They sat in comfortable silence. She could hear Em moving inside the cabin. This was the fifth family they had found. Inside, a husband and wife and a six-month-old babe rested in a rope bed. They were so poor that their mattress was made of grass ticking and they only owned two tattered blankets. Jenny was glad she had thought to have Em bring extra linens.

A warm south wind blew across the grassy land. Flowers peeked out among the drier older grasses as if suspended in mid-air. The bright blue sky showed no sign of changing. No sign of rain.

The smell of dust and awakening earth warmed her senses. Jenny had left Texas only once, to go to medical school back east. She found she missed it terribly.

"What do you think of Texas so far?" she asked.

"There's certainly something about it. I can't quite put my finger on it, but I can see how it would get under a man's skin."

"People come to Texas looking for freedom and a better life. Some find it, but some like this family only find sickness and disappointment."

"The plot he's homesteading is too dry," Shay said. "I had to go to the neighbors to get the water."

"Em said she thought they were from New York. He must have read one dime novel too many. He thought he'd bring a couple head of cattle out here and become a cattle baron in a year."

"On land without a clear source of water?"

"He bought the homestead sight unseen. The owner told him there was a stream that cut through the middle."

"He lied."

"Not really," Jenny said. "If you look at the horizon you can see a small creek bed. It dried up a few years ago, but I bet it still flash floods when the weather's right."

"Why didn't he sink a well?"

"He spent all his money on cattle." Jenny hugged her knees. "Bawling cattle who eventually died of thirst."

"There's not enough time in the day for a man to carry the amount of water it takes to nurture a herd."

"You know something about cattle."

"My family owns the Bar M near Amesville, Wyoming. Before the blizzards, we had the third largest spread in the state."

"What happened?"

"We lost three quarters of our herds that year."

"Oh, no. What did your family do?"

"Fell apart." Shay picked up a rock and tossed it across the yard. It skipped along the tufts of grass. "My pa struggled to keep the ranch on its feet. He worked night and day and pushed my brothers beyond their boundaries."

"What about you?"

"I was too young. My ma protected me from most of it." Shay leaned back and studied the sky. "Eventually my brother Matt couldn't take it any more. He was convinced he was nothing but a disappointment to pa, so he ran off. Trey stayed and worked side by side with pa, but it wasn't enough."

"What happened?"

"Ma used to say pa died of a broken heart." Shay paused. "He was a man with big dreams. It didn't matter that ma was happy with what we had. It didn't matter that we had a warm home, a good community and enough food. Pa dreamed of better and killed himself trying to get it."

Jenny's heart went out to Shay. It was clear he still hadn't forgiven his father. She knew what that was like. "I see a lot of that out here," she said softly. "I figure God made dreamers and realists. The dreamers are here to discover, explore, and reach beyond our wildest imaginations. The realists take what the dreamers give them and make it, well, something you can actually do."

"So which are you, Doc? A dreamer or a realist?"

"I guess a bit of both." She tapped her toes against the grayed wood of the steps. "I mean I must be a dreamer to be a doctor." She shrugged. "But I'm also realistic enough to know I can't change everything. If I could we wouldn't be sitting here now."

Shay seemed to accept her answer. He looked out over the overgrown yard. "So, are they going to be okay?"

"This family?"

Shay nodded.

"I don't know," Jenny said. "The baby is the worst we've seen so far."

"The wife?"

"The next few hours will tell. She's running a very high fever."

"They may not make it."

"It's not looking good, but we're doing the best we can."

Shay's hands balled into fists. "Whoever sold him the land should be shot."

Jenny reached over and put her hand on his fist. "I know it's frustrating, but shooting people isn't the answer."

"It was just an expression," he said darkly. "There has to be some kind of recourse for this guy."

Jenny patted his hand absently in an attempt to comfort him. His hands were large, the skin warm and callused by the sun and work. She stroked it absently. "When they come through this illness, we'll see what he wants to do. If he wants to go home, we'll buy the land from him. If he wants to stay, we'll send out a dowser and find him a good well."

"Whose we?" Shay asked, his tone curious but gentle.

Jenny realized she had been practically holding his hand. She returned to hugging her knees. "Me." She glanced at him. "Not me. It's a bit hard to explain."

"I'm listening."

"I was left a large trust by one of Doc Beckman's patients. I guess she saw potential in what I wanted to do."

"Which is?"

"Help people help themselves."

"Admirable."

"Not really," she said. "Just practical. For instance, whether he decides to go or stay, we'll put in a good well and that should prevent this situation from happening again."

"Just like training your nurses gives them something to fall back on."

"Education is something you can never lose."

"And you do this all by yourself?"

"I have Em," Jenny said. "It works. That's why I picked Johnstown. A place like Tyler would be too big."

"So you aren't interested in saving the world."

Jenny smiled. "No, just a small corner of it."

"You sure are something, Jenny Edwards."

The sound of her name caused a shiver to run down her back. She stood. "I'd better go check on the baby."

He caught her by the wrist. "I'm staying as long as you need me." His blue eyes were dark with a sincere emotion.

Jenny swallowed hard. "Thank you."

"You're welcome."

She escaped into the dim small cabin. The intimacy of their conversation crumbled the protective walls around her heart. If she wasn't careful, she was going to forget her rules when it came to charming men.

Chapter Six

Shay primed yet another pump and worked the handle up and down. It took a long time for any water to be drawn. Still he pumped. The epidemic was clustered around one area of the county. Shay figured it was due to the drought and the water supply sinking to dangerous levels.

Knowing why it was happening didn't make the reality of the work any less bitter. They had been working around the clock for four days.

Shay had cut wood, and brought up bucket after bucket of water to wash and bathe the stricken. He'd spent hours wrestling nearly wild farm animals back into their corrals where they could be tended more readily.

As hard as he'd worked, Jenny had worked harder. She was amazing—cleaning, delegating, and moving from homestead to homestead checking on the nurses. She was always in the right spot at the right time to lend a hand wherever it was needed.

Shay knew she hadn't slept since he'd brought back Em and that worried him. She had to be dead on her feet. The door creaked open and slammed shut. He straightened and glanced toward the house. Jenny rushed out, tears rolling down her cheeks.

Shay sat the bucket down. His heart moved into his throat. "What happened?"

"I need you to . . . I'm sorry."

Her expression was so stricken that he reached out and drew her into his arms. She was so tired, she didn't protest. Instead she buried her face in his chest and leaned into him.

She was slender as a whip, yet he felt her heart beat against him and was uncomfortably aware of the softness of her skin.

"I told you I'd do whatever you need," he said, his tone gruff.

"I need . . ." She took a deep breath and he waited for her to finish. "I'm sorry. It's so hard to say this."

"It's okay, darlin'," he said and stroked her back. Her body warmed the linen on her dress. She smelled sweet like rose water and woman. "Take your time."

"Mrs. Harris and the baby." She shook her head and sighed. "They didn't make it."

"I'm so sorry."

She put her hand to her forehead and stepped back. "I, we, can't just leave them. Mr. Harris is too weak to get out of bed."

"You need me to dig graves."

"Awful, isn't it?" She hugged herself. "Yes, we need graves dug, but you don't have to do it. I need you to take Katie into town. She needs to check on her ma. I thought while you were there you could let Mr. Tiner know we need his services."

"Mr. Tiner?"

"He's the undertaker," she said. "He has a couple of men who dig graves. Tell him I sent you. He'll send them out."

"The trust pays for this too?"

"Sometimes," she admitted. "When we arrive too late."

He wrapped his hands around her arms and studied her expressionless face. "This is not your fault."

She looked up at him, her big eyes filled with emotion. "I should have come out here the moment I heard about these families."

"You came as quickly as you could," he said. "Now, I want you to listen to me. You're exhausted and soon you aren't going to do anyone any good."

"There's so much to do."

"There's also a lot of people doing it," he replied. "So, come back to town with me."

"But Em—"

"Em has been back to town twice. It's your turn."

"He's right," Em said as she stepped out of the shadow of the porch. "You need rest."

"But—"

"No, buts," Shay said. "If you don't come back into town, I won't go either."

"What about Katie?"

"She can take Mr. Harris' horse, if she has to."

"That's ridiculous. Katie can't ride."

"Then you have to come back to town with me."

When she looked like she would waver more, Shay did the most prudent thing. He picked her up and tossed a glance in Em's direction. "Send Katie out."

"What are you doing? Put me down."

"No."

Em sent him a smile and a nod. "Katie will be right there." Em disappeared back into the darkness.

"Shay Morgan, put me down!" Jenny ordered. She crossed her arms over her chest and frowned up at him.

"Nope," Shay said. "If you won't take care of yourself then I will."

"This is simply ridiculous."

"No more ridiculous than you going five days without any real sleep."

She might be frowning, but she rested her head in resignation against his shoulder. The movement did something to his heart.

"I know there's a word for this and if you'll give me a minute I'll remember what it is."

"Prudence?"

"No."

"Guidance?"

"No!"

"Caring?"

"Definitely not."

He tossed her up on the wagon seat, then turned and helped Katie up beside her.

"Kidnapping!" Jenny said triumphantly.

Shay shook his head and sent a sideways glance to Katie. "Kidnapping? Katie, is anyone here being kidnapped?"

The little seventeen-year-old with the long brown hair and big brown eyes giggled. "No, sir."

"See?" Shay said, and climbed up on the driver's side of the wagon. He turned to where Em stood on the porch. "Is there anything you need me to bring back?"

"Just send the Tiner boys out," Em said, and wiped her hands in the immaculate apron tied around her waist.

"I'll be back in the morning," Doc said.

"I won't need you that early," Em replied. "Come back day after tomorrow."

"I'll need to check on Teresa at the Purdy place."

"We were just out there yesterday. She has a good head on her shoulders. She'll be fine."

"Face it, Doc," Shay said, "you did a good job and the crisis is over."

"If I did such a good job, why do we have to have graves dug?"

Shay shared a look with Em. It wasn't like Doc to be so down on herself. She was exhausted and needed taking care of. Em was counting on him to see that it got done. He nodded in silent agreement.

Katie patted Doc's hand. "You can only do your best, no more. Remember? That's the first lesson you teach us as nurses. Sometimes all you can do is make people comfortable."

"That's what we're going to do right now," Shay said and snapped the reins. "Right, Katie?"

"Right," Katie said and sent him an adoring smile.

"Maybe I should move over and let her sit beside you," Doc said under her breath.

Shay's heart lifted. His charm was finally starting to work on Jenny Edwards. She had to be dead tired, but hey, he would take whatever he could. He leaned toward her and answered in a low voice. "Now that just wouldn't make any sense. Katie's home is first."

Jenny was so tired she had to fight to keep her eyes open. The wheels of the wagon churned in a constant drone underneath her, and Katie chatted away. Her voice was soft, sweet and monotone.

The angel was back. Goodness, how she missed him. He smiled at her and pulled her up on his lap. She snuggled into his shoulder and relished the comfort and safety she always felt when she was in the angel's arms. She never felt this way with anyone but the angel in her dreams.

She didn't have to talk to him. He simply understood the heaviness of her heart, the bitterness and anger that her father had placed there. The loneliness she often felt, and the deep, deep wound of not being good enough. Never being good enough. Somehow she knew it was the real reason her father abandoned her. The real reason her mother died.

The angel saw all of it and still he came and pulled her into his arms and gave her safe haven. It was as if here, she was good enough to be loved just the way she was.

The wagon stopped with a lurch. Startled, Jenny opened her eyes and sat up. They were at Katie's house. Shay eased out of the seat beside her and helped Katie down.

Jenny blushed in embarrassment when she realized she must have been using Shay's shoulder as a pillow. The corner of her mouth was damp and she said a silent prayer that she hadn't been drooling. She moved as if to get down, but Shay held up his hand to stop her.

"Stay there," he ordered. "I'll walk Katie to her door."

It was late in the afternoon and Katie's brother came out of the barn when he heard the wagon. Jenny watched as Shay greeted the young man. It was clear that Katie had a crush on Shay by the way she introduced him to her older brother. The boy shook Shay's hand. Jenny could see that Shay's charm worked on men as well as women.

The boy was as pleased to meet him as the girls had been. It wasn't beneath Jenny to notice how all the girls stopped for a moment whenever Shay walked by. She swore they held their breath until he smiled or nodded at them, and he always smiled or nodded. All the time he worked he was never too busy to acknowledge the girls or the children.

Over time he'd stripped off his work shirt. It was an unconscious thing. The sheer beauty of him almost brought the nurses to their knees. Jenny shook away her own feeling and tapped each on the shoulder, gently reminding them that they had sick people to tend.

It was bad enough that the girls watched him with hungry

eyes. Jenny hated the fact that she wanted to do the same. Just looking at Shay Morgan reminded her of her angel, and stirred a hunger in her she hadn't known existed. A hunger for love.

Jenny shook herself mentally. She was over tired. That was all. Shay Morgan was not her angel. The angel existed only in her dreams and Shay was real-life flesh and blood. The evidence of it was in the dirt on his boots, the dried sweat marks on his shirt.

He even smelled real, like a fierce summer wind. He smelled of heat and life and possibilities. Possibilities that were not hers.

Shay shook the boy's hand again and headed back to the wagon. Jenny waved at Katie and her brother. They waved back and headed into the two-story clapboard home her father had built before he died.

Shay climbed up beside Jenny and clicked the horses into action. "Katie's brother seems like a nice kid."

"He's smart as a whip," Jenny said, and scooted over so that there was space between them. "He's doing a fine job with the homestead. Katie tells me the herd has doubled since her brother took over."

"What happened to her father?"

"There was a wagon accident," Jenny said. Her heart hurt at the memory. "The horses took off and when he went to stop them, the wagon fell over on top of him. It crushed him."

"I'm sorry."

Jenny glanced at Shay and fought the tired tears that came to her eyes. "It happened three years ago. Katie's fine now. Her brother is doing very well."

"What about her mom?"

"She's a bit of a worrier. So we make sure Katie doesn't go out on long nursing assignments."

"What about you?"

"What do I have to do with it?"

"It's obvious you haven't gotten over the death."

Jenny closed her eyes and took a deep breath in a poor attempt to get a hold of her wildly swinging emotions. "Doc Beckman used to say I wasn't tough enough for the job." The admission cost her something, for deep down inside she was afraid he was right. She wasn't good enough for the job and if she wasn't a doctor what was she?

"You're about the toughest woman I've ever met," Shay said.

Jenny sent him a self-deprecating smile. "My teachers said I care too much. They said it wasn't healthy."

He studied the road and pondered that. "Seems to me that that's what makes you so good," he said, and glanced at her. "The way you care about people. They can tell it's genuine."

"But I can't help them all."

"They know that."

"Do they? They come to me for help, and some I can, and some are beyond my ability. Those people are the ones I remember."

"Ah," he said wisely. "I see how you are."

"What?" She didn't like the way he said that and it got her back up. "What do you see? You barely know me."

"I may barely know you but I see you quite clearly," he said smugly. "It's a gift."

"Oh, right, I forget, Mr. Attorney at Large, you are all knowing and wise beyond your years."

"Of course."

She snorted at his arrogance. "What if I don't care what you see?"

"Oh, you care," he said and grinned. "That's the whole thing. You care deeply about what I see when I watch you."

"That's ridiculous," she said and crossed her arms over her chest.

"Of course. But that doesn't change it."

"I'm not having this conversation."

"Want me to tell you why?"

"No."

"I'm going to anyway."

"I'm sure there is no way to stop you."

"Nope."

Jenny started humming.

Shay laughed out loud. The sound brightened her tired heart. She turned her head away from him and grinned. At the same time she hummed louder.

He leaned over until his shoulder touched hers and whispered in her ear. "You are a stubborn thing, aren't you?"

He said it like it was a good thing. The tone of his voice caressed her and caused shivers to race down her spine and stirred the hunger in her soul. She squashed the feeling and looked at him. "What is wrong with being stubborn?"

"Nothing, if you're a mule."

She gasped in outrage.

"Since you're not a mule, then being stubborn doesn't really work for you."

"You have some nerve."

"I like you Jenny Edwards," he said, and smiled at the horses. "You're fun to tease."

Jenny blinked. She was still affronted by his mule comment. "You know what I think?"

"What do you think?"

"I think you are spoiled."

"Spoiled? Whatever gave you that idea?" He sent her a look that was wholly tongue in cheek. The arrogant man knew he was spoiled and he didn't seem to care much.

"I've been watching you too," she said. "I've seen the way everyone reacts to you and that angel smile of yours."

"You think I have an angel smile?"

"What I think about your smile is neither here nor there, Shay Morgan. What I've seen is how you use the impact of that smile to get everyone to do exactly what you want when you want it."

"I see," he said and nodded his head. "You're jealous."

"What?!"

"You want me to save all my smiles for you."

"I don't think so," she said. She realized that she was tired and had boxed herself into a conversational corner.

"Then, you don't want me to smile at anyone?"

"I didn't say that either. Stop putting words in my mouth."

"It is a cute mouth," he said.

Jenny shook her head. "I can't believe you just said that."

"Did I offend you?"

"No, the words weren't offensive, but the way you used them was." He didn't look like he understood so she explained. "You used them to distract me."

"Did I?"

"Yes, you did," she said. "I'm sure that works well in a courtroom, but I don't like it."

"I beg your pardon," he said, a grin teasing the corners of his mouth.

"See you're doing it again."

He looked at her.

"You're distracting me. What I'm trying to say is that you can't use that smile and your sweet words to get by me, Shay Morgan."

"No?"

"No," she replied. A smug feeling came over her when he studied the road.

"You are something, Doc," he said and turned the corner into town. He glanced at her. "I still like you."

Jenny shook her head. "You are incorrigible."

"Yep," he said. "Can I let you in on a secret?"

"I guess."

He leaned over again and she held her breath in anticipation. Would he whisper again? Would she feel the delicious shivers that raced over her the last time?

"They say I'm the black sheep of the family."

He whispered and Jenny felt the shivers again. She had to keep from leaning into him like a snake leaned into a snake charmer. "You are?" she whispered back.

"Umhmmm," he said and winked at her.

Jenny swallowed hard. "Why do they say that?"

"When you meet my brothers you'll find out why."

"But your brothers are in Wyoming."

He pulled the wagon around to the back of the clinic and got out. "They'll be down to visit."

"They will?" Somehow she couldn't imagine three more like Shay Morgan in little Johnstown.

"Oh, yeah," he said, and held out his hand to help her down. "I'm going to send a telegram back letting them know that I've decided I like Texas. They'll come down just to see what's keeping me here."

Jenny put her hand in his and stepped out of the wagon. Shay caught her around the waist and pulled her against him. He was solid and secure and smelled wonderful. She had the strange feeling of coming home.

Tired, Jenny closed her eyes and took a moment to relish the feeling.

"Are you okay?"

She opened her eyes and realized that she had leaned just a tad too long for propriety. Embarrassed, she felt a flush rise over her cheeks. "Yes, I'm fine. I just stood up too fast and felt dizzy."

Concern came over his face. "You aren't getting sick, are you?"

"No, no," she reassured him. Moving away from him was like walking away from her favorite piece of candy. She knew it wasn't good for her to indulge in the sweetness of it, but it tempted her beyond reason. Time to change the subject. "Can I ask you a personal question?"

"Sure." He pulled her medical bag out of the wagon.

"What is keeping you in Johnstown? It can't be the warm reception or even the active social life. I mean, so far you've been threatened by the men, stabbed by a crazy old woman, and overworked when you were kind enough to volunteer. It would seem to me that a sane person would be running away from here."

He laughed out loud. The sound brought a skip of joy to her tired heart. He put his hand on her back and steered her to the steps that led to her apartment above the clinic. "You're right, it has been a challenge, but I'm the kind of guy who loves a challenge."

She lifted the edge of her skirt and climbed the stairs. He took her key and unlocked the door. A quick check of the inside and he waved her through. The action was unconscious as if it were the normal thing for a man to do. As if he were protecting her.

She stepped inside and turned quickly. He hadn't come in behind her. She knew it was because he was waiting for her to invite him in and she realized suddenly she wanted to invite him in. If only to share a cup of tea and some sandwiches.

Jenny mentally shook herself. What was she thinking? The last thing she needed in her life was a man. "Thank you for everything you did."

He handed her her medical bag. "You're welcome."

It was awkward. He just stood there and looked at her as if it made him happy just to look at her. She fought a blush of excitement at the idea. "So—"

"I'll—"

They spoke at the same time and then they both stopped. She waited a moment and tried again. "Did—"

"I—"

This time they both laughed. "Please," she said, offering to let him speak first.

"No, you first," he said, and leaned against her door jamb. The motion brought him closer to her. It was then she noticed that his eyes had turned an amazing shade of blue. He had a three-day growth of beard and his mouth lifted at the corners as if he knew something no one else did.

"Doc?"

She'd been caught staring. "Oh, um . . ." She swallowed and collected her thoughts. "We didn't stop by the undertaker."

"I'll take care of it," he assured her.

"You don't have to. I can do it."

"No," he said. "I'll do it. You are supposed to get some sleep."

"But it's the middle of the afternoon."

"You haven't slept in days. That was part of the deal. I brought you back to sleep." He raised an eyebrow. "Do I have to come in and make sure you go to bed?"

It was a question that seemed to cause the air to suddenly become heavy between them. Her mind flitted from the idea that he would come in, to the idea that he would watch over her while she slept, to having him in the bed beside her. She looked into his eyes and saw danger and something else. Something that made her mouth go dry and tingles rush down her back.

"No," she said when she realized he was waiting for her to decide. "No, I'll get some rest."

He straightened away from her door jamb and took a step back. "Okay. Good." The air seemed to exhale around them. She wondered if her tired mind had created the strange emotions. "I do have one thing to ask of you."

"What?"

"I believe that after all my hard work, you at least owe me dinner."

"Dinner?"

"Yep," he said lightening the mood. "How about you meet me at the hotel restaurant around seven. If I remember right, they make a delicious fried chicken dinner."

"Fried chicken?" She felt like a thoughtless nitwit, but she couldn't seem to wrap her mind around having dinner with Shay. Maybe it was because she had never had dinner in a restaurant with a man. It was too close to courting.

"If you don't like chicken, they have roast and a divine lemon pie."

"I don't know," she said as she fought fear and uncertainty.

"Oh," he said as if he realized what she struggled with. "Don't worry, it's not a courting thing. You told me from the start that you weren't interested in that. This would just be dinner company. I don't want to eat alone, and I haven't been in town long enough to find a dinner companion."

"Just dinner company," she repeated, strangely disappointed. "Okay, I would be happy to keep you company over dinner."

He grinned his angel grin. "Good, I'll see you at dinner then. Around seven?"

"Around seven," she said.

"Great!" He turned and hurried down the stairs, hopped into the wagon and moved the team out. He waved up at her. She waved back and watched until he disappeared around the corner.

For the first time in her life she was meeting a man for dinner.

Chapter Seven

Shay was energized. He had been truthful when he told Jenny that he liked a challenge. Right now, Doctor Jenny Edwards was a big challenge.

His respect for her grew as he observed her work. She was no pushover. He found he liked the banter between them, and he'd been truthful when he told her that he liked the Texas town. There was something about a town that refused to have a lawyer that made the lawyer in him want to settle in just to see what would happen.

Shay left the undertaker's office and walked down to the telegraph office where he discovered that Johnstown had a telephone that was connected for long distance service. Shay smiled to himself. A phone was even better than a telegram. He'd get a hold of Bess, the operator in Amesville, and ask her to connect him to Matt. Shay's brother Matt was the sheriff of Amesville and he had access to one of the new telephones.

The telegraph office had two telephone booths inside. Shay paid the man and stepped into the walnut-paneled booth. Inside, a shiny new telephone was attached to the

wall. Made of wood, it was quite large. He took the earpiece off the handle and cranked the metal handle.

"Connection to Amesville Wyoming," Shay said into the
mouthpiece of the phone. "Alpha-Baker-Nine."

"One moment, please," the operator said.

With satisfaction, Shay settled onto the padded stool that
was provided for the customer's convenience.

"Amesville operator."

"Hey, Bess," Shay said. "How's my favorite telephone
operator."

"Shay? Shay Morgan is that you?!"

"Of course it's me," he said. "You aren't two-timing me
by flirting with someone else are you, sweetheart?"

"I haven't heard from you in so long, I about gave up
on you, honey."

"Sorry, Bess, I've been out of town."

"That's no excuse," she scolded. "You have my number."

"I'm sorry, darling, I won't let it happen again."

"Good," she said, and Shay could tell by her tone she
was smiling. "Now, who can I connect you to?"

"Connect me to Matt, please."

"Is it urgent?"

"Oh, no," Shay said. "Just checking in."

"I'll dial him, but there's been a bit of a thing going on
in town today. Seems that Doug Horton got drunk and shot
up the stables. Samantha is out of town doing a story on
some guy in Cheyenne, and Matt's got Lillian taggin'
around with him. So it might take him a while to answer."

"I'm sure you'll do your best."

"I always do," Bess said.

The thing Shay loved the most about Amesville was that
everyone knew everything about everyone else.

"Hello?" Matthew Morgan's deep voice carried across the telephone line.

"Hey, big brother. I hear you're busy."

"Shay?"

"Yeah, it's me."

"Where are you?"

"Can I talk, Daddy?" Shay's heart lifted as Lillian's voice carried across the line. Matt had to be holding her.

"Is that Lillian? Put her on."

"Shay, I'm a bit busy. Where are you?"

"I'm in Johnstown, Texas."

"Still?" Matt didn't sound very happy and Shay thought he heard Lillian start to scream in the background.

"I want to talk!"

"Hold on, Shay, Lil needs to say hi."

The receiver went dead a moment, then a small voice said, "Hi, Uncle Shay."

"Hi, Lilly."

"Where are you?"

"I'm in Texas."

"Is that very far?"

"Far enough, baby girl."

"Ma's gone to Cheyenne."

"I heard."

" 'Bye, Uncle Shay."

More silence until Matt was able to pull the receiver back. "Okay, what's the call for?" Matt asked.

"I've decided to move to Texas," Shay said. "Johnstown is in need of a lawyer and I'm the man to do it."

"What?!" Matt's voice resonated disapproval. "Stop fooling around, Shay. I've got my hands full here."

"I'm not fooling," Shay said, and shifted in his chair. "There's a challenge down here and I've decided to stay and see it through."

Silence drifted across the line.

"Are you in trouble?" Matt asked.

"Not with the law."

"Now, Shay if this is about a woman—"

"I met Jenny Edwards," Shay interrupted his brother.

"Cold-hearted Jenny?"

"She's a doctor, Matt."

"What?"

"We only got part of the story, Matt. I'm going to stay until I get the whole story."

"You're expected back in town in three weeks," Matt said. "If not, there's a handful of men who will be showing up in Texas looking for their money."

"I've got it under control," Shay reassured him.

"Is that what you want me to tell Edwards?"

"Look," Shay said. "I have to go, but I really called because I want you to tell Trey to have Brianna pack up my law books and ship them down here."

"Shay . . ."

"Trust me, Matt. I know what I'm doing."

"I've heard that before."

"Now, Matt, you have to admit that I've always managed to land on my feet. Haven't I?"

"There was that time you broke your leg—"

"That was a slight miscalculation on my part. This is different."

"All right, I'll tell Trey, but if you aren't back in twenty-one days, expect a few visitors."

Shay grinned with family pride. "I wouldn't expect anything less from you brother. Give Sam and Lilly a big kiss for me."

"I mean it, Shay. Twenty-one days."

"Bye, Matt." Shay hung up the phone and whistled to himself. It didn't matter what his brothers thought. Shay knew in his gut he was doing the right thing. He glanced at his pocket watch. He had an hour and a half until dinner. He rubbed the hard beard on his chin. It was enough time to get a shave and a haircut and see if there was any place in town that sold fresh flowers. He had a doctor to charm.

A few hours of sleep and a hot bath left Jenny feeling like a real person. She got out a pencil and a piece of paper and made a list of things she needed to do. To begin with she needed to restock her supplies, file her patient notes, and then she needed to put that sign back up in the grocery. She needed a driver and she refused to let Shay Morgan charm his way into the job permanently.

She chewed the end of her pencil and thought how hard he worked this week. She knew the boys she had thought to hire would not have been able to do half of what Shay had done.

But, any future driving would not entail an epidemic, she reassured herself. Jenny believed that if she made regular rounds she would be able to keep control of these little outbreaks.

Which would mean that she wouldn't need a man of Shay's caliber. She wouldn't need someone to tirelessly chop wood and haul bucket after bucket of water.

Her mind drifted over the picture of Shay without his shirt. His glorious tanned skin glistened with sweat and gleamed like gold in the sunlight. His muscles had strained with each stroke of the axe. He moved with efficient strokes as if he'd been cutting wood all his life. Jenny sighed. It had been as beautiful as a ballet.

A little egg timer dinged, and Jenny glanced at the watchpin she wore. It was time to head over to the hotel for dinner. Butterflies seemed to come to life in her stomach. She shook her head and stood. "Calm down, Jenny

Edwards," she muttered to herself. "It's only dinner with a business acquaintance."

She put on her best hat, pushed the hatpin through it and glanced at her reflection in the wavy mirror in her office. Her thick auburn hair was fixed in a Gibson-girl style. The little hat attached neatly and gave her an air of competence. She tugged her small green jacket down over her cream-colored blouse and put on a pair of wrist-length gloves.

She convinced herself the nervousness wasn't excitement to see Shay and have dinner with him. No, she was nervous because, after all he had done for her this week, she had to fire the man.

She picked up her pocketbook and stepped out of the clinic, pausing only long enough to lock the front door.

"Hey Doc," Bill Watts said as he passed by. "I heard about the epidemic. Do you think it'll spread to town?"

"I don't think so," Jenny said, and put her key in her pocketbook and closed it. "We have a good source of water here in town. I think we'll be fine."

"That's good to hear," Bill said and tipped his hat. "Just let me know if things start to spread. I'll be happy to gather up the boys and give you a helping hand."

"Thank you, I'll keep that in mind." Jenny stepped along the walk. People called their hellos to her. She greeted each with a smile. There was some question as to when the clinic would reopen. Jenny assured them she'd reopen this week.

"Hey Doc, you going to have dinner at the hotel?" Joe asked from his seat outside the barbershop.

"Yes, I haven't had time to cook," she replied.

"Have the chicken. It's the best ever."

"I just had a piece of their peach pie," Elmer said, looking up from the chessboard. "Dorothy said she had the peaches shipped over from California."

"I'll keep that in mind," Jenny said and entered the hotel.

Shay was in the lobby area waiting for her. He rose the moment she walked in and the butterflies really kicked loose in her stomach. She smoothed her matching green wool skirt to hide the confusion she felt.

"Hello, Doc," Shay said. He took her hand and put it in the crook of his arm. "You look like you got some rest."

"Thank you," she said. "I feel better. My mind's clearer."

"Good." Shay escorted her into the dining area. The waitress smiled with joy when she spotted Shay. She was in front of them in an instant.

"Welcome back, Mr. Morgan," she said. "Your favorite table is open."

"Thanks," Shay said.

"Right this way." Somehow the young girl managed to navigate the dining area without taking her eyes off Shay. She took them to a table in a back corner. It was small enough to be comfortable for one, or intimate for two.

"Thanks, Evie," Shay said and pulled out a chair for Jenny. Jen sat and Shay took the chair opposite her.

Evie stood at the table smiling at Shay. "Can I bring you something to drink?"

"Do you have any of that wonderful lemonade?"

"Sure do. Dot's made it every day just for you. She'll be happy to hear you're back."

"Well, tell her I'll be happy to have some of her fantastic cooking." He glanced at Jenny. "The lemonade is good."

"No thanks," she said and pulled off her gloves. "I would like a cup of tea, please, with milk and sugar."

"I'll bring it right out," Evie said. She leaned toward Shay. "It's so nice to have you back tonight, Mr. Morgan."

"It's good to be back."

Jenny watched as the pretty waitress walked back to the kitchen. She noted that the waitress wasn't the only one looking at Shay. It seemed the whole room was observing them.

"You draw a crowd," Jenny said and nodded toward the others.

"Ignore it," Shay said, and turned his chair and attention on her. "It'll eventually go away."

"Eventually?" Jenny raised a questioning eyebrow. "You make it sound like a natural occurrence."

"It's been like this my whole life. People seem to be fascinated with me." He shrugged elegantly. "I use it when I need to but for the most part I ignore it."

"What did your mother say about that?"

"She used to tell me that if I weren't careful my head would grow to such a size it wouldn't fit through the doorway."

"I like your mother."

"Yeah. She would have liked you too."

Evie brought a tray with the tea and lemonade. She set the lemonade in front of Shay. "Dot said to tell you she saved a peach pie in case you came in."

"Wonderful," Shay said with a smile.

"I hear the peaches were shipped in from California," Jenny said. Both Shay and Evie turned to her. Evie blinked as if she just now realized that Jenny was in the room.

"Hi, Doc," Evie said, a nice shade of pink flushing over her cheeks. "Yes. Dorothy had a friend send her a bushel on the train."

"Then we'll have to try it," Jenny said. "Won't we, Mr. Morgan."

"Of course," Shay said. He sat back as if intrigued by the interaction between Jenny and Evie.

"How's your mother these days, Evie?"

"She's fine, Doc. She'll be needing to see you come October though."

"Let her know I'll be by to check on her next week."

"I heard you are making housecalls now."

"That's right. I'll be making calls in the morning and opening the clinic after lunch."

"I heard Mr. Morgan was driving you," Evie said, her adoring gaze going back to Shay. "Does that mean you'll be coming by the house next week too?"

"No." Jenny said at the same time Shay said, "Yes."

Evie glanced from one to the other a bit confused. "Mr. Morgan is a busy man," Jenny said. "I'm going to find a new driver."

Shay turned to Jenny and raised an eyebrow. "You are?"

"Yes," Jenny said, and clasped her hands together on top of the table. "I thought we'd talk about that over dinner." She glanced pointedly at Evie.

"Oh," Evie said and blushed. "Well, then you'll want to order."

"I think we need a moment to look at the menu," Shay said. His tone was gentle.

"Okay," Evie said and turned to go.

"My tea?" Jenny said.

Evie's blush grew, and she pulled the teapot off the tray along with a small server of cream and sugar. "Sorry."

"It's all right," Shay said and put his hand on Evie's to reassure her. "Why don't you come back in five minutes. We'll be ready to order then."

"Okay." Evie looked as if she would melt into a little puddle.

Jenny could not believe the effect the man had on people. It was as if they took one look at him and lost their minds. Then she noticed the small square bandage that covered the stitches in his hand and remembered that he hadn't charmed Mrs. Dewitt.

Jenny hid her sudden grin behind the tall menu sheet. She pretended to read the selections as Evie stumbled her way out of the room. Jenny sat the menu down on the table. "She isn't going to wash that hand for a month."

Shay sent her a look of disbelief. "What?"

"Never mind," Jenny said, resigned to the obvious. The man was indeed a snake charmer. She had to be very careful around him if she didn't want to get caught up in his charm like everyone else around here. "I'll have the pot roast."

"Good choice," Shay said. "I had that last week and it was delicious."

Jenny picked up the small silver sugar tongs, and put a single cube of sugar in her tea. She followed it with a bit of cream and stirred. "You certainly have a way with the staff here." She eyed him over the top of her teacup and took a sip.

"It's something I learned when I went away to college. If you have the staff on your side, you're more likely to get the best cuts in the kitchen."

"I see," Jenny said and wrapped her hands around her cup. "So, you flirt and flatter your way into the biggest piece of cake."

Shay sat back in his chair. "Why not?"

"Why not indeed," Jenny said. "Is that the plan then? I mean, do you plan on charming your way into the heart of the townsfolk?"

"If it works," he said simply. "What's the harm?"

She put down her teacup. "The harm comes when people begin to count on you. When they think you are really their friend. When they believe they are important to you, and then you simply leave. Why? Because their problems don't suit your best interests or because you are bored with the same smiles, the same admiration. The harm comes when you move on to charm the next town, the next waitress into believing you might actually stay."

Shay picked up his fork and twirled it on its end on the white table cloth. "Who hurt you, Jenny?" he asked softly. "Who left you with such a bitter outlook on life."

Jenny stiffened, affronted by his words. "I am not bitter," she stated. "You've spent a week with me, you should know that I'm not a bitter person."

"When it comes to doctoring, you're not bitter," he said.

"Thank you."

"When it comes to men, you are. So tell me Jenny Edwards, who hurt you so bad that you keep all men at a distance?"

"I think that's a pretty personal question. One an employee should not ask his boss."

"I thought I volunteered."

"It still doesn't give you a right to get so personal."

"I see. So you want to keep the conversation to that of strangers. For instance, the weather was lovely today, don't you think?"

"Exactly," Jenny said relieved not to have to consider the other conversation. She picked up the sugar tongs and put another cube in her tea. "I think the weather was lovely," she replied. "Although we could use some more rain. We are in a bit of a drought."

"A bit of a drought is an understatement, don't you think?"

Jenny had the strangest feeling that he was talking about something other than the weather, but she refused to explore it further.

The meal was delicious. Shay was careful to keep the conversation flowing while adhering to Doc's rules of casual talk.

Evie brought coffee and two slices of hot peach pie. It smelled sweet with a slight scent of nutmeg. Shay took a forkful and tasted it. The fruit burst in his mouth and he closed his eyes to savor the experience.

"That good, huh?"

He opened his eyes and grinned. "Better," he said. "Try it." He waved his fork in the general direction of the piece in front of her.

She picked up her fork and took a bit. "Wow."

"Exactly," Shay said and scooped up another forkful.

"Dorothy has outdone herself," Jenny said. "Didn't Evie say they saved a whole pie for you?"

"What are you thinking?"

"I'm thinking we should purchase the whole pie and take it back to the icebox in the clinic."

"Now Doc, I'm amazed at you. Didn't your mother teach you to share?"

"I've shared," she said and took another bite. "You've got a piece. That's sharing."

"Are you saying the rest of the pie is yours?"

"All mine," she said.

"Not if I get to it first." Shay liked the way her eyes lit up when she was teasing. He wondered if she realized that she was flirting, then decided it wasn't his place to tell her. He doubted she got out very often.

"Evie," Jenny called as she swallowed her mouthful and dabbed her lips with her napkin.

"Yes, Doc?" Evie said as she cleared another table.

"Have Dorothy wrap up the rest of the pie. I'm going to take it back to the clinic."

Evie glanced at Shay.

"Evie," Jenny said, her tone more sincere. "Wrap up the pie."

"Mr. Morgan?"

Jenny's eyes widened when Evie looked to Shay to see what she should do. Shay decided he'd better behave before Doc made a public scene. "Go ahead. Doc deserves it."

Evie glanced at Jenny and then took her stack of dirty dishes back to the kitchen.

Doc forked up another bite of her pie. "I can't believe she did that," she said around a mouthful of warm pie. "She's supposed to be my friend. I'm the one who talked her ma into letting her work here."

Listening to her talk, Shay realized how involved Jenny was in the lives of these people. He had the sinking feeling that it may be impossible to get Doctor Jenny Edwards to leave Johnstown, even if only to see her dying father.

Chapter Eight

"Are you going to eat that?"

Astonished, Shay looked at Jenny. She pointed toward his piece of pie. Her plate was empty except for a couple of crumbs and some juice.

"Yes, I'm going to eat it," he said and forked up a piece to prove it. He chewed the treat and swallowed. "After all, this might be the only piece I'm going to get."

As if on cue, Evie emerged from the kitchen with a small box tied with string. She put it on the table in front of Jenny.

"Thank you," Jenny said. "Please tell Dot that it was wonderful."

"Yes, ma'am." Evie refilled their cups and moved back to the kitchen.

A comfortable silence danced around them. Shay savored the last bite of his pie and put his fork down. "Delicious," he said and patted his stomach.

Jenny smiled.

"What?"

"You have peach juice on your chin."

"I do?"

"Yep."

"Where?"

She pointed in the general direction. Shay reached up and wiped his chin, but he didn't feel peach juice. "Did I get it?"

"No," she said her eyes lighting up as if she were party to a private joke. The look did something to his guts.

"Well, you need to be more specific in your directions."

"It's right there," she said and leaned closer.

He wiped a spot, but felt nothing.

"No, there," she said again, this time her hand hovering near his chin.

He tried again, but obviously wasn't getting it.

"I'll get it," she said and picked up her napkin. Moving in even closer, she wiped the juice from the corner of his mouth.

Heat lightning filled the room, scattering down his spine. Her gaze laughed at him as she held up the napkin to produce the tiny bit of peach. "See?"

Shay swallowed hard. "Thanks," he said his voice low and gravely.

"It's still a bit sticky," she said, and put a corner of her napkin in the finger bowl and got it wet. "May I?"

"Sure." Shay held on to his control as she eased a breath away and wiped the corner of his mouth with the cool linen. He could smell the pie on her fingers and the rose water on her heated wrist.

Her touch was warm under the linen and gentle. It made him crave more.

"There," she said with satisfaction. "All better." She went to pull away and Shay reached out and snagged her wrist. She was so small in his grip, so sweet and soft.

He bent down and kissed the small exposed area on the inside of her wrist. "Thank you."

Her gaze darkened and she pulled away slowly. "You're welcome."

The air was so thick he could barely breathe.

"It wouldn't do to have a professional lawyer seen with peach pie on his chin." He could tell she was trying to be nonchalant, but it fell flat.

Shay's heartrate skipped a beat. She was feeling the tension as much as he was.

He walked on very thin ice here. He had to get her to trust him enough to explain about her father. If he got close enough for her to trust him, he would have to be careful not to fall himself. Doctor Jenny Edwards was a woman one could easily love.

She was so beautiful in the candlelight, but it was more than her beauty that attracted him. It was her warm and stubborn heart. Her quick mind. The sheer mystery in the depths of her gaze.

Indeed, it was a double-edged sword. He pushed away from the table and held out his hand. "May I have the pleasure of a short walk before you retire?"

"A walk?"

"A walk, you know, around the town square to enjoy the balmy April air."

She looked skeptical.

"Come on, I promise only simple conversation. For example, are Aprils usually this lovely in Johnstown?"

She took him at his word and rose. He waited for her to put her gloves on, and then he took her hand and slid it in the crook of his arm. "May I?" he asked and pointed at the pie box.

"Only if you promise to give it back."

"I promise to see that it gets inside your icebox."

"That's all a girl can ask," she said and waved at the box. "Please."

Shay picked up the box by the strings, paid the tab, and left Evie a generous tip, before he walked Jenny out of the hotel and into the cool night air.

They strolled for a while, each lost in their own thoughts. Since he had kissed her wrist, the silences were more awkward. The conversation seemed more strained.

"I really do want to know about the weather," he said as he led her onto the small path that crossed the grassy park in the middle of the square.

"Do you mind if I make an observation about you?"

"Certainly not. Be my guest."

"You certainly are a curious fellow. It would seem you stepped right out of the sky and want to know everything all at once."

He laughed at the comment. It sounded so absurd, but in a way he felt as if he had stepped out of Wyoming and found a world he didn't know existed. "I know you are just as curious," he replied. "Perhaps you are more polite than I am about it."

"Perhaps," she said and strolled farther.

The night air was clear and brisk, but most people didn't seem to mind. They weren't the only couple strolling along the walkway. He watched her wave and speak to the people they passed. It was more than clear that she was an integral part of this town. He wondered if he would ever become so important to anyone.

"I've been meaning to ask," Jenny said, breaking into his thoughts. "Where did you go to school?"

"The University of Kansas," he said with pride.

"I hear only good things about the school."

"I enjoyed my years there."

"I bet it was a change from Wyoming."

"Definitely a change from ranching."

She glanced at him. "Do you like ranching?"

"There's something to be said for working with your hands."

"Sounds like you miss it."

"The only reason I went to college was because my brothers made me."

"Now you're a lawyer."

"It seemed like the right thing to do at the time." He caught her studying him in the starlight. "What?"

"What brings you to Johnstown, Texas, Shay Morgan?"

"I told you," he said with a shrug. "I have a client who needed me to do some business for him here."

"Is that business done?"

"No," he said softly. "Not yet."

"Then you need to get to it," she said with resignation in her voice. "It would be selfish of me to let you continue to volunteer as my driver."

"But—"

"No, I need to find a driver and you need to finish this business you've got for your client."

"I can drive and take care of my business."

"Lawyers should not be driving for doctors. It simply doesn't look right."

"I suppose you have a point."

"Of course I do."

"Fine. I'll drive you out tomorrow to check on everyone. That will give you a day or two to review your applicants."

"Thank you," she said. "It's late and we need to get an early start tomorrow."

Shay knew when he was dismissed. He didn't like it much either. He walked beside her through the park and back to the clinic. "May I ask you a question?"

"Sure."

He stopped at the bottom of the steps that led to her apartment. "Do you always order people about?"

"What do you mean?"

"I wonder if you order everyone about, or if you're just ordering me around."

"I'm not ordering you."

"Yes, you are. You're telling me that I can't work for you. Then you're telling me to get busy with my client's work."

"Well you should—"

He reached up and put a finger to her lips to silence her. When he touched her, the air crackled with something close to madness. The hairs on the back of his neck stood on end. All his danger signals screamed.

He was only partially aware of that. What he was aware of was the softness of her lips and the sweet startled look in her eyes.

He stepped in close enough to crowd her. "This isn't about what I should or shouldn't do, Jenny Edwards." His voice deepened as it softened, and he touched her cheek. "This is about what you want."

She closed her eyes and tilted her cheek into his touch. The action was at once unconscious and telling. It did something to his guts. "Jenny?"

She opened her eyes.

"Is it me that you are wary of, or men in general?"

"Both," she whispered back. Her face was filled with hurt and sadness as she took a step away from him. "Men promise so much, but the moment a woman grows old or fat or sick they abandon them." She took his hand. "Like you, they charm with heated looks and capable hands, but when times are bad . . ." She shrugged and let go. "I've seen too many women struggle while their man spends time in the saloon or leaves the farm to find better work and never returns. Women with babies forming inside them are out doing the work of ranch hands."

"Not all men are like that," Shay protested. "I'm not like that."

"You have been nothing but kind and charming," Jenny agreed. "But so are most men. They come with charming grins and sweet talk." She shook herself and backed toward her stairs, fear and uncertainty in her gaze.

"This is about your father, isn't it?"

She sent him a soft sorrowful smile. "It's about me, Shay. It's about me. I don't have anything to give a good man and I don't have time for a bad man."

"Don't you ever get lonely, Jenny Edwards?" Shay asked and stepped within reach.

"Sure, doesn't everyone? Even married people get lonely." She avoided looking at him.

"You don't need to do all this alone," he said and rested her chin between his fingers. He gently turned her until he could stare into her eyes.

"I don't have a choice," she whispered.

"Yes," he said, and drew her into his arms. "Yes, you do." He kissed her forehead. Her skin was smooth and warm. She sighed and leaned against him. He kissed her cheeks, the corner of her eyes and finally, finally he kissed her full on the mouth.

She tasted of peach pie and pure magic. She did not pull away. Instead she buried her hands in his shirt and pulled him toward her.

She was light and darkness, sweetness and danger. He deepened the kiss, drawing her against him until they touched the full length of their bodies. He spanned her corseted waist. Her clothing was linen and wool, softened by multiple washings.

Shay's plans to charm her crumpled at his feet. Her kiss was more than he had ever imagined. Filled with mystery and danger, he was buoyed by the challenge. He never felt this way before, and he'd been finessing kisses out of women ever since he was five years old.

For some reason, here, surrounded by a star-filled sky, he found a depth of his soul he never knew existed. He pulled away at that thought. It frightened him.

"Jenny," Shay said when he could speak. They clung to each other in the moonlight, shaking from the power of their emotions.

"Yes, Shay?"

"I'm not like other men."

She didn't say anything. Her silence worried him. He was not going to let it end with one earth-shaking kiss. No. He wanted, no, needed to find out more about her.

"If you can't trust me," he said, and took her hand and placed it on his chest just over his racing heart. "Trust this."

She looked up at him with liquid eyes. "I don't know if I can." Tears welled up. "Don't you see. I don't know if I can."

He pulled her back against him and held her close. "Okay. Okay. Shhhh. It's okay,'darling."

"Why did you come here?"

Shay ignored the danger that question held. "Maybe it was fate," he replied. "Maybe you're not supposed to spend your life alone."

She pulled away from him as if what he said scared the daylight out of her. "It's late," she said and scooted up three steps until she loomed over him. "I'm tired."

"Do you want me to open your door and check the place for you?"

"No," she said a bit too sharp. "I mean, no, thank you. Good night." She turned and raced up the stairs.

"Good night," he called as he watched her enter. The wind was colder now that she was gone. He watched her apartment. A lamp came to life in the window of her tiny kitchen. She came to the window. The lamp cast her as shadow against the wavy glass.

Shay blew out a breath and turned to leave. He couldn't charm her and he found that he didn't want to be able to charm her. What he wanted was for her to look at him and see the man he really was, the man that hid beneath the slick surface.

If he let her see him, truly see him, she would see the truth. She would know that he was there to betray her. His loyalty to her father was stronger, maybe stronger than the need he had for her to see into his soul.

He realized he still held the pie box. For a moment he thought about climbing the stairs and knocking on the door, but ultimately dismissed the idea. Shay was a good poker player. He knew when it was best to walk away.

He hooked the string over his wrist and shoved his hands in his pockets. He'd keep the pie until morning, then make sure it got placed in her icebox. Of course that didn't mean he couldn't have a little piece when he got back to his room. Maybe that would ease the odd ache that her kiss had caused.

Jenny could not sleep. She stood in her kitchen and heated a cup of milk on her stove. Her hair hung in a long braid down her back and she wore a simple cotton nightgown and thick flannel robe. Leaving her feet bare was the biggest indulgence in her life. She glanced at her toes. They were clean from the bath she had taken earlier. Her feet rarely saw daylight and the skin was so pale she could see the blue blood in her veins.

The cool floor soothed the heated flush of her skin. She

felt utterly decadent. She stirred the milk as steam slowly rose into the cool April air.

Her thoughts went back to Shay and the kiss that had shattered her world. Just thinking about it made her stomach flip, and yet, she wanted more.

Who would have thought that a real-life, flesh-and-blood man made her feel safer and more alive than the angel in her dreams? Jenny sighed.

It was easy to stand at the stove in the middle of the night and imagine warming milk for a baby. Imagine returning to lie beside Shay. To have him wrap his arms around her and hold her all night long. To have a family and to never be alone again.

The very idea kept her awake and staring at the ceiling. It was not an idea she could really entertain. She had other goals, other responsibilities.

His mouth had been firm, yet gently demanding. He smelled of bay rum and heated male. Her hands had run over his shoulders, measuring the breath and form of him. She had reached up and wrapped her arms around his neck.

The motion allowed her to lean more fully into him to feel the solid presence of another human being. He had been solid and sunwarmed and she had wanted nothing more than to climb inside him where it was safe. She was so tired of being the strong one, so tired of caring for everyone while no one cared for her.

She shook herself free of the emotion and poured the milk in a mug. This odd realization of how alone she really was had come about so suddenly. Perhaps it was due to how tired she was. The few hours of sleep she had gotten this afternoon were only a drop in the bucket to what she really needed.

She banked the small fire and covered her burner with the cast iron cover. Then she picked up her mug and padded her way back to the tiny bedroom. The small bed was covered in papers. She often used her insomnia to work on the patient records. Usually that was enough to put her right to sleep. Tonight it wasn't working.

She stacked up the papers and put them in a leather case and closed it. She climbed into the bed, tucked the covers around herself and wrapped her fingers around the warmed ceramic mug.

Her traitorous thoughts went back to Shay. The way he kissed as if she were the only woman he'd ever wanted, the only woman he ever needed.

She took a sip of the milk and made a face. She hated warm milk, but she knew that it would help her sleep. She put the mug on the night table and blew out her oil lamp.

Darkness surrounded her as she snuggled into her covers. *"Trust me," Shay had said. "Trust this."* The beating of his heart melted something cold inside her. Something she had lived with for so long, she hadn't even remembered it was there.

It melted the bitter wall of ice that protected her from getting hurt. Jenny closed her eyes. If that wall melted, then she would be vulnerable again. At the age of eight she had vowed never to be that vulnerable again.

How can she reckon with that small child? The child that she was when she built the wall. The child that had taken on the care of her dying mother and the loss of her father.

If she allowed herself to be vulnerable, she would open the door to having to relearn the lesson that small child had learned. It was a lesson she didn't want to have to learn again.

But Shay's kiss had upset everything, absolutely everything. It had made her realize the price she paid to save herself from hurt. Suddenly, that price seemed far too costly.

Chapter Nine

"You know we don't like lawyers here," Bill Watts said, and spit just outside the door.

Unconcerned, Shay continued to put his law book up on the shelf behind his new desk. "Now, Bill, I told you what you needed to do about that squatter that's been living on the edge of your back forty. Did you do it?"

"Yep."

"It worked, didn't it?"

"Yep."

"Then I'd like to believe this town needs a lawyer." Shay stood and took in the beauty of a full set of law books. It gave the tiny office a sense of authority.

"Didn't say we didn't need one," Bill said. "I said we didn't like them."

Shay let that comment go. He had plans for this town that went above and beyond why he originally came here. In Amesville people came to see him because they knew his family, or because old man Edwards sent them.

Johnstown would be different, very different. If Shay was going to make it as a lawyer here, it would be strictly based on his skill as a lawyer. He grinned. He loved a challenge and this seemed perfect.

"So," Bill said, breaking the silence. "I hear you're sparking our doc."

That got Shay's attention. He turned, leaned against his desk and crossed his arms. "What if I am?"

"I don't know why, but I've taken a likin' to you, son. I don't want to see you run out of town on a rail."

"That isn't very likely."

"You hurt Doc and it will be more than likely. It will be a sure thing." Bill spit again and wiped his mouth on the back of his hand. "In fact, I could guarantee that you'd be tarred and feathered to boot."

"That's a chance I'm willing to take."

Bill laughed out loud. "Yep, I heard that about you. You're a gambler, a good gambler." He sobered. "It's okay to gamble with high stakes when you're the only one who could git hurt."

"I won't hurt her," Shay swore with soft resolve. "She's had enough of that in her life."

"No kidding," Bill agreed. "You be sure and keep that in mind at all costs."

"Are you giving me your blessing?"

"Ain't up to me. It's up to Doc." Bill squinted at Shay. "You got her blessing?"

"I won't do anything without her blessing."

"Be sure and don't."

Suddenly there was a large rumbling noise. Thunder on a clear day. Shay and Bill both looked at each other as if to ask if they both heard the sound.

"Hey, Mr. Morgan," Tommy McQuire hollered as he burst past Bill. "The stable just exploded and there's a big fire."

Shay followed the boy out into the street. Sure enough

thick black smoke rolled out from the big building on the corner. Dread snaked down Shay's back and he took off at a run.

People poured into the streets. Noise and confusion followed. The entrance to the stable spewed flames, and the sound of screaming horses and shouting humans filled his ears. The air smelled of burning hay and singed hair.

Shay pulled off his coat and held it up to his mouth as he stormed his way into the fire pit. The smoke nearly filled the building. A few feet to his left lay the blacksmith. The explosion must have knocked him out. Dropping his coat, Shay grabbed the big man by the shoulders and dragged him out into the middle of the street.

Jenny ran up to him, her doctor's bag in hand. "What happened?"

"The stables exploded. Probably from wet hay," Shay said and eased the smith down. "I think he's still breathing, but he inhaled a lot of smoke."

"Are you okay?" Her gaze was so terrified that Shay wanted to grab her and hold her, but now was not the time.

"I'm fine." He put his hand on her shoulder. "I need to go back in and see who else is in there." He willed her to understand.

She nodded and turned her attention to the unconscious man at their feet.

Bill, Albert and a few of the barbershop men had formed a fire line. They passed bucket after bucket of trough water down the line, dousing what they could of the flames. It was like spitting into the wind.

"You're wasting your time," Shay shouted. "Soak down the building beside it. We don't want the fire to spread." He pointed at the two nearest buildings. The older men nodded.

Shay studied the burning building a moment. It was going up fast. The screaming sounds of horses had died down, but the smell of burning flesh had grown. The roof smoldered. Still there appeared to be some time left.

Shay hid his mouth and nose in the crook of his arm and rushed back inside. The thick smoke made it near impossible to see. He felt his way to the first stall and opened it. A terrified horse pawed at him. Shay tore off his shirt and tied it around the animal's eyes to calm it and led it out of the building.

Once outside, Shay pulled his shirt off the horse and plunged back inside. He worked his way through the first three stalls, helping the animals out one by one.

When he turned to go back in the fourth time, Bill stopped him. "It's too late. If you go back in there you won't be coming out." He pointed toward the roof. "It's about to go."

Shay's gaze followed Bill's finger. The fire licked wildly at the roof.

Someone hollered, "It's going to collapse!"

The crowd moved back and watch in horror as the building fell into itself. Flames shot high in the air as if in a dance of triumph. Sparks flew toward the surrounding buildings.

Shay grabbed the bucket out of Bill's hand and tossed it on the side of the feed and tack building. He handed the bucket back to Bill and took another from Albert.

They worked for nearly an hour, pouring bucket after bucket of water onto the nearby buildings. The smoke stung Shay's eyes, clogged his nose, and made breathing an effort.

He ignored it and determinedly continued to douse any sparks that flew loose of the main fire. Finally, the water ran out. Shay and the other men took shovels and threw dirt on what was left of the stable building. Foot by foot they smothered the remaining fire.

Occasionally, Shay would get a glimpse of Jenny ministering to the men, cleaning burns, wrapping salve on blistered hands or pounding soot out of their lungs. She was a little powerhouse.

He recalled the sheer terror in her gaze when she had first come out. Then he realized that it was a fire that had caused her life to fall apart. Fire that made her father desert her and eventually killed her mother.

Yet, she didn't run and hide. No, she bravely stayed in the middle of the chaos—the fire leaping, the smoke choking, the awful sight and smells of burning creatures.

She faced it as bravely as the men did. Shay's heart swelled. Old man Edwards had lost out when he abandoned Jenny. It was clear that she was more than beautiful, she was brave and determined and caring. Shay felt more than admiration for her.

He was falling in love with her.

The smell was the worst. Jenny tried to ignore it as she bandaged Mr. Calier's right forearm. But the burning black smoke was something she often smelled in her nightmares.

At least the screaming had stopped. She shuddered at the thought of the pain the animals had been in before they died. Jenny had known some of that pain first hand. Her own leg had been badly burned. There was no relief from the pain. The very air seemed to scorch her.

It had been worse for her mother who had been burned over thirty percent of her body. The only thing that Jenny could do was feed her laudanum and keep the burns covered in cooling save and clean bandages.

In many ways her mother was burned to death, but instead of it being quick, the burning had been slow and laborious over four years. Infection had set in and her mother's flesh had never healed.

Jenny on the other hand had been saved. She didn't know if it was because her burns had been only on one leg, or if it was because she had been forced to get out of bed and care for her mother. Her wounds had healed. The constant walking and working had stretched her scars until the skin on her leg was pulled enough that she could walk without a hitch.

Only the scars buried deep inside her remained.

She had lived with those scars for so long, she barely knew they were there—until something happened that would rip the scabs off and expose the pain she kept hidden underneath.

When she had come out of her clinic to see Shay dragging Mr. Kenner out of the fiery building, her heart had been ripped right out of its protective shell. Shay was covered in black soot. His golden hair near black. His eyes vivid blue against his soot-covered face.

She had thought for one terrible moment that he was badly burned. That she would have to nurse yet another person she loved, and watch them slowly die.

Jenny stopped short, her hands hovering in mid air over her patient.

She loved Shay.

The very idea terrified her and yet made her smile. She looked over to where he worked, his bare back gleaming with sweat as he shoveled foot after foot of dirt on the building. She loved him.

"Doc? You okay?" Mr. Calier asked, pulling her out of her thoughts.

"Yes," she said and tied his bandage tight. "How about you?"

"I'll be fine," he said and patted her hand. "You did a bang up job on my arm."

"Now, it'll hurt for a few days when you expose it to air. I want you to go see Em at the clinic and tell her you need a small pot of burn salve. You take that home and tell your wife to gently rub it on the burn twice a day for the next week and whatever you do, keep it bandaged."

"Yes, ma'am."

Jenny smiled at him. "I want to see you in the clinic next week. Then I'll be able to tell if we've managed to keep any infection out."

"Thanks," he said and tugged his hat. He stood and watched the men as they finished off the fire. "Guess I'm not any more help here."

"Go home," Jenny said, and snapped her medical bag closed. "You need to heal properly and you can't do that if you're shoveling dirt."

"Yes, ma'am," he said and saluted her.

"Tell Penny I said hi."

"I will, thanks, Doc."

Jenny stood and looked around. She had triaged the people who had been hurt from the fire or explosion. She had gotten two teenage boys to carry Mr. Kenner to the clinic. She had a small room there with a cot for patients who needed to be watched for a while.

Her gaze settled back on Shay. It was as if she were starved and Shay was a feast. She could not get enough of the sight of him.

"He is something beautiful to watch."

Jenny jumped at the sound of a voice nearby. Em stood beside her. "Goodness, you startled me."

"It ain't like I come up on you quiet," Em chided. "I think you were preoccupied."

Embarrassed, Jenny felt the heat of a blush rush up over her cheeks. "I was thinking about the wounded."

"Sure you were."

"I assure you, I was," she said and straightened. "I was wondering how Mr. Kenner was, and thinking about how much he had lost today."

"Right, and my aunt is the queen of England," Em said. "When I came up on you, you were standing there stone stunned by that man of yours working without his shirt on."

"I was not."

"Don't say as I blame you," Em said. "Every other pair of female eyes in town is doing the same."

Jenny looked around and realized Em was right. The thought made her angry. She didn't want other women eyeing Shay as if he were some kind of candy. "I'm sure there's something more important to do," she said and looked pointedly at Katie. "Why don't you get some of Dot's lemonade and take it to the men."

Katie dropped her head in shame and left.

"You can bring a plate of sandwiches," she said to Mary Olsen and her sister Sue. "These men have been working for hours. They need something to eat."

The rest of the girls got the hint and scrambled to get the men something. Jenny knew it would be a race and she was right. Within minutes, girls offering food and water surrounded Shay.

Jenny looked up from where she worked on pounding the smoke out of Mr. Harrison's lungs. "Em, see if you can't get the girls to offer food to someone other than Shay Morgan."

Em sent her a smile and tied the bandage she had placed around a curious young boy's burned palm. "Sure, wouldn't want to see the boy get a big head from all that attention."

"I'm more concerned that the other men are looking for an excuse to run him out of town on a rail. It's bad enough he's a lawyer. Let's not give them any further encouragement."

"You like him, don't you?"

Jenny glanced up at Em's smiling face. "How can you help but not like him?"

Jenny gave Mr. Harrison a final rub. "Now, Mr. Harrison, I want you to go home and have your wife put some of this herb in a pot of boiling water. When it's really boiling, I want you to set it on the table where you can breathe the steam."

"Breathe the steam."

"Gently," she added. "Don't get too close, your throat is burned enough. If you aren't feeling any clearer in a couple of days come see me, okay?"

"Okay, Doc."

Mr. Harrison pocketed the packet of eucalyptus and headed down the street. It was late and most everyone who had been hurt was gone. The only people who remained were the final four men, standing around with shovels, putting out any flare-ups.

Em ordered the young girls about making sure every soot-covered man had something to eat and drink. A camaraderie had sprung up among the men. They shared laughter and hard work. It heartened her to see the way they included Shay. It was as if he had been part of the town all along.

Jenny realized that Em was right. She spent a lot of time simply standing and watching Shay. Embarrassed, she glanced around to see if anyone else noticed. The streets were clear except for the usual bustle of people going about their daily lives.

Jenny knew that she should go back to the clinic and get

cleaned up. She had patients waiting too. Mrs. Ambrose had a boil that needed to be lanced and Ayla Perkins would be waiting with her twelfth ailment in six days.

Jenny brushed the hair out of her face and stood, picking up her medical bag.

"Hey, Doc."

Shay came toward her. The blue of his eyes intense in his darkened face.

"Mr. Morgan."

He stopped just inches from her and she felt the lightning in the air. It was as if her skin came alive the moment he got close. She was unusually aware of everything about him.

"You packing up?"

"I believe I've helped everyone here," she said and wrapped her hands around the handles of her bag. "Unless you need medical attention."

"Oh, I need attention all right," he said with a wink. "We can call it medical if you like."

Jenny blinked. The heat in his gaze left her speechless. She swallowed. "Are you hurt?"

He leaned closer. "Maybe a little scorched here and there, but I'll live."

"Do you want me to take a look at it?" He was so close and he wore only his pants and boots. She tried to keep her gaze off his beautifully muscled chest. When that didn't work, she told herself she was checking for injuries.

He glanced down. "Don't see anything here," he said. "How about my back?"

He turned his back to her and she allowed her gaze to hungrily run over his broad shoulders and well defined back. Streaks of black covered portions of his burnished skin. He was like a golden statue that had just survived a dust storm.

"Anything?" he asked and glanced over his shoulder at her.

She backed away. "You look fine," she said when she could speak. Her voice was a tad too wobbly. She cleared her throat. "You'll need a good bath before you'll know for sure, but I don't think you're burned."

He turned and leaned on his shovel. Putting his hands on the top of the shovel and his chin on his hands he contemplated her. "How are you?"

She had never been under such scrutiny before and she squirmed with discomfort. "I'm fine, thank you."

"You did a fine job helping today. Thank you."

"You're welcome." It was hard to take the thank you and simply accept it. Before, she would have said something about how little she had done compared to the men, but she bit her tongue. It was her current goal to learn to take a compliment.

One thing about Shay Morgan, he was full of compliments. She wasn't used to it.

"Well."

"I suppose you need to get back to the clinic," he said.

"Yes." She didn't budge. She liked standing this close to him. She liked being the center of his attention. The last thing she wanted to do was walk away.

"Come to think of it, there is a spot on my shoulder that hurts."

Concern filled her. "There is?"

"Yeah," he said. "Maybe I should come by later and have you check it out."

"I didn't see anything."

"Might be covered in soot," he said in a serious tone. "How about I stop by the clinic after I've bathed. Then you can do a quick check."

"Okay."

"Hey Shay, quit sparking and get over here. We've got another flare-up," Bill shouted behind them.

Jenny's blush deepened. "Sparking?"

"I think Bill's hoping we'll have a romance," Shay said and winked. "He wants to live vicariously."

"Oh."

"I know it's ridiculous," Shay said. "After all, you've insisted on more than one occasion that we keep any thoughts of courting out of our friendship. Right?"

"Right," she agreed.

"Then as long as we know we're not courting, who cares what anyone else thinks. So, I'll come by later. Say in two hours?"

"That will be fine," Jenny said.

He grinned and lifted his shovel. "Better get back to work before they decide they want to run this lawyer out of town."

Jenny smiled back. His grins were so infectious. She watched in fascination as he returned to the ranks of the men. They teased him about talking to her, but they all seemed not to be put off by it.

Jenny turned and walked toward her clinic. Shay had yet to do anything that would disappoint. Maybe she was being silly by keeping him at arm's length. Maybe, just maybe she should let him in. Maybe she could explore the feelings she had for the man. It could be all right.

And she could be the queen of England.

Chapter Ten

A bath and a fresh shave had Shay feeling like himself again. The smell of the fire still clung in his nostrils, but for the most part he was back to normal. He whistled as he made his way toward the clinic.

Somewhere along the way he'd decided that he would bring old man Edwards his daughter, but not before Shay made her his wife. Excitement filled him. He liked the way that felt. The thought of Doctor Jenny Edwards becoming his bride. It would be like winning the biggest prize of all.

He stopped in front of the clinic door and hid the handful of flowers he'd purchased behind his back. He hoped she wouldn't say no when he asked her to dinner. Then after dinner maybe another walk and, even better, another kiss.

Shay pushed open the clinic door. Two female faces turned his way. "Hello, Em," Shay said as he entered.

"Mr. Morgan," Em said. "You don't look any worse for wear."

"I clean up well, don't I?" He nodded at the woman who sat in a chair and stared at him open-mouthed. "Hello."

"Hello," she said and continued to stare.

120

"Beth Snow, this is Shay Morgan. He seems to think he's going to settle here in Johnstown," Em said.

"Oh," was all Beth could say.

"Beth is going to be one of our nurses."

"Congratulations," Shay said and took her hand. "It's very nice to meet you."

"Oh," was all the young girl could say again.

"Is Doc in?"

Em looked around him. "Are those for me?" she teased.

"Now, Em," Shay said and leaned against the desk. "You know you are my favorite nurse."

"But they're not for me," she said and gave him the silliest fallen face.

"You are very good at that," he said. "You should think about taking up the stage."

She smiled brightly. "I thought about it in my youth, but I've found it gets me farther in real life."

"I see how you are," Shay said, and pulled a single flower out of the arrangement and handed it to her. "In appreciation of your talent."

"Em, have you seen my—"

Shay stood up straight and tried to hide the rest of the bouquet behind him.

Jenny tilted her head and narrowed her eyes. "Mr. Morgan, are you trying to steal away my best employee?"

"Just showing my appreciation," Shay said and pulled out the flowers. "These are for you."

"Oh." Jenny took the flowers and studied them. "Spring wildflowers," she said and buried her nose in the arrangement. "How thoughtful."

"I paid the younger Lefert boys to collect them."

Jenny's eyes grew wide. "I certainly hope they didn't rob anyone's flower gardens."

"They assured me they found them all near the creek and away from anyone's gardens."

"I've seen these lilies growing down by the creek," Em said. "I'm sure Jared and Brandon didn't steal them."

"Well, now that we've established the fact that they are lovely and quite unattached, I think I need to take them in the back and get them in some water." She turned to the door that led to the examination room.

Em caught Shay's eye and motioned for him to follow Jenny. He didn't need a second hint. He followed her and closed the door behind him.

"Thank you," Jenny said as she pumped water into a glass-canning jar and then proceeded to arrange them. "What's the occasion?"

"I thought if I bribed you, you might take out the stitches in my hand."

Jenny turned to him with an expression of deep concern. "Your stitches," she said. "I forgot about them." She put the flowers on the counter, rushed to his side and grabbed his hand. "You shoveled all day. That had to have hurt."

Her hands were damp from the flowers. She gently turned his palm over and examined it. Shay inhaled the fresh scent of her hair and relished the way she touched him.

She glanced up at him. "You're right, they are ready to come out."

"I heal fast."

"You're lucky," she said and ran her fingers along the row of stitches. The touch did something to his guts. She might not know it, but, as she caressed his palm, she sent dangerous signals up his arm and down his spine. He pulled his hand away before he was tempted to caress her back.

The touch must have effected her as well. She took a step back and clutched the apron that was tied neatly around her waist. Then she put on her professional demeanor. "Please, have a seat and I'll take care of that right away."

"Thanks," Shay said and sat down. She busied herself gathering up scissors and tweezers. Then washed and dried her hands. "I suppose I could have done it myself," he said when she sat down next to him. "But I thought it was best to leave it to a professional."

She draped the end table with a clean white cloth and laid out her instruments. "Please put your hand here, palm up." He did what she said.

Jenny studied the stitches a moment and then picked up the scissors. "This shouldn't hurt," she said. "Let me know if it does and I'll try to be more gentle."

"Honey, you can manhandle me all you want," he said, his tone low. "I won't mind."

She looked at him with innocent eyes and then they widened. Her pupils grew darker and she bent her head quickly. "You need to stop that," she scolded and clipped the stitches.

"Stop what?"

"You know what," Jenny said, and put the scissors down. Then she picked up the tweezers and holding his palm in one hand pulled the stitches out with the tweezers in the other.

"Being honest?"

"I wouldn't call that honest, I would call that . . ."

"What? Sounded honest to me."

She tugged the third stitch out rather roughly.

"Ow."

"Sorry."

Although Shay didn't think she sounded too apologetic. He watched her work in silence and wondered how he could make his wishes known without scaring her away. It was probably the toughest bit of negotiating he'd ever en-countered.

"The guys at the barbershop think that I'm courting you."

"Really?" She kept on working.

"Well, you heard them out at the fire."

"I thought you were going to set them straight."

"I opened my mouth to do just that, but it would have been a lie."

"No, it wouldn't," she argued and looked at him.

"Yes it would," he said gently.

She blinked. "But I told you from the start I wasn't the courting kind."

"That doesn't mean I haven't been trying to change your mind." He tipped his head, and waited for that to sink into her thoughts.

"Oh," she said and sat back. "I see."

"I realized today that I have strong feelings for you, Jenny Edwards. I think it's only fair that I tell you."

She didn't look at him as she got up and washed her hands. "Your stitches are out. As long as you didn't get scorched out there being a hero today, you should be good to go."

He stood and moved to within inches of her. He wanted nothing more than to crowd her up against the sink until she leaned into him. "I think there's something between us, Doc," he said in a low whisper that he allowed to caress the side of her neck.

She closed her eyes. Her fingers clenched the edge of the cast iron sink.

He took the opportunity to plant kisses just behind her ear and along her neck. She sighed and leaned into his arms. He turned her and lifted her chin. "Look at me, Jenny," he commanded. "Tell me you feel nothing."

She opened her eyes. He thought he would drown in the depth of mystery he saw inside. It was a mystery he wanted to spend a lifetime discovering.

"Shay." His name was sweet on her lips and he dipped his head to kiss her.

It started off gentle and undemanding. He wanted to ease her into the idea, but Jenny put her arms around his neck and scorched him with her heat and intensity. Her emotion seared his soul, and he put his hands around her waist and drew her closer.

"Jenny." Filled with joy and desire and passion he kissed her again. "Jenny."

"Wait!" she said and put her hand on his chest. She stepped out of his arms. "Wait. This is not what I expected."

He held onto her forearms with a gentle grasp. He was desperate for her not to get too far away from him. "It's not sudden, Jenny. I've had you on my mind since the day I walked in here with my poor hand in need of healing." He caressed her arms with his thumbs, being careful not to let her slip away. "I liked Texas the moment I stepped off the train, but then when I met you, I knew I was going to stay."

"Shay," she said and lifted her gaze to his. "I'm afraid."

"I know. It's hard to trust after so much has happened."

"I don't want you to leave me."

"I would never leave you."

She pulled away. "How can you know that? My father thought he would never leave my mother. So many men make that promise in the heat of passion only to slip away when things get hard."

Fear twined down Shay's back. He didn't want to lose her. He took her hand. "I will never leave you."

"You don't know how much I want to believe that."

"Believe it, sweetheart," he said, and tugged her back into his arms. "Believe it."

"I want to believe it so bad." She framed his face with her hands. "I've dreamed of you, but I never thought you were real."

"I'm real. I'm very real."

"I know," she said and dropped her hands. "That's what scares me. When you were just a dream you were always with me. Now that you're real you are free to go whenever you wish."

"I know this is hard for you," he said and pulled her into his arms. He caressed her back. She was so fragile and soft, but he knew she had steel-like determination. It was one of the few things that could get around his charm. "I have an idea. I know you need some time to really trust me. Why don't you come back to Wyoming with me for a week? You can meet my family and see where I grew up. Get to hear from the people who know me best, then you can make a solid decision."

"I can't leave Johnstown. You know these people need me."

"I need you too."

"How do you know? How do you know you need me? You've only known me for a few weeks."

"I know that you are beautiful and brave. I know that for the first time in my life I feel like I'm home."

"I'm scarred," she said, shaking her head.

"I know."

"Do you? Do you know that my left leg is no longer whole and beautiful?" She lifted her skirt and rolled down her stocking. "Did you know about this?"

Pain shot straight to Shay's heart when he saw the scars. She had to have been in such pain, and yet, instead of wallowing in pity she got up and took care of things. "I had no idea." He looked her in the eye. "But I know now, and I can tell you that it makes me love you more."

She dropped her skirt and stepped back against the sink. "Who are you Shay Morgan? Why should I believe you want to court me?"

"I'm a man who likes what he sees when he watches you move. I like what I hear when you give your speeches about helping others. Heck, I even like to hear your ideas of how men and women should work together."

"You don't agree with my ideas."

"Doesn't mean I don't like to hear them. It just means I'm looking at things from another point of view. A second pair of eyes helps in any situation." He cocked his head and contemplated her. "If you ask me, that's what's missing from your life."

"What?"

"A second pair of eyes. A second pair of hands. Someone to hold you in the darkest nights. I want to be that for you Jenny Edwards. If you'll let me."

"You scare me."

He sent her his most charming smile. "So, will you consider it?"

"Consider what?"

"Consider letting me court you."

"I suppose this means you want me to go to Wyoming and meet your family."

"It would make me the happiest man on earth."

She shook her head. "Really, the happiest man?"

"Okay, so I might like to embellish things a bit." Then he took her hand and covered it with his. "Marry me Jenny, and I swear I'll never leave you."

"What if I get fat?"

"I like cushy women."

"What if I lose my teeth and go gray and have so many

wrinkles you can barely see my eyes." She made a face to show him what she meant.

He laughed and never took his hand off hers. "I will never leave you. Even if you lost all your limbs and were blind and deaf. I would take care of you, Jenny. Now it's my turn. Can you see yourself loving me when I'm bald?"

"Bald?"

"Well, I have an uncle who is as bald as a pool ball." He shrugged. "It could happen to me."

Jenny laughed with pure joy. It was a sound that warmed Shay's heart. "I suppose I could love you even if you were bald."

"What if I lost my teeth and took up smacking my gums? Would you leave me?"

Jenny was really laughing now. He smacked his gums at her and chased her around the room. She squealed and tried to get away, but he caught her.

She smacked his arms. "Stop that. You frighten me."

Shay waggled his brows at her and pretended to twist his mustache in a perfect imitation of a villain in a bad melodrama. "Don't be frightened, my sweet. I won't hurt you."

There was a knock at the door and Em stuck her head in. "Is everything all right? I thought I heard something."

Stunned, Jenny stepped away from Shay. She felt a sudden rush of heat as embarrassment hit her. "I'm sorry we were . . . playing."

"It's my fault entirely," Shay said, and stepped between Em and Jenny as if to shield her from any bad opinions Em might have. "Seems I frightened her. Unintentional, of course."

"Of course," Em said. Her old blue eyes twinkled as she looked from Shay to Jenny. "I suppose this means you are going to let him court you."

"I—"

"Jenny has promised to come back to Wyoming with me to meet my family and find out all she can about me before she makes any decision," Shay informed her.

"Really? How wonderful."

"It all depends on when we can get Doc Beckman to cover for me," Jenny said.

"Done," Em said, the twinkle growing. "You can leave on the next train."

"The next train, but—"

"No buts," Em said and stepped into the room. "I believe the next train leaves in two days. That is plenty of time to square things away here." She took Jenny's hand and put it in the crook of Shay's arm. "Now, go to dinner. You both need your nutrition if you're going to be packed and ready. I'll tell Stewart at the station to send over your ticket."

Jenny could not believe that Em would change on her. Em knew how Jenny felt about men and marriage, and still she was practically baking a cake and calling the preacher. "Em—"

"Go," she said, and made shooing motions with her hands. "Go, git, eat before the restaurant closes."

Shay gave her a buzz on the check. "I told you you were my favorite nurse," he said, and escorted Jenny out of the office.

Jenny went half-afraid that Em would smack her if she didn't. She couldn't help the smile that wreathed her face or the excitement that filled her heart. Shay Morgan wanted to court her and Em thought enough about him that she was encouraging the match.

Maybe, just maybe it was time for Jenny to let go of her fear and trust destiny.

* * *

"I'm bringing Jenny home," Shay shouted into the phone. There was some static and a lot of noise on the other end before he heard his eldest brother's voice.

"You don't have to marry her just to get her back here," Trey said. His voice sounded concerned.

"I want to marry her. Even if we never came back. I want to marry her."

"Give me the phone," Brianna said. "Shay, are you in love?"

"Yes, ma'am, I believe that I really am this time. Wait until you meet her. You'll like her. She's a doctor and she helps mostly poor women."

"She sounds wonderful. When are you coming?"

"We're taking the train out on Wednesday. We should be there Thursday. There's a stop in Denver first."

"I'll let the family know. The weather has been decent, perhaps we can have a picnic. I know Samantha is dying to bake you her new cake recipe. Please just smile and nod and tell her it tastes good."

"That bad?"

"It's that bad," Brianna said cheerfully. "But it's made with love."

"Always," Shay said. "I can't wait for everyone to meet her."

"I'm sure she's wonderful."

"Perfect."

"Just one question."

"What?"

"What did she say when you told her that her father sent you out to get her?"

Shay was quiet.

"Shay, you did tell her, didn't you? You know the whole town will want to see her. I've heard that she ran the last man off with a rifle and a big dog. Why they even say she tried to poison the one before that. Did she?"

"I have to go now," Shay said. Dread filled him. He didn't want Jenny to know what Amesville thought of her. They didn't know her. "Look, do me a favor," Shay said. "Tell everyone the rumors aren't true. Tell them I'll personally whip the first man who repeats any of the rumors because they're lies. Can you do that for me, Bri? Can you make sure everyone knows that it would kill Jenny if she knew what they thought?"

Silence crackled along the phone line. "Okay, Shay, I'll tell everyone, but on one condition."

"What's that?"

"You tell her the truth about her father first."

"I will."

"Tell her before she gets to Amesville."

" 'Bye, Bri." Shay hung up the earpiece and stared at the phone. Telephones were interesting inventions. He knew that there were at least two operators listening in on their conversation; one in Amesville and one here in Johnstown. If he knew small-town life, his secret wouldn't be a secret much longer.

Tomorrow he'd have that talk with Jenny.

Chapter Eleven

"**H**ey, Doc," Bill said as he stuck his head in the door of the clinic. "Stagecoach is in and there's some guy looking for Shay Morgan."

"Does he look like Shay?" she asked. "He told me once that his brothers might be coming to town."

"I don't think he's related to this one," Bill said and spit across the sidewalk. "He looks squirrelly."

Uncertain, Jenny smoothed her hair and pulled off her apron. "He said that he was a bit different from his brothers. I'd better come see."

"Shay's over at the Eckerts' place this afternoon. He was helpin' them with their last will and testament. Seems they got some hoity toity property back east and they don't want their relatives to fight over it."

Jenny grabbed her gloves and put her hat on her head. "Let's find out if this man is one of Shay's relatives, then we can either offer him tea or the way out of town, depending on what he wants from Shay."

"I'm for that," Bill said with a twinkle in his eye. "It's been a while since we had us a tar and feather party."

Jenny slapped his arm. "You will do no such thing to the poor man. I swear you are bloodthirsty."

Bill grew serious. "Just protecting our own, Doc," he said. "Just protecting our own."

Jenny crossed the street quickly. Her stomach was in complete butterflies. What if he was Shay's brother? What would he think of her? It wasn't as if there were a whole lot of lady doctors. Maybe he would think she wasn't good enough for their brother. Maybe he had come to convince Shay to go back to Wyoming for good.

Jenny frowned and purposely slowed her steps. It wasn't as if she were going to a fire. She would just wait until she met the man before she started to worry. After all they were scheduled to take the train to Wyoming in the morning. There wasn't much damage to be done in one afternoon. Was there?

"He's in the saloon," Bill said. He stopped just outside the window and put his hand on Jenny's shoulder. "See, the one near the bar."

Jenny peered in the window. The man Bill pointed out was short and thin as any wiry cowboy. Right down to his bowed legs and thick leathery skin. "Well, he certainly doesn't look like Shay, does he? But Shay did say his oldest brother had inherited his father's ranch. So, I guess it could be him."

"Won't know until we meet him, I expect," Bill said and spit. He wiped his hand across his mouth. "You up for a trip into the saloon?"

"I suppose," Jenny said and bravely squared her shoulders. "It's been a while since I've had a root beer."

"That's the spirit." Bill held the swinging door open for her. "After you, Doc."

Jenny picked up her skirts and stepped into the saloon as if she were a grand lady attending a ball. She knew that first impressions meant everything and if this man was Shay's brother, then she wanted to make a good impression.

"Doc," the bartender called. "Wonderful to see you. Why don't you come in? This here gentleman was just regaling us with some stories of Shay Morgan."

"Hello, George," Jenny said and strode to the bar with as much confidence as she could muster.

"I'll get you a soda," George said.

"Thank you," she said and turned to the newcomer. He was smaller than she was and still held the dust of his long trip on his skin and clothing. "Hello, are you Shay's brother?"

"Shoot, no," the man said and took a long swig of his draft. He put the mug down and wiped his mouth. "I'm more like a friend."

"Really. What brings you to Johnstown?" Jenny said. George handed her a small glass of the bubbly soft drink she preferred.

"Well, now, pretty lady, I came to check on Shay. I've got a bet going and since Shay seems to have been delayed, I came myself to find out what's going on."

Jenny took a thoughtful sip of her beverage. The usual sweetness seemed flat on her tongue. "It must be some bet for you to come all the way to Texas, Mr . . . ?"

"Williams, Pete Williams," the man said and took another swig. "It's a big bet all right. I've got near a hundred dollars riding on it myself."

"Funny, Mr. Morgan never mentioned a bet to me," Jenny said. "Did he mention a bet to you, George?"

"Nope."

"Well, that Shay, he's got him one of the best poker faces in the west," Pete said. "He never gives away his hand. That's why I couldn't take it any longer. I had to find out how he's doing."

"What exactly is Shay Morgan supposed to be doing?" Jenny asked. She didn't like this man one bit. She had no idea why Shay would make a bet with him. She knew Shay was a gambler, but this man's words didn't make sense.

"Now, I shouldn't be talkin' about things like gamblin' to a nice lady like you," he said. "I cain't see how it would be right."

"Is it illegal?"

"Heck, no," the man said. He set down his empty mug and waved to the bartender. George filled the mug with more draft. The man paid his two bits and drank half the mug in one swallow. "I mean it ain't like kidnapping or anything. 'Cause Shay would lose the bet if he resorted to kidnapping. Not that he'd have to, shoot, with his looks the gals are just swooning around him."

Jenny's stomach flipped at the ominous turn the conversation was taking. She straightened to her full height. "What exactly is this bet about?"

"Well, shoot, you're gonna make me tell you, ain't ya?"

"Yes, I am," Jenny said. She put her hands on her hips and tapped her toe. She only knew him for a few minutes, but already the man annoyed her.

"I can always run him out of town on a rail, Doc," Bill said with just a bit too much anticipation.

Jenny put her hand out to stop him. "Hang on, let's see what Mr. Williams has to say first."

"It ain't that bad," Pete said and swallowed hard. "I mean it's just that ain't no one else been able to do it. So when Shay said he was gonna, we just had to bet that he couldn't do it."

"Do what?" Jenny's patience had run thin. She was very close to letting Bill have his way when the man spoke.

"Why, bring home old man Edwards' daughter, of course," he said quickly and then drank down the rest of the beer in case they were going to throw him out.

Jenny just stared at the man. "What did you say?"

Pete slammed the mug down and belched loudly. "That's some good drink."

"Bill, take him away," Jenny ordered, her anger flaring at his impertinence.

"No," the man protested as Bill wrapped a meaty hand in the man's flannel shirt. "Wait. Let me explain."

"Doc?"

"Fine," she said. "You have two minutes to explain yourself."

"It's simple really," Pete said. "Old man Edwards was Shay's pa's best friend. After Shay's pa died, Edwards took Shay under his wing. He's been Shay's mentor for years. Helped him through law school, got him clients when he opened his office. Basically treated Shay like the son he didn't have."

"Old man Edwards?" Jenny asked. She felt the hairs on the back of her neck stand on end.

"Ben Edwards, you all should know him. He says he's from here."

"I know Ben Edwards," Jenny whispered. The pit of her stomach sank deeper. "Go on."

"Well, Shay, he feels like he owes Edwards, and since the old man is dying—"

"He's dying?"

"Yep, Doc says it's cancer. There's nothing much to be done now but keep the pain down."

Jenny leaned against the bar for support. Her father was dying.

"You okay, Doc?"

"Yes," Jenny said. She wrapped her arms around her

waist. "What has Shay Morgan got to do with Ben Edwards?"

"Edwards tells Shay his dying wish is to see his daughter. So Shay tells him not to worry. He'll bring her to Amesville. What Shay didn't know is that Edwards' daughter is a heartless wench. Why the last man Edwards sent to get her came back tarred and feathered. The man hasn't been the same since. Ain't nobody else willing to come for Edwards' daughter. Nobody, but Shay. Ol' Shay, he's a slick one. When he heard the stories, was he worried? Nope," Pete said with pride. "He just smiled that angel smile of his and said he loves a good challenge."

Jenny had to work to keep her stomach from revolting. "A good challenge. Is that how he saw her?"

"Yep, and to prove how confident he was, he bet all of us he'd have her back within a month even if he had to marry her to do it."

All the blood rushed out of Jenny's head. Someone grabbed her before she keeled over. "I'm fine, I'm fine," she said fiercely and hurried toward the door. "I just need some fresh air."

"What about this guy?" Bill called.

"Send him home," Jenny said. "There's no bet to be won here." She struggled through the saloon. Why did it seem so crowded all of a sudden? Finally she pushed out of the saloon and down the street. She scurried away until she could turn a corner where curious eyes could no longer watch. Then she ran blindly, trying to erase the words that ate at her. He would even marry her if he had to, to get her back to see her father.

Shame, embarrassment and betrayal filled her. He didn't mean any of it. Not one word. He was simply doing a job for her father.

She found herself in the patch of woods that surrounded

the creek, which fed the town. It was well hidden and Jenny quit running. Out of breath, she hung onto a tree. The rough, bark dug through her gloves and into her palms.

She fell to her knees and wept. Wept for her father who was dying. Wept for a dream that she had thought would come true. Wept for the loss of her angel.

Shay rode back into town, whistling. One of the things he loved best about being a lawyer was helping people. The new trust he had put together for the Eckerts was going to help a lot of poor children in Philadelphia.

He grinned. Their relatives won't know what hit them. The contracts had been duly witnessed and signed. They were as iron clad as a contract could get. The Eckerts could rest easy knowing that needy people would benefit.

Shay stopped his horse in front of his office and hopped down. He wrapped the reins around the hitching post and straightened. Bill leaned against Shay's storefront. His hat was pulled low over his eyes and he didn't look happy. Bill never looked happy, but this moment was different. This moment Bill appeared to be bunched up and ready to strike.

" 'Bout time you got back," Bill said and spit.

"Something bothering you, Bill?" Shay asked as he stepped up on the wooden walk.

Bill pushed off the wall. "I'd say there's something bothering me. It appears there's a snake in our midst. A snake that has some serious explaining to do."

"Whoa there, Bill. Why are you looking at me like I just killed your best friend?"

"Maybe you didn't kill her, but you broke her and that's more than I can tolerate." He took a menacing step toward Shay.

"Wait, what are you talking about?"

"Seems you had a visitor today. Some gent from Amesville, Wyoming." Bill spit. "Ain't nothin' worthwhile come out of Wyomin' ever."

Dread creeped down the back of Shay's neck. "Who?"

"Some guy, named Williams. He comes off the stage as pretty as you please. Tells everyone he knows you. So we go git Doc. She said she wanted to meet him and welcome him like he was family."

Shay swallowed. "Doc went to see Pete Williams?"

"Found him in the saloon, downing beer and telling stories about you."

"What kind of stories?"

"The most interesting kind," Bill said and put his arm around Shay's shoulders. It was not a friendly move. "Seems there's this story about how you made a bet to bring Ben Edwards' daughter home. You bet you'd do it in a month."

Shay didn't like where this was going. Bill squeezed him tight and dragged him out into the street.

"The real kicker was when this Pete guy tells Doc how you said you'd even marry Ben Edwards' daughter if that's what it took to bring her home."

Shay stopped in his tracks and shrugged Bill off. "Wait."

"No, you wait," Bill said and turned on Shay. Bill's eyes glared fire and brimstone and Shay considered how he had every right to feel that way. "Doc turned a very nasty shade of white when she heard that."

"Is she okay?"

"I imagine she tossed her supper somewhere, but our doc's a strong lady. She'll recover."

"I've got to go see her."

"You ain't going nowhere," Bill said. "Not before you explain to me and the boys exactly what you think you're doing."

"I think I need to explain things to Jenny first," Shay argued.

Bill crossed his arms across his chest. He glared at Shay like an angry genie. "If you think we're going to let you anywhere near our doc, then you got another thing coming."

"I'm sorry Bill, but I'll go through you and the rest, in fact I'll go through the gates of hell if I have to to see Jenny."

"Then you'd better get started. 'Cause I'm in the mood to oblige you." He took a fighter's stance. "When I'm done with you, you'll wish you were the last guy. 'Cause bein' eaten alive by ants is going ta be a lot less painful than what you're gonna get."

"Look, Bill, this is ridiculous," Shay said and started to roll up his sleeves. "It's all a misunderstanding."

"Yeah, well you didn't see the tears running down her cheeks. I should beat you just for that."

Shay felt his stomach turn. In his entire life he'd never caused a woman to cry with anything other than joy. It angered him to think that Jenny had cried. He put up his fists. "Then let's get on with the beating," Shay said. "I feel a terrible need to whack something myself."

They danced around each other. Bill took a poke at Shay. Shay dodged the blow and landed one of his own on Bill's jaw. In return Bill swung hard connecting with Shay's eye. Pain shot through his head, stirring the anger deep inside Shay and the fear that he had lost the best thing that ever happened to him.

Shay took a step forward and landed a flurry of blows. Bill was a big man and took the beating well. He countered with a blow that caught Shay's jaw. Shay shook his head and tried to get rid of the ringing in his ears.

"Stop it!"

Shay brushed the cry off with a shrug and took another step into the fight. Punches flew and Shay gave as good as he got. The beating was painful and filled with anger. In a word it was utterly satisfying.

Until a wave of very cold water washed over him. The water stole his breath and his concentration. "What the?!!"

"I said stop it."

Shay turned to find Jenny standing a yard away. Her hands were on her hips and a bucket sat at her feet. She looked mad as hell and more beautiful than he remembered.

"Jenny."

"Don't you 'Jenny' me," she said. She pointed at Bill. "That is enough from you. Em, take him to the clinic and get some salve on his cuts."

"But, Doc—"

"Go."

Shay wiped the blood from the corner of his mouth. "Honey, we need to talk."

She looked him up and down in a slow manner that portrayed disgust more than anything else. It was something Shay had never experienced before and it hurt more than a lashing. "There is no need to call me by a pet name. My name is Doctor Jenny Edwards and I'm the daughter of your client Ben Edwards."

Shay cringed at the ice in her tone. From the sounds of it, he was in more trouble than he ever thought he'd be. "I heard you spoke to Pete."

Jenny picked up the bucket and turned her back to him. "He was an unsavory fellow. I have no idea why you would be friends with him."

"Amesville's a small town. It's like a very large family. You have your good members and your bad members. Living in a large family you learn tolerance."

"Tolerance," she repeated, and headed back to the clinic. "Interesting choice of words."

Shay could tell he wasn't handling her right. She became more distant with each step she took away from him. He rushed around her and put a hand on her arm to stop her. "Jenny, Doc, please hear me out."

Her gaze turned on him and he saw a deep sadness in their depths, a sadness that tore at his heart and scared him to the bone. "Don't worry, Mr. Morgan, you won't lose your bet. I've decided to go with you to Amesville to see my father and the good news is you don't have to marry me to get me to go." She gave him a fake smile. "You don't even have to be charming. I'm sure that is a burden lifted off your shoulders."

"Jenny, don't."

"Don't what? Don't tell the truth? Don't be hurt that you lied to me? That you had loyalty to my father?"

"Okay, sure, I came here to find you and tell you that your father was dying." He caught a flash of pain in her gaze and he knew that she still loved her father. His admission hurt her, and he wanted to kick himself for not being more sensitive. "I came here to convince you to go and see him."

"Well, then you've managed to do just that," she said and shrugged him off. "I will see you on the train in the morning."

"Jenny, everything changed when I saw you," Shay said, scrambling to put together the words that would make everything better. He was normally so good at that.

"Good day, Mr. Morgan." She lifted her skirt and walked away.

He blocked the door to the clinic. "When I got here I had no idea why you weren't with your father. Honey, I had no idea that you had been abandoned."

"Please step aside, I have patients inside who need me."
She pinned him with her gaze. "People who are honest
about what they need."

"I was honest, Jenny. I am honest. Everything I feel for
you is honest."

"And a bit too convenient," she said sadly. "I thought
you were serious. I even humiliated myself and showed you
my scars." She shook her head at him. "I should have
known that you were lying when you said it didn't matter."

"Jenny, please. I meant everything I said."

"I told you," she said with sad resignation. "You don't
have to marry me. You've won your bet." She turned on
her heel and walked away.

Shay watched as she went around the building to the
back entrance. His head pounded. His heart felt like it had
been chewed on by a wolf. He reached up and touched his
face. No wonder he couldn't charm his way out of this one.
He must look like hell.

"She loves you, you know."

Shay turned at the sound of Em's voice. "I've obviously
ruined that."

"She's hurting right now," Em agreed. "But she still
loves you. She strictly forbid the men from hurting you.
It's the first time that ever happened."

"Not much comfort in that."

Em reached up and gently touched the knot that was
forming on Shay's face. "You look like death warmed
over."

"I feel like death."

"Come on, let me patch you up." Em waved him into
the clinic.

Shay eyed the door. "Are you sure?"

"I'm sure, I sent everyone else home. She knows it. She
won't come down."

Shay followed Em into the clinic.

"Sit right here, I'll get something to clean you up with."

Shay sat and watched Em gather her stuff. She dipped a rag into a basin of cool water and applied it to his face. He winced at the sharp sting it created. "She still loves her father, doesn't she?"

"Yes, she does."

"Then why didn't she go see him when he sent his other men?"

"When the first man came out, Jenny sent him back to her father with a message. If Ben Edwards wanted to see his daughter he needed to come and see her himself." She dipped the rag again and wiped the blood from the corner of Shay's mouth.

"I take it he didn't like that."

"Nope. In many ways they are a lot alike. Both stubborn and autocratic."

"In other words, they bumped heads."

"Her father thought he'd force her hand. He sent a lawyer out here and tried to close down the clinic. I guess he figured if she had no place of employment she'd have to go to him."

"Ouch, I doubt Jenny took that lying down."

"It darned near killed her, but she fought like a lioness over her cubs. The lawyer was unscrupulous."

"No wonder she hates lawyers."

"She studied the law and found a loophole. If she legally put the clinic under the control of the trust, then it couldn't be shut down."

"Tell me about the trust."

"Not much to tell. One of Doc Beckman's patients willed Jenny property and stock. Jenny was worried that if anything happened to her the trust would be lost, so she set it up as a separate entity. Then she named me, and Doc Beckman as board members."

"So the three of you run the trust."

"No, Jenny runs the trust, we just put in our point of view."

"She must trust you very much."

Em paused and looked him in the eye. "We're the only family she knows."

Shay winced. "So, she got to keep her clinic."

"Yes, but the price was almost more than she could bear. So the next time her father sent a man in to get her—"

"The men in town took care of him."

Em dabbed iodine on the cut on his cheek. "Jenny is very important to everyone here in Johnstown."

"Yeah, I figured that out my first day here."

"The way I figure it, you fell in love with her too, didn't you?"

Shay didn't know what to say to that. "Not that it matters. It took weeks to get her to consider letting me court her. Now, I doubt she'll ever forgive me enough to hear me out."

Em stood and patted his shoulder. "Whatever you do, don't give up on her."

Curious, he looked at Em.

"When Jenny loves she loves deeply. Even after all he's done to her, she still loves her father. I believe she loves you too."

"She made me promise once to never leave her," Shay said and stood. "I guess this is a good test of that promise."

Em smiled. "Go home and pack. Your train leaves early. I expect that you'll be here to see that she makes it on time."

"I'll be here," Shay vowed. "No matter what. I'll always be here."

"I wouldn't expect anything less."

Chapter Twelve

"**Y**our father will be waiting for us at the train station."
Jenny had trouble calming the flutter in her stomach. Her father. Her dying father. She stared out the window and watched the landscape roll by. It was the first time she had been this close to mountains in her life. They rose up from the rolling plains, tall and majestic. Their peaks were still capped with snow. Jenny felt a chill run through her.

She wore her best wool suit. It was deep green with rickrack trim. The matching hat and gloves made her look smart and stylish. She couldn't have her father seeing her any other way. The last thing she wanted was for him to judge her and find her lacking.

She swallowed her uncertainty. In truth she didn't know what to expect from him. Her current emotional state was frighteningly raw. Shay sat beside her, trying to make conversation. She told him he didn't have to pretend any more. He said he wasn't pretending, but she didn't believe it. Experience had taught her differently.

"I understand your father got out of his bed to greet you."

She glanced at Shay. "He's gloating over the fact that he won." She turned back to the window. "I'm coming to him."

"He's not a bad man, Jenny. He's just made some bad choices."

She let that comment go.

Shay took her hand and squeezed it. It was then that she realized she had been twisting her gloves around her fingers. She pulled out of his reach.

"I want you to know that things aren't done between us," Shay said. "I'm just giving you some time to resolve things with your father first."

She didn't know what to say to that. Just thinking about how he had lied and deceived her cut her to the bone. She had the horrible suspicion that once he collected his bet he wouldn't be back. The suspicion didn't fit with the Shay she thought she knew, but then again, everything she thought she knew about Shay had been based on a series of lies.

She realized that she was being petulant. "I suppose your family will be excited to see you."

"Yes. They miss me."

"What's it like to have a large family?"

"It can be more bother than it's worth somedays," he said. "But I wouldn't give it up for the world."

"You're a lucky man."

He glanced at her, pain in his eyes. "Not so lucky. I've lost you."

"You never truly wanted me," she pointed out. "You lied to me from the start."

"I wanted you to get to know me for me first," he said. "I didn't want your father to come between us."

She shook her head. "So what? You thought if you married me then I couldn't run when you brought me here?"

"It's not like that," Shay said. "I asked you to come here first."

"Yes. You didn't have to marry me to convince me to come, did you?"

He blew out a breath. "I was going to tell you."

"When? When I stepped off the train?"

"I was going to tell you last night."

"Sure, sure you were."

"Jenny, please. I never meant to hurt you. I'm not playing with your heart." He put his hand on her arm. "You asked me once to swear I would never leave you. I did. Remember? I swore I would never leave you."

"You have no reason to stay now," she said and turned to the window. "You have no more reasons to lie."

The train pulled into Amesville around 5 P.M. Shay escorted Jenny out the door. The scent of high country air filled his nostrils, comforting the pain in his heart.

"Uncle Shay, Uncle Shay!" Lilly yelled and raced through the crowd to give him a big hug.

"Hey, Sugar Lil." Shay grabbed the girl up and hugged her tight, burying his nose in the sweet spot between her shoulder and neck. Lilly always smelled like sweetness and light.

Lilly giggled and hugged him tight. "Ma says you're going to bring home my new aunt." Lilly peered around him. Then she put her pudgy hands on his face and looked him square in the eyes. "Is that her?" she asked in a whisper loud enough to be heard across country.

"I hoped so," Shay whispered back, "but right now it ain't looking too good."

Lillian frowned and put her hands on her hips. "Did you mess it up, Uncle Shay?"

"Yep," Shay said. "I'm afraid so."

"Men," Lilly said, her tone disappointed. It was clear she'd been taking lessons from her mother. "Put me down." Lilly pushed and Shay set her down. Then she marched up to Jenny and stuck out her hand. "Hello, I'm Miss Lillian Morgan," she said and shook Jenny's hand and curtsied. "What's your name?"

"My name is Jenny Edwards," Doc replied solemnly. "It is a pleasure to meet you Miss Lillian."

"Lilly's Matt and Samantha's youngest," Shay explained.

"I'm four," Lilly said proudly. She took Jenny's hand. "Come on, I want you to see my ma," Lillian said and tugged.

"Whoa there, princess," Shay said and pulled his niece aside. "Jenny didn't come to meet the family."

"She didn't?"

"No, she didn't. She came to see her father."

Lillian looked from Shay to Jenny and back. "You really messed up, didn't you? Really Uncle Say. I expected better from you."

Shay felt the heat of embarrassment rise up over his cheeks. "Yes, well, so did I," he agreed. "Now scoot. Go tell your ma and pa I'll be at the ranch for dinner. Right now I have other things to do."

"You going to take Miss Jenny to see her father?"

"He doesn't have to," came the deep reply.

Shay turned to see Ben Edwards standing nearby. He was pale with pain and gaunter than Shay remembered him being. He leaned heavily on a cane. His eyes never leaving Jenny.

"Hello, Ben."

"Shay, I see you kept you word."

"Father," Jenny said. She stood frozen to the spot. Her shoulders rigid, her chin held high as if to ward off a blow. It was all Shay could do not to put his arm around her. He touched her arm, but she ignored him and kept her face on her father.

"Jenny," Ben said. "I'm glad you came."

"I was told you're dying," she said dispassionately.

"Yes, little girl," he said and sighed into the cane. "They tell me the same thing."

Jenny softened then. Shay watched as she took two steps toward her father. "You should be in bed," she said. Shay recognized her tone as the same one she used on a particularly troublesome patient.

"It's not everyday that my daughter comes for a visit. It gave me a reason to get out of that darned bed. I'm not ready to go back there."

"You need rest and care," she said sternly.

"People die in bed," Ben said, his tone commanding. "Come, I have dinner reservations for us at the tearoom."

"I should settle my bag—"

"It's already taken care of," Ben said and pointed to a porter who placed Jenny's bags in a wagon. "Come, there is so much to talk about. It does me good to escort a lovely young woman to dinner." He put his arm out, but Jenny didn't take it.

Shay put his hat on and followed behind them. Ben looked over his shoulder and raised an eyebrow.

"I promised her I wouldn't leave her." Shay said as way of explanation.

"I've got her, she'll be fine." Shay refused to budge. "The reservations are for two," Ben added pointedly.

"That's fine. I'll wait in the entry."

"Go home, young man," Ben ordered. "I'm sure your family has something planned for your welcome home."

Uncertain, Shay looked at Jenny. She stood and twirled her velvet purse by the silk cord. He couldn't tell what she was thinking. In fact at this moment she had the best poker face he'd ever seen. "I'm not leaving her."

"Fine, suit yourself," Edwards said, and waved him away with a dismissive gesture.

Shay noted that while the porter loaded Jenny's things up on a wagon, Shay's own bag was left on the depot floor. He mentally shrugged. He'd come get it later. Right now, he could tell Jenny was afraid.

She stood straighter than he'd ever seen her. Her shoulders stiff and square, her chin lifted. She was so brittle it looked as if she'd break into a thousand pieces if she wasn't handled just right.

He vowed that he was going to be there if she needed him. Heck he was going to be there if she didn't.

They walked across the street, passed the saloon and the mercantile to the new hotel on the corner. It boasted a fine restaurant and a third-story tearoom for the more genteel. The silence that surrounded them was fraught with tension and mistrust.

Shay wanted to kick himself. If he had been honest with Jenny from the start, then this would not have been so awkward. He could have come between them and helped negotiate their relationship back to where Jenny was comfortable.

Now, all he could do was stand in the shadows and offer any support she would reluctantly take.

Jenny waited while the waiter pulled out her chair. Once she was seated, her father eased into the chair across from her. The exertion from the walk across the street made him break out in a fine sweat. He looked gray with pain. If he were her patient she would have bullied him back into his bed.

But he wasn't her patient. He was her father. The man

who abandoned her. The man who didn't love her or her mother enough to stay when times got tough. She watched him wipe his forehead with a kerchief.

"I've never seen Shay so concerned about a woman before," he said and stuffed the kerchief back into his breast pocket. "I believe the boy fancies himself in love."

She glanced over to where Shay sat. He'd taken up a seat in the small entryway. He sat there on a small hard chair with his hat in his hands. In a strange way it comforted her to have him so close.

"The boy looks uncomfortable as hell," Ben said.

Jenny turned her attention back to her father. He had taken off his hat and put it on the chair next to him, along with his gloves and cane. Her father had a full head of silver-white hair. He must be vain about it, for it was brushed back with a bit of pomade. From the silver of his hair to the tops of his boots, her father radiated charm, charisma and wealth.

"You look as if life has treated you well," Jenny pointed out. She took off her gloves and sipped the lemonade the waitress brought. The drink was tart and sweet and cold.

"I've made some good investments," he said and studied her with eyes the same color as hers. "You look like your mother."

"Funny, I don't remember what she looked like without scars," Jenny said with more pain in her voice than she wanted to reveal. She folded her hands together in the preceding awkward silence. "I've been told I have your stubborn streak."

He laughed. It was a sad sharp laugh that ended with a deep cough. She waited for him to finish. She'd learned that the last thing dying patients wanted was for her to remind them that they were dying.

She reached over and traced a pattern in the condensation on the glass. "Why did you send all those men?"

"Why didn't you come see me the first time?"

She shrugged. "I was angry with you I suppose. All those years I was alone I dreamed that someday you'd come to find me. I never dreamed you'd want me to find you."

"I suppose you imagined that I would come crawling back, begging you to forgive me."

She gave a short sad laugh. "When it comes to you, I don't even try to imagine any more. It keeps the disappointment away."

"Ouch, I deserve that, I suppose. I wanted to be part of your life."

"You tried to take away my life," she accused him. "Your lawyer, Mr. TP Billings I believe it was, nearly took away my only means of support."

"That was a long time ago," Ben said dismissively. "You kept your precious clinic. Why can't you let bygones be bygones?"

"If this is about forgiveness, you're not off on the right foot."

He gave a short snort. "Forgiveness. You think I need you to forgive me? No," he said. "No. I didn't ask Shay to bring you here so that I could find forgiveness."

"Then why am I here?"

He contemplated her a moment. She folded her hands on her lap and waited for his answer. If he were going to continue to be stubborn then by goodness so was she.

"I just wanted to see you," he said and took a swallow of the whiskey that he'd been served. "I wondered how you turned out."

"Well, here I am. So much to be proud of," she said. "I'm a doctor. I repair broken people and broken lives. Thanks to you, I help others find hope."

"I didn't do that, baby girl, you do that all on your own."

"Yes," she said. "Yes, I do do that on my own."

He ran his finger around the edge of his whiskey glass. "So, here we are."

"Yes, here we are."

"How was your trip?"

"Long. Hard."

"Yes, I've heard that about that trip."

"You made it once."

"I don't remember much of it. I was out of my head."

"From everything I've heard, you didn't stay that way long." She sipped her drink and eyed him "I understand from Mr. Billings that you are a highly successful businessman, one of the most important men in the state of Wyoming."

"I did all right for myself."

She put the lemonade down and decided to take off her kid gloves. "It took her three years to die."

"I know."

"Three years of constant nursing care, constant pain." When a shadow of something like shame brushed over his face, she pushed on. "I took in laundry and sewing. Any work that I could do while I nursed her. We were so poor that there were times when my stomach ate itself for dinner."

He tossed the contents of his drink down and waved the waiter to bring on another. "Look how strong it made you."

"What doesn't kill you only makes you stronger," she recited under her breath. The waiter came and placed their lunch of delicate sandwiches in front of them. The plate was pretty with soft white bread that had the crust cut off. The sandwiches were made with cold cuts and cheese, watercress and cucumber.

Jenny realized she wasn't very hungry, and from the way

her father eyed the meal, neither was he. "I can't imagine you went through all this trouble to see me just to pretend to eat cucumber sandwiches." She eyed him. "Why am I here?"

He swallowed more of the whiskey, his gaze running across the room to where Shay sat, hat in hand. "What do you think of Shay Morgan?"

Jenny sighed. Her father was deliberately being obtuse. "Mr. Morgan is very charming. From what I understand he's an excellent poker player. Now, why am I here?"

"Shay's going to be the executor of my will."

"I'm sure he'll see that everything you want will get done. He's been very good about that."

"I'm having everything split between you and him."

"If that is what this is all about, you should have saved yourself the time and effort," she said and stood, placing her napkin on the table. "I don't need your money."

"I know, you've made excellent use of what I've given you so far."

That stopped her. "What?!"

"Sit down, Jenny."

She sat to avoid causing a scene. "Tell me what you meant by that. I've never taken a cent from you and I don't intend on starting now."

"Pride," he said as he sipped his whiskey. "It runs in the Edwards family." He contemplated his glass. "It's not the best of traits."

Jenny took a deep breath and worked to control her temper. "Explain yourself, Mr. Edwards."

He sent her a self-deprecating grin. "I'm the widow Banks."

"I beg your pardon?"

"I said I was the widow Banks. I'm the one who left you that big trust fund."

Jenny sat back against her chair. "You gave me the trust fund?"

"Yep." He finished off his drink. "I figured you'd never take money from me. It'd been too long, and being an Edwards I knew you'd be hardheaded. So I made up the widow. I figured you'd take the money and move back east. Maybe buy yourself some pretty dresses and catch yourself a rich husband."

Jenny didn't know what to say. It was Mrs. Banks' trust fund that had gotten her through college and medical school. She'd found that when one had money there were fewer barriers. It hadn't mattered that she was one woman in a class of a hundred men. She had money and as long as she was paying, they educated her. "I guess your plan backfired."

"I must say you did a good job investing it. You must have inherited my head for business."

"Is there nothing I inherited from my mother?" She had to ask. He acted as if she were just like him. That was something she didn't want to believe. She would never abandon the people she loved.

"You inherited your mother's good looks," he admitted. "I knew you the moment you stepped off the train. It was like looking at your mother." He smiled a soft faded smile of memory. "I fell in love with her the moment I first saw her. She was about your age and had just stepped off the train from St. Louis. She was so lovely and had a heart of gold. I fell hard."

"Not hard enough," she muttered then stopped herself. She had always vowed not to let his betrayal and abandonment make her bitter. Sometimes it was a hard thing to remember. "So, you gave me the trust fund."

"Yes."

"I used it to fight your lawyer and keep my clinic."

"Yes."

"Not very smart of you was it?"

He looked down at his empty glass and waved for another. "I underestimated you." He shrugged. "It happens. I forgot I was dealing with an Edwards."

"I'll repay you," she said. "I still have the principal balance you gave me."

He laughed then ended in a fit of coughing. She waited for him to catch his breath. It was clear he was deteriorating.

"Perhaps you should quit drinking."

"It dulls the pain." He wheezed. Finally he caught his breath. "I don't want the money back, baby girl. I'm a walking dead man. I have no need for it."

"I don't want your money."

"Don't be a little fool," he said. "Use the money to help your nurses. Send that young Miss Ambrose to medical school. You could use the help."

"How did you know about Mary?"

"I've been keeping tabs on you for years," he said and pushed his plate away. "You have no secrets from me. I know that you waste your life on doctoring women who can't pay. I know that you live alone and have rebuffed every man who has ever considered loving you." He took her hand. "Don't do it, Jenny."

"Don't do what?"

"Don't make the same mistake I did. Don't run out on love. Life is too short." He coughed and shook his head. "I'm dying and I've come to realize that money isn't everything. It doesn't warm your bed at night. It doesn't laugh at your bad jokes or comfort you when you're down. It certainly doesn't buy you freedom."

"I would never do what you did," Jenny said, affronted by the very idea that she would abandon anyone, let alone a burn victim and a small child.

"But you are," he said, his tone bleak. "You are running away from your future just as I did."

Jenny stood up. "I don't have to listen to this."

"No. You don't have to listen. I gave up my right to advise you years ago."

"That's right, you did. Now, if that is all, I am worn out and would like to go to my hotel."

The waiter replaced her father's empty whiskey glass. He stared at the amber liquid as he rolled it in the glass. "Yes," he said wearily. "That is all."

"Then good day, sir." She moved away from the table.

"Jenny," he called after her. She stopped and glanced back at him. He looked every inch a dead man. Pain and plain old exhaustion covered his pale skin. If he were anyone other than her father, she would have been making sure he made it back to bed and that his family would be there to care for him. "Thank you for coming."

Jenny didn't know what to say. Her heart hurt in too many places. It hurt to see this man alone and dying. It hurt to know that he didn't ask for her to forgive him, that he didn't seem to care what she thought of him. It hurt to know he'd tried to buy her off.

The biggest sting of all was the fact that he judged her and found her lacking. After all she had been through, after all she did to prove her worth. He still had the gall to tell her not to make the same mistake he did.

As if she would.

Chapter Thirteen

Shay followed Jenny out of the tearoom. He could tell she was upset. She fairly sizzled with emotion. He put his hat on and walked quietly beside her.

"I would like to be alone," she said, her voice edged with tears.

"I'm not leaving you."

She stopped and stomped her foot. "You cannot follow me around for the rest of my life."

"I can and I will," he said simply. "I promised and I'm not a man to go back on my word."

"No, but you sure will lie to a person if you need to," she spit out.

"I did not lie," he countered.

She cocked her head and stared at him. He shrugged. "I may have misled you."

"My point exactly."

"I never lied about how I feel about you, Jenny."

She rolled her eyes. "I can't do this right now."

"Then don't."

She strode down the sidewalk. He kept up with her. She

was beautiful when she was angry. She fairly shimmered with passion. It made him want to hold her and divert it all in his direction. Shay had sense enough to know that making a scene in the middle of Amesville was the last thing Jenny would want. So he simply followed her.

Right now he knew that the one thing Jenny needed was someone to listen. He figured he was the one to do it. Sooner or later she was going to start talking, and when that happened he wanted to be the one to hold her.

Jenny stepped off the sidewalk and crossed the wide dusty street. She had no idea where she was going, but she knew she had to move. Otherwise she would explode with the emotions that coursed through her. Unfortunately, she couldn't make Shay understand that he wasn't wanted. The faster she walked the faster he did. It wasn't fair that he could easily keep up.

Maybe if she just kept walking he would eventually get tired and give up. So she headed down the road that pointed out of town.

She walked hard until she was out of breath. Shay kept up as if they were going for a leisurely walk in the park. There was nothing leisurely about her feelings. When they were well out of town she turned on him.

"What gives you the right to follow me? What gives you the right to think you could just come into my life and charm me into doing what you want? Did you even think about what would happen to me if you did? Did you even think about how difficult it was for me to face that man?" She pointed back at the town and then, didn't wait for a response. She went back to pushing herself down the road.

Shay didn't answer her. He just stayed beside her. In a way it irritated the heck out of her, but in another way it comforted her to know that she couldn't chase him away with a few tart words.

After a while, she slowed her pace. The sky was crystal blue in Wyoming. The air was thinner than Texas and drier. The scent of snow blew on the breeze, while the dry hot scent of sun-warmed earth rose up from her feet.

It was a beautiful place. These grass-covered foothills. The huge rolling Teton Ranges on the horizon stood as sentinels, watching all that happened. She took a deep breath and understood why her father stayed here. It was one of the most beautiful places she'd ever been.

She shook her head. Her life was in Texas—that was where she planned to live and die. How could she let the scenery seduce her this easily? Jenny told herself it was just exhaustion from her trip playing with her mind.

Maybe it was because this is where Shay lived. Even though her mind knew he had misled her, her heart still warmed at the sight of him. Her feet crunched on the road. Shay stayed beside her. She was aware of his even breathing and the solid warmth of him beside her.

It comforted her.

Sheesh, that was a feeling she had to learn to live without. "My father told me that he wants his estate split between you and me."

"I didn't know that," Shay said, his hands in his pockets. "I'll do my best to talk him out of it."

"Don't."

"Why not?"

"I don't want anything from my father. Did you know he was the widow Banks?"

"I beg your pardon?"

"You're his lawyer. Did you know that he left the trust fund to me under the assumed name of the widow Banks?"

"No," Shay said, his angel face solemn. "I didn't know. How long ago was it?"

"Ten years."

"I wasn't even in college then. I have to assume his previous lawyer set it up."

"Billings," she said. "How odd."

They walked in silence. Birds chirped as they flew low over the awakening prairie, gathering insects. "Tell me about my father."

"What do you want to know?"

"Tell me about him from your point of view. It's clear you have some respect for him."

"Edwards was a good friend to my father," Shay said. "They were like two peas in a pod. Together they ruled the county. But there was always something reserved about him."

"What do you mean?"

"I don't know for sure. There was some sadness that always rested on his shoulders. He would come to the Bar M and watch us playing with each other. He would watch my mother with something close to envy. After my father died, my mother became very sick. Edwards sent in a nurse and came to visit almost every day." Shay picked up a rock and flung it across the grass. "I suppose in some way he was trying to make up for abandoning your mother. I didn't know it. I just knew I could look to him for support."

"Your mother must have been very special."

"Yes, she was."

"Was she beautiful?"

Shay laughed. "I don't know about physical beauty, but my ma had a quality about her that could soothe the most savage of hearts. It was just after her death that your father sent out the first man to get you."

"So, everyone knew about me?"

"Not at first. In fact it was only recently that they even discussed you."

"Your friend told me what this town thinks of me."

"They don't know you."

"No, they don't," she agreed. "There's a lot they don't know. I doubt they would hold my father in such high regard if they knew what he did."

"I suppose that's true."

Jenny walked along the road. The heat of the sun loosened the tightness in her shoulders. "I promised myself early on that no matter what he did to me I would not become bitter. But I had no idea how angry I was."

"Holding on to so much anger takes a lot of energy."

"True," she said wryly. "Sitting across from him at the restaurant brought it all out. It was difficult, but I did it."

Shay picked up another rock and skipped it along the road. He glanced at the horizon with squinted eyes and avoided looking at her. "So, are you glad you came?"

Jenny thought about it. The rush of anger had left her and she realized that her father was nothing more than a regretful, bitter old man. Neither his love nor his approval made any difference in who she was. "Yes," she said. "I'm glad I came. He always made me feel as if his leaving were somehow my fault."

"Now hold on—"

"No," she said and held out her hand. "I told myself it wasn't my fault that he abandoned us, but that didn't get rid of the doubt. It's a lingering doubt that maybe just maybe it was my fault."

"It wasn't," Shay said, his tone tinged with anger.

"No, it wasn't," she agreed. "He chose to leave us, and he's lived the rest of his life paying for it in one way or another."

"Unfortunately, you had to pay as well."

She glanced at Shay. "I think I'm done paying." It felt

good to be free of the anger and sadness that had been part of her for so many years. It made the scenery all the more beautiful. "What a lovely country."

"We're on the Bar M," Shay said.

Startled, she looked at him. "This is your brother's ranch?"

"Yes."

"It's so lovely. You must be glad you aren't really moving to Texas."

"I am moving to Texas."

"But there's no need to go back to Johnstown."

"Are you going back?"

"Of course, my clinic is there. My patients are there."

"Then I'm going."

Jenny stopped. "Stop being ridiculous, Shay."

"I'm not."

"Yes, you are. Look, I forgive you for misleading me. I think you had what you thought were good reasons. So, I'm not upset with you any more."

"That's a relief."

"You can stay here in this beautiful place. Really, take my father's things. I don't need them. Take it all guilt-free and with my blessing. He was more father to you than he will ever be to me. It's okay. I can accept that."

"You still don't get it, do you? I want to be with you Jenny Edwards. I love you."

"What?"

"I said I love you."

Fear rushed over Jenny as if she had been doused in a bucket of ice water. "Why?"

"Because of who you are," Shay said. "Because my life made sense after I met you."

Jenny turned and walked fiercely back toward town. "You can't love me."

"Why not?"

"It has to be guilt or pity." She nearly ran away from him.

"Jenny stop." Shay grabbed her by the arm. "Stop and listen to me. I know the difference between love and pity. What I feel for you is far from pity." He reached up and brushed her hair out of her eyes. "I admire you, Doc."

"Admiration is not enough," she said. Tears filled her eyes. "Don't you see? I don't believe that love is enough to sustain a lifetime of trials."

"If love isn't enough, then what is? What keeps people together, Jenny? Not all people end up alone."

"You're right. Not all people end up alone, but a lot of people do. Right now I would guess the odds are fifty-fifty that a marriage will last. You're the gambler, Shay, not me. I'm not up to those odds."

"I won't leave you, Jenny."

"I'm sure you feel that way right now. You're a good man, Shay, but people change. Let me remember you like you are today. It would break my heart if you left me in twenty years when I was old and fat, or worse in six months when you get restless and tired of my headstrong ways." She shook her head. "No, I won't spend the rest of my life apologizing for who I am, or worse wondering when you're going to leave. Good-bye, Shay," she whispered with her heart in her throat.

The look in his eyes pierced her through and through. She doubted he'd ever been rejected. She shook her head. Only a crazy person would turn away from Shay Morgan. She knew then that she was crazy, but she couldn't bring her torn heart to trust his angel smile.

"I'm sorry," she said and headed back to town. This time he didn't follow her.

The walk back was long and lonely. Jenny realized one

thing her father said was true. She was like him. She didn't have the courage to hold on to love.

Shay watched her as she stormed away. His heart was heavy and laced with anger. For the first time in his life he could not charm his way into what he wanted. He'd gambled big and lost.

He couldn't make her need him. He couldn't charm her into loving him. He couldn't shake sense into her. All he could do was love her even though she didn't want anyone to love her.

A pounding at her door brought Jenny to her feet. "Who is it?" she called as she grabbed for her robe and crossed the small hotel room.

"Miss Edwards, it's your father," said a voice from the other side of the door. "He needs you."

Jenny turned the key in the lock and opened the door. A young man stood there with his hat in his hands. "Shay Morgan sent me," the teen said. "He said that you should come quick. Your father has taken a turn for the worse."

"Does he need a doctor?" Jenny asked and grabbed her medical bag.

"Doc Adams is with him," the boy said. "But he's asking for you."

Jenny followed him out into the dark hallway. Fear raced through her. Her father had not looked good at lunch, but she hadn't thought he might actually die tonight.

The steps in the hotel were cool against her bare feet. Her robe barely kept her warm as they rushed out into the dark of night.

"Shay sent a carriage," the boy said, and helped her into a small two-seater. He ran around the front of the vehicle and climbed up beside her. "I'm sorry not to give you time to dress, but Uncle Shay thought it was important that you be there now."

"Uncle Shay?"

The boy flicked the reins and the carriage took off down the street. "I'm Josh Morgan," he said. "I was adopted into the Morgan family by Trey Morgan and his wife Brianna." The boy glanced at her. "I'm sorry about your pa and all. I know what it's like to be the only one left. At least you got this time to say your good-byes."

Jenny clutched the handle of her medical bag. "I didn't think he was that sick."

"Put up a good show for you, did he? My ma did the same thing. 'Course I was ten at the time, but it seemed like she was fine one day and dead the next. Turns out she had been sick a long time. I was just too young to see it."

"How old are you, Josh?"

"I'm seventeen, ma'am."

"How long have you been a Morgan?"

"Since I was fourteen. Best thing that ever happened to me."

"Why's that?"

" 'Cause when you're an orphan you get used to being alone. You know what I mean? After a while you forget that there's such a thing as family. That rain or shine, you work together, play together, and count on each other. I was awfully used to doing things by myself and for myself. Let me tell you that's one tough way to live."

Jenny nodded. Her heart constricted as she thought about her father living his life alone. How he'd abandoned himself when he'd abandoned his family.

"We're here," Josh said, and pulled the carriage up to a big two-story brick home. It was a large Georgian structure. There were glass windows ablaze in light across the front of the house. Josh jumped down and came around to help her out of the carriage.

The oak door opened as she stepped onto the brick walk. Shay stood in the hall and waited for her. Jenny clutched her throat at the sight of him. He looked as if he were losing his best friend or worse, his father.

"Jenny," Shay said, his tone whiskey rough. "He's asking for you."

Jenny followed Shay up a wide staircase to the second floor. Shay opened the second door on the right. Inside, candles blazed on every surface. A large four-poster bed stood in the center. Her father lay still in the center of the bed.

"Pa." Jenny willed her feet to move forward, past the strangers that stood in the shadows.

"Jenny? Is that you, baby girl?"

"I'm here, Pa," Jenny said and set her bag down on the floor. She took her father's hand. It was cold and nearly lifeless. "I'm here."

"Jenny," her father said through cracked lips.

"It's okay, Pa, I'm here."

"I was wrong."

"Shush, it's okay," she said, and sat next to him on the bed. "It's okay Pa."

"No," he croaked. "No, I . . . I was wrong at lunch. I didn't bring you here just to advise you."

"Pa."

"No, let me speak. I know it's probably too late, baby girl, but I . . . I need your forgiveness."

Tears welled up in Jenny's eyes. Her father, this big man dying before her, needed her to open her heart to him.

"Forgive me, Jenny."

"I forgive you," she said, her voice choking in her throat. "I love you, Pa."

"I love you, baby," he said, and coughed long and deep. His chest rattled.

Jenny reached around and held him up so that he could catch his breath. The light in her father's eyes dimmed. He couldn't catch his breath.

Shay eased in beside her and took her place. Jenny held her father's hand as he took his last few breaths.

"Jenny."

"I'm here, Pa."

"Remember what I said at lunch," he whispered, and dragged in one last breath.

"Shhh," Jenny said. "Save your energy."

A final coughing spasm took him. A look of peace came over his face. "Evelyn," was the last thing he said.

Jenny felt the chilblains rising on her arms. Her mother's name was the last thing her father would ever say. Perhaps her mother had come to take her father home. It was something she desperately needed to believe.

The room went quiet. Tears of loss welled up in her eyes and spilled down her cheeks. Now, she was truly alone in the world. She hadn't realized that she had counted on her father to be with her always. She had planned on fighting him forever.

In two short days all that had changed forever. Jenny bent down and kissed her father's cool cheek. At least now he no longer suffered.

Someone took her arm and gently pulled her out of the room. Jenny went along into the dark hall. The woman was small with pale blond hair and a pixie face. "Come on," she said. "The boys will take care of your father now."

Jenny followed her through the hall and down into what had been her father's library. Inside, a fire burned hot and bright in the fireplace. Two walls were stacked with books.

A winged back chair sat in one corner next to a small table. On the other side of the room was a large walnut desk.

The woman eased Jenny into the chair. "I'm Lana Morgan," she said gently. "Let me get you something. Which would you like, tea or brandy?"

Jenny wiped her cheeks with her hand and curled up in the chair. "Whatever you think is best." She hadn't felt this kind of grief and loss since her mother died all those years ago. Maybe it had been less then. After all, she had her father to hate and blame.

Now there was only grief and regret.

Lana pressed a glass into her hand. Jenny thanked her and took a sip. The drink took away her breath and burned all the way down. "What?"

"Whiskey," Lana said with a smile. "Your feet are bare and you look as pale as death. I thought you needed something to warm you up fast."

Jenny took another sip. It did warm her. "Thank you."

"You're welcome," Lana said and pulled up another chair. "You've come a long way. It can get to be too much."

"I knew he was sick, but I didn't expect him to go so fast."

"He should have been dead weeks ago."

"But he didn't die."

"No, he didn't die. He believed that Shay would bring you here and he suffered unduly to make sure he was alive when you came."

Jenny twirled the amber liquid in her cup. "He should have come to see me himself years ago."

"Yes," Lana said and put her hand on Jenny's knee. "Yes, he should have, but he didn't. Pride kept him away. Pride lost him the opportunity to really know you."

Tears welled up again, and Jenny let them flow. It was

just her and this pretty little woman. "I don't know what to do," she admitted.

"What do you mean?"

"All my life I've fought the image I had of my father." She sniffed and Lana handed her a handkerchief. Jenny used it to wipe her nose. She crumpled the linen in her hand. "I built my whole life around proving to that man that I was worth loving."

"You did it," Lana said. "He loved you so much."

"He told me I was just like him," Jenny said with a watery smile. "The very idea would have made me cringe before, but now . . ."

"Now, you can see the positive qualities."

"What he did was terrible," Jenny said. "He abandoned my ma when she needed him most. He abandoned me."

"Something he will never be able to undo," Lana said. "I was young when my ma died. My father abandoned me too. He didn't leave like your father did; instead he hid in a bottle for years."

Jenny reached out and squeezed the woman's hand. "I'm sorry."

"I'm not," Lana said. "I was lucky. That adversity made me the woman I am today."

"Is your pa dead?"

"No. I'm lucky. He realized his mistake and sobered up about a year ago."

"I'm glad."

"Difficult things happen to everyone. Your character is determined by how you act in these situations."

"I used my anger to help others."

Lana patted her hand. "I used mine to go after my dreams."

"Did you find them?"

"Yes," Lana said. "Yes. I found them."

Lana had a look of confident contentment. Jenny envied her. "You said your name was Lana Morgan."

"I'm married to Shay's brother Taggart. We own a horse ranch north of Amesville."

"Why are you here?"

"It's a family thing. Whenever there's trouble the Morgans rally." She smiled. "At first I didn't understand that either, but now I wouldn't have it any other way."

"Did you know my father?"

"He was considered part of the family."

Jenny chewed her bottom lip. "I'm glad," she finally said. "I'm glad my father found family."

"We could never take your place. He wouldn't let anyone that close. He loved you that much."

"He had a strange way of showing it."

"Yes, he did," Lana said and stood. "Well, I need to get back to the others. It was nice meeting you, Jenny."

"Thank you for your kindness."

"That's what family's for. Don't worry, you'll get use to it."

"To what?"

"To being included in the Morgan family."

"But—"

"But you aren't going to marry Shay, yes, we know. It doesn't make you any less family. Remember, Jenny, you are Ben Edwards' daughter. He was part of this family and so are you. You need anything, anything at all, you just holler. One of us will be there."

Lana left humming a beautiful tune. Jenny curled up in the chair and hugged her knees. Her linen night rail billowed about her. Her soft robe acted as a blanket. She sipped the whiskey and tried to sort everything out. But she couldn't. It was simply too much to ask of one person. Jenny rested her head in the corner of the winged chair and closed her eyes. Tomorrow would be a better day.

Chapter Fourteen

"Welcome back, Doc," Bill Watts said, and picked up Jenny's bags from the train station. "We missed you."

"Thank you, it's good to be home."

He tossed her bags into the wagon and helped her up. "I hear Sarah Jones has tied her knees together so that baby didn't come out until you got back."

Jenny laughed. "Goodness, I hope that's a tall tale."

Bill climbed up on the seat beside her and grinned. "Sounded good, didn't it?"

"Yes, it did." The town rolled by slow and certain. The sights and smells were all familiar, bringing back memories of the person she was, the person she would never be again.

"So, does it look smaller now that you've been back out in the world?"

"No. It looks just right."

"I have to tell you it was all I could do not to run that Morgan feller out on a rail."

"I don't want to hear of anyone being run out of town ever again," Jenny said sternly. "If you hadn't been so crazy, Shay may have told me the truth from the start."

"Hey, it ain't my fault he misled you."

"No," Jenny said and put her hand on his arm reassuredly. "No, Bill, it's not your fault."

"So how was it? Was your pa contrite? Did he crow to the world about how beautiful and smart you are? Heaven knows I would if you were my daughter."

Jenny smiled, but her heart hurt. "He died. They say he was only holding out to see me."

"Gee, I'm sorry, Doc. Are you okay?"

"Yeah. I'm going to be all right."

"Of course you are. You got us. This town might be small, but we're mighty when it comes to taking care of our own."

Jenny felt her heart warm. People waved as they rode by. Em waited outside the clinic with a couple of the nursing students. They had great big welcoming smiles on their faces.

She was home. So why did her heart feel so heavy? Maybe because she no longer dreamed of a fair-haired angel that held her in his arms.

"You're going after her, aren't you?"

Shay glanced over at Trey. His eldest brother leaned against the porch rail of the Bar M's main house. He squinted out at the cool dusky sky. It was a small moment of quiet in the boisterous ranch life.

"Yes," Shay said. "I am."

"Can't say as I blame you. She sure is something."

Shay felt the oddest bit of jealousy rise up inside him. "She's my something," he said, emotion crawling into his tone.

Trey nodded and crossed his arms. "Now you know how it feels."

"It feels like hell," Shay admitted. "I can't eat, I can't

sleep and worse. She's immune to my charm. Can you figure? All those women, and I fall for the one who sees right through me."

"Yeah. That's how it works."

They stood in silence and listened to the crickets singing in Brianna's flowerbed. "The way I see it, you're going to need some help."

"What makes you say that?"

"Hmmm, maybe because you're here and she's in Texas."

"She's stubborn."

"Admit it, you bungled it just like the rest of us."

"Shoot, must be something in the Morgan blood."

Trey grinned and clapped him on the back. "Why don't you come on in. Matt and Tag are waiting inside."

"What are they doing here?"

"We got us a foolproof plan."

"Oh, no, I've heard that one before."

"This time it'll be different. This time we've got smart women to see that it all works out."

Two weeks went by and Jenny settled back into her work. Although she was warmed by the way the town rallied behind her, her heart was oddly empty. She found a reason to walk by Shay's old office every day. Sometimes twice. She didn't know what she expected, but it was always the same. The door was locked. A small sign read that the office was temporarily closed. The sign said temporary yet she knew he wouldn't be back.

Em stuck her head into the now empty exam room. "Doc, there's something outside you need to see."

Jenny finished washing her hands and dried them on a towel. "What is it?"

"Come look. You won't believe it."

Jenny stepped out into the warm spring air. The sun shone down on the streets, baking them into rock. A small crowd had gathered around. "What's going on?"

Em took her hand. "Look."

The crowd parted and in the middle stood Bill holding the bridle of a beautiful horse and buggy. "It's for you Doc," Bill said with a grin. "It arrived today."

"Oh my goodness," Jenny said and reached up and petted the animal. Her head was dainty, her eyes wide and liquid. She was the most beautiful thing Jenny had ever seen.

"Beautiful, ain't she?" Bill asked. "Did you see the buggy?"

Jenny let them lead her around the horse to the snappy black buggy. It had a curtain canopy and cushioned seats. There was room in the back to carry medical supplies, but it was small enough that Jenny could handle it herself if she wanted to.

"Who? Where?" Jenny asked as she ran her hands along the leather seat.

"There's a note," Em said and handed Jenny a card.

She opened the note. Inside it said simply: *Every doctor needs to make housecalls, especially one with a heart as big as yours.*

Jenny looked up. The crowd seemed to smile at her. "It's not signed. Did you all do this?"

"No, ma'am," Bill said. "It arrived today with that note. I was instructed to bring it by."

Jenny glanced around at the familiar welcoming faces of the town. "I need to know who did this so that I can thank them."

"He brought it," Bill said and pointed. "Maybe he can tell you more."

Jenny watched a big man with dark hair straighten from

the porch post. He nodded in acknowledgement.

"Thank you," she said. "It's wonderful."

"It's not from me," he said.

"Then who sent it?"

"You'll find out in due time. I'm here to ensure you accepted it."

"Thank you," she said and patted the horse. "Please thank whoever sent it, Mister . . . ?"

"Morgan, Taggart Morgan," the man said. "I can attest that she's a fine filly with good bloodlines."

Jenny's heart took a leap at the sound of Taggart's name. "Your wife is Lana."

"Yes, ma'am."

"Did she send it?"

"Nope."

Jenny's hopes grew. Shay hadn't spoken to her since her father's funeral, and then it was simply to express his sorrow. Perhaps, just perhaps, he sent this gift. Perhaps he still thought about her.

"Well, please send her my regards. If this horse came off your ranch then it is indeed a prize. Bill, why don't you take her to the corral."

"There's no need."

"Why?"

"You need to go around back and find out."

Jenny's heart pounded as she led the crowd around the building to the back. Behind the clinic a full crew of men worked. Already she could see the outline of a large carriage house being erected. Two men were nailing boards into place while a third laid down posts for a small corral. "I don't understand," Jenny said.

"That's my brother, Matt," Taggart said. "Trey's laying the posts. You remember Josh, and that's his brother Cordell."

"Oh my," Jenny said. "How can I ever repay you?"

"Ain't from us," Taggart said. "So there's no reason to repay us."

"But all this work and the supplies."

"Have all been taken care of, don't worry your pretty little head over it."

"This is too much," Jenny protested.

"Just practical. I understand the stables burned last month, and you needed some place to keep your buggy and house your animal."

"I suppose you're right." Jenny looked around. With all these Morgans around she hoped to find Shay in the mix.

"He ain't here," Taggart said low.

She glanced at the big man. "I beg your pardon?"

"If you're looking for Shay, he ain't here."

"Oh," she said, and felt the heat of a blush warming her cheeks. "Well, thank you very much. All of you." She turned to Em. "Why don't we get them some lemonade and some lunch."

Bill hitched the animal to the back porch post and went to join the men in construction. The crowd dispersed and Jenny went inside to help Em make them all something to eat.

"Those Morgans sure are a passel of lookers," Em said as she squeezed lemons into a pitcher. "I bet they're a force to be reckoned with."

"Hmmm," Jenny said as she sliced up a ham. "I can't believe they're here putting up a carriage house. For that matter, I can't believe how fast it's going up."

"Never been to a barn raising, have you?"

"No, I can't say as I have."

"It's a sight for sure. From the looks of things, they'll have the place up and ready by the time the sun sets."

"That quickly?"

"That quickly. My guess is soon the whole town will come out to pitch in."

"I don't think we have enough to feed the whole town." Jenny buttered thick slices of homemade bread and piled them with ham and cheese. Then she sliced them in half and placed them on a platter.

"Not to panic," Em said with a grin. "There will be enough food."

She was right. As the afternoon wore on, more people came. The men carried hammers and nails and work belts. The women brought salads, beans, sandwiches and prized desserts.

Jenny had Em put out two tables, and her backyard took on a party atmosphere. It warmed her heart to see how much the town thought of her. She caught herself looking for Shay. She thought she saw him going around to the back of the building. So, she excused herself and hurried after, but he was nowhere to be found.

In the middle of all this joy, she felt disappointment creeping in. If Shay was behind this, why wasn't he here?

"Hello, Jenny."

She whirled around to find Shay standing behind her. Joy filled her at the sight of him. He stood there so beautiful, and so determined. "Hello," she said, suddenly shy. "Did you do all this?"

"If I say yes, will you send it all back?"

She swallowed. "No, no I would not send it back."

"Then yes. I did all this."

"Thank you. It means more than you can ever know."

He took a step toward her and her heart rate sped up. "Jenny."

"Yes?"

"Come here."

"You come here," she countered.

"Let's go together."

"Okay." She met him somewhere in the middle. She eyed him with longing and hunger, but she knew that she had hurt him when she had turned her back on him.

"Shay—"

"Jenny—"

"You first," they said together.

Shay smiled and her heart melted. He handed her a bouquet of flowers. "I got these for you."

"Thank you, they're beautiful."

"Jenny—"

She reached up and touched his mouth. His lips were warm under her fingertips and a small thrill ran up her arm at the touch. "Please," she said, "let me."

He nodded.

She pressed on. "My father told me that I was just like him. He said I ran away from love out of fear. It hurt to hear it, but I've realized that he was right."

"Jenny."

"No, please, let me finish. I pushed you away because I knew that I loved you. From the moment you knocked on my door I loved you. But you are so wonderful, handsome, and kind, I thought there was no way you could truly love me."

"You're wrong," he said, his voice low and gravely.

"It wasn't you I doubted. It was me. I thought I was unlovable, but you and your family showed me that I was wrong. Even after I pushed you away, you still came back."

He took her hand. "Of course I came back. I told you I would never leave you." He reached up and brushed a hair out of her face. "I won't ever leave you, Jenny."

"But Wyoming is your home. It is so beautiful. You

belong there, Shay, you belong with your wonderful family. I belong here. Johnstown is my home. I can never leave these people. I owe them my love and my respect."

"I would never ask you to leave," he said. "I told my family to get used to the train trip." He pulled her into his arms. "Jenny, Jenny," he whispered against her temple. "Don't you know that you are my home? Wherever you live, I'll live. Wherever you go. I'll go."

"But—"

"No, buts," he said. Then he got down on his knees. "Jenny Edwards, I love you. Will you marry me?"

She held the bouquet tight and knelt down with him. "Can you live with me? Can you let me be the doctor I am? Do you understand that there will always be emergencies and late-night happenings?"

"I know that I can't live without you."

"Are you sure?" she whispered.

He laughed. "As sure as the sky is blue and the grass is green."

Tears of joy welled up in her eyes. "Yes," she said. "Yes."

"Good!" he said, and jumped up pulling her with him. "Because we're getting married now."

"What?"

He pulled her around and into the crowd. "Ladies and gentlemen, I have an announcement. Doctor Jenny Edwards has said she will marry me. If you all will stick around, there's going to be a wedding."

The crowd cheered.

"But—"

"No, buts, Doc," Shay said and squeezed her hand. "I'm not giving you another chance to change your mind."

"Miss Jenny! Miss Jenny!" little Lillian shouted as she

came running around the corner. She stopped when she saw Jenny and put her hands on her hips. "Did Uncle Shay do it right this time?"

Jenny felt a huge grin cross her face. She glanced at Shay. "Yes, Lilly, he did it right this time."

"Good," she said and took Jenny's hand. "Come with me." Jenny glanced back at Shay.

"It's okay," he said. "See those three lovely ladies over there?"

Jenny looked where he pointed. There stood Lana and two others smiling and waving. "Yes."

"Those are your new sisters. They are going to be your bridesmaids."

"But."

"No buts, Em gave them your measurements. They had a gown made especially for you."

"Em did what?"

"You can thank me later," Em said and took Jenny's other hand. "Come on, it's time for you to get dressed." Together Em and Lilly pulled Jenny into the small group of women. Her last glance at Shay showed him smiling like a Cheshire cat.

They were married that night in the small chapel at the end of the town square. The party afterward made the barn raising look like a small affair. It seemed the whole town knew what Shay had planned. Jenny smiled as they danced their first dance together as husband and wife. Every single soul there knew that she loved Shay.

It was destiny.

He pulled her into his arms and twirled her. She was safe. She was loved and her father was wrong. She was brave enough to fight for what was right.

"Happy?" Shay whispered.

"Very," Jenny said. "There's just one thing."

"What's that?"

"We didn't get married in your home town. I'm sorry it wasn't a Wyoming wedding."

Shay glanced around. "All the people I love in the world are here. That makes it Wyoming enough for me."

"I love you, Shay Morgan."

"Of course you do," Shay said with a grin. "No one can resist the Morgan charm."

"Arrogant man." She smacked him playfully on the arm. He held her tight against him.

"I will never leave you," he vowed.

"Even if I'm old and wrinkled?"

"Even if you're bald and have lost all your teeth," he replied and smacked his gums.

Jenny giggled. Her heart swelled with emotion, and somehow she felt like her father looked down with approval. With the Morgans as family, Jenny would never be alone again.